# Rigging Engineering Basics

Revised & Expanded 2nd Edition

J. Keith Anderson

# Copyright

## RIGGING ENGINEERING BASICS
### *A practical guide for rigging engineers and lift planners*

## About the Author

Keith Anderson is a native of Newcastle U.K., a Chartered Engineer and Fellow of the Institution of Mechanical Engineers. After graduating in 1975 with a BSc in Mechanical Engineering, he was engaged in designing high pressure vehicle braking systems. In 1979, he joined the world of heavy lifting at Kramo Montage, engineering and overseeing specialist lifting applications using hydraulic gripper type climbing jack systems.

Over the next 12 years, he rose to Chief Engineer and was responsible for many complex, heavy and innovative lifting operations and for the further expansion and development of the heavy lift systems used. In 1991, Keith was appointed Chief Engineer for Van Seumeren UK (now Mammoet UK), responsible for engineering and proposal preparation for heavy lift and specialist transport operations.

For 2 years from 1996, Keith managed Sarens heavy road haulage company in the UK, after which he rejoined Van Seumeren as Contracts Manager in Utrecht, Netherlands. In 2000, Keith joined Bechtel as Senior Rigging Engineer based in London, transitioning to the US in 2001 as Rigging Manager / Chief Rigging Engineer, the position he currently holds. Keith is a Bechtel Distinguished Engineer and an ASME P30 Lift Planning Standard Committee Member. He lives in Louisville Kentucky.

# FUNDAMENTALS OF RIGGING ENGINEERING

**Rigging Engineering Basics** was the catalyst for the development of the **Fundamentals of Rigging Engineering** Training Program offered through **Industrial Training International** (iti.com). Mr. Anderson serves as the ITI Program Manager for this ASME approved online course taught by over 20 of the world's leading engineers. Mr. Anderson's hope is to elevate the skill and profession of the world's lift planners and rigging engineers through this book and training program.

**ASME** has audited and approved all courses in ITI's **Fundamentals of Rigging Engineering** Program for **Continuation Education Units** (CEUs) in compliance with the **IACET** (International Association for Continuing Education and Training) Standard.

**Fundamentals of Rigging Engineering** is fully accredited by the **Lifting Equipment Engineers Association**.

## Fundamentals of Rigging Engineering Introduction

The Fundamentals of Rigging Engineering Program is a comprehensive introduction to the science and art of the engineering behind heavy rigging, lifting, and transport activities.

This program was built to prepare key personnel with foundational knowledge in rigging engineering, exposing students to what they need to consider, and provide them with the resources to solve a challenge when it arises.

The Program is designed for lift planners, crane and rigging managers, and other non-engineers who conduct lift planning activities. Additionally, the Program is designed for engineers needing formal training for heavy crane, rigging and lifting activities.

## Fundamentals of Rigging Engineering Instructors & Contributors

**J. Keith Anderson, CEng FIMechE**
· FORE Program Manager
· Chief Rigging Engineer, Bechtel

**Kyle Adams, P.E.**
· Sr. Project Manager, Barnhart Crane

**Fernando Ferraz Alves, P.E.**
· Managing Director, ITI Latin America

**Jeff Dacey, P.E.**
· Rigging Manager

**David Duerr, P.E.**
· Owner, 2DM Associates

**Brandon Hitch, P.E.**
· CEO, CICA, CraneSafe

**Ron Kohner, P.E.**
· Owner, Landmark Engineering

**Richard Krabbendam**
· Owner, Heavy Lift Specialist

**Joseph Kuzar**
· Asst. Technical Director/
Training Manager, ITI

**Jim Lory**
· Rigging Engineering Manager,
Fluor Corporation

**Don Mahnke, P.E.**
· Owner, Hydra-Slide

**Larry Means, P.E.**
· Owner, Means Engineering

**Roger "Skip" Ohman, Jr., P.E.**
· Technical Adviser, The Crosby Group

**Jonathan Parnell, P.E.**
· Project Manager, Barnhart Crane

**Mike Parnell**
· Technical Director & CEO, ITI

**Don Pellow, P.E.**
· Owner, Pellow Engineering

**Bill Rigot**
· Senior Consultant, Fluor

**Larry Shapiro, P.E.**
· Partner, Howard I. Shapiro & Assoc.

**Sammy Suggs**
· Project Manager, Technip

**Paul Sweeney, P.E.**
· Fmr. Manager of Cranes & Lifting Equipment,
General Dynamics Electric Boat

**Marco van Daal**
· Owner, The Works Int'l

**Jim Wiethorn, P.E.**
· Chairman & Principal Engineer, Haag Engineering

**Jim Yates, P.E.**
· SVP of Engineering & Technical Services,
Barnhart Crane & Rigging

For more information on the Fundamentals of Rigging Engineering Program visit:
**riggingengineering.com**

# CONTENTS

# 1 Introduction

When you pass a construction jobsite, what do you invariably see? Crane booms. When someone wants to illustrate "construction", pictures of what do they reach for? Cranes. Cranes are the visible indicator of lifting activities. Lifting is everywhere in construction, everything you remove or add has to be handled, sometimes multiple times. Then there is lifting in general industry, in steel works, in fabrication, in routine handling at docks and so on. As well as being universal, lifting is also one of the most hazardous activities routinely encountered on a construction job.

Advanced as we are in safety culture, there are way too many accidents happening (actually one is one too many). Daily we see reports of crane accidents; mostly these are what should have been routine lifts, although the occasional high profile failure occurs to feed the sensation hungry media.

How do we address this? Key to the success of any work activity is that it is well thought through and properly planned, never more so than when lifting things. There are multiple pitfalls to catch the unwary or the unprepared and multiple opportunities to mess up big time. Unlike say welding where a defect can be detected and corrected, with lifting there are few second chances to get it right - it has to be done right first time; lifting is an unforgiving discipline. With that understood, if the task is approached methodically the pitfalls can be identified and eliminated or managed; good planning is the solid foundation on which success is built. ALL LIFTING OPERATIONS MUST BE PLANNED!

Who does this and what qualifies them to do so?

Traditionally, much of lift planning was the preserve of skilled crafts-persons and there was not a lot of formal documentation. More complex lifting operations might have used the support of a civil/structural engineer and maybe a draftsman to lay it out on paper. A relatively few crafts-persons and engineers specialized and became rigging engineers; in the main however planning lifting operations was just part of the regular day job. Much of the required knowledge was hard won over the years in the field and passed down through the generations. It evolved from some formal training in rigging and crane operations coupled with experience gained in the field, a "feel" for what is right and wrong, rules of thumb, old-wives tales and a smattering of witchcraft.

That piece-meal approach served well enough over the years and much impressive work was undertaken with what we would now consider meager resources; much ingenuity was brought to bear and many developments made that we now take for granted and have built on. However, industry has moved on, and this approach no longer totally addresses the need to lift safely and efficiently. At the same time as we need enhanced skills, we are losing the old-timers with the hard-won knowledge.

In recent years, many good people and forward thinking companies have been responsible for pushing the bounds of lifting in the construction industry forward, developing lifting capabilities and technologies we never could have dreamed of in the past, taking on ever greater lifting challenges and putting this discipline on a more professional footing. We have seen a rapid expansion in lifting technology with cranes becoming ever more complex and their capabilities greater; in parallel, there are now ever more sophisticated "alternative" technologies filling specialist niches in the market. These developments have supported the demand to lift ever larger and heavier items. Cost and schedule pressures are driving companies towards "modularization" techniques, building and handling large and heavy pieces and/or planning ever more complex lifts. These more complex operations require skilled engineering input from people with specialized knowledge and skills.

So, given these drivers, lift planning has rightly come much more center stage at a time when there appears to be a decline in the numbers of skilled "old-timers" brought up through the "school of hard knocks".

This has resulted in the emergence of the rigging engineer as a job in its own right rather than a part-time activity for a field engineer or supervisor. There is however, so far as I am aware at least, no rigging engineering degree you can take to become a "rigging engineer"; most rigging engineers are structural / civil or mechanical engineers or maybe have construction management degrees; some rigging engineers have excelled on the craft side and have gone on to get additional technical education. Some companies do an excellent job of training graduate engineers through in-house training programs requiring formal education and field time with mentors.

Strange then that given the safety-critical nature of the job and given how ubiquitous lifting is that it is rarely considered as a discipline or profession in its own right. Often it is just seen as an adjunct to another job, pipe-fitters rig, steel erectors rig, scaffolders rig; engineered lifting operations are routinely planned by structural engineers or mechanical engineers not formally qualified rigging engineers. True, there is training for riggers, but what about rigging engineers? How do they get the knowledge and skills?

In my view it is time that this discipline needs to come of age and be recognized for what it needs to be, a stand-alone profession in its own right, supported by quality education and training.

So what knowledge and skills are required to plan a lift, be a rigging engineer? That of course depends on the field you are working in, and the complexity of the operation.

Typically, a rigging engineer who plans lifting and other heavy rigging operations such as load-outs and heavy transportation, skidding, jacking and so on would be required to have knowledge of some elements of many traditional engineering disciplines such as:

- Civil (inc geotech)
- Structural
- Mechanical
- Hydraulics
- Marine
- Electrical

and of course would also need knowledge of the operating characteristics of, and be able to design for the use of:

- Cranes and other lifting equipment
- Rigging materials
- Heavy trailers
- Barges / tugs

and possibly more.

So where is a raw rigging engineer to get the required knowledge to plan a lift successfully?

First, you are not going to get it all from books, you need to get in the field and see it in action, work alongside good riggers, supervisors, crane operators and of course engineers. You will however need a good source of reference to support you, and that's where I think the problem lies at the moment.

There is a wealth of information out there for riggers, excellent training courses on the selection and use of rigging equipment, slinging techniques and so on; there are excellent riggers guides produced by a number of individuals and organizations. There is good training for crane operators and great literature and support from manufacturers. If you want a learned tome on cranes themselves there is "Cranes and Derricks" by Shapiro. There are industry standards such as the ASME or EN standards, there are publication by the Lifting Equipment Engineers Association in the UK, the SC&RA in the USA and many more. To design a lift beam you can take a structural engineering course; to figure ground loadings out you can take a geotech course; to understand mechanisms become a mechanical engineer. The rigging engineer doesn't need to be an expert in all these areas, but needs to know some of all of them. I can't operate a crane but I understand the modes of operation and can plan for the use of one.

The problem as I see it is that there is no one-stop shop for those who would plan lifts, bringing together relevant bits from all these sources and explaining it in a practical manner. To cover the entire subject is of course a huge (and impossible) task but I have attempted in this book to hit many of the major topics and I hope it goes some way to filling the gap. I am sure there are many glaring omissions and areas that could (and should) be expanded or corrected. Maybe in time those within the rigging community who are experts in their specific field will be motivated to contribute sections / offer improvements.

If you want to know more about specifics hopefully the included references will guide you to sources of additional or more-in-depth information. I have included photos gleaned over the years from projects I (and others) have been associated with. I have attempted to give credit where I was able to ascertain who owned the copyright. If I failed to give you due credit, I apologize. Contact me and will correct that when re-issued.

As a Brit who has grown up through various systems of units and who now lives in the USA, I have freely mixed units up through the book. To those who would rather I had done it all in one or the other system, I would defend myself by saying that it doesn't hurt to know a foreign language.

I don't know it all, and even if I did, couldn't possibly cover everything relating to this topic. Hopefully what is included will be of help to you. Feel free to contact me to correct my errors or suggest where improvements could be made.

For all the cautionary tone of the above, I heartily recommend rigging engineering as a career for those who are detail orientated and thrive on responsibility. You will daily be thrown varied engineering challenges that you have to solve through your ingenuity and expertise as safely and efficiently as possible. To see a complex lifting (or other load handling) operation being successfully undertaken by the team in the field in the manner you devised is incredibly satisfying.

Disclaimer

This book is intended to inform people planning rigging operations and point them in the direction of best practice (as I see it); to alert them to pitfalls and how to avoid them; to instruct in how to do certain basic rigging engineering tasks. It is not all the information that will be needed; reading this will not on its own make a rigging engineer / lift planner of anyone.

At all times lift planners must fully inform themselves and comply with manufacturer's ratings, manuals and requirements and with applicable legislation / contractual and other requirements. They should also recognize their own limitations and seek guidance when faced with a situation beyond their skills and knowledge.

I intend the content to be as accurate as possible but errors are sure to have crept in; I will happily correct those brought to my attention.

Guidance is offered in the spirit of improving standards of lift planning and execution. I cannot be held responsible for any negative consequences of following guidance or resulting from errors contained herein.

Opinions expressed are mine alone.

# 2   Fundamentals of lifting

Lifting operations may appear very diverse but at heart they all share a very few fundamentals.

All lifting operations from the lightest to the heaviest, from the simplest to the most complex, are either pushed or pulled to height and all require:

Figure 2-1

- Provision of a suitably strong, stable surface below the load to push (jack) against or a strong anchor point above to suspend from.
- A suitably strong lifting mechanism, capable of changing length under load, to either push the load up from a supporting surface or to pull it up towards an anchor point.
- A sufficient number of adequately strong, suitably located, lifting / jacking points on the load enabling it to be lifted and manipulated as required in a stable manner without being overstressed or deflecting excessively.
- Suitably rated lifting accessories (rigging) to attach the load to the lifting mechanism (if suspending the load).
- Appropriate lifting and rigging techniques.

The requirements need to be addressed in a well-considered plan that takes into account the working environment and puts the safety of the participants (and others who may be affected) at its core. If the plan is communicated to all the participants and is executed by skilled persons using well maintained equipment in good prevailing conditions, monitoring throughout, risk will be minimized and the likelihood of success maximized.

In planning a lifting/rigging operation in accordance with the above, there are many options, factors to consider and choices to make; there is no one "right" answer. A right answer will be one that is safe, efficient and cost-effective.

The contents of this volume will hopefully assist you in planning your lifts safely through:

- Advice on the characteristics and use of the many differing types of cranes and other lifting devices available, their advantages and disadvantages, scope of application and so on
- Advice on the characteristics and use of the more commonly used items of rigging tackle
- Discussion of considerations to be made re stability of loads, location of lift points.
- Discussion of various rigging techniques.
- Discussion on how to assess imposed ground loadings and pressures and load-spreading techniques.
- Discussion of lifting plan content.
- Direction to reference information.

Before we can do that though, an over-view of some engineering basics <u>may</u> be required by some. Those who don't need this recap can skip this section.

# 3 Some engineering basics

## 3.1 Mass, gravity & weight

In lifting it is fundamental to know what an object "weighs" as this determines how much force we need to apply to it to support it and to get it to move (and that drives everything). Weight is measured in units of force e.g. lbs, kips (1000 lb) or US tons (2000 lbs). We talk correctly about something weighing 50 lbs or 500 kips or 10 tons, but also talk somewhat incorrectly about things weighing 50 kg or 10 t (metric tonnes) in the S.I. (metric) system. Kgs and metric tonnes are actually measures of mass, whereas lbs and tons are measures of force.

Aren't mass and weight basically the same thing and the terms interchangeable? After all, aren't crane charts quoted in either US tons or metric tonnes, sling safe working load limits quoted in lbs or kg?

They are related but not interchangeable. Mass in its own right is a relatively meaningless concept for us until it is acted on by gravity when that mass exerts a force, its weight. The afore-mentioned metric crane charts are basically saying that the crane can safely support the force exerted by a certain mass when acted on by standard earth gravity. This works well enough when considering "weights" of loads in kg versus crane capacities in kg, but when you start getting into calculating stresses and the like in the metric S.I. system, you need to convert units of mass into forces (newtons N or kN) by multiplying by standard gravitational acceleration. A quick review is in order.

*Mass* - mass is the property of an object that causes it to have weight in a gravitational field. It is a measure of the amount of matter an object has and is independent of the environment – a mass of 50 kg for instance is the same on earth as on the moon. A body's mass also determines the degree to which it generates or is affected by a gravitational field.

*Gravity* - objects are attracted to each other in proportion to the product of their masses and in inverse proportion to the square of the distance between them. i.e. 2x the distance, 1/4$^{th}$ of the attraction.

The most massive thing in our environment is the earth itself; being so massive, it's attraction for objects overwhelms all other effects and it is all we need concern ourselves about in figuring weight. The attraction it exerts on other objects is "gravity" and the Earth's gravitational field causes items near the Earth having mass to have "weight". As we are operating on the surface of the earth which, for what we are doing, can be considered to be a fixed distance from its core, the only variable in calculating "weight" is the mass of the object in question. Gravity can be taken as a constant = 9.81 m/s² (or 32 ft/s²). Note that gravity is measured in units of acceleration m/s² or ft/s². As all matter is attracted to the center of the earth, the weight of an item is a force that always acts directly downwards.

*Weight* - weight is a measure of the force which must be applied to support an object (i.e. hold it at rest) in a gravitational field. As we are concerned with forces when lifting, it is weight rather than mass we want to deal in. To determine weight from mass, we use Newton's second law which relates the force F exerted in a body of mass "m" to the body's acceleration "a" by the equation:

$$F = m.a$$

In this case, substituting into the above where acceleration "a" is the acceleration due to the Earth's gravity "g" and , the force "F" is W, the weight, we can say that on the surface of the Earth, the weight "W" of an object is related to its mass "m" by the equation:

$$W = m.g$$

Where, for our purposes, Earth's gravity g can be considered to be uniformly equal to 9.81 m/s²; (or 32 ft/s²). We can easily determine weight, by measuring the force an object exerts; mass we can't measure directly.

Note: an item in the open expanse of zero-gravity deep space still has the same mass but doesn't have the same weight. The same item on the moon weighs about $^1/_6$th (17%) of its weight on earth – keeps the crane and rigging tackle requirements down!

The more an item <u>weighs</u>, the more force is required to hold it at rest against the attraction of gravity.

***Density*** - density is mass per unit volume (kg/m³ in the S.I. system). The average density of an object equals its total mass divided by its total volume. A denser object (such as iron) will have less volume than an equal mass of some less dense substance (such as water). If you have a piece of uniform density, you can determine its weight by calculating the volume of material from the dimensions then multiplying by the density which you look up in reference sources.

(i) How much would a piece of 50 mm steel plate 2 m x 0.75 m weigh?

> The volume = 2 x 0.75 x 0.05 = 0.075 m³

> The density of steel is approximately 7850 kg/m³ (it varies a little by grade).

> The mass = 7850 x 0.075 = 589 kg. Note: 1 t (metric tonne) = 1000 kg.

(ii) How much concrete do I need to make a 5 t deadman (anchor block)?

> Concrete of the type we are going to use weighs approximately 2400 kg/m³ (145 lbs/ft³)

> Volume required = 5x1000 / 2400 = 2.1 m³, say a block about 1.5 x 1.5 x 1 m

## 3.2   Work, power and energy

***Energy*** – energy is the capacity of a physical system to perform Work.

***Work*** – work is the amount of energy transferred by a force acting through a distance in the direction of the force; when lifting, that equates to weight x height lifted.

The units of Work and Energy are the same, i.e. Nm (equivalent to Joules) or ft-lbs.

A load at height has potential (or stored energy). The more it weighs, and the higher it is, the more potential energy it has. You gave it that stored energy when you did work in lifting it up there.

A load at height (even a relatively light one) has considerable potential energy. If a load is freely released at height, the potential energy it has changes to kinetic energy as it gains speed and loses height. Arresting that load from speed suddenly, by it striking the ground for instance, converts that kinetic energy into other forms of energy (heat, sound etc) in an uncontrolled manner can cause enormous damage.

- Even light loads when lifted have the potential to destroy property and maim / kill people.
- All lifts including light, routine, lifts must be treated with respect and must be properly planned.

***Power*** - is the rate at which Work is done.  Units are Nm/s or J/s or W (watts); in customary units ft-lb/sec. If you want to lift something quickly, you have to provide more power.

## 3.3   Forces, moments & pressures

In lifting, we are often concerned with:

***Forces***: the weight of the load, the self-weight of the crane, rigging weight, wind forces and the like and the manner in which they are handled and transferred through the lifting system to the ground; lift lug loads, sling and shackle forces, spreader compression, load line tension etc.

***Moments***: rotational effects deriving from these forces such as the overturning effect that they have on a crane or bending moments in lift beams.

**Pressures**: for example the pressures imposed beneath crane tracks / outrigger pads as a result of the track loadings / outrigger forces.

Following, we will discuss forces; how they can be represented, summed and factored; how moments are derived. Means of calculating imposed ground pressures are discussed in a later chapter.

### 3.3.1 Forces & Vectors

Forces have magnitude and direction and, for analysis and summation, can conveniently be represented as vectors. Vectors are indicated by arrows whose direction is that of the force and whose length is proportional to the magnitude of the force. Vectors can be summed graphically.

Vectors can be summed or broken down to equivalent constituent vectors.

e.g. A force of 10t in a sling pulling on a lug at 60° can be represented by a vector of scale length equivalent to 10t, starting at the lug and acting at 60°.

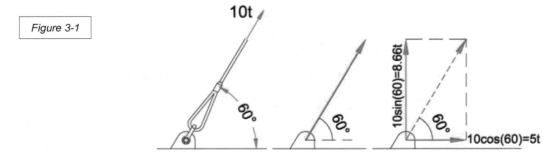

Figure 3-1

We may want to know how much vertical lift the sling tension is providing and how much horizontal force it is imposing on the lug. The single vector representing the tension force can be replaced by equivalent horizontal and vertical vectors whose magnitudes are equivalent to the scaled lengths of the sides of the enclosing rectangle; i.e. if the diagonal length represents 10 t, then the vertical and horizontal loads are 10sin(60) and 10cos(60) respectively. Taken together those two forces are directly equivalent to the 10 t sling force and can replace it in analysis.

Similarly if you know how much vertical force is required (say 8.66 t in this example) and the angle at which the sling is pulling (say 60°), the tension (10 t) and the horizontal component (5 t) can be derived by drawing a horizontal line from the head of the vertical vector to intersect the line of action of the sling and completing the rectangle and scaling the diagonal and horizontal lengths.

Using vectors, two forces acting from a point can be replaced by a single equivalent (resultant) force by summing them using vector analysis. e.g. a 10 t tension acting from a connection at 60° to the horizontal and a 5 t tension acting directly downwards from the same point can be analyzed as follows.

Figure 3-2

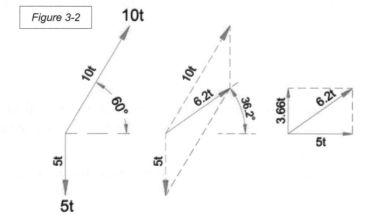

Construct a parallelogram whose sides scale to the magnitudes of the two forces, the diagonal is a vector representing the resultant in magnitude and direction. In this example, the two forces can be replaced by a single equivalent 6.2 t force acting at 36.2° to the horizontal. It in turn is equivalent to 3.66 t acting vertically and 5 t acting horizontally; that may be a more useful way for you to look at it.

### 3.3.2 Vector examples in basic lifting applications

Let's consider how the forces work in some basic arrangements. If, for example, you take a 10 t load suspended by a sling from a hoist. The weight can be represented by a vector whose length is equivalent to 10 t acting directly downwards. If no lateral restraint force is applied, it needs to be opposed by an equal and opposite vector of length equivalent to 10 t acting directly upwards – the sling tension.

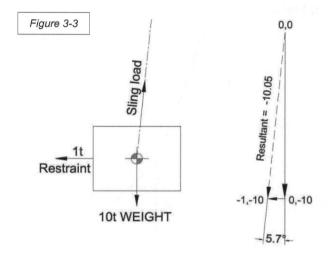

Figure 3-3

If a 1 t lateral force as shown above is then applied to the load, to what does the sling force increase?

You can sum the 10 t weight and the 1 t restraint to combine them into a single <u>equivalent</u> vector. The sling force required to hold the load static against the weight and restraint is a vector directly equal and opposite to the resultant equivalent vector.

Start by drawing an arrow of length equivalent to 10 t from an origin point directly down the page. From the head of the arrow, now draw an arrow sideways in the direction of the force of length equivalent to 1 t.

The single equivalent vector can be represented by a line from the origin to the head of the 2nd arrow. Its length is equivalent to the magnitude of the resultant force and its direction is the direction of the force.

You can either:

- measure the length to the scale you used (it represents 10.05 t) and measure the angle using a protractor (it is about 6 degrees), or
- use Pythagoras to determine the length = $\sqrt{(10^2 + 1^2)}$ = $\sqrt{101}$ = 10.05 t; then by calculus the angle = $\tan^{-1}(1/10)$ = 5.71°, or
- figure the angle per above, then use calculus, the force = 10 t / cos(5.71°) = 10.050 t

#### Example – telecommunications tower

Figure 3-3a

Consider a lifting operation such as this. In the telecommunications industry, it is often required to lift antennas, dishes, frames etc to the top of a tower; these items are usually not particularly heavy (a few hundred lbs typically) but the towers can be high. To avoid the need for a large crane just for the height, a common technique is to use a small capstan winch. This would be anchored at ground level and equipped with (say) a 1/2" double braid polyester rope led over a single sheave headblock (e.g. 3" McKissick 418) anchored to the top of the tower. The load is attached to the live end of the rope (hoist line) and is hoisted using the winch under manual control.

Typically these loads have to pass by obstructions on the tower such as existing antennae. To do this, a "tag" line is attached to the load allowing it to be pulled away from the tower (often by hand). This induces a "fleet" angle in the line from the headblock (out of plumb).

Let's assume that we want to calculate the magnitude of the tag line force required to pull the load out a known distance (standoff) past an obstruction. How can the forces in the system be assessed? The principles outlined above can be applied.

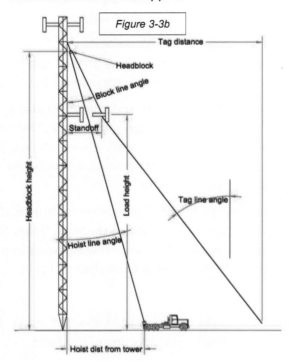

Figure 3-3b

Tag distance

Headblock

Block line angle

Standoff

Headblock height

Load height

Tag line angle

Hoist line angle

Hoist dist from tower

The system can be considered schematically as shown left. The forces acting on the load can be represented as below.

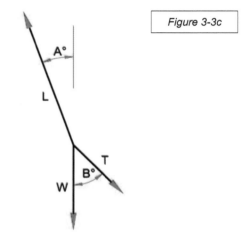

Figure 3-3c

The force in the load (hoist) line is "L", the weight of the load is "W" and the tag line force is "T".

The block line angle "A" can be determined knowing the standoff needed to clear the obstruction and the height below the headblock at which the obstruction is.

$$A° = \tan^{-1}\left(\frac{standoff}{dist\ below\ headblock}\right)$$

The tag line angle "B" can be determined knowing the height of the load and the horizontal distance the tag line handler is away from the load.

$$B° = \tan^{-1}\left(\frac{horizontal\ tag\ distance\ from\ load}{load\ height}\right)$$

For static equilibrium, the forces acting on the load have to balance out, i.e. there must be no nett force acting in any direction; as much acts down as acts up and as much acts left as right etc.

Vertically, there is the weight W plus the vertical component of the tag line force acting downwards and the vertical component of the load line force acting upwards. Horizontally, there is the horizontal component of the load line force acting to the left and the horizontal component of the tag line force acting to the right.

So, it can be stated that:

$L\cos(A) = W + T\cos(B)$ (i)

$L\sin(A) = T\sin(B)$, hence

$$L = \frac{T\sin(B)}{\sin(A)}$$

Substituting in (i),

$$\frac{T\sin(B).\cos(A)}{\sin(A)} = W + T\cos(B)$$

Rearranging

$$W = T\left(\frac{\sin(B).\cos(A)}{\sin(A)} - \cos(B)\right)$$

or

$$W = T\left(\frac{\sin(B).\cos(A) - \sin(A).\cos(B)}{\sin(A)}\right)$$

$$T = \frac{W.\sin(A)}{\sin(B).\cos(A) - \sin(A).\cos(B)}$$

If say, W = 100 lbf (or your units of choice), A=20° and B=45°

$$T = \frac{100 \sin 20°}{\sin 45°.\cos 20° - \sin 20°.\cos 45°}$$

$$T = \frac{100 \times 0.342}{0.707 \times 0.940 - 0.342 \times 0.707}$$

<u>T = 80.9 lbf</u> (or whatever units you used)

$$L = 80.9 \sin 45°/\sin 20° = 80.9 \times \frac{0.707}{0.342} = 167.3 \; lbf$$

So, <u>L = 167.3 lbf</u>

You can however, do the same thing graphically using vectors. If you have basic hand drawing skills or CAD ability, this approach will give you the answer a whole lot quicker.

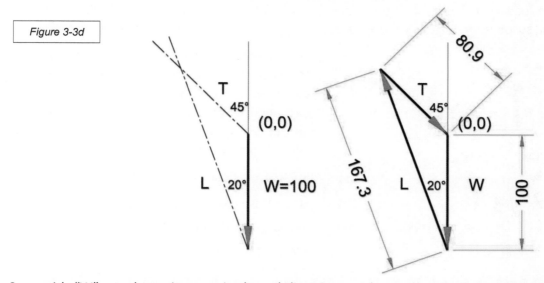

Figure 3-3d

Start with "W", you know its magnitude and direction, so draw a line from an origin point to a known scale with a length representing 100 units of force. Working (say) clockwise around our node point, the next force L has an unknown magnitude, but a known direction (up and to the left). Draw a line in that direction from the tail of the first vector. Similarly with the final vector, you know its direction but not its magnitude (down and to the right). For equilibrium, that vector has to conclude at the origin, completing the diagram, so working back from 0,0 establishes the line of that vector. The intersection of the two chain lines gives the previously unknown lengths of the sides. By measuring them to the same scale, the magnitude of L and T can be determined. The answer is the same. You have actually done the exact same thing whichever method you use.

## Example – spreader bar

Let's consider a simple spreader bar arrangement and apply the above concepts to figuring out the loads in the system.

Figure 3-4

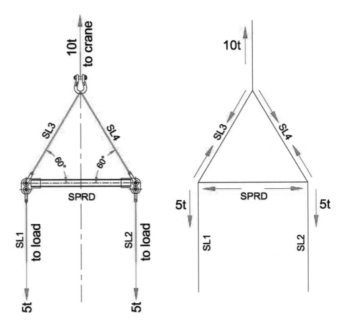

A 10 t load is lifted with a simple spreader arrangement, the lift points are equidistant about the C of G and the inclined sling lengths equal the spreader span giving a 60° suspension.

The problem can be broken down into a force diagram as shown on the right. Slings 1 and 2 each have a tension of half the load = 5 t. The axes of the inclined slings, the spreader and the vertical slings meet at a common point. The suspension slings SL3 and SL4 are under tension and the spreader is under compression.

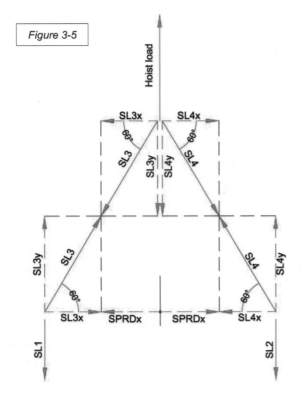
Figure 3-5

Considering the node point at the LHS of the spreader and drawing the vectors. The vertical component SL3$_y$ of vector SL3 must equal SL1=5 t. Knowing that and the direction of SL3 at 60° to the horizontal we can figure out the magnitude of SL3 and SL3$_x$ graphically or by calculus.

SL3 = SL3$_y$ / sin60° = 5 t / 0.866 = 5.77 t

SL3$_x$ = SL3 x cos60° = 5.77 x 0.5 = 2.89 t

We now know all the forces acting at the end of the spreader. As the C of G is in the center, the forces are mirrored equal and opposite at the other end. SL3$_x$ = SL4$_x$, balancing each other out and acting to compress the spreader which must be capable of resisting the 2.89 t load without crushing or buckling.

The slings SL3 and SL4 are in tension and pull up and in at the end of the spreader and pull down and out at the crane hook.

Considering the crane hook or shackle; resolving SL3 at the hook gives us $SL3_y$ = 5 t acting down on the hook and $SL3_x$ = 2.89 t acting out at the hook. $SL3_x$ is directly opposed by $SL4_x$, so they cancel each other out. The vector SL3y can be directly added to the vector SL4y = 5 t + 5 t = 10 t balanced by the force provided by the hoist. Therefore the crane has to provide 10 t which equals the sum of SL1 and SL2 as we would expect.

Graphical methods work well if using CAD as vectors are proportional to lengths and angles both of which are readily measured. In a 60° spreader arrangement such as this, each of the inclined slings will always have a tension 15.5% greater than the tension in each of the vertical slings. The compression force in the spreader will always be 50% of the inclined sling tension (equivalent to 58% of the load in one of the vertical slings).

If the suspension sling angles are reduced to 45°, by similar process you can show that the inclined sling tension is 41.4% greater than the vertical sling tension and the spreader compressive force = 100% of the load in one of the vertical slings.

### 3.3.3   Moments

The moment a force induces is a measure of its tendency to rotate an object about some point – loosely speaking (in mechanical terminology) it is torque. To evaluate it we need to know the force vector (force magnitude and direction) and the location of the point we want to calculate the moment about relative to the vector.

The moment = the force x the perpendicular distance from the point in question to the line of action of the force. Units are ft-lb, Nm (or stretching the definition), kgm.

In a static situation, for equilibrium all the clockwise moments have to balance all the anti (counter) clockwise moments. (Otherwise there would be a nett tendency for the load to want to rotate). More on equilibrium later.

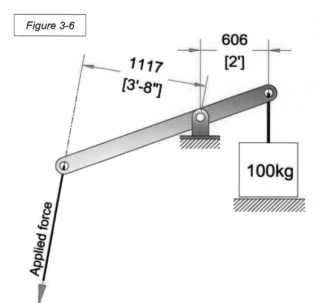

Figure 3-6

Here a lever is used to raise a load; consider moments about the pivot.

When the load is clear, the force it applies is vertical, so the perpendicular distance is horizontal = 606 mm. The applied force is not vertical; its perpendicular distance = 1117 mm.

For balance,

Applied load (kg) x 1117 mm = 100 kg x 606 mm

Applied load = 100 x 606 / 1117 = 54.3 kg

*What if the applied force was vertical?*

*The left hand moment arm (perpendicular distance from the pivot to the line of action of the force) would be greater, so the applied force required would be reduced.* <u>*Maximum mechanical advantage is gained when the line of the applied force is tangential to a circle centered on the pivot.*</u>

### 3.3.4   Moment examples in basic lifting applications

*Example (a):* two unequal loads (5 t and 10 t) are lifted using a balance beam as shown following. To account for the difference in weight, the lift is taken off-center on the beam, 5 m from the 5 t load and 2.5 m from the 10 t load. Is the load in balance?

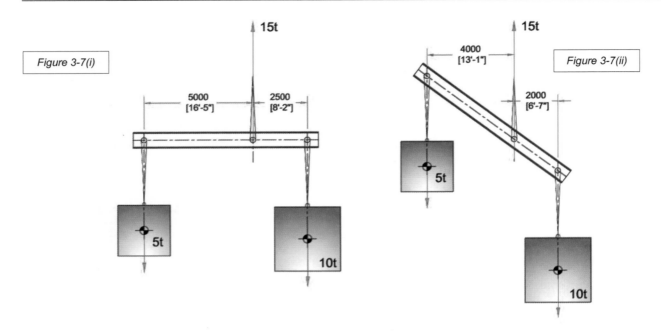

Figure 3-7(i)

Figure 3-7(ii)

First, consider the moments about the main suspension point on the beam (which acts as a pivot point). (Refer to the left hand figure). As the loads all act vertically, the moment arms (which are always taken from the pivot point normal to the directions of the forces, will be horizontal distances. The clockwise moment about the pivot is 10 t x 2.5 m = 25 t.m; the counter (anti) clockwise moment is 5 t x 5 m = 25 t.m. As they are equal the load is in balance.

However, being in balance is not enough in itself; it would equally be in balance at the attitude shown on the Figure to the right. At the angle indicated (which is arbitrary), the clockwise moment = 10 t x 2 m = 20 t.m; the anti-clockwise moment = 5 t x 4 m = 20 t.m. It is in balance; in fact it would be in balance at any angle, and could adopt any angle. We will likely want it to lift level, what can be done?

The problem arises because all the pivot points are on the same axis. <u>To provide some stability in the arrangement, the central pivot point (main suspension) must lie above the other two.</u>

What happens if we add a lug to give some offset?

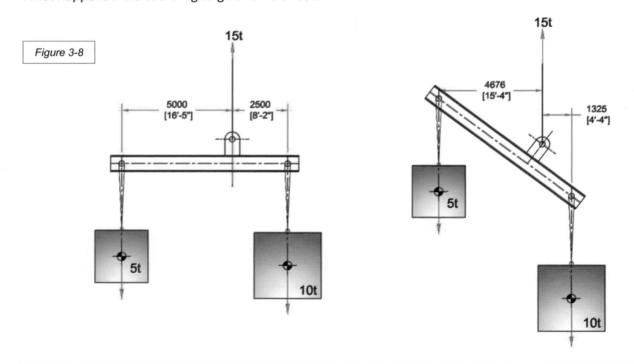

Figure 3-8

In the LH Figure above, the moment arms are again 5 m and 2.5 m, the load is in balance. Let's see what happens if it tries to rotate to a situation such as shown in the RH Figure. As a result of the vertical offset of the central pivot point, the ratio of the moment arms has changed. It is no longer 2:1. At this notional angle; the clockwise moment = 10 t x 1.325 m = 13.25 t.m; the anti-clockwise is 5 t x 4.676 m = 23.38 t.m. There is a nett anti-clockwise moment of 10.13 t.m. Under the influence of this moment, the arrangement will rotate anti-clockwise about the pivot, lowering the 5 t load and raising the 10 t load. As it does this, the ratio of the moment arms comes back closer to 2:1 and the out-of-balance moment reduces until it arrives at the situation shown in the LH Figure at which angle there is no longer an out-of-balance moment and the beam comes to a stable level attitude. The arrangement is stable and self-correcting. More on stability later.

*Example (b):* what happens if your weights or distances are slightly off?

Consider a situation such as the preceding. The lift is planned to be level on the basis that the loads weigh 5 t and 10 t, however say the heavier load actually weighs 10.25 t. What will happen?

As we start to lift, the clockwise moment = 10.25 t x 2.5 m = 25.625 t.m and the anti-clockwise moment = 5 t x 5 m = 25 t.m. There is a small nett clockwise moment of 0.625 t.m. This will rotate the beam clockwise, lowering the 10 t load and raising the 5 t load. Eventually the beam will stabilize out at about 2.1° off level at which time the moment arms are 5.038 m and 2.457 m.

At this angle; the clockwise moment = 10.25 t x 2.457 m = 25.19 t.m; the anti-clockwise is 5 t x 5.038 m = 25.19 t.m. They are equal. <u>Having this vertical offset provides a self-correcting effect; the greater the offset, the less angle the beam will adopt for a given initial out-of-balance.</u>

*Note: suspending the beam from a matched pair of inclined slings as shown in the R.H. figure may be a good solution if height isn't an issue. The pivot point is now effectively the point "P" where the slings intersect. This arrangement won't be very sensitive to small discrepancies in weight. If you lift and find it wanting to hang unacceptably out of level, it is relatively easy to add an extra shackle in one of the inclined legs to throw the pivot point across slightly to better balance the load. (Add it on the lighter side to increase the moment arm on that side and reduce it on the heavier).*

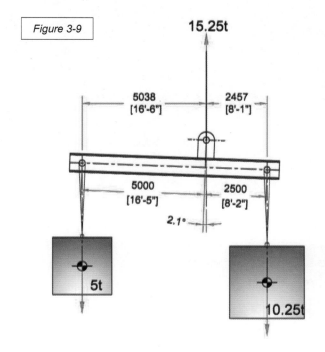

Figure 3-9

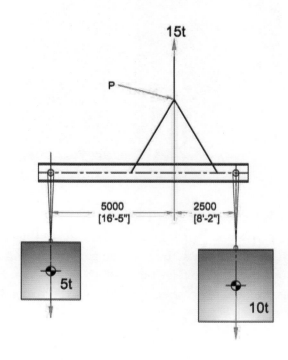

### 3.3.5 Practical application of counterbalanced rigging arrangement

These photos show how Barnhart has used this principle in an innovative rigging arrangement. Their design has a beam suspended from the main crane hook; the payload is supported at one end of the beam and balancing counterweight is suspended from the other. Fixed length slings are used from the hook-block at the load end.

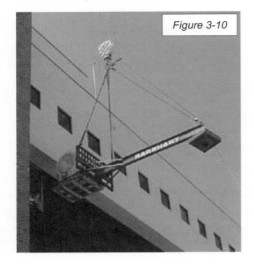

*Figure 3-10*

At the counterweight end, the whip line is taken vertically alongside the main hoist lines and is led over a diverter sheave anchored to the main block to the beam end, around a pulley block to a dead end at the hook-block. This allows independent adjustment of the suspension length at the counterweight end. By this means the suspension can be maintained stable and level. After the load is released the combined C of G will shift towards the counterweight beam and it will be necessary come up on the whip line and swing to bring the C of G under the suspension. Once clear, the counterweight end can be lowered off to allow it to hang off the main hook. The picture to the left shows the rig being used to place a package inside a building. The following pictures show replacement of a vessel inside a structure with limited headroom.

*Figure 3-11*

*Figure 3-12*

### 3.3.6 Moment balance in a basic derrick

e.g. A simple derrick system consists of a mast supported in an "ink-well" bearing at its base and restrained back from its head by a reeved guying system attached to a ground anchor (deadman). This allows the mast to be luffed and to raise the load which is suspended from the head of the mast. The mast itself weighs 25 t, what is the required restraint force when the load is at 9.317 m from the mast?

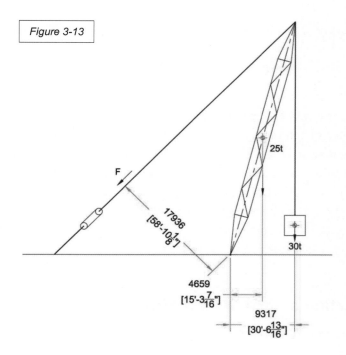

Figure 3-13

The clockwise moments trying to overturn the mast derive from the payload and the self-weight of the mast. These forces are vertical; therefore the moment arms are horizontal distances from the bearing to the line of action of the forces:

$M_{clock}$= (30 t x 9.317 m) + (25 t x 4.659 m) = 396.0 t.m

The restraining force does not act vertically but at an angle of about 45° when the mast is luffed out to this particular radius; the moment arm is the distance from the bearing normal to the line of action of the reeved guy wire = 17.936 m.

The anti-clockwise restraining moment thus = the force in the wire F x 17.936 and it equals the clockwise overturning moment = 396 t.m.

Therefore F = 396 / 17.936 = 22.1 t

## 3.4  Buoyancy

There are a couple of points to note when lifting loads out of the water. Per Archimedes, a load that is partially or completely submerged in a liquid will be buoyed up by a force equal to the weight of water displaced. i.e. it will appear to weigh less by an amount equal to the weight of water displaced. If the object is completely submerged, the weight of water will be the weight of a volume of water equal to the volume of the object. If the object is partially submerged, the weight of water will be the weight of a volume of water equal to the submerged volume of the object. An object will float if it can be partially submerged to a depth where the volume of water displaced equals the weight of the object.

If you start lifting with the object submerged in water the buoyancy will progressively disappear as it breaks the surface; when lifted clear, the load will attain its true weight. You may have had adequate capacity initially, but have inadequate capacity at the true weight.

You also need to be cautious of suction if lifting a flat-bottomed object clear of water or mud. Bear in mind that if two surfaces are in close contact, air pressure of 14.7 psi (1 bar or 100 kN/m$^2$, about 10 t/m$^2$) acting on the contact area is holding the two surfaces together. That can amount to a considerable force if say lifting a barge off a muddy river bed. You have to ensure the air can get between the surfaces to break the suction.

Finally, if the object can contain water, you need to be sure it can all drain clear as you lift; that you are not trying to lift water with the load.

# 4   Center of gravity

As important as knowing what an object weighs is to know the location of the C of G; i.e. the center of mass, the point the weight appears to act from.

## 4.1   What is the Center of Gravity?

The Center of Gravity of an object is a theoretical point (x,y,z) that can be considered to be the center of mass of the object. It is not necessarily the geometric center of the object. If the object could be supported at its C of G, it would be in perfect balance, regardless of orientation. The C of G location derives from the weights and centers of mass of all the constituent parts of the assembly and their location within the whole. At the C of G, there is no nett tendency for the object to rotate under the effect of gravity; all the individual elements making up the piece are in balance with each other. The weight of the entire object can thus be considered to act from that point, which is a useful concept when trying to analyze support reactions. This concept applies best when the load is relatively rigid and acts as a single entity; it is less useful if the load is "floppy" and bits of it can act somewhat independently of others.

## 4.2   Why is it important to know the location of the Center of Gravity?

Once you have determined the location of the C of G, you can treat the entire compound object as one item, whose weight acts from the C of G location with magnitude equal to the total weight of the constituent parts. You need to know where the C of G is to locate support / lifting points, figure out a stable, level lifting arrangement, determine reactions, assess how reactions change (during upending for instance) and so on. It is required also to determine transport arrangements, ensure stability on trailers and on barges. If elements of the load can move, e.g. liquid in a tank, then the C of G can shift during (say) upending.

## 4.3   Calculating support reactions

If the location of the C of G is known relative to say a pair of lifting lugs, the support reactions at those lugs can be determined by applying the principle of moments.

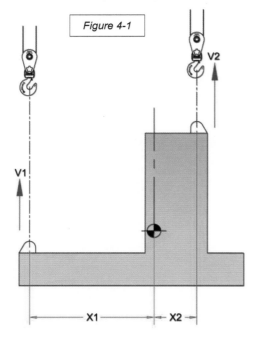

Figure 4-1

Case (i) vertical lines of support

The forces are all vertical, the moment arms are therefore all horizontal distances. For equilibrium, the moments have to balance; so, taking moments about the C of G:

V1.X1 = V2.X2

therefore V1 / V2 = X2 / X1

or V2:V1 = X1:X2

i.e. the load is shared in inverse proportion to the horizontal distances the lines of action of the support forces are from the C of G.

e.g. if X1 = 1800 mm and X2 = 600 mm, the ratio of load sharing (V2:V1) is 3:1.  V2 = 3 x V1.

If the weight is 10 t, V1 = 2.5 t and V2 = 7.5 t. (Nearest gets most).

Alternatively, $V_1 = Wt\left(\frac{X2}{X1+X2}\right) = 10\left(\frac{600}{1800+600}\right) = 2.5\,t$

*When the support forces are vertical, the heights of the attachments are unimportant as it does not affect the moments. The lugs could be anywhere along the lines of action.*

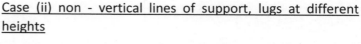

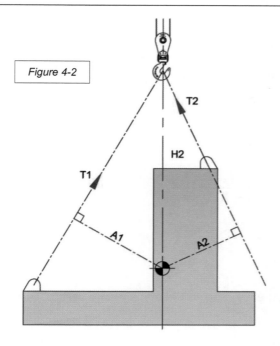

Figure 4-2

## Case (ii) non - vertical lines of support, lugs at different heights

What if the lines of support are not vertical and the attachment points are not at the same elevation, how is the load shared?

The moments have to balance; so, taking moments about the C of G:

$$T1.A1 = T2.A2 \text{ or } T1:T2 = A2:A1$$

This does not help us much. We really need to relate the problem back to the x and y locations of the lift lugs relative to the crane hook.

Luckily the ratio A2:A1 is the same as the ratio of the (X) lengths either side of the C of G of any horizontal line drawn intersecting the lines of action of the forces. e.g. taken through one of the lift lugs.

The H and V components of T2 can be resolved at any point along the line of action of T2 and will be the same. Let's consider a horizontal line through the LH lug intersecting the line of action of T2 and treat the problem as though the RH lug was at that intersection. This eliminates the vertical component of the problem.

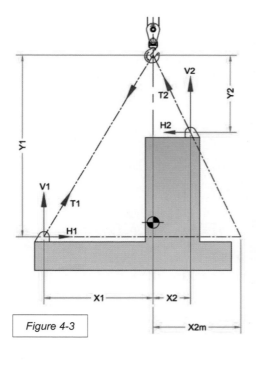

### Vertical forces

For moment balance, taking moments about the LH lug,
$$V_2(X_{2m} + X_1) = Wt. X_1$$

$$\therefore V_2 = \frac{Wt. X_1}{(X_{2m} + X_1)}$$

By proportion, $\quad X_{2m} = \left(\frac{Y_1}{Y_2}\right) X_2$

Substituting, $V_2 = Wt\left(\dfrac{X_1}{\left(\frac{Y_1}{Y_2}\right) X_2 + X_1)}\right)$

$$V_2 = Wt\left(\frac{X_1 Y_2}{X_2 Y_1 + X_1 Y_2)}\right)$$

Figure 4-3

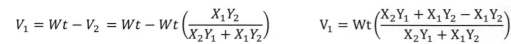

$$V_1 = Wt - V_2 = Wt - Wt\left(\frac{X_1 Y_2}{X_2 Y_1 + X_1 Y_2}\right)$$

$$V_1 = Wt\left(\frac{X_2 Y_1 + X_1 Y_2 - X_1 Y_2}{X_2 Y_1 + X_1 Y_2}\right)$$

$$V_1 = Wt\left(\frac{X_2 Y_1}{X_2 Y_1 + X_1 Y_2}\right)$$

## Horizontal Forces

$$\left(\frac{H_1}{X_1}\right) = \left(\frac{V_1}{Y_1}\right)$$

$$\left(\frac{H_2}{X_2}\right) = \left(\frac{V_2}{Y_2}\right)$$

Substituting,

$$H_1 = Wt\left(\frac{X_2Y_1}{X_2Y_1 + X_1Y_2}\right)\frac{X_1}{Y_1}$$

$$H_1 = Wt\left(\frac{X_1X_2}{X_2Y_1 + X_1Y_2}\right)$$

$$H_2 = Wt\left(\frac{X_1Y_2}{X_2Y_1 + X_1Y_2}\right)\frac{X_2}{Y_2}$$

$$H_2 = Wt\left(\frac{X_1X_2}{X_2Y_1 + X_1Y_2}\right)$$

Note that $H_1 = H_2$, they are the same value and balance each other; $V_1 + V_2 = Wt$ balancing the vertical forces.

## Sling Tensions

By Pythagoras.

$$T_1 = \sqrt{(V_1^2 + H_1^2)} \quad \text{and} \quad T_2 = \sqrt{(V_2^2 + H_2^2)}$$

*From the above it can be seen that, when inclined slings are used to a single suspension point (e.g. crane hook), the reactions and sling tensions are determined not only by the horizontal distances from the attachment points to the C of G (as is the case with vertical slings), but also by the vertical distances from the attachment points to the hook.*

## Example

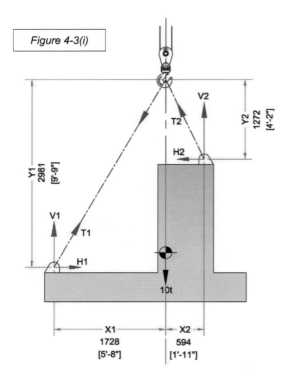

Figure 4-3(i)

$$V_2 = Wt\left(\frac{X_1Y_2}{X_2Y_1 + X_1Y_2}\right)$$

$$V_2 = 10\left(\frac{1728 \times 1272}{594 \times 2981 + 1728 \times 1272}\right)$$

$$V_2 = 5.538\,t$$

$$V_1 = 10 - 5.538 = 4.462\,t$$

$$H_1 = Wt\left(\frac{X_1X_2}{X_2Y_1 + X_1Y_2}\right)$$

$$H_1 = 10\left(\frac{1728 \times 594}{594 \times 2981 + 1728 \times 1272}\right)$$

$$H_1 = H_2 = 2.586t$$

$$T_1 = \sqrt{(V_1^2 + H_1^2)} = 5.157\,t$$

$$T_2 = \sqrt{(V_2^2 + H_2^2)} = 6.112\,t$$

Alternatively, if you have drawn the slinging arrangement accurately you can work out the lug reactions and the tensions simply knowing the weight and the angles the two slings make to the vertical. This is probably a more convenient method if using CAD.

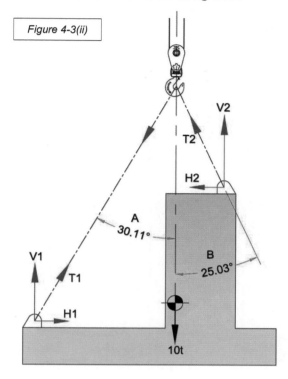

Figure 4-3(ii)

The horizontal distances from the line of suspension to the slings at any level are proportional to the tangents of the angles the slings make to the vertical. The vertical forces F1 and F2 are inversely proportional to those distances so:

$$\frac{V_1}{V_2} = \frac{\tan B}{\tan A} \quad \text{and we know} \quad V_1 + V_2 = Wt$$

Example

$$\frac{V_1}{V_2} = \frac{\tan B}{\tan A}$$

$$\frac{V_1}{V_2} = \frac{\tan(25.05)}{\tan(30.11)} = 0.806, \quad V_1 = 0.806V_2$$

$$0.806V_2 + V_2 = 10\,t, \quad \mathbf{V_2 = 5.537\,t} \text{ so } \mathbf{V_1 = 4.463\,t}$$

$$\mathbf{H_1 = H_2} = V_1\tan(30.11) = 4.463 \times 0.58 = \mathbf{2.588\,t}$$

Using Pythagoras, the tensions can now be derived as previous.

## 4.4   Calculating the location of the C of G

If we want to know where the C of G is located in something that has uniform shape, say a concrete block or a steel beam, pipe or a piece of plate, we can say confidently that it will be at the center of volume; in the geometric center of the block, in the middle of the beam or pipe on its axis, or in the center of area of the plate at half height and so on. However, most things we lift are not uniform and are constructed from many constituent parts, each of which has its own mass and location within the whole. How do we figure it out? One way is to consider all of the constituent parts and their location and do (x,y,z) moment calculations in order to find the one point at which there is no nett moment.

Example – moment method

A duct section is formed from two separate pieces D1 (60 t) and D2 (40 t) of the same width. Each is uniform in its own right, so the C of G of each will lie in the geometric center of each. The assembly is uniform in the "y" direction (into the page) so it's C of G will lie in the center in that direction. However the assembly is non-uniform in the X, Z elevation shown, so we will just consider this view. See the Figure 4-4.

The forces acting on the assembly are the two "weights" of the two constituents acting vertically downwards from their individual centers of gravity balanced by a support force equal to the total weight acting vertically upwards through the C of G of the total assembly – location unknown, to be calculated.

We want to find an X, Z location where the load is in balance & the sum of the clockwise moments thus equal the sum of the anti-clockwise. The C of G is at that point. We need to choose a point as an origin to measure from – any point will do, but it's best to choose an extreme corner where all the constituent parts act to rotate the same way, say clockwise. This keeps all the X's +ve and avoids confusion.

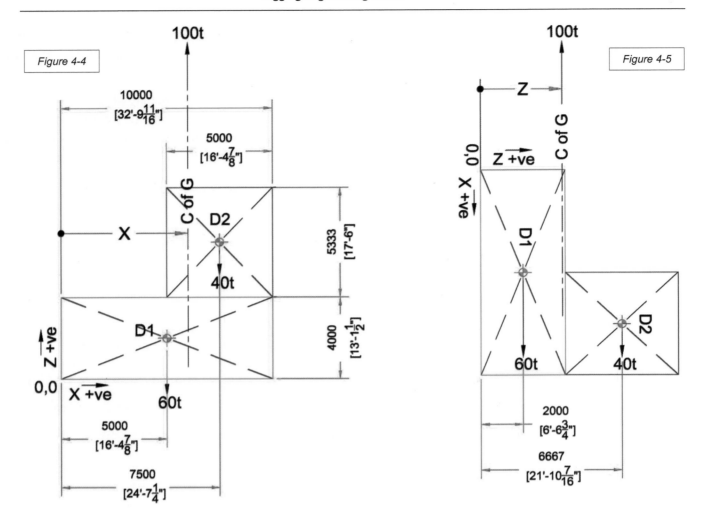

To determine the location of the C of G in the X direction, take moments about the origin.

The forces are vertical; therefore the moment arms (which are always at 90° to the line of the force) are the horizontal X dimensions.

The clockwise moments about our 0,0 origin = D1.X1 + D2.X2 = (60 t x 5 m) + (40 t x 7.5 m) = 600 t.m

As there has to be zero nett moment, it has to be balanced by the anti-clockwise moment derived from the total weight of 100t acting with a moment arm equal to the unknown X distance.

Therefore 100x = 600; x = 6 m

The location of the C of G in the X direction is 6m from the origin, i.e. 1 m horizontally from D1 and 1.5 m from D2.

To prove the load is balanced in the x-direction at the C of G location, take moments about the C of G:

Clockwise = 60 t x 1 m = 60 t.m,   anti-clockwise = 40 t x 1.5 m = 60 t.m; proved !

To determine the location of the C of G in the Z direction.

Consider the whole problem turned through 90 degrees, use Z dimensions as the moment arms & take moments about the origin. See Fig 4-5.

The clockwise moments about our 0,0 origin = D1.Z1 + D2.Z2 = (60 t x 2 m) + (40 t x 6.667 m) = 386.667 t.m.

As there has to be zero nett moment, it has to be balanced by the anti-clockwise moment derived from the total weight of 100 t acting at the unknown Z distance.

Therefore $100z = 386.667$; $z = 3.86$ m

The location of the C of G in the Z direction is 3.86 m from the origin, i.e. 1.86 m vertically above D1 and 2.81 m vertically below D2.

<u>Example – by proportion method</u>

In cases where there are only a relatively few pieces, it is probably easier to figure out where the C of G is by proportion. When considering a combination of 2 pieces we know that the C of G of the assembly must lie somewhere on a 3D direct line joining the centers of gravity of the two constituent parts. Logic says that it will lie closer to the heavier end of that line. That is so and in fact <u>its location divides the line in inverse proportion to the weights.</u>

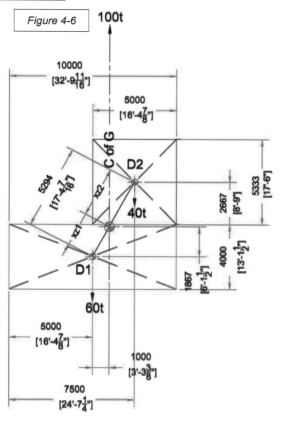

Figure 4-6

Looking at the duct section again (in the X,Z sense only in this case as we know Y is central), we can draw it to scale (by hand or CAD), mark the centers of gravity and measure the length of the line joining them. It is 5.294 m long. We know D1 weighs 60 t and D2 weighs 40 t; the total is therefore 100 t. D1 thus represents 60% of the total weight; D2 represents 40%.

By inverse proportion, the C of G therefore lies 40% of the line length from D1 and 60% of the line length away from D2. Therefore xz1 = 40% x 5.294 = 2.12 m and xz2 = 60% x 5.294 m = 3.18 m. Knowing this we can measure the X and Z dimensions, which come out at 1 m to the right of D1 and 1.86 m above it.

Alternatively, by calc.n, ΔX =40% x (X1-X2) = 0.4x2500 = 1000 mm. ΔZ=40% x (Z1-Z2) = 0.4 x 4667 = 1867 mm.

This directly agrees with the moment method.

If using CAD this graphical method can be quicker for simple assemblies than summing moments on a spreadsheet. If you have a 3rd component, you can then add that by similar method to the assembly of two so on. Much beyond 3 or 4, I would suggest you use a spreadsheet.

## 4.5 Weight control & report

To calculate the theoretical weight and C of G location of say a process skid comprising a structural box with a few items of plant, pipe and so on, a more sophisticated approach is needed.

First, it is necessary to establish a datum and co-ordinate system and identify everything in the skid or module, its weight and where it is (x,y,z) in reference to the datum. Using a spreadsheet (or a piece of paper and a calculator), the moment each component induces about the reference point can be calculated by multiplying its weight by its x,y,z coordinates. A running total can be kept of the weight and the three moments.

To determine the location of the C of G, the three cumulative moments are each divided by the cumulative weight to give the co-ordinates of the C of G referenced from the datum point.

You can design your spreadsheet to add steel members by length and wt/length, plate by some much volume at such a density, items by individual weights and so on.

Let's consider a structural box that looks something like the following schematic.

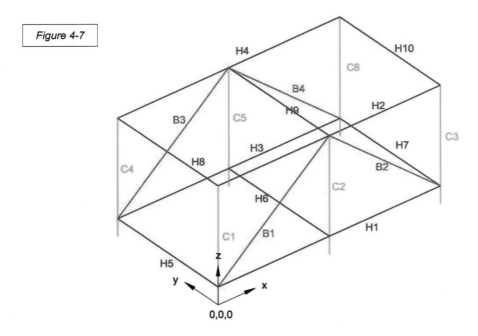

Figure 4-7

In this simple example, the calculation might well look like an expanded version of the following:

| | L(m) | kg/m | wt (kg) | x (m) | y (m) | z (m) | Mx (kg-m) | My (kg-m) | Mz (kg-m) |
|---|---|---|---|---|---|---|---|---|---|
| **Members** | | | | | | | | | |
| H1 | 12.2 | 238 | 2903.6 | 6.10 | 0.00 | 0.61 | 17711.96 | 0.00 | 1771.20 |
| H2 | 12.2 | 179 | 2183.8 | 6.10 | 0.00 | 5.80 | 13321.18 | 0.00 | 12666.04 |
| H3 | 12.2 | 238 | 2903.6 | 6.10 | 6.10 | 0.61 | 17711.96 | 17711.96 | 1771.20 |
| H4 | 12.2 | 179 | 2183.8 | 6.10 | 6.10 | 5.80 | 13321.18 | 13321.18 | 12666.04 |
| H5 | 6.1 | 149 | 908.9 | 0.00 | 3.05 | 0.61 | 0.00 | 2772.15 | 554.43 |
| H6 | 6.1 | 149 | 908.9 | 6.10 | 3.05 | 0.61 | 5544.29 | 2772.15 | 554.43 |
| H7 | 6.1 | 149 | 908.9 | 12.20 | 3.05 | 0.61 | 11088.58 | 2772.15 | 554.43 |
| H8 | 6.1 | 149 | 908.9 | 0.00 | 3.05 | 5.80 | 0.00 | 2772.15 | 5271.62 |
| H9 | 6.1 | 149 | 908.9 | 6.10 | 3.05 | 0.61 | 5544.29 | 2772.15 | 554.43 |
| H10 | 6.1 | 149 | 908.9 | 12.20 | 3.05 | 5.80 | 11088.58 | 2772.15 | 5271.62 |
| C1 | 6.1 | 198 | 1207.8 | 0.00 | 0.00 | 3.05 | 0.00 | 0.00 | 3683.79 |
| C2 | 6.1 | 198 | 1207.8 | 6.10 | 0.00 | 3.05 | 7367.58 | 0.00 | 3683.79 |
| C3 | 6.1 | 198 | 1207.8 | 12.20 | 0.00 | 3.05 | 14735.16 | 0.00 | 3683.79 |
| C4 | 6.1 | 198 | 1207.8 | 0.00 | 6.10 | 3.05 | 0.00 | 7367.58 | 3683.79 |
| C5 | 6.1 | 198 | 1207.8 | 6.10 | 6.10 | 3.05 | 7367.58 | 7367.58 | 3683.79 |
| C6 | 6.1 | 198 | 1207.8 | 12.20 | 6.10 | 3.05 | 14735.16 | 7367.58 | 3683.79 |
| B1 | 9.5 | 80 | 760 | 3.05 | 0.00 | 10.50 | 2318.00 | 0.00 | 7980.00 |
| B2 | 9.5 | 80 | 760 | 9.15 | 0.00 | 10.50 | 6954.00 | 0.00 | 7980.00 |
| B3 | 9.5 | 80 | 760 | 3.05 | 6.10 | 10.50 | 2318.00 | 4636.00 | 7980.00 |
| B4 | 9.5 | 80 | 760 | 9.15 | 6.10 | 10.50 | 6954.00 | 4636.00 | 7980.00 |
| | **A (m2)** | **kg/m2** | | | | | | | |
| **Deck plate** | 74 | 60 | 4440 | 6.10 | 3.05 | 0.91 | 27084.00 | 13542.00 | 4040.40 |
| **Equip.t** | | Valve V1 | 5000 | 8.00 | 2.1 | 4.1 | 40000.00 | 10500.00 | 20500.00 |
| **TOTALS** | | | 35355 | | | | **Moments** 225165.50 | 103082.75 | 120198.57 |
| | | | **Tot wt (kg)** | | | | /tot wt 35355.00 | 35355.00 | 35355.00 |
| | | | | | | | C of G 6.37 | 2.92 | 3.40 |
| | | | | | | | x (m) | y (m) | z (m) |

In instances such as lifting an oil rig module offshore with a floating crane, knowing the weight and C of G location is particularly vital and a sophisticated weight control program will be instigated during the design and fabrication of the module. Everything that goes into the module will be tracked and they will weigh the module several times including immediately before loadout. Normally weight control will include allowances for rolling tolerances and the like and reality may differ slightly from the prediction.

Note: If modeling a structure in a structural design program such as TEKLA or STAAD PRO, it will likely be able to give you the C of G location of your design directly.

## 4.6   Determining C of G location by weighing

If we decided to weigh our skid using strain gauge load cells, we might have got support reactions similar to this.

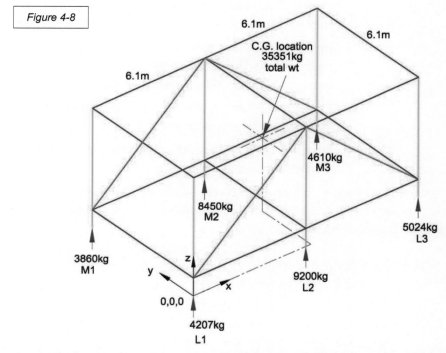

Figure 4-8

If we do a moment calculation about our origin in the x and y directions using our measured support reactions as shown below, we can calculate the X and Y coordinates of the C of G.  ($X = m_x / wt$,   $Y = m_y / wt$).

|     | x (m) | y (m) | wt (kg) | mx | my |
|-----|-------|-------|---------|----|----|
| L1  | 0     | 0     | 4207    | 0       | 0     |
| L2  | 6.1   | 0     | 9200    | 56120   | 0     |
| L3  | 12.2  | 0     | 5024    | 61292.8 | 0     |
| M1  | 0     | 6.1   | 3860    | 0       | 23546 |
| M2  | 6.1   | 6.1   | 8450    | 51545   | 51545 |
| M3  | 12.2  | 6.1   | 4610    | 56242   | 28121 |
|     |       |       | 35351   | 225199.8 | 103212 |
|     |       |       |         |         |       |
|     |       | X(m)  | **6.37** | **2.92** |

Note: If the structure is stiff and the supports also stiff, the load reactions can jump around between supports. It is important to raise the load very evenly; ideally remote reading stroke indicators are used at each support. The C of G calculation will yield the same answer but you can overstress the module or overload the jacks / strain gauges if not careful.

Short of turning the module on its side and weighing it again, you can't determine the Z coordinate by weighing. However, this is usually not as critical to know accurately.

# 5  Lifting Principles

## 5.1  Unassisted lifting

### 5.1.1  Direct lifting

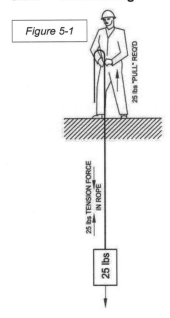

Figure 5-1

If you want to lift a relatively light load up to a working platform, it may be sufficient for you to position yourself on the platform, suspend a rope, tie it to the load and pull it up by hand.

Say you want to lift a 25 lb bag of scaffold clips. The tension in the rope will equal the weight of the bag (25 lbs); you will need to support that load. The platform supports you and the load. If you pull the rope up 1', the load will rise 1'. There is no mechanical advantage or speed change. You have done a certain amount of Work in lifting that bag up to the platform and there are no losses in the system.

Note: Work is the amount of energy transferred in moving a force through a distance. Work done = (force x distance) in units of Nm (also termed joules) or ft-lb. (Energy has the same units).

Power is the rate at which you do Work in units of Nm/s or watts; ft-lb/sec in U.S. customary units.

Energy is power x time which equates back to work. In electrical terms often measured as kWh.

The option of unassisted manual lifting is going to be severely limited; it won't work for you if the load gets a whole lot heavier than the example as you won't be able to pull that much. It won't be long before you start looking for some assistance to make life easier.

### 5.1.2  Making life easier with a diverter sheave.

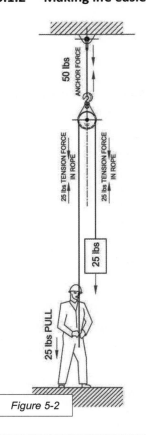

Figure 5-2

If you are going to lift 25 lb bags repetitively up to a platform by hand using a rope it may be easier and safer to use a pulley (single sheave block) attached to a suitably strong point above the platform and lead a rope from the ground over the pulley back to the ground to attach to the bag. This is like the system used in old barns where the ridge beam is extended to provide a point to attach a pulley allowing bales or whatever to be lifted up to a loading door on the raised storage floor.

By hauling in one end of the rope manually, you can raise the other end to which the load is tied. The tension in the rope is again the weight of the load (25 lbs in this case); the rope is continuous and the system assumed frictionless, so the tension is constant along the length of the rope. You need to pull a force equal to the weight of the load. If you pull the rope 1', the load rises 1'. There is no mechanical advantage or speed change. You have redirected your pulling effort from where you choose to stand to a point directly above where you want the load to go by use of a Diverter Sheave.

Although you have no mechanical advantage in lifting the load, what about the force required to anchor the pulley? Assuming the load is hanging plumb and you are pulling directly downwards, there is a tension in the rope equal to the load weight acting downwards on both sides of the sheave, therefore for the pulley to be in equilibrium, there has to be a resisting force acting directly upwards = 2 x the rope tension (provided by the anchor point and whatever it is attached to).

The anchor point has to support the 25 lbs load pulling down plus the 25 lbs you are pulling down = 50 lbs. The platform supports your weight (minus the 25-lbs uplift when you are pulling on the rope).

Note that in order to make sure the unloaded rope doesn't run up (and possibly through) the pulley block after you have detached the load at height you need to ensure that there is enough weight in shackles or whatever remaining on the "load" end of the rope.

## 5.2 Magnifying your manual effort

There are a number of ways in which the relatively puny effort (force) you can apply can be magnified to lift heavy objects.

### 5.2.1 Using levers

Levers are an ancient concept used from time immemorial to lift heavy blocks of stone etc.

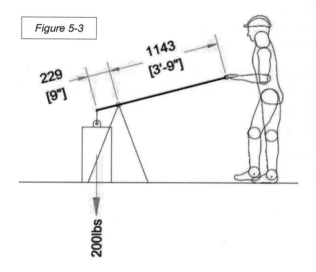

Figure 5-3

Archimedes apparently commented "Give me a place to stand and with a lever I will move the whole world". Of course he'd need something to react against, a suitable pivot (fulcrum), like Mars maybe.

Mind you, on the other hand Joseph Conrad apparently said, "Don't talk to me of your Archimedes' lever. He was an absentminded person with a mathematical imagination. Mathematics commands all my respect, but I have no use for engines. Give me the right word and the right accent and I will move the world."

This guy is using a lever supported on a pivot on a tripod to lift a 200 lb (990 kN) load. His lever has a 5:1 mechanical advantage, i.e. he is 5x further away from the pivot than the load is. He only has to apply 1/5th of the weight of the load to lift it.

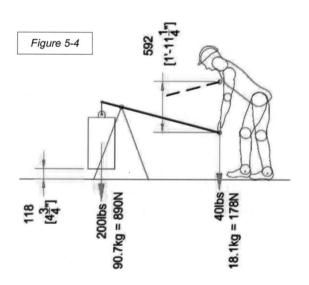

Figure 5-4

The load required is 40 lbs (178 N). Of course you get nothing for nothing and there is a downside – the load only lifts 1/5th of the distance he moves the handle end. He moves the handle about 2' to lift the load less than 5". This makes sense when you think in terms of the work done.

The work done at the handle end = 178 N x 0.592 m = 105 Nm. The work done at the load end = 890 N x 0.118 m = 105 Nm (equivalent to about 77.5 ft-lb).

The load only lifts at 1/5th the speed of the handle end, so the rate of doing work, i.e. the power requirement is reduced; the payback is slower lifting.

You'll find plenty of "levers" in use on cranes. In fact the whole mechanism of most construction cranes is basically a lever.

## 5.2.2  Gearing

Gears are simply rotary levers and another old principle.

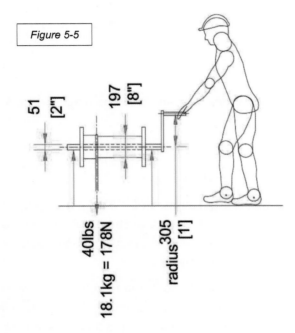

Figure 5-5

The cranked winding handle on a well is an example of leverage applied to a rotary application. The full bucket weighs say 40 lbs. The effective diameter of the winding shaft, given the rope stored on it at this time, is 8" (equivalent to a radius of 4"). The radius of the handle about the shaft is 12". This gives the worker a 3:1 mechanical advantage.

The torque applied to the shaft by the rope is 40 lbs x 8" = 26.7 ft-lbs. The torque the operator has to apply is this 26.7 ft-lbs = his effort x 1'. He therefore has to apply a force of 26.7 lbs. His hand though has to move through 3x the distance the rope pulls up.

When (nearly) all the rope is down the well, the shaft is virtually empty and the effective diameter may be only 2". He has to turn furiously at that time to get any rope pulled, but with little effort.

This is a primitive winch.

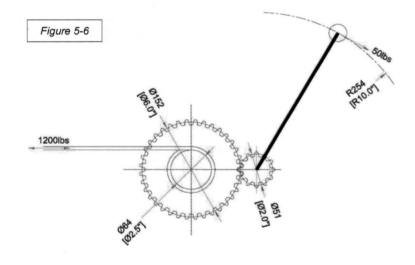

Figure 5-6

This represents a simple geared hand winch. The torque applied on the handle to the first gear = 50x10 = 500 lb-in. The 3:1 gear ratio increases the torque to 3x50 = 1500 lb-in. With an effective drum diameter of 2.5" (= 1.25' radius) you can pull 1500/1.25 = 1200 lbs.

Although you have amplified your effort 24x, you only pull in $1/24^{th}$ of the distance you move the handle; it's a lot of hard work. Before long you've decided to dispense with the handle and fit a drive motor. This is the basis of all winches fitted to cranes.

### 5.2.3 Hydraulics

Hydraulics are another ancient concept for amplifying effort; there's really nothing fundamentally new in lifting.

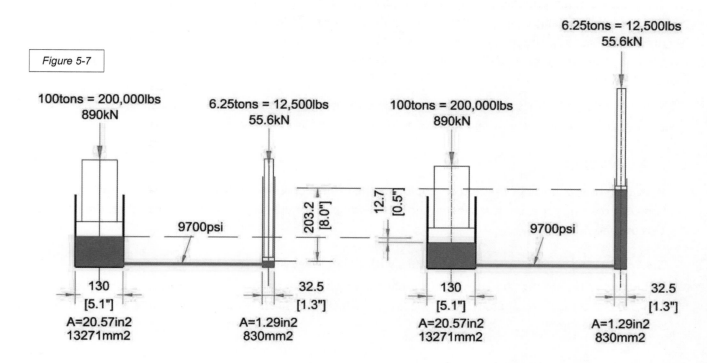

Figure 5-7

A hydraulic cylinder jack (left of each graphic) comprises a cylinder (closed at one end) in which a sealed plunger operates. Hydraulic fluid introduced (or released) under pressure into the closed volume beneath the plunger head will cause the plunger to extend or retract. Cylinder jacks may be single acting i.e. extends under pressure – retracts under external load; double acting – may be pressurized to extend or retract (plunger rod end is also sealed to cylinder) or single acting spring return. The static pressure supporting the plunger = the load / the effective area of the cylinder.

In this example, a 100 ton capacity single-acting jack has a diameter of 5.1" and an effective area of 20.57". The pressure in the system to support a load of 100 tons (200,000 lbs) = 200,000/20.57, approximately = 9700 psi. High tonnage rams are typically rated at about 10,000 psi.

In metric, 100 tons (U.S.) = 90.7 t or 890 kN; pressure = $890 \times 10^3 / 13271 = 67.1$ N/mm$^2$ = 671 bars.

Note: 1 bar = 14.5 psi. Atmospheric pressure is about 14.7 psi (1.013 bars). It varies a bit as we know.

To raise the load, fluid is pumped into the ram. The pump can be thought of as a smaller cylinder jack – somewhat like a bicycle pump. The pump and ram are piped together with a fixed volume of oil in the system. The pump has a diameter ¼ the diameter of the jack and thus an area $1/16$th of the jack area. The load required to develop 9700 psi in the pump is therefore only $1/16$th the load supported on the jack. i.e. 6.25 tons or 12,500 lbs. Check, 12,500 lbs / 1.29 in = 9,700 psi.

So 6.25 tons supports 100 tons, but as usual there is a downside. The work in the system is constant; when pumping, the displaced volume only results in the load rising $1/16$th of the stroke of the pump. e.g. 8" stroke of the pump results in the load lifting ½". Ignoring losses, the work is the same.

When working a jack with a hand pump, the pump will have a lever to amplify the load applied to the pump piston and there will be a check valve in the system to hold the load as the pump is retracted for another stroke and a valve to allow fresh fluid from a reservoir into the system prior to the next stroke.

This of course is a lot of hard work. For anything more than a slow inch or two, you are likely going to use a motorized pump. High pressure pumps often use a swash plate design using multiple pistons. The swash plate is inclined relative to the shaft of the pump and affixed to it, so that as the shaft rotates the plate "wobbles". The individual pump elements (typically six) are arranged around the shaft bearing on the swash plate. The wobble (which is angle dependent) causes the pistons to stroke back and forth in their cylinders developing pressure. Typically, the pistons are finger sized and don't individually contribute huge volumes per stroke, but the speed of operation makes up for that. Volume flow can often be adjusted by altering the angle of the swash plate.

You will find high pressure hydraulics and rams on most cranes these days. Transmission of energy is an advantage of hydraulics; you can do work one place and readily use it somewhere else.

## 5.3   Reeving

Reeving a rope is another method of amplifying the effort applied – as extensively used on sailing ships. If the rope is a running rope, i.e. it moves rather than a static rope such as a stay or guy wire, then the pay-back is a loss of speed.

### 5.3.1   Getting some mechanical assistance with a simple reeving arrangement.

If the load is heavier than you can comfortably & safely manage to lift using your unassisted muscle power, you can use some mechanical assistance. One way in which you might do this is by adding an additional sheave block as shown here.

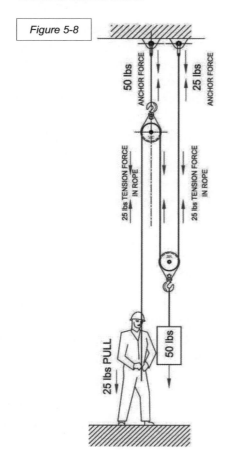

Figure 5-8

Going back to the man with his scaffold clips, in this case he wants to lift a 50 lb load but keep the pull down to 25 lb. As previously the rope (load line) is led over an anchored diverter sheave; now however the load line is fed through a second single sheave block attached to the load; the end of the load line is anchored adjacent to the diverter sheave anchor which acts as a Traveling Block. Considering the forces acting on the traveling block; the 50 lb load is supported by 2 parts of line. As the sheave is free to rotate, the tension in the line must be constant at 50% of the load = 25 lbs. This tension is constant throughout the "frictionless" system. Therefore, the dead end of the wire applies a load of 25 lbs to its fixed anchor point. The load line passes over the diverter sheave applying 2 x 25 lb downwards forces that require a single 50 lb anchor for that sheave. The man pulling the rope has to apply 25 lbs which will lessen his apparent weight by the same amount.

It is necessary to make sure that he, or the equivalent lifting machine performing that function, is anchored down by deadweight or tie-downs sufficient to resist the uplift with generous reserve.

50 lbs is now lifted by applying 25 lbs of pull, doubling the applied effort. However, nothing is free; every 1' that he hauls in on the rope shortens the suspension length by 1' / 2 parts of line = 6". The effort is doubled, but the height raised is halved.

### 5.3.2 Multi-sheave arrangements

To lift heavier and heavier loads while keeping the pulling force (winch effort) relatively low, this principle can be continued adding more and more sheaves and parts of line creating a reeving system.

The load that can be raised = the number of parts of line supporting the traveling block x the load line tension.

The distance lifted = the amount of load line pulled in / the number of parts of line supporting the traveling block.

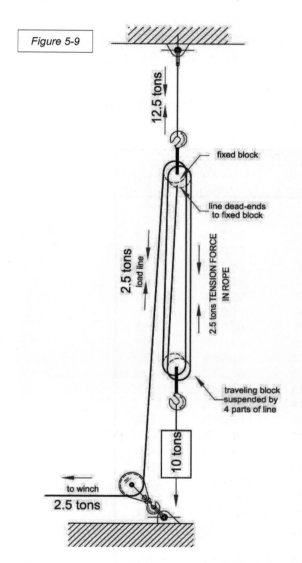

Figure 5-9

12.5 tons

fixed block

line dead-ends to fixed block

2.5 tons load line

2.5 tons TENSION FORCE IN ROPE

traveling block suspended by 4 parts of line

10 tons

to winch
2.5 tons

In this case 10 ton loads are to be lifted using a 3 ton winch. To keep the tension in the line less than 3 tons, it is decided to use 2 double-sheave blocks and 4 parts of line. The load line is dead-ended to the fixed block. The traveling block is suspended by 4 parts, so the line tension is 10 tons / 4 = 2.5 tons (nominally). This is adequately conservative for a winch rated at 3 tons.

The traveling block is in equilibrium, 4 parts of line x 2.5 tons acting upwards, 10-tons acting downwards. No side loads or moments.

The fixed block has 4 parts of line x 2.5 tons acting downwards PLUS 2.5 tons acting almost vertically = 12.5 tons acting downwards; therefore the required anchor force for the fixed block is 12.5 tons. The rigging self-weight is ignored for the example.

Note when counting parts of line to figure line tension, it is only the parts supporting the traveling block you count, the load line from the winch to the fixed block is not counted as it is not contributing to supporting the traveling block.

The load line is diverted at ground level to approach the winch horizontally. The winch has to pull 2.5 tons; therefore its fixings are subject to a horizontal shear of 2.5 tons. There will be some overturning to account for in designing the winch fixings too as the 2.5 tons acts some distance above the base.

As there are 4 parts of line, the load lifts $1/4^{th}$ of the amount of line winched in.

The method of determining the lower diverter sheave restraint force and its direction is discussed later.

### 5.3.3    Losses in reeving systems

In practice, when a reeving system is active with line running through it, there are losses deriving from friction in the sheave bearings and from the energy expended in bending the wire / internal friction in the wire. No reeving system is 100% efficient i.e. in a running system you don't get as much useful work out of it as you put into it. Assuming your max winching effort to be fixed, because of losses, you will need to use more parts of line to get the lifting effort you want.

The loss of efficiency may not be significant when only considering a few parts of line, but the losses are cumulative. With bronze-bushed sheaves, leading the line over 1 sheave, i.e. 1 part of line, you get about 96% of your input force as output. Thereafter, every time you add another part, you get 98% or so output to input. So with 2 parts, your output is 98% x 96% = 94% of your original input; bend it again to give 3 parts and your output is 98% x 94% = 92% of original input and so on.

The results for blocks using bronze bushes and for those using low friction bearings are tabulated below.

| Figure 5-10 | BRONZE BUSHES | | | LOW FRICTION BEARINGS | | |
|---|---|---|---|---|---|---|
| | actual parts | cumulative efficiency | force multiplier | actual parts | cumulative efficiency | force multiplier |
| | 1 | 96.00% | 0.96 | 1 | 98.00% | 0.98 |
| | 2 | 94.08% | 1.88 | 2 | 97.07% | 1.94 |
| | 3 | 92.20% | 2.77 | 3 | 96.15% | 2.88 |
| | 4 | 90.35% | 3.61 | 4 | 95.23% | 3.81 |
| | 5 | 88.55% | 4.43 | 5 | 94.33% | 4.72 |
| | 6 | 86.78% | 5.21 | 6 | 93.43% | 5.61 |
| | 7 | 85.04% | 5.95 | 7 | 92.54% | 6.48 |
| | 8 | 83.34% | 6.67 | 8 | 91.67% | 7.33 |
| | 9 | 81.67% | 7.35 | 9 | 90.79% | 8.17 |
| | 10 | 80.04% | 8.00 | 10 | 89.93% | 8.99 |
| | 11 | 78.44% | 8.63 | 11 | 89.08% | 9.80 |
| | 12 | 76.87% | 9.22 | 12 | 88.23% | 10.59 |
| | 13 | 75.33% | 9.79 | 13 | 87.39% | 11.36 |
| | 14 | 73.83% | 10.34 | 14 | 86.56% | 12.12 |
| | 15 | 72.35% | 10.85 | 15 | 85.74% | 12.86 |
| | 16 | 70.90% | 11.34 | 16 | 84.93% | 13.59 |
| | 17 | 69.48% | 11.81 | 17 | 84.12% | 14.30 |
| | 18 | 68.09% | 12.26 | 18 | 83.32% | 15.00 |
| | 19 | 66.73% | 12.68 | 19 | 82.53% | 15.68 |
| | 20 | 65.40% | 13.08 | 20 | 81.74% | 16.35 |
| | 21 | 64.09% | 13.46 | 21 | 80.97% | 17.00 |
| | 22 | 62.81% | 13.82 | 22 | 80.20% | 17.64 |
| | 23 | 61.55% | 14.16 | 23 | 79.44% | 18.27 |
| | 24 | 60.32% | 14.48 | 24 | 78.68% | 18.88 |

i.    To determine the lifted load knowing line pull and parts of line used,

Output (load on traveling block) = Winch line pull x parts of line x cumulative efficiency

For example, if using a bronze-bushed sheave block with 10 t line pull & 10 parts of line; with 10 parts, mechanical efficiency is 80%, therefore the load that may be lifted on traveling block = 10 x 10 x 80% = 80 t (as against 100 t if it were frictionless).

ii.    To work out the required parts of line, knowing the required lift load and the line pull, firstly figure out by how much you want the input line multiplied.

Required force multiplier = Load to lift / winch line pull

To lift 100 t with a winch line pull of 10 t requires a force multiplication of 10. If using bronze bushes, look down the force multiplier until a multiplier greater than 10 is found. That will show 14 parts are required. If using low-friction bearings, 12 parts are needed.

iii. To figure out the required line pull when the payload and parts of line are known, look up the parts of line in the first column, and then look up the appropriate force multiplier. Divide the load by the force multiplier.

For example, if lifting 100 t with 14 parts of line and bronze-bushed blocks, the multiplier is 10.34; the required line pull = 100 t / 10.34 = 9.7 t.

If lifting 100 t with 14 parts of line and low-friction blocks, the multiplier is 12.12; the required line pull = 100 t / 12.12 = 8.3 t.

### 5.3.4 Calculating anchor forces for diverter sheave (fairleads)

Whenever the direction of a loaded wire or rope is changed using a diverter sheave aka a fairlead, there is a force required to divert it; the wire would rather take the direct path between its two ends. The wire is trying to pull the fairlead into line and the fairlead and its anchor is holding the wire out of line in an equal and opposite manner. It is important to figure out the magnitude of the force to specify a suitably rated sheave block & associated rigging and to design the required anchor point.

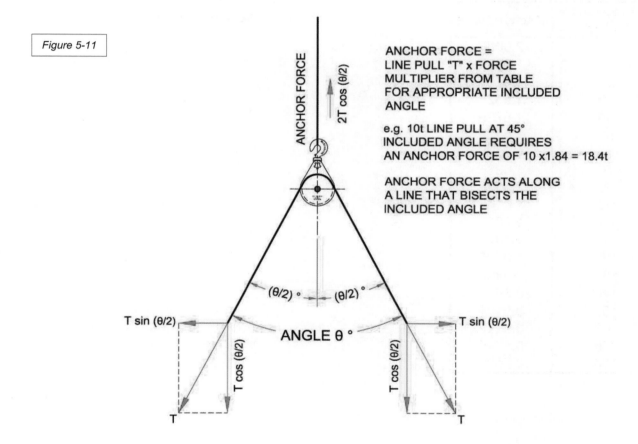

Figure 5-11

ANCHOR FORCE =
LINE PULL "T" x FORCE
MULTIPLIER FROM TABLE
FOR APPROPRIATE INCLUDED
ANGLE

e.g. 10t LINE PULL AT 45°
INCLUDED ANGLE REQUIRES
AN ANCHOR FORCE OF 10 x1.84 = 18.4t

ANCHOR FORCE ACTS ALONG
A LINE THAT BISECTS THE
INCLUDED ANGLE

The tension in the wire "T" is a constant through the pulley, equal either side. Under tension, the pulley will align itself and find equilibrium when the line of the anchor force equally bisects the included angle as shown above.

Considering the forces acting on the system;

> T (on either side) can be resolved into a component aligned with the anchor (shown vertical in this case)

> $= T \cos(\theta/2)$ and a component at 90° to that (horizontal here) $= T \sin(\theta/2)$ .

> The horizontal components are equal and opposite and cancel each other out; the two vertical components are opposed by the anchor force. Therefore the anchor force $= 2 T \cos(\theta/2)$

The anchor force is calculated for a range of included angles from 0° to 180° and is tabulated and shown graphically below.

If the included angle is 180°, the wire is not being diverted and the required force is zero. If the included angle is 0°, the 2 parts of wire are parallel and pulling directly in line with the anchor which therefore has to resist 2x the tension.

If the angle is 90°, then the anchor force is 1.414x the tension and the anchor force is aligned centrally at 45° to each.

Figure 5-12

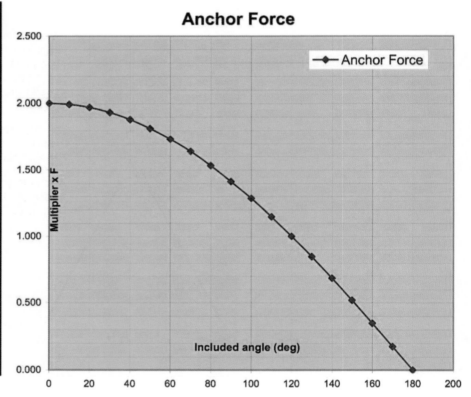

| Included angle θ (deg) | Anchor Force |
|---|---|
| 0 | 2.000F |
| 10 | 1.992F |
| 20 | 1.970F |
| 30 | 1.932F |
| 40 | 1.879F |
| 50 | 1.813F |
| 60 | 1.732F |
| 70 | 1.638F |
| 80 | 1.532F |
| 90 | 1.414F |
| 100 | 1.286F |
| 110 | 1.147F |
| 120 | 1.000F |
| 130 | 0.845F |
| 140 | 0.684F |
| 150 | 0.518F |
| 160 | 0.347F |
| 170 | 0.174F |
| 180 | 0.000F |

# 6 Powered lifting

As noted earlier, lifting things manually will only get you so far, and it won't be long before you want to apply some powered assistance to the issue. Powered winches with reeving arrangements are at the heart of most construction cranes. The most basic form applied to lifting is the "tugger" or base mounted drum hoist / winch.

## 6.1 Winch "tugger" basics

Figure 6-1

*Typical Ingersoll Rand air-driven "tugger".*

- Materials are sometimes lifted with base-mounted drum hoists / winches (commonly known as tuggers). Basic features of tuggers used for lifting are:
- a bed
- a flanged drum on which wire rope is stored
- a geared drive system powered by a prime mover such as an internal combustion engine, electric motor, compressed air or hydraulics to pay the wire out from the drum under load / pull it in
- a clutch (usually) to disengage the drive
- a brake mechanism
- a ratchet or pawl system to hold loads independent of the brake
- controls

Tuggers simply provide a hoisting mechanism; they need to be used in conjunction with a suitably strong support structure. Using diverter sheaves, the load line (wire rope) needs to be led (diverted) from wherever the tugger is installed over a sheave block anchored to a suitably strong anchor point at height directly above where the load is to be suspended. The load line will typically be terminated with a wedge socket to which the load can be attached using suitable rigging. It may be necessary to reeve the load line in order to get sufficient lifting effort in which case a stationary block will be used at height and a (multi)sheaved travelling block used at the load.

Tuggers are typically used in applications such as the construction of power station coal-fired boilers where they can be used to lift components high up into the boiler structure to locations inaccessible by crane. As most of the boiler elements hang from the structure there is usually plenty of strength at height to anchor to. The tugger would typically be installed at a lower level or at grade where it can conveniently be anchored.

Every application is unique and requires engineering to ensure adequacy of the system and the structure(s) to which it is applying load.

In the USA, ASME B30.7 is the relevant industry standard applying to their design and use. Note particularly the testing requirements therein, note also that this standard does not apply to hoists or winches used exclusively in horizontal pulling applications or personnel hoisting systems, to which special provisions apply. See ANSI A10.4.

### 6.1.1 Unreeved systems

In its simplest form, the arrangement may be something like the following sketch.

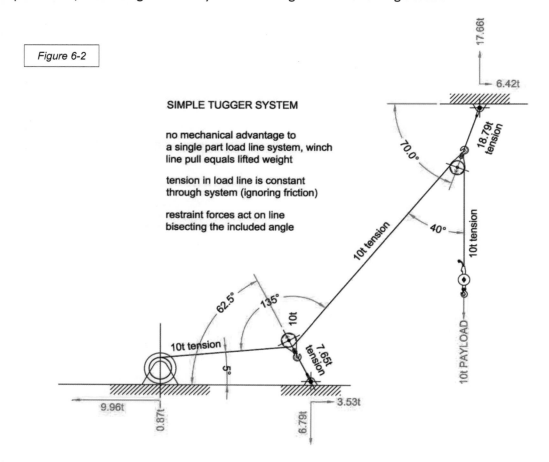

Figure 6-2

SIMPLE TUGGER SYSTEM

no mechanical advantage to
a single part load line system, winch
line pull equals lifted weight

tension in load line is constant
through system (ignoring friction)

restraint forces act on line
bisecting the included angle

In this case, a 10 t payload is to be lifted into a boiler using a single drum base-mounted hoist (tugger) system. The tugger is rated to lift 11 t at all layers at 5:1 Safety Factor, the 1.125" wire to be used is rated for 13 t at 5:1 S.F.

The tugger is installed on a lower floor and anchored down. A fairlead (lead sheave) is provided at the specified distance from the winch to ensure the wire spools correctly on the drum; this fairlead doubles as a diverter sheave to divert the wire high up into the boiler where an anchor point is provided on the boiler structure directly above the required installation point. A suitably rated ball and hook is attached to the end of the single unreeved line using a wedge socket.

Note the need for adequate weight (or alternative tension) on the line sufficient to overcome friction and provide adequate tension at the drum to ensure that the wire remains taut and spools on correctly. The weight of the block and hook is not considered for the purposes of illustration above, but in real life, you do need to consider it as load on the system.

The included angle at the fixed block (single sheave block in this case) is 40°. The line tension is 10t from the load (ignoring the block weight for the example) therefore, referring to the above table, the required anchor force is 1.879 x 10 = 18.79 t. It will act at ½ x 40° from vertical = 70° to the horizontal.

The sheave block, shackles & restraint sling all need to be rated for say 20 t min. The lug should also be rated for say 20 t acting at the angle shown and the structure checked for this load (at this angle). (Lug design and required factors are discussed elsewhere). The diverter sheave has an included angle of 135°, therefore the required restraint force and rating of the sheave and associated rigging = 0.765 x 10 t = 7.65 t acting at 62.5° to the horizontal. Here 10 t design rating would be reasonably conservative.

The tugger fixings need to withstand the 10 t line pull plus deal with rotation of the skid on which it is mounted deriving from the line of action of the rope being above the base.

As this is a lifting application, allowances for dynamic factors need to be considered and a greater degree of conservatism over those included in "normal" structural steel codes generally applied. Wrapping it up into one action, I'd recommend use of a 2x design factor then apply regular structural codes to give an adequate design basis for attachments and anchorages. This will give about 3:1 on yield on structural components.

### 6.1.2    Fleet angle

Note that for wire rope to spool evenly onto a winch drum in uniform layers with each wrap snug against the preceding, the angle at which the rope approaches the drum needs to be controlled within close limits by feeding the rope over a fixed guide (lead) sheave. The angle by which the rope deviates from being perpendicular to the drum face is called the Fleet Angle. If the fleet angle is too great, the rope will be crushed and abraded, whilst too small an angle will cause the rope to pile up. Experience has shown that keeping the fleet angle within the range 1.5° – 0.5° on smoothed drums and in the range 2.0° to 0.5° on grooved drums works best.

| Figure 6-3 |

### Fleet angle smooth & grooved drums

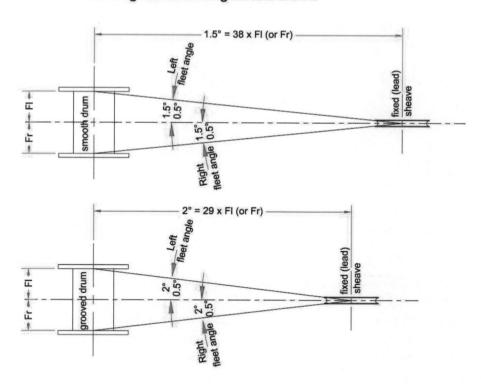

You should aim to locate the lead (fixed) sheave nominally centrally on the drum face and aligned perpendicular to it so that distances $F_l$ and $F_r$ are somewhat equal. It is recommended that the fleet angle to the left or right should not exceed 1.5° which requires the sheave to be at least 38x $F_l$ or $F_r$ (whichever is greater) away from the drum. It should not be more than 114x the greater of those distances away. In practice, keep it closer to the nearer end of the spectrum.

### 6.1.3   Reeved tugger systems

Air-driven tuggers are typically available up to about 10 t (11 ton) lifting capacity. To lift greater loads it is necessary to use a reeved system.

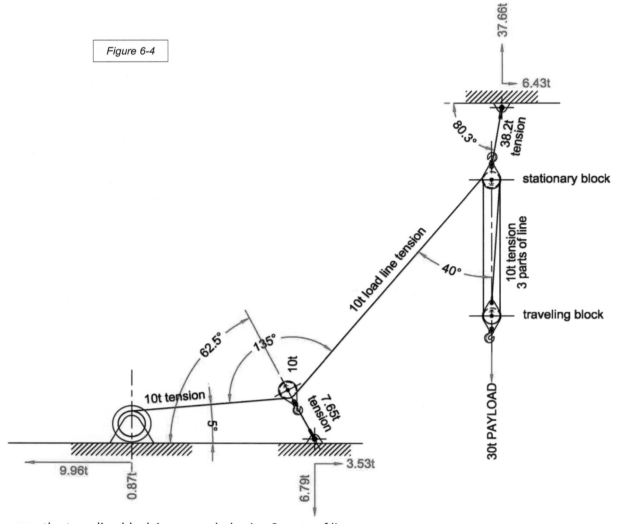

Figure 6-4

In this case, the traveling block is suspended using 3 parts of line.

In the above case, we have taken our basic system and substituted 2-sheave stationary and traveling blocks. We have reeved the two blocks to give us 3 parts of line to the traveling block with the load line dead-ended at the traveling block. The tension in the line (rope) is equal along its length, so with three parts supporting 30 t, the load line tension = 30/3 = 10 t (ignoring friction). To raise the load, each part of line supporting the block has to be shortened by the required amount, so the winch has to spool an amount of line equal to 3x the required lift height. i.e. 3x the lifting effort, $1/3^{rd}$ the lifting speed

The forces on the stationary block are the 30 t acting directly downwards and the 10 t lead line acting at 40° to the vertical. They can be resolved to an equivalent single force of 38.2 t acting at 9.7° off vertical. An equal and opposite restraint is required. Therefore the block, restraint sling, shackle, lug and structure all need to be rated for at least 40 t. The loads to the fairlead and winch are unchanged as the load line tension and geometry is unchanged.

## Example

The following is an extract from an arrangement used to lower a vertical pump down an access shaft in a power plant.

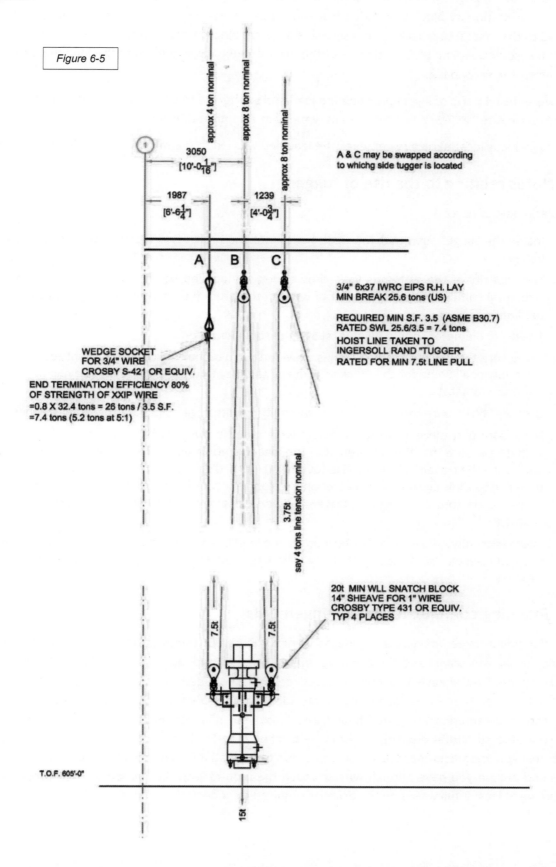

Figure 6-5

The pump weighed 15 tons and had two lift lugs; there was a 7.5 ton capacity tugger already located on a lower level, equipped with sufficient ¾" wire rope to 4-part the suspension from the roof to the ground.

Rather than using single multi-sheave stationary and traveling blocks, we elected to take the load line over a single sheave stationary block suspended from a roof beam directly over one lift lug, round a travelling block attached to the first lift lug, back up to a second stationary block located centrally over the pump's drive shaft, back to a second traveling block attached to the other lift lug and dead-ended the load line at the roof beam directly over the second lug.

There were thus 4 parts of line supporting the load and so the line tension was nominally 3.75 tons. The tugger and wire were rated at 7.5 tons which meant working at a comfortable 50%.

As the tugger was located on a lower level, the load line was led to the roof level over diverter sheaves.

## 6.2 Notes relating to the use of tuggers

Particular points of note:

- Install the tugger such that the fleet angle onto the drum is correct so that it spools correctly – see below
- The capacity of the system is limited by either, the applied power, rope or rigging capacity, reeving, structural competence, the amount of wire on the drum (i.e. effective diameter of the drum). Rate to the limiting factor.
- The drum diameter should be at least 18x the rope diameter.
- Make sure the drum can store (and is provided with) sufficient rope to account for the falls of wire in the reeving, allowing for the block to come all the way to the ground whilst leaving adequate wraps on the drum (at least 2).
- Use 6x37 IWRC wire rope, rated at 5:1 when <u>lifting</u> with tuggers (3.5:1 is permissible only for pulling).
- Make sure that there is always sufficient weight in the traveling block and the falls of rope associated with it to ensure that the self-weight of the load line going up to the stationary block can't overcome it and cause the traveling block to rise (overhaul), particularly when there is no load on the block and the traveling block is close up to the stationary block – it could run on you and rise uncontrollably, it may be necessary to use a weighted traveling block – but of course that weight comes off your useful lift capacity.
- There must always be adequate tension on the load line to ensure the rope spools correctly and tightly onto the winch drum, noting that the self-weight of the traveling block comes out of your useful capacity.

## 6.3 Planning complex tugger arrangements

When planning a tugger lift, you are going to want to figure out the location of the tugger(s), the location of the load suspension points and the anchor points to be used, the location of the fairleads, the path the load line takes to the fixed sheave & diverter sheaves required, the required reeving to support the loads. You need to evaluate the loads in the various components, identify & specify the rigging tackle required, identify anchor points and their required rating, and finally sketch out your plan schematically. A competent person such as the responsible structural engineer, may need to check the loadings you intend to impose into the points (structures) you are anchoring to, to ensure you don't overload it locally or globally. Check the winch and wire ratings and ensure you have enough wire to reach the ground with the number of falls proposed whilst still maintaining at least 2 full wraps on the drum as required by code, (preferably several more than that).

The following sketch schematically represents <u>one half</u> of a tugger arrangement used in a boiler to raise a wall panel. The North side is shown; the South (not shown) is the mirror image. One each side of the boiler, a double drum air hoist is provided. Each drum is rated for a line pull of 22,000# (10 t). The hoists are located on one of the lower levels of the boiler and the skid on which it is mounted is bolted down to the permanent steel. Each load line is led over a fairlead, then via various diverter sheaves to a stationary sheave high in the boiler directly over the wall panel header. The line is then taken to a single sheave traveling block shackled to the header and then back to a separate anchor point where it is dead-ended. Each of the four lines of support thus has 2 parts of line associated with it, giving 80 t total hoisting effort. The panels weighed 50 t. The "I" sections shown represent permanent steel. The restraint anchor forces need to be evaluated at each point where the load line is diverted or anchored and the permanent structure checked out for those forces. At some points, suitably "softened" slings may be basketed around the steel; at others welded lugs are required.

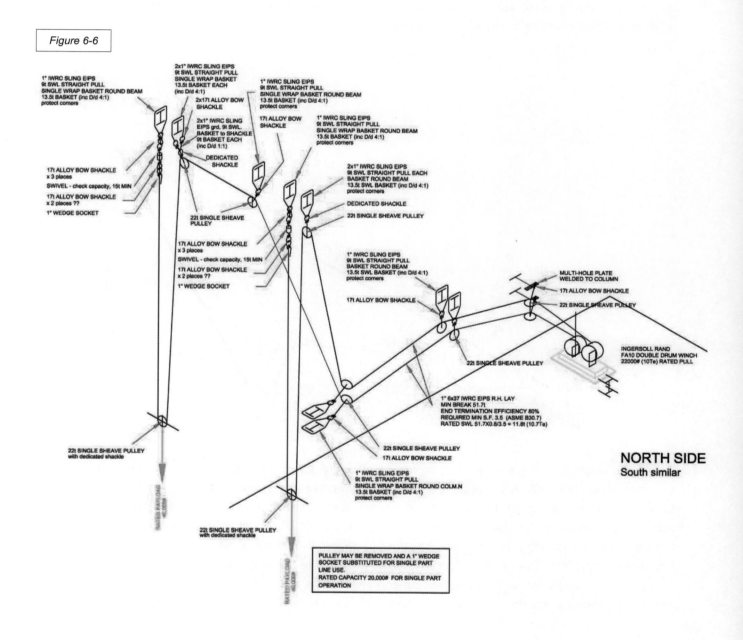

Figure 6-6

# 7 Basics of cranes and derricks

## 7.1 Fundamentals

As lifting machines, all Construction Cranes and Derricks share two basic features:

a) A structure that provides a suitably strong point at height from which a pay load can be suspended. This point is usually movable in space under load allowing the suspended payload to be relocated.

b) A powered hoisting mechanism, typically one or more winches, allowing the payload to be hoisted towards / lowered from, the strong point.

The simplest construction crane or derrick is basically just a reeved tugger system in which the tension anchor point for the stationary block is replaced by a stayed compression member (boom in crane parlance). A back stay is required to resist the clockwise moment on the compression member deriving from the 18.79 t resolution of the load line forces acting on a line outside the base pivot point.

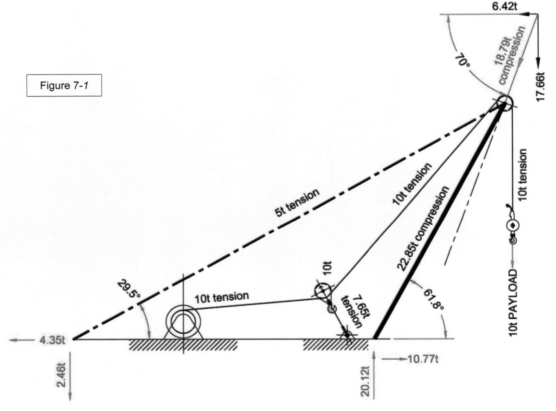

Figure 7-1

The above arrangement is such as you might find on a wrecker or tow truck; the winch, fairlead and load line are unchanged from the first tugger example. However, we don't have a suitable anchor point in the sky. Instead, a boom is provided; the boom head incorporates a sheave over which the load line is led. The boom acts as a compression member and (in this case) is fixed at 61.8° restrained by a back stay. The resolution of the two 10 t forces acting on the head sheave is a single 18.79 t force acting at 20° off vertical (70° to the horizontal). Note that this resolved force needs to act outside the angle formed between the boom and back stay in order to keep the back stay in tension and ensure that the boom is not pulled over backwards. For this particular geometry, for the 10 t payload shown, the force in the back stay is 5 t and the boom compression is 22.9 t.

More sophisticated designs have adjustable length back stays allowing the boom angle to be altered under load changing the distance of the load from the "crane". If the whole arrangement is mounted on a carrier on a large bearing, it can be designed to swing (slew) under load to relocate the suspended payload.

## 7.2 Evolution

*Basic crane* - from the very basic arrangement shown above it's a fairly short evolution to a basic strut-boom derrick or crane.

The fundamental elements are:

- A boom structure (typically lattice and adjustable in length by means of fixed length inserts), pivoted at its base.

- A means of tying back the head of boom to prevent it overturning. The length of this tension element is usually variable to allow the boom to luff up and down (change its operating angle) under load, thus altering the distance of the load from the crane. Typically a boom luffing arrangement incorporates fixed pendant ropes attached to a reeving system allowing adjustment of the boom angle using one of the crane's winches.

- A hoisting system comprising multiple parts of load line reeved between a stationary block on the boom head and a travelling block to which the load is attached. The load line is led down the boom to a winch mounted on the crane's superstructure; by operating the hoist winch, the load is raised / lowered; hoisting effort is adjusted using more or less parts of line in the reeving.

- A counterweight system; the whole mechanism is subject to overturning as the imposed load is outside the base of the machine, hence there is uplift to the rear of the machine and a down-thrust at the front; counterweight (or some form of tie-down system) is required to oppose this.

- Some form of superstructure to carry the base of the boom, carry the counterweight, provide mounting points for the various winches and reeving systems; it has to resist the moments and forces induced.

- If the crane is required to swing with the load (slew), then the superstructure (upper works) will be mounted on the carrier (lower works) via a slew ring (bearing) with a geared drive system to provide the slewing motion. The carrier may be static and use outriggers to transfer the loads and moments into the ground or, if the whole machine is required to move under load, crawler tracks or wheels may be used – or even skids. The carrier has to distribute the loads imposed by the crane into the surroundings, often crane mats or other forms of load distribution systems will be required to further distribute them down to pressures that the ground can withstand.

Figure 7-2

The above vintage photo of an early Bigge rig lifting what is believed to be a Steam Generator vessel for the Palisades project (origin of photo unknown, please accept my apologies for lack of credit) shows the basic elements referred to in a specially designed heavy lift rig. I'm not sure whether to call it a luffing gin pole system, crane, derrick or gallows frame.

There are twin lattice booms each hinged in an "ink-well" type bearing (per gin pole practice); each ink-well is supported on the center of a crawler track, the boom feet are located and spaced apart using a lattice frame; each boom is stayed back from the head using reeved wire ropes to winches located on a rear tracked carrier; the rear carrier is located to the boom feet with a triangular lattice frame that takes out the horizontal compression forces from the boom feet and the luffing gear. Spanning the heads of the booms is a lifting beam supported via bearings that allow it to find its own line while loading the booms axially. A stationary block is suspended from the center of the lifting beam via a swivel; a travelling block is reeved to the stationary block, the load line(s) are taken back to winch(es) on the rear carrier.

The load can be hoisted with the hoist line, luffed up and down by adjustment of the boom hoist reeving and crawled directly forward using the tracked carriers. It can't easily slew (swing).

*Lampson Transi-Lift* - many elements of the preceding can be seen in the evolution of the Lampson Transi-Lift heavy lift cranes.

Figure 7-3

Figure 7-4

To the left, there is a single main boom, lattice construction, adjustable length (using pinned insert sections). The boom foot is carried on a crawler carrier; counterweight is carried on a trailing carrier, the two carriers are connected by a lattice spar frame. In this case instead of the luffing gear going directly from the rear carrier to the boom head at a flat angle, a back mast is provided to obtain better leverage. The tip of the back mast is directly over the counterweight carrier and is attached to it; the luffing gear works between the tip of the back mast and the boom head. For better reach for lighter loads, a fixed fly jib is fitted to the boom head; back stays allow for fixed length pendants to secure the jib. The whole machine can be crawled under load. Slewing of the load is possible to a limited extent by orientating the crawler carriers in different directions and driving them independently. See the photo on the right; the main carrier is tracking along the mats, whilst the rear carrier is moving basically left to right.

*Heavy lift "cranes" using strand jacks*

Figure 7-5

Figure 7-6

Another direction taken in the evolution of heavy lift machinery was the development of ring mounted "cranes" using strand jacks to lift. The Mammoet MSG is such a case. Twin booms arranged as an A-frame sit on slide bogies on a ring track support. Counterweight sits on the rear of the ring and is suspended from the tip of the two back masts. Luffing of the A-frame is by strand jacks from the tip of the back masts to the head of the A-frame. A fixed fly jib is fitted.

Lifting is not by winches but by strand jacks mounted on the jib head. The whole machine can slew by jacking the bogies around the track. This machine has elements of derricks, gin poles, luffing strand jack rigs, cranes.

Figure 7-7

ALE's SK190 and AK350 are heavy lift machines operating on these principles.

To lift between 4000 t and 5000 t, they use strand jacks (max. 4 x 1250 t strand jacks); for loads up to 4000 t, conventional winches may be used.

Again it has an A-frame boom and is mounted on skid tracks, but radically, the entire machine rotates about its own counterweight which is static. You may use only a segment of track if you do not require the full 360° of slew (swing).

It is not the intent to discuss cranes themselves in detail, that is covered well elsewhere, but to show that most construction cranes from the humblest to the mightiest rely on some basic principles of physics. This leads us to a basic comprehension of how the mechanism works, what types of loads act where and an understanding of what needs to be dealt with in distributing those loads into the surroundings.

## 7.3   Strut booms v telescoping (hydraulic) booms

### 7.3.1   Fundamentals

As we have looked at the basic elements of a crane and the evolution of construction cranes, we have so far only considered strut booms, i.e. booms that work in compression. There is another type in common use – the telescopic (hydraulic boom). This works in a different manner.

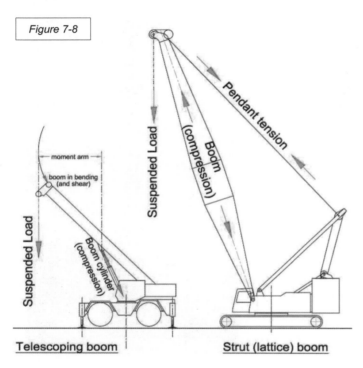

Figure 7-8

On a strut boom, the boom is restrained against overturning by pendants at its head. The resolution of forces acting at the boom head is opposed by the boom in compression. Forces are essentially axial. A lattice construction (sectional) boom is usually used as you make a very efficient long compression member that can be broken down for transport.

A telescopic boom is supported by its base hinge pin and an extendible ram pinned towards the top of base section. The boom sections telescope out from the base section to the required length. The entire boom beyond the boom cylinder is subject to bending and shear. In addition to those considerations, the designer has to limit boom tip deflection.

Telescopic booms are required to be light but relatively stiff with adequate strength. A lot of effort has been (and is being) expended to optimize this and there has been much evolution in boom design through the years.

Crawler mounted telescopic boom

Rough Terrain Crane with telescopic boom

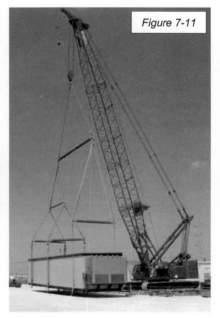

Lattice boom Crawler Crane

Telescopic booms are most usually found on wheel-mounted carriers (RTs, ATs, truck cranes) where mobility and speed of set up are important. Lattice booms are typically used on all other types of carriers such as crawlers, pedestals, rings. This is not exclusively so – as explained later.

### 7.3.2   Comparing capacity charts

If you are relatively new to lifting, you might imagine:

- That the nominal quoted capacity of a crane represents what it can lift, that for instance if you want lift 800 t, you need an 800 t crane
- That the rating charts for a telescopic boom crane are going to be somewhat similar to the rating charts for a lattice boom crane (all else being like-for-like)
- That one manufacturer's 90 t telescopic crane (say) is going to have very similar duty charts to another's 90 t telescopic crane, i.e. that if you have figured a certain manufacturer's 90 t machine will do the job, that procurement can find the cheapest "90 t crane" and it will be assured of being an equivalent substitute.

None of the above is likely to be true.

The first two bullets can be examined by looking at (and comparing) selected capacity charts for an outrigger mounted telescopic crane and a crawler mounted lattice boom crane. I've chosen to look at a Liebherr LTM1800 (800 t telescopic crane) and a Liebherr LR1800 (800 t crawler crane). This is an arbitrary choice for illustrative purposes and is not intended to imply anything good or bad about this manufacturer versus any other. As noted above, while you mostly find telescopic booms on wheel mounted carriers (using outriggers), they can be fitted to crawler carriers. Vice versa, lattice booms may be found sometimes on (usually older) wheel mounted carriers. I've chosen to compare what is more typical.

The charts selected are DIN standard charts based on 75% tipping criteria (more on this later) in basic lift crane configuration with full machine counterweight, without Superlift or any other enhancement accessory. I've looked at two boom lengths, the minimum and one of the longer telescopic boom lengths with a similar strut boom length. Note that the LR1800 can carry up to 112 m boom versus 60 m for the LTM1800, which may be a significant consideration.

This comparison exercise is only going to be meaningful to illustrate some fundamental differences and general trends from which we can derive some guidelines to help you in choosing an appropriate crane – at the end of the day you need to read the charts!

Note firstly that Liebherr chose to give an indication of their nominal capacity class in naming these machines. Both include "1800", both are considered to be 800 metric ton machines. Other manufacturers such as Demag have in the past attempted to give a more meaningful indication of capacity by naming their cranes by their nominal moment capacity. Note also that Liebherr indicate the greatest load-moment on the LR1800 is 12100 t-m (with Superlift) against 2750 t-m for the LTM1800 – a large difference.

# Lifting capacities on telescopic boom.

**LTM 1800**

19,3 m – 60 m | 360° | 160 t | DIN ISO

| m | 18 m | 19,3 m | 26 m | 31,6 m | 38,4 m | 44 m | 50,7 m | 56,4 m | 60 m | m |
|---|---|---|---|---|---|---|---|---|---|---|
| 3 | 800 | | | | | | | | | 3 |
| 4 | 550 | | | | | | | | | 4 |
| 5 | 450 | | | | | | | | | 5 |
| 6 | 390 | | | | | | | | | 6 |
| 6,5 | 360 | 350 | | | | | | | | 6,5 |
| 7 | 340 | 340 | 335 | | | | | | | 7 |
| 8 | 310 | 303 | 297 | 296 | | | | | | 8 |
| 9 | 278 | 268 | 263 | 262 | 260 | | | | | 9 |
| 10 | 250 | 240 | 235 | 234 | 233 | 210 | | | | 10 |
| 12 | 205 | 197 | 193 | 192 | 191 | 181 | 159 | | | 12 |
| 14 | 170 | 165 | 162 | 161 | 161 | 158 | 139 | 120 | 107 | 14 |
| 16 | 148 | 142 | 139 | 137 | 137 | 139 | 124 | 109 | 97 | 16 |
| 18 | 130 | 124 | 121 | 119 | 119 | 121 | 110 | 99 | 87 | 18 |
| 20 | | | 106 | 104 | 105 | 106 | 99 | 90 | 79 | 20 |
| 22 | | | 94 | 92 | 93 | 94 | 89 | 82 | 71 | 22 |
| 24 | | | 84 | 82 | 83 | 84 | 81 | 74 | 64 | 24 |
| 26 | | | | 73 | 74 | 75 | 74 | 67 | 58 | 26 |
| 28 | | | | 66 | 67 | 68 | 68 | 62 | 53 | 28 |
| 30 | | | | 60 | 60 | 61 | 63 | 57 | 49 | 30 |
| 32 | | | | | 55 | 56 | 58 | 53 | 45 | 32 |
| 34 | | | | | 50 | 51 | 53 | 49 | 42 | 34 |
| 36 | | | | | 45 | 46 | 49 | 46 | 38,5 | 36 |
| 38 | | | | | | 41,5 | 44,5 | 43 | 35,5 | 38 |
| 40 | | | | | | 37,5 | 40,5 | 40 | 33,5 | 40 |
| 42 | | | | | | | 37 | 37,5 | 31 | 42 |
| 44 | | | | | | | 34 | 35 | 29 | 44 |
| 46 | | | | | | | 31 | 32,5 | 27 | 46 |
| 48 | | | | | | | | 29,8 | 25 | 48 |
| 50 | | | | | | | | 27,3 | 23,5 | 50 |
| 52 | | | | | | | | | 22 | 52 |
| 54 | | | | | | | | | 21 | 54 |

Figure 7-12

TAB 79018

# Lifting capacities on L boom.

**LR 1800**

L 21 m – 112 m | 11,08 m x 10,8 m | 360° | 238 t | 142 t

| m | 21 m | 28 m | 35 m | 42 m | 49 m | 56 m | 63 m | 70 m | 77 m | 84 m | 91 m | 98 m | 105 m | 112 m | m |
|---|---|---|---|---|---|---|---|---|---|---|---|---|---|---|---|
| 6 | 650 | | | | | | | | | | | | | | 6 |
| 6,5 | 605 | | | | | | | | | | | | | | 6,5 |
| 7 | 580 | 520 | | | | | | | | | | | | | 7 |
| 8 | 520 | 510 | 500 | | | | | | | | | | | | 8 |
| 9 | 480 | 480 | 480 | 440 | 400 | 360 | | | | | | | | | 9 |
| 10 | 440 | 440 | 440 | 420 | 388 | 347 | 312 | 280 | | | | | | | 10 |
| 11 | 410 | 410 | 410 | 400 | 370 | 332 | 300 | 271 | 235 | 200 | | | | | 11 |
| 12 | 385 | 385 | 385 | 380 | 352 | 319 | 288 | 262 | 228 | 194 | 178 | 165 | | | 12 |
| 14 | 340 | 340 | 340 | 334 | 320 | 294 | 266 | 242 | 214 | 184 | 169 | 157 | 136 | 120 | 14 |
| 16 | 300 | 300 | 300 | 295 | 288 | 270 | 245 | 224 | 200 | 174 | 160 | 150 | 130 | 114 | 16 |
| 18 | 260 | 260 | 260 | 258 | 256 | 244 | 226 | 207 | 185 | 164 | 152 | 142 | 125 | 109 | 18 |
| 20 | 225 | 225 | 225 | 223 | 222 | 220 | 207 | 190 | 173 | 155 | 143 | 136 | 120 | 104 | 20 |
| 22 | | 200 | 200 | 198 | 197 | 196 | 190 | 177 | 161 | 146 | 137 | 129 | 114 | 99 | 22 |
| 24 | | 178 | 178 | 176 | 176 | 175 | 174 | 163 | 150 | 139 | 130 | 123 | 109 | 95 | 24 |
| 26 | | 160 | 160 | 158 | 158 | 158 | 157 | 152 | 140 | 131 | 122 | 117 | 104 | 90 | 26 |
| 28 | | | 147 | 146 | 146 | 145 | 145 | 142 | 131 | 125 | 116 | 112 | 99 | 86 | 28 |
| 30 | | | 137 | 135 | 135 | 134 | 134 | 132 | 123 | 119 | 110 | 107 | 95 | 82 | 30 |
| 32 | | | 130 | 127 | 126 | 125 | 125 | 122 | 116 | 113 | 106 | 103 | 91 | 79 | 32 |
| 34 | | | | 118 | 117 | 117 | 116 | 114 | 110 | 108 | 101 | 99 | 87 | 76 | 34 |
| 36 | | | | 112 | 112 | 111 | 109 | 109 | 104 | 102 | 96 | 95 | 83 | 73 | 36 |
| 38 | | | | 106 | 105 | 104 | 102 | 100 | 98 | 95 | 92 | 91 | 80 | 70 | 38 |
| 40 | | | | | 100 | 98 | 95 | 94 | 91 | 89 | 88 | 86 | 77 | 67 | 40 |
| 44 | | | | | 89 | 86 | 84 | 82 | 80 | 77 | 76 | 74 | 71 | 63 | 44 |
| 48 | | | | | | 77 | 74 | 72 | 70 | 68 | 66 | 64 | 62 | 59 | 48 |
| 52 | | | | | | | 66 | 64 | 62 | 60 | 58 | 56 | 54 | 51 | 52 |
| 56 | | | | | | | 60 | 58 | 55 | 53 | 51 | 49 | 47 | 45 | 56 |
| 60 | | | | | | | | 52 | 50 | 47 | 46 | 44 | 41 | 39 | 60 |
| 64 | | | | | | | | | 45 | 42 | 41 | 39 | 36 | 34 | 64 |
| 68 | | | | | | | | | 40 | 38 | 36 | 34 | 32 | 30 | 68 |
| 72 | | | | | | | | | | 34 | 32 | 30 | 28 | 26 | 72 |
| 76 | | | | | | | | | | | 29 | 27 | 24 | 22 | 76 |
| 80 | | | | | | | | | | | 26 | 24 | 21 | 19 | 80 |
| 84 | | | | | | | | | | | | 21 | 19 | 16 | 84 |
| 88 | | | | | | | | | | | | | 16 | 14 | 88 |
| 92 | | | | | | | | | | | | | 14 | 12 | 92 |
| 96 | | | | | | | | | | | | | | 10 | 96 |

Figure 7-13

Traglasten über 520 t nur mit Zusatzausrüstung
Lifting capacities above 520 t only with special equipment
Forces de levage plus de 520 t seulement avec équipement supplémentaire

TAB 57185

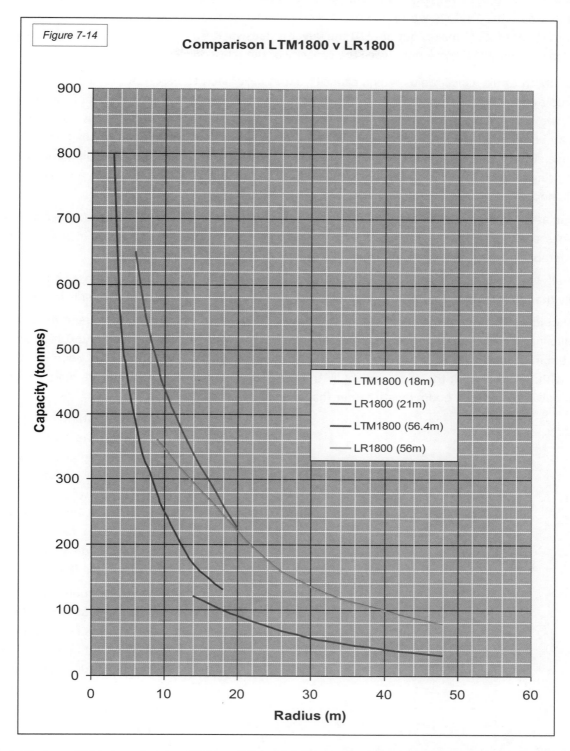

*Figure 7-14*

**Comparison LTM1800 v LR1800**

There is in fact an 800 t duty for the LTM machine with 160 t of machine counterweight at minimum boom length (18 m) and minimum radius (3 m) - the dark blue line above. However, apart from say tailing applications, there is nothing that weighs 800 t that is small enough to be lifted at 3 m radius; even if you could, what would you do with it? Capacity drops off rapidly with increase in radius; at 4 m, it has reduced to 550 t. At a relatively useful 10 m, it is only 250 t.

Generally speaking, when using a telescopic boom crane, to do anything useful you probably need to start looking at cranes with a "class" rating of at least 3x the load you need to lift.

Looking at the strut boom crane, the only place an 800 t duty can be found is when the crane is used with Superlift (that chart not shown here). The basic lift crane with minimum boom length of 21 m and machine counterweight of 238 t maxes out at 650 t, however it does so at 6 m rather than at 3 m. Its max radius is 20 m and it can still lift 225 t, more than twice the capacity of the telescopic boom crane.

If you intend to use close radius – high capacity duties, you need to be careful to check that crane (whether telescopic or strut) is equipped with a boom head (and hook-block) rated for the part of the chart you want to use. It would not be surprising to find that the 800 t telescopic crane in particular is equipped with a lesser capacity boom head (and less sheaves); after all why would they fit a heavy boom head for a duty you won't ever use.  In fact, the small print indicates that to lift over 520 t requires "special equipment". Also make sure when using long booms with maximum reeving that the crane is actually fitted with enough rope (hoist line) for the hook to reach the ground.

Looking at the curves for the longer boom lengths, (I used 56 m), you'll note that the lattice boom crane (red line) has a closer minimum radius of 9 m as against 14 m for the telescopic boom (brown line) and has considerably greater capacity across the board for like radii (about 2.5x as great).

Generally speaking the capacity of the telescopic boom crane drops off with increase in radius much more rapidly than that of the strut boom crane but it has the advantage of being quick to ready for work.

You should also note that the capacities of the cranes reduce with increase in boom length; however increase in radius has a much greater effect. e.g. the telescopic crane with 18 m boom can lift 250 t at 10 m radius, with 44 m boom it can still lift 210 t at 10 m radius; the strut crane can lift 225 t with a 21 m boom at 20 m radius and 220 t with 56 m boom at the same radius. If struggling to reach over the parapet of a building for instance, it might better to increase boom length rather than increase radius.

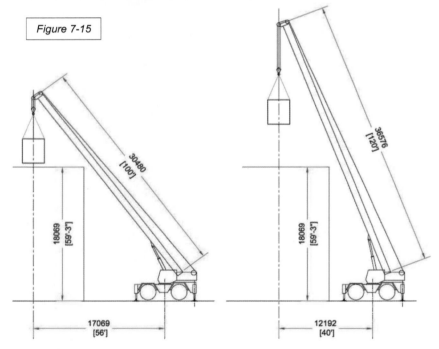

Figure 7-15

Here for instance a load has to be lifted onto the roof of a building and we can't make it using a jib. The least boom length we can make it with is 100' (33 m); we have to stand back at about 56' (17 m) radius to clear the parapet by a fairly minimal 3' (1 m) (neglecting deflections). Capacity is 20,900 lbs (9478 kg).

If we trade boom length for radius we can come in to 40' (12.1 m) radius and have greater clearance to the building. Although we lose capacity when increasing the boom length, we more than make it up by decreasing radius. Capacity is now 28,000 lbs (12698 kg).

It is always better to concentrate on minimizing radius and take the hit on boom length. There is an optimum there somewhere, find it!

Sometimes, paradoxically, with lattice booms you might find a better duty with a slightly longer boom. If so, it is likely due to the mix of "heavy" and "light" boom sections required to achieve those lengths. Check it out, it might save you!

### 7.3.3 Importance of understanding boom extension modes

If you are preparing a plan involving the use of a telescopic boom crane you need to know if the boom on that particular crane can be extended according to different modes as that can radically affect the capacity of the crane at a particular boom length.

As an example, on this particular chart the (5-section) boom can be extended according to three different modes, EM1, EM2 and EM3.

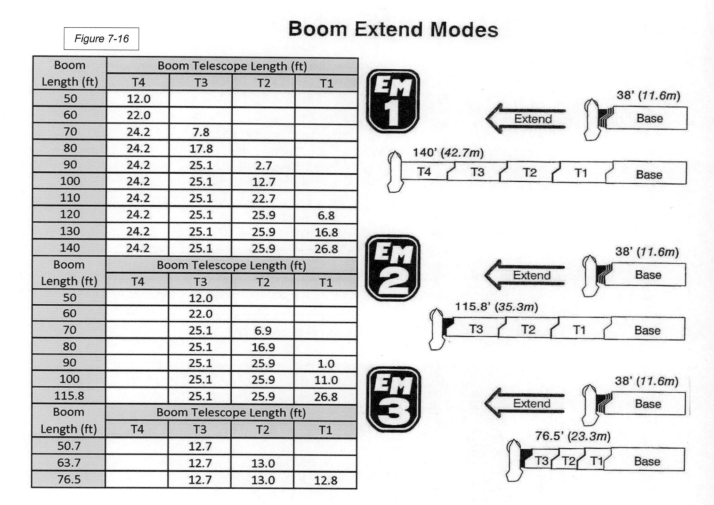

Figure 7-16

**Boom Extend Modes**

| Boom Length (ft) | Boom Telescope Length (ft) | | | |
|---|---|---|---|---|
| | T4 | T3 | T2 | T1 |
| 50 | 12.0 | | | |
| 60 | 22.0 | | | |
| 70 | 24.2 | 7.8 | | |
| 80 | 24.2 | 17.8 | | |
| 90 | 24.2 | 25.1 | 2.7 | |
| 100 | 24.2 | 25.1 | 12.7 | |
| 110 | 24.2 | 25.1 | 22.7 | |
| 120 | 24.2 | 25.1 | 25.9 | 6.8 |
| 130 | 24.2 | 25.1 | 25.9 | 16.8 |
| 140 | 24.2 | 25.1 | 25.9 | 26.8 |

| Boom Length (ft) | Boom Telescope Length (ft) | | | |
|---|---|---|---|---|
| | T4 | T3 | T2 | T1 |
| 50 | | 12.0 | | |
| 60 | | 22.0 | | |
| 70 | | 25.1 | 6.9 | |
| 80 | | 25.1 | 16.9 | |
| 90 | | 25.1 | 25.9 | 1.0 |
| 100 | | 25.1 | 25.9 | 11.0 |
| 115.8 | | 25.1 | 25.9 | 26.8 |

| Boom Length (ft) | Boom Telescope Length (ft) | | | |
|---|---|---|---|---|
| | T4 | T3 | T2 | T1 |
| 50.7 | | 12.7 | | |
| 63.7 | | 12.7 | 13.0 | |
| 76.5 | | 12.7 | 13.0 | 12.8 |

Looking at (say) 60' extension; in EM1 mode (a telescoping mode) it is arrived at by combination of the base section (38') plus 22' extension of the T4 (head section) only, which is the lightest. In EM2 mode, which is also a telescoping mode, it is arrived at by the base section (38') plus 22' extension of the T3 only (which is stronger). In EM3 mode, which is a fixed non-telescoping mode, 63.7' extension is arrived at by the base section (38') plus 12.7' extension of the T3 section and 13' of the T2 section. It makes a big difference to the capacities, particularly at close radii (as we'll see below). e.g. EM3 mode has twice the capacity compared to EM1 at 10' radius.

For the purpose of illustration I have prepared a capacity comparison (lbs) at approximately 60' boom extension for 360° duties, with full outriggers and full counterweight.

Following is a summary of the chart capacities (lbs) to be compared.

| Rad (ft) | 60' boom EM1 | 60' boom EM2 | 63.7' boom EM3 |
|---|---|---|---|
| 10 | 58000 | 96400 | 117900 |
| 12 | 53700 | 89500 | 108800 |
| 15 | 48400 | 79900 | 106500 |
| 20 | 41300 | 67800 | 87900 |
| 25 | 36100 | 58800 | 69000 |
| 30 | 32000 | 51700 | 56100 |
| 35 | 28700 | 46300 | 46800 |
| 40 | 26100 | 40100 | 39700 |
| 45 | 23900 | 34200 | 33600 |
| 50 | 22100 | 28500 | 28000 |

Note: the hatched areas are "structural", so nearly all of the duties here are governed by structural considerations (I'll explain that later). Where that isn't so, the duties converge – see EM2 and EM3 above 35'.

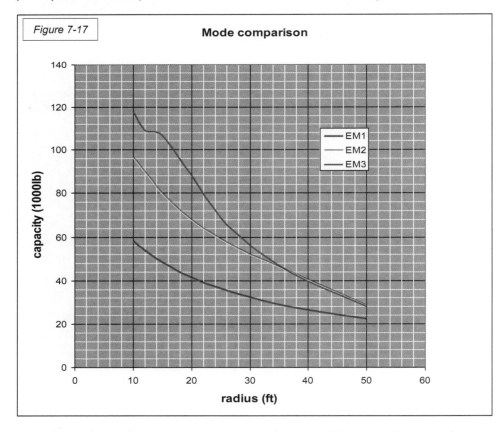

Figure 7-17 — Mode comparison

The message to take from this is that it is very important that your lift plan reflects the boom extension mode (where there are options) and whether it is "fixed" versus "telescoping" and/or the boom percentage extensions you planned on using to get to the boom length you want as it can radically alter the capacity.

Note: before you prepare a plan that requires the crane to telescope out with the load, check whether it is possible / permissible with the crane you have in mind, whether restrictions apply.

### 7.3.4    Comparison between manufacturers

You may find yourself in the situation where you have prepared a plan using say a Link-Belt RTC-8090 SII Rough Terrain crane – 90 ton (US) capacity but, for whatever reason, that crane is not available and someone takes it on themselves to send over a Grove GMK4090 All-Terrain crane – 90 ton (US) capacity in the belief that it is a direct substitute.

Comparing them physically, they have similar (but not identical) outrigger bases, the Grove carries a little more machine counterweight and they are both 5-section booms; the Link-Belt has a slightly greater tail swing.

If you want to use say 63' of boom, you can use the best duties of the Link-Belt (EM3 mode); comparing them with the basic duties of the Grove as below, you'll see that they are in fact very similar, (which somewhat destroys my argument). You might come up a little shy with the Grove if working at say 16' radius.

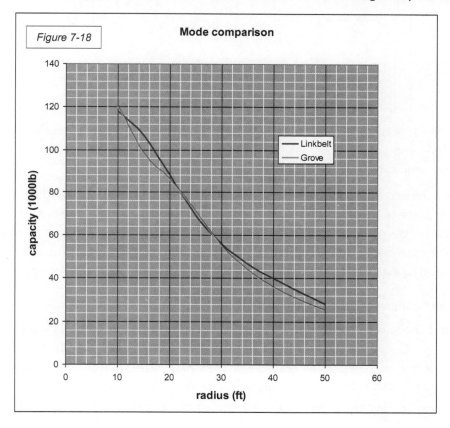

If however, your (Link-Belt) study calls for 140' of boom, to use the Grove you would have to use its maximum boom length of 142'; those charts of the two manufacturers do vary in areas that may be critical to you.

The following graph compares the 140' EM1 capacity of the Link-Belt (that is the required mode at that boom length) with the 142' capacity of the Grove (all else being as like-for-like as possible).

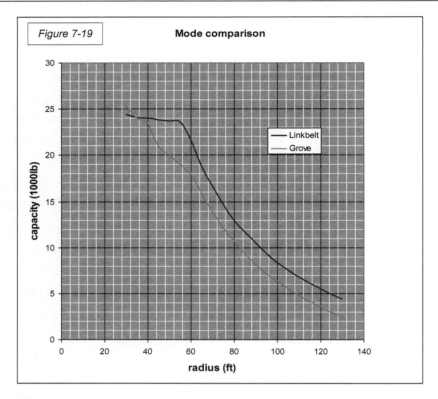

Figure 7-19    Mode comparison

If your plan for the Link-Belt calls for 55' radius, you would have 23,600 lbs capacity, but only 19,000 lbs with the Grove. By the time you take similar fixed deductions for the hook-block etc, the difference in useable capacity could be significant.

Note that I chose these cranes arbitrarily because I have their charts and can use them to illustrate a point. It's not to say either crane is better or worse than the other, it's just that they have differences that need to be understood and which could be critical to you. The point is simply that you can't assume that two manufacturer's similar cranes will be a direct substitute one for the other. If a substitution is proposed by someone, you need to dig into the charts to verify that the proposed substitute will do what you need.

### 7.3.5    What can be learned from the preceding?

- The name of the crane or its nominal class is not a good indication of its useful capacity – refer to the chart
- Lattice boom crawler mounted cranes will likely have much better duties, particularly at longer radii, than telescopic boom outrigger mounted cranes of the same nominal class
- There is no correlation between the capacities or operating ranges of telescopic booms and strut booms
- Cranes might not be fitted with boom heads or hook-blocks sufficient to achieve the max chart capacity, check the small print on the charts for words like "extra equipment may be required"
- The nominal rating of the crane may be based on a radius / boom length at which it would be practically impossible to lift something of that weight
- Telescopic boom capacities drop off relatively quickly with radius
- Boom length does affect capacity but not as dramatically as radius does
- Increase in boom length has less negative effect on the capacity of strut jib cranes than it does on telescopics
- Telescopic cranes on wheels are relatively quick to mobilize and assemble, compared to crawler mounted strut boom cranes but are expensive and static

- Crawler mounted strut boom cranes can move carrying load, are costly to mobilize and assemble but are much cheaper on the daily / monthly rate
- One manufacturer's crane is not necessarily a direct substitute for another manufacturer's similarly rated crane. Charts vary!

### 7.3.6 Options to enhance telescopic crane duties

In order to improve the capacities of their telescopic boom cranes at longer extensions, some manufacturers have devised systems of stays and guys to take out some of the bending in the boom and to limit deflection.

Terex-Demag have a system they call the "Sideways Superlift", Liebherr have what they refer to as the "Y-guy boom system", Grove have a similar system they call "Mega WingLift.

*Figure 7-20*

*Terex Sideways Superlift*

*Figure 7-21*

*Liebherr Y-guy boom system*

*Figure 7-22*

*Grove Mega WingLift*

What effect does this have on capacity? Let's look at the Liebherr LTM-1500 as an example. The crane can boom out from 16.1 m to 50 m – see left. Between 31.7 m and 47.3 m an option exists to "guy" the boom – see right. Capacities are shown on each of the curves.

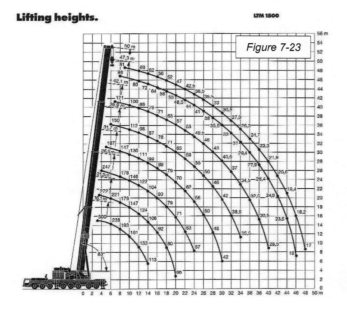

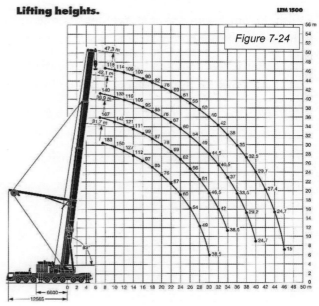

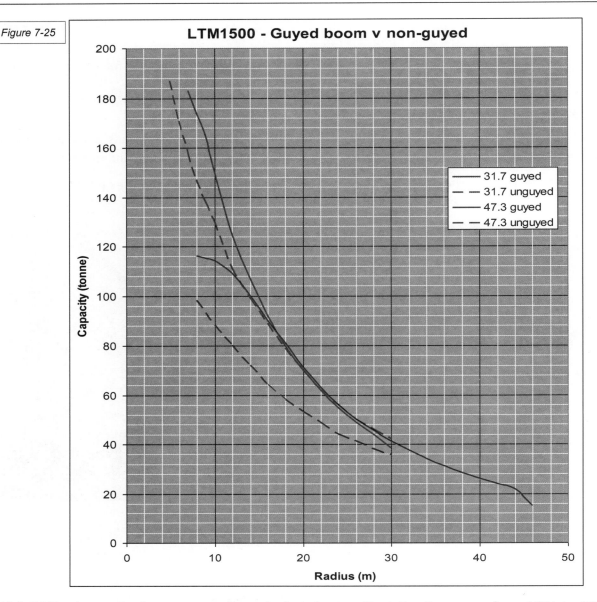

Figure 7-25

**LTM1500 - Guyed boom v non-guyed**

With 31.7 m boom the improvement is marked at short radii, at 7 m it goes up from 158 t to 183 t; at and above 16 m there is very little difference; at max radius, the guyed option is slightly worse.

Note that when unguyed the minimum radius is 5 m at which the capacity is 187 t, which is greater than the 183 t you get with the guyed option at its minimum radius of 7 m.

With 47.3 m boom the improvement is marked across the range (+40% at 16 m) and guying the boom extends the operating radius from 30 m to 46 m, (albeit you don't get much capacity out at 46 m).

It is another case of reading the chart carefully.

If you do intend to use these accessories, make sure to account for the width of the "Y" varieties and for the back swing of the stays on all varieties.

## 7.4   Cranes as structures

Let us just consider the crane as a support structure to start with and deal with the hoisting mechanism later. We'll be looking at the basic structural mechanisms of the cranes, the stability of the crane and how the loads and moments and distributed through outriggers and crawler tracks.

### 7.4.1   Goliath type cranes

Figure 7-26

Figure 7-27

Figure 7-28

Gantries and goliath cranes span the load they are lifting, keeping the load within their support "legs". The crane seen here spans an inlet of the river and a quayside unloading zone. It is a permanent fixture and is used to receive heavy equipment such as generators and turbines directly off barges at a power plant. It is seen here under test prior to lifting a 400 ton Generator.

The picture left shows it receiving a 200 ton transformer.

Such cranes may be fixed or mounted on rails; larger goliath cranes will typically have a "fixed" leg and a "pinned" leg so that one end of the crane girder is unrestrained and can move / articulate. All the lifting loads pass down the legs and there are no overturning effects to consider.

### 7.4.2 Moments acting on construction cranes

Unlike Goliath cranes, most construction cranes are designed to lift loads outside their support base; there are therefore overturning moments acting on the crane. Some cranes such as tower cranes may be bolted down to a foundation or otherwise secured such that uplift can be resisted. Carrier mounted cranes such as crawlers or RTs are not tied down to the ground in any way and rely on deadweight to resist overturning. On those types of cranes, if the combined C of G of the crane and load were to move outside the support base of the crane it would overturn (tip).

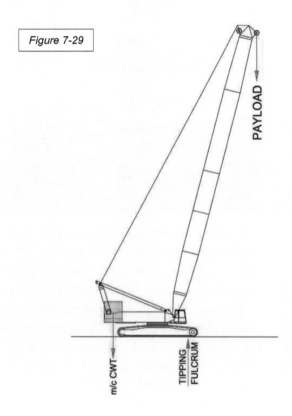

Figure 7-29

Figure 7-30

### 7.4.3 Superlift

To increase the lifting capacity and / or radius, (in addition to having the required structural strength), it is necessary to increase the restoring (backwards) moment. Crane designers can do this by providing more weight behind the crane and preferably putting it as far as practical from the fulcrum. However, there are practical limits to adding weight to the crane upper works and carrying it on the crane itself. It is undesirable to impose a very large moment on the slew ring when the crane is unloaded or carry all that extra weight on the crane. Additionally, the combined C of G has to be maintained within the support base of the crane which would require increasing the size of the crane base.

An advance that avoided a lot of these issues was the introduction by American Hoist of the Skyhorse attachment for their crawler cranes. This development has the additional counterweight supported independently of the crane on a wheeled carrier following the crane. The crane reacts against this counterweight relieving weight from it as required to balance the suspended load. It is a kind of moveable anchor point for the crane to pull against. The restoring moment is variable and is maintained appropriate to essentially balance the overturning moment from the lift being made.

This principle was taken up by others and has evolved into what we generically think of as "Superlift"; strictly that term probably applies only to the Demag-Terex version of the concept using a derrick mast with auxiliary counterweight carried on a carrier or tray.

Figure 7-31

Figure 7-32

The crane shown is an American Hoist 11320 with Skyhorse attachment. The auxiliary counterweight is carried on a wheeled carrier. In Super Skyhorse configuration the operating radius of the wheeled carrier can be considerably increased from that shown here to improve crane reach / capacity.

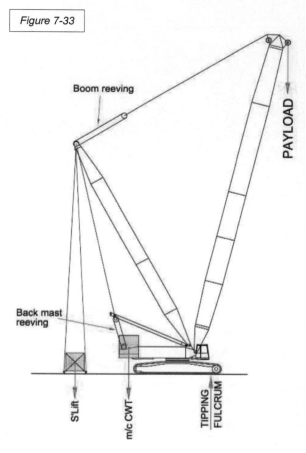

Figure 7-33

The basic "Superlift" principle is that a rearward facing back (derrick) mast is fitted to the crane and the boom is reeved to the tip of the back mast instead of to the A-frame. The A-frame reeving controls the back mast angle (and thus tip height). Auxiliary counterweight is located on either a tray or a wheeled carrier attached by pendants to the tip of the back mast. The design of many cranes allows the Superlift radius to be altered. Luffing the main boom is now achieved using reeving between the tip of the back mast and the head of the boom.

The payload and boom cause a forwards moment, the back mast and machine counterweight provide a rearwards (restoring) moment. Additional restoring moment is provided as required by adjusting the tension in the back mast reeving; this allows the back mast to pull against the auxiliary counterweight (Superlift) tensioning the pendants, better balancing the crane. There is a range that the operator has to maintain the reeving tension within.

The nett forward moment is transferred through the slew ring into the lower works and then into the ground. Note that the weight relieved from the Superlift is now carried through the crane but the ground loadings are more uniform.

Figures 7-34 and 7-35 show a wheeled carrier fitted to a CC-8800 crawler crane.

The carrier is attached to the upper works with a tubular spar incorporating a hydraulic ram allowing the Superlift radius to be adjusted. The wheels on the carrier can be orientated to rotate around the center of the crane's slew ring (Fig 7-34) or to align with the tracks (Fig 7-35) in follow mode. It can therefore slew (swing) freely with the load or crawl with it. Note that the upper works (in the figure) are not directly aligned with the tracks but at about 10° to it. The carrier wheels can adjust for this allowing a crab type movement, which can be useful.

Figure 7-36 shows a CC-2800 fitted with a tray (note it is floating). Figure 7-37 is a detail of the Superlift tray option on a CC-8800 (at rest). As noted, there are options to use either a wheeled carrier or a tray; there are advantages and disadvantages to both. Neither is better or worse.

The main disadvantage of a tray is that it only comes clear of the ground when the crane is operating at about 85% of capacity (it varies by model). Note that it is very important that the SL tray is correctly pre-positioned under the tip of the back mast so it does not impose significant side loads on the crane as the tension comes on. Trays would also normally be restrained from the upper works with a frame or wires to restrict lateral movement as the tray "floats". The crane can only swing when the tray is clear of the ground. If you pick a load at close radius but want to place it at long radius, the load may have to be pushed out to long radius before it can be swung. Once the load is released, the tray comes down on the ground again and has to be detached before the crane can be relocated. The advantage is that it is easily detached and attached. A possibility is to preposition the tray, but not attach it, lift a load at close radius, swing it, attach the Superlift, boom out (which lifts the tray), then swing as required.

With the carrier, the crane is always ready for use. Generally it will not be necessary to adjust the weight on the carrier. The crane can swing (slew) at mid-range percentages of capacity. Disadvantage is that everywhere the crane goes the carrier goes too. This requires a very level, load-carrying pathway for the carrier. Detaching the carrier is not a quick job. The tray only requires matting where it sits and it doesn't have to be absolutely level with the crane. If you don't need the capacity, the tray does not have to be fitted.

As a lift planner, you need to decide which option best suits, noting the type lifts to be made, crane relocations required, matting and ground preparation needs etc.

The following is an example of a Superlift chart. Example only, do not use!

| Figure 7-38 |
|---|

```
Mannesmann
DEMAG Baumaschinen

CC 4800      Tragfähigkeiten am Hauptausleger          SSL/LSL        75%

             Tragfähigkeit (t) = Last + Unterflasche                  360°

                                                        Gegengewicht  160 t
                                                        Spur          10.5 m

             Hauptausleger  90.0 m   Typ 820/717

             SL-Mast        42.0 m   Typ 717/714

             Mastradius     22.0 m
```

| Radius (m) | Superlift-Gegengewicht (t) | | | | |
|---|---|---|---|---|---|
| | 0.0 | 100.0 | 200.0 | 300.0 | 400.0 |
| 14 | 320.0* | – | – | – | – |
| 16 | 300.0* | – | – | – | – |
| 18 | 247.0* | – | – | – | – |
| 20 | 209.0* | 320.0* | – | – | – |
| 22 | 179.0* | 287.0* | – | – | – |
| 24 | 156.0 | 258.0* | 320.0* | – | – |
| 26 | 138.0 | 234.0* | 304.0* | – | – |
| 28 | 122.0 | 211.0* | 279.0* | – | – |
| 30 | 109.0 | 191.0* | 257.0* | 317.0* | – |
| 34 | 89.0 | 160.0 | 221.0* | 274.0* | – |
| 38 | 74.0 | 136.0 | 193.0* | 240.0* | 287.0* |
| 42 | 62.0 | 117.0 | 170.0* | 213.0* | 255.0* |
| 46 | 52.0 | 102.0 | 152.0 | 191.0* | 229.0* |
| 50 | 43.0 | 90.0 | 135.0 | 172.0* | 208.0* |
| 54 | 37.0 | 80.0 | 121.0 | 157.0 | 189.0* |
| 58 | 31.0 | 71.0 | 109.0 | 143.0 | 174.0* |
| 62 | 26.0 | 64.0 | 99.0 | 132.0 | 160.0 |
| 66 | 22.0 | 57.0 | 91.0 | 121.0 | 148.0 |
| 70 | 18.0 | 51.0 | 83.0 | 113.0 | 138.0 |
| 74 | – | 46.0 | 77.0 | 105.0 | 129.0 |
| 78 | – | 42.0 | 71.0 | 98.0 | 120.0 |

```
Hubseileinscherung
                          * 2x11
                            1x11
```

| DS | *0542 | *0552 | *0562 | *0572 | *0762 |
|---|---|---|---|---|---|
| | 0642 | 0652 | 0662 | 0672 | 0862 |

```
DS = Kodierschalter an PAT-Konsole

* Doppel Unterflasche erforderlich!

Bei angebautem Runner (6 m) sind die Tragfähigkeiten um 4 t zu reduzieren.

8316, 29.09.1994  21,5,22                          397 860 40 - 2
```

How is this to be interpreted?

It is a chart for a specific Demag CC-4800 II crawler crane in SSL/LSL configuration, i.e. Superlift with 90 m main boom (mixture of heavy and light sections) and a 42 m back mast whose tip is at 22 m radius from the axis of rotation of the upper works. There are charts for different back mast radii and different boom lengths. It is a 360° chart based on 75% tipping (and structural) criteria. Machine counterweight is 160 t and the track width (center to center) is 10.5 m. Lifting capacities are from the main boom. Capacities shown are payload plus hook-block weight, i.e. hook-block weight has to be accounted for as weight on the crane and added to the payload weight, it is not included in the chart.

Operating radii (m) are down the LHS of the chart, Superlift counterweight is shown across the top. The intersection of the appropriate radius with the appropriate Superlift quantity gives the rated capacity in metric tonnes. Note "0t" Superlift still uses the backmast; duties are likely a little better than the SH (main boom - no back mast) chart duties as the weight of the backmast contributes a rearward moment. This can be a consideration when deciding how to configure the machine, plus it opens up the possibility of using SL at some later stage.

Capacities are indicated for every approved combination of radius and Superlift weight, e.g. 172 t with 300 t of SL ballast at 50 m radius. At that payload, with the correct tension on the backmast, the tray will float. It will likely float at some figure less than 172 t, but probably not at say 136 t, thus when operating between chart intervals, some reduction in ballast may be required, the manufacturer may provide a calculation method to determine that. See below.

Interpolation of the SL weight may be permitted, or when between intervals it may be a question of fitting the next highest amount allowed in the chart, then removing some ballast slabs if the tray doesn't float, (all else being with prescribed limits) until it does. Make sure you have the correct weight on the tray, correct back mast radius, correct SL tray pendant lengths, correct back mast tension etc first. Note also that if you start the lift at say 34 m radius, the tray with 300 t SL ballast won't float until you push the radius out to close to 50 m.

Another point to note is that when upending something, the head load doesn't reach its maximum until the load is freely suspended from the head crane, so if using a head crane in SSL configuration with a tray, you won't be able to swing that crane anywhere until it has the full load at the intended radius for which you have specified the required SL ballast.

The next area says that where a "*" is indicated, the double hook-block is required, i.e. 2 winches working in unison. You must use 2 x 11 parts of hoist line. Where not indicated, 1 x 11 parts is sufficient.

The DS numbers are the codes to be entered into the PAT control system, appropriate to the particular modes.

Finally, when the optional 6 m "runner" is fitted to the boom head, you need to reduce the capacity by 4 t.

Note that when using Superlift on a tray, you may need to use a load case between quoted Superlift rows and would not have adequate lift capacity at the lower SL figure and not be able to get the Superlift off the ground to swing at the higher SL figure. In such cases an interpolation may be required to calculate the appropriate amount of Superlift. The following illustrates conceptually the methodology. This is for illustration only, every case is different, consult the crane charts/ crane manual to see how it has to be done in a specific case.

Example – Terex Demag Method for interpolating SL ballast for CC2800. For example only – do not use; contact the manufacturer for guidance.

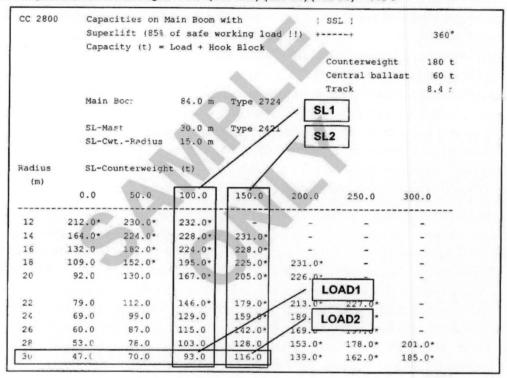

**Interpolating SL-Counterweights**

Figure 7-39

To interpolate the necessary SL-Counterweight for a load case between two superlift rows use the following formula (linear interpolation):

$$SL = SL1 + (SL2 - SL1) * (LOAD - LOAD1) / (LOAD2 - LOAD1)$$

For Example:

The required Loadcase is 30m x 100t => SL1=100, SL2=150, LOAD1=93, LOAD2=116, LOAD=100

**The required SL-counterweight = 100+(150-100)\*(100-93)/(116-93) = 115 t**

### 7.4.4 Limiting rating conditions – "structural" v "tipping"

Regarding the crane as a support mechanism and ignoring its hoisting abilities (winches, parts of line etc) for the moment, code requires that a crane's rated capacity (in a given configuration when lifting at a particular radius) is limited to the lesser of:

the load that would result in the moment on the crane reaching a limiting percentage of the moment that would cause it to tip (in the least stable direction) – "tipping" criterion

the load that would any element of the machine to reach a limiting design condition – "structural" criteria

Note that code requires there to be a margin of stability when rating a crane, you cannot work it right up to the point of tipping. The permitted percentage of tipping is typically up to 75%, although it does vary somewhat by locale. (In the USA when lifting on fully extended outriggers, the limiting percentage per ASME B30.5 is 85%). Crane charts ought to state the design code used and the limiting percentage of tipping used.

In the USA, charts are required to differentiate those capacities limited by tipping and those limited by structural considerations (all conditions other than tipping). Capacities at close radii and short boom lengths (like the example) will likely be "structural". Some long boom, long radii duties may also be structural.

### 7.4.5 Examining "tipping" criteria in load chart preparation

Introduction

I have long argued that if crane users and lift planners live within the ratings provided by the crane manufacturers in the crane charts there should be no need for them to be concerned with what lies behind the preparation of those charts – which particular rating is determined by which criterion; in my view that is the crane manufacturer's business. Compliance of a crane's rating chart with an approved industry safety code should be totally sufficient assurance of the safety of those ratings.

However it is evident there are still people out there who second guess the manufacturer and will push beyond approved ratings in the mistaken belief that they understand what they are doing, that there is really no increased risk and if there is, they are managing it. This is done on the basis of an imperfect understanding of the real-world implications of the code criteria when translated into actual crane charts. It is not helped by the fact that there is still currently a requirement in the USA to indicate those areas of the crane charts that are governed by factors other than stability and therefore, by default, those that are governed by tipping criteria. I wish this was not so; once "tipping criteria" is mentioned or quoted on a crane chart, people naturally want to know what it means and many times the true meaning is actually misunderstood. Further, many people are confused when they see reference to "75%" or "85%" on a crane chart. Given that the implications of misunderstanding the crane charts (and the basis on which they are prepared) can be serious, an explanation of what "tipping criteria" in crane chart preparation really means is in order.

As will be discussed, I have a concern that ASME B30.5 (in particular) is inadequate in addressing the all-important aspect of forward stability (especially when cranes are fitted with long booms and operating at shallow boom angles). As currently written, I believe the basis by which "margin of stability" is to be assured is flawed and it effectively leaves the ultimate margin of forward stability to the discretion of the manufacturers. This is not immediately obvious until one examines how the standard translates in a particular instance. I think many people would be shocked if they realized just how unstable a crane can be and still be within code. Take this "hidden" fact together with the "don't worry, I know what I'm doing mentality" and it's not surprising that we daily see examples of cranes overturning. Following I would like to examine margins of stability derived from following the B30.5 safety code, show the inadequacy of the code and reinforce the absolute need to comply with manufacturers ratings.

Background

As we've seen, cranes used in construction typically comprise a lower works or carrier providing a support base for the rotating upper works. The upper works carries the engine, winches, machine counterweight and it provides a hinged mounting point for a boom from the head of which the load is suspended. By varying the boom angle, the reach can be altered.

Commonly the carrier is crawler or outrigger mounted although wheeled carriers, rings or rail mounted arrangements are also available. Lifting loads (totaling the weight of the crane and supported load) are imposed onto the foundation (supporting surface) through the crawler tracks or outriggers.

As these types of cranes are designed to lift loads outside their own support base at varying radii (measured from the center of rotation of the crane) they are subject to greater or lesser overturning effects arising from the magnitude of the load being lifted and the radius of operation. The proportion of the total load carried by each support point varies according to the moment balance of the crane i.e. the magnitude of the overturning moment (forwards or backwards). The foundation load distribution under a crane is evenly distributed when the combined C of G and load lies centrally between the outriggers or crawler tracks – a position that often approximates to the center of rotation of the crane. To remain stable, the combined C of G has to remain securely within the support base of the crane.

A construction crane's capacity is dependent on its configuration and the reach being used (measured as radius from the center of rotation); as boom length or operating radius increases, capacity reduces as a result of structural, mechanical, hydraulic or other considerations or the greater propensity of the crane to overturn. The capacity of a crane in a given situation is found in the charts produced by the manufacturer - there will be a chart for every approved configuration and operating radius. Operation is only permitted where there is a rated capacity shown and there is often a radius beyond which operation is not rated or approved even though the crane could physically reach out there (albeit with the boom very horizontal).

<u>Criteria for load chart preparation</u>

So, what criteria does the manufacturer use in developing these charts?

As noted earlier, there are two primary considerations:

- The strength of the crane.
- The stability of the crane.

The rated capacity is the lesser of:

- A defined percentage of the load that would cause the crane to tip when the boom is in the least stable direction - STABILITY.
- The load that will cause one of the components of the crane to reach a limiting condition. Such a condition is often generically referred to as "STRUCTURAL COMPETENCE" when in fact it encompasses a number of possible factors such as mechanical limitations (e.g. clutches and brakes), hydraulic limitations (e.g. pumps, motors, valves), pneumatic limitations (e.g. compressors, cylinders, valves), electrical limitations (e.g. resistor capacity) or other arbitrarily imposed limits (e.g. competitor capacities or test limitations) as well as the more universally assumed "structural competence" These limiting conditions are more properly referred to as "factors other than stability" .

*Note that rated capacity is the maximum total vertical load that is permitted to be imposed at the crane's boom or jib point <u>under ideal conditions</u>.*

Regardless of the standard used, "Factors Other Than Stability" will usually govern at close radii whereas Stability will govern at longer radii. We know this because US crane charts are (currently) required to indicate which capacities are governed by "structural" criteria. You may find that some load ratings at longer radii (when the boom is at small angles to the horizontal) are also governed by factors other than stability.

<u>Design standards</u>

Naturally, cranes must be designed with sufficient reserves of strength and stability and be rated such that they are safe in use, <u>so long as they are operated within approved parameters</u>. To that end, safety standards such as ASME B30.5 (USA) and EN13000 (Europe) have been developed laying down standards for the construction and characteristics of construction cranes. Included are stability criteria with which cranes made to those standards must comply.

*Note that globally, crane design standards are not created equal; regarding load charts; they differ in some key areas including tipping percentages and methodology for determining ratings. There may be several differing load charts for the same machine depending on where it is being used geographically and the associated governing code.*

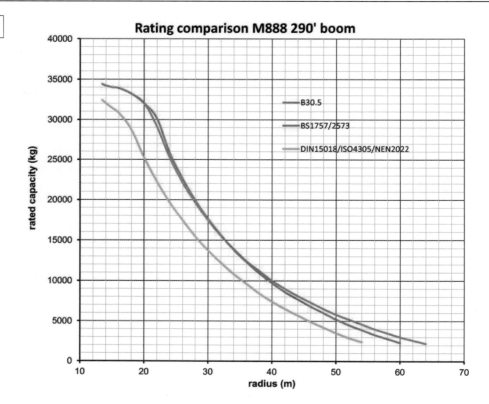

*Figure 7-40*

The above chart compares three rating charts produced by Manitowoc for the M888-S2 with 290' of boom. One to ASME B30.5, another to British Standards (BS1757 & BS2573) and finally one to European standards (DIN15018, ISO 4305 & NEN 2022); they differ significantly. B30.5 and BS charts are close, but the BS ratings are less at longer radii and the chart stops at 60 m, whereas the B30.5 chart goes out to 64 m. The European chart stops a full 10 m shorter at 54 m. All three are rated similarly at these three different max radii. The B30.5 chart goes to tipping criteria at 20 m, the European at 18 m and the British at 22 m. The European ratings are universally less. This is the exact same crane!

ASME B30.5 stability criteria and their origins

Re stability, ASME B30.5 says the following:

"5-1.1.1 Load ratings – Where Stability Governs Lifting Performance

a) The margin of stability for determination of load ratings, with booms of stipulated lengths at stipulated working radii for the various types of crane mountings, is established by taking a percentage of the loads that will produce a condition of tipping or balance with the crane in the least stable direction relative to the mounting." "....the load ratings shall not exceed the percentages for cranes given in Table 5-1.1.1-1."

Table 5-1.1.1-1, in essence says that if mounted on fully extended outriggers, the percentage is 85%, otherwise 75%.

The traditional methodology for determining the Balance Point, i.e. "the condition of crane loading wherein the load moment acting to overturn the crane is equal to the maximum moment of the crane available to resist overturning", is contained in SAE J765. Tipping loads are derived by manufacturers across the operating range for each approved configuration. From those results, rated capacities are developed using the ASME defined permitted percentages of tipping load.

Note that the afore-mentioned criteria in ASME B30.5 apply only to forward stability – backward stability is defined by limiting the approach of the C of G of the crane to the rear tipping fulcrum (crawler cranes) or by requiring a minimum percent of the crane's weight to be maintained on the front outriggers. This approach is, in my view, a meaningful measure of stability.

Regarding the origins of the ASME B30.5 criteria, I believe that they are derived from the Power Crane and Shovel Association Standard #4 (previously #1 & #2) – Mobile Power Crane and Excavator and Hydraulic Crane Standards. (PCSA No 1 was copyrighted in 1968).

Section 4.01.2 of that document states:

"Lifting crane rated loads at specified radii shall not exceed the following percentages of tipping load at specified radius:

a) Crawler Machines          75%
b) Wheeled Machines          75%
c) Machines on Outriggers    85%

Rated loads shall be based on the direction of minimum stability, unless otherwise stated."

Section 6.02.1 Rated Load states:

"Rated loads at specified radii are the lesser of a specified percentage of tipping loads or the machine's hydraulic or structural competence as established by the manufacturers rating charts and are the maximum loads at those radii covered by the manufacturer's warranty."

Backward stability is not addressed in this standard.

<u>What are the implications of the tipping criteria in the real world?</u>

We know that there are 75% and 85% charts and those figures relate to limiting tipping criteria, but what do we understand by that? Let's try a small quiz based on ASME B30.5 and 75% criteria.

1) ASME B30.5 provides mandatory criteria for crane chart preparation that will ensure safe ratings with ample reserve against forward tipping. True or False?
2) Rated capacities in crane charts prepared to ASME B30.5 result in the same percentage of instability when in the tipping regions of the charts. True or False?
3) A 75% chart results in ratings that will take you to a 75% tipping condition. True or False?
4) When in the tipping region of a 75% chart, the crane would be brought to a point of balance if you were to apply 25% more than the rated capacity to the crane (Warning: This is a theoretical exercise which would overload the crane and should never be attempted by anyone other than the manufacturer). True or False?

All these statements are false – at least as I view it.

1) A crane chart prepared (solely) to ASME B30.5 tipping criteria results in a crane becoming progressively less stable as radius increases and, with a long boom, could bring the crane right to the point of tipping at the radius at which zero capacity is first indicated.
2) As noted above a crane chart prepared to ASME B30.5 tipping criteria results in a crane becoming progressively less stable as radius increases according to any reasonable measure of what stability is.
3) With a long enough boom, a 75% chart could take you right to tipping due to the self-weight of the boom. Manufacturers of course do not to rate their cranes right to that limiting radius but they do rate cranes to the point where 95% or so of the weight is to the front supports (outriggers or track). Nothing in the code sets a limit for that point; it is the manufacturer's judgment that results in safe charts (on that point at least) – not the Code. What does 75% of tipping mean in any event?
4) Ratings in the tipping region of a chart are based on 75% of the additional vertical load applied at the boom head required to tip the crane – IN THE SPECIFIED DIRECTION. 25% over chart will not tip the

crane, it takes 1 / 75% = 1.33x chart, i.e. 33% over chart. However it is very misleading to measure stability in this manner. As the radius increases, the overturning effect of the boom weight reduces the overall stability of the crane against overturning and it takes progressively less applied overturning moment from the payload to tip it. To say the stability margin it is 33% over chart load rating when that rating is a very small figure does not give a true measure of stability. Only a moment-based approach is meaningful.

Note that taking a crane to the point of tipping could result in overloading the crane by more than 33% if the boom is not in the least stable direction. What that translates into in terms of loads and stresses in the crane is unknown to the user.

## ASME B30.5 as a basis for load chart preparation

The result of ASME B30.5 defining forward stability criteria only in terms of percentage of applied load to tip the crane is that a crane designed only on that basis would become progressively less stable (in real terms) with increase of radius. The fact that US crane charts are adequately safe is because the manufacturers do not rate their cranes right up to the limiting radius at which tipping would occur – code does not establish a moment limitation in the forwards direction. The fact that this is at the manufacturer's discretion in the code is, in my view, a major oversight.

It is my contention that defining forward stability only in terms of applied load at the boom head (and not in terms of moments) ignores the overturning effect of the self-weight of the boom and is fundamentally flawed as a basis for safe design.

ASME B30.5 may have adopted the PCSA (load-based) methodology for forwards stability but they also addressed backwards stability using, in this case, a moment based approach. This effectively defines a maximum percentage of the crane load that can be applied at the fulcrum (and thereby a minimum percentage that must be maintained on the opposite track or outriggers). Another way to express this is that it defines how closely the C of G of the crane can approach the fulcrum (tipping point) as a percentage of the width of the support base (track or outrigger centers). That is a rational basis for considering stability and an approach that I would urge ASME B30.5 to also adopt in addressing forward stability.

So why are we stuck with this flawed methodology? I think it goes back to the decision to adopt the existing Power Crane and Shovel Association standard when first developing the ASME B30.5 standard. It was probably considered to be working well enough for cranes of the day (which didn't have particularly long booms) and it's likely the committee would not have wanted to make a change. While crane manufacturers recognize the deficiency of this methodology in the modern age and deal with it in house, they likely don't want to open the can of worms that it would now be to change the code. I advocate that the manufacturers (who are well represented on the ASME committee) should agree a limiting forward moment criterion (say 95% max of the total load to the highly loaded line of support) and lobby for it to be added over the current ASME B30.5 requirements. They should also throw out all mention of "structural" v tipping on crane charts. It wouldn't hurt to try to reach global consensus on the approach either. Without knowing exactly what manufacturer's in-house practices are, I believe a revised soundly based code could be written that is no more onerous than their current practices.

## How better to define stability?

Comprehending when a limiting condition of pressure, function, stress or deflection is reached can present complex issues and I have no issue with that aspect of load chart preparation. You might imagine that comprehending stability would be far more straightforward. In fact understanding the stability criteria in B30.5 is not that difficult – basically find out what load is needed to tip the crane, multiply by (say) 75% and call that the rated capacity. The margin of stability is the difference in load between the rating and the load to tip. Clear enough? That gives 33% margin of stability right? That depends how stability is defined, but basically no it doesn't.

With that said, what is meant by forward stability margin and how should it be measured? It has to basically be a meaningful measure of how close a crane comes to overturning (tipping).

Per ASME B30.5 it is true that there is a minimum of 33% of load over the chart capacity before the crane tips, but in the limiting condition with a long boom that could be 33% of zero = zero reserve over tipping. *i.e. If you reach the point where the boom weight alone is sufficient to tip the crane, you will arrive at a limiting radius where the additional load to tip the crane is zero, the capacity is zero and stability is non-existent. Percentage load over chart capacity is therefore not a good measure of stability.*

So, defining margin of stability in terms of how much extra load it takes to tip it is not a very useful concept and doesn't give a meaningful measure of how close the crane is to tipping. What would a better way to look at it be? Let's go back to basics.

A crane will be in theoretical balance and on the point of tipping when the total overturning moments are equal to the total restoring moments.

First a quick reminder of what a "moment" is. It is the rotational effect a force has about a particular point. It is equal to the magnitude of the force x the perpendicular distance (the moment arm) from the rotation point to the line of the force. All our forces are vertical, so all our moment arms are horizontal distances. The rotation point is the fulcrum about which the crane would tip. In the case of a crane, it will want to tip about a theoretical line connecting an adjacent pair of outriggers or about the track rollers in the case of a crawler crane. It is not forces we are so much concerned about as the rotational effects (moments) that they cause.

Analyzing "tipping"

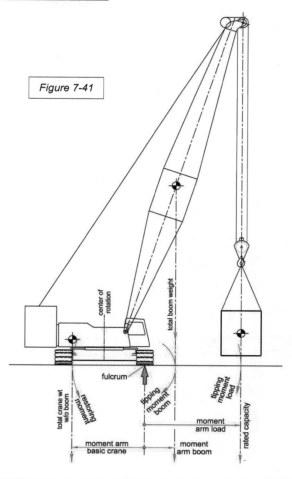

Figure 7-41

To examine tipping it is necessary to consider what moments act to overturn the crane and what provide the restoring effect. For analysis, I am going to locate the boom (of a crawler crane) directly over the side and boom it up and down to change the radius. That will generally be the least stable direction and will govern the chart ratings for 360 degree operation. The crane can be considered in two parts; a) those components that move when the radius is altered and b) those components whose relation to the fulcrum is unchanged as the radius is changed i.e. the rest of the crane. The hook block is not considered because it is part of the payload.

Regarding the components that move, I'm going to consider just the boom as being significant and combine the pendant weights in with that; the boom weight x the horizontal distance from its C of G to the fulcrum equates to a moment acting about the fulcrum. As the C of G of the boom is outside the fulcrum at all but the shortest radii, this moment will act to overturn the crane at longer radii. Its magnitude is a variable figure dependent on boom angle.

The other effect acting to overturn the crane is of course the vertical load acting on the boom head (i.e. the rated capacity at any given radius); it acts at a moment arm equal to the horizontal distance from the boom head to the tipping fulcrum.

The restoring moment is provided by the weight of all the other crane components (upper works, counterweights, lower works etc) acting on the other side of the fulcrum at a moment arm equal to the horizontal distance from the combined C of G of those components to the fulcrum point. For a given configuration, this is a fixed figure independent of operating radius.

The net restoring moment provided by the crane = the fixed restoring moment − the overturning moment of the boom.

As the boom angle (to the horizontal) reduces, the boom weight moment increases and the net restoring moment provided by the crane reduces. In fact with very long booms the overturning effect of the boom when horizontal may approach or exceed the fixed restoring moment (on its own with no applied payload). Another way to view that situation is that the C of G of the crane is directly over or outside the fulcrum with no load on the boom. An assist crane may be required in such cases to raise the boom to a minimum operating angle at which the C of G of the crane is securely inside the support base.

You can see how the crawler loads alter and the location of the combined C of G shifts with increase of load & radius in the following sequence; the crane examined is a Manitowoc M888-S2 with 80' of boom. Capacities quoted are based on a US ASME B30.5 compliant chart (i.e. 75% tipping criteria).

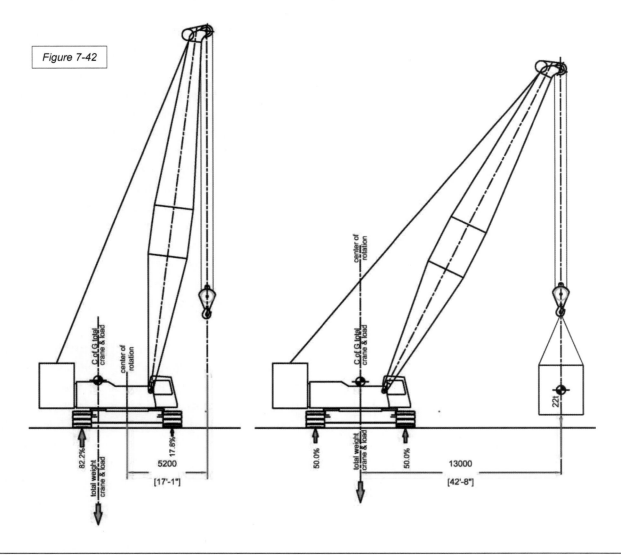

Figure 7-42

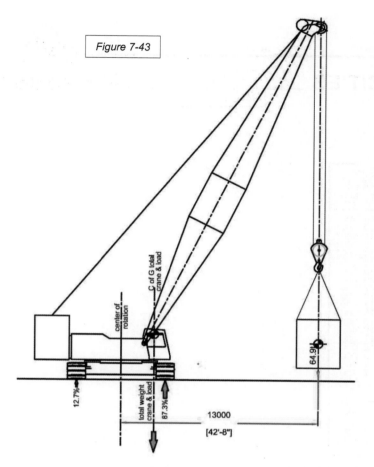

Figure 7-43

At minimum radius when lifting over the side with zero load to the boom head (ignore the hook-block in the graphic), the rear crawler carries about 82.2% of the load. (Figures derived from the Manitowoc ground bearing pressure estimator). The C of G of the unloaded crane therefore lies well to the rear as indicated.

If we (say) lift 22 t (total inc hook-block) at 22 m radius, the combined C of G has moved forward and now lies on the center of rotation; each track supports 50% of the total load. If we increase the weight at the same radius to the chart max of 64.9 t, the percentage applied to the most highly loaded track becomes 87.3%. The C of G now lies further forward and is approaching the fulcrum.

To take the crane beyond chart to the point of tipping (in theory only!), where the C of G lies over the fulcrum, would require about 84 t.

Note that with this "75%" rating chart and 80' of boom, 87% of the crane's weight is on one crawler when operating at max radius with full rated load. As we'll see later, it is an even greater percentage when using the maximum boom length.

In conclusion, when the overturning moments equal the restoring moments, the crane is at the balance point (and is dramatically overloaded). It is the same as saying that the combined C of G of the crane and load lies directly over the fulcrum. If the overturning moment is increased, the C of G moves outside the support base of the crane and it overturns. If the overturning moment is reduced, the C of G will move back inside the support base and the crane will not overturn. The true measure of stability is by how much the combined C of G of crane and load lies within the crane's support base. The closer it gets to the fulcrum the less stable the crane is.

Let's look at a typical crawler crane to see how this all works out in developing a crane chart per ASME B30.5. I'll analyze the Manitowoc M888-S2 for no other reason than good information is available for that machine. I'll reference a US metric ANSI/ASME B30.5 compliant chart and will examine the chart for the longest boom (290' – 88.4 m) as that is likely to be the worst tipping case. My choice of crane should not be taken as implying anything about Manitowoc's design practices – I have high regard for them as a company. My concern is with analyzing ASME B30.5 as a design basis.

To reverse engineer this chart I'll need some data to start with. The M888 crane charts contain a lot of useful weight data; the Manitowoc ground bearing pressure estimator also yields some useful information and is a good basis for verifying the analysis.

Figure 7-44

# MANITOWOC ENGINEERING CO.
Division of the Manitowoc Company, Inc. Manitowoc, Wisconsin 54220

# LIFTCRANE BOOM CAPACITIES

| MEETS ANSI B30.5 REQUIREMENTS | 888 SERIES 2 |

BOOM NO. 22EL
81 240 kg CRANE COUNTERWEIGHT
19 960 kg CARBODY COUNTERWEIGHT
360 DEGREE RATING

| BOOM LENGTH METERS | BOOM LGTH. FEET | OPER. RADIUS METERS | BOOM ANG. DEG. | BOOM POINT ELEV. METERS | BOOM CAPACITY CRAWLERS RETRACTED KILOGRAMS | BOOM CAPACITY CRAWLERS EXTENDED KILOGRAMS |
|---|---|---|---|---|---|---|
| 88.4 | 290 | 13.4 | 82.7 | 90.1 | 34 400* | 34 400* |
| | | 14.0 | 82.3 | 90.0 | 34 200* | 34 200* |
| | | 15.0 | 81.7 | 89.8 | 34 000* | 34 000* |
| | | 16.0 | 81.0 | 89.7 | 33 900* | 33 900* |
| | | 18.0 | 79.7 | 89.3 | 32 600 | 33 200* |
| | | 20.0 | 78.4 | 88.9 | 28 100 | 32 000 |
| | | 22.0 | 77.1 | 88.4 | 24 200 | 29 100 |
| | | 24.0 | 75.7 | 87.9 | 21 100 | 25 200 |
| | | 26.0 | 74.4 | 87.4 | 18 400 | 22 100 |
| | | 28.0 | 73.0 | 86.8 | 16 200 | 19 600 |
| | | 30.0 | 71.7 | 86.1 | 14 300 | 17 400 |
| | | 32.0 | 70.3 | 85.4 | 12 700 | 15 500 |
| | | 34.0 | 68.9 | 84.7 | 11 300 | 13 900 |
| | | 36.0 | 67.5 | 83.9 | 10 000 | 12 400 |
| | | 38.0 | 66.1 | 83.0 | 8 900 | 11 200 |
| | | 40.0 | 64.6 | 82.0 | 7 900 | 10 000 |
| | | 42.0 | 63.2 | 81.0 | 7 000 | 9 000 |
| | | 44.0 | 61.7 | 80.0 | 6 200 | 8 100 |
| | | 46.0 | 60.2 | 78.8 | 5 500 | 7 300 |
| | | 48.0 | 58.7 | 77.6 | 4 800 | 6 500 |
| | | 50.0 | 57.2 | 76.4 | 4 200 | 5 800 |
| | | 52.0 | 55.6 | 75.0 | 3 600 | 5 200 |
| | | 54.0 | 54.0 | 73.6 | 3 100 | 4 600 |
| | | 56.0 | 52.4 | 72.1 | 2 600 | 4 000 |
| | | 58.0 | 50.7 | 70.5 | 2 200 | 3 500 |
| | | 60.0 | 49.0 | 68.7 | | 3 000 |
| | | 62.0 | 47.3 | 66.9 | | 2 600 |
| | | 64.0 | 45.5 | 65.0 | | 2 200 |

I ran the Manitowoc ground bearing pressure estimator for this crane with the maximum 290' of boom at various radii up to the maximum permitted 64 m, lifting the published chart capacities over the side (the least stable direction) at those radii. The estimator yields the pressure distribution under the crawler crane tracks. From this I can derive:

- The proportions of the total load carried by each track.
- The total weight of crane and load.
- The crane self-weight.

Following is a representative output for the longest boom length of 290' (88.4 m).

Collating the results for a range of radii from 20 m (which is the minimum radius at which the capacity is governed by tipping) to the max chart radius of 64 m yields the following table. You can see that the self-weight of the crane calculates to a fairly constant 207 t, which agrees fairly well with the figure for the crane with 290' of boom derived from the crane weights in the crane charts. Note as well that at the max radius, the most heavily loaded track supports 95.6% of the total weight of the crane and load.

**Figure 7-45**

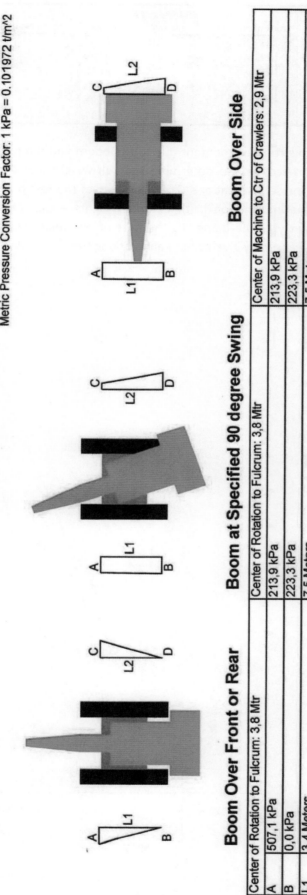

## Ground Bearing Pressure Estimator

GBPressure ver: 1.0.6.0
7/3/2012 10:37 AM

| | |
|---|---|
| Project: | Operating Surface: Soft – Tread Contact Width 1,2 Meters |
| Model: 888 Series 2 | Primary: 290FT (88.4M) #22EL BOOM |
| Machine Counterweight: 179,100-LB (81,150-KG) | Secondary: 0FT (0M) No Attachment |
| Crawler: Extended, Position: Gantry Up | Load: From Boom 2 200 kGf @ 64 M radius |

Metric Pressure Conversion Factor: 1 kPa = 0.101972 t/m^2

### Boom Over Front or Rear

| Center of Rotation to Fulcrum: 3,8 Mtr | |
|---|---|
| A | 507,1 kPa |
| B | 0,0 kPa |
| L1 | 3,4 Meters |
| C | 507,1 kPa |
| D | 0,0 kPa |
| L2 | 3,4 Meters |

### Boom at Specified 90 degree Swing

| Center of Rotation to Fulcrum: 3,8 Mtr | |
|---|---|
| A | 213,9 kPa |
| B | 223,3 kPa |
| L1 | 7,5 Meters |
| C | 5,4 kPa |
| D | 14,8 kPa |
| L2 | 7,5 Meters |

### Boom Over Side

| Center of Machine to Ctr of Crawlers: 2,9 Mtr | |
|---|---|
| A | 213,9 kPa |
| B | 223,3 kPa |
| L1 | 7,5 Meters |
| C | 5,4 kPa |
| D | 14,8 kPa |
| L2 | 7,5 Meters |

| radius | chart | boom side | | | | c'weight side | | | | total | crane wt |
|---|---|---|---|---|---|---|---|---|---|---|---|
| (m) | (t) | track pressure (kPa) | average | percent | | track pressure (kPa) | average | percent | | load (t) | (t) |
| 64 | 2.2 | 213.9 | 223.3 | 218.6 | 95.6% | 5.4 | 14.8 | 10.1 | 4.4% | 209.8 | 207.62 |
| 58 | 3.5 | 212.2 | 221.6 | 216.9 | 94.2% | 8.6 | 17.9 | 13.3 | 5.8% | 211.1 | 207.65 |
| 48 | 6.5 | 210.7 | 220.1 | 215.4 | 92.3% | 13.3 | 22.7 | 18.0 | 7.7% | 214.1 | 207.63 |
| 38 | 11.2 | 211.0 | 220.4 | 215.7 | 90.4% | 18.1 | 27.5 | 22.8 | 9.6% | 218.8 | 207.61 |
| 28 | 19.6 | 215.1 | 224.5 | 219.8 | 88.8% | 23.1 | 32.5 | 27.8 | 11.2% | 227.2 | 207.56 |
| 20 | 32.0 | 220.1 | 229.5 | 224.8 | 86.1% | 31.6 | 40.9 | 36.3 | 13.9% | 239.5 | 207.50 |

To determine the overturning moment due to the boom and the fixed restoring moment provided by the rest of the crane, it is necessary to determine the self-weight and C of G location of the boom (and related components) and the self-weight and C of G location of the rest of the crane. The weights can be derived and summated from the information in the Crane Weights – the C of G locations can be estimated from the weights and geometry of the crane. To the best of my ability, it looks somewhat like the following. I can't guarantee absolute accuracy given what I am working from, but I don't believe it is far off.

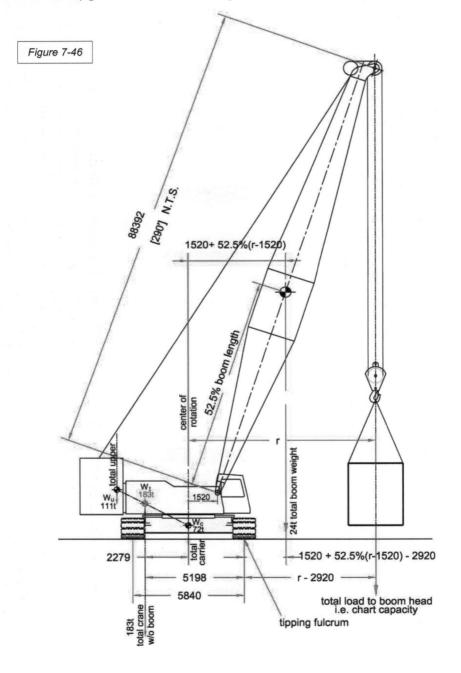

Figure 7-46

# M888-S2 crawler crane - 290' of boom

Figure 7-47

| radius (m) | chart capacity (t) | fixed restoring moment (t-m) | boom overturning moment (t-m) | nett restoring moment (t-m) | load to tip (t) | 75% x load to tip (t) |
|---|---|---|---|---|---|---|
| 13.4 | 34.4 | 951.6 | 116.1 | 835.5 | 79.7 | 59.8 |
| 14 | 34.2 | 951.6 | 123.6 | 828.0 | 74.7 | 56.0 |
| 15 | 34.0 | 951.6 | 136.2 | 815.4 | 67.5 | 50.6 |
| 16 | 33.9 | 951.6 | 148.8 | 802.8 | 61.4 | 46.0 |
| 18 | 33.2 | 951.6 | 174.0 | 777.6 | 51.6 | 38.7 |
| 20 | 32.0 | 951.6 | 199.2 | 752.4 | 44.0 | 33.0 |
| 22 | 29.1 | 951.6 | 224.4 | 727.2 | 38.1 | 28.6 |
| 24 | 25.2 | 951.6 | 249.6 | 702.0 | 33.3 | 25.0 |
| 26 | 22.1 | 951.6 | 274.8 | 676.8 | 29.3 | 22.0 |
| 28 | 19.6 | 951.6 | 300.0 | 651.6 | 26.0 | 19.5 |
| 30 | 17.4 | 951.6 | 325.2 | 626.4 | 23.1 | 17.3 |
| 32 | 15.5 | 951.6 | 350.4 | 601.2 | 20.7 | 15.5 |
| 34 | 13.9 | 951.6 | 375.6 | 576.0 | 18.5 | 13.9 |
| 36 | 12.4 | 951.6 | 400.8 | 550.8 | 16.6 | 12.5 |
| 38 | 11.2 | 951.6 | 426.0 | 525.6 | 15.0 | 11.2 |
| 40 | 10.0 | 951.6 | 451.2 | 500.4 | 13.5 | 10.1 |
| 42 | 9.0 | 951.6 | 476.4 | 475.2 | 12.2 | 9.1 |
| 44 | 8.1 | 951.6 | 501.6 | 450.0 | 11.0 | 8.2 |
| 46 | 7.3 | 951.6 | 526.8 | 424.8 | 9.9 | 7.4 |
| 48 | 6.5 | 951.6 | 552.0 | 399.6 | 8.9 | 6.6 |
| 50 | 5.8 | 951.6 | 577.2 | 374.4 | 8.0 | 6.0 |
| 52 | 5.2 | 951.6 | 602.4 | 349.2 | 7.1 | 5.3 |
| 54 | 4.6 | 951.6 | 627.6 | 324.0 | 6.3 | 4.8 |
| 56 | 4.0 | 951.6 | 652.8 | 298.8 | 5.6 | 4.2 |
| 58 | 3.5 | 951.6 | 678.0 | 273.6 | 5.0 | 3.7 |
| 60 | 3.0 | 951.6 | 703.2 | 248.4 | 4.4 | 3.3 |
| 62 | 2.6 | 951.6 | 728.4 | 223.2 | 3.8 | 2.8 |
| 64 | 2.2 | 951.6 | 753.6 | 198.0 | 3.2 | 2.4 |
| 66 | | 951.6 | 778.8 | 172.8 | 2.7 | 2.1 |
| 68 | | 951.6 | 804.0 | 147.6 | 2.3 | 1.7 |
| 70 | | 951.6 | 829.2 | 122.4 | 1.8 | 1.4 |
| 72 | | 951.6 | 854.4 | 97.2 | 1.4 | 1.1 |
| 74 | | 951.6 | 879.6 | 72.0 | 1.0 | 0.8 |
| 76 | | 951.6 | 904.8 | 46.8 | 0.6 | 0.5 |
| 78 | | 951.6 | 930.0 | 21.6 | 0.3 | 0.2 |
| 80 | | 951.6 | 955.2 | -3.6 | 0.0 | 0.0 |
| 82 | | 951.6 | 980.4 | -28.8 | -0.4 | -0.3 |
| 84 | | 951.6 | 1005.6 | -54.0 | -0.7 | -0.5 |
| 86 | | 951.6 | 1030.8 | -79.2 | -1.0 | -0.7 |
| 88 | | 951.6 | 1056.0 | -104.4 | -1.2 | -0.9 |
| 90 | boom flat | 951.6 | 1081.2 | -129.6 | -1.5 | -1.1 |

Using the weights and moment arms above, the net restoring moment can be calculated all the way down to the boom being horizontal. From that, the load to tip can be calculated; finally the load being 75% of the tipping load can be derived. This is the calculated capacity per ASME B30.5.

First, you can see that at about 79 m – 80 m, there is no net restoring moment, the crane is in balance, therefore there is no capacity. From 82 m – 90 m you would need an assist crane as there is uplift on the lightest loaded track – the red figures are nonsense. The amber figures are calculated beyond the manufacturer's chart (which cuts off at 64 m). The grayed out areas are limited by considerations other than stability – I have to believe them and have no issue with that.

*Figure 7-48*

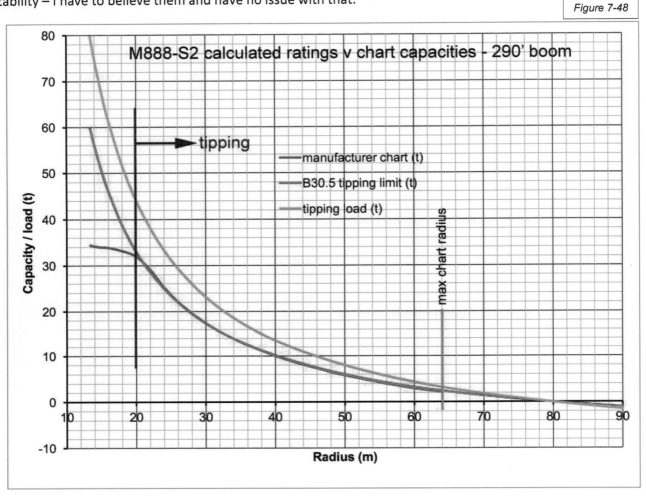

Plotting my calculated capacities versus the manufacturer's charts shows very good agreement over the tipping range.

I have also included the load that would be required to tip the crane. You can see that because the rated capacity is a fixed percentage of the tipping load, the two lines trend closer and closer together and converge at the point of tipping, which is at about 79 m – 80 m radius. The margin of stability is indeed the difference in load between the red and green lines with the green line being 1.33x the red line. This difference is an ever smaller load which eventually becomes zero. The problem I have with this approach is that the stability in any meaningful measure is getting less with increasing radius until it becomes unstable at 79 m. There is nothing in ASME B30.5 that prevents a manufacturer from going all the way to that point when rating your crane; Manitowoc has chosen to stop their chart at 64 m radius at which point they have 2.2 t capacity. There is little point in going further as by the time you get a hook-block and some load lines and some rigging there would be nothing left for payload. It is however a safety issue; we have seen earlier that at max radius, the most heavily loaded crawler is seeing 95.6% of the total load. It doesn't take a lot of imagination to see how easily that slim margin could be overcome if the crane is out of level or the load weighs more than it should or the wind gets hold of it. Manitowoc stop where they do as their choice, the code does not dictate it; they could have chosen to rate up to 98% or more. The code won't keep you safe, Manitowoc does that. Who is to say all manufacturers stop at the same point? The code needs to define safe margins of forward stability and it currently doesn't.

If you plot the percentage of load going to the most heavily loaded track it increases from about 86% when the tipping determined capacities start to about 96% where Manitowoc stopped the chart to 100%. As noted there is nothing in ASME B30.5 to stop you going all the way to 100%.

Figure 7-49

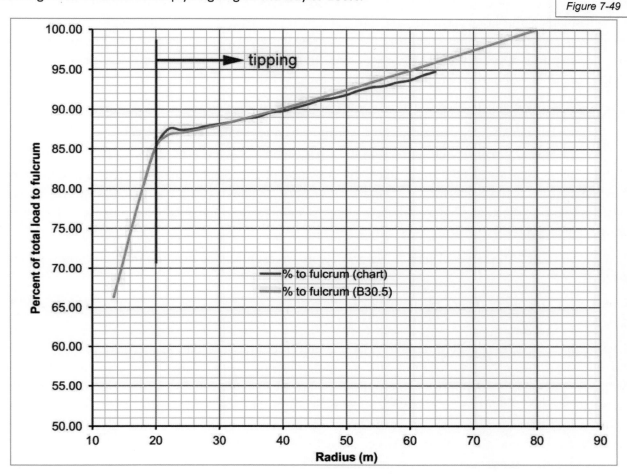

## Conclusion

In conclusion, as noted I picked the M888-S2 to analyze (relatively randomly) in order to demonstrate how ASME B30.5 forward tipping criteria can (and to some extent are) applied to load chart development and why I believe ASME B30.5 is flawed as a safety code. I hope I've done so. I'm sure the manufacturer could pick multiple holes in the analysis but I think it is good enough to show the general principles. I do believe that crane manufacturers add their own internal design and rating criteria in addition to those of the ASME code.

I do not believe that crane manufacturers are making unsafe products, but I think it is important to realize just how close to instability a crane can be at long radii.

I have shown that crane charts derived from different codes vary; I'm aware for instance that EN13000 (which I have not analyzed) has a different calculation method that includes consideration of part of the boom head weight. The crane industry is global; products are sold worldwide and are moved around the globe. It is ridiculous that different standards apply and we aren't big enough to agree. It is time that we adopted meaningful global crane safety standard that includes a meaningful moment-based limit on forward tipping. If need be, grandfather in older cranes and set a standard going forwards that reflects modern cranes and is sufficient as a basis for keeping people safe.

Do not use this analysis for anything more than comprehension of the basic principles behind crane chart development; never knowingly overload a crane - STICK TO THE CHART!!

Note that the opinions expressed are mine alone.

### 7.4.6    Assessing crane support loadings

When using a crawler or outrigger mounted crane, it is critical that it is supported on a surface that is capable of withstanding the imposed loads and pressures without reaching a limiting failure condition or settling excessively. It is also very important that the crane remains level in use; the loadings into the crane outriggers or crawler tracks are rarely uniform, so you need to be concerned that you don't get significant differential deflection across support points that would cause the crane to tilt out of tolerance.

There are two elements to assessing the support, you need to estimate:

A.   the peak loads / pressures the crane will impose under its tracks or outriggers

B.   the loads / pressures the supporting surface is capable of safely accepting

Determining crane loadings is very much the province of the rigging engineer, whereas determining soil bearing capacity is not something for the average rigging engineer, it is a highly specialist subject and it is a topic on which, wherever possible, you are going to want to seek guidance from a geotechnical specialist, a soils engineer typically.

Looking firstly at "A", we'll deal with "B" later. How do we estimate the loadings that the cranes will impose in use?

There are a number of means of estimating crane loadings and note I say "estimate" as this subject has few absolutes.

Luckily, these days there is little need to work it all out from first principles as there are programs packages to do all the hard work for you for most of the common cranes in use. Many of the crane manufacturers offer software packages in support of their products in which you can input the crane configuration and characteristics of the lift to be made; they will typically output the outrigger loads (or peak track pressures) with the load over the side, with it over the front/rear and with it at the worst swing (slew) angle which usually be with the boom directly over an outrigger or over the corner of the tracks. Some independents offer similar as part of a lift planning package. Some crane rental companies have their own proprietary programs for the cranes in their fleets. All of these will yield figures; it is important to note that they are estimates; crane loadings provided by software packages are based on best case, rigid support, level crane, (possibly) no wind forces acting on the crane, no mechanical or structural deflections and all the software inputs being exactly mirrored in the real world.

Rather than blindly entering data and accepting the output, I think it is important that you understand what lies behind these program and their limitations.  For that reason, we will examine the concepts below.

If you can't (or don't want to) work out the actual loadings, in the crane manual you should be able to find the maximum outrigger load (crawler track pressure) that the crane can ever impose. Use that figure if you can live with it (economically).

To make a worst case assessment, you can note that if the crane were actually at the point of tipping, the combined loads on two outriggers / front track pads would be 100% of the total weight of crane plus load.  It cannot exceed that figure and of course should be less as chart does not permit you to go right up to tipping. So how would they be shared if the boom is not centered but over one outrigger? I would suggest that using say 65% of the total load to any one outrigger will be about as bad as it gets in service and would be a realistic figure to use in the absence of any better data.

It is noted that the CSCS advice in the UK used to be to take 65% of the total weight of the crane plus load to be lifted as an outrigger load; I believe they now advise 100% which, if so, seems very unrealistic to me.

Noting the preceding, for interest a review of a number of RT cranes from several suppliers was conducted to see what they quoted in the crane manuals as being the max outrigger loads.

The results showed surprising consistency, indicating that RT cranes in the range 30 tons – 130 tons generally put down a max outrigger load of about 40% of the sum of the crane self-weight plus max payload and (a little less predictably) will put down about 25-28 ksf under the outrigger floats. In general terms, using mats 5x the float area could be expected to get you down to 5 or 6 ksf.

Anyway, I digress, back to the theory, and then we'll look at some software packages based on it.

<u>Outrigger based cranes, boom over the front</u>

Knowing that there are loads and moments acting on a crane, how does the crane work as a mechanism to resist tipping and how do loads and moments on the crane alter the loads into the outriggers or crawlers? Let's look firstly at a crane mounted on outriggers.

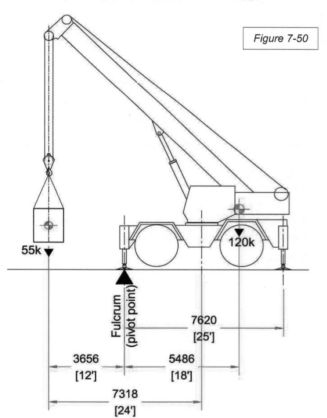

Figure 7-50

As seen here, this RT crane is sitting on its outriggers and is lifting a 55 kip load at 24' radius. (24.94 t at 7.3 m).

We will first consider the boom to be directly over the front of the crane.

The crane itself weighs a total of 120 kips (54.42 t) and its combined C of G lies 18' (5.486 m) from the front outriggers. The outriggers are on a nominally 25' (7.6 m) square grid centered on the center of rotation.

The mechanism acts like a lever with the front outriggers being the fulcrum.

The overturning moment is 55 kips x 12' = 660 kip-ft (24.94 t x 3.656 m = 91.2 t.m), whereas the restoring moment is 120 kips x 18' = 2160 kip-ft (54.42 t x 5.486 m = 298.5 t.m).

The crane is working at 30.6% of tipping.

To determine the outrigger loadings in the example above, the easiest approach is to consider what is happening about the center of rotation, taking moments about that axis. If the combined C of G of the crane and load lies on that line, then the crane is perfectly balanced and the outriggers loads will be all equal (assuming the outriggers are on a rectangular grid centered about the center of rotation and assuming level support). If the combined C of G of crane and load lies to the front, there will be a forward moment and the front outriggers will be more highly loaded (and vice versa to the rear); similarly side to side.

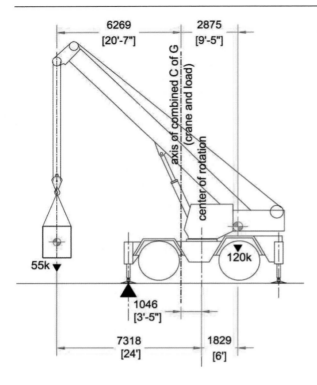

If in our example, we consider the boom to be directly over the front, then taking moments about the axis of rotation:

- the forward moment = 55 x 24 = 1320 kip-ft (24.94 x 7.318 = 182.5 t.m).
- the restoring moment = 120 x 6 = 720 kip-ft (54.42 x 1.829 = 99.5 t.m).

There is therefore a nett forward moment of 600 kip-ft (83 t.m).

This moment is equivalent to considering the total load acting at an eccentricity "e" from the axis of rotation.

The total load x it's eccentricity (e) from the center of rotation thus = 600 kip-ft (83 t.m).

e = 600 kip-ft / 175 kips = 3.43 ft (or 3'-5"), (83/79.4 = 1.05 m).

i.e. the combined C of G of the crane and load is at 3'-5" (1.05 m) in front of the center of rotation.

Figure 7-51

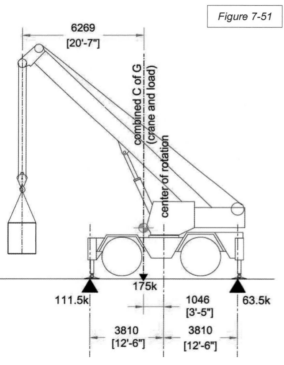

Considering the combined weight and C of G of the crane and load together as 175 kips (79.36 t) acting at 3'-5" (1.05 m) in front of the center of rotation:

The load to the two front outriggers

= 175 kips x 15'-11" / 25'-0", (79.36 t x 4.86 m / 7.62 m)

= 111.5 kips (50.6 t) shared equally between the two front outriggers as the boom is directly over the front.

The load to the two rear outriggers

= 175 kips x 9'-1" / 25'-0", (79.36 t x 2.76 m /7.62 m)

= 63.5 kips (28.8 t) shared equally between the two rear outriggers as the boom is directly over the front.

Alternatively, you can look at it this way.

If the crane were perfectly balanced under load, the outrigger loads would be split 50/50 front to rear

= the total load / 2 = 175/2 = 87.5 kips, (79.36/2 = 39.68 t) to the front and to the rear.

The moment about the center of the crane = 600 kip-ft (or 83.0 t.m) - see above.

This moment is opposed by a couple derived from a down-thrust on the front outriggers and a similar uplift to the rear outriggers acting at a spacing equal to the span of the outriggers.

The increase / decrease in load = +/-(600/25) = +/- 24 kips, (or +/- 83.0/7.62 = +/- 10.9 t).

Thus the front outriggers see 87.5 + 24 = 111.5 kips (or 39.7 + 10.9 = 50.6 t).

The two rear outriggers see 87.5 − 24 = 63.5 kips (or 39.7 − 10.9 = 28.8 t).

There is no side moment as the boom is over the front so the loads are shared equally side to side.

<u>Outrigger based cranes - boom not over the front</u>

When a crane is supported by four outriggers on a rectangular grid, the moment arms of the applied load (acting forwards) and of the crane's upper works (acting backwards) change as the upper works are rotated (swung / slewed) with the load at a constant radius. As the moments acting on the crane thus vary, stability is not constant around the crane.

A 360 degree chart gives ratings that can be applied anywhere around the crane and are based on the worst geometry for stability purposes. You might find charts that give you different duties when the upper works is over different sectors around the crane, say "over the rear", or "over the side".

Generally, "over the side" refers to sectors on either side of the crane bounded by lines from the center of rotation through the outriggers; similar principles apply to "over the front" or "over the rear". This definition isn't necessarily always the case, particularly with older cranes. To see what the specific manufacturer means by these terms refer to the crane charts.

How are the outrigger loads assessed when the boom is not over the front?

Given that a particular crane (basic RT or similar) is in a particular configuration with a certain amount of boom and a fixed amount of counterweight, what can change in operating the crane that would affect the base loadings?

Typically those things would include:

- the load being lifted
- the radius at which the load is being lifted
- the angle of the upper works relative to the base
- the vertical angle of the boom relative to the upper works (this is a function of the radius)

Let's look at this somewhat simplistically in order to illustrate the concepts. To analyze the problem, it is necessary to divide up the primary elements that can move relative to each other.

Considering firstly the upperworks; the moment $M_u$ acting on it (relative to the center of rotation of the crane) is given by:

$$M_u = M_w + M_b - M_c$$

where,

$M_w$ is the moment due to the payload (inc hook-block, rigging etc) acting at "r" where r is the radius,

$M_b$ is the moment due to the weight of the boom assembly acting at a moment arm that is a function of the boom angle and it's C of G

$M_c$ is the moment due to the weight of the upper-works (including machine counterweight) acting at a fixed moment arm determined by its rearwards C of G location

$M_u$ acts in the plane of the boom is considered +ve if it acts forwards.

$M_u$ can be resolved into component moments $M_{uf}$ acting front to rear and $M_{us}$ acting to one side or the other.

If the C of G of the lower works (the carrier part) does not lie on the center of rotation (and it likely won't on say a truck crane) then there will be a moment Mc acting front to rear due to the weight of the lower works x the eccentricity of its C of G from the center of rotation. There is unlikely to be much lateral offset to cause a side moment of any concern.

The total forward moment $M_f = M_{nf} + M_c$ (noting sign of $M_c$)

The total sideways moment $M_s = M_{us}$

Knowing the outrigger base in both directions, these moments can be resolved into outrigger loads.

*Note that it is not unknown on more modern cranes for one outrigger (directly opposite the load) to be completely unloaded and for the crane to still be operating within chart. Apparently this is a result of manufacturers using high strength steel which allows the use of lighter sections resulting in the crane being as strong but not being as stiff. This does not mean that it is always OK if an outrigger goes light. It may not be an indication of anything wrong for a specific crane under specific conditions – verify! Better still, note that this could happen on the lift study if it is known to be a possibility.*

These basic concepts are used in the analysis of crawler crane loadings following.

Determining pressures under crawler crane tracks

The weight of a crawler crane (plus any load suspended from it) is distributed via the crawler tracks into the supporting surface.

Note that track pads are normally profiled in section, flat in the center and tapered towards the edges. On a hard surface such as concrete, only the flat part will be in contact, whereas on a soft surface the pad can settle slightly into the surface and the entire width is considered effective. Similarly along the length of the crawlers, the profile of the track may taper up towards the ends and thus less length is considered effective on a hard surface. For these reasons, the contact area is considered less on a hard surface and the imposed pressure is corresponding higher. Manitowoc for instance recognizes this in their software and gives you a choice of "hard" or "soft" supporting surface. Note that if you are intending to locate your crawler crane on concrete (that you care about), you should soften the contact pad - concrete interface by using plywood or matting or similar under the tracks to avoid local high contact pressures damaging the concrete or cracking it. Avoid supporting a crane partly on concrete or other non-compliant surface and partly on a compliant surface such as compacted ground. You may get differential settlement and could crack the edge of the slab. Avoid loading slabs close to their edges.

If the crane is perfectly balanced, i.e. the combined C of G of the crane plus load is central to the tracks, the loads can be considered to be distributed evenly along the tracks. There is no nett moment acting on the crane - the two pressure profiles will be equal and rectangular.

However cranes are generally designed to be tail-heavy when lightly loaded and front-heavy when loaded to their maximum. There is therefore in most cases a nett front or rear moment on the crane; as the moment increases, the pressure profile changes to trapezoidal with less pressure at one end than at the other; with further increase the pressure becomes zero at one end of the track and the profile is then triangular (occupying the whole length of the track). With yet further increase in moment, part of the track becomes unloaded – the profile is a shorter triangle. The peak pressure is the max height of the pressure profile. Note that the area of the pressure profile represents the total load carried by that track. If the boom is parallel to the tracks and you are merely booming up and down, the load carried by each track will remain the same, but the pressure profile changes with the moment. The area of the profile remains the same regardless of the shape. A vertical line through the center of area of the pressure represents the axis about which the crane is balanced and therefore passes through the location of the C of G of the crane and load combined.

### 7.4.7 Example of changing pressure profiles (crawler crane)

How the pressure profiles change can demonstrated by looking at this spreadsheet. I'll explain the formulae that lie behind the spreadsheet in a moment. Let's consider a representative crane with 200' of boom fitted. The weights and C of G locations of the various components can be gleaned from manufacturer's data and inputted. We'll consider lifting 50,000 lbs. The minimum radius is 34' at which the crane is rated for 157,200 lbs.

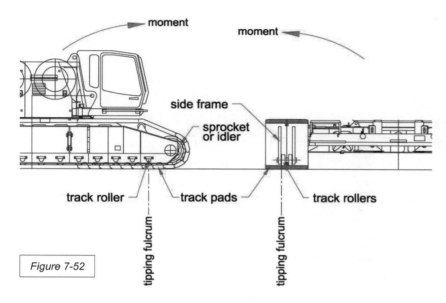

Figure 7-52

Note the track length $d_L$ is the effective track length for bearing purposes which will usually be the "flat" distance between extreme track rollers not the distance between track sprockets. Track pads which often rise slightly towards the sprockets.

Note as well that the actual tipping fulcrum across the tracks is not likely to be the actual center of the track pads (as used in the analysis below), but a line closer to the outside of the pads.

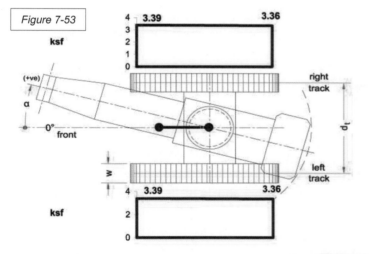

Figure 7-53

| | | | |
|---|---|---|---|
| W | load being lifted | 50000 | lb |
| r | load radius | 34 | ft |
| $W_b$ | weight of boom | 35100 | lb |
| $L_b$ | dist to C of G of the boom | 104.4 | ft |
| θ | angle of boom to ground | 76.7 | ° |
| t | boom offset | 4 | ft |
| $W_u$ | weight of superstructure + counterweight | 230050 | lb |
| $d_u$ | upper (superstructure + counterweight CG from rotation axis | 11.63 | ft |
| $W_c$ | weight of crane undercarriage | 186822 | lb |
| $d_c$ | dist of undercarriage CG behind centerline of bearing | 0 | ft |
| $x_o$ | dist from centerline of bearing to axis of rotation (+ve towards rear) | 0 | ft |
| $d_t$ | distance between centerlines of tracks | 17.7 | ft |
| $d_L$ | track length | 18.6 | ft |
| w | track effective width | 4 | ft |
| α | angle of upper works (0° to front, measured clockwise) | 0 | ° |

As it happens, lifting 50,000# at 34' results in a very well balanced crane (the blue rectangles represent the pressure profiles under the tracks). With the boom over the front (represented by the blue "dumbbell"), both tracks are equally loaded and the pressure is fairly constant at about 3.39 ksf along the entire length of the tracks.

As the combined C of G of the crane plus load obviously lies near directly over the axis of rotation, swinging the crane will have next to no effect on the pressure distribution.

The areas of the pressure profiles (multiplied by track width) represent the load carried by each track.

If we were lifting less than 50,000#, the crane would be tail-heavy and the pressure profiles trapezoidal (skewed to the rear).

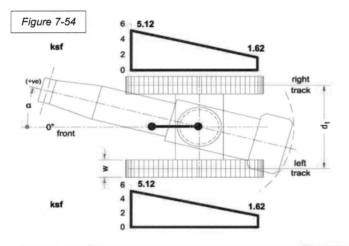

Figure 7-54

| W | load being lifted | 50000 | lb |
|---|---|---|---|
| r | load radius | 50 | ft |
| $W_b$ | weight of boom | 35100 | lb |
| $L_b$ | dist to C of G of the boom | 104.4 | ft |
| θ | angle of boom to ground | 76.7 | ° |
| t | boom offset | 4 | ft |
| $W_u$ | weight of superstructure + counterweight | 230050 | lb |
| $d_u$ | upper (superstructure + counterweight CG from rotation axis | 11.63 | ft |
| $W_c$ | weight of crane undercarriage | 186822 | lb |
| $d_c$ | dist of undercarriage CG behind centerline of bearing | 0 | ft |
| $x_o$ | dist from centerline of bearing to axis of rotation (+ve towards rear) | 0 | ft |
| $d_t$ | distance between centerlines of tracks | 17.7 | ft |
| $d_L$ | track length | 18.6 | ft |
| w | track effective width | 4 | ft |
| α | angle of upper works (0° to front, measured clockwise) | 0 | ° |

If we push the 50,000# load out to 50' radius and keep the boom over the front, the pressure profile changes to trapezoidal. Each track still carries 50% of the total load.

The areas under the pressure profiles still represent the load carried by the tracks. As the loads haven't changed, the areas of the profiles remain the same although the shape has changed. The peak pressure is higher.

The center of gravity of the combined crane and load lies on the center of area of the pressure profile. It is actually 1.6' forward of the axis of rotation at this point.

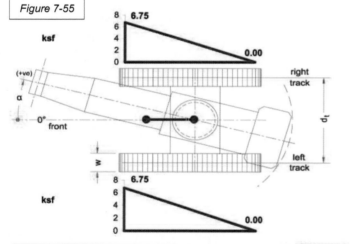

Figure 7-55

| W | load being lifted | 50000 | lb |
|---|---|---|---|
| r | load radius | 65 | ft |
| $W_b$ | weight of boom | 35100 | lb |
| $L_b$ | dist to C of G of the boom | 104.4 | ft |
| θ | angle of boom to ground | 76.7 | ° |
| t | boom offset | 4 | ft |
| $W_u$ | weight of superstructure + counterweight | 230050 | lb |
| $d_u$ | upper (superstructure + counterweight CG from rotation axis | 11.63 | ft |
| $W_c$ | weight of crane undercarriage | 186822 | lb |
| $d_c$ | dist of undercarriage CG behind centerline of bearing | 0 | ft |
| $x_o$ | dist from centerline of bearing to axis of rotation (+ve towards rear) | 0 | ft |
| $d_t$ | distance between centerlines of tracks | 17.7 | ft |
| $d_L$ | track length | 18.6 | ft |
| w | track effective width | 4 | ft |
| α | angle of upper works (0° to front, measured clockwise) | 0 | ° |

If we push the 50,000# load out to 65' radius and keep the boom over the front, the pressure profile becomes triangular with the whole track length loaded. Each track still carries 50% of the total load. The peak pressure is higher still.

This change in profile will always happen when the combined C of G of the crane and load lies at an eccentricity = track length / 6 from the axis of rotation. In this case, the eccentricity is 3.1 ft, which is indeed 18.6/6.

Why is this so? We know the C of G lies on the center of area of the pressure profile; the center of area of the triangle lies horizontally at track length $d_L/3$ from the LH end (when the whole track is loaded); the center of rotation is at $d_L/2$ from the LH end. The difference = the eccentricity "e" = $d_L/6$

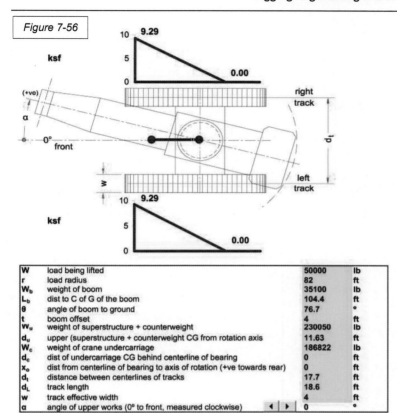

Figure 7-56

| W | load being lifted | 50000 | lb |
|---|---|---|---|
| r | load radius | 82 | ft |
| $W_b$ | weight of boom | 35100 | lb |
| $L_b$ | dist to C of G of the boom | 104.4 | ft |
| θ | angle of boom to ground | 76.7 | ° |
| t | boom offset | 4 | ft |
| $W_u$ | weight of superstructure + counterweight | 230050 | lb |
| $d_u$ | upper (superstructure + counterweight CG from rotation axis | 11.63 | ft |
| $W_c$ | weight of crane undercarriage | 186822 | lb |
| $d_c$ | dist of undercarriage CG behind centerline of bearing | 0 | ft |
| $x_o$ | dist from centerline of bearing to axis of rotation (+ve towards rear) | 0 | ft |
| $d_t$ | distance between centerlines of tracks | 17.7 | ft |
| $d_L$ | track length | 18.6 | ft |
| w | track effective width | 4 | ft |
| α | angle of upper works (0° to front, measured clockwise) | 0 | ° |

If we push the 50,000# load out to 82' radius (which is the max chart radius for this load) and keep the boom over the front, the pressure profile remains triangular but part of the track length is unloaded. As each track still carries 50% of the total load but the profile is shorter, the peak pressure has to be higher. Through all this the area of the profiles has not changed, just the shape.

The eccentricity "e" = 4.8' which is as much as the manufacturer wants it to be. We are using 360° charts here and are in a "tipping" region of the chart. i.e. one governed by tipping criteria rather than by structural considerations. As the track base is slightly narrower than it is long, it is likely that the limiting "tipping" condition is not actually over the front but when the boom is over the side.

You may in fact be able to obtain a better duty chart from the manufacturer for lifting directly over the front with blocking under the front of the tracks. This may be needed when raising a long boom for instance.

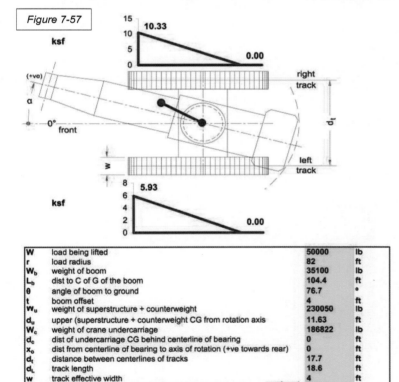

Figure 7-57

| W | load being lifted | 50000 | lb |
|---|---|---|---|
| r | load radius | 82 | ft |
| $W_b$ | weight of boom | 35100 | lb |
| $L_b$ | dist to C of G of the boom | 104.4 | ft |
| θ | angle of boom to ground | 76.7 | ° |
| t | boom offset | 4 | ft |
| $W_u$ | weight of superstructure + counterweight | 230050 | lb |
| $d_u$ | upper (superstructure + counterweight CG from rotation axis | 11.63 | ft |
| $W_c$ | weight of crane undercarriage | 186822 | lb |
| $d_c$ | dist of undercarriage CG behind centerline of bearing | 0 | ft |
| $x_o$ | dist from centerline of bearing to axis of rotation (+ve towards rear) | 0 | ft |
| $d_t$ | distance between centerlines of tracks | 17.7 | ft |
| $d_L$ | track length | 18.6 | ft |
| w | track effective width | 4 | ft |
| α | angle of upper works (0° to front, measured clockwise) | 30 | ° |

If we maintain the 50,000# load at 82' radius and swing (slew) clockwise till the boom is at (say) 30° relative to the lower works, the pressure profiles both remain triangular with part of the track length unloaded. However as part of the moment acting on the crane is now acting across the tracks, the track to that side is the more highly loaded of the two.

The sum total of the areas under the pressure profiles represents the total load on the crane.

At 30° of swing, the peak pressure is now pretty much at a maximum (as you might expect as the boom lies over the front pads of one of the tracks).

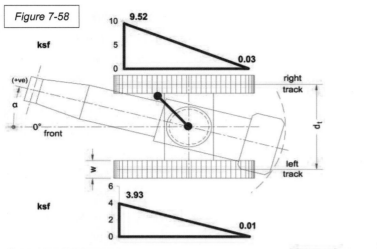

Figure 7-58

| W | load being lifted | 50000 | lb |
|---|---|---|---|
| r | load radius | 82 | ft |
| $W_b$ | weight of boom | 35100 | lb |
| $L_b$ | dist to C of G of the boom | 104.4 | ft |
| θ | angle of boom to ground | 76.7 | ° |
| t | boom offset | 4 | ft |
| $W_u$ | weight of superstructure + counterweight | 230050 | lb |
| $d_u$ | upper (superstructure + counterweight CG from rotation axis | 11.63 | ft |
| $W_c$ | weight of crane undercarriage | 186822 | lb |
| $d_c$ | dist of undercarriage CG behind centerline of bearing | 0 | ft |
| $x_o$ | dist from centerline of bearing to axis of rotation (+ve towards rear) | 0 | ft |
| $d_t$ | distance between centerlines of tracks | 17.7 | ft |
| $d_L$ | track length | 18.6 | ft |
| w | track effective width | 4 | ft |
| α | angle of upper works (0° to front, measured clockwise) | 50 | ° |

As we continue to swing the load clockwise, the length of track loaded increases as the location of the C of G along the length of the tracks more closely approaches the axis of rotation until at about 48.8°, the whole track length is once again loaded.

The peak pressure has passed its maximum and is starting to decrease as the crane gets better balanced.

The actual radial eccentricity is still 4.8'. It's resolution along the track = 4.8 cos(48.8°) = 3.16' which is the critical eccentricity at which the profile is fully-loaded triangular and after which it turns trapezoidal.

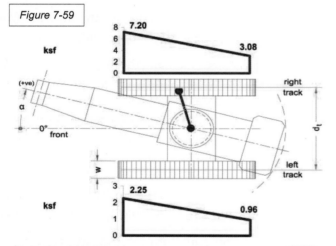

Figure 7-59

| W | load being lifted | 50000 | lb |
|---|---|---|---|
| r | load radius | 82 | ft |
| $W_b$ | weight of boom | 35100 | lb |
| $L_b$ | dist to C of G of the boom | 104.4 | ft |
| θ | angle of boom to ground | 76.7 | ° |
| t | boom offset | 4 | ft |
| $W_u$ | weight of superstructure + counterweight | 230050 | lb |
| $d_u$ | upper (superstructure + counterweight CG from rotation axis | 11.63 | ft |
| $W_c$ | weight of crane undercarriage | 186822 | lb |
| $d_c$ | dist of undercarriage CG behind centerline of bearing | 0 | ft |
| $x_o$ | dist from centerline of bearing to axis of rotation (+ve towards rear) | 0 | ft |
| $d_t$ | distance between centerlines of tracks | 17.7 | ft |
| $d_L$ | track length | 18.6 | ft |
| w | track effective width | 4 | ft |
| α | angle of upper works (0° to front, measured clockwise) | 75 | ° |

At say 75°, the profiles are trapezoidal and tending to rectangular. The RH track is considerably more heavily loaded than the LH track but the peak pressures are dropping as the forward moment decreases.

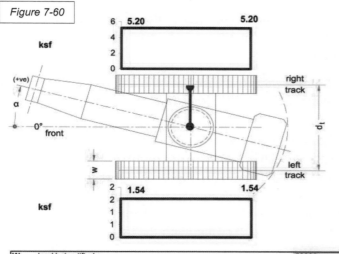

Figure 7-60

| W | load being lifted | 50000 | lb |
|---|---|---|---|
| r | load radius | 82 | ft |
| $W_b$ | weight of boom | 35100 | lb |
| $L_b$ | dist to C of G of the boom | 104.4 | ft |
| $\theta$ | angle of boom to ground | 76.7 | ° |
| t | boom offset | 4 | ft |
| $W_u$ | weight of superstructure + counterweight | 230050 | lb |
| $d_u$ | upper (superstructure + counterweight) CG from rotation axis | 11.63 | ft |
| $W_c$ | weight of crane undercarriage | 186822 | lb |
| $d_c$ | dist of undercarriage CG behind centerline of bearing | 0 | ft |
| $x_o$ | dist from centerline of bearing to axis of rotation (+ve towards rear) | 0 | ft |
| $d_t$ | distance between centerlines of tracks | 17.7 | ft |
| $d_L$ | track length | 18.6 | ft |
| w | track effective width | 4 | ft |
| $\alpha$ | angle of upper works (0° to front, measured clockwise)  ◄ ► | 90 | ° |

At 90°, there is no forward component of the moment acting on the crane, so the pressure profiles are rectangular. They are however different as there is a moment and it acts directly over the side.

This is probably the worst situation for tipping and the one on which the manufacturer based the chart capacities.

The tipping moment is restricted by code to 75% of that which would actually cause it to tip.

This spreadsheet is somewhat simplistic and data plugged in won't necessarily agree absolutely with estimation aids provided by manufacturers for their machines. It does however illustrate the principles and the manner in which the pressure profiles change. These days, there should be little requirement to calculate crane loadings from scratch, but if you do need to do so, follow along through the next section. For background reading you are recommended to "Cranes and Derricks" by Shapiro.

### 7.4.8    How are the pressure profiles calculated?

As noted above, there are software packages available to do this, but what are the principles that lie behind them and what if I want to work it out manually? To illustrate the concepts, we will consider a basic lattice boom crawler crane w/o jib or back mast / Superlift. There are many theories as to how this all works in practice and in truth there are so many variables that an exact answer isn't realistic. The best that can be hoped for is a sound method for estimation supported by long term positive results using that methodology. The method below for instance assumes enough compliance in the ground to cope with say deflections due to twisting in the lower works. The relative stiffness of crane and supporting surface has a major effect in how the loads are actually distributed. The method following has served well in practice and is probably most accurate when the crane is relative stiff and the ground not so. Note that the software packages don't necessarily follow this exact methodology and they don't necessarily all calculate in similar manner.

*You may see reference to the PCSA (Power Crane and Shovel Association) method of calculating pressures. "Ground pressure" in PCSA terms is an average pressure derived by dividing the total working weight of the machine (but without load), by the crawler assembly bearing area. It assumes uniform support and will yield much lower pressures than the methods discussed here. It is not representative of the loadings imposed by construction cranes in use.*

To calculate the pressure profiles, we need to determine the weights and moments acting on the crane.

Every component of the crane has its own weight and location causing a moment on the crane. For the purpose of analysis, it is easiest to group components together mathematically and consider the crane as a number of assemblies which can move relative to each other:

- The Undercarriage (lower works) – although not always the case, we will assume it is symmetrical about the center of rotation and we will assume it's C of G lies on the center of rotation. Its weight includes any central ballast fitted.

- The Upper Works – this is mounted on, and can swing (slew) relative to, the lower works. Its weight includes machine counterweight; its C of G is going to be behind the center of rotation.

- The Boom – this will be an assembly of boom head and boom butt with insert sections and will include pendants and any accessories fitted; it's C of G will lie somewhere close to the axis of the boom at approximately mid length. The boom foot is pinned to the Upper Works forward of the center of rotation and it can boom up and down on that hinge point. It swings with the upper works.

- The Load – this is suspended from the boom head and includes the payload, hook-block and rigging; it's radius changes as the crane booms up and down. It swings with the upper works and its C of G lies directly under the boom head.

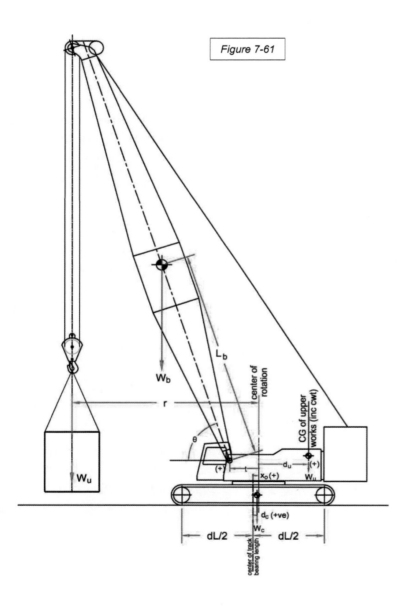

Figure 7-61

You'll need enough weight and location information to be able to sum the weights of the components that constitute each of the above assemblies and to be able to calculate the location of the C of G of the assembly.

It is first necessary to calculate the moments acting on the crane, the positive (forward) moments due to the boom and to the load lifted, and the balancing negative (backwards) moment due to the upper works and machine counterweight. Moments are calculated relative to the center of rotation. As the C of G of the lower works is considered to lie on this line, it contributes weight but zero moment one way or the other.

If the C of G of the lower works does not lie on (or very close to) the axis of rotation, it would be necessary to consider the moments induced by the lower works front - rear and side - side and include them in the summations.

The following inputs are required, let's input some sample (representative) data.

| | | | |
|---|---|---|---|
| W | load being lifted | 50000 | lb |
| r | load radius | 50 | ft |
| $W_b$ | weight of boom | 35100 | lb |
| $L_b$ | dist to C of G of the boom | 104.4 | ft |
| θ | angle of boom to ground | 76.7 | ° |
| T | boom offset | 4 | ft |
| $W_u$ | weight of superstructure + counterweight | 230050 | lb |
| $d_u$ | upper (superstructure + counterweight C of G from rotation axis | 11.63 | ft |
| $W_c$ | weight of crane undercarriage | 186822 | lb |
| $d_c$ | dist of undercarriage C of G behind centerline of bearing | 0 | ft |
| $X_o$ | dist from centerline of bearing to axis of rotation (+ve towards rear) | 0 | ft |
| $d_t$ | distance between centerlines of tracks | 17.7 | ft |
| dL | track length | 18.6 | ft |
| w | track effective width | 4 | ft |
| α | angle of upper works (0° to front, measured clockwise) | 0 | ° |

As noted above, for our purposes it will be assumed (as this is generally the case), that the tracks are symmetrical about the center of rotation and the C of G of the undercarriage is coincident with the center of rotation. i.e. $X_o$ and $d_C = 0$, taking moments about the center of rotation:

Moment due to boom weight

$M_b = W_b(t+L_b\cos\theta)$

$M_b = 35,100(4+104.4\cos76.7)$ = _983,403 lb-ft_

Moment due to payload

$M_w = W.r$ = 50,000 x 50

$M_w = 2,500,000$ lb-ft

Moment due to upper works (inc counterweight)

$M_c = W_u.d_u$ = 230,050 x 11.63 lb-ft

Mc = _2,675,481 lb-ft_ (acts backwards)

From this we can sum the total upper moment acting on the crane's upper works (+ve is forwards)

$M_u = M_b+M_w-M_c$ = 983,403 + 2,500,000 − 2,675,481 lb-ft

**$M_u$ = 807,922 lb-ft**      this acts forwards in the plane of the boom

To determine the components of the moment acting along the tracks and across the tracks, we need to resolve the upper moment considering the rotation angle relative to the undercarriage.

*Note that the weight of the undercarriage does not contribute an overturning moment (about the center of rotation) if, as assumed, the C of G lies at the center of rotation.*

Over the front of the crane, the net applied moment, $M_{nf}$, is:

$M_{nf} = M_u\cos\alpha$

at α=30 degrees (say)

$M_{nf} = 807,922 \cos(30°)$ = 699,681 lb-ft

Over the side of the crane, the net applied moment, $M_{ns}$, is:

$M_{ns} = M_u\sin\alpha$

at α=30 degrees

$M_{ns} = 807,922 \sin(30°)$ = 403,961 lb-ft

Having figured moments acting on the crane, we need to derive the vertical loads acting.

Total vertical load excluding weight of undercarriage

$V_u = W + W_b + W_u = 50,000 + 35,100 + 230,050$

$V_u = 315,150$ lbs

Total vertical load including weight of undercarriage

$V = V_u + W_c = 315,150 + 186,822$

$V = 501,972$ lbs

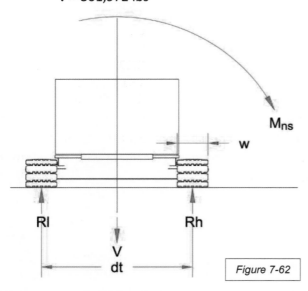

Mns

w

Rl          Rh

V

dt

*Figure 7-62*

For a perfectly balanced crane with respect to the track-bearing surfaces, $M_{nf} = M_{ns} = 0$ and the load would be equally shared between the tracks with each track carrying V/2 (250,986 lbs) However, if $M_{ns} \neq 0$ then the distribution of loads between the tracks cannot be even, and the difference in track loading must produce a ground reaction moment equal and opposite to $M_{ns}$.

The couple $M_{ns}$ produces an uplift on one track and a corresponding downthrust on the other of +/- $M_{ns}/d_t$ = 22,823 lbs.

If the reaction under the more heavily-loaded track is termed $R_H$ and under the more lightly-loaded track is termed $R_L$, then:

$R_H = V/2 + M_{ns}/d_t = 250,986 + 22,823 = 273,809$ lbs (= 273,809 / 501,972 or 54.5%)

$R_L = V/2 - M_{ns}/d_t = 250,986 - 22,823 = 228,163$ lbs (= 228,163 / 501,972 or 45.5%)

We now need to consider the effect of the moment over the front, $M_{nf}$. This moment determines the pressure profile along the track.

Rectangular pressure distribution

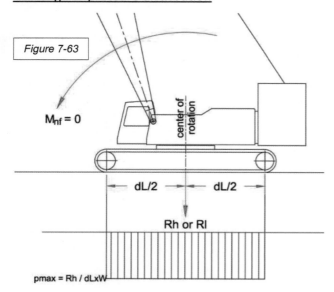

*Figure 7-63*

$M_{nf} = 0$

center of rotation

dL/2      dL/2

Rh or Rl

pmax = Rh / dLxW

If $M_{nf} = 0$, then there is no overturning effect (about the center of the crane) in the longitudinal direction and the pressure will be constant along each track; i.e. there will be a rectangular pressure distribution = $R_H$ (or $R_L$ as appropriate) / the full bearing area of the track;

$P_H = R_H / (d_L \times w)$

The total area under the pressure profile (multiplied by the track width) equals the load on that track.

The pressure distribution profile under the tracks of a crawler crane is rectangular only when the forward (or rearward) moment on the crane is zero. If there is a moment across the tracks (only), the track pressures will be rectangular but different.

In our example, $M_{nf}$ is NOT zero, so the distribution is not rectangular

Trapezoidal pressure distribution

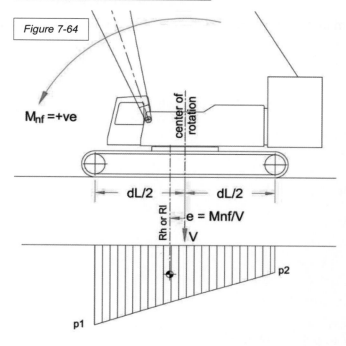

Figure 7-64

$M_{nf}$ =+ve

center of rotation

dL/2          dL/2

Rh or Rl    e = Mnf/V

V

p2

p1

If the combined C of G of the crane and load does not lie on the axis of rotation, then $M_{nf} \neq 0$ and there is an overturning effect on the crane in the longitudinal direction (either forwards or backwards) about the center of rotation. This causes the loads in the track pads to increase in the direction of the moment and correspondingly decrease away from it, skewing the pressure profile. The pressure distribution profile changes initially from a rectangular to a trapezoidal shape. Note however that as the total load carried by each track is unchanged, the area under the pressure profile remains the same.

The moment shifts the effective center of application of the vertical loads forwards or backwards relative to the center of rotation according to whether it is a forward or backwards moment (+ve or –ve). Note the combined C of G acts through the geometric center of area of the pressure profile.

To determine the eccentricity of application of the vertical reactions in the two tracks, moments are taken about the center of rotation yielding $M_{nf} = V.e$, where $M_{nf}$ is the forward moment, V is the total weight and e is the eccentricity of the combined C of G from the axis of rotation.

$e = M_{nf}/V = 699,681 / 501.972 = 1.4$ ft

i.e. the C of G of the loaded crane and thus the center of pressure is 1.4 ft in front of the center of rotation (in this example).

Knowing this, how do we determine $p_1$ and $p_2$?

With zero moment, as noted above:

$p_1 = p_2 =$ track load ($R_H$ or $R_L$ as applicable) / (track length ($d_L$) x track width (w))

i.e. the mean (uniform) track pressure = ($R_H$ or $R_L$) / $d_L$.w

An applied forward or rearward moment increases the pressure at one end and reduces it by the same amount at the other whilst maintaining the same area under the profile.

The amount by which $p_1$ and $p_2$ vary from the mean is given by: +/- $(p_1-p_2)/2$

For analysis, the trapezoidal pressure profile can be broken down into a rectangular area and a triangular area. The center of area of the rectangular part lies on the center of rotation and the loads carried by that portion of the profile are thus balanced and contribute nothing to resisting the moment.

The center of area of the triangular portion lies at $d_L/3$ from the base of the triangle, the eccentricity of the center of area of the triangular portion from the center of rotation is thus = $d_L/6$. The load represented by the triangular part of the profile x its eccentricity must equal the imposed moment $M_{nf}$.

Therefore the moment carried by 1 track, say the most highly loaded track, $M_{nfH}$ is given by:

$$M_{nfH} = 0.5 \ w \ (p_{1H}-p_{2H}) \ d_L.d_L/6$$

Re-arranging yields

$$6M_{nfH} /w.d_L^2 = (p_{1H}-p_{2H})/2$$

As we know from above that +/- $(p_{1H}-p_{2H})/2$ is the amount by which $p_1$ and $p_2$ vary from the uniform pressure distribution, we can say that:

$$p_{1H} = R_H/d_L.w + (6M_{nfH} /w.d_L^2)$$

$$p_{2H} = R_H/d_L.w - (6M_{nfH} /w.d_L^2)$$

$$p_{1L} = R_L/d_L.w + (6M_{nfL} /w.d_L^2)$$

$$p_{1L} = R_L/d_L.w - (6M_{nfL} /w.d_L^2)$$

In our example, we know from above that,

$$M_{nf} = 699,681 \text{ lb-ft, and}$$

$$R_H = 273,809 \text{ lbs (54.5\%)}$$

$$R_L = 228,163 \text{ lbs (45.5\%)}$$

therefore

$$M_{nfH}= 54.5\% \times 699,681 = 381,326 \text{ lb-ft}$$

$$M_{nfL}= 45.5\% \times 699,681 = 318,355 \text{ lb-ft}$$

Substituting in the equations above, yields:

$$p_{1H} = (273,809 / 18.6 \times 4) + (6 \times 381,326 / 4 \times 18.62) = 5334 \text{ lb/ft}^2$$

$$p_{2H} = (273,809 / 18.6 \times 4) - (6 \times 381,326 / 4 \times 18.62) = 2027 \text{ lb/ft}^2$$

$$p_{1L} = (228,163 / 18.6 \times 4) + (6 \times 318,355 / 4 \times 18.62) = 4447 \text{ lb/ft}^2$$

$$p_{1L} = (228,163 / 18.6 \times 4) - (6 \times 318,355 / 4 \times 18.62) = 1686 \text{ lb/ft}^2$$

Triangular pressure distribution – entire track loaded

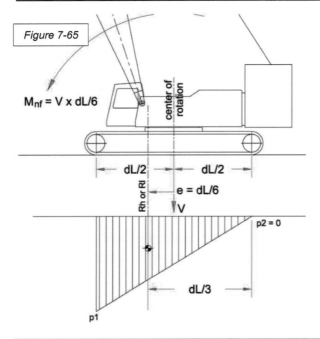

Figure 7-65

$M_{nf} = V \times dL/6$

As $M_{nf}$ further increases, $p_1$ increases and $p_2$ decreases until $p_2=0$ and the distribution changes to triangular with the whole length of the track loaded.

At this point the combined C of G lies at $d_L/3$ from the LH side of the profile (which is where the center of area is) and the axis of rotation is fixed at $d_L/2$ from the LH side. The eccentricity "e" is given by: $e = d_L/2 – d_L/3 = d_L/6$

The pressure profile under the crawler crane tracks will be triangular, with the whole track length loaded, when the eccentricity of the combined C of G of crane and load is located at a distance front or rear from the axis of rotation equal to the effective track/6.

At this point, when the boom is over the front,

$M_{nf} = V.d_L/6$, where V is the total vertical load

$p_1 = 2.R_H$ (or $R_L)/(d_L.w)$  &  $p_2 = 0$

The pressure distribution profile on a crawler crane changes from trapezoidal to triangular when the forward (or rearward) moment on the crane divided by the total weight of crane plus load = the track length / 6. At that point the whole track length is loaded.

i.e. the critical eccentricity $e = d_L/6$.

In our example, the critical eccentricity = 18.6 / 6 = 3.1 ft, the actual eccentricity e = 1.4 ft, therefore the distribution is trapezoidal in our example.

Triangular pressure distribution – only part track loaded

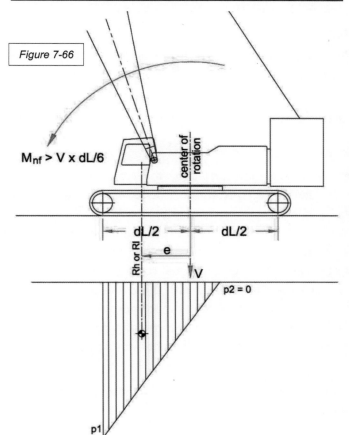

Figure 7-66

$M_{nf} > V \times dL/6$

If $M_{nf}$ further increases the eccentricity becomes larger and the center of area of the pressure profile moves left to coincide with it.

As the area under the pressure profile "curve" has to remain the same (equivalent to the load on the track $R_H$ or $R_L$), for this to happen the effective length of the pressure profile has to shorten and $p_1$ has to increase further; $p_2$ cannot decrease any further as it is already zero and cannot be negative.

The result is higher peak pressures and part of the track being unloaded.

To determine the effective length of bearing, Le; we know that:

- the center of area of the distribution profile lies on the line at which there is no nett moment; i.e. at an eccentricity $e = M_{nf} / V$
- also, the center of area lies at $L_e/3$ from the base ($L_H$ side) of the pressure triangle.

The axis of rotation is at $d_L/2$ from the base ($L_H$ side), so the eccentricity e is given by:

$e = d_L/2 - L_e/3$;

hence, when the distribution is triangular, the contact length, Le is given by:

$L_e = 3(d_L/2 - e)$

or

$L_e = 3(d_L/2 - M_{nf}/V)$

The area under the curve x the effective track width is equivalent to the load on the track.

$p_1 \times L_e.w / 2 = R_H$ (or $R_L$)

The peak pressures under the tracks are given by:

$p_{1H} = 2 R_H / L_e.w$ (heavy)

$p_{1L} = 2 R_L / L_e.w$ (light)

Summary

Start by determining the total weight of crane plus load and the moments acting on the crane. Resolve the moments to the front and to the side.

Knowing that, calculate the front/rear eccentricity of the combined C of G from the center of rotation, it is the forward moment / the total weight

- If the (longitudinal) eccentricity = 0, the distribution is rectangular
- If the eccentricity lies between +/- dL/6, the distribution is trapezoidal.
- If the eccentricity is = dL/6 the distribution is triangular with the whole track loaded.
- If the eccentricity is > dL/6 (+ or -) the distribution is triangular with part track loaded.

*The eccentricity cannot be greater than dL/2 as the crane would overturn at that point. In practice, design codes limit how close the crane ratings can approach the tipping condition and thus when operated within ratings "e" will never be allowed to reach dL/2.*

Knowing the distribution pattern, use the formulae in the appropriate sections to determine peak pressures.

## 7.4.9 Effect of Superlift use on crawler crane track pressures

When using Superlift, the additional counterweight is initially not carried by the crane but is supported independently through the tray or wheeled carrier (as fitted) directly from the ground. As the crane is loaded and the overturning (forward) moment on it increases, the tension restraining the back mast is adjusted to load the SL pendants relieving some of the weight on the tray or carrier from the ground and adding it to the crane. At, or close to full rated capacity, the entire weight of the Superlift ballast will be taken through the crane's back mast. This extra weight acting behind the crane provides additional restoring moment, keeping the combined C of G of the crane, payload and imposed Superlift securely with the crane base support and better balancing the machine.  By adjusting the amount of Superlift weight supported by the crane (within prescribed bounds), you can often balance the crane very well, albeit at the expense of carrying more weight in total on the crane tracks. How well it is balanced of course, also relies on the operator operating the crane optimally.

Working the crane at the extremes of the range of permitted back mast tension may not result in the pressures being quite as favorable as you may have planned it.

### 7.4.10  Calculating loads and pressures using software packages

As noted earlier, there are a number of software packages available to you to assist in coming up with estimates of loads and pressures imposed by construction cranes in use.  I can't guarantee that they calculate in the exact same manner as outlined above, you may not get exactly the same answers doing it manually. Even though they may differ a bit, using these various estimators in conjunction with reasonably conservative judgments on ground bearing capability has served well over the years. The problems really start when no reasonable assessment is made as to loads imposed or the ground's ability to withstand them. Let's look at a few packages and note some of the key features.

Liebherr-LICCON

This is the sort of output you will get if you use Liebherr's LICCON lift planner to determine outrigger loadings. The crane used for illustrative purposes is a Liebherr LTM1300/1 truck mounted telescopic boom crane. (The crane operator gets a similar display on the crane's computer system).

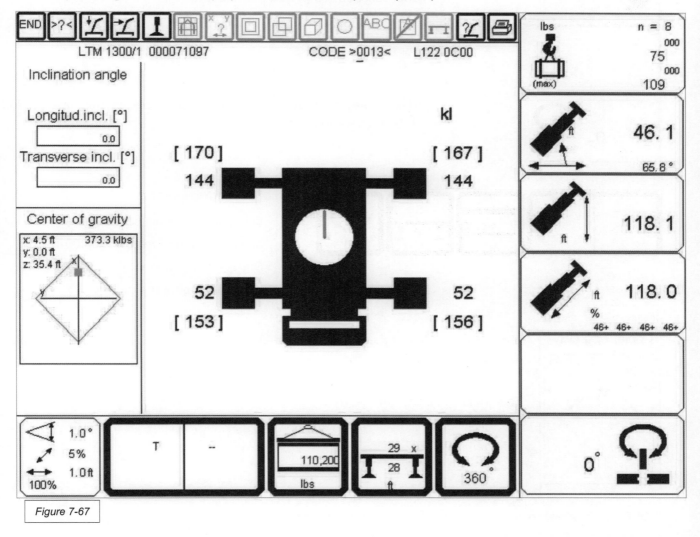

Figure 7-67

Key to understanding any of Liebherr's crane-related information is to understand the icons. Some explanation here may help; so, starting with the boxes on the right hand side.

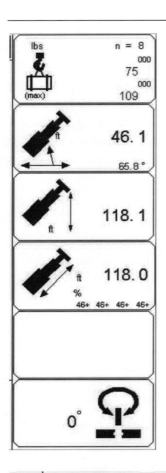

This box is concerned with loads on the hook. 75000 is the actual intended payload (lbs) – user inputted.

109000 is the chart capacity (lbs) defined by the inputs.

n=8 indicates 8 parts of hoist line are required (can be changed by user).

46.1 ft is the operating radius (user inputted) and 65.8° the calculated boom angle at that radius with the boom length selected below.

This box shows the calculated boom lower sheave height.

This indicates user selected boom length and percentages of the boom sections employed to achieve it.

For the jib where used.

This is the boom swing angle (user selected); in this case 0°, i.e. directly over the front.

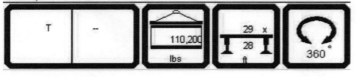

Figure 7-68

These boxes indicate:

Configuration (main boom only)

Machine counterweight (110,200 lbs)

Outrigger base (29' x 28')

360° rated operation

Figure 7-69

Center of gravity

x: 4.5 ft    373.3 klbs
y: 0.0 ft
z: 35.4 ft

This graphic indicates the location (in green) of the combined C of G of the crane plus load (with coordinates) relative to the center of the crane.

The red box indicates the permitted boundary for the location of the C of G.

Top right is the total weight of crane plus load (in kips).

"CODE" is a number corresponding to the particular configuration of the crane.

The small icons are program control buttons.

The bracketed numbers by the outriggers are the maximum loads (in kips) that any outrigger would see as the boom is swung through 360°. The un-bracketed figures are the outrigger loads with the boom at the specific rotation specified bottom right (over the front in this case). Best bet for planning is to go with a conservative approach and use the maximum bracketed figure even if you only intend restricted slewing (swinging).

## Manitowoc Ground Bearing Pressure Estimator

Manitowoc makes a ground bearing pressure estimator for their products available via their web site or on disc. Included is a disclaimer which, to paraphrase, makes the very valid points that the software is an "aid" only and is not a substitute for load chart requirements and safe practices; the user has to confirm that the inputs are accurate and permitted by the charts. Following is a typical output for a Manitowoc crawler crane, a M14000-S2.

*Figure 7-70*

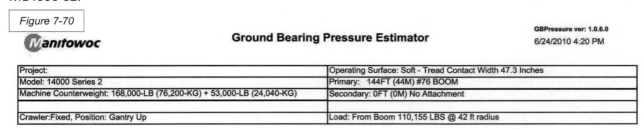

| | | | | |
|---|---|---|---|---|
| **Manitowoc** | **Ground Bearing Pressure Estimator** | | GBPressure ver: 1.0.6.0 6/24/2010 4:20 PM | |

| Project: | | Operating Surface: Soft - Tread Contact Width 47.3 Inches |
|---|---|---|
| Model: 14000 Series 2 | | Primary: 144FT (44M) #76 BOOM |
| Machine Counterweight: 168,000-LB (76,200-KG) + 53,000-LB (24,040-KG) | | Secondary: 0FT (0M) No Attachment |
| | | |
| Crawler:Fixed, Position: Gantry Up | | Load: From Boom 110,155 LBS @ 42 ft radius |

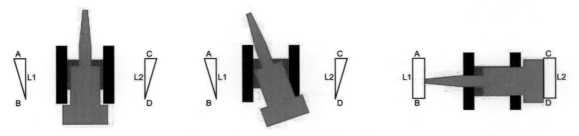

| **Boom Over Front or Rear** | | **Boom at Critical 24 degree Swing** | | **Boom Over Side** | |
|---|---|---|---|---|---|
| Center of Rotation to Fulcrum: 141.83 inch | | Center of Rotation to Fulcrum: 141.83 inch | | Center of Machine to Ctr of Crawlers: 109.7 inch | |
| A | 46.3 psi | A | 49.0 psi | A | 30.8 psi |
| B | 0.0 psi | B | 0.0 psi | B | 30.8 psi |
| L1 | 243.3 inch | L1 | 281.4 inch | L1 | 283.7 inch |
| C | 46.3 psi | C | 39.0 psi | C | 8.9 psi |
| D | 0.0 psi | D | 0.0 psi | D | 8.9 psi |
| L2 | 243.3 inch | L2 | 223.8 inch | L2 | 283.7 inch |

This program estimates crawler or outrigger reaction loads which are estimates of expected actual loads but are not exact, due to assumptions in mechanical deflection, support rigidity, machine levelness and crane manufacturing tolerances. Additionally, loads are calculated for static conditions only and do not include dynamic effects of swinging, hoisting, lowering, traveling, wind conditions, as well as adverse operating conditions. For these reasons, sufficient design tolerances should be used to ensure adequate support structure design. Also please verify that all machine configurations and total lifted loads selected correspond to appropriate capacity charts. This Program will not run and may not be used after its Sunset Date of 12/31/2010. Please load a newer version of this Program prior to the Sunset Date.

First to note; there is the option of calculating based on the crane being located on a "hard" or a "soft" surface. Most crawler tracks are profiled and taper up towards the outsides – Manitowoc tracks are certainly like this. The hard calculation assumes rigid support with only hard contact between track and supporting surface; it is based on only the flat central portion being in contact - similarly along the length, that only the flat length (usually between extreme track rollers) is used. The "soft" calculation assumes sufficient compliance in the supporting surface to be able to consider the entire track width as being supportive. It also assumes a slightly greater track length is effective. You'll need to make a judgment call on which to use; to one extreme it can certainly be said that locating on concrete or on a steel plate or steel mat is "hard" whereas at the other extreme, sitting on graded and compacted dirt is "soft". There is always the option of using a layer of compliant material over a hard surface and then using the soft calculation.

The pressures obtained when using the "hard" calculation are very much greater than those obtained when using the "soft" calculation (one calculation I ran indicated up to 4x as much at peak). The difference is much more than can be explained simply by the slightly lesser track area and would probably suggest a more sophisticated approach in their calculation methodology, taking account of stiffness. Noting that, you would generally be well advised to takes steps that would allow you to use the soft calculation.

As noted elsewhere, you really want to avoid locating your crane partly on a compliant surface and partly on a non-compliant one.

The program allows you to select the crane model and configuration, boom length, jib (if fitted), jib offset and so on. The user inputs the payload and radius. Metric or imperial units can be selected.

This sample output is for a Manitowoc M14000-S2 in main boom configuration (144') with full counterweight, lifting 110,115 lbs at 42' radius, located on a soft operating surface.

The program will calculate the pressure profiles over the front/rear, over the side and at the critical angle of swing giving the highest loadings. It will tabulate pressures to both ends of the profiles and the effective bearing lengths along the tracks.

<u>Demag – Cranimation</u>

For Demag crawler cranes such as the CC-2600 here, you might use Cranimation and will get a result like so.

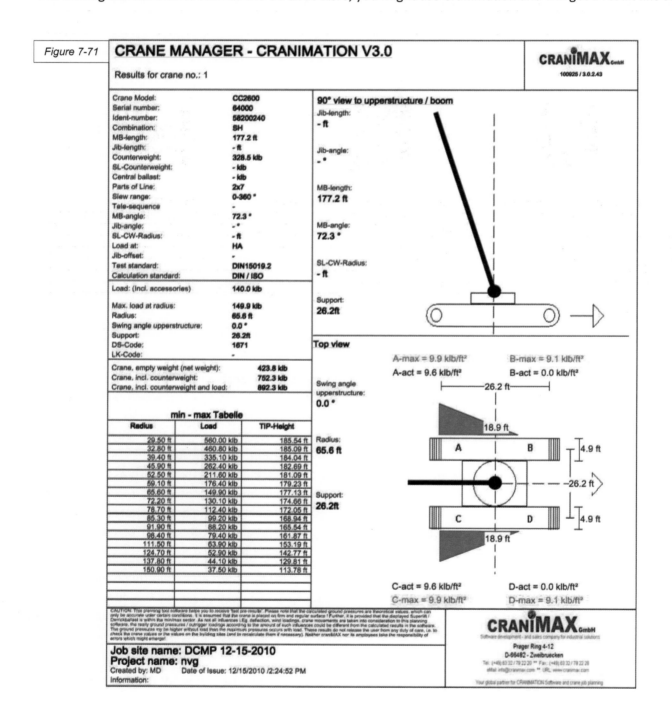

Link-Belt

For Link-Belt cranes, you might well use 3D Lift Plan by A1A software.

The outrigger loading output might look something like the following for an HC-238H.

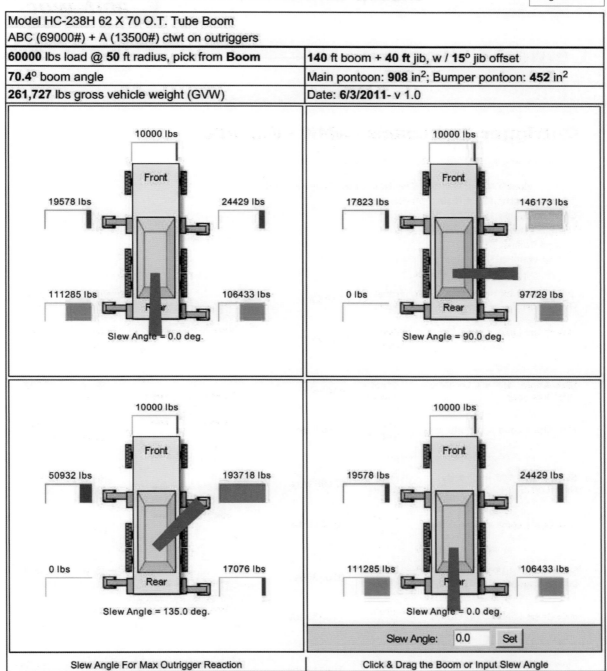

**Link-Belt Constructon Equipment Co., Lexington, Kentucky - HC-238H**

Figure 7-72

| Model HC-238H 62 X 70 O.T. Tube Boom | |
| --- | --- |
| ABC (69000#) + A (13500#) ctwt on outriggers | |
| **60000** lbs load @ **50** ft radius, pick from **Boom** | **140** ft boom + **40 ft** jib, w / **15°** jib offset |
| **70.4°** boom angle | Main pontoon: **908** in²; Bumper pontoon: **452** in² |
| **261,727** lbs gross vehicle weight (GVW) | Date: **6/3/2011**- v 1.0 |

Slew Angle = 0.0 deg.

Slew Angle = 90.0 deg.

Slew Angle = 135.0 deg.

Slew Angle = 0.0 deg.

Slew Angle For Max Outrigger Reaction

Click & Drag the Boom or Input Slew Angle

Slew Angle: 0.0   Set

**CAUTION: DO NOT USE FOR CAPACITIES!**

User to consult the crane rating manual or capacity plate supplied with the machine for input values used in these ground bearing reaction calculations. Do not exceed allowable lifting capacities for configured machine setup.

Grove Cranes

For Grove cranes (part of the Manitowoc group), Compu-Crane can be used. Below is a sample result for a GMK5275.

Figure 7-73

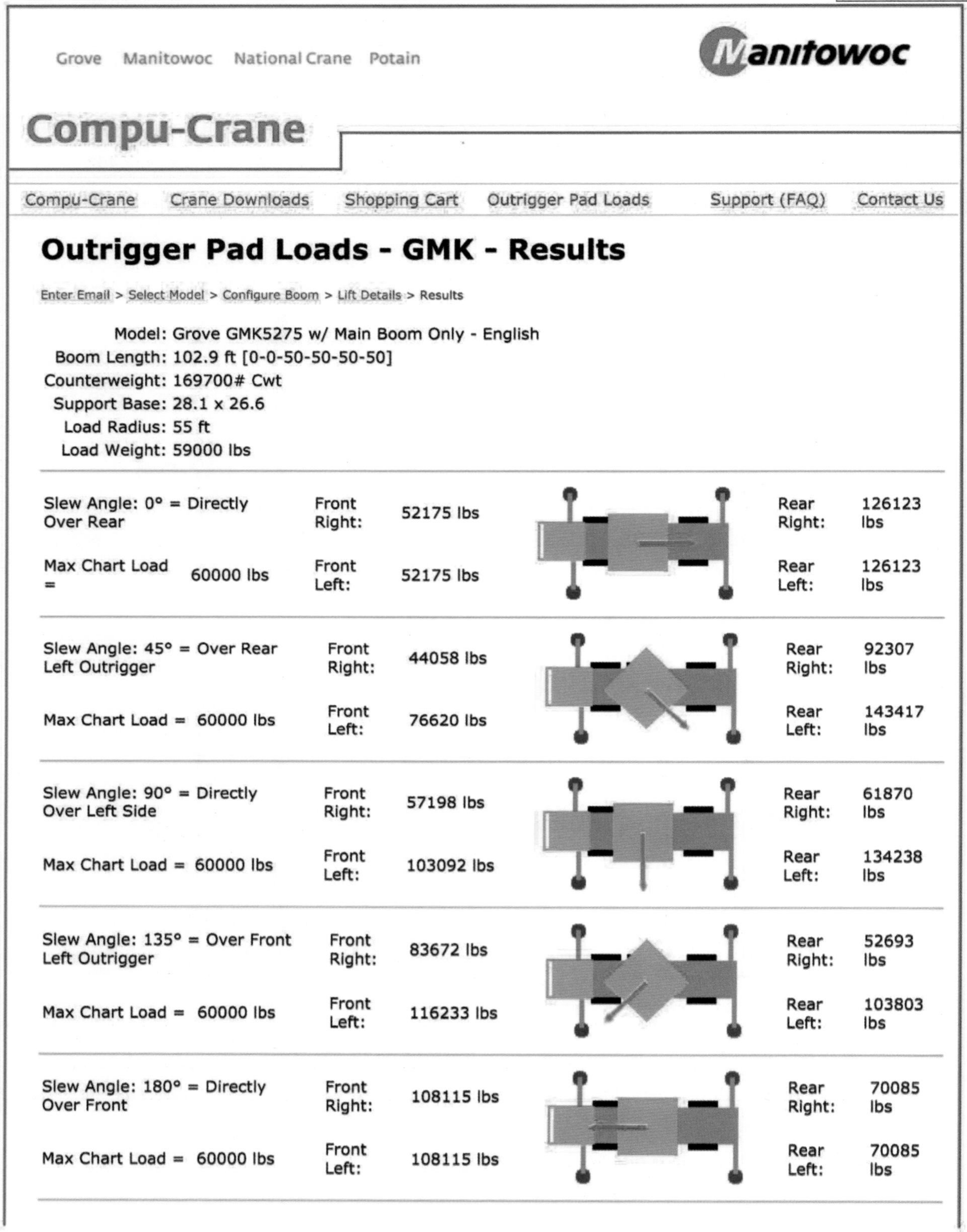
Grove Manitowoc National Crane Potain

Manitowoc

Compu-Crane

Compu-Crane | Crane Downloads | Shopping Cart | Outrigger Pad Loads | Support (FAQ) | Contact Us

**Outrigger Pad Loads - GMK - Results**

Enter Email > Select Model > Configure Boom > Lift Details > Results

Model: Grove GMK5275 w/ Main Boom Only - English
Boom Length: 102.9 ft [0-0-50-50-50-50]
Counterweight: 169700# Cwt
Support Base: 28.1 x 26.6
Load Radius: 55 ft
Load Weight: 59000 lbs

| | | | | | |
|---|---|---|---|---|---|
| Slew Angle: 0° = Directly Over Rear | | Front Right: | 52175 lbs | Rear Right: | 126123 lbs |
| Max Chart Load = | 60000 lbs | Front Left: | 52175 lbs | Rear Left: | 126123 lbs |
| Slew Angle: 45° = Over Rear Left Outrigger | | Front Right: | 44058 lbs | Rear Right: | 92307 lbs |
| Max Chart Load = | 60000 lbs | Front Left: | 76620 lbs | Rear Left: | 143417 lbs |
| Slew Angle: 90° = Directly Over Left Side | | Front Right: | 57198 lbs | Rear Right: | 61870 lbs |
| Max Chart Load = | 60000 lbs | Front Left: | 103092 lbs | Rear Left: | 134238 lbs |
| Slew Angle: 135° = Over Front Left Outrigger | | Front Right: | 83672 lbs | Rear Right: | 52693 lbs |
| Max Chart Load = | 60000 lbs | Front Left: | 116233 lbs | Rear Left: | 103803 lbs |
| Slew Angle: 180° = Directly Over Front | | Front Right: | 108115 lbs | Rear Right: | 70085 lbs |
| Max Chart Load = | 60000 lbs | Front Left: | 108115 lbs | Rear Left: | 70085 lbs |

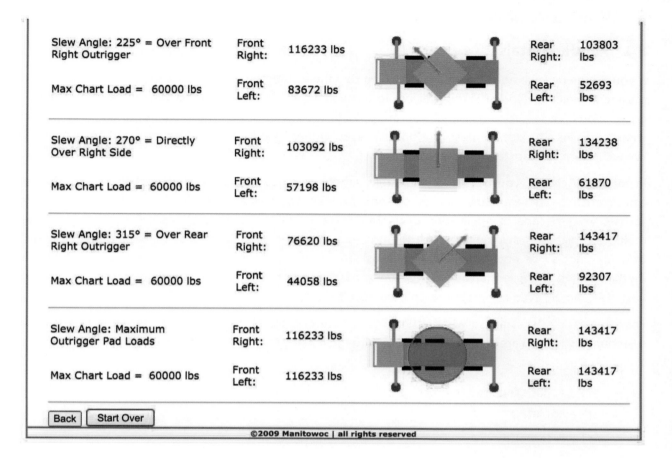

| Slew Angle: 225° = Over Front Right Outrigger | Front Right: | 116233 lbs | | Rear Right: | 103803 lbs |
|---|---|---|---|---|---|
| Max Chart Load = 60000 lbs | Front Left: | 83672 lbs | | Rear Left: | 52693 lbs |
| Slew Angle: 270° = Directly Over Right Side | Front Right: | 103092 lbs | | Rear Right: | 134238 lbs |
| Max Chart Load = 60000 lbs | Front Left: | 57198 lbs | | Rear Left: | 61870 lbs |
| Slew Angle: 315° = Over Rear Right Outrigger | Front Right: | 76620 lbs | | Rear Right: | 143417 lbs |
| Max Chart Load = 60000 lbs | Front Left: | 44058 lbs | | Rear Left: | 92307 lbs |
| Slew Angle: Maximum Outrigger Pad Loads | Front Right: | 116233 lbs | | Rear Right: | 143417 lbs |
| Max Chart Load = 60000 lbs | Front Left: | 116233 lbs | | Rear Left: | 143417 lbs |

Back    Start Over

## Others

There are other crane manufacturers who have similar programs; there are also crane companies such as Mammoet who have developed in-house lift planning software for the cranes in their fleet. Any of these tools will give you a maximum figure for track pressures or outrigger loads to work from. Their methodologies aren't necessarily all the same and the answers you get are only as good as the data you entered and take no account of out-of level, wind forces and so on. Treat the results with caution, they are only an estimate. If circumstances dictate, use engineering judgment and err on the conservative side in establishing a design figure from this data.

# 8   What sort of crane to use?

## 8.1   Fundamentals

If you are being called on to prepare a lift plan to handle something on a construction site, when it comes to making a choice of type of Lifting Devices to use you are most likely going to think in terms of "what sort of <u>crane</u> should I use". Assuming that you are outside the realm of lifts that could be made manually or with something like a forklift; in most (but not all) cases, cranes <u>would</u> be the logical type of Lifting Device to use. We will return to that statement later!

In making a choice, you have a considerable variety of <u>types</u> of cranes to choose from; each has its own characteristics - we've already touched on some of them. You may also have multiple choices of configurations to use. As the scope of application of various crane types and configurations can overlap, you may have multiple choices in how you approach the problem. Although your lift may be made in many different ways, they may not all be equally as efficient or as safe. Your task is to make an informed choice of a least-risk method that is as efficient and cost-effective as possible. Bear in mind that your first idea isn't necessarily your best idea, maybe even using a crane isn't the best idea.

Your first task is to establish what Lifting Devices are capable of making the lift; the next task is to make a selection. Things you are going to want to consider in making that decision include:

- Availability
- Time / space required to erect
- Speed of lifting
- Ground preparation / foundation requirements
- Whether this is required for a one-off lift or for a series of lifts
- Required space / sterilization required
- Ground conditions
- Cost (direct and indirect)

That exercise may take you back to the starting point and you might want to revisit the lift concept and ask yourself:

- Whether (for instance) a 2-crane pick with available machines might be a better option
- Whether the lift can be modified to fall within the range of readily available machines

## 8.2   Characteristics of crane types

The following brief oversight should assist you in understanding the basic characteristics of different types of cranes; capacities and boom/jib combinations quoted are representative only to give you an indication. Manufacturers are constantly pushing the boundaries and coming up with innovations.

*Figure 8-1*

<u>Rough Terrain Crane with telescopic boom</u>

Quick to bring into use. Mobile around a job site, quick to relocate. Relatively compact. Generally not suitable for travel on public roads, so has to be brought in on a low-boy. As name implies suitable for rough terrains. May have limited pick and carry duties, but generally static on outriggers when lifting. Great site cranes for general duties.

The Grove RT9150E is the largest Grove currently makes with 150 tons (136 t) capacity, boom lengths to about 197 ft (61 m), max tip heights (with jib) up to about 310 ft (95 m). Tadano now make a 160 ton RT.

Figure 8-2

## All-Terrain Crane with telescopic boom

Suitable for travel on public roads, so can drive to the job site. Relatively quick to bring into use. Fully articulating independent suspension allows it to be mobile around a job site, even on relatively rough ground. Quick to relocate.

Figure 8-3

Liebherr considers its flagship LTM11200-9.1 to be an all-terrain crane. It has a capacity of 1320 tons (1200 t) capacity at 2.43 m, boom lengths to about 328 ft (100 m), jib length up to about 413 ft (126 m). Great for lifting not only heavy loads close to, but fairly significant loads to great height and reach.

Figure 8-4

## Truck-mounted crane – telescopic boom

Can travel on public roads and relatively good site roads. Not suitable for rough terrains. Quick to bring into use. Cannot pick and carry. Available up to about 110 tons (90 t). A telescopic boom mounted on a truck carrier. The Grove TMS9000E is a 90 t crane with 142' (43 m) max boom and 56' (17 m) max jib. Cost effective for a one-off lift on a well prepared site.

## Truck-mounted crane – lattice boom

Can travel on public roads and relatively good site roads. Not suitable for rough terrains. Cannot pick and carry.

Figure 8-5

Figure 8-6

The Linkbelt HC-278H II is a 300 ton crane designed to be assembled quickly. It can be rigged with up to 200' of luffing boom plus 200' of luffing jib and 30' of fixed jib for reaching high up and over buildings. It will have better duties and greater height and reach than a 300 ton telescopic boom crane.

Figure 8-7

## Carry deck crane

Available up to about 25 tons (23 t). Compact and maneuverable. e.g. the Grove Shuttlelift 7725 carries a max boom of 71' (22.6 m) and a jib of 17' (5.2 m). It can carry up to 15 tons (13.6 t) on its own deck, then lift and place the load. Very suitable for confined spaces and low-headroom applications such as placing pipe in pipe racks.

Broderson make them to 15 tons, with a max 8.5 ton pick and carry duty.

Figure 8-8

Figure 8-9

## Pick and carry type cranes

Franna cranes (not seen much outside of Australia) are compact units designed for pick and carry duties and range from 10-25 t capacity. Unusually, the carrier pivots in the center for maneuverability. Radius is measured from the front wheels in this case. Franna describes them as all-terrain. Useful for light handling duties and minor lifts.

See also Mobilift cranes which are somewhat similar, but do not articulate. They steer about their front wheels. They are described as low-headroom rough terrain cranes; used in mines and for heavy maintenance work in factories etc with restricted head room.

## Basic crawler crane with lattice boom

Figure 8-10

Crawler cranes such as this Manitowoc are basic work horses on many construction sites. They are rugged, have good lifting duties, are relatively compact, can relocate easily on rough ground, can carry suspended loads, are relatively cheap to rent over long periods and can be configured in numerous configurations. They cannot transport themselves to site and need to be assembled on arrival, although some of the more modern cranes can pretty much self-assemble. A lattice boom crawler crane would most likely not be your first choice for a one-off lift.

Cranes up to and including the 440 ton (400 t) Manitowoc 16000 or Liebherr LR1400 or even 600 t class machines such as the Demag CC-2800 might be considered workhorses on major jobsites these days.

## "Superlift" attachment

Figure 8-11

Extra ballast carried on a tray or wheeled carrier (as shown here). Together with an extra back (derrick) mast, this attachment will improve reach and may improve capacity. This arrangement is not as compact obviously as the basic lift crane as you require space for the swing of the carrier; often the SL radius can be varied which helps. The tray or carrier may be detached when the basic crane suffices.

Figure 8-12

The Liebherr LR13000 is currently one of the largest conventional crawler cranes available. Shown here under test, it is rated at 3000 t at 12 m radius (3300 tons at 40') with Superlift (tray fitted). It can be fitted with a max main boom of 144 m or a maximum boom/jib combination of 120 m/126 m. Will lift extremely heavy loads such as heavy reactors at close radius or, fitted with a long boom and jib, heavy loads at great height and long reach. It is of course very large and expensive to ship and rent. Assembly is not quick but it could well pay for itself in the savings it allows, particularly if making multiple lifts. Better still if you can make them from one central location as you save relocation time and multiple set ups.

*Figure 8-13*

## Crawler crane with ring attachment

Some cranes like the Manitowoc M888 crawler crane can be fitted with a ring attachment to enhance capacity and reach. The (heavy duty) boom foot is supported on the front of the ring, the normal main boom does duty as a back mast and additional counterweight is carried on the rear of the ring. The ring is supported on multiple pedestals.

Compact for its capacity, it spreads the lifting loads well. It is relatively economic & well suited to multiple lifts from one fixed lifting location. Requires a well leveled solid matted (or custom piled) foundation.

*Figure 8-14*

## Ring crane with luffing jib

Not an attachment to a crane, but one designed originally as a ring mounted crane. Mammoet now has a PTC ring crane variant rated at a nominal 3200 t. Cranes such as these can make extreme lifts, e.g. a 1600 t x 100 m high Splitter Column. Not cheap to transport (although the PTC is designed to ship on a conventional container handling ship) or to erect, it may never the less be a cost-effective solution for the extreme lift. Ideally you want to make multiple lifts once you have it there erected. Given its capacity and reach, you can do a lot at extreme radius. There are options to move some of these cranes on crawlers or SPMT transporters essentially fully erected.

*Figure 8-15*

## Crane with luffing jib

We have noted above that many cranes can be fitted with luffing jibs. These crawler cranes were configured with long booms and long jibs to reach up and over this coal fired boiler, serving the entire unit from both sides. The boiler roof here is about 300' above grade. The main booms are set at about 85° to keep the booms near vertical and allow the crane to keep close to the structure minimizing operating radii. You need a fairly high capacity crane in order to get a machine that can carry a lot of boom and jib. Capacities are fairly restricted at extreme heights.

Flare tips or windmills are instances where you might use such an arrangement.

*Figure 8-16*

## Crane with fixed jib or runner

In many cases, a crane boom can be fitted with a short jib, the angle of which to the main boom is fixed. A single or possibly 2-part auxiliary hoist line from a separate winch would be used from the jib point. The "crank" provided by the offset jib gives reach over an obstruction such as the corner of a building or structure; the auxiliary hoist line provides quicker hoisting speeds than if the main hoist were used.

This option can be a great advantage in structural steel erection for instance.

The short cranked boom extension shown here would typically be referred to as a runner.

Figure 8-17

## Basic crawler crane with telescopic boom

This arrangement combines the ability to traverse rough ground, to pick and carry and is quick to set up. It won't have the capacity or reach of a lattice boom crane, but that may not be needed. It combines many of the advantages of an all-terrain crane without having to have a costly sophisticated carrier and without having to engage outriggers. It has the major advantage of being able to pick and carry. Its disadvantage is that it is not public road-going. It is suited more for construction sites where you want to move quickly from lift to lift, where speed of set up is important. Several manufacturers including Mantis offer this arrangement. The Liebherr LTR1100 is rated at 120 tons, and can extend to 171' of boom plus 63' jib; it has a max hook height of 272'.

## Tower cranes

Primarily suited to serving a large area of a construction site with relatively light lifts at long radii from a fixed location. May sometimes be rail mounted to increase working area. Two basic types, the flat-top type with the horizontal boom (Fig 8-18) or the luffing jib type (Fig 8-19).

Conventional flat top (hammerhead) tower cranes are typically good for up to about 30 t at close rad; you may get up to about 2.5 t at 90 m radius. You can get them stronger, Favelle Favco make a 275 t luffing crane that will do 9 t at 90 m; Kroll make a huge hammerhead crane that can lift 100 t at 100 m radius.

Figure 8-18

Figure 8-19

Figure 8-20

Locating a tower crane on a structure at height (as shown left for example) may be a very cost-effective solution compared with say using a crawler crane with a long boom and jib.

## Pedestal construction cranes

Figure 8-21

These types of crane have no carrier; they are static and assembled in-situ. The central "pot" carrying the slew ring and upper works is supported on four outriggers. This Deep South crane has a main boom, back mast and "spar" in which the winches are carried and from which additional counterweight can be carried. These cranes are robust with good duties and are relatively cost effective once delivered and assembled. A number of combinations are possible. They are ideally suited to serving a number of heavy lifts from one location.

# 9 Alternatives to cranes

When you think of lifting something beyond what you can manage manually or with say a forklift, you are likely going to think instinctively of using one of the many varieties of crane. In most cases, that would be the best solution, however you need to be aware that there are alternatives that might suit better from either a technical, financial or safety perspective. This topic justifies a thick book in its own right; I am going to aim to do nothing more than give you a brief overview and describe some of the more common "alternative" systems, their basic characteristics, scope of use, advantages / disadvantages. Many of the major lifting companies have alternative lifting systems to offer, some of them proprietary and exclusive to them only. You are advised to search the web and see what is available that could be of use and contact them for details.

## 9.1 What types of "alternative" lift systems are there?

There are a great number of alternative lift systems and techniques available; they can be generally grouped as follows:

- Jack and pack techniques using regular spring return or double-acting cylinder jacks with hardwood packing
- Proprietary jack and pack systems using elephant's foot jacks and hardwood packing
- Heavy duty proprietary jack and pack systems using long stroke rams and locking steel inserts (such as the Mammoet JS500 lift system)
- Telescoping hydraulic gantries (such as those made by Lift Systems Inc, Riggers Manufacturing, J&R Engineering and Hydrospex)
- Strand jacks either used on a suitable existing load-carrying structure or in conjunction with proprietary mast (tower) structures
- Mast systems using climbing jacks (such as those operated by Dorman Long Technology)
- Mast systems using base mounted jacks with inserts (such as the Sarens Sarlift system)
- Static or mobile gantries using strand jacks, winches or chain jacks to provide the lifting effort (see ALE, Mammoet, Sarens, Barnhart's MLT, Rigging International and many others

Many of these rigs can be made mobile; they can often incorporate lateral / longitudinal skidding or skating facilities to move/adjust the supported load, swivels may be incorporated and so on. The possibilities are pretty much limitless as they are all engineered applications.

## 9.2 What market niches do "alternative" lift systems fill?

The situations in which alternative lift systems come into their own include:

- Exceptionally heavy loads beyond available cranes
- Extreme height
- Where space to locate a crane is limited or would require an extreme radius
- Remote locations where heavy cranes are not available or where it would be impractical to mobilize one to
- Where a load needs to be held securely at height or worked beneath
- Inside buildings or where adequate overhead access is not available
- Occasional lifts over a prolonged period
- When a heavy load requires lifting only a relatively small height and does not require relocating far

## 9.3 Over-view of some systems

### 9.3.1 Jack and packing (conventional)

This involves providing double-acting (or sprung return) cylinder jacks between the load to be raised and the supporting surface below. Adequate numbers of support points need to be used to support the load properly without overstressing it. The number and capacities of the jacks used at each support point will be dictated by the support reactions noting that loads can jump around between supports if the load is stiff and is not maintained very level during jacking. Obviously each support point needs to be a "strong point".

The jacks are extended in unison to raise the load from its supports. Better systems will have central monitoring of load and extension. When at full stroke the load is repacked from its supports, the load is released back onto the supports (higher by the amount of the pack added) and the jacks will be fully retracted. A similar thickness pack will be placed under (or maybe over) each jack and the process repeated jacking and packing. As clearances are required, if the stroke is say 6", you may only be able to add 4" packs each time; you won't get gain the full jack stroke.

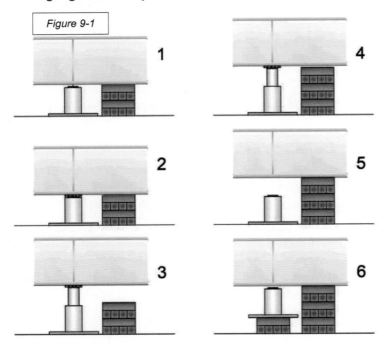

Figure 9-1

1. The load to be lifted is supported at a height that allows the jacks to be located under suitably strong jacking points. The jacks are positioned on a prepared support surface with plate for distribution if needed.
2. Each jack head is hard shimmed to the underside of the bearing point and extended to "nip up".
3. The jacks are extended in unison to full stroke raising the load, monitoring pressure, extension and load level throughout.
4. Additional hardwood packing is added under the load support points.
5. The jacks are retracted to lower the load to the support packs, the shims are removed and the jacks fully retracted.
6. An equal amount of extra hardwood packing is added under each jack bringing the process back to the start point with the load higher. Repeat as necessary. Lowering if required is by similar reverse process.

Cautionary notes

- You have to be concerned about the stability of the packs; timbers need to be crossed at each level. Higher packs may need to be strapped and stabilized.
- The timbers "squash" a bit and this builds cumulatively; eventually you lose significant stroke, to the point where you may not be able to get the packs in (particularly so if the timbers are not quality hardwood).
- Be careful of the bearing stresses in the timbers and make sure you have adequate contact area at support points (and in the stack).
- You need to use good quality, dimensionally similar hardwood wood packs.

- With stiff loads you can throw load around between supports and possibly overload your design if you develop different jack extensions (think of the 4-legged stool that rocks on only two legs when on an uneven floor).

- Consider whether you are going to feed the jacks independently hydraulically (and control and monitor them individually and simultaneously) or whether you are going to divide them into hydraulic groups; if so, how many groups, three or four, arranged like what? A lot comes down to the stiffness of the load when making this call. It can sometimes be better with a 4-point support to take one end up at a time (going end to end) rather than lifting the whole thing bodily each stroke. This keeps one end stable of a fixed hinge at all times – you do need to ensure that the slope you induce is insignificant.

Advantages / disadvantages

- With heavy duty cylinder jacks available as standard up to about 1000 t per unit, capacity is not an issue; by providing enough jacks you can lift nearly anything.

- You cannot lift very high using this method, 2 or 3 m (10' or so) would be about as far as you would go without seriously considering some other method. That said, I've seen where buildings have been jacked much higher than this during relocations.

- This is a very slow operation and is highly labor intensive; it is however relatively cheap.

- You might use this technique in association with say a lateral movement to get the load high enough to get the skidding or transport equipment beneath.

- Where you have hydraulic platform trailers available, and you have the necessary area / height / strength under the load, you might be able to use the trailers under the load to provide the jacking function.

*Figure 9-2*   *Figure 9-3*   *Figure 9-4*

*This 3600 t bridge was jacked up through about 300 mm using this technique – see difference in parapet height left. Jacks were located beside the bridge bearings at the parapets and piers – strong points. Steel shim packs were inserted above the bearings as the bridge deck was progressively raised in small increments.*

### 9.3.2 Proprietary jack and pack systems using elephant's foot jacks and hardwood packing

Some lifting companies have proprietary "climbing" jacking systems that are an improvement over basic jacking and packing in that the jack does not require removal and replacement after each step and the pack is not separate but surrounds the jack unit. The ALE version is shown in the following graphic. The jack unit incorporates an inverted double acting hydraulic cylinder jack, the ram of which terminates in a foot. The foot can be drawn up into the unit and extended out below it. You alternately pack under the foot and the body of the unit as shown. The unit bears directly under the load and climbs as the operation proceeds. Various capacities are available.

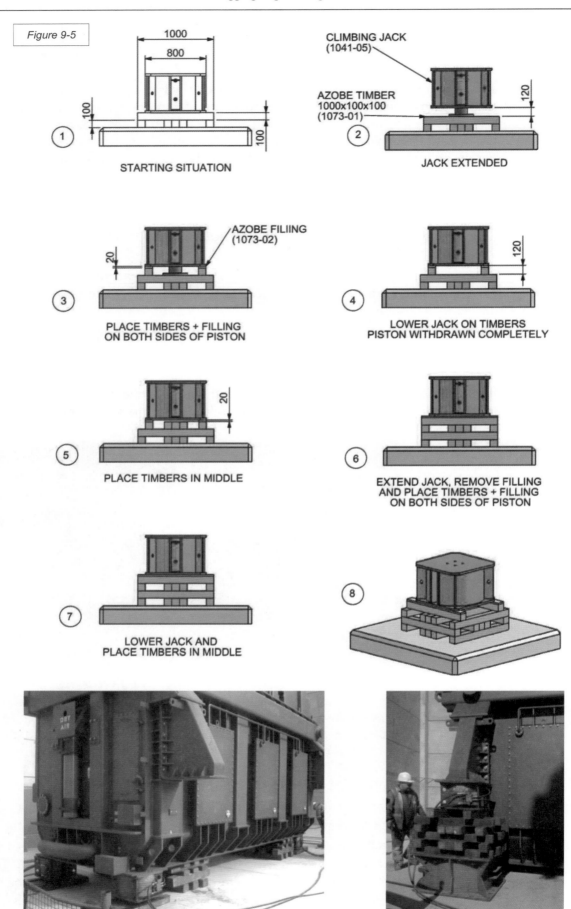

Figure 9-5

1 STARTING SITUATION

CLIMBING JACK (1041-05)

AZOBE TIMBER 1000x100x100 (1073-01)

2 JACK EXTENDED

AZOBE FILIING (1073-02)

3 PLACE TIMBERS + FILLING ON BOTH SIDES OF PISTON

4 LOWER JACK ON TIMBERS PISTON WITHDRAWN COMPLETELY

5 PLACE TIMBERS IN MIDDLE

6 EXTEND JACK, REMOVE FILLING AND PLACE TIMBERS + FILLING ON BOTH SIDES OF PISTON

7 LOWER JACK AND PLACE TIMBERS IN MIDDLE

8

Figure 9-6

Figure 9-7

### 9.3.3  Heavy duty proprietary jack and pack systems

The Mammoet JS500 lift system is a further development of the jack and pack principle; it is a heavy duty automated push up system. Each jacking unit comprises a base frame incorporating four synchronized (inverted) hydraulic jacks with a combined capacity of 500t bearing on the lower part of the frame. The upper movable part of the frame, attached to the jacks, can be jacked up and down through approximately 600 mm and surrounds a stack of steel inserts on the top of which the load is supported. To lift, the movable upper section is pinned to the lowest insert section and the rams extended raising the upper part with the inserts and load. This creates a clear gap beneath into which the next insert can be slid. The stack is lowered back onto the newly inserted section and it is attached. The moveable section is released and relocated and pinned to what is now the lowest insert and the process repeated. Appropriate numbers of these jack units can be used to suit the size and weight of the load to be lifted; they are fed from external hydraulic power packs and are centrally controlled by one person. The process is automated. The max freestanding height is about 10 m. Check with Mammoet for official specifications. Other companies have similar variations on the theme.

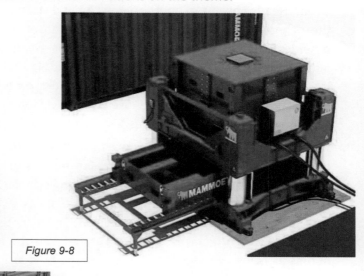

Figure 9-8

These types of systems are heavy duty, robust and stable; they are relatively quick in operation compared with other jacking systems. They can be used in conjunction with lateral jacking and skidding techniques to translate loads

A load supported in this manner would not be considered a suspended load and would be safe to work beneath once lifting had finished and the area made safe.

### 9.3.4　Telescoping hydraulic gantries

There are a number of companies such Lift Systems Inc, Riggers Manufacturing, J&R Engineering and Hydrospex (now Enerpac) who make varieties of telescoping hydraulic gantries. They differ in detail but have basic elements in common.

ASME B30.1 (2009) lays down American National standards for these types of gantries. You are also advised to read the Specialist Carriers and Riggers Association publication "Recommended Practices for Telescopic Hydraulic Gantry Systems Manual". There is also a companion video available.

You are also recommended to refer to David Duerr's comprehensive book "Telescopic Hydraulic Gantry Systems" ISBN 978-0-615-75016-3.

The gantry consists of pairs of jack units each of which comprises a wheel mounted base and a vertically mounted extending "leg". Early versions used single exposed (bare) multi-stage hydraulic cylinders, later versions used multiple bare cylinders per jack unit; other designs use a single cylinder inside a telescoping boom. Header beams of appropriate span and strength span between the pairs of jacks and are supported on the heads of the legs via (usually) some kind of articulating bearing. The payload is suspended from (or otherwise supported on) the header beams using conventional rigging techniques. The suspension may incorporate cross-sliding facilities to move loads laterally. Longitudinal movement can be achieved by mounted the jack units on tracks along which the entire rig and load can be slid or rolled. Some arrangements use push/pull cylinder jacks, others use hydraulic motor drive to the wheels in the base; if required powered swivels can be provided in the suspension to allow the suspended load to be rotated.

Typically, the capacity of these systems reduces with height. I can illustrate that (and some basic features of one specific rig) by looking at a system; for the sake of example only, a J&R LIFT-N-LOCK T-1400 series. This is a telescopic octagon boom gantry, i.e. the lifting cylinder is enclosed in a telescoping boom made of square steel tubing with solid steel bars attached at two sides. Two powered stages and an optional use pinned manual section are provided; the sections slide within each other using Nylatron bearings to maintain low friction and a close fit. Eccentric cams are incorporated into the heads of the sections; these bite into the walls of the booms allowing the booms to be locked and held at any extension independent of the lift cylinder. They are engaged automatically whenever the controls are returned to neutral or if there is a loss of pressure for whatever reason.

The gantry closed or in the 1$^{st}$ stage extension (with or without the manual stage extended) has a capacity of 700 tons (635 t) at the max pressure of 3000 psi (about 200 bars); in the 2$^{nd}$ stage (with or without the manual section extended), the capacity reduces to 470 tons (425 t). (These figures are total for a 4-legged arrangement). The units are hydraulically fed from a self-contained power module that incorporates the pump, controls and instrumentation. Fluid flow is volumetrically equal to each unit independent of pressure. This gantry uses a planetary self-propel drive system.

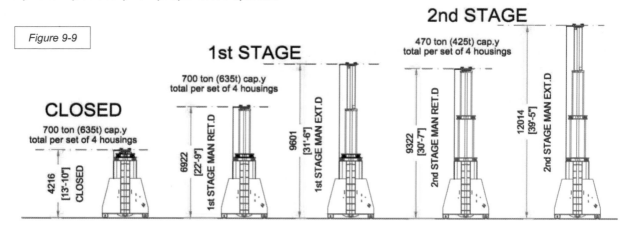

Figure 9-9

Some of these features can be seen on the following photos.

Figure 9-10

Figure 9-11

Shown here is the upending of a large cooling water circulation pump at a power plant using a four-leg system with two header beams and a swivel (rotator) from which the head is rigged; the tail is taken by crane. The rig is mounted on tracks spanning the shaft into which the pump is to be lowered. Initially (left) only the manual is extended.

On completion, the rig is at full stretch, the pump has been rotated and the rig centered over the opening. This method had major cost and schedule advantages over use of a very large crane.

Figure 9-12

Figure 9-13

The same rig used at a rail spur to lift a 300 t stator off a rail car and on to road transport. Hydraulically powered links to allow lateral movement of the load are also available.

A TBM being handled by a 4-legged rig. Such arrangements are cost-effective alternatives to the use of large cranes.

Figure 9-14

This Hydrospex SBL1100 gantry is being used to lift and place a 350 t Generator stator inside a turbine hall. Shown here being turned at turbine block level after raising through the loading bay. The capacity of this rig ranges from 1172 tons (1063 t) fully closed at 14'-4" (4370 mm) to 440 tons (400 t) fully extended at 30'-4" (12000 mm), the 3rd stage. This gantry features a fold down boom to minimize transport height and uses wireless remote operation with automatic synchronization and overload protection. Here a powered rotator spins the stator 90° to align it.

You are advised to contact the aforementioned manufacturers and research their product lines, capabilities and features to find gantries that best serve your needs. Information contained here is for illustrative purposes only and cannot be relied upon for lift planning purposes.

## Advantages / disadvantages

- Of great advantage when needing to lift and move heavy loads such as generators, press crowns etc inside buildings and other confined spaces, particularly where headroom is limited.
- Small plan area.
- Relatively cheap to mobilize and operate.
- Good at places like rail spurs to provide a long term but temporary offloading / reloading facility.
- Not good where extreme height is required.
- Capacity reduces with extension.
- Very poor stability, particularly when fully extended; only 1.5% lateral is required by code.
- Requires meticulous set up and has to be very well supported.
- Needs skilled, well trained persons to operate.

### 9.3.5    Strand jacks

Strand jacks are hydraulically powered heavy duty pulling devices; they are a development of the gripper jacks used to preload the steel strands incorporated in pre- and post-tensioned concrete structures. Mounted horizontally they are used in construction to tow loads during (say) skidding operations; mounted vertically on a suitable load-carrying structure they can be used to hoist loads. How do they work?

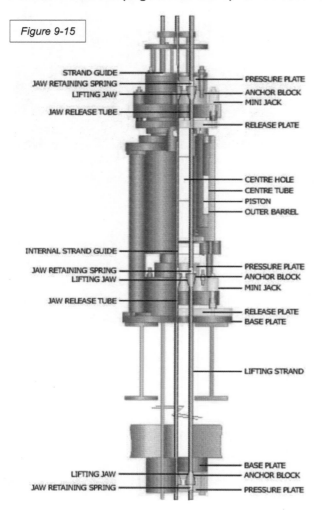

Figure 9-15

STRAND GUIDE
JAW RETAINING SPRING
LIFTING JAW
JAW RELEASE TUBE

PRESSURE PLATE
ANCHOR BLOCK
MINI JACK
RELEASE PLATE

CENTRE HOLE
CENTRE TUBE
PISTON
OUTER BARREL

INTERNAL STRAND GUIDE
JAW RETAINING SPRING
LIFTING JAW
JAW RELEASE TUBE

PRESSURE PLATE
ANCHOR BLOCK
MINI JACK
RELEASE PLATE
BASE PLATE

LIFTING STRAND

LIFTING JAW
JAW RETAINING SPRING

BASE PLATE
ANCHOR BLOCK
PRESSURE PLATE

A strand jack comprises a double-acting hollow-ram hydraulic cylinder separating an upper (moveable) and lower (static) grip head. A bundle of individual high tensile dyformed strands are "threaded" through the jack passing through individual holes in the lower grip head, through the ram, through equivalent individual holes in the upper grip head and out through a guide. A strand is typically 18 mm diameter and rated (for lifting purposes) at about 16 t with a FOS of 2.5. Jacks using up to 54 strands (900 t rated capacity) are available. (Some designs use 15.2 mm diameter strands with a rated capacity of about 12 t / strand).

Each individual strand is gripped in the grip heads by split collets (jaws or grippers) with inner serrated teeth. The holes in the grip heads are conical to match the collets; when the collets are pushed or drawn down into the seating , the cone angle forces the three sectors of the collets together causing the teeth to bite into the dyformed surface of the strand, locking it in the grip head. The greater the seating force, the greater the grip.

When lowering, the collets are unseated (when unloaded) using small cylinder jacks operating a release plate which actuates release tubes bearing on the underside of the collets. Their effort is insufficient to release the collets when loaded. The sequence is explained later.

The live end of the bundle of strands terminates in an anchor block in which the strands are locked using similar collets. The anchor typically incorporates a lug to which the payload is attached. The dead end of the strand bundle exiting the jack can be either re-coiled, looped or diverted back towards the ground.

Seen right is a piece of strand with a set of collets (grips)

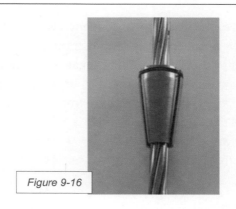

Figure 9-16

Figure 9-17

Figure 9-18

The yellow item (left) is a 45 t, 3-strand jack, one of several located on the top of a coal-fired boiler structure to lift a water wall inside the boiler. The wheel-like item is the recoiler for the dead end of the strands. Right, the yellow items are the strand anchors pinning the live end of the strand bundle to the water-wall header down inside the boiler. Unusually clearances through the boiler required an in-line arrangement rather than the conventional triangular pattern.

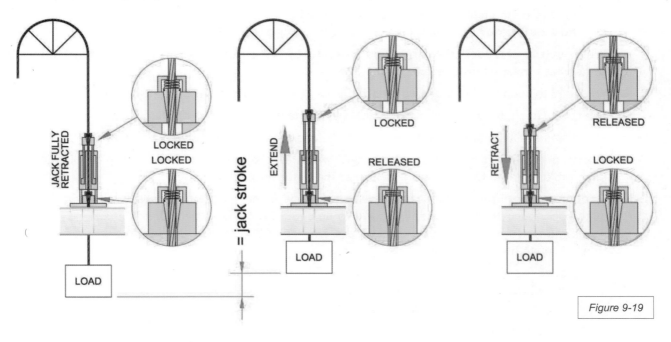

Figure 9-19

So how does the operational sequence work? We can look at that with a simplified graphic showing only one strand. When you commence the strand is under load and the upper and lower grips are engaged. Note the spring acting to keep the collets engaged. As the cylinder is extended, the upper grip head moves upward and takes the strand with it, pulling it up through the jack and the lower grip. The grip of the collets is uni-directional, the strand is prevented from moving down relative to the collets, but it is free to move upwards. At the end of the stroke, the cylinder is retracted; the initial lowering movement causes the lower grip head to lock the strand and prevent it lowering. Further retraction releases the grip of the upper collets and allows the jack to be reset for another stroke. Stroke length is driven by cylinder design and varies by manufacturer and model.

To lower, the jack is initially retracted with the load on the lower grips, the upper mini-jacks (not shown on the sequence drawing) are used to unseat the upper grips. The cylinder is then extended with the load static and the upper grips released. Towards the end of the stroke, the mini-jacks set the upper collets which allows the upper grips to lock the strand and raise the load slightly relieving it from the lower grips which are then unseated by the lower mini-jacks. The cylinder can then be retracted with the upper grips locked and the lower grips held free. Towards the end of the retract stroke, the lower grips are allowed to engage, this locks the lower grip head to the strand and the upper grips release allowing another lowering stroke to be initiated.

Most systems use load and stroke monitoring devices on the strand jacks and utilize a centralized computerized control system to operate the jacks in unison while maintaining them within close height differential tolerances. Load limits can be set to automatically shut down the operation should one jack be taking more load than permitted. After checking and adjustment, the operation can be reset and recommenced. Typically, the pump units (which may be electrically or engine driven) are located close to the jacks. Jacking speeds are dependent on the volumetric output of the pumps versus the volumetric requirements of the jacks; speed of lifting is therefore dependent on the power input you are prepared to provide. Working pressures are typically up to about 400 bars (5800 psi). An overall lifting speed of about 12 m/hr (40 ft/hr) would be typical. The height of lift is not limited by the jacks or strand; if towers (masts) are used to support the jacks, it is their strength that is likely to be the governing factor.

Advantages / disadvantages

- Strand is very stiff and comes coiled. You need to be extremely careful handling / uncoiling / cutting it.
- You need to be meticulous when threading the jacks to get each strand through the matching holes in top and bottom grip heads, particularly with jacks using a lot of strands.
- When you've threaded the jacks, you need to try to ensure that all the individual strands are somewhat similarly tensioned.
- You need to keep the grips clean of debris and oil/grease and replace them regularly.
- The strand itself, once cut to length, is not easy to move on to another job unless recoiled as a bundle.
- The strand has a limited life and may need to be replaced over the duration of a long project.
- If a strand breaks, it can cause a "birdcage" which can be difficult to clear. It can be difficult, if not impossible to get to the grips in the center of the pattern to work on them.
- If you don't recoil the strand as it comes out of the jack and choose to loop it or lead it back over the edge back towards the ground, you have to be careful that the weight of the dead end of strand is never enough to overcome the weight on the live side of the jack, otherwise the entire bundle will run freely through the jack and drop to the ground.
- Lifting speeds are not very fast by comparison with cranes, a high lift can take a long working day to complete, which can leave you possibly vulnerable to unexpectedly high winds
- This equipment is very well suited to lifting extremely heavy loads to extreme height if necessary with a high degree of control and precision.

Figure 9-20

This 8500 t airport hanger roof was assembled at ground level and raised to height using strand jacks. The majority of the jacks were supported from temporary steelwork located on top of the permanent roof support columns; the exceptions were the jacks at the hanger door opening (the face nearest us) where two temporary support structures (grey items in the center of the photo here) were provided. Once at height, the roof was held until the bolted connections to the permanent steel were made, after which the load was released and the temporary works removed.

Where there is an existing structure capable of taking the lifting loads this can be a viable cost-effective alternative for lifting heavy loads.

### 9.3.6    Mast (tower) systems using strand jacks

Figure 9-21

Where there is no suitable existing structure, you can provide a temporary one. Most of the major project lifting companies and a number of specialists have mast (tower) systems that can be used to support strand jacks. Typically the masts arrive in knock-down form and are assembled into lattice mast sections (often 12 m or 6 m high) which are stacked one on another and pinned together to the required height. Suitably strong header beams are supported on the mast heads and span the required erection zone. The jacks are located on the header beams; options include swivels and cross-slide facilities.

If required, the mast bases may be located on skids to allow relocation of the assembled rig (sometimes while loaded). Max mast height v capacity is dependent on the individual design; typically you may be able to go 120 m, possibly 150 m.

In many cases, it may be possible to avoid the use of guys and make the rig free-standing; there are of course significant stability and wind forces to consider. If upending, as with this 730 t reactor in Canada, there are forces induced as a result of tailing. The Mammoet rig used double sections to mid height to handle these considerations; a single 900 t strand jack, computer controlled from the ground provided the lifting effort. A Demag CC-2600 was used on the tail of the Reactor.

Advantages / disadvantages

- The bases are compact and may possibly be located on foundations incorporated into the reactor foundation.

- It can be an economic cost-effective solution where you only have one or two heavy vessels on a project avoiding mobilizing a very heavy crane for only a very few lifts. The tail crane can be the main lift crane for all the other lifts.

- By spanning an item to be lifted (rather than it being outside the support base of your rig), you avoid the need to mobilize huge quantities of balancing counterweight.

- It takes time, manpower and support craneage to assemble and erect the masts (but a very large crane needs it too).

- Guys or stays, if required, can be a disadvantage.

- You typically have a short suspension length at the end of the lift, which isn't very forgiving of inaccurate tailing (if that's what you are doing) at the very end of the lift and can induce some sizeable lateral forces if say a tilt-up frame is used on the tail (as may be the case with a very heavy vessel).

### 9.3.7 Cranes using strand jacks

Figure 9-22

This heavy duty lifting machine is the Mammoet MSG (Mammoet Sliding Gantry); it may look like a ring crane and it does perform many of the same functions but it differs from cranes such as the Mammoet PTC ring cranes in some important areas. Firstly, the hoisting mechanisms are not winches but strand jacks mounted on the tip of the fly jib. It has no slewing ring but is mounted on a ring track on skid pads (rather than rollers) and is hydraulically jacked around the ring to swing (slew). It can luff up and down, but uses strand jacks to perform that function.

It is therefore more like a luffing strand jack gantry than a conventional crane. However, whatever you call it; it can lift up to about 3000 t at 22 m radius which makes it a very strong contender for extremely heavy / tall lifts.

Many of the major crane companies can offer super-heavy lifting "cranes" working on somewhat similar principles.

Figure 9-23

This is the ALE SK190 lifting a 3680 t load.

This crane has 4300 t capacity (190,000 t.m) with a maximum 140 m main boom.

The similar ALE SK350 is (at the time of writing) the strongest land based crane in the world with a 350,000 t.m load moment capacity and 5000 t lifting capacity.

Ultra heavy loads are lifted using up to 4 x 1250 t strand jacks; for lighter loads conventional winches are used. Luffing is by means of hydraulic chain pendants.

Interestingly these machines swing around their ballast (which is static), allowing the use of only a part of the ring, sufficient for the need.

The self-propelled hydraulic skid shoes under the base have hydraulic cylinders installed with 450 mm stroke. These cylinders level the crane in case of settlement of the ground. This is an important safety feature of the crane which most of the latest generation ring cranes don't have.

Special designed shipping containers are used to hold 4000 t of locally sourced ballast.

For economy of shipping, the components are all 20'/40' container sized and weigh a maximum of 36 t.

The details on these machines are indicative only to illustrate the concept, features and capabilities; they constantly evolve. You are advised to contact the major manufacturers to see what they currently can offer and get accurate and complete details.

## Advantages / disadvantages

All these machines have the benefits and disadvantages of strand jacks, plus:

- They are relatively slow to operate and use more basic technology.
- They take considerable resources to assemble and erect; however, unlike a mast system, the boom can be built on the ground and reared up.
- Unlike a mast system, the load is outside the support base of the machine, so counterbalancing ballast is required. Unlike a crane, many of these rigs allow the use of locally available materials as ballast.
- Although they claim relatively low imposed pressures, a large firm well leveled base is required which involves a considerable amount of civil work and may need piling.
- They take up a reasonable amount of real estate but don't need guys or stays like mast rigs which take even more space.
- They can lift enormous loads reasonably quick, at considerable radii. The SK cranes also have a 600 t runner system installed for miscellaneous smaller lifts.
- They are best suited to one or more extremely heavy lifts from one location; however, the SK cranes have the possibility of relocation using their own skid system or by SPMTs.
- They can be an economic cost-effective solution where you only have one or two very heavy vessels on a project avoiding mobilizing a very heavy crane for only a very few lifts. The tail crane can be the main lift crane for all the other lifts.

Figure 9-24

A 1300 t Splitter Column being lifted in India using a Mammoet MSG with a Demag CC8800 tailing.

### 9.3.8 Strand jacks on hydraulic telescopic gantries

One of the issues you can face with hydraulic gantries is the restricted lift height available, and of course the reduction in capacity and stability when fully extended. This can often be the case when, for instance, handling generators in Turbine Halls. Typically, you'd have the gantry on rails supported on the Turbine Block level; the generator / stator comes in at loading bay level and needs to be raised up to above block level before the rig can be tracked along to place the item on the block. This lift height is usually in excess of the amount of useful lifting you can get out of the gantry by simply extending it. If you could find (or develop) a gantry with sufficient telescoping range, it would then likely be too high when fully extended considering the usually restricted overhead space and the requirement to maintain the overhead traveling crane(s) in the building. So how to keep the advantages of the gantry including travel facilities while keeping the arrangement compact but providing enough lift height. One answer is to mount strand jacks up on the header beams of the gantry and use them rather than the telescoping ability of the gantry to do the major lifting.

Figure 9-25

This 4-legged J&R 1400 series gantry is being used to set a generator inside a building. It is set up on tracks supported on the Turbine block and on four temporary support towers spanning the loading bay. The header beams support lift beams at centers corresponding to the lateral centers of the lift trunnions on the generator. Four 105 t 7-strand strand jacks are located on the beams at centers corresponding to the longitudinal centers of the trunnions. The strand bundles are led through the lift beams to fixed anchors shackled to basketed slings around the lift points. The dead end of the strands is led over guides. Overall height is below the overhead crane (just).

Figure 9-26

The generator is lifted to height in the loading bay at the end of the block using the strand jacks until the fixed anchor approaches the underside of the lift beams (left). The remaining lifting is done with the gantry. Once above block height, the gantry with suspended load is "driven" along the tracks until over the hole in the block where the generator is lowered to location using the gantry.

Figure 9-27

<u>Advantages / disadvantages</u>

Using the strand jacks with the gantry combines the advantages of the travel of the gantry and the unlimited lifting height of the strand jacks. It keeps the rig compact and stable. One disadvantage is that the strand has to leave the jacks linearly and the exit curve cannot be too sharp so there is a height to the guide which detracts from the available jacking height (assuming you need to keep below the crane or building roof steel). A disadvantage is that you are doubling up the gantry and the strand jacks costs.

### 9.3.9 Shark-Link system used with hydraulic telescopic gantries

A recently developed patented alternative to the use of strand jacks to extend the lifting range of the gantry is the Shark-Link system developed by HLI and marketed by J&R. The two gantry header beams are each fitted with two link plates from each of which a chain of pinned plate links is suspended. The lowest link of each "chain" is shackled to a basketed sling fitted around one of the trunnions. Each link is profiled to form a buttress shape either side under which anchor blocks can be slid allowing the load in the chain to be transferred from the gantry to a support structure at a time when the gantry is as extended as you wish it to get; this design then allows the unloaded chain to be shortened by removing and storing links as the gantry is retracted. The shortened chains can then be re-pinned to the loaded chain sections beneath, the weight taken off the support structure back onto the gantry, the anchor blocks slid back to disengage from the chain and lifting continued with a shortened chain. By extending the gantry, locking the raised suspension, retracting the gantry, shortening the suspension and repeating, you can progressively raise the load through distances greater than the gantry stroke (up to 3x), keeping gantry extension relatively low. This arrangement does not project much above the top of the gantry header beams. The support structure comprises beams spanning the gantry track in turn supporting longitudinal beams arranged in pairs with a gap between through which the links pass. The locking anchors are located on these secondary beams and are moved laterally to engage / disengage the links. When moving the gantry, the support structure is slung from the header beams, lifted clear with the gantry and carried with the gantry and load to the new lowering location.

Figure 9-28

# Hydraulic gantry lift extension system
## Lifting Sequence

1. Attach load with lowered gantry

2. Extend gantry to lift the load

3. Engage anchors
Remove Shark-Links as gantry is lowered

4. Reconnect Shark-Links, diisengage anchors
lift load & platform beam

Figure 9-29

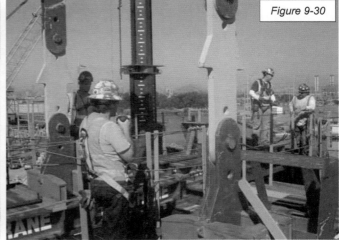

Figure 9-30

Figure 9-31

Link Removal Sequence

Figure 9-32

Figure 9-33

The photos show the first application of the Shark Link attachment by Bay Crane in New York.

### 9.3.10 Strand jacks used with fixed height mobile gantries

It is not a very complex task to design a braced frame based on standard structural components pinned or bolted together to form a gantry on which you can mount some form of hoisting device such as a winch or strand jack. The gantry can be static or can be mobile by mounting it on wheeled carriages or skid pads on tracks. Accessories such as swivels can be incorporated. Such arrangements can be very effective in lifting and placing items such as the turbine below.

Figure 9-34

This gantry by ALE is being used to place a Combustion Turbine on a power plant. The inter-braced tubular structure is skid mounted and supports header beams and cross beams on which four strand jacks (yellow items) are mounted. It is a relatively simple matter to deliver the piece, connect up, lift to height and skid the rig over the foundation, then lower to place.

The rig is relatively cheap, robust and stable and has ample capacity. It uses simple components and is easy to assemble.

Figure 9-35

This gantry by Mammoet is being used to place a 410 t Generator on a power plant. A temporary structure is assembled outside the building; it supports (red) skid beam / track on which a movable braced gantry (formed from similar components) is located. Strand jacks are used to raise the Generator from ground transport to track height. The upper moveable gantry is slid into the building where the Generator is staged and handed off to a telescoping gantry for final location on the turbine block.

Figure 9-36

Figure 9-37

## 9.3.11  Barnhart Modular Lift Tower (MLT)

The Barnhart Modular Lift Tower (MLT) is a custom designed modular gantry system using standardized structural components.  The pin connected nodal design offers ease of erection without any bolted connection; preassemblies may be readily formed at ground level and offered up to the rig using standard cranes allowing relatively speedy erection.  The modular design of the MLT allows arrangements configured to meet the site specific needs of the project; rigs stable to 250' (75 m) can be designed without guy wires. The gantry supports header beams on which the hoisting mechanism is mounted. Barnhart offers strand jacks for capacities up to 1600 tons; alternatively, Barnhart self-contained hoist modules (winches) can be used for quicker lifts up to 500 tons.

If required, it is possible to mount the MLT on skid tracks at grade allowing the loaded system to be moved using Barnhart hydraulic slide system. Cross-sliding arrangements and swivel suspension can also be incorporated.

The design of this system allows its use in confined spaces and flexible solutions; gantries such as these can be a viable cost-effective alternative where cranes are impractical.

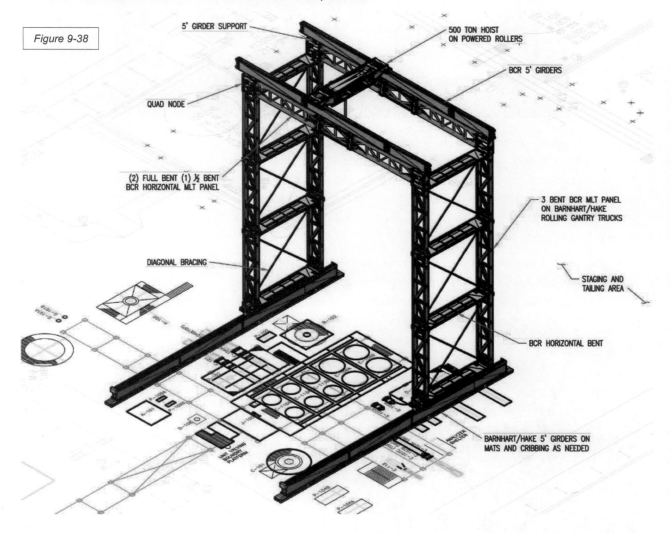

Figure 9-38

The modular nature of this system can be seen in this conceptual arrangement reproduced by permission of Barnhart.

### 9.3.12  Rigging International (now Sarens) chain jack system

Figure 9-39

Rigging International have a proprietary design chain jack that they use extensively in nuclear related lifting works. Here a steam generator has been uplifted, lowered to the horizontal inside the containment and skidded outside onto a platform. A gantry (the white item) is assembled spanning the platform and a lowering zone beyond. The gantry is fitted with a "trolley" incorporating four chain jacks for hoisting / lowering. Suspended from those are chains supporting a carrier with a swivel from which the load is suspended using conventional rigging.

The generator is uplifted from the skids using the chain jacks and the trolley with suspended load is moved along the gantry beams to the left where the generator is rotated 90° at which point it can be lowered to waiting transport at ground level. This replaces the need for a very substantial crane.

Figure 9-40

The chains are somewhat like over-sized bicycle chain. The jacks incorporate dogs which can be engaged to lock or release the chain links; hydraulic jacks are used to provide the lifting effort. The lifting sequence is raise – lock the chain with the lower dogs – release the uppers & retract the jack – re-engage the uppers – extend to release the lowers and raise etc etc. Lowering is by reverse process.

This is a relatively low-tech design for a heavy lifting device but that is an advantage in this case as it has very little to go wrong with it and it is effective (if slow).

### 9.3.13  Push-up mast systems

An alternative to mast systems using strand jacks is to use a push-up mast system such as the Sarens SARTOWER system. This system uses a pair (or pairs) of lattice mast assembled at site from easily transported knock-down components and erected to the required height. The masts are rectangular in plan and comprise box section rear members and "C" section front members braced with hollow section braces. Sections pin and bolt together. Each mast is built on a substantial steel base in which are incorporated 2 x 500 t double acting hydraulic rams. A lifting yoke (small lift beam) spans the two front members and is engaged in the "C" shape. Tubular inserts (pistons) with a lower enlarged base are located in the front members and are guided within its C-shape. They support the lifting yoke. A locking plate supports the column of inserts on the base at a height that allows subsequent inserts to be inserted sequentially from the sides of the base. To lift, the rams are extended, raising the guided column of inserts and elevating the yoke. A lifting beam spans between the masts and is supported at its ends by the yokes. When at full stroke, the locking plate is engaged around the jack ram beneath the head of the lowest piston insert. The load is lowered onto the plate and the jack retracted. A new insert is slid in at each location. The jacks extend taking the load and the locking plate is retracted. This process is repeated to progressively raise the lift beam. Conventional rigging is used from the lift beam to the load. It can include swivels, cross slide facilities or the load may be supported directly from beneath depending on application.

A two mast rig has a basic jacking capacity of 2000 t. Actual capacity is dependent on a number of factors including height, wind loads and so on. Multiples of masts may be combined. At lower heights, the arrangement may be free-standing but at greater heights, braces or guys may be required.

*Figure 9-41*

*A Sarens Sartower system being used on an LNG plant to lift an Absorber Column.*

### 9.3.14 Climbing jack systems

There are a number of companies offering hydraulic gripper type climbing jack systems. The technology is a development of gripper jacks developed by Bygging in Sweden for slip forming purposes. The original jack was static and pulled up a solid square bar whose lower end was attached to the form. For lifting purposes, the jack was inverted and arranged to climb a static bar. The bar now being in compression rather than tension needed to be stabilized against buckling; this was achieved by providing "T"- shaped attachments to the bar at regular intervals. The head of the T was clipped to a suitable structure to provide lateral restraint whilst allowing unrestricted vertical movement. This ensures the lifting loads go down the bar into the base and not into the support structure which is provided primarily to keep the bar straight. Climbing jacks of capacities from 25 t (operating on a 50 mm square bar) to 400 t (using a 200 mm square bar) are available. 100 t jacks and 100 mm square bars are often used for lifting purposes. Various lattice mast designs allowing the use of up to 3x400 t jacks per mast and maximum heights in the order of 150 m are available.

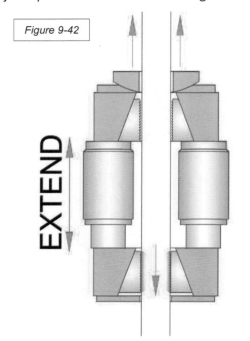

Figure 9-42

The jack units at the heart of this technology comprise an upper and a lower head-block separated by a pair of double-acting hydraulic rams. The jacks are vertically mounted on a solid steel square bar up which they climb. A pair of tool steel wedge shaped grips are located in angled recesses in each head-block; when the head-block is subject to a downwards force, the wedge angle forces the wedges against opposite side faces of the square bar clamping onto it using serrated teeth and locking the head-block to the bar. The payload is supported on the jack head – more on this later.

The illustration shows the lower wedges gripping and the uppers released as the jack is extending (and lifting). Gripping is indicated red for ease of understanding the mode of operation.

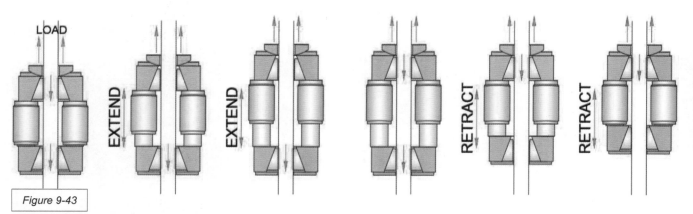

Figure 9-43

The jack climbs the bar by firstly extending the jack; the lower wedges grip locking the lower head-block to the bar; this forces the upper head-block (and load) to rise. At the end of the stroke, the jack is retracted which causes the upper head-block to grip transferring the load onto it and allowing the lower head-block to be retracted ready for another stroke. As noted, the lifting loads are all transferred vertically down the bars into the mast base for distribution into the foundation.

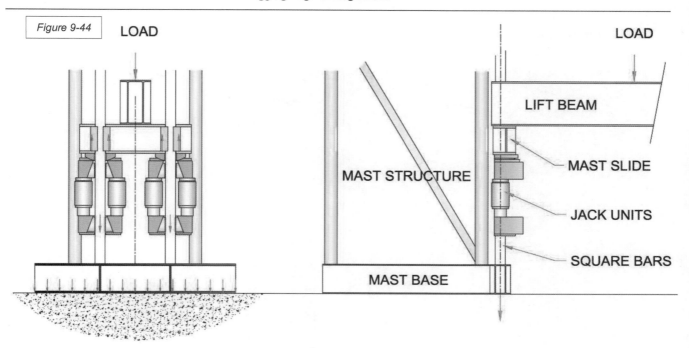

Typically, a lattice mast system is used to stabilize the bars against buckling. For economy of transport, the more heavy-duty systems usually arrive at site in "knock-down" form; they are assembled at site into 6 m or 12 m sections which are stacked vertically on a steel base to the required height using pinned or bolted connections. Lifting systems are built in pairs of masts; at lower elevations they may possible be free-standing; at greater heights they will likely need to be stayed or guyed. Each mast may support multiple bars/jacks; in such cases, a mast sliding chair (yoke) may be used to unify the lifting effort. Where multiple jacks are used, load equalizing single-acting cylinder jacks may be provided between the climbing jacks and the yoke to equalize the jack loads hydraulically. Usually lift beams of appropriate span and strength will span between opposite masts and the load will be suspended or otherwise supported from the lift beams. Cross slide and swivel facilities are possible. Control of the system is usually from ground level using a computerized control system similar to that used for strand jacks.

*2 x 400 t climbing jacks fitted to 200 mm square bars on a Bidlift type mast.*

This schematic shows a two-mast 1600 t guyed arrangement with x-slide and swivel being used to upend a vessel using a tilt-up frame. The base is on skids allowing relocation (unloaded) to the next vessel foundation.

Figure 9-47

Advantages / disadvantages

These systems always require a supporting mast unlike strand jacks which may be used independently of a mast when a suitable load carrying structure exists. However when there isn't a suitable structure, these rigs go head-to-head with strand jack systems. The lift beam and all the rigging starts low on climbing jack systems and rises with the lift; in many cases, you can design to lower it down again on completion. This is a major advantage in assembly and disassembly time and cost. There aren't the problems of handling strand, bird-caging or strands breaking; the bars have a long life unlike strand. The masts are not load carrying and are much lighter than strand jack rigs. They can be made guy-less to some extent, but not as readily as strand jack rigs which use heavier masts. Where you can't start with the lift beam low, you have to have a long suspension which makes the masts higher than an equivalent strand jack rig, so it wouldn't be a good choice there. Like strand jack rigs or push up systems, these rigs are compact and can often be located in very tight spots; they may need guys though, as noted above, which can be a significant disadvantage. The smaller versions of these rigs are very useful inside buildings and provide much better capacity than telescoping gantries and are very much more stable.

Figure 9-48

This rig used 4 x 24 m high "Standard" Masts fitted with 2 x 100 mm square bars, each using a 100 t capacity climbing jack to form an 800 t capacity rig supporting two 30 m span lifting beams. The upper deck of the module was transported beneath the beams and slung from them using 4 basketed grommet slings. By operation of the climbing jacks the deck was raised allowing the lower assembly to be transported beneath for mating. This approach allowed parallel fabrication under cover in two construction halls and avoided the need for heavy cranes.

### 9.3.15  Gin pole systems (heavy duty)

Figure 9-49

Essentially the precursor to strand jack tower systems – used in past times to lift heavy/large chemical vessels beyond the ability of the existing cranes. Not seen much these days, except possibly in the Far East. The gin pole is basically a vertically mounted crane boom. The base is mounted in a universal bearing (the ink well). Often guyed and used in pairs with a lift beam spanning the head, this is a 4-pole braced arrangement with external guys.  A winch line is run up the pole to the head and reeved to traveling blocks from which the load is suspended. The static blocks may be on the lift beam or on the head of the pole as here. By synchronized winch operation, the load is raised, with the lifting loads going down the pole to the ground. They can often be accommodated in the vessel foundation design. As the rig spans the load, balancing counterweight is not required; the whole rig is very compact. Guys where required may be a negative consideration – lifting is slow.

Guyed arrangements in which a pair of gin poles luffs with the suspended load are possible.

The low-tech nature of these rigs makes them relatively cheap and (if you can find one) worth considering for a one-off lift outside the range of a readily available crane.

## 9.4  Summary

Although cranes are generally quick, convenient, versatile and "standard", they are not always the best solution to a lifting task, either technically, financially, physically or on safety grounds. No matter what you can imagine to lift, there is usually a solution and it's not always a crane. There are very many alternatives that can be considered when confronted with a lifting task and I have just touched on a few with which I am somewhat familiar. The aim is really to open your eyes to the possibilities; if you are confronted with a lifting task that is somewhat out of the norm, review alternative lifting systems and talk to the companies that offer this service. I've mentioned a few, there are many more; apologies to all those companies with ingenious lifting techniques and equipment that I didn't cover. They may have something to offer that meets your needs well or something that can be adapted or a great idea for a new solution. Today's great idea is tomorrow's standard technique.

# 10 Loadspreading

## 10.1 Adequacy of support

As noted earlier, it is critical for capacity and stability that construction cranes whether crawler, outrigger ring (or otherwise) mounted, are supported on a surface that is capable of withstanding the imposed loads and pressures without reaching a limiting failure condition or settling excessively. A limiting failure condition would be general shear, local shear or punching shear failure. On soft soils, large settlements could occur without shear failure occurring, in which case, the allowable bearing capacity would be limited by settlement considerations.

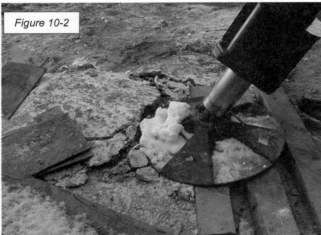

Punching failure – surface was a very hard crust, ground beneath loose & sandy. No mats used.

Not the way to mat under an outrigger!

It is also very important that the crane remains essentially level in use. Typically you are restricted to being within 1% of level (or even less, 0.5% in some cases) – read the manual, it varies by manufacturer and crane configuration! As settlement is load dependent and the loadings in crane outriggers or crawler tracks are rarely uniform, so you need to be concerned to ensure that there isn't significant differential deflection across support points (or a rotation of the crane foundation) that would cause the crane to tilt out of tolerance.

Why is the level tolerance so tight? Operating a crane out of level (across the boom) induces lateral loads in the boom and structure that the crane is not designed to accept. Cranes are not designed to accept much lateral loading and capacities drop off dramatically when tilted. To get a feel for the order of magnitude of the possible loss, a crane that is 3° out of level could lose up to 50% of its capacity when lifting with a long boom at minimum radius. Operating a crane out of level in the plane of the boom will result in the radius of a freely suspended load being greater or less than it should be and can increase the overturning moment on the crane.

As noted earlier, in order to confirm adequacy of support, it is necessary to:

- A. Establish a best estimate of the peak loads / pressures the crane will impose under its tracks or outriggers, and
- B. Confirm the integrity of the supporting surface and establish the maximum loads / pressures that it is capable of safely accepting. There are two parts to this:
    - a. Identifying subsurface (invisible) hazards - are there any sinkholes / voids, subservice utilities such as water/sewer lines or buried objects under the ground in the area in which it is intended to impose loads; is the ground saturated.
    - b. Investigating the make-up of the ground in the area and establishing its load-carrying ability

With the answers to the above, an assessment can be made as to whether further distribution of the support loads and pressures is needed using crane mats or similar and/or improvements to the ground are required.

Figure 10-3

This pipe is only just below the surface. OK, you can see it here, but say 20' away you may be unaware of its existence. Sit an outrigger directly over that and you will likely be in trouble.

## 10.2 Who is responsible?

Generally speaking, the company operating the crane is in the best position to know its operating characteristics and has the necessary information to determine the loads it will impose. Further, they often will be in the best position to provide load-spreading materials (wooden/steel mats, plate etc) to distribute those loads. However, the crane operator (entity that is, not individual) is not necessarily in the best position to know about the ground conditions on the site on which the crane is to be operated. The crane operator is however ultimately responsible to ensure the stability of the crane in use.

The ''Controlling entity'', i.e. ''an employer that is a prime contractor, general contractor, construction manager or any other legal entity with overall responsibility for the construction of the project & it's planning, quality and completion'' is generally the entity that is best placed to know about the ground conditions at the job site and is generally the entity that will be conducting (or having conducted) civil work to improve those ground conditions (if required).

OSHA in the USA advocates this division of responsibility and imposes specific duties on both the entity responsible for the project (the controlling entity) and the entity operating the crane to ensure that the crane is adequately supported. It places responsibility for ensuring that the ground conditions are adequate on the controlling entity, while also making the employer operating the crane responsible notifying the controlling entity of any deficiency in the ground conditions, and having the deficiency corrected before operating the crane. (OSHA notes that the controlling entity, due to its control of the worksite, has the requisite authority and is in the best position to arrange for adequate ground conditions).

Accordingly, OSHA requires the controlling entity to inform the user of the equipment and the equipment operator of the location of hazards beneath the equipment set-up area (such as voids, tanks, and utilities, including sewer, water supply, and drain pipes) that are identified in documents (such as site drawings, as-built drawings, and soil analyses) that are in the possession of the controlling entity. If the controlling entity is aware of underground hazards by means other than documents it is also required to communicate that knowledge to the crane operator. If the controlling entity does not possess the information, it is not required to obtain it from another source.

In the event that no controlling entity exists, the requirements must be met by the employer that has authority at the site to make or arrange for ground preparations needed to meet the requirements. For example, if the employer who hires the crane has the authority to get the ground prepared in the absence of a controlling entity, the responsibility for complying would fall to that employer.

So, the default position is that the crane company has to ensure the crane is properly supported and the controlling entity needs to inform the crane company of hazards identified on information it has in its possession or otherwise knows of. Responsibility for sub-surface investigation is not well defined; that together with matting and ground preparation is generally a contractual matter; often the crane company will mat and the employer will investigate & prepare/improve the ground. Of course the crane "operator" and the controlling entity may be the same entity. Divisions of responsibility may be different by law or by contract in different locales.

## 10.3 What ground conditions am I dealing with?

The ground conditions you may be faced with at the job site, and how you have to assess them, are extremely varied and are very dependent not only on the general locale but on the type of site. Work locations can be generally classified as:

- Green-field construction sites
- Brown field construction sites
- Existing facilities
- Public or private locations

### 10.3.1 Green-field construction sites

A large green-field construction site is probably the best situation for the lift planner. There will be a controlling entity. The site conditions have been evaluated, the site has likely been graded, the organic material has been removed, fill has been brought in and compacted (or the ground improved by soil mixing or some other technique). There are no unknown voids; services are well identified and there is likely to be a geotechnical engineer around to determine a permissible ground bearing pressure in the work area. (Make sure he/she gives you a figure for temporary construction purposes and not for permanent buildings). There should be a level, stable, well drained supporting surface to work from, good for a certain figure. You just need to be aware of what may be been constructed subsurface and consider proximity to trenches and the like. On green-field projects, the controlling entity should consider lifting and site transportation requirements in preparing the site. Where lifting imposes particularly heavy loads, they may be able to cater for them in a foundation design, provide special piled foundations or construct "heavy load" crane pads.

### 10.3.2 Brown-field construction sites

A brown-field construction site is one that is being redeveloped and has been used before for industrial purposes. What was there has likely been demolished and the ground graded; it may have been "improved". The additional hazards include:

- Unidentified services such as water and sewer pipes, voids, buried objects and the like
- Previously disturbed ground with possibly soft spots, maybe saturated ground possibly from leaking services

Again, there will be a controlling entity. They should have conducted a sub-surface survey using techniques such as metal detectors, pipe and cable locators, ground penetrating radar, electromagnetics or magnetrometry to determine what is down there (possibly unknown and undocumented). This would be followed by soil borings to determine the ground make-up. They may have removed material and "improved" the ground.

Again this is not too bad a situation for the lift planner given the presence of a controlling entity who is going to do this investigation and improvement and given that there is likely to be a geotechnical engineer involved who can determine a permissible ground bearing pressure for you to design to in the area in which you are going to work. Again, you just need to be aware of new subsurface construction and consider proximity to trenches and the like.

### 10.3.3 Existing facilities

Lifting during say maintenance or minor construction projects inside an existing working facility, whether contracted by the owner or a general contractor can present hazards that you don't have on a construction site. It could be a chemical plant, steel works, wharf, lay-down yard, building or whatever. There will likely be a controlling entity, but the quality of the information available may be poor. Services may not be documented, they may be shown incorrectly, modifications may have been made, voids could have formed from leaking pipes and so on. If there is a concrete slab, you aren't going to know how thick it is, what reinforcement it has or how well supported beneath it is.

In an ideal world, if the conditions are not well known, there would be a sub-surface survey followed by test borings and a geotechnical engineer to make a determination. Reference may be made to facilities engineers / original designers where available. Some or all of this would likely happen if conducting a major lift but would be unlikely to happen for what is seen as a relatively "light" lift, say removal of a 5 t pipe spool during maintenance using a 40 t telescopic crane. The fact is however, that the majority of crane tipping incidents occur in those sorts of situations and not with the major lifts – they always get plenty of attention in the planning stage.

Figure 10-4

Figure 10-5

So, what do you do in such cases? First you should make a visual inspection of the area. Settlement of an asphalt area or of a concrete slab would raise concern as would cracked concrete. You would want to look for man-holes, cable trench covers, drains, fire-water monitors and so on; they are all possible indicators of underground services.

If any concerns are raised by your investigation, have them checked out or, if possible, relocate the crane to avoid the problem areas.

Having established that there is little or no probability of subsurface hazards, the problem is to determine a working design figure for the ground (probably without the expertise of a geotechnical engineer to help you). In this case, it's generally a question of working with what you have – see later.

### 10.3.4 Public or private locations

You may be called upon to prepare a plan for a one-off lift at a site that is neither a construction site nor a working facility, say:

- lifting an HVAC unit onto the roof of a building from a public road
- lifting a communications antenna onto a tower in a field
- lifting a boat over a building from the parking lot

In the case of public property such as a road, you may be working under stipulations given to you (particularly if in somewhere like New York), or there may be persons to guide you, there again maybe not. The road will have been prepared for the sort of traffic it carries. There could be services there.

In a field, you may be dealing with virgin undisturbed ground, or someone may have dumped some roadstone there and rolled it out when the tower was constructed. There could be organic matter and the ground could be saturated.

If located in an asphalt parking lot, the ground will have been leveled and some sort of sub-base laid, but won't generally be capable of very high pressures.

Figure 10-6

If lifting a tree out of the back yard of a house over the house you will likely not want to locate the crane with any of the outriggers in the front yard as the ground will likely have been disturbed and have very poor bearing capability. The street will not be particularly good either.

This overturn is actually likely to have been overload at the required long radius.

## 10.4 Establishing permissible ground loadings

### 10.4.1 Construction sites – available geotechnical engineer

The best advice I could give you in this complex area is to seek the advice of a geotechnical engineer. You should find such a person engaged somewhere on any major construction project. He/she will determine an allowable bearing capacity based on either soil strength or settlement as applicable, noting the short term duration of the loading. If the ground conditions are somewhat uncertain, investigation, sampling and testing (possibly plate testing) may be required before the geotechnical engineer can make a determination.

On a large construction project different areas may be prepared to different capacities e.g. haul road, laydown areas, unit xxx, unit yyy, heavy crane pad and so on. The info may be presented in the form of a hatched map of the worksite.  Note that you may be given a lower bearing capacity when the area over which the load is applied is larger. To keep things simple, you may decide for your fleet of outrigger based cranes that, knowing the ground capacity and the max loadings each crane could put down, each crane must always use a particular size mat. That would guarantee keeping within the permissibles at all times and avoid having to recalculate every time.

### 10.4.2 Construction sites – presumptive bearing capacities

As noted earlier, having an available geotechnical engineer and/or a working pressure provided to you may be a luxury you don't have. In that case, I would suggest that you use the bearing capacities that Shapiro proposes in "Cranes and Derricks". The following table is based on that (with my conversions).

| Soil type | | Bearing capacity (presumptive) | | | |
|---|---|---|---|---|---|
| | | tons/ft$^2$ | ksf | kN/m$^2$ | t/m$^2$ |
| Rock (not shale unless hard) | Bedrock | 60 | 120 | 5746 | 586 |
| | Layered | 15 | 30 | 1436 | 146 |
| | Soft | 8 | 16 | 766 | 78 |
| Hardpan (cemented sand or gravel) | | 10 | 20 | 958 | 98 |
| Gravel, sand and gravel | Compact | 8 | 16 | 766 | 78 |
| | Firm | 6 | 12 | 575 | 59 |
| | Loose | 4 | 8 | 383 | 39 |
| Sand, coarse to medium | Compact | 6 | 12 | 575 | 59 |
| | Firm | 4.5 | 9 | 431 | 44 |
| | Loose | 3 | 6 | 287 | 29 |
| Sand, fine, silty or with trace of clay | Compact | 4 | 8 | 383 | 39 |
| | Firm | 3 | 6 | 287 | 29 |
| | Loose | 2 | 4 | 192 | 20 |
| Silt | Compact | 3 | 6 | 287 | 29 |
| | Firm | 2.5 | 5 | 239 | 24 |
| | Loose | 2 | 4 | 192 | 20 |
| Clay | Compact | 4 | 8 | 383 | 39 |
| | Firm | 2.5 | 5 | 239 | 24 |
| | Loose | 1 | 2 | 96 | 10 |

Figure 10-7

The above presumes that organic material has been removed and the soil is graded down to an undisturbed natural stratum and the ground is well drained.

### 10.4.3 Public / private sites – presumptive bearing capacities

What do you do if planning to lift at a quay or from a roadway, in a field or a parking lot or a transport company yard? These are not construction sites but public / private facilities and there is not likely to be a geotechnical engineer to help (if there is, proceed as above). The employing entity may not have a presence at the job site, or may have no knowledge of site conditions or expertise in geotechnical matters – the judgment as to what the ground can take and what matting (if any) is required falls on the crane company. If you are on asphalt, concrete or lifting in someone's yard, the above table may not really apply too well.

This situation is primarily an issue with truck and other outrigger mounted cranes. You rarely use a crawler crane on anything other than a construction site; if you did use one elsewhere, there would likely be considerable effort put into establishing a suitable support arrangement for it.

Further, this is usually, but not exclusively, an issue restricted to "jobbing" truck cranes below about 120 tons. Above that size, you are likely talking project work or something of sufficient significance that people would consider justifies some ground investigation. So the issue is mainly one of planning for the use of smaller outrigger mounted cranes conducting routine lifts. The person planning the lift on behalf of the crane company (could be the crane driver or a rigger) has to make a call regarding ground conditions. All he/she has to go on is what is observed, what sort of dent can be made with the heel of a boot and experience; there is little or no guidance out there. It is no wonder that the majority of tipping incidents are with "jobbing" truck cranes conducting routine lifts (particularly when you note how close a crane fitted with a long boom / jib can be to tipping when at chart capacity at long radii).

One of the reasons there is no guidance / rules of thumb is that every case is different and it is very difficult (and potentially dangerous) to generalize. So, what sort of guidance can I offer? It is an instance where bad advice is worse than no advice, but no advice is no answer either. The best I can do is to offer some conservative figures that historically have proved sufficient. First however, do the following:

## Observe

Have a good look around, has this ground been prepared for a purpose, if so what. That may give you a clue. Is it well consolidated e.g. has it had a lot of heavy traffic over it for years. What is it made of? Has it settled? Is it saturated?

## Local knowledge

Conditions vary tremendously – lifting on rock in Norway is a whole lot different to lifting on reclaimed swamp in Louisiana. Frozen ground may be good for a lot more than the same ground when thawed. Local building codes can help. Ask locals engaged in similar work, what works for them.

## Design codes

A quayside will likely have been designed for road traffic, a road will likely have been designed to a standard such as AASHTO (American Association of State Highway and Transportation Officials) or similar.

## Be conservative

Cover the extent of your lack of knowledge with conservatism. If you don't know anything of the ground conditions, err on the side of caution, go for a very conservative figure and extensive matting.

What would a reasonably conservative figure to use if you have no better information, I would suggest the below – treat these figures with extreme caution!

| Figure 10-8 | ksf | ton/ft$^2$ | t/m$^2$ | kN/m$^2$ |
|---|---|---|---|---|
| Road (highway) concrete | 4 | 2 | 20 | 200 |
| Road (highway) asphalt | 3 | 1.5 | 15 | 150 |
| Quayside | 3 | 1.5 | 15 | 150 |
| Laydown yard (compacted stone fill) | 5 | 2.5 | 25 | 250 |
| Field (undisturbed ground) | 2 | 1 | 10 | 100 |
| Reclaimed swamp land | 0.6 | 0.3 | 3 | 30 |
| House front yard | 0.6 - 1 | 0.3 – 0.5 | 3 – 5 | 30 - 50 |
| Parking lot (cars) asphalt | 2 | 1 | 10 | 100 |
| Steel works (similar heavy industrial) roads | 5 | 2.5 | 25 | 250 |

## 10.5 Bridging the gap between crane loads and ground capacity

When you have determined the maximum loads (and therefore the pressures) that the crane will impose beneath its outrigger pads (or crawler tracks) in use and you have arrived at a limiting figure for the ground bearing capacity, you will in most cases find that the crane loads exceed the ground capacity requiring some action on your part.

There are two things that can be done:

- Reduce the pressures imposed into the ground by increasing the contact area to the ground using crane mats or similar load spreading materials
- Improve the bearing capacity of the ground locally by incorporation of a layer of gravel/crushed stone reinforced with geogrid or similar. In some cases with poor ground and high crane loads, it may be necessary to provide a piled foundation.

It might make sense to do one or the other or a bit of both.

Figure 10-9

River banks are notoriously poor for accepting high loadings. This Manitowoc 4100 ringer was being used long term at a river dock to unload oversize and overweight components from barges direct at the job site. The crane loadings were provided to the project civil group and a piled foundation was designed and installed.

The pile cap is the circular light grey concrete at grade directly below the timber blocking. A stiff foundation is highly desirable under a ring crane as significant differential settlement cannot be tolerated.

Piling on a job where piling is already being conducted is not as frightening a prospect as you might imagine.

It would be unusual not to need to use some form of load distribution matting beneath a crane outrigger pad. The mats used as standard by truck cranes in the areas of the world I am most familiar with will typically be sized to get the outrigger loads into the ground at about 5 ksf (2.5 tons/ft$^2$ or 25 t/m$^2$) – it varies a bit, do NOT assume it will necessarily be so where you are. That figure may well be OK in the majority of cases, but not in all. Further matting may be required or the ground will need to be improved.

With crawler cranes, the figures might show that you are OK without using mats on cranes up to about 250 t capacity if the ground is good. However, using mats is always a good idea when lifting on crawlers. Even if the figures work, mats will even out the loadings over the area, will minimize and even out settlement and minimize the likelihood of the crane tipping because of an unforeseen soft spot under say the front of a crawler track. I would always use them on cranes over 250 t unless there was overwhelming evidence that they were unnecessary.

*Figure 10-10*

The exception to my rule! Lifting a conveyor section in the mountains of Chile. The ground is beautifully prepared over solid rock. Mats are not required in this case. You rarely get it as good as this.

*Figure 10-11*

This would be more typical. Lifting on a petrochemical site in S-E Texas on the Gulf Coast. The site was reclaimed and prepared with about 3' of compacted structural fill and geogrid. The geotechnical engineer determined the bearing capacity for crane operation purposes was 1.6 ksf (0.8 tons/ft$^2$ or approximately 8 t/m$^2$) in this case.

Note that the bearing capacity figures that the geotechnical engineer provided on this site were dependent on the matted area, e.g. 2.1 ksf for a 20'x20' matted area, 1.5 ksf for a 20'x40' matted area, 1.2 ksf for a 40'x40' matted area.

Crane mats were universally required when lifting.

## 10.6 Load distribution using crane mats

### 10.6.1 Mat construction

Crane mats as used under crawler crane tracks are typically of wooden or steel construction.

Wooden mats

Wooden mats are typically 8" - 12" (200-300 mm) deep, 4' or 5' (1200-1500 mm) wide and about 20' (6 m) long. They are made from quality hardwood such as beech, hickory, oak or Douglas Fir; the variety used will be dependent on locale. In some parts of the world, exotic hardwoods such as Mora or Ekki may be used.

There are a considerable number of companies making wood mats, Quality Mat Company being one, Dixiemat another. Mats can be purchased or often rented.

The following pictures (courtesy of Dixiemat) show typical construction details. The individual timbers are solid and free of major defects, with straight grain; typically they would be 8" or 12" deep x 12" wide. Steel tie rods passing through them tie 4 or 5 of them tightly together to form a mat. Mats are laid side by side on prepared ground (possibly on a leveled sand bed) to cover the required area. Individual mats are not connected to each other in any way.

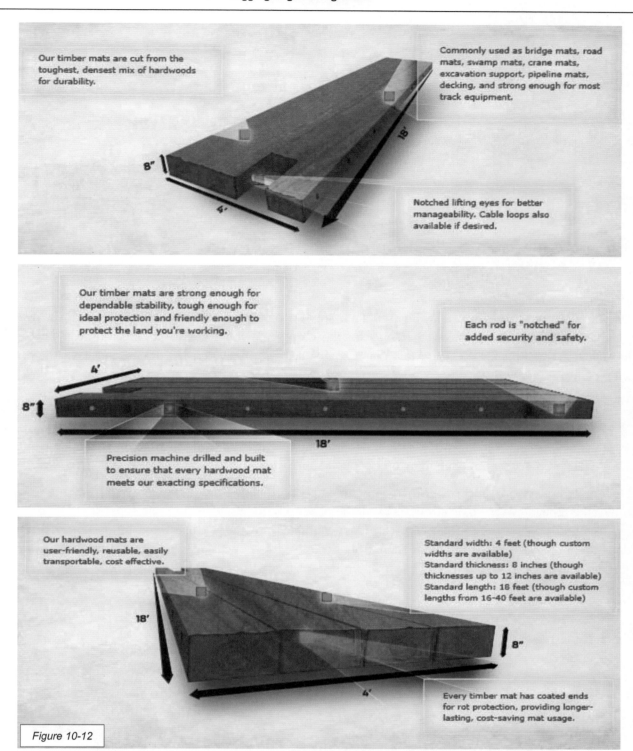

Our timber mats are cut from the toughest, densest mix of hardwoods for durability.

Commonly used as bridge mats, road mats, swamp mats, crane mats, excavation support, pipeline mats, decking, and strong enough for most track equipment.

Notched lifting eyes for better manageability. Cable loops also available if desired.

8"

4'

18'

Our timber mats are strong enough for dependable stability, tough enough for ideal protection and friendly enough to protect the land you're working.

Each rod is "notched" for added security and safety.

4'

8"

18'

Precision machine drilled and built to ensure that every hardwood mat meets our exacting specifications.

Our hardwood mats are user-friendly, reusable, easily transportable, cost effective.

Standard width: 4 feet (though custom widths are available)
Standard thickness: 8 inches (though thicknesses up to 12 inches are available)
Standard length: 18 feet (though custom lengths from 16-40 feet are available)

18'

8"

4'

Every timber mat has coated ends for rot protection, providing longer-lasting, cost-saving mat usage.

Figure 10-12

There are laminated mats available. e.g. Emtek mats made by Anthony Hardwood Composites are vertically laminated mats. Boards the full depth of the mat are glued together side by side using thermoset polymer resins to form billets which are then clamped together using threaded steel tie rods. AHC claims that by eliminating or distributing natural defects, Emtek mats are superior to solid drawn material. They claim a 6" deep x 12" Emtek beam has the 10% greater strength than a 12" x 12" #2 grade White Oak timber and is half the weight. It is not however necessarily stiffer (for the same depth), and stiffness as we shall see is as important as strength.

Horizontally laminated mats such as the below (by Dixiemat) are primarily intended for creating temporary roadways rather than being used as crane mats.

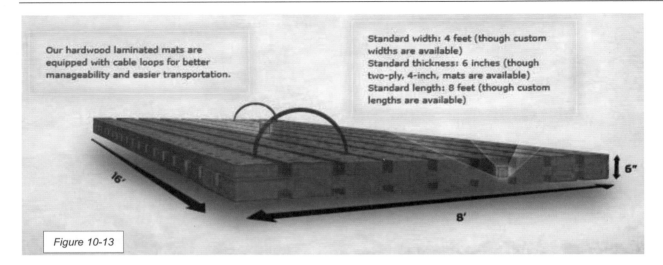

Our hardwood laminated mats are equipped with cable loops for better manageability and easier transportation.

Standard width: 4 feet (though custom widths are available)
Standard thickness: 6 inches (though two-ply, 4-inch, mats are available)
Standard length: 8 feet (though custom lengths are available)

Figure 10-13

## Steel Mats

On poorer grounds steel mats may be used. I am not aware of there being a standard line of these available to purchase commercially although that may be the case somewhere. They may be rented from companies including LGH (Lifting Gear Hire). Most crane companies with heavy cranes design and have them made to their own specification.

Typically they are formed from a number of rolled steel I-sections arranged side by side and stitch welded toe-toe looking something like that shown below with or without top and bottom plates.

Width is usually about 5' (1.5 m), length varies from about 10' - 20' (3 m – 6 m) and the section size between 8"-12" (200 mm – 300 mm) depending on intended application.

Steel mats are considerably stiffer than wooden mats and thus are more effective at getting the loads out to their ends; they have bending strength so can be used to span between available support points or span over an area you don't want to load; you can form a bridge with them / use them in load-out operations. All dependent on the sections you make them from of course; the down side is weight.

Figure 10-14

## Other options

There are companies such as DuraDeck offering crane outrigger pads made from plastic with a honeycomb construction. They also make temporary access roadways along similar lines. MaxGlyde make all-polymer outrigger pads. Aluminum outrigger pads are available from others.

### 10.6.2 Recommended reading

Note that this topic is somewhat subjective and reliant on the professional judgment of engineers. As regards crane matting, there are a number of different approaches used in the industry in an attempt to simplify the complexities in order to provide a structured way to design a safe arrangement. Not rules of thumb exactly, but simplified approaches based on some reasonable real world (but adequately conservative) generalizations. By and large these have been vindicated over the years.

On the whole topic of crane matting I have found the approach and analysis methods proposed by David Duerr of 2DM Associates (TX) in his paper "Effective Bearing Length of Crane Mats" and his related presentation "Crane Mats and Ground Bearing Issues" to be the most practical and comprehensible on the subject. The following leans heavily on that material and is my attempt to explain it. You are advised to go to David's web site to read the source material. Note that David has now released a book "Mobile Crane Support Handbook" *ISBN 978-0-692-31382-4* that incorporates and expands upon his material – it is highly recommended.

You are also advised to read Shapiro – Cranes and Derricks on the subject.

If you want to know more about the theory and practice of foundation design (not specifically crane matting), you are recommended to read Bowles – Foundation Analysis and Design (1996). Note that our application is temporary so we are not as concerned about long term settlement; also note that limited settlement is OK.

### 10.6.3 How do mats distribute load?

A crane mat is effectively a temporary above-grade spread footing. It distributes the load horizontally. A piled foundation by comparison distributes the load vertically. As with any foundation, a mat has to interface with the ground at a safe stress level and has to limit settlements to an acceptable amount.

In addition to compressive strength considerations, the foundation system (mat and ground on which it sits) must be safe against overturning and sliding. As noted earlier, on construction sites the ground may well have been "improved" by the introduction of structural fill and geogrid or by other means. The function of the improved layer(s) is to distribute loads imposed at construction grade down to pressures that can be withstood by the underlying "unimproved" ground. In such cases, the function of the mats is to distribute concentrated track or outrigger loads into the improved layer at pressures that layer can safely accept.

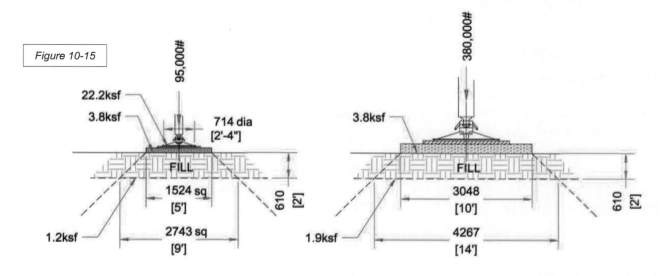
Figure 10-15

If the basic ground at the job site is good for say 1.5 ksf, the ground may well have been improved with say 2' of structural fill to get the capacity at construction grade up to 5 ksf. (All these figures are totally arbitrary to illustrate a principle). A 65 ton RT putting down an outrigger load of 95,000# will impose a pressure of 22.2 ksf under the pontoon. Using a 5' x 5' wood mat with a plate between it and the pontoon (to ensure the full width of the mat is loaded), the pressure into the prepared ground will be about 3.8 ksf. (It is reasonable to take the full area of the mat as being effective given those dimensions). If we presume the prepared fill to distribute the load at 45° (it's not really that simple), the effective area 2' down at the level of the underlying natural ground will be 9' x 9' = 81', therefore the pressure to that layer will be 1.2 ksf, which is OK.

If we consider a much larger crane that puts down 380,000# through its outrigger and use 10' x 10' mats so that the pressure into the ground is the same 3.8 ksf, you might imagine the situation is the same and all is well. In fact, assuming the same 45° distribution gives you an area of 14' x 14' at the underlying layer. This results in a pressure of 1.9 ksf at that level, which is too high. The analysis is crude, but should give you the concept.

This is why you may be restricted to lower contact pressures when you apply them over larger areas. Conversely it is why very high pressures imposed through small contact areas such as you get with loaded tires rolling across a job site may be OK. Tires on heavy trailers and the like put down about 120 psi (equivalent to 17 ksf) which would appear way too high for the average road, but the pressure is applied over patches of relatively small area, quite some distance from each other and quickly dissipates with depth. You may see some local settlement but you won't get a general failure of your (say) 5 ksf site road.

### 10.6.4  Importance of mat stiffness

Whilst the mat has to have adequate strength to withstand the shear and bending stresses induced in it in distributing loads, it is its stiffness relative to the stiffness of the ground that determines how effective it is in spreading load along its length.

Stiffness is a measure of how much something deflects under load; strength is the ability to withstand a load without failing. A mat could be strong enough but not adequately stiff. The extent by which a beam (as a mat basically is in this situation) deflects for a given load is a function of the modulus of elasticity of the material and of the moment of inertia (2nd moment of area) of the section. That in turn is a function of the breadth of the mat x the cube of its thickness. As the load is a given, the material is a given and the breadth likely fixed, the only variable you have in limiting deflection is the mat thickness. Thus mat thickness is a critical element in making a mat "stiff" and ensuring its effectiveness in distributing load along its length. Of course steel mats are much stiffer than wood mats as the modulus of elasticity of steel is so very much greater.

Note as well that 2 x 6" mats (stacked) do not equate to 1 x 12" mat either in strength or stiffness. (50% of the bending strength and 25% of the stiffness).

### 10.6.5  Pressure profiles

The conventional way to analyze foundation behavior of the mat/ground is to treat the ground as being linearly elastic up to the ultimate bearing capacity and perfectly plastic thereafter. Load carried (in the elastic range of the ground) is considered to be proportional to deflection, so can be mathematically modeled as a series of springs beneath the mat at say 1' centers. As the shape of the ground follows the deflection of the mat, ground support is proportional to the deflection of the mat at that point. A mat loaded in the center and supported continuously beneath is going to want to sag in the center. Therefore the ground deflection is greatest there and the load is going to be highest in the center. As the deflection decreases as you move away from the center, the load decreases. If the ends of the mat lift clear of the ground, the load carried there (and beyond) will be zero as the ground is not displaced. The amount by which the mat "sags" is dependent on how stiff it is and how stiff the ground beneath is. Therefore the shape of the pressure profile is determined by the relative stiffnesses of mat and ground. The area under the profile x the mat width = the load carried.

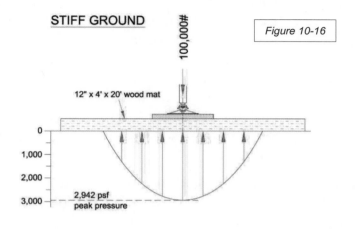

Figure 10-16

If the mat is stiff and ground is relatively stiff, then the load in the center of the mat will be supported with minimal deflection of the mat and ground (equivalent to a high spring rate). The pressure profile will be narrow and deep. The ends of the mat will carry no load.

The figures are after Duerr.

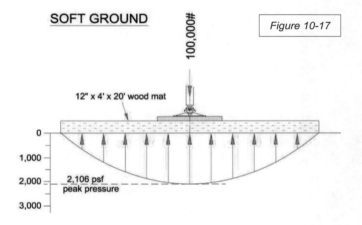

Figure 10-17

If the mat is stiff and ground is soft, then the center of the mat will need to deflect a lot more to get the required support (equivalent to a low spring rate). As the mat takes on more of a curve, the more pronounced sag engages more of our little "springs" into contributing support. The pressure profile will be wide and shallow. At this particular ground stiffness the whole mat is engaged with the pressure zero at the ends.

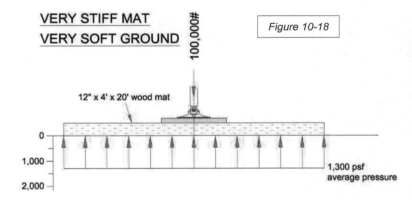

Figure 10-18

If the mat is infinitely stiff and ground is infinitely soft, then the mat would not deflect at all and would move down bodily with uniform deflection of the ground and thus uniform support. This is not truly feasible in the real world.

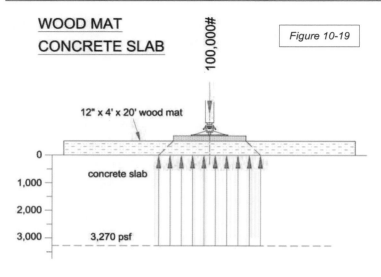

WOOD MAT
CONCRETE SLAB

Figure 10-19

12" x 4' x 20' wood mat

100,000#

0

1,000

2,000

3,000

concrete slab

3,270 psf

What happens if you put your wood mat on a thick concrete slab and both are flat and in contact? The slab can be considered as being infinitely stiff. The mat is somewhat stiff but has some elasticity, so will "squish" some locally. There will be some lateral distribution but not a lot. Best bet would be something like 30° - 45°. That gives you a high pressure of about 3,270 psf, but there again the slab can probably take it. The mats are really protecting the concrete and assuring uniformity of contact.

With a steel mat on a concrete slab, it is worse as steel deflects even less; a 45° distribution is probably the best you can expect.

One thing you can do is lay a thin bed of sand (maybe 2" - 4") on the concrete before laying the mat. This provides uniform contact and provides a bit of compliance in the system allowing the mat to deflect a bit which will help lateral distribution.

An option is to use Dow Ethafoam polyethylene foam sheets between the mat and concrete. Lifting Gear UK for instance offer 2" thick sheets on a rental basis as an alternative to sand. See the white layer in the photograph.

Figure 10-20

Note that if you want to be able to consider the whole width of your lower level wood mats as effective, you need the upper level steel mat to be laid cross-ways catching the whole width. You can't rely on the steel tie bars to transmit load laterally between individual members of a wood mat.

### 10.6.6  Basis of calculation

Mr Duerr suggests that to conduct a rigorous analysis using a program such as FADEMLP, an analysis program packaged with the Bowles (1996) text is usually not practical as one of the required inputs, the soil elastic property or the modulus of subgrade reaction is generally not known reliably.

Instead he proposes a simplified practical approach to mat design that uses the concept of determining an "effective length" for the mat over which the pressure can be considered to be uniform. The effective length is calculated through consideration of the soil bearing capacity and stiffness and the mat bending strength and stiffness. It does not require you to know the soil's elastic properties.

The analysis quantifies:

- The maximum load that can be imposed on the mat without exceeding the allowable bending stress
- The maximum load that can be imposed on the mat without exceeding the allowable shear stress
- The maximum load that can be imposed on the mat without exceeding an established deflection limit.

To find the three limiting conditions and simplify the analysis, he proposes that the pressure distribution under the mat is considered to be uniform and equal to the maximum allowable pressure. This allows the limiting load carried by the mat to be simply expressed as a function of the allowable pressure (a constant) and an effective length over which the allowable pressure is applied (a variable). That in turn then allows the bending stress, shear stress and deflection all to be expressed in three equations in terms where $L_{eff}$ is the only variable, allowing a solution for $L_{eff}$ for each of the three criteria. The least $L_{eff}$ governs. Knowing that, and the maximum allowable pressure, the maximum allowable load to the mat may be calculated.

The actual imposed load can then be compared against the allowable load. The "actual" averaged pressure is the actual load / $L_{eff}$ x the mat width.

The true pressure distribution is not likely to be uniform & rectangular but somewhat parabolic with a slightly greater peak pressure and a greater applied width.

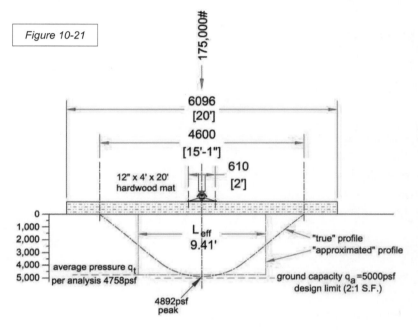

Figure 10-21

The rectangular profile is considered adequately equivalent to the true profile for the purpose of mat/ground evaluation.

For instance, the worked example we will be going through yields a ground pressure (uniform) of 4758 psf (as we will see later). This compares with a "true" peak pressure calculated using FADEMLP of 4892 psf and an allowable (based on a 2:1 safety factor) of 5000 psf.

The bending and shear stresses and the deflection calculated using the approximation do not differ markedly from those calculated from complex analyses for the real world conditions which we are likely to encounter.

### 10.6.7 Effective length based on mat bending and ground bearing

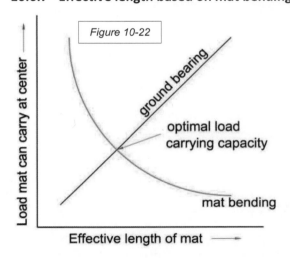

Figure 10-22

If you draw a graph of load carrying capacity v effective length of mat based on the maxing out the permissible ground bearing pressure, it will be a straight line relationship. The longer the effective length, the more load can be carried.

If you draw a graph of load carrying capacity v effective length of mat based on maxing out the bending capacity of the mat, it will be a curve. The shorter the effective length of the mat, the more load it takes to bring the mat to its maximum bending capability. Conversely, the longer the effective length, the less load it takes to bring the mat to its maximum bending capacity.

There is an optimal effective length at which those two lines cross. At that point, both the mat bending and ground pressures are at the max permissible and the load that can be imposed is at a maximum.

Per Mr Duerr's approach, the first step is to find that optimal point.

The second step is to calculate a maximum effective length based on limiting shear of the mat. This calculation is determined from the allowable ground bearing pressure (and the dimensions and weight of the mat) only.

The third and last effective length calculation is to figure the length at which a predetermined deflection limit is met. The calculation is based on allowable ground bearing pressure; the modulus of elasticity, width and moment of inertia of the mat and a limiting deflection of $0.0075L_c$ where $L_c$ is the cantilevered (effective) length of the mat beyond the stiff bearing on top.

The least of these three calculated effective lengths governs; that in turn allows determination of the maximum load which can be safely imposed which can then be compared to the actual load. So long as the actual is less than the maximum, the mat is considered good. You can then determine what percentage of allowables you are actually operating at and fill in the blanks.

### 10.6.8 "Duerr" methodology with worked example

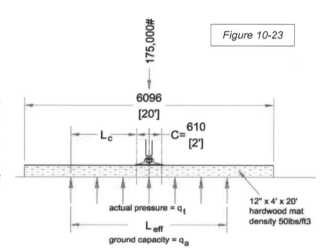

Figure 10-23

Let's consider the approach through an example; say a load of 175,000 lbs is applied to a 1' x 4' x 20' hardwood mat. The ultimate ground bearing capacity is 10,000 psf, so applying a FOS of 2 (note 2 not 3), gives a maximum allowable bearing pressure of 5000 psf.

From various industry sources, David proposes the following allowable stresses for timber mats.

| Allowable stresses for timber mats | | Oak/Fir | Mora | Emtek | |
|---|---|---|---|---|---|
| Bending stress | $F_b$ | 1,400 | 2,500 | 4,123 | psi |
| Shear stress | $F_v$ | 200 | 200 | 379 | psi |
| Bearing stress | $F_c$ | 750 | 1,000 | 750 | psi |
| Modulus of elasticity | E | 1,200,000 | 2,960,000 | 1,600,000 | psi |
| Generally suitable for mixed hardwoods oak, beech, hickory or Douglas Fir | | | | | |

Note: 1 psi = 6.895 x 10$^{-3}$ N/mm$^2$

Figure 10-24

The mat in this case is hardwood, so we will use the values in the first column. Density is 50 lb/ft$^3$, which gives a self-weight of 1'x20'x4'x50 = 4000 lbs.

Mat bending / ground bearing criterion

The allowable moment in the mat $M_n$ = the permissible bending stress x the elastic modulus ($Bd^2/6$).

For the example $M_n$ = 1,400 x 46 x 122/6 = 1,612,800 lb-in or 134,400 ft-lb.

The allowable moment in the mat $M_n$ equals the allowable pressure beneath the mat due to the imposed load q x the breadth of the mat B x the cantilevered length $L_c$ x the moment arm $L_c/2$

**Eq.n 1** $$M_n = \frac{qBL_c^2}{2}$$

The allowable ground pressure q due to the imposed load = the ground capacity $q_a$ – the pressure imposed due to the self-weight of the mat, i.e.

**Eq.n 2** $$q = q_a - \frac{W}{L_{eff}B}$$

Where q is the pressure due to the imposed load P, $q_a$ is the ground capacity, W is the self-weight of the mat, $L_{eff}$ is the effective length of the mat and B is its breadth.

**Eq.n 3** $$L_c = \frac{L_{eff} - C}{2}$$

Substituting Equations 1 & 2 into Equation 3 gives:

**Eq.n 4** $$M_n = \left(q_a - \frac{W}{L_{eff}B}\right)\frac{B}{2}\left(\frac{L_{eff} - C}{2}\right)^2$$

Expanding this yields:

$$(q_a B)L_{eff}^2 + (-2q_a BC - W)L_{eff} + (q_a BC^2 + 2CW - 8M_n) - \frac{C^2 W}{L_{eff}} = 0$$

The last term can be shown to be insignificant, so the formula becomes:

$$(q_a B)L_{eff}^2 + (-2q_a BC - W)L_{eff} + (q_a BC^2 + 2CW - 8M_n) = 0$$

This is a quadratic that can be solved for $L_{eff}$ using the standard solution:

$$L_{eff} = \frac{-b \pm \sqrt{b^2 - 4ac}}{2a}$$

Where:

$$a = (q_a B) = 5000 \times 4 = 20000 \text{ lb/ft}$$

$$b = (-2q_a BC - W) = -(2 \times 5000 \times 4 \times 2) - 4000 = -84000 \text{ lb}$$

$$c = (q_a BC^2 + 2CW - 8M_n) = (5000 \times 4 \times 2^2) + (2 \times 2 \times 4000) - (8 \times 134400) = -979200 \quad \text{lb-ft}$$

$$L_{eff} = \frac{--84000 \pm \sqrt{-84000^2 - 4 \times 20000 \times (-979200)}}{2 \times 20000} = 9.41 \text{ ft}$$

i.e. The optimal effective length of the mat based on mat bending and ground bearing is 9.41 ft. The mat can carry the greatest load at that length; if the effective length were greater, that load would cause the bending stress to be exceeded; if the effective length were less, the bearing stress would be exceeded at that load.

$L_{eff}$ of course cannot exceed the actual length of the mat. If the calculation gives a result greater than the actual length, use the actual length!

## Shear in the mat

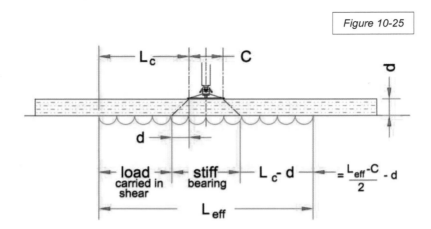

Figure 10-25

The allowable shear force in the mat (each side)
$$V_n = \frac{(F_v Bd)}{1.5} = \frac{200 \times 48 \times 12}{1.5} = 76800 \text{ lb}$$

(The 1.5 factor applies to wood only, do not use for steel mats).

The allowable shear load $V_n$ (each side of the mat) is the allowable pressure beneath the mat due to the imposed load "q" x the breadth of the mat "B" x the length of mat carrying that load. That is considered to be the distance from the end of the effective length to the start of stiff bearing under the outrigger = $L_c$- d. (Stiff bearing at 45° is assumed).

$$V_n = (qB)(L_c - d)$$

Substituting for q and $L_c$

$$V_n = \left(q_a - \frac{W}{L_{eff}B}\right) B \left(\frac{L_{eff} - C}{2} - d\right)$$

Expanding this yields:

$$(q_a B)L_{eff}^2 + (-2V_n - q_a BC - 2q_a Bd - W)L_{eff} + (CW + 2Wd) = 0$$

Again, this is a quadratic that can be solved for Leff using the standard solution

$$a = (q_a B) = 5000 \times 4 = 20000 \text{ lb/ft}$$

$$b = (-2V_n - q_a BC - 2q_a Bd - W)$$

$$= (-2 \times 76800 - 5000 \times 4 \times 2 - 2 \times 5000 \times 4 \times 1 - 4000) = 237600 \text{ lb}$$

$$c = (CW + 2Wd) = (2 \times 4000 + 2 \times 4000 \times 1) = 16000 \text{ lb-ft}$$

$$L_{eff} = \frac{--237600 \pm \sqrt{-237600^2 - 4 \times 20000 \times 16000}}{2 \times 20000} = 11.81 \text{ ft}$$

i.e. The optimal effective length of the mat <u>based on mat shear and ground bearing</u> in this example is 11.81 ft. The mat can carry greatest load at that length; if the effective length is greater, that load would cause the shear stress to be exceeded; if the effective length is less, the bearing stress would be exceeded at that load.

$L_{eff}$ of course cannot exceed the actual length of the mat.

## Note

Regarding the 1.5 factor noted above and the deduction of d from the effective length contributing to shear, Dave clarifies thus:

> "the term d and the coefficient 1.5 are based on design provisions in the National Design Specification for Wood Construction (NDS). For beams loaded by a uniformly distributed load (the ground bearing pressure, in our case), the NDS allows calculation of the maximum shear stress at a distance from the face of the support equal to the depth of the beam. The critical shear stress in a wood beam isn't vertical shear stress, as is the case for steel beams, but horizontal shear stress. The maximum value occurs at the neutral axis and is equal to 1.5 times the average vertical shear stress".

## Deflection of the mat / ground

The final check is for deflection of the mat. Mats that are not adequately stiff may display excessive deflections on softer grounds without reaching a limiting bending or shear stress condition. In such cases, it would be necessary to reduce the load carried (which is effective length dependent for a given permissible pressure). Mr Duerr proposes a deflection limit of 0.75% $L_c$ based on examination of numerous mat designs (approximates to about ¾" on a 20' long mat).

Deflection of a crane mat is commonly treated as a cantilever beam of length $L_c$ loaded by an upward uniform pressure equal to q. Deflection $\Delta$ is given by:

$$\Delta = \frac{(qB)L_c^4}{8EI}$$

This deflection criterion will only control effective bearing length with softer ground when the actual pressure q due to the imposed load approximates to 90% of the ground bearing capacity $q_a$. Plugging this into the above equation and using the above proposed deflection limit ($\Delta$=0.75%Lc), gives:

$$L_c = \sqrt[3]{\frac{0.06EI}{0.9(q_aB)}}$$

$I = Bd^3/12 = 48 \times 12^3/12 = 6912 \text{ in}^4$

$q_a = 5000\text{psf} = 5000/144 = 34.72 \text{ lb/in}^2$

$$L_c = \sqrt[3]{\frac{0.06 \times 1,200,000 \times 6912}{0.9(34.72 \times 48)}} = 69.2" = 5.77'$$

$L_{eff} = 2L_c + C$ (up to a maximum of the actual length)

$L_{eff} = (2 \times 5.77) + 2 = 13.5 \text{ ft}$

Thus the effective length (subject to maximum bearing pressure) at which deflection would reach the defined limit in this example is 13.5'.

## Governing condition

The governing (least) $L_{eff}$ is that calculated from mat bending / ground bearing considerations and = 9.41' (which is less than the actual length of 20', so is valid). So, using this figure in the expressions,

$L_c = (9.41-2)/2 = 3.705'$

$$q = \frac{P}{L_{eff}B} = \frac{174000}{9.41 \times 4} = 4649 \text{ psf}$$

The bending moment in the mat $\qquad M_n = \dfrac{qBL_c^2}{2} = \dfrac{4649 \times 4 \times 3.705^2}{2} = 127634 \quad$ lb-ft

This is equivalent to 127,634 x 12 = 1531607 lb-in

The bending stress in the mat $\qquad f_b = \dfrac{M}{bd^2/6} = \dfrac{1531607}{48 \times 12^2/6} = 1330 \text{ lb/in}^2$

This compares to the max allowable of 1400 lb/in$^2$ (95%)

The shear in the mat $\qquad V = (qB)(L_c - d) = (4649 \times 4)(3.705 - 1) = 50302 \text{ lb}$

The shear stress in the mat $\qquad f_v = \dfrac{1.5V}{Bd} = \dfrac{1.5 \times 50302}{48 \times 12} = 131 \text{ lb/in}^2$

This compares to the max allowable of 200 lb/in$^2$ (65%)

The imposed pressure $q_t$ is given by:

$$q_t = \frac{P + W}{L_{eff}B} = \frac{175000 + 4000}{9.41 \times 4} = 4756 \text{ psf}$$

This compares to the max allowable $q_a$ of 5000 lb/in$^2$ (95%)

Mat deflection works out at a mere 0.23"; that may not be 100% accurate, but does not a good indication of order of magnitude. It is not difficult to imagine the ground conditions you will usually encounter could accommodate figures of that order.

Notes:

- In most cases, when the mat is made of the most common hardwood species and the allowable ground bearing pressure is not unusually high, the bending strength usually governs mat design.
- All else being equal, using Emtek mats would have increased the effective length to 14.6' and reduced the pressure to 3060 psf (bending governs).
- MORA mats would be governed by shear (just); the effective length would be 11.8' and the pressure would be 3790 psf.
- If you had made a steel mat from 4 x W12 x 65 column sections welded toe to toe, and all else being equal, the effective length would be 18.8' and the pressure 2400 psf.

## Summary

The stated objective of Mr Duerr's paper is "to develop a practical means of calculating the effective bearing length of a crane mat that relies on readily available values and that produces an acceptably safe and reliable result"; I believe that it does so. For those with spreadsheet skills, it is a relatively easy task to automate the analysis (in US customary units or in metric units), which really speeds up figuring mats out. When considering steel mats, don't forget to dispense with the 1.5 factor in the shear calc.

Mr Duerr concludes (and you should note) that:

- this methodology provides a practical method for calculating the effective bearing length  of a crane mat loaded with a single outrigger or crawler track (and hence pressure imposed)
- the true behavior is more complex than is implied
- a theoretically "exact" approach is usually not practical due to the difficulty in determining the elastic properties of the soil
- sometimes engineering judgment is required in the solution of a crane support problem, users of the preceding should possess the engineering background and experience to exercise that judgment

I recommend that you visit the 2DM Associates website and access the latest revision of the source material and/or research Mr Duerrs "Mobile Crane Support Handbook".

## 10.7 Matting under crawler crane tracks

When you mat under a crawler crane's tracks, what load should be used to analyze the mat?

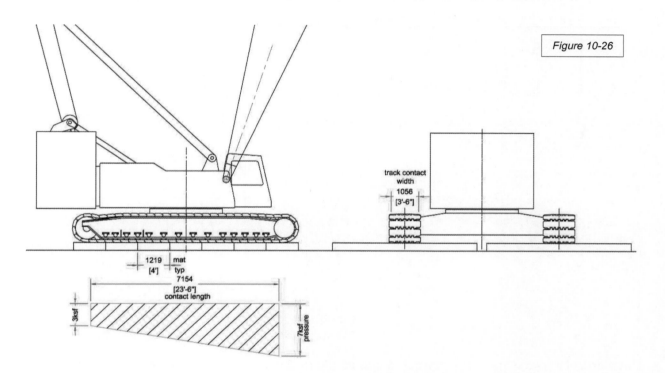

Figure 10-26

To be in any way effective in spreading load, the mats have to be laid across the tracks, not in line with them. The mats are usually not connected to each other in any way. The timbers forming one mat can be presumed to act together so the mat works as a single member. The pressure profiles under the tracks are determined using one of the methods described in the preceding chapter. The most highly loaded mat is the one subject to the maximum pressure, in this case the one under the front of the most highly loaded track. The mats are presumed to be level and providing their apportioned share of support, i.e. you don't have a huge hollow in the level of the matting under the tracks with the tracks bridging it and the central mats doing nothing. The peak pressure (in this example 7 ksf) can conservatively be considered to be applied uniformly over the entire contact area between track and mat; in this case over 3'-6" x 4'. The most highly loaded mat can be analyzed on the basis of supporting 7,000 x 3.5 x 4 = 98,000 lbs using the method described earlier (or other method).

## 10.8 Matting under outriggers

When you mat under the outrigger of a large crane such as this pedestal crane you can be confronted with a large outrigger load and low ground bearing pressures; in such cases, you may need to double mat. I will look at this in metric units.

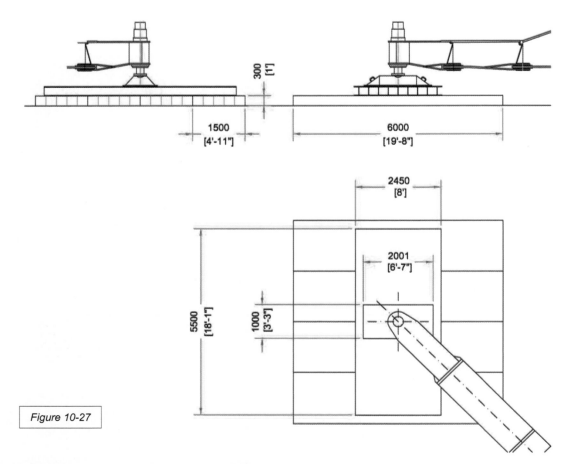

Figure 10-27

This particular crane has an outrigger pontoon (float) 2 m x 1 m. It can impose say 250 t (equivalent to approximately 250 kN). The crane comes with a standard steel mat 2450 mm x 5500 mm whose construction is 9 x HEA280 column sections stitch welded toe to toe. The ground is rated at 10 t/m$^2$ (permissible).

The properties of the mat are;

- width = 280 mm
- depth = 270 mm
- individual webs = 8 mm
- combined shear area = 9 x 8 x 270 = 19440 mm$^2$
- combined $I_{xx}$ = 9x13670 x 104 = 1230.3 x 106 mm$^4$
- combined elastic modulus = 9 x 1010 x 10$^3$ = 9090 x 10$^3$ mm$^3$
- modulus of Elasticity = 200 x 10$^3$ N/mm$^2$

Regarding the steel mat, the initial presumption is that the wooden mats can settle enough to ensure that the loading into the steel mat is essentially uniform on its underside.

The intensity of loading on the underside = 2500kN / 5.5m = 454.5 kN/m

The cantilevered length for bending purposes = (5.5-1)/2 = 2.25 m

The load carried by that section = 2.25 x 454.5 = 1022.6 kN

The moment arm = 1.125 m, therefore $M_{max}$ = 1.125 x 1022.6 = 1150.1 kNm

The bending stress $f_{bc/t}$ = 1150.1x10$^6$ / 9090 x 10$^3$ = 126.6 N/mm$^2$. Steel is a 36 ksi grade, BS 4360 grade 43 or similar, $p_{bc}$ = 165 N/mm$^2$, therefore OK. *In this application, I would consider normal structural steel permissible stresses to be adequate.*

The mat deflection = $WL^3/8EI$, where W is the load carried by the cantilevered length L

$$= (1250 \times 10^3 \times 1125^3) / (8 \times 200 \times 10^3 \times 1230.3 \times 10^6) = 0.9 \, mm$$

It is quite reasonable to accept that the wood mats / ground beneath could allow the steel mat to deflect by 0.9 mm in the center.

For shear purposes, the stiff length in the center of the beam = the width of the pontoon plus a 45° distribution through the mat either side = 1000 + 270 + 270 = 1540 mm. The length either side of the mat carrying load in shear = (5500-1540)/2 = 1980 mm. The shear load = 1.980 x 454.5 = 900 kN

The shear stress $f_q$ = 900x10³ / 19440 = 46 N/mm². Steel is a 36 ksi grade, BS 4360 grade 43 or similar, $p_q$ = 100 N/mm², therefore OK.

So the steel mat checks out OK and can be considered to distribute load into the wood mats uniformly.

The steel mat pretty much catches every timber of all of the mats, so we can assume that each of the four mats carries 25% of the imposed load = 625 kN.

You can take this and use the Duerr method to calculate the wood mat situation. It indicates the critical criterion to be mat bending and the effective length is only a theoretical 100 mm less than the actual length. The mat bending stress is 73% of that permitted. The mat deflection works out at about 2.5 mm. The imposed pressure (ignoring self-weights of mats) is 7.2 t/m². We are permitted up to 10 t/m².

## 10.9 Using plate under an outrigger

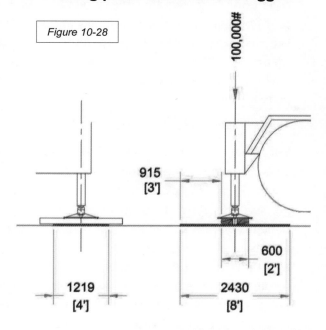

Figure 10-28

How about using a steel plate under an outrigger? Steel is strong; it should do the job, right?

Let's consider a situation. The permissible ground capacity at the job site is 17 t/m² (3.5 ksf). A 65 t RT crane is to be used; its maximum outrigger load is say 45.4 metric tons (100,000#). The guys at the job figure they need 100,000/3500 = 29 ft² effective; they have some 8' x 4' steel plates 1.5" thick, quality unknown and have a number of railroad ties. (Equivalent to 2.43 m x 1.22 m x 38 mm plate plus railway sleepers). They arrange them as shown.

How will it work? Looks not too bad? You see this kind of thing all the time.

By inspection, the rail ties will do an adequate job at spreading the load laterally over the plate width.

To get down to the required figure, pretty much the whole plate has to be effective and therefore has to remain in contact with the ground. The true pressure profile will likely be somewhat parabolic, but I will consider it as being uniform over the plate and see how that works for a start. If it isn't somewhat uniform you won't achieve your goal of 3.5 ksf (17 t/m²).

The plate sizes yield the following properties:

- Elastic modulus $Z_{xx}$ = 294.9 cm³
- Moment of inertia $I_{xx}$ = 561.8 cm⁴
- Shear area A = 464.4 cm²

The pressure at a UDL would be (100,000 / 8x4) = 3.125 ksf (15.3 t/m²)

The load/m assuming UDL = 183.1 kN/m

The load carried by the cantilevered section = 0.915 x 183.1 = 167.6 kN

The moment arm for bending = 0.4575 m

$M_{max}$ = 167.5 x 0.4575 = 76.7 kNm

$f_{bc/t}$ = 76.7 x $10^6$ / 294.9 x $10^3$ = 260 N/mm$^2$

Shear stresses at 3.6 N/mm$^2$ are minimal for any sort of steel.

First problem; we don't know what the steel is good for. A 36 ksi steel (A36 or BS4360 grade 43) is going to be right at or about yield (250 – 275 N/mm$^2$ maybe). Something of lesser quality would yield.

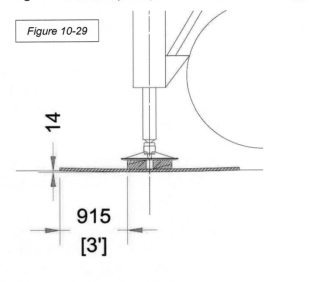

Figure 10-29

14

915
[3']

Next question would be how much does the plate deflect under this loading?

Deflection = $WL^3$ / 8EI = 167.6x$10^3$ x $915^3$ / 8 x 200x$10^3$ x 561.8x$10^4$ = 14.3 mm (9/16")

i.e. the plate has to deflect 14.3 mm (9/16") over the cantilevered length (and still be completely supported) in order to achieve this loading condition. That requires the ground to settle (dish) by that amount differentially and stabilize like that without continuing to settle bodily. Is that reasonable given the ground conditions you have? Will the ground dish and the ends of the plate lift clear?

The averaged uniform pressure is 3.125 ksf.

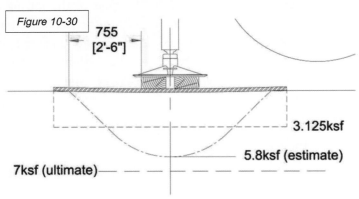

Figure 10-30

755
[2'-6"]

3.125ksf

5.8ksf (estimate)

7ksf (ultimate)

But, what is really happening? Let's assume a situation where the ground settles such that about 7' of the plate is in contact with the ground; the ends of the plate curl up clear; it depends on how soft the ground actually is. Let's also assume a curved pressure profile something like that indicated. The peak pressure would actually be in the order of 5.8 ksf, which exceeds our permissible of 3.5 ksf, but likely would not exceed the actual ultimate capacity of the soil.

Note that the extent by which the plate dishes is a function of the ground stiffness. The harder the ground, the more concentrated the load will be in the center of the plate. It needs to deflect to shed. If the ground is very soft, it will deflect so much that the ends come clear and that will concentrate the load too. The plate needs to be stiff relative to the ground for it to work and that is going to be difficult if the plate is relatively thin as shown here. Note as well that if the ground deflects, it likely will stay deflected when the load comes off. That might not be a problem to you on a job site, but could be a problem in an asphalt parking lot if you leave dished depressions after you. If on a thin concrete slab, you don't want the slab to crack to accommodate the shape the plate has to achieve. Using plate directly over a thick concrete slab does nothing useful; the loads go in one side and virtually directly out the other at similar magnitude.

If you must use plate rather than a proper mat on prepared ground, make sure it is thick enough (considering the length) that the ground deflections are reasonable and achievable and result in enough of the plate being in contact with the ground to get the pressures down to where you need them. Of course check the bending stresses too. Plate shear is unlikely to be an issue. If the supporting surface is hard, consider locating the plate on a sand bed or other semi-compliant medium such as foam.

Figure 10-31

If using loose timbers under an outrigger pad, ensure they are sound, structural hardwood and of uniform size. Make sure the float is fully supported and arrange layers in opposed directions. You do not want the timbers to be able to move independently of each other.

Do not use bits of old dunnage you found on the job site.

Ensure the ground is level and well compacted.

To re-iterate, this is a complex subject; if in doubt when designing a load spreading arrangement, seek some expert help!

# 11 Reading crane load charts

## 11.1 Introductory notes

As noted earlier, the rated capacity of a crane varies according to how it is configured and being used. Factors influencing the capacity include such things as:

- Boom length / extension / extension mode being used
- Boom type – heavy/light etc
- Jib type (where fitted) / length / offset angle / extension (if telescopic) / whether stowed or not
- Machine counterweight used
- Track width or outrigger span, whether lifting "on rubber"
- Derrick mast (where fitted) and it's radius
- Amount of Superlift (where used)
- Zone / quadrant of operation (over front / side / rear or 360°)

The chart capacity is the <u>maximum</u> load that can be suspended from the boom or jib head (as applicable) in a particular configuration; the provisions of the crane chart may require you to take a reduction to account for factors such as operating wind speed, size (sail area) and shape of the load, level of the crane, condition etc.

Note also that capacity may be limited by the number of parts of hoist line provided in the hook-block reeving or the capacity of the hook-block itself.

Load charts are the instrument to determine the capacity of the crane in a given configuration; crane manufacturers provide load charts giving rated load capacities for all approved configurations and operating ranges. As cranes get ever more complex, the number of possible combinations has become ever greater and the paper crane charts can be several inches thick in some cases. Some modern cranes now calculate the capacity seamlessly for the particular combination of boom extension / radius / back mast radius / superlift etc etc in play at the time and will ensure that you keep within the overall envelope of permitted combinations. Rather than providing paper charts, similar software to that fitted to the crane is available to lift planners. Paper crane charts may eventually become a thing of the past.

<u>Whichever way you do it, it is vital that you make sure that you are looking at the correct chart for the machine in question and the configuration being used; it is equally vital that you understand it.</u> Note that generic load charts for a particular crane model can give a preliminary capacity indication, but the only chart you should be using for detailed lift planning is the chart that is specific to the individual machine, (preferably referencing the crane serial number).

As noted elsewhere, by code manufacturers develop crane charts showing rated payload v operating radius for each crane configuration based on the <u>lesser</u> of the two following conditions:

- **Stability criteria**. The load that would result in the moment on the crane reaching a limiting percentage of the moment that would cause it to tip (in the least stable direction). Typically the percentage is set at 75% – in the USA it is 85% for carrier mounted cranes on outriggers.
- **Structural criteria**. The load that would cause any element of the crane to reach its limiting condition per the applicable design code.

Many people are confused by the "75%" or "85%" that they see on the charts. They either think that this means they have margin left to play with or alternatively that they have to multiply the capacities quoted by 75% or 85% to get to useable capacity. Neither is the case! It merely defines the limiting tipping criteria of the design code used in preparing the chart; you are not required to do anything about it other than note it and make sure it is the applicable design standard for the locale in which you are operating (or which you are otherwise mandated to follow by say contract or company standard or whatever).

Personally, as noted earlier, I would much rather that crane charts did not quote 75% (or whatever of tipping); I believe it confuses and I don't think that it should be any concern of the crane operator whether the crane is being operated in a "tipping" or a "structural" area of the chart – he/she just needs to operate within the chart capacities with reserve sufficient for the application. I would rather that the charts merely quote the design code basis on which the charts are prepared. e.g. ASME B30.5, DIN15018/15019, or whatever.

The chart capacities are the chart capacities and you may not exceed them. To quote OSHA, "no crane shall be loaded beyond its rated load".

Circumstances may require you to set yourself a lesser percentage limit of chart capacities to account for conditions as apply to your particular situation. Your company may have a policy that for instance states that you will not exceed 90% of chart capacity without review.

Notes:

i.    the same crane may have different charts applicable to different regions; make sure you use the right one

ii.   crane design codes around the world are not directly comparable; e.g. a crane designed to ASME B30.5 does not necessarily have some of the allowances built in to the chart that a crane designed to a DIN/ISO standard has. Read the small print in the crane chart and understand the codes!

If you require slightly better duties than are standard on a crane designed to DIN standards, you may be able to get the crane manufacturer to give you a one-off dispensation for a few extra percent if you give them with specifics of the lift you want to make. They will put restrictions on you, say only one movement at a time, crane truly level, low wind speed and so on and will return you some of the allowances they had included in the standard chart. You likely won't get that from a crane designed to ASME B30.5 as those allowances weren't included in the design in the first place.

## 11.2 Operating quadrants

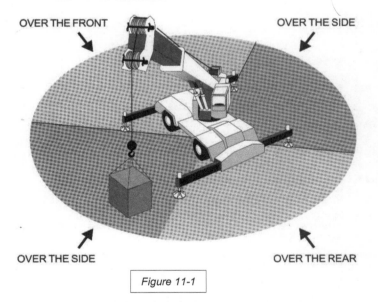

OVER THE FRONT

OVER THE SIDE

OVER THE SIDE

OVER THE REAR

Figure 11-1

Note that the manufacturer may rate the crane differently as it swings through different quadrants, particularly with older truck cranes. This is a result of the tipping fulcrum changing. In such cases, an over-the-side capacity will be different from an over-the-rear or over-the front capacity. Typically these quadrants are defined by lines from the center of rotation through the outriggers as shown. Check the charts to make sure what the manufacturer intends if using one of these charts.

Most often charts will be 360 degree charts meaning that the capacity applies anywhere around the crane.

## 11.3 Information contained in crane charts

There is no standard for how information is presented in a crane chart and there is great variety in how it is actually done, even within companies within the same group. It has to be said that some are much easier to follow than others. In one form or another however, they all contain the following (as a minimum):

–    Range Diagrams

- Rated Loads (Gross Capacities)
- Jib/ Boom Extension Capacities
- Travel Capacities (if available feature)
- Capacities based on outrigger/track/counterweight combinations
- Weight Reductions for Load Handling Devices
- Special operating notes for Lifting Capacities
- Hoist Line Capacities (Line Pull)
- Wind restrictions

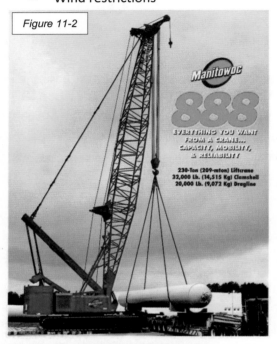

Figure 11-2

To explain the contents, let's look at the crane chart for a typical basic crawler crane - the 230 ton (209 t) Manitowoc 888 in lift-crane mode.

As you can see from the screen-shot below there are numerous crane chart options (this isn't all of them); different booms, jibs, different design codes, barge operation, US and metric versions.

For variety, we'll look at a metric version (to ASME B30.5 design code).

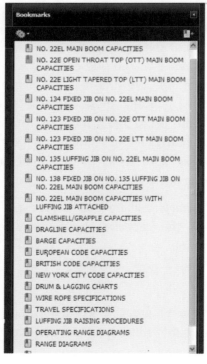

Figure 11-3

888_Crawler_Crane_Released_Chart_Index.doc                                    10/31/00

**Bookmarks**

- NO. 22EL MAIN BOOM CAPACITIES
- NO. 22E OPEN THROAT TOP (OTT) MAIN BOOM CAPACITIES
- NO. 22E LIGHT TAPERED TOP (LTT) MAIN BOOM CAPACITIES
- NO. 134 FIXED JIB ON NO. 22EL MAIN BOOM CAPACITIES
- NO. 123 FIXED JIB ON NO. 22E OTT MAIN BOOM CAPACITIES
- NO. 123 FIXED JIB ON NO. 22E LTT MAIN BOOM CAPACITIES
- NO. 135 LUFFING JIB ON NO. 22EL MAIN BOOM CAPACITIES
- NO. 138 FIXED JIB ON NO. 135 LUFFING JIB ON NO. 22EL MAIN BOOM CAPACITIES
- NO. 22EL MAIN BOOM CAPACITIES WITH LUFFING JIB ATTACHED
- CLAMSHELL/GRAPPLE CAPACITIES
- DRAGLINE CAPACITIES
- BARGE CAPACITIES
- EUROPEAN CODE CAPACITIES
- BRITISH CODE CAPACITIES
- NEW YORK CITY CODE CAPACITIES
- DRUM & LAGGING CHARTS
- WIRE ROPE SPECIFICATIONS
- TRAVEL SPECIFICATIONS
- LUFFING JIB RAISING PROCEDURES
- OPERATING RANGE DIAGRAMS
- RANGE DIAGRAMS

| Chart # | Date | Description |
|---|---|---|
| | | **NO. 22EL MAIN BOOM CAPACITIES** |
| 7813-A | 03/07/97 | Liftcrane Boom Capacities, Boom No. 22EL, 179,100 Lb. Crane Counterweight, 44,000 Lb. Carbody Counterweight, 360 Degree Rating - [888 S2] |
| 7813-AM | 03/07/97 | Liftcrane Boom Capacities, Boom No. 22EL, 81 240 kg Crane Counterweight, 19 960 kg Carbody Counterweight, 360 Degree Rating - [888 S2] |
| 7813-B | 03/07/97 | Liftcrane Boom Capacities, Boom No. 22EL, 179,100 Lb. Crane Counterweight, 44,000 Lb. Carbody Counterweight, 28' 2" Crawlers Extended, Rating Over Front of Blocked Crawlers, No Travel - Limited Swing - [888 S2] |
| 7813-BM | 03/07/97 | Liftcrane Boom Capacities, Boom No. 22EL, 81 240 kg Crane Counterweight, 19 960 kg Carbody Counterweight, 8 585 mm Crawlers Extended, Rating Over Front of Blocked Crawlers, No Travel - Limited Swing - [888 S2] |
| 7811-A | 03/07/97 | Liftcrane Boom Capacities, Boom No. 22EL, 144,100 Lb. Counterweight, 360 Degree Rating - [888 S1] |
| 7811-AM | 03/07/97 | Liftcrane Boom Capacities, Boom No. 22EL, 65 360 kg Counterweight, 360 Degree Rating - [888 S1] |
| 7811-B | 04/03/97 | Liftcrane Boom Capacities, Boom No. 22EL, 144,100 Lb. Counterweight, 28' 2" Crawlers Extended, Rating Over Front of Blocked Crawlers, No Travel - Limited Swing - [888 S1] |
| 7811-BM | 04/03/97 | Liftcrane Boom Capacities, Boom No. 22EL, 65 360 kg Counterweight, 8 585 mm Crawlers Extended, Rating Over Front of Blocked Crawlers, No Travel - Limited Swing - [888 S1] |
| 7811-C | 08/25/96 | Liftcrane Boom Capacities, Boom No. 22EL, 109,100 Lb. Counterweight, 360 Degree Rating - [888 S1] |

## Range Diagram

One of the first things you find in any crane chart is a range diagram like this. It is a planning tool indicating ranges of height and reach for possible boom and jib combinations; it is used to make initial assessment of the boom (or boom/jib/offset combination) and radius combination required to make the lift. I've sketched a typical lift on it. e.g. a column lifted at 15 m (50') radius from crane center to a height of 43 m (140') above grade requires a boom length of about 64 m (210') to give enough head height for the hook block anti two block (ATB) distance and rigging. Boom clearances also need to be checked.

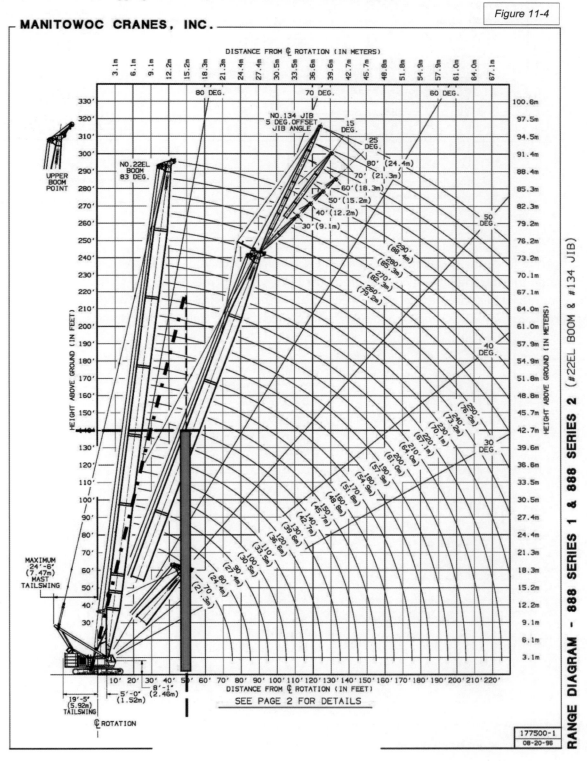

Figure 11-4

## Dimensions

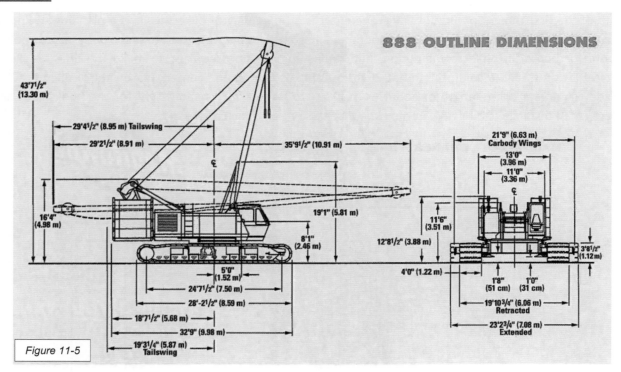

*Figure 11-5*

To prepare a lift study, you'll need to draw the crane for which you'll need the dimensions; of key interest is going to be the track length / width / spread (or outrigger base), the location of the boom mounting and the tail swing. In many cases these days, the crane will be modeled in a CAD program or other lift planning software. For many lifts a simple hand sketch will suffice to check heights, radii and clearances.

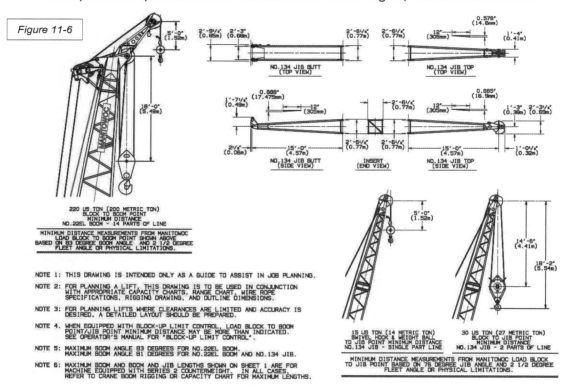

*Figure 11-6*

The above shows the minimum distances from the various hook-blocks (that can come as standard with the machine) to the boom or jib point.

## Crane weights

There follows several pages of crane component weights (of which this is only one). These are mostly of interest for shipping purposes rather than lift planning.

**MANITOWOC ENGINEERING CO.**
Division of the Manitowoc Company, Inc. Manitowoc, Wisconsin 54220

Figure 11-7

# CRANE WEIGHTS _____ 888 SERIES 1
# 888 SERIES 2

NOTE: WEIGHTS MAY FLUCTUATE ± 3% DUE TO MANUFACTURING TOLERANCES

| DESCRIPTION: | WEIGHT POUNDS | KILOGRAMS |
|---|---|---|
| LIFTCRANE - BOOM NO. 22E: UPPERWORKS AND LOWERWORKS COMPLETE, COUNTERWEIGHT, GANTRY, BACKHITCH, MAST, FULLY RIGGED 70' (21.3m) BOOM NO. 22E WITH OPEN THROAT TOP (INCLUDING SINGLE SHEAVE UPPER BOOM POINT, 230 TON (209t) BLOCK, AND 15 TON (14t) HOOK AND WEIGHT BALL), BOOM STOPS, AND MAXIMUM LENGTH HOIST AND WHIP LINES - 888 SERIES 1 | 339,685 | 154 078 |
| 888 SERIES 2 | 418,835 | 189 980 |
| UPPERWORKS MACHINERY MODULE WITH CARBODY: CARBODY, UPPERWORKS WITH TWO FULL POWER DRUMS, OPERATOR'S CAB, GANTRY, BACKHITCH, MAST, BOOM HOIST WIRE ROPE, AND MAXIMUM LENGTH HOIST AND WHIP LINES | 85,535 | 38 798 |
| CRAWLERS: 28'2" (8 585 mm) CRAWLER ASSEMBLY WITH 48" (1 219 mm) TREADS (EACH) | 40,845 | 18 527 |
| COUNTERWEIGHT - UPPER: | | |
| BOX - SIDE (6 ON 888 SERIES 1, 8 ON SERIES 2) (EACH) | 17,500 | 7 938 |
| BOX - CENTER | 18,000 | 8 165 |
| TRAY - LOWER COUNTERWEIGHT | 21,050 | 9 548 |
| TOTAL UPPERWORKS COUNTERWEIGHT - 888 SERIES 1 | 144,100 | 65 363 |
| TOTAL UPPERWORKS COUNTERWEIGHT - 888 SERIES 2 | 179,100 | 81 238 |
| COUNTERWEIGHT - LOWER: | | |
| CARBODY COUNTERWEIGHT (2 ON SERIES 2) (EACH) | 22,000 | 9 979 |
| CARBODY COUNTERWEIGHT STEPS (EACH) | 65 | 29 |

The page shown below however, has information of interest to the lift planner. As we will see later, the crane charts do not make allowance for the self-weight of the hook-blocks. The capacity of the crane is quoted at the boom or jib head and the weight of the hook-blocks is considered to be weight on the crane. To determine the total lift weight, you therefore need to know which hook-block you are going to use and what it weighs. The table below lists self-weights of the various standard blocks that may be available to use (weights in lbs and kg). Note that a hook-block supplied with an older crane may not necessarily be original equipment and could weigh differently; that might be significant at longer radii.

**MANITOWOC ENGINEERING CO.**
Division of the Manitowoc Company, Inc. Manitowoc, Wisconsin 54220

# CRANE WEIGHTS _____ 888 SERIES 1
# 888 SERIES 2

NOTE: WEIGHTS MAY FLUCTUATE ± 3% DUE TO MANUFACTURING TOLERANCES

| DESCRIPTION: | WEIGHT POUNDS | KILOGRAMS |
|---|---|---|
| LOAD BLOCK AND HOOK AND WEIGHT BALL OPTIONS: | | |
| 15 TON (14t) HOOK AND WEIGHT BALL | 1,250 | 567 |
| 30 TON (27t) LOAD BLOCK WITH 500 LBS (227 kg) OF WEIGHT PLATES | 2,000 | 907 |
| 60 TON (54t) LOAD BLOCK | 2,825 | 1 281 |
| 155 TON (141t) LOAD BLOCK | 4,660 | 2 114 |
| 200 TON (181t) LOAD BLOCK | 5,600 | 2 540 |
| 230 TON (209t) LOAD BLOCK (BOOM NO. 22E) | 6,550 | 2 971 |
| 220 TON (200t) LOAD BLOCK (BOOM NO. 22EL) | 5,450 | 2 472 |
| WIRE ROPE: | | |
| BOOM HOIST - 1060' (323m) OF 22 mm WIRE ROPE - 1.46 LB/FT (2.17 kg/m) | 1,550 | 703 |
| LOAD LINES - 26 mm ROTATION RESISTANT WIRE ROPE 2.13 LB/FT (3.17 kg/m) | | |
| HOIST LINE - 1600' (488m) BOOM NO. 22E | 3,410 | 1 547 |
| HOIST LINE - 1625' (495m) BOOM NO. 22EL | 3,460 | 1 569 |
| HOIST LINE - 1200' (366m) LUFFING JIB NO. 135 | 2,555 | 1 159 |
| WHIP LINE - 950' (290m) BOOM NO. 22E WITH OPEN THROAT TOP | 2,025 | 919 |
| WHIP LINE - 1040' (317m) BOOM NO. 22E WITH LIGHT TAPERED TOP | 2,215 | 1 005 |
| WHIP LINE - 1010' (308m) BOOM NO. 22EL | 2,215 | 1 005 |
| AUXILIARY LINE - 1900' (579m) BOOM NO. 22EL | 4,045 | 1 835 |
| AUXILIARY LINE - 2200' (671m) BOOM NO. 22E | 4,685 | 2 125 |

Figure 11-8

## Boom capacity charts

The following section relates to the boom capacity charts. The first page contains notes relating to the charts; this is important information and needs to be read carefully.

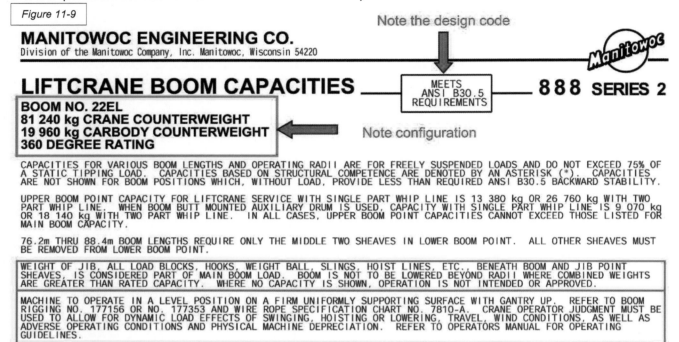

Figure 11-9

Note the design code

**MANITOWOC ENGINEERING CO.**
Division of the Manitowoc Company, Inc. Manitowoc, Wisconsin 54220

**LIFTCRANE BOOM CAPACITIES** —— MEETS ANSI B30.5 REQUIREMENTS —— **888** SERIES 2

**BOOM NO. 22EL**
**81 240 kg CRANE COUNTERWEIGHT**
**19 960 kg CARBODY COUNTERWEIGHT**
**360 DEGREE RATING**

Note configuration

CAPACITIES FOR VARIOUS BOOM LENGTHS AND OPERATING RADII ARE FOR FREELY SUSPENDED LOADS AND DO NOT EXCEED 75% OF A STATIC TIPPING LOAD. CAPACITIES BASED ON STRUCTURAL COMPETENCE ARE DENOTED BY AN ASTERISK (*). CAPACITIES ARE NOT SHOWN FOR BOOM POSITIONS WHICH, WITHOUT LOAD, PROVIDE LESS THAN REQUIRED ANSI B30.5 BACKWARD STABILITY.

UPPER BOOM POINT CAPACITY FOR LIFTCRANE SERVICE WITH SINGLE PART WHIP LINE IS 13 380 kg OR 26 760 kg WITH TWO PART WHIP LINE. WHEN BOOM BUTT MOUNTED AUXILIARY DRUM IS USED, CAPACITY WITH SINGLE PART WHIP LINE IS 9 070 kg OR 18 140 kg WITH TWO PART WHIP LINE. IN ALL CASES, UPPER BOOM POINT CAPACITIES CANNOT EXCEED THOSE LISTED FOR MAIN BOOM CAPACITY.

76.2m THRU 88.4m BOOM LENGTHS REQUIRE ONLY THE MIDDLE TWO SHEAVES IN LOWER BOOM POINT. ALL OTHER SHEAVES MUST BE REMOVED FROM LOWER BOOM POINT.

WEIGHT OF JIB, ALL LOAD BLOCKS, HOOKS, WEIGHT BALL, SLINGS, HOIST LINES, ETC., BENEATH BOOM AND JIB POINT SHEAVES, IS CONSIDERED PART OF MAIN BOOM LOAD. BOOM IS NOT TO BE LOWERED BEYOND RADII WHERE COMBINED WEIGHTS ARE GREATER THAN RATED CAPACITY. WHERE NO CAPACITY IS SHOWN, OPERATION IS NOT INTENDED OR APPROVED.

MACHINE TO OPERATE IN A LEVEL POSITION ON A FIRM UNIFORMLY SUPPORTING SURFACE WITH GANTRY UP. REFER TO BOOM RIGGING NO. 177156 OR NO. 177353 AND WIRE ROPE SPECIFICATION CHART NO. 7810-A. CRANE OPERATOR JUDGMENT MUST BE USED TO ALLOW FOR DYNAMIC LOAD EFFECTS OF SWINGING, HOISTING OR LOWERING, TRAVEL, WIND CONDITIONS, AS WELL AS ADVERSE OPERATING CONDITIONS AND PHYSICAL MACHINE DEPRECIATION. REFER TO OPERATORS MANUAL FOR OPERATING GUIDELINES.

MACHINE TO TRAVEL ON A FIRM, LEVEL AND UNIFORMLY SUPPORTING SURFACE AND BOOM WITHIN BOOM ANGLE RANGE SHOWN IN CAPACITY CHART. REFER TO MAXIMUM ALLOWABLE TRAVEL SPECIFICATION CHART NO. 7808-A.

OPERATING RADIUS IS HORIZONTAL DISTANCE FROM AXIS OF ROTATION TO CENTER OF VERTICAL HOIST LINE OR LOAD BLOCK. BOOM ANGLE IS ANGLE BETWEEN HORIZONTAL AND CENTERLINE OF BOOM BUTT AND INSERTS, AND IS AN INDICATION OF OPERATING RADIUS. IN ALL CASES, OPERATING RADIUS SHALL GOVERN CAPACITY. BOOM POINT ELEVATION IS VERTICAL DISTANCE FROM GROUND LEVEL TO CENTERLINE OF BOOM POINT SHAFT.

Hitting the high points:

- Firstly, these are Liftcrane <u>Boom</u> Capacities, i.e. the capacities of the crane at the boom head for a M888 series 2. These charts comply with ASME/ANSI B30.5 (which limits the capacities to 75% of tipping); there are other charts to other design codes.

- The charts are valid only for a specific configuration, i.e. a specific boom type (22EL) with full machine counterweight and full series 2 carbody counterweight (fitted to the lower works between the tracks). Make sure this is your configuration!

- The weight of all <u>hoist lines,</u> load blocks, hooks, weight balls, and rigging materials suspended from the boom or jib is considered load on the crane. If a jib is fitted but you are lifting from the main boom, then the weight of the jib and associated pendants etc has an overturning effect on the crane that has to be considered. Manitowoc quote an equivalent weight you need to use as load on the crane in such cases to allow for this; it is not the actual deadweight of those components but a weight applied at the boom head that produces a similar effect to the jib being fitted. Don't forget the weight of an unused headache ball or jib hook-block is also weight on the crane.

- You are not to operate the crane at a radius at which the total load to the boom head exceeds the capacity.

- "Machine to operate in a level position on a firm uniformly supporting surface". We've talked about what constitutes a firm uniformly supporting surface; level likely means within 1%, but could be less at longer boom / jib combinations, check! Capacity drops off very rapidly when the crane is not level.

- "Crane operator judgment to be used to allow for dynamic load effects of swinging (slewing), hoisting or lowering, wind and adverse operating conditions and machine depreciation". The B30.5 design code (and the manufacturer) does not allow for those things – you are required to make a judgment call, which is why it is not good practice to operate cranes rated to B30.5 right up to their rated capacity; a reserve is required to cater for all these factors. Typically you'd restrict yourself to 85% or 90% of chart capacity unless you have all the above variables (and the lift weight) under very tight control.

- Operating radius is the horizontal distance from the axis of rotation to the center of vertical hoist lines, which, in a static stable condition, will be where the C of G of the load is for a freely suspended single point pick.

## Jib and other capacity "deductions"

As noted above, if a jib is fitted to the crane but you are lifting from the main boom, you use the main boom charts (as that is where you are lifting from) but there is a capacity deduction to be taken to account for the overturning effect of the weight of the fitted jib and related components. The small table below gives the deductions Manitowoc wants you to take for all the possible jib lengths. Note, although you might imagine it would do, the jib offset angle does not change the required deductions. These deductions are not the actual weights of the jibs.

Figure 11-10

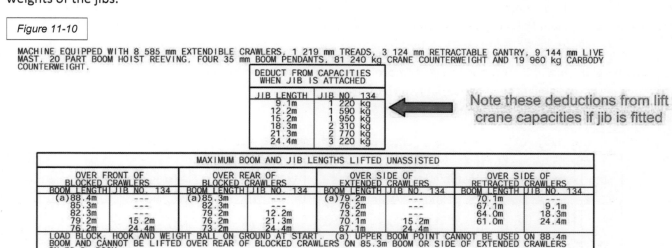

I often get asked "why if they are capacity deductions am I required to add them to the lift weight"?

You can look at the situation two ways, you either:

- Take the chart capacity, subtract the deductions, and then consider what is left to be useful capacity at the hook. The total suspended weight can then be compared to that figure to see what capacity reserve is left, or
- The deductions can be considered to be load on the crane and be added to the suspended loads to arrive at a total load that can be compared to the chart capacity to determine capacity reserve.

Either approach does basically the same thing. The most common way of looking at it is the latter (it is a little easier to figure). However, the capacity reserve (in lbs or kgs) is the same amount in either case. Personally, I think there is more logic in the former approach, but it really doesn't matter until you start talking percentages of capacity.

The two approaches will yield slightly different percentages of capacity at anything less than 100%. This is because the one method is looking at percentages of gross capacity (at boom head) and the other percentages of net capacity at the crane hook. The methods converge at 100%; if you use all the capacity, it is the same whichever way you look at it. Where a difference is more apparent is where a light load is lifted with a crane that has a large capacity. If your company policy defines lifting risk thresholds by percent of capacity, you may come down on a different side of the divide according to what method you are using and thereby be required to treat planning differently. Physically it makes no difference, so long as you know what "percent capacity" means per the method selected you will be fine.

## Boom capacities

The next area starts the boom capacity charts proper. They are tabulated, grouped by boom length with escalating radius. Boom length, radius and capacity are the most important pieces of information (marked in red). Column 1 is the boom length (m); Column 2 is the equivalent in feet. Column 3 is the operating radius (m). Column 4 is the boom angle that boom length at that radius represents; Column 5 is the Boom Point Elevation above grade; this information can also be determined from the range diagram. Column 6 is the boom capacity (kg) for each operating radius permitted for that boom length when the crane is configured with the crawlers retracted (i.e. the narrow track width option). Where a capacity is not indicated, operation is not permitted. Column 7 is the boom capacity (kg) for each operating radius permitted for that boom length when the crane is configured with the crawlers extended (standard operating mode). The asterisks indicate capacities limited by structural competence – it is mandated by ASME B30.5 that this information is shown; I see little reason for you to know this fact if you keep well within chart as you should do. If you are getting up to 90% or more of chart, you should go the extra mile in determining the payload weight to a greater degree of accuracy than would be required if well within capacity.

Caution: Always be very conservative when dismantling something in situations where you can't put the load down again should it turn out to weigh more than expected. It can be difficult to accurately assess weights in such cases and weights given invariably turn out to be heavier.

Figure 11-11

CONSULT JIB CHART FOR JIB CAPACITIES.   UPPER BOOM POINT CANNOT BE USED WHEN JIB IS ATTACHED.

| BOOM LENGTH METERS | BOOM LGTH. FEET | OPER. RADIUS METERS | BOOM ANG. DEG. | BOOM POINT ELEV. METERS | BOOM CAPACITY CRAWLERS RETRACTED KILOGRAMS | BOOM CAPACITY CRAWLERS EXTENDED KILOGRAMS |
|---|---|---|---|---|---|---|
| 21.3 | 70 | 4.9 | 82.8 | 23.5 | | 200 000* |
| | | 5.0 | 82.5 | 23.5 | | 194 000* |
| | | 5.5 | 81.1 | 23.4 | | 175 000* |
| | | 6.0 | 79.7 | 23.3 | | 161 000* |
| | | 7.0 | 77.0 | 23.1 | | 138 700* |
| | | 8.0 | 74.2 | 22.8 | | 121 600* |
| | | 9.0 | 71.3 | 22.5 | | 108 000* |
| | | 10.0 | 68.4 | 22.1 | | 95 900 |
| | | 11.0 | 65.5 | 21.6 | | 82 700 |
| | | 12.0 | 62.5 | 21.1 | | 72 800 |
| | | 13.0 | 59.3 | 20.5 | | 64 800 |
| | | 14.0 | 56.1 | 19.8 | | 58 300 |
| | | 15.0 | 52.7 | 19.0 | 45 100 | 52 900 |
| | | 16.0 | 49.1 | 18.1 | 41 300 | 48 300 |
| | | 18.0 | 41.3 | 16.0 | 35 100 | 40 900 |
| | | 20.0 | 31.9 | 13.2 | 30 200 | 35 300 |

| BOOM LENGTH METERS | BOOM LGTH. FEET | OPER. RADIUS METERS | BOOM ANG. DEG. | BOOM POINT ELEV. METERS | BOOM CAPACITY CRAWLERS RETRACTED KILOGRAMS | BOOM CAPACITY CRAWLERS EXTENDED KILOGRAMS |
|---|---|---|---|---|---|---|
| 24.4 | 80 | 5.2 | 83.0 | 26.6 | | 183 800* |
| | | 5.5 | 82.2 | 26.5 | | 174 600* |
| | | 6.0 | 81.0 | 26.4 | | 160 700* |
| | | 7.0 | 78.6 | 26.2 | | 138 300* |
| | | 8.0 | 76.2 | 26.0 | | 121 300* |
| | | 9.0 | 73.8 | 25.7 | | 107 700* |
| | | 10.0 | 71.3 | 25.3 | | 95 900 |
| | | 11.0 | 68.8 | 24.9 | | 82 800 |
| | | 12.0 | 66.2 | 24.5 | | 72 800 |
| | | 13.0 | 63.5 | 24.0 | | 64 900 |
| | | 14.0 | 60.9 | 23.4 | 49 600 | 58 400 |
| | | 15.0 | 58.1 | 22.8 | 45 100 | 52 900 |
| | | 16.0 | 55.2 | 22.1 | 41 200 | 48 300 |
| | | 18.0 | 49.1 | 20.4 | 35 000 | 40 900 |
| | | 20.0 | 42.4 | 18.4 | 30 200 | 35 300 |
| | | 22.0 | 34.5 | 15.7 | 26 400 | 30 800 |
| | | 24.0 | 24.5 | 11.9 | 23 200 | 27 100 |

7813-AM, 3-7-97/L
PAGE 1 OF 6

**Figure 11-12**

| BOOM LENGTH METERS | BOOM LGTH. FEET | OPER. RADIUS METERS | BOOM ANG. DEG. | BOOM POINT ELEV. METERS | BOOM CAPACITY CRAWLERS RETRACTED KILOGRAMS | BOOM CAPACITY CRAWLERS EXTENDED KILOGRAMS |
|---|---|---|---|---|---|---|
| **27.4** | **90** | 5.8 | 82.5 | 29.6 | | 165 500* |
| | | 6.0 | 82.0 | 29.5 | | 160 400* |
| | | 7.0 | 79.9 | 29.3 | | 138 100* |
| | | 8.0 | 77.8 | 29.1 | | 121 900* |
| | | 9.0 | 75.6 | 28.9 | | 101 800* |
| | | 10.0 | 73.4 | 28.6 | | 95 800 |
| | | 11.0 | 71.2 | 28.2 | | 82 900 |
| | | 12.0 | 69.0 | 27.8 | | 72 900 |
| | | 13.0 | 66.7 | 27.4 | 55 100 | 64 900 |
| | | 14.0 | 64.4 | 26.9 | 49 600 | 58 400 |
| | | 15.0 | 62.0 | 26.4 | 45 100 | 52 900 |
| | | 16.0 | 59.6 | 25.8 | 41 200 | 48 300 |
| | | 18.0 | 54.5 | 24.4 | 35 000 | 40 900 |
| | | 20.0 | 49.1 | 22.7 | 30 200 | 35 300 |
| | | 22.0 | 43.2 | 20.7 | 26 400 | 30 800 |
| | | 24.0 | 36.4 | 18.2 | 23 300 | 27 200 |
| | | 26.0 | 28.3 | 14.9 | 20 600 | 24 100 |
| **30.5** | **100** | 6.1 | 82.7 | 32.6 | | 157 900* |
| | | 7.0 | 80.9 | 32.5 | | 138 000* |
| | | 8.0 | 79.0 | 32.3 | | 120 900* |
| | | 9.0 | 77.1 | 32.0 | | 107 300* |
| | | 10.0 | 75.1 | 31.7 | | 95 800 |
| | | 11.0 | 73.2 | 31.4 | | 83 000 |
| | | 12.0 | 71.2 | 31.1 | | 73 000 |
| | | 13.0 | 69.2 | 30.7 | 55 100 | 65 000 |
| | | 14.0 | 67.1 | 30.3 | 49 700 | 58 400 |
| | | 15.0 | 65.1 | 29.8 | 45 100 | 53 000 |
| | | 16.0 | 62.9 | 29.3 | 41 300 | 48 300 |
| | | 18.0 | 58.6 | 28.1 | 35 000 | 41 000 |
| | | 20.0 | 54.0 | 26.7 | 30 300 | 35 400 |
| | | 22.0 | 49.1 | 25.0 | 26 400 | 30 900 |
| | | 24.0 | 43.8 | 23.1 | 23 300 | 27 200 |
| | | 26.0 | 37.9 | 20.6 | 20 700 | 24 200 |
| | | 28.0 | 31.0 | 17.6 | 18 500 | 21 700 |
| | | 30.0 | 22.2 | 13.4 | 16 600 | 19 500 |
| **33.5** | **110** | 6.7 | 82.3 | 35.6 | | 143 700* |
| | | 7.0 | 81.8 | 35.5 | | 138 000* |
| | | 8.0 | 80.0 | 35.4 | | 120 600* |
| | | 9.0 | 78.3 | 35.2 | | 107 100* |
| | | 10.0 | 76.5 | 34.9 | | 95 600 |
| | | 11.0 | 74.8 | 34.6 | | 83 000 |
| | | 12.0 | 73.0 | 34.3 | | 73 000 |
| | | 13.0 | 71.2 | 34.0 | 55 000 | 64 900 |
| | | 14.0 | 69.3 | 33.6 | 49 600 | 58 400 |
| | | 15.0 | 67.5 | 33.2 | 45 100 | 52 900 |
| | | 16.0 | 65.6 | 32.7 | 41 200 | 48 300 |
| | | 18.0 | 61.7 | 31.7 | 34 900 | 40 900 |
| | | 20.0 | 57.7 | 30.4 | 30 200 | 35 300 |
| | | 22.0 | 53.5 | 29.0 | 26 300 | 30 800 |
| | | 24.0 | 49.1 | 27.3 | 23 200 | 27 100 |
| | | 26.0 | 44.3 | 25.4 | 20 600 | 24 100 |
| | | 28.0 | 39.0 | 23.0 | 18 400 | 21 600 |
| | | 30.0 | 33.1 | 20.2 | 16 500 | 19 400 |
| | | 32.0 | 25.8 | 16.5 | 14 800 | 17 600 |

The next pages are charts of capacities for boom lengths up to the maximum that the crane carries 88.4 m (290').

If for instance you want to read the chart capacity for 30.5 m (100') boom at 15 m radius with the crawlers extended, find the table that relates to 30.5 m (Column 1), scroll down to 15 m in Column 3 and read the capacity in Column 7 = 53000 kg (53.0 t).

Boom angle and boom point elevation (if you need to know those), can be read on the same line.

## Jib capacities

The next area concerns jib capacities, to be used whenever lifting from the jib point. Again, the first page contains similar notes relating to the charts; this is important information and needs to be read carefully.

Figure 11-13

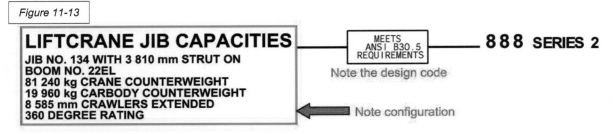

**LIFTCRANE JIB CAPACITIES**
JIB NO. 134 WITH 3 810 mm STRUT ON
BOOM NO. 22EL
81 240 kg CRANE COUNTERWEIGHT
19 960 kg CARBODY COUNTERWEIGHT
8 585 mm CRAWLERS EXTENDED
360 DEGREE RATING

MEETS ANSI B30.5 REQUIREMENTS — **888** SERIES 2

Note the design code

Note configuration

CHART SUPPLEMENTS BOOM CAPACITY CHART NO. 7813-AM. CAPACITIES FOR VARIOUS BOOM LENGTHS, JIB LENGTHS AND JIB OPERATING RADII ARE FOR FREELY SUSPENDED LOADS AND DO NOT EXCEED 75% OF A STATIC TIPPING LOAD. CAPACITIES BASED ON STRUCTURAL COMPETENCE ARE DENOTED BY AN ASTERISK (*).

76.2m THRU 88.4m BOOM LENGTHS REQUIRE ONLY THE MIDDLE TWO SHEAVES IN LOWER BOOM POINT. ALL OTHER SHEAVES MUST BE REMOVED FROM LOWER BOOM POINT.

WEIGHT OF ALL LOAD BLOCKS, HOOKS, WEIGHT BALL, SLINGS, HOIST LINES, ETC., BENEATH BOOM AND JIB POINT SHEAVES, IS CONSIDERED PART OF JIB LOAD. BOOM AND JIB ARE NOT TO BE LOWERED BEYOND RADII WHERE COMBINED WEIGHTS ARE GREATER THAN RATED CAPACITY. WHERE NO CAPACITY IS SHOWN, OPERATION IS NOT INTENDED OR APPROVED.

MACHINE TO OPERATE IN A LEVEL POSITION ON A FIRM UNIFORMLY SUPPORTING SURFACE WITH CRAWLERS FULLY EXTENDED AND GANTRY UP. REFER TO BOOM RIGGING NO. 177156 OR NO. 177153, JIB ASSEMBLY NO. 177062, AND WIRE ROPE SPECIFICATION CHART NO. 7810-A. CRANE OPERATOR JUDGMENT MUST BE USED TO ALLOW FOR DYNAMIC LOAD EFFECTS OF SWINGING, HOISTING OR LOWERING, TRAVEL, WIND CONDITIONS, AS WELL AS ADVERSE OPERATING CONDITIONS AND PHYSICAL MACHINE DEPRECIATION. REFER TO OPERATORS MANUAL FOR OPERATING GUIDELINES.

MACHINE TO TRAVEL ON A FIRM, LEVEL AND UNIFORMLY SUPPORTING SURFACE AND BOOM WITHIN BOOM ANGLE RANGE SHOWN IN CAPACITY CHART. REFER TO MAXIMUM ALLOWABLE TRAVEL SPECIFICATION CHART NO. 7808-A.

OPERATING RADIUS IS HORIZONTAL DISTANCE FROM AXIS OF ROTATION TO CENTER OF VERTICAL HOIST LINE OR LOAD BLOCK. BOOM ANGLE IS ANGLE BETWEEN HORIZONTAL AND CENTERLINE OF BOOM BUTT AND INSERTS, AND IS AN INDICATION OF OPERATING RADIUS. IN ALL CASES, OPERATING RADIUS SHALL GOVERN CAPACITY. JIB POINT ELEVATION IS VERTICAL DISTANCE FROM GROUND LEVEL TO CENTERLINE OF JIB POINT SHAFT.

MACHINE EQUIPPED WITH 8 585 mm EXTENDIBLE CRAWLERS, 1 219 mm TREADS, 3 124 mm RETRACTABLE GANTRY, 9 144 mm MAST, 20 PART BOOM HOIST REEVING, FOUR 35 mm BOOM PENDANTS, AND 81 240 kg CRANE COUNTERWEIGHT AND 19 960 kg CARBODY COUNTERWEIGHT.

MAXIMUM CAPACITY ON 26 mm OR 1" WIRE ROPE IS 13 380 kg PER LINE (9 070 kg WHEN AUXILIARY DRUM IS USED).

Again, to expand on the important points:

— Firstly, these are Jib Capacities, i.e. the capacities of the crane at the jib point sheaves for a M888 series 2. It is a 360° rating chart, it applies anywhere around the crane.

— The charts are valid only for a specific configuration, i.e. a specific jib type (134) with 3.8 m (10') strut fitted to a specific boom type (22EL) with full machine counterweight and full series 2 carbody counterweight (fitted to the lower works between the tracks). Make sure this is your configuration!

— Other operating notes are as for the main boom

— The maximum capacity on the hoist line is limited to 13.38 t (per part of line) or 9 t if the auxiliary drum is used. This may be more of a restriction than the crane chart capacity.

There are charts for every standard jib length fitted to each permissible boom length. e.g. this chart is for a 30' (9.1 m) jib fitted to a 90' (27.4 m) boom. There are 3 possible jib offset angles (the angle by which the jib is offset to the main boom), i.e. 5°, 15° and 25°. Each has a different set of capacities. You can see that the jib is limited structurally to a maximum of 26,700 kg (30 tons).

Figure 11-14

Note capacities for different offsets

9.1m (30 FT.) JIB

| BOOM LGTH. METERS | BOOM LGTH. FEET | JIB OPER. RADIUS METERS | 5 DEGREE OFFSET | | | 15 DEGREE OFFSET | | | 25 DEGREE OFFSET | | | JIB OPER. RADIUS METERS |
|---|---|---|---|---|---|---|---|---|---|---|---|---|
| | | | BOOM ANG. DEG. | JIB POINT ELEV. METERS | JIB CAPACITY KILOGRAMS | BOOM ANG. DEG. | JIB POINT ELEV. METERS | JIB CAPACITY KILOGRAMS | BOOM ANG. DEG. | JIB POINT ELEV. METERS | JIB CAPACITY KILOGRAMS | |
| 27.4 | 90 | 9.1 | 79.2 | 38.2 | 26 700* | | | | | | | 9.1 |
| | | 10.0 | 77.8 | 38.0 | 26 700* | | | | | | | 10.0 |
| | | 12.0 | 74.6 | 37.5 | 26 700* | | | | | | | 12.0 |
| | | 14.0 | 71.3 | 36.8 | 26 700* | 77.1 | 37.3 | 26 700* | | | | 14.0 |
| | | 16.0 | 67.9 | 36.1 | 26 700* | 73.7 | 36.6 | 26 200* | 76.2 | 36.1 | 20 700* | 16.0 |
| | | | | | | 70.3 | 35.8 | 25 600* | 72.8 | 35.3 | 19 300* | |
| | | 18.0 | 64.4 | 35.1 | 26 400* | 66.9 | 34.9 | 25 100* | 69.2 | 34.3 | 18 200* | 18.0 |
| | | 20.0 | 60.9 | 34.0 | 25 800* | 63.3 | 33.8 | 24 700* | 65.6 | 33.2 | 17 200* | 20.0 |
| | | 22.0 | 57.2 | 32.8 | 25 200* | 59.5 | 32.5 | 24 000* | 61.8 | 31.9 | 16 300* | 22.0 |
| | | 24.0 | 53.3 | 31.3 | 24 800* | 55.6 | 31.0 | 22 600* | 57.8 | 30.4 | 15 600* | 24.0 |
| | | 26.0 | 49.2 | 29.6 | 24 400 | 51.5 | 29.3 | 21 300* | 53.5 | 28.7 | 14 900* | 26.0 |
| | | 28.0 | 44.8 | 27.7 | 23 000 | 47.1 | 27.4 | 20 200* | 49.0 | 26.6 | 14 400* | 28.0 |
| | | 32.0 | 34.8 | 22.7 | 18 900 | 36.9 | 22.3 | 18 400* | | | | 32.0 |

*Figure 11-15*

**9.1m (30 FT.) JIB**

| BOOM LGTH. METERS | BOOM LGTH. FEET | JIB OPER. RADIUS METERS | 5 DEGREE OFFSET BOOM ANG. DEG. | 5 DEGREE OFFSET JIB POINT ELEV. METERS | 5 DEGREE OFFSET JIB CAPACITY KILOGRAMS | 15 DEGREE OFFSET BOOM ANG. DEG. | 15 DEGREE OFFSET JIB POINT ELEV. METERS | 15 DEGREE OFFSET JIB CAPACITY KILOGRAMS | 25 DEGREE OFFSET BOOM ANG. DEG. | 25 DEGREE OFFSET JIB POINT ELEV. METERS | 25 DEGREE OFFSET JIB CAPACITY KILOGRAMS | JIB OPER. RADIUS METERS |
|---|---|---|---|---|---|---|---|---|---|---|---|---|
| 30.5 | 100 | 9.1 | 80.1 | 41.4 | 26 700* | | | | | | | 9.1 |
| | | 10.0 | 78.8 | 41.2 | 26 700* | | | | | | | 10.0 |
| | | 12.0 | 75.8 | 40.7 | 26 700* | 78.1 | 40.4 | 26 700* | | | | 12.0 |
| | | 14.0 | 72.8 | 40.1 | 26 700* | 75.1 | 39.8 | 26 500* | 77.4 | 39.3 | 21 200* | 14.0 |
| | | 16.0 | 69.7 | 39.3 | 26 700* | 72.0 | 39.1 | 25 900* | 74.2 | 38.6 | 19 900* | 16.0 |
| | | 18.0 | 66.5 | 38.5 | 26 700* | 68.8 | 38.2 | 25 400* | 71.0 | 37.7 | 18 700* | 18.0 |
| | | 20.0 | 63.3 | 37.5 | 26 200* | 65.5 | 37.3 | 24 900* | 67.7 | 36.7 | 17 700* | 20.0 |
| | | 22.0 | 60.0 | 36.4 | 25 700* | 62.2 | 36.1 | 24 500* | 64.3 | 35.5 | 16 900* | 22.0 |
| | | 24.0 | 56.5 | 35.1 | 25 200* | 58.7 | 34.8 | 23 700* | 60.8 | 34.2 | 16 100* | 24.0 |
| | | 26.0 | 53.0 | 33.6 | 24 700 | 55.1 | 33.3 | 22 400* | 57.1 | 32.7 | 15 500* | 26.0 |
| | | 28.0 | 49.2 | 31.9 | 22 900 | 51.3 | 31.6 | 21 200* | 53.2 | 30.9 | 14 900* | 28.0 |
| | | 32.0 | 40.8 | 27.8 | 18 800 | 42.8 | 27.4 | 19 000 | 44.5 | 26.6 | 14 000* | 32.0 |
| | | 36.0 | 30.6 | 22.0 | 15 700 | 32.5 | 21.5 | 15 800 | | | | 36.0 |
| 33.5 | 110 | 9.1 | 80.8 | 44.5 | 26 700* | | | | | | | 9.1 |
| | | 10.0 | 79.6 | 44.3 | 26 700* | | | | | | | 10.0 |
| | | 12.0 | 76.8 | 43.8 | 26 700* | 79.0 | 43.6 | 26 700* | | | | 12.0 |
| | | 14.0 | 74.0 | 43.3 | 26 700* | 76.2 | 43.0 | 26 600* | 78.3 | 42.5 | 21 700* | 14.0 |
| | | 16.0 | 71.2 | 42.6 | 26 700* | 73.3 | 42.4 | 26 200* | 75.4 | 41.8 | 20 300* | 16.0 |
| | | 18.0 | 68.3 | 41.8 | 26 700* | 70.4 | 41.6 | 25 700* | 72.5 | 41.0 | 19 200* | 18.0 |
| | | 20.0 | 65.4 | 40.9 | 26 700* | 67.5 | 40.7 | 25 200* | 69.5 | 40.1 | 18 300* | 20.0 |
| | | 22.0 | 62.4 | 39.9 | 26 000* | 64.4 | 39.6 | 24 800* | 66.4 | 39.0 | 17 400* | 22.0 |
| | | 24.0 | 59.2 | 38.7 | 25 500* | 61.3 | 38.5 | 24 400* | 63.2 | 37.8 | 16 600* | 24.0 |
| | | 26.0 | 56.0 | 37.4 | 25 100 | 58.0 | 37.1 | 23 400* | 59.9 | 36.5 | 16 000* | 26.0 |
| | | 28.0 | 52.7 | 35.9 | 22 600 | 54.7 | 35.6 | 22 300* | 56.5 | 35.0 | 15 400* | 28.0 |
| | | 32.0 | 45.5 | 32.3 | 18 600 | 47.4 | 32.0 | 18 800 | 49.0 | 31.2 | 14 400* | 32.0 |
| | | 36.0 | 37.1 | 27.6 | 15 500 | 38.9 | 27.2 | 15 700 | | | | 36.0 |
| | | 40.0 | 26.6 | 20.9 | 13 100 | | | | | | | 40.0 |
| 36.6 | 120 | 10.7 | 79.4 | 47.2 | 26 700* | | | | | | | 10.7 |
| | | 12.0 | 77.7 | 47.0 | 26 700* | | | | | | | 12.0 |
| | | 14.0 | 75.1 | 46.4 | 26 700* | 77.1 | 46.2 | 26 700* | 79.1 | 45.7 | 22 000* | 14.0 |
| | | 16.0 | 72.5 | 45.8 | 26 700* | 74.5 | 45.6 | 26 400* | 76.5 | 45.0 | 20 800* | 16.0 |
| | | 18.0 | 69.8 | 45.1 | 26 700* | 71.8 | 44.9 | 25 900* | 73.7 | 44.3 | 19 700* | 18.0 |
| | | 20.0 | 67.1 | 44.3 | 26 700* | 69.1 | 44.0 | 25 400* | 71.0 | 43.4 | 18 700* | 20.0 |
| | | 22.0 | 64.4 | 43.3 | 26 400* | 66.3 | 43.1 | 25 000* | 68.1 | 42.5 | 17 900* | 22.0 |
| | | 24.0 | 61.5 | 42.3 | 25 900* | 63.4 | 42.0 | 24 700* | 65.2 | 41.4 | 17 100* | 24.0 |
| | | 26.0 | 58.6 | 41.1 | 25 000 | 60.5 | 40.8 | 24 300 | 62.3 | 40.2 | 16 400* | 26.0 |
| | | 28.0 | 55.6 | 39.7 | 22 500 | 57.4 | 39.4 | 22 900 | 59.2 | 38.8 | 15 800* | 28.0 |
| | | 32.0 | 49.2 | 36.5 | 18 500 | 51.0 | 36.2 | 18 700 | 52.6 | 35.5 | 14 800* | 32.0 |
| | | 36.0 | 42.0 | 32.5 | 15 400 | 43.8 | 32.1 | 15 600 | 45.2 | 31.3 | 14 000* | 36.0 |
| | | 40.0 | 33.7 | 27.2 | 13 000 | 35.3 | 26.7 | 13 100 | | | | 40.0 |
| | | 44.0 | 22.7 | 19.4 | 11 000 | | | | | | | 44.0 |
| 39.6 | 130 | 10.7 | 80.1 | 50.4 | 26 700* | | | | | | | 10.7 |
| | | 12.0 | 78.5 | 50.1 | 26 700* | | | | | | | 12.0 |
| | | 14.0 | 76.1 | 49.6 | 26 700* | 78.0 | 49.4 | 26 700* | 79.8 | 48.8 | 22 400* | 14.0 |
| | | 16.0 | 73.6 | 49.0 | 26 700* | 75.5 | 48.8 | 26 600* | 77.4 | 48.2 | 21 200* | 16.0 |
| | | 18.0 | 71.2 | 48.4 | 26 700* | 73.0 | 48.1 | 26 100* | 74.8 | 47.5 | 20 100* | 18.0 |
| | | 20.0 | 68.6 | 47.6 | 26 700* | 70.5 | 47.3 | 25 700* | 72.3 | 46.8 | 19 200* | 20.0 |
| | | 22.0 | 66.1 | 46.7 | 26 600* | 67.9 | 46.5 | 25 300* | 69.7 | 45.9 | 18 300* | 22.0 |
| | | 24.0 | 63.5 | 45.7 | 26 200* | 65.3 | 45.5 | 24 900* | 67.0 | 44.9 | 17 600* | 24.0 |
| | | 26.0 | 60.8 | 44.6 | 24 900 | 62.6 | 44.4 | 24 500 | 64.2 | 43.7 | 16 900* | 26.0 |
| | | 28.0 | 58.0 | 43.4 | 22 400 | 59.8 | 43.1 | 22 800 | 61.4 | 42.5 | 16 300* | 28.0 |
| | | 32.0 | 52.2 | 40.5 | 18 300 | 53.9 | 40.2 | 18 600 | 55.5 | 39.5 | 15 200* | 32.0 |
| | | 36.0 | 45.9 | 37.0 | 15 300 | 47.6 | 36.6 | 15 500 | 49.0 | 35.8 | 14 400* | 36.0 |
| | | 40.0 | 38.8 | 32.4 | 12 900 | 40.4 | 32.0 | 13 000 | | | | 40.0 |
| | | 44.0 | 30.3 | 26.4 | 11 000 | 31.8 | 25.9 | 11 100 | | | | 44.0 |

If you want to say determine the jib capacity when using a 30′ (9.1 m) jib with a 15° offset on a 120′ (36.6 m) boom at 26 m radius, look for the 9.1 m (30′) jib charts, search out the 36.6 m boom area and scroll down to 26 m radius and across to the 15° capacities; this will yield 24,300 kg (24.3 t).

<u>Hoist reeving</u>

In addition to the ability of the crane to support the load, you need to ensure that you have adequate hoisting capability. The front and rear drums use 1.125″ (28 mm) wire rope and the maximum line pull is restricted to 40,000 lbs (18.14 t). To obtain more hoisting ability, it is necessary to reeve the hook-block and use more parts of hoist line.

The following table gives the load capacity for different numbers of parts of line. The largest standard block is a 6-sheave block which may be reeved with 12 parts max. Actual lift capacity is limited to the lesser of either the hoist block reeving or the crane load chart capacity.

Figure 11-16

| Hoist Reeving for Main Load Block - Rear Drum (3 Layers Maximum) | | | | | | |
|---|---|---|---|---|---|---|
| No. Parts of Line | 1 | 2 | 3 | 4 | 5 | 6 |
| Maximum Load Lbs. | 40,000 | 80,000 | 120,000 | 160,000 | 200,000 | 240,000 |
| Maximum Load kg | 18 140 | 36 290 | 54 430 | 72 570 | 90 720 | 108 860 |
| No. Parts of Line | 7 | 8 | 9 | 10 | 11 | 12 |
| Maximum Load Lbs. | 280,000 | 320,000 | 360,000 | 400,000 | 440,000 | 441,000 |
| Maximum Load kg | 127 010 | 145 150 | 163 290 | 181 440 | 199 580 | 200 000 |

## Wire rope specifications

Next the crane charts include a section on wire rope on wire rope specifications.

Figure 11-17

| Wire Rope Specifications |
|---|

3.5 : 1 Safety Factor

Hoist Line:            1-1/8 in. -    6 X 31 Warrington-Seale, Extra Extra Improved Plow Steel,
                                      Regular Lay, IWRC (MCC Part No. 719284)
                                      Minimum Breaking Strength 143,000 Lbs. (64 860 kg)
                                      Approx. Weight = 2.34 Lbs. Per Ft. (3.48 kg/m)

Whip Line:            1-1/8 in. -    6 X 31 Warrington-Seale, Extra Extra Improved Plow Steel,
                                      Regular Lay, IWRC (MCC Part No. 719284)
                                      Minimum Breaking Strength 143,000 Lbs. (64 860 kg)
                                      Maximum Load = 40,000 Lbs. (18 140 kg)
                                      Approx. Weight = 2.34 Lbs. Per Ft. (3.48 kg/m)

**Note:** Block Spin May Occur With 6 X 31 Construction Wire Rope Under Certain Operating Conditions.

**Warning!** Single part whip line is maximum for upper boom point application with 1-1/8 in. wire rope (greater than 29,500 Lbs. [13 380 kg]) for liftcrane service. Two part whip line not allowed with 1-1/8 in. wire rope.

Jib capacity with single part whip line is limited to 29,500 Lbs. (13 380 kg) or 59,000 Lbs. (26 760 kg) with two part whip line for 1-1/8 in. wire rope. 40,000 Lb. (18 140 kg) line pull not allowed.

Notes:

i.    Hoist line and whip lines are both $1^1/_8$" 6x31 EEIPS IWRC and weigh approximately 2.34 lbs/ft (3.48 kg/m); you need to know this to determine the total lift weight because the weight of the hoist lines is considered part of the lift weight.

ii.   Jib capacity with single part whip line is limited to 29,500 lbs (13,380 kg) per part of line.

## Wind warnings

There next follows a section on wind effects, starting with warnings. Read and understand them! Note the requirement for job planners (and others) to compensate for the effects of wind by reducing ratings or operating speeds or a combination of both.

Figure 11-18

**General**

Wind adversely affects lifting capacity and stability as shown in Figure 1. The result could be loss of control over the load and crane, even if the load is within the crane's capacity.

### WARNING

**TIPPING CRANE HAZARD!** Judgment and experience of qualified operators, job planners, and supervisors must be used to compensate for affect of wind on lifted load and boom by reducing ratings, reducing operating speeds, or a combination of both.

Failing to observe this precaution can cause crane to tip or boom and/or jib to collapse. Death or serious injury to personnel can result.

Wind speed (to include wind gusts) must be monitored by job planners and supervisors.

*Beware that wind speed at the boom or jib point can be greater than wind speed at ground level. Also beware that the larger the sail area of the load, the greater the wind's affect on the load.*

As a general rule, ratings and operating speeds must be reduced when:

***Wind causes load to swing forward past allowable operating radius or sideways past either boom hinge pin.***

## Max wind speeds and capacity reductions

Operation of the crane is always permitted up to 15 mph (6.7 m/s) and is never allowed above 35 mph (15.5 m/s); between the two limits, there may be a capacity deduction to take dependent on boom or total boom plus jib length – see below.

**Manitowoc Recommendations**

**Operation Permitted**

Figure 11-19

Operation is permitted in steady winds or wind gusts up to 35 mph (56 km/hr). However, ratings must be reduced the amount given in Tables 1 through 4 when the corresponding wind speed is reached.

For boom or boom and fixed jib in steady winds or wind gusts above 25 mph (40 km/hr) *at front of boom*, do not operate boom higher than 70° with loads less than 6,000 lb (2 722 kg). ***Boom and jib could be blown over backwards if this precaution is not observed***.

For boom and luffing jib in steady winds or wind gusts above 15 mph (24 km/hr) *at front of boom*, do not operate luffing jib higher than 55° with loads less than 2,800 lb (1 270 kg). ***Boom and jib could be blown over backwards if this precaution is not observed***.

**Table 1**
**Rating Reductions for Various Wind Speeds and Wind Gusts**
WHEN EQUIPPED WITH #22E OR 22EL BOOM ONLY

| Boom Length ft (m) | | 70 – 180 (21.3 – 54.9) | 190 – 240 (57.9 – 73.2) | 250 – 290 (76.2 – 88.4) |
|---|---|---|---|---|
| Maximum Wind Speed | | Percent Rating Reduction | | |
| (mph) | (m/s) | | | |
| 15 | 7 | 0 | 0 | 0 |
| 20 | 9 | 0 | 0 | 10 |
| 25 | 11 | 0 | 0 | 20 |
| 30 | 13 | 0 | 10 | 40 |
| 35 | 16 | 0 | 20 | 60 |
| Above 35 mph (16 m/s) | | OPERATION NOT PERMITTED | | |

**Table 2**
**Rating Reductions for Various Wind Speeds and Wind Gusts**
WHEN EQUIPPED WITH #22E OR 22EL BOOM AND #123 OR 134 FIXED JIB

*Figure 11-20*

| Fixed Jib Length ft (m) | | 30 – 60 (9.1 – 18.3) | | | 70 – 80 (21.3 – 24.4) | |
|---|---|---|---|---|---|---|
| Boom Length ft (m) | | 90 – 200 (27.4 – 61.6) | 210 – 250 (64.0 – 76.2) | 260 – 270 (79.2 – 82.3) | 90 – 200 (27.4 – 61.0) | 210 – 250 (64.0 – 76.2) |
| Maximum Wind Speed | | Percent Rating Reduction | | | | |
| (mph) | (m/s) | | | | | |
| 15 | 7 | 0 | 0 | 0 | 0 | 0 |
| 20 | 9 | 0 | 0 | 0 | 0 | 0 |
| 25 | 11 | 0 | 0 | 10 | 0 | 0 |
| 30 | 13 | 0 | 10 | 40 | 0 | 30 |
| 35 | 16 | 0 | 30 | OPERATION NOT PERMITTED | 10 | |
| Above 35 mph (16 m/s) | | | OPERATION NOT PERMITTED | | | |

## 11.4 Summary

Before planning a lift you need to fully read and understand the crane charts for the crane in question including all the warnings and caveats; that does not mean simply looking up the generic promotional literature on the web, but using the comprehensive crane charts from the crane itself. The preceding should give you a taste of some of the things you can come across in the small (and large) print. They are important!

If working as a rigging engineer on a project, I'd advise you to get a copy of the actual crane charts for every crane on the project for which you will be planning as they come onto the job site. Scan them or keep hard copies. If working in an office supporting a crane fleet, make sure the office has copies of crane charts for all the cranes in the fleet available to you.

*Figure 11-21*

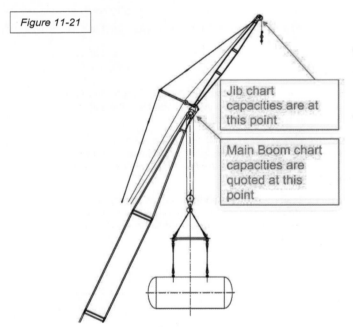

Jib chart capacities are at this point

Main Boom chart capacities are quoted at this point

## Crane chart capacities

- Crane chart capacities are the gross capacities at the main boom or jib point sheaves (according to which configuration you are using)

- There is a specific crane chart provided by the manufacturer quoting gross capacity v operating radius for every approved crane configuration

*Note: Chart capacities are not the max payload that can be lifted but the max load that can be applied to the boom or jib point*

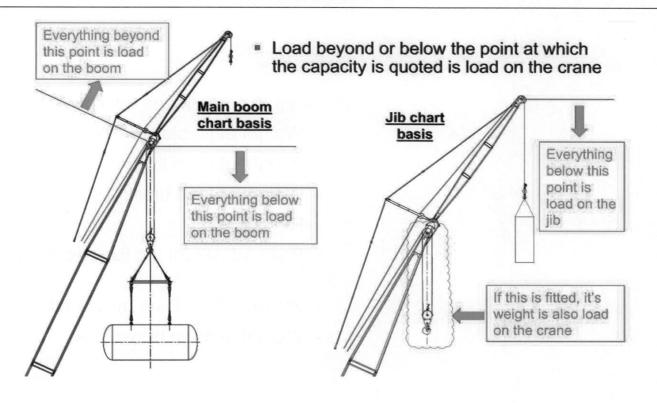

Everything beyond this point is load on the boom

**Main boom chart basis**

Everything below this point is load on the boom

- Load beyond or below the point at which the capacity is quoted is load on the crane

**Jib chart basis**

Everything below this point is load on the jib

If this is fitted, it's weight is also load on the crane

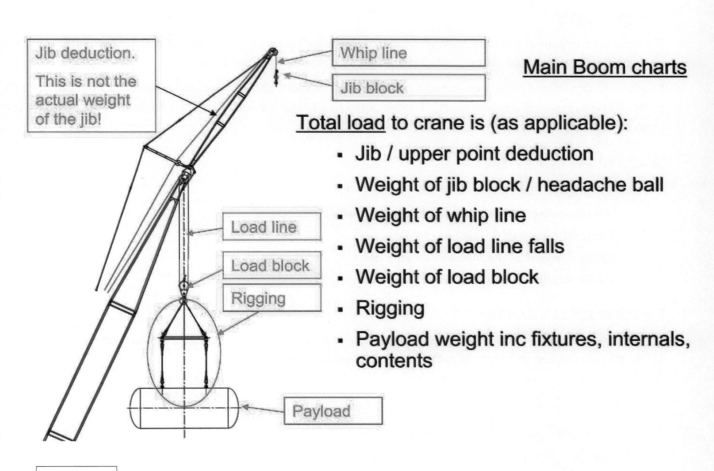

Jib deduction. This is not the actual weight of the jib!

Whip line

Jib block

Load line

Load block

Rigging

Payload

## Main Boom charts

**Total load** to crane is (as applicable):

- Jib / upper point deduction
- Weight of jib block / headache ball
- Weight of whip line
- Weight of load line falls
- Weight of load block
- Rigging
- Payload weight inc fixtures, internals, contents

*Figure 11-22*

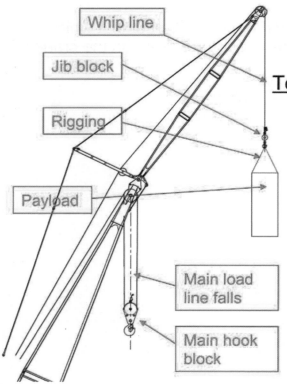

## Jib charts

Total load to crane is (as applicable):

- Weight of jib block / headache ball
- Weight of whip line
- Weight of load block
- Rigging
- Payload weight inc fixtures, internals, contents
- Weight of load line falls (if fitted)
- Weight of main hookblock

Figure 11-23

Load line capacity

The load line winching capability usually needs to be amplified by reeving up the hook-block with sufficient parts of line to support the suspended load with adequate reserve of capacity.

Manitowoc provides a table showing the capacity that different parts of line will give you, (others quote min parts of line to be used on each chart). The block may be better balanced and less likely to twist up if you use even parts of line.

Suspended load

The load suspended on the hoist line reeving is the sum of:

-     — The total weight of the payload (inc fixtures and contents)
-     — The total weight of the rigging
-     — The self-weight of the load block being used
-     — The weight of the load line reeving

Percentage of load line capacity

The percentage of load line capacity is: (total suspended load / hoisting capacity of the parts of line used) x 100%. You should aim to keep this below about 90% where possible.

Example 1 – part A

What is the maximum radius at which you can lift an Exchanger weighing 10,200 kg from the **Main Boom** of a Manitowoc 888 Series 2 crane at ground level? What radius would you recommend using?

Crane is configured as follows:

- Manitowoc Crane 888 Series 2, (note Series 2 counterweight installed)
- 57.9 m of #22EL boom
- 141 t capacity main load block used, reeved with 4 parts of line
- Crawlers extended
- 9.1 m lattice jib #134 rigged on main boom (at 15° offset)
- 15 t capacity auxiliary hook and ball (Headache Ball) fitted on single whip line from jib
- Total rigging weight hook to load is 200 kg

**Calculate Total Load to crane**

**– Lifting from Main Boom**

Payload

- Exchanger            10,200 kg
- Rigging              200 kg

           Load to hook    10,400 kg

Fixed weight deductions

- 141t Load Block       2,114 kg
- Load line 4x57.9x3.48    806 kg
- Jib deduction (9.1m')    1,220 kg
- Whip line 1x6x3.48       21 kg
- Headache ball (15t)      567 kg

       Total capacity deductions    4,728 kg

**Total load to crane**         **15,128 kg**

This is the right chart!

Figure 11-24

| BOOM LENGTH METERS | BOOM LGTH. FEET | OPER. RADIUS METERS | BOOM ANG. DEG. | BOOM POINT ELEV. METERS | BOOM CAPACITY CRAWLERS RETRACTED KILOGRAMS | BOOM CAPACITY CRAWLERS EXTENDED KILOGRAMS |
|---|---|---|---|---|---|---|
| **57.9** | **190** | 9.8 | 82.5 | 59.8 | 82 100* | 82 100* |
| | | 10.0 | 82.3 | 59.8 | 79 300 | 81 500* |
| | | 11.0 | 81.3 | 59.6 | 69 100 | 79 200 |
| | | 12.0 | 80.3 | 59.4 | 60 900 | 72 900 |
| | | 13.0 | 79.2 | 59.2 | 54 300 | 64 400 |
| | | 14.0 | 78.2 | 59.0 | 48 900 | 57 800 |
| | | 15.0 | 77.2 | 58.8 | 44 300 | 52 300 |
| | | 16.0 | 76.2 | 58.5 | 40 300 | 47 600 |
| | | 18.0 | 74.2 | 58.0 | 34 100 | 40 100 |
| | | 20.0 | 72.1 | 57.3 | 29 300 | 34 400 |
| | | 22.0 | 70.0 | 56.6 | 25 400 | 29 900 |
| | | 24.0 | 67.8 | 55.8 | 22 300 | 26 300 |
| | | 26.0 | 65.7 | 54.9 | 19 700 | 23 300 |
| | | 28.0 | 63.5 | 54.0 | 17 500 | 20 800 |
| | | 30.0 | 61.2 | 52.9 | 15 600 | 18 600 |
| | | 32.0 | 58.9 | 51.7 | 14 000 | 16 700 |
| | | 34.0 | 56.6 | 50.4 | 12 600 | 15 100 |
| | | 36.0 | 54.1 | 49.0 | 11 300 | 13 700 |
| | | 38.0 | 51.6 | 47.4 | 10 200 | 12 400 |
| | | 40.0 | 49.0 | 45.7 | 9 200 | 11 300 |
| | | 42.0 | 46.3 | 43.9 | 8 300 | 10 300 |
| | | 44.0 | 43.5 | 41.8 | 7 500 | 9 400 |
| | | 46.0 | 40.5 | 39.6 | 6 700 | 8 500 |
| | | 48.0 | 37.3 | 37.0 | 6 100 | 7 800 |
| | | 50.0 | 33.9 | 34.2 | 5 400 | 7 100 |
| | | 52.0 | 30.0 | 30.9 | 4 900 | 6 400 |
| | | 54.0 | 25.7 | 27.0 | 4 300 | 5 800 |
| | | 56.0 | 20.5 | 22.1 | 3 800 | 5 200 |

- The maximum radius at which the load can be lifted is 32 m, capacity 16700 kg; (at 34 m the capacity is insufficient at 15,100 kg). <u>You are not permitted to interpolate between radii unless specifically permitted to do so by the manufacturer.</u>

- The percentage of chart capacity at this radius = 15,128 / 16,700 = 90.6%

- If it is possible to do so, you'd be better to restrict your radius to not more than 30 m, at which the capacity is 18600 kg.

- The percentage of chart capacity at this radius = 15,128 / 18,600 = 81.3%

- What is the maximum hoisting capacity for the crane in this configuration? 72,570 kg

- From the reeving table, 4 parts of line is good for 72,570 kg; the required capacity = load to hook (10,400#) plus weight of hook-block (2,114 kg), plus wire (806 kg) total = 13,320 kg, so OK (18.4%).

Example 1 – part B

What is the maximum radius at which you can lift the same Exchanger weighing 10,200 kg from the jib of a Manitowoc 888 Series 2 crane at ground level?

Crane is configured as follows:

- Manitowoc Crane 888 Series 2, (note Series 2 counterweight installed)
- 57.9 m of #22EL boom
- 141t capacity main load block fitted, reeved with 4 parts of line
- Crawlers extended
- 9.1 m lattice jib #134 rigged on main boom (at 15° offset)
- 15t capacity auxiliary hook and ball (Headache Ball) fitted on single whip line from jib

Total rigging weight hook to load is 200 kg

**Calculate Total Load to crane – Lifting from Jib**

Payload

| | | |
|---|---:|---|
| Exchanger | 10,200 | kg |
| Rigging | 200 | kg |
| Load to hook | 10,400 | kg |

Deductions

| | | |
|---|---:|---|
| 141t load block | 2,114 | kg |
| Load line 4x6x3.48 | 84 | kg |
| Jib deduction (30') | 0 | kg |
| Whip line 1x67x3.48 | 233 | kg |
| Headache ball (15t) | 567 | kg |
| Total capacity deductions | 2,998 | kg |
| **TOTAL** | **13,398** | **kg** |

9.1m (30 FT.) JIB    This is the right chart!    Figure 11-25

| BOOM LGTH. METERS | BOOM LGTH. FEET | JIB OPER. RADIUS METERS | 5 DEGREE OFFSET | | | 15 DEGREE OFFSET | | | 25 DEGREE OFFSET | | | JIB OPER. RADIUS METERS |
|---|---|---|---|---|---|---|---|---|---|---|---|---|
| | | | BOOM ANG. DEG. | JIB POINT ELEV. METERS | JIB CAPACITY KILOGRAMS | BOOM ANG. DEG. | JIB POINT ELEV. METERS | JIB CAPACITY KILOGRAMS | BOOM ANG. DEG. | JIB POINT ELEV. METERS | JIB CAPACITY KILOGRAMS | |
| 54.9 | 180 | 13.7 | 79.7 | 65.3 | 26 700* | | | | | | | 13.7 |
| | | 14.0 | 79.4 | 65.2 | 26 700* | | | | | | | 14.0 |
| | | 16.0 | 77.6 | 64.8 | 26 700* | | | | | | | 16.0 |
| | | 18.0 | 75.8 | 64.3 | 26 700* | 79.0 | 64.5 | 26 700* | 78.6 | 63.5 | 21 800* | 18.0 |
| | | 20.0 | 73.9 | 63.7 | 26 700* | 77.2 | 64.0 | 26 700* | 76.7 | 62.9 | 20 900* | 20.0 |
| | | 22.0 | 72.0 | 63.1 | 26 700* | 75.3 | 63.5 | 26 500* | 74.8 | 62.2 | 20 100* | 22.0 |
| | | 24.0 | 70.1 | 62.4 | 26 500 | 73.4 | 62.8 | 26 200* | 72.9 | 61.5 | 19 400* | 24.0 |
| | | 26.0 | 68.2 | 61.6 | 24 000 | 71.5 | 62.1 | 25 900* | 70.9 | 60.7 | 18 700* | 26.0 |
| | | 28.0 | 66.3 | 60.7 | 21 500 | 69.6 | 61.3 | 24 500 | 69.0 | 59.8 | 18 100* | 28.0 |
| | | 32.0 | 62.3 | 58.7 | 17 500 | 67.6 | 60.5 | 21 800 | 64.9 | 57.8 | 17 100* | 32.0 |
| | | 36.0 | 58.1 | 56.4 | 14 400 | 63.6 | 58.5 | 17 800 | 60.7 | 55.4 | 14 900 | 36.0 |
| | | 40.0 | 53.7 | 53.6 | 12 000 | 59.4 | 56.1 | 14 700 | 56.2 | 52.6 | 12 400 | 40.0 |
| | | 44.0 | 49.1 | 50.3 | 10 100 | 55.0 | 53.3 | 12 200 | 51.5 | 49.2 | 10 400 | 44.0 |
| | | 48.0 | 44.1 | 46.5 | 8 500 | 50.4 | 50.0 | 10 200 | 46.4 | 45.3 | 8 800 | 48.0 |
| | | 52.0 | 38.6 | 41.8 | 7 100 | 45.4 | 46.1 | 8 600 | | | | 52.0 |
| | | 56.0 | 32.4 | 36.1 | 6 000 | 39.8 | 41.4 | 7 200 | | | | 56.0 |
| | | 60.0 | 24.7 | 28.5 | 5 000 | 33.5 | 35.6 | 6 100 | | | | 60.0 |
| 57.9 | 190 | 13.7 | 80.2 | 68.4 | 26 700* | | | | | | | 13.7 |
| | | 14.0 | 79.9 | 68.3 | 26 700* | | | | | | | 14.0 |
| | | 16.0 | 78.2 | 67.9 | 26 700* | | | | | | | 16.0 |
| | | 18.0 | 76.4 | 67.5 | 26 700* | 79.6 | 67.7 | 26 700* | 79.2 | 66.6 | 22 000* | 18.0 |
| | | 20.0 | 74.7 | 66.9 | 26 700* | 77.8 | 67.2 | 26 700* | 77.4 | 66.1 | 21 200* | 20.0 |
| | | 22.0 | 72.9 | 66.3 | 26 700* | 76.0 | 66.7 | 26 700* | 75.5 | 65.4 | 20 400* | 22.0 |
| | | 24.0 | 71.1 | 65.6 | 26 300 | 74.2 | 66.0 | 26 300* | 73.7 | 64.8 | 19 700* | 24.0 |
| | | 26.0 | 69.2 | 64.9 | 23 800 | 72.4 | 65.4 | 26 000* | 71.9 | 64.0 | 19 000* | 26.0 |
| | | 28.0 | 67.4 | 64.1 | 21 300 | 70.6 | 64.6 | 24 300 | 70.0 | 63.2 | 18 400* | 28.0 |
| | | 32.0 | 63.6 | 62.2 | 17 200 | 68.7 | 63.8 | 21 700 | 66.2 | 61.3 | 17 300* | 32.0 |
| | | 36.0 | 59.7 | 60.0 | 14 200 | 64.9 | 61.9 | 17 600 | 62.2 | 59.0 | 14 700 | 36.0 |
| | | 40.0 | 55.6 | 57.4 | 11 800 | 61.0 | 59.7 | 14 500 | 58.0 | 56.4 | 12 300 | 40.0 |
| | | 44.0 | 51.3 | 54.3 | 9 800 | 56.9 | 57.1 | 12 000 | 53.7 | 53.3 | 10 200 | 44.0 |
| | | 48.0 | 46.8 | 50.8 | 8 200 | 52.6 | 54.0 | 10 100 | 49.0 | 49.6 | 8 500 | 48.0 |
| | | 52.0 | 41.8 | 46.6 | 6 900 | 48.0 | 50.4 | 8 400 | 43.9 | 45.3 | 7 100 | 52.0 |
| | | 56.0 | 36.3 | 41.6 | 5 800 | 43.0 | 46.2 | 7 100 | | | | 56.0 |
| | | 60.0 | 30.0 | 35.3 | 4 800 | 37.4 | 41.1 | 5 900 | | | | 60.0 |
| | | 64.0 | 21.9 | 26.8 | 3 900 | | | | | | | 64.0 |

- The maximum radius at which the load can be lifted is 36m at which the capacity is 14,500 kg.
- The percentage of chart capacity at this radius = 13,389 / 14,500 = 92.4%
- If possible, you would want to reduce the lift radius to say 32 m, at which the chart capacity is 17,600 kg
- What is the percentage of chart capacity at this radius = 13,389 / 17,600 = 76.1%
- The maximum line pull for the crane in this configuration is 13,380 kg (note the jib whip line capacity is less)
- 1 part of line is good for 13,380 kg, load on line = 10,400 + 233 + 567= 11200 kg, (83.7%). You could use a single sheave hook-block fitted with 2 parts of line to reduce this if you wanted.

You will note that counter-intuitively, you can actually lift the load safely at a greater radius when using the jib. All else being equal and you didn't say need to reach over anything, I'd stick with the main boom option as my first choice, particularly when at relatively high percentages of chart.

Example 2

What is the maximum pay load that can be lifted with this crane when lifting off the jib at 28 m radius in order not to exceed 85% of the gross rated capacity of the crane at the hook?

Chart

| | | | | |
|---|---|---|---|---|
| Jib capacity at 28m rad | 21,700 | kg | | |
| | 85% of chart capacity | | 18,445 | kg |

Deductions

| | | | | |
|---|---|---|---|---|
| 141t load block | 2,114 | kg | | |
| Load line 4x6x3.48 | 84 | kg | | |
| Jib deduction (30') | 0 | kg | | |
| Whip line 1x67x3.48 | 233 | kg | | |
| Headache ball (15t) | 567 | kg | | |
| Total capacity deductions | | | -2,998 | kg |
| 85% gross capacity minus fixed deductions | | | 15,447 | kg |
| Minus rigging weight | | | -200 | kg |
| **Remaining capacity for payload** | | | **15,247** | **kg** |

This is the sort of situation you might find if your company policy regarding "standard" lifts restricts you to using not more than 85% of chart capacity. If say operating in a laydown yard at not more than 28 m radius, configured as above, you would be limited to receiving and unloading items weighing not more than 15 t using this crane (in order to stay within policy for routine, standard lifting operations).

# 12 Lifting tackle

It is not proposed to discuss standard proprietary items of rigging tackle in great depth other than to highlight important aspects of their scope of application and considerations that need to be taken in engineering for their use within rigging arrangements. We will however spend some time on custom engineered tackle.

If you want to get into greater depth, there are some excellent industry association publications and much good information in codes such as the ASME B30 series. Most rigging tackle manufacturers have excellent web sites and technical support.

## 12.1 Terminology

Terminology varies around the world and similar terms are often used to designate rated capacity. Regardless of terminology, there is a difference between what a piece of rigging is rated at in ideal conditions and it's rating as used. e.g. a sling has different ratings according to the hitch used.

Traditionally, as applies to rigging tackle, the term Safe Working Load (SWL) was used to denote the design rated capacity of a sling, shackle, lifting beam or whatever. Rigging items were marked by their manufacturer with their "SWL". It was a maximum to apply under specific ideal conditions of use. e.g. a shackle marked with a 55 t SWL was rated at that figure in a straight line pull, between certain temperatures; a 25 t spreader bar might only be good for 10 t at its maximum span and so on; the SWL of a sling is in a straight line pull. In recent years, it has been felt that, considering the useable capacity of many of these items depends on the manner of their use, using "SAFE" in defining rated capacity of rigging is misleading and the term Working Load Limit (WLL) has largely superseded SWL. e.g. ASME B30.9 now uses only Rated Load, Rated Capacity or Working Load Limit when referring to the maximum rated capacity of a sling. The term SWL is now effectively retired in the USA. In the UK, the Lifting Equipment Engineers Association uses the following definitions (to paraphrase):

Working load limit (WLL) or Rated Load

> "The working load limit of a piece of rigging equipment, sling, shackle or whatever is the maximum load that piece of equipment is designed to be rated to lift / lower / suspend when used as intended in ideal conditions."

Safe Working Load (SWL)

> "The Safe Working Load is the maximum load (as assessed by a Competent Person) that a piece of equipment may lift / lower / suspend when used in the particular manner and actual conditions that prevail."

So in the UK (at least) the term SWL has not been retired as a term, but its meaning has been adjusted subtly. To avoid confusion I suggest that you do not use "SWL", but talk in the following terms:

- WLL – the maximum rated capacity of a piece of rigging tackle, as determined by the designer/manufacturer, when used under ideal conditions in a specific configuration. e.g. a 1.5" dia sling might be rated with a WLL of 21 tons. i.e. It has a rated capacity of 21 tons in a straight line pull.

- Rated Capacity – the same 1.5" x 21 ton WLL sling might be rated by the manufacturer at 42 tons when used in a basket hitch with the legs vertical, so long as it is not bent more tightly than 25:1.

- Assessed Capacity – if the same (21 ton) sling is basketed over a 6" diameter pin, the Competent Person (i.e. maybe you if you are planning the lift) should de-rate the sling to 73% of its (basket) Rated Capacity as a result of the tightness of the 4:1 bend ratio (see later for details); this would give an Assessed Capacity of 30.7 tons when used in that manner. If the same sling is used in a basket hitch, bent over a 6" dia pin with the legs at 60°, the Assessed Capacity would be 20.7 tons. (OK, maybe not a great example as it is not actually physically feasible to do that, but you get the principle).

At the very least, you need to be clear what the terms used commonly in your locale actually mean and rate your rigging tackle correctly noting the manner and conditions of use. Read the manufacturers documentation carefully.

## 12.2 Lifting beams

### 12.2.1 Suppliers

There are a number of prominent suppliers of proprietary lift beams and spreader bar systems (including these):

| | | |
|---|---|---|
| – | Tandemloc | http://www.tandemloc.com |
| – | Modulift | http://www.modulift.com/ |
| – | Versabar | http://www.vbar.com/ |
| – | Holloway Houston | http://www.hhilifting.com/ |
| – | Bishop Lifting Products | http://www.lifting.com/ |
| – | Caldwell | http://www.caldwellinc.com |

You may also need to design a beam for specific needs and we'll run through a simple example.

### 12.2.2 What is a lifting beam?

What is a lifting beam (as against a spreader bar?)

Figure 12-1

A lifting beam is a means of splitting lifting effort provided by one (or sometimes two) hoisting devices such as a crane into two or more lines of suspension by means of shear through a rigid beam.

- It is subject to bending and shear
- By use of offset suspension points, it can allow for lines of suspension not being equidistant about the C of G
- It may have multiple holes to allow for adjustment and/or multiple lines of support
- It can have a short suspension length making it good in restricted headroom situations
- It's self-weight will be greater than the equivalent spreader

This yellow beam is being used in an LNG plant to lift a replacement Combustion Turbine off a transport cart using an overhead crane. Only vertical slinging is permitted. Note: As the vertical offset between the upper and lower holes is not great, the location of the C of G needs to be known to a fair degree of accuracy and the load slung so that the C of G lies directly under the upper hole if the load is to lift relatively level.

On the telescoping gantry system shown on the left below, the beams spanning across the page supported on the heads of the gantry legs are lifting beams, as are the beams they in turn support from which the load is suspended. The loading conditions are static and the shear and bending moments can be readily determined.

On the similar system shown on the right, the load is suspended directly from the primary lift beams using mobile links that can be hydraulically powered along the beams. Thus the shear loads and bending moments change as the load moves laterally. You would need to figure out an envelope of the maximums to determine the design parameters.

Figure 12-2

Figure 12-3

Figure 12-4

This yellow lift beam is being used to provide multiple lines of support to a large boiler wall panel on a coal fired power project. The panel has been upended and walked in by the single crane and will be handed off to a strand jack system for raising to full height in the boiler (forming part of the front wall).

Figure 12-5

To clarify Figures 12-2 and 12-3. The beams indicated are indeed lifting beams, but are gantry header beams and BTH-1 does not apply to their design. Refer to ASME B30.1 and the SC&RA publication "Recommended Practices for Telescopic Hydraulic Gantry Systems". See also "Telescopic Hydraulic Gantry Systems" by David Duerr for guidance and information.

### 12.2.3   Design standards

Below-the-hook lifting beams are structural lifting devices and as such, in the USA, are covered under ASME B30.20 – 2006 "Below the hook lifting devices" and its related design code BTH-1.

BTH-1 is a self-contained design code that leans heavily on AISC practice but, recognizing the service conditions when lifting, uses more conservative design factors than are used for regular structural design of structures.

Regardless of where you are located in the world, and noting other standards may well apply and take precedence, these documents are probably the most practical and comprehensive on the subject and I would recommend that you design in accordance with their principles.  You are recommended to thoroughly study ASME B30.20 and its accompanying design code BTH-1 and be familiar with AISC, 1989 Specification for Structural Steel Buildings - Allowable Stress Design and Plastic Design, or an equivalent elastic or plastic design code. See also EN 13155, Cranes - Safety - Non-fixed load lifting attachments.

BTH-1 requires the designer to select a Design Category (based on static strength criteria) and a Service Class (based on fatigue life criteria) for the lifter considering its intended application. Design Category A applies only to controlled applications when the magnitude and variation of the loads are predictable, where the loading and environmental conditions are accurately defined or not severe. There is the presumption of rare and only minor unintended overloading and only mild impact loads during routine use (max multiplier 50%). The load cycles are <20,000. All other applications should be treated as Design Category B. (Read the small print in BTH-1). To paraphrase, general use and abuse "lifters" are "B", engineered and closely controlled applications might be "A". (My words).

BTH-1 stipulates that design factors for Design Category A lifting devices shall be not less than 2.00 for limit states of yielding or buckling and 2.40 for limit states of fracture and for connection design; for Category B lifting devices they shall be not less than 3.00 for limit states of yielding or buckling and 3.60 for limit states of fracture and for connection design. This compares with AISC specifying (for structural steel design), nominal design factors of 1.67 for yielding and buckling and 2.00 for fracture and connections. i.e. for lifting purposes a structure has to be 1.25x stronger (Category A lifters) or 1.8x stronger (Category B) than it would have to be as regular structural steel in say a building.

### 12.2.4   Design process

Code to be used

Start by considering what design code you will use. It is strongly preferable that you use a self-contained design code such as ASME B30.20 BTH-1 as this is written specific to the application. If you have to use a structural steel design code you should at least lower the permissible stress levels in line with BTH-1 to reflect the nature of the lifting application.

Applying an "impact factor" of 1.25x to the load to which you wish to rate Category A devices, then using AISC as a design basis will give you 1.25x1.67 = 2.08 on yield or buckling and 1.25x2.0 = 2.5, which is generally in line with BTH-1.

Applying an "impact factor" of 1.8x to the load to which you wish to rate Category B devices, then using AISC as a design basis will give you 1.8x1.67 = 3.0 on yield or buckling and 1.8x2.0 = 3.6, which is generally in line with BTH-1.

Allowable stress design computes actual stresses and compares them to allowable stresses (often tabulated for convenience) that will keep the element in question within the elastic range with an appropriate factor of safety. Allowable bending stresses might typically be 0.66 x yield, shear may be 0.5 x yield. When considering bending of beams, the tables will prescribe lesser allowable stresses with increasing $l/r_{yy}$ and D/T ratios; the effective length "l" used will take into account the end fixity and so on. If using an elastic structural design code, the best way to be more conservative (as is appropriate for lifting) is to apply a factor upfront to the actual load you intend to rate the item at, to allow you to calculate design working stresses that you can compare to the normal structural steel allowable stresses. As recommended, BTH-1 can be used for guidance on an appropriate degree of conservatism; use 1.25x or 1.8x factors (according to Design Category) factors over the required SWL and then apply the normal elastic structural steel design code. If you are not a manufacturer and are designing for a particular application or low frequency in-house use, you are likely not designing for absolute economy of steel use, nor are likely to be running right up to the maximum permitted stress in your design. You may well be making use of readily available sections and somewhat over-designing. Designing lifting beams using elastic design codes will normally serve adequately for these applications and are generally easier to work within for those who don't make their full time daily living in such areas.

As with everything, know your own limits and have a competent person check your work. That said, designing a simple lifting beam or spreader should not be beyond the ability of a competent engineer with basic structural design expertise.

### Establish required rating

— Ensure that your lifting device is designed and rated with adequate reserve of capacity to allow for unexpected eventualities, like the weight "growing" as the project develops for instance.

— Consider the possibility that the C of G may not be exactly where you expected it to be. Do you want to provide some alternative suspension points to provide some adjustment or flexibility of application?

— Do you want it to serve more than one purpose? Is it to be a general piece of rigging tackle or a special one off?

### Application

— How is this to be used? e.g. suspended from an overhead crane; lugs and Crosby G2130 shackles at all suspension points; vertical slings to the load equidistant about the center at 12' centers.

### Loading

— Knowing the design loads and the lift centers, figure out the BM and SF diagrams and hence the design Max Bending Moment and Shear load.

### Preliminary beam section selection

— Decide what steel grade is to be used and using conservative permissible stresses, make a first assessment of the minimum section modulus and shear area required.

— It may be that for what you are doing a built up section from plate is going to work best. For long spans you will likely need good lateral properties, so a box beam may be a better choice. Very large beams may work best as lattice sections, with pick points at nodes. For small general use lift beams, rolled sections provide a convenient readymade section with minimal welding required.

— On the assumption that a rolled section is the way forward, using a sections book evaluate the section options available that meet the criteria. In selecting a beam or column section, you'll have a few to choose from. You don't want a beam that is too shallow as it will deflect excessively, somewhere about span/10 to max span/20 usually works well; neither do you want a beam that is too narrow for its depth as the compression flange is less stable laterally (particularly at longer lengths) and you can't run the beam at such high stress levels. Don't pick odd size sections that are difficult to obtain. Try to pick sections of weight somewhat central in the weight range as they are more obtainable.

## Attachment lug design

The design of lift lugs is subject to much debate. In my opinion, ASME standard Design of Below-the-Hook Lifting Devices BTH-1 (although not intended specifically for that purpose) is probably as good a basis for designing lugs for general lifting purposes as any. This code is based on analysis of stress values derived from classical strength of materials methodology being compared to allowable stresses defined in the Standard. Alternative codes to consider using are: DNV 2.7.1 (lug section), EN 12079 or API 17D Appendix K.

Design for standard shackles from manufacturers such as Crosby, Van Beest, Skookum or other reputable manufacturers to a recognized international quality standard; have the shackle type in mind right from the outset. Design to accommodate a range of manufacturers offering similar styles; comparable pattern shackles don't vary much in size, but they can vary some and that can make all the difference – check that out.

For a lug to be to be properly proportioned to fit a standard shackle, designing it according to the following principles will give you a starting point with a good chance that it will check out adequately when analyzed for strength in accordance with BTH-1. Shackles of a given type are designed somewhat proportional to WLL, they maintain similar shape but are scaled up or down according to WLL. Their proportions are compatible with their use and the lug to which they will fit, so these principles apply well across the size ranges for standard shackles.

- Do not use a shackle excessively larger than the beam is rated at unless the slings to be used require a large amount of room in the bow. People have a tendency to assume that the beam will be at least as good as the shackles fitted. (The beam should be marked with WLL but still it happens).
- Size the lug initially to the following guidelines as though the shackle was to carry its full rated WLL.
- Do not design excessively strong (as the self-weight comes out of your lift capacity) but design conservatively; cover the level of your ignorance, but do not design down to the last pound (kg); this is not permanent structure where every kg counts, but a one off.
- Hole diameter should be approximately $^{1}/_{8}$" (3 mm) larger than the pin diameter up to about 35 t capacity and about ¼" (6 mm) for shackles larger than that. Do not make holes too large as you will get high local bearing stresses that could cause local yield. If provided with a lift lug that has an excessively large hole that can't be adequately filled with an excessively large shackle, consider bushing the hole out.
- The radius of the head of the lug should be about 1.75x the diameter of the hole. It should be centered on the hole.
- Locate the center of the hole above the flange at a distance at least equal to the radius of the head to provide adequate room for the shackle to fit and operate.
- To keep lug bearing stresses within AISC permissible limits at the full capacity of the shackle (when using a 1.8x "impact" factor per Cat B lifters), you will need the lug width to fill about 75% of the jaw width of the shackle. This also adequately locates the shackle without being too tight.
- If proportioned per these guidelines, the basic plate from which the lug is constructed will likely only needs to be 50% or so of the width you derived from bearing considerations. Thus, if for example 2" (50 mm) is required for bearing, you could consider making the lug out of 1" (25 mm) plate and adding ½" (12.5 mm) doublers (donut plates) for bearing considerations.
- If using donuts, make their outside diameter approximately 2.5x the hole diameter.
- There needs to be sufficient weld to transmit the force you have in the donuts into the base plate. In the example about 25% of the load is carried in each donut.
- It is unlikely you will need to consider the donuts for shear or tension in the lug.
- Ensure the holes in donuts are in-line drilled / bored through the lug assembly, or otherwise adequately located to ensure that all three holes are all in line and supporting load. Do not flame cut holes.

- Make sure the donuts will not cause access problems that would prevent you welding the lug to the beam.

- Lug plates should not be thinner than the web of the beam to which they are attached and not excessively thicker.

- Unless the beam or plate to which you are welding your lug to has guaranteed through-thickness properties, welding directly to that plate or flange runs the risk of welding to only a lamination. As you are relying on that weld to carry your lifted load in tension into the body of the beam, you could end up pulling that lamination off and losing the load. It is better to carry the lug plate through the flange and use it to form part of the web. In fact you may decide to make the lugs and the web one plate and weld longitudinal stiffener plates to that plate to provide the major and minor axis bending strength. This provides a continuous path for the shear loads through the beam. The yellow beam in the first picture was constructed this way.

- Consider the angle the slings will operate through (if any) and ensure adequate room in the shackle eye for the sling when considering the lug metal. (If you make the body of the lug wider than 2x the radius of the head and flare the head of the lug out to that width, the available gap for the sling diminishes as the shackle rotates and the sling eye may be trapped).

### 12.2.5  Example beam design using structural code (SI units)

Many old-timers in the UK will be familiar with the now-retired structural steel design code BS449 or the crane design code BS2573. If you know your way around these codes, there is nothing fundamentally wrong with their use for straight-forward low-use applications so long as adequate conservatism (such as outlined above) is applied.

Example

Let us consider a lifting beam such as the one shown in Figure 12-1 lifting the small Turbine.

The turbine weighs 35 t (77,175#). To give some reserve, I will choose to conservatively design the beam for a rated Safe Working Load of 40 t. This gives some reserve should the weight "grow" as the project develops. This often happens – do not rate your designs too closely to weights given to you!

The location of the C of G for the combined lifting beam and Turbine is known; the Turbine is provided with lift attachments 2 m to one side (6'-7") and 3 m (9'-10") to the other. The material we are going to use has 250 N/mm$^2$ (36 ksi) yield.

This beam is assessed as falling within the criteria for Category A lifters so factors of 2.0 for yielding and buckling and 2.4 for fracture and connections are required. The easiest way to obtain those, given the approach we are using, is to apply a factor of 1.25 to the required rating up front and use the regular code permissible stresses thereafter. Call it an impact or dynamic factor if you want!

As noted above, a structural steel code using allowable stress approach will not be as conservative, so if you intend to use such codes, one way to arrive at a similar degree of conservatism is to add a "dynamic" factor to the required rated load to give a more conservative design load for calculation purposes; then apply your intended structural steel code.

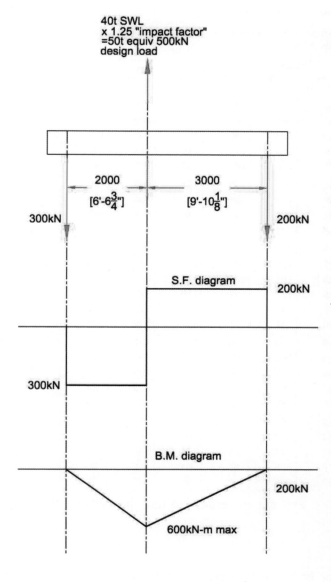

40t SWL
x 1.25 "impact factor"
=50t equiv 500kN
design load

2000
$[6'-6\frac{3}{4}"]$

3000
$[9'-10\frac{1}{8}"]$

300kN

200kN

S.F. diagram

200kN

300kN

B.M. diagram

200kN

600kN-m max

Figure 12-6

## Loads

To arrive at BTH-1 design conservatism when using an elastic code, a 1.25x factor is applied to the required rated load up front; the calculated stresses are then compared to BS449 allowable stresses.

The design load = 40 t SWL x 1.25 = 50 t

50 x 9.81 = 490.5 kN, say 500 kN.

As the lift points are offset, the lift load will be split unequally between the "slings" in inverse proportion to the horizontal distances = 300 kN to the left and 200 kN to the right. (Shortest distance = greatest load).

The max Shear "Q" = 300 kN

The max BM = 300 kN x 2 m = 600 kNm

## Bending

Per BS449, the max bending stress $p_{bc}$ or $p_{bt}$ in a rolled section for Grd 43 (A36) material is 180 N/mm$^2$ for thickness ≤ 40 mm or 165 N/mm$^2$ for thickness > 40 mm. As a starting point, I will use $p_{bc}$ = 120 N/mm$^2$.

M/I = f/y, therefore f = My/I, where

F = actual bending stress (N/mm$^2$)

I = moment of inertia (mm$^4$)

y is dist from neutral axis (NA) to extreme fiber (mm)

I/y = Z, where Z = elastic modulus (mm$^3$),

Therefore f=m/z,

Inverting that, Z required = M/f

Z req'd = $600 \times 10^6$ / $120 \times 10^3$ cm$^3$ = 5,000 cm$^3$

A beam with a $z_{xx}$ of about 5000 cm$^3$ is needed.

As noted above, in selecting a beam or column section, you'll have a few to choose from. A 610x305 UB 179 kg/m with an elastic modulus of 4911 cm$^3$ appears a good compromise for the basic section.

Using that beam section, $f_{bc}$ and $f_{bt}$ = $600 \times 10^6$ / $4911 \times 10^3$ = 122 N/mm$^2$.

We now need to check the permitted bending compressive stress $f_{bc}$. For that we need to know the D/T ratio (total depth of beam to flange thickness) and the $l/r_{yy}$ (ratio of effective length of the beam to radius of gyration in the YY direction). Together, these determine the lateral stability of the beam and will limit the maximum allowable stress in the compression flange at longer spans.

D/T for this beam is 26.1, $r_{yy}$ is 7.08 cm; the effective length is the span x an effective length factor determined by the end conditions. As the beam is effectively held in position, but not restrained in direction, the factor is 1.00.

Therefore the effective length is 5 m = 500 cm. The $l/r_{yy}$ ratio = 500 / 7.08 = 70.6

Figure 12-7

## BS 449-2:1969

### Table 3a — Allowable stress $p_{bc}$ in bending (N/mm²) for case A of Clause 19 *a*) 2) for grade 43 steel

| $l/r_y$ | D/T | | | | | | | | | |
|---|---|---|---|---|---|---|---|---|---|---|
| | 5 | 10 | 15 | 20 | 25 | 30 | 35 | 40 | 45 | 50 |
| 40 | 180 | 180 | 180 | 180 | 180 | 180 | 180 | 180 | 180 | 180 |
| 45 | 180 | 180 | 180 | 180 | 180 | 180 | 180 | 180 | 180 | 180 |
| 50 | 180 | 180 | 180 | 180 | 180 | 180 | 180 | 180 | 180 | 180 |
| 55 | 180 | 180 | 180 | 178 | 176 | 175 | 174 | 174 | 173 | 173 |
| 60 | 180 | 180 | 176 | 172 | 170 | 169 | 168 | 167 | 167 | 166 |
| 65 | 180 | 180 | 172 | 167 | 164 | 163 | 162 | 161 | 160 | 160 |
| 70 | 180 | 177 | 167 | 162 | 159 | 157 | 156 | 155 | 154 | 154 |
| 75 | 180 | 174 | 163 | 157 | 154 | 151 | 150 | 149 | 148 | 147 |
| 80 | 180 | 171 | 159 | 153 | 148 | 146 | 144 | 143 | 142 | 141 |
| 85 | 180 | 168 | 156 | 148 | 143 | 140 | 138 | 137 | 136 | 135 |
| 90 | 180 | 165 | 152 | 144 | 139 | 135 | 133 | 131 | 130 | 129 |
| 95 | 180 | 162 | 148 | 140 | 134 | 130 | 127 | 125 | 124 | 123 |
| 100 | 180 | 160 | 145 | 136 | 129 | 125 | 122 | 119 | 118 | 117 |
| 105 | 180 | 157 | 142 | 132 | 125 | 120 | 116 | 114 | 112 | 111 |
| 110 | 180 | 155 | 139 | 128 | 120 | 115 | 111 | 108 | 106 | 105 |
| 115 | 178 | 152 | 136 | 124 | 116 | 110 | 106 | 103 | 101 | 99 |
| 120 | 177 | 150 | 133 | 120 | 112 | 106 | 101 | 98 | 96 | 95 |
| 130 | 174 | 146 | 127 | 113 | 104 | 97 | 94 | 91 | 89 | 88 |
| 140 | 171 | 142 | 121 | 107 | 97 | 92 | 88 | 85 | 83 | 81 |
| 150 | 168 | 138 | 116 | 100 | 92 | 87 | 82 | 79 | 77 | 75 |
| 160 | 166 | 134 | 111 | 96 | 88 | 82 | 77 | 74 | 72 | 70 |
| 170 | 163 | 130 | 106 | 92 | 84 | 77 | 73 | 69 | 67 | 65 |
| 180 | 161 | 126 | 102 | 89 | 80 | 73 | 69 | 65 | 63 | 60 |
| 190 | 158 | 123 | 97 | 85 | 76 | 70 | 65 | 61 | 59 | 56 |
| 200 | 156 | 119 | 95 | 82 | 73 | 66 | 62 | 58 | 55 | 53 |

As our beam design has an $l/r_{yy}$ = 70.6 and D/T = 26.1, and our materials are less than 40 mm thick, $p_{bc}$ = 158 N/mm². Therefore $f_{bc}$ = 122 N/mm2 is OK.

### Web shear

Per BS449, for hot rolled sections such as this is, we can go to a max average shear stress on the gross section of the web of 110 N/mm² (thickness ≤ 40 mm) or 100 N/mm² (thickness > 40 mm) for unstiffened webs. Note we can use an unstiffened web if the d/t ratio (clear depth / web thickness) is less than 85; d = 537.2, therefore d/t = 537.2/14.1 = 38, so no web stiffeners are required.

For rolled sections, the gross section is the total depth of the beams x the web thickness = 617.5 x 14.1 = 8707 mm². Therefore $f_q$ = 300x10³ / 8707 = 35.5 N/mm² (versus $p_{bc/t}$ = 100 N/mm²) OK.

### Lugs

As we are rating the beam for 40 t, I am going to use a 55 t shackle to the crane and, noting the division of load, 2 x 35 t shackles to the load. In this case, we will design suitable for the use of Crosby G2130 or Green Pin (Van Beest) G4163 standard type shackles - they are virtually identical at these sizes but may vary slightly at the larger sizes. You are advised to check pin diameters and jaw widths using manufacturer's catalogues if you want to ensure versatility of design (note also manufacturing tolerances and allow for them). Note high alloy and wide body shackles have smaller sizes / different proportions for a given capacity. Select the pattern(s) to be used and stipulate it on the drawing.

Crosby          *http://www.thecrosbygroup.com*

Van Beest       *http://www.vanbeest.nl/products/catalogue_en*

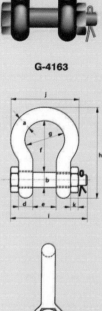

G-4163

Figure 12-8

# Green Pin® Standard Shackles
## bow shackles with safety bolt

- **Material** : bow and pin high tensile steel, Grade 6, quenched and tempered
- **Safety Factor** : MBL equals 6 x WLL
- **Standard** : EN 13889 and
  meets performance requirements of US Fed. Spec. RR-C-271 Type IVA Class 3, Grade A
- **Finish** : hot dipped galvanized
- **Temperature Range** : -20°C up to +200°C
- **Certification** : at no extra charges this product can be supplied with a works certificate, certificate of basic raw material, manufacturer test certificate and/or EC Declaration of Conformity

| working load limit | diameter bow | diameter pin | diameter eye | width eye | width inside | length inside | width bow | length | length bolt | width | thickness nut | weight each |
|---|---|---|---|---|---|---|---|---|---|---|---|---|
| | a | b | c | d | e | f | g | h | i | j | k | |
| tons | mm | mm | mm | mm | mm | mm | mm | mm | mm | mm | mm | kg |
| 0.5 | 7 | 8 | 17 | 7 | 12 | 29 | 20 | 54 | 43 | 37 | 4 | 0.06 |
| 0.75 | 9 | 10 | 21 | 9 | 13.5 | 32 | 22 | 61 | 51 | 42 | 5 | 0.11 |
| 1 | 10 | 11 | 23 | 10 | 17 | 36.5 | 26 | 71 | 61 | 49 | 8 | 0.16 |
| 1.5 | 11 | 13 | 26 | 11 | 19 | 43 | 29 | 80 | 68 | 54 | 11 | 0.22 |
| 2 | 13.5 | 16 | 34 | 13.5 | 22 | 51 | 32 | 91 | 83 | 63 | 13 | 0.42 |
| 3.25 | 16 | 19 | 40 | 16 | 27 | 64 | 43 | 114 | 99 | 79 | 17 | 0.74 |
| 4.75 | 19 | 22 | 47 | 19 | 31 | 76 | 51 | 136 | 115 | 94 | 20 | 1.18 |
| 6.5 | 22 | 25 | 53 | 22 | 36 | 83 | 58 | 157 | 131 | 107 | 23 | 1.77 |
| 8.5 | 25 | 28 | 60 | 25 | 43 | 95 | 68 | 176 | 151 | 124 | 25 | 2.58 |
| 9.5 | 28 | 32 | 67 | 28 | 47 | 108 | 75 | 197 | 167 | 137 | 28 | 3.66 |
| 12 | 32 | 35 | 74 | 32 | 51 | 115 | 83 | 218 | 179 | 154 | 31 | 4.91 |
| 13.5 | 35 | 38 | 80 | 35 | 57 | 133 | 92 | 240 | 198 | 170 | 34 | 6.54 |
| 17 | 38 | 42 | 89 | 38 | 60 | 146 | 99 | 262 | 202 | 183 | 19 | 8.19 |
| 25 | 45 | 50 | 104 | 45 | 74 | 178 | 126 | 314 | 244 | 226 | 24 | 14.22 |
| 35 | 50 | 57 | 111 | 50 | 83 | 197 | 138 | 358 | 270 | 250 | 27 | 19.85 |
| 42.5 | 57 | 65 | 134 | 57 | 95 | 222 | 160 | 414 | 302 | 287 | 30 | 28.33 |
| 55 | 65 | 70 | 145 | 65 | 105 | 260 | 180 | 463 | 330 | 329 | 33 | 39.59 |
| 85 | 75 | 83 | 163 | 75 | 127 | 329 | 190 | 556 | 376 | 355 | 40 | 62 |

## Draft design

Using the above principles, the following draft design was arrived at.

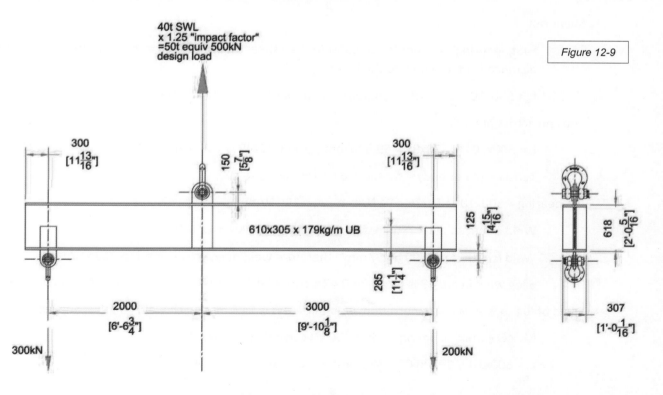

Figure 12-9

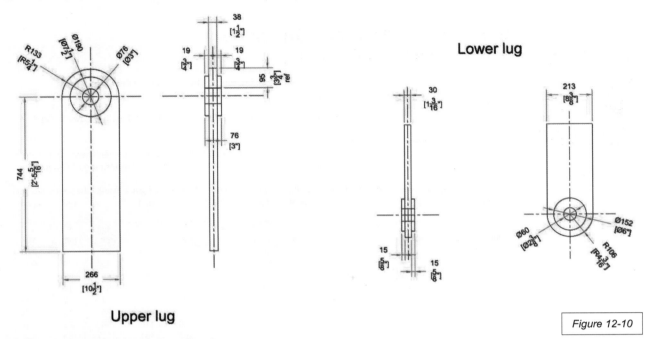

Lower lug

Upper lug

Figure 12-10

<u>Simple analysis of draft design to BS449</u>

There are 3 major failure modes of the lug itself (refer to Figures 16-27), they are:

- shear out of the head of the lug parallel to the line of action of the force
- tensile failure normal to the line of action of the force
- tensile failure of the body of the lug

plus it is necessary to check

- pin bearing
- attachment of the lugs to the beam

*Upper lug*

Shear out

First, ignoring the donuts, we consider two shear planes of area = the plate thickness x the min distance from the hole to the head

$f_q$ = 500x10³ / 2x38x95 = 69.3 N/mm², $p_q$ per BS449 is 100 N/mm² OK

Tension across pin hole

$f_t$ = 500x10³ / 2x38x95 = 69.3 N/mm², $p_t$ per BS449 is 155 N/mm² OK

Tensile area of body < tensile area across hole, so OK

Pin bearing = 500x10³ / 70x76 = 94 N/mm², $p_b$ = 190 N/mm²

Weld donut to plate requires to carry ¹/₄ th of 500 kN = 125 kN

Weld length is π x 190 = 597 mm², therefore weld needs to be good for 0.2 kN/mm,

6 leg weld in grd 43 is rated for 0.48 kN/mm (at 115 N/mm²), use 6 mm (1/4" leg fillet weld)

Weld of lug to web is full penetration, web thickness is 14.1 mm, each weld length is approx 600 mm.

Max Q coming from one side = 300 kN carried by one weld

$f_q$ = 300x10³ / 14.1x600 = 35.5 N/mm², $p_q$ = 100 N/mm² OK.

*Lower lug*

Shear out

Firstly ignoring the donuts, we consider two shear planes of area = the plate thickness x the min distance from the hole to the head

$f_q$ = 300x10$^3$ / 2x30x77 = 64.9 N/mm$^2$, $p_q$ per BS449 is 100 N/mm$^2$ OK

Tension across pin hole

$f_t$ = 300x10$^3$ / 2x30x77 = 64.9 N/mm$^2$, $p_t$ per BS449 is 155 N/mm$^2$ OK

Tensile area of body < tensile area across hole, so OK

Pin bearing = 300x10$^3$ / 60x57 = 87.7 N/mm$_2$, $p_b$ = 190 N/mm$^2$

Weld donut to plate requires to carry $^1/_4$$^{th}$ of 300 kN = 75 kN

Weld length is π x 152 = 477 mm, therefore weld needs to be good for 75 kN / 477 mm = 0.16 kN/mm,

4 leg weld in grd 43 is rated for 0.32 kN/mm (at 115 N/mm$^2$), use 4 mm ($^5/_{32}$" leg fillet weld)

Weld of lug to web is full penetration, web thickness is 14.1 mm, each weld length is approx 285 mm.

Max Q = 300 kN carried by two welds

$f_q$ = 300x10$^3$ / 2x14.1x285 = 37.3 N/mm$^2$, $p_q$ = 100 N/mm$^2$ OK.

*Conclusion*

The draft design checks out to BS449 and can be detailed on this basis.

Note: The consequence of not line boring the hole through the complete lug.

Figure 12-11

Figure 12-12

The holes in the three plates (web and 2 extra shear plates/doublers) this shackle pin had to fit through in this load test frame were not in-line machined and didn't (quite) line up. The big hammer wasn't enough to solve it. After much hand grinding of the hole (and lost time) it was made to fit. Note wide-body shackle used.

### 12.2.6 Example beam design to ASME B30.20 BTH-1

Working the above example in U.S. Customary Units (USCU) to BTH-1.

Let us consider a lifting beam such as the one used above to lift the small Turbine. It weighs 77.175 kips (35 t). To give some reserve, we'll choose to conservatively design the beam for a rated Safe Working Load of 88.2 kips. We know where the C of G is and the Turbine is provided with lift attachments 6'-6¾" (78.75") to one side and 9'-10⅛" (118.125") to the other. The material we are going to use is A36 with 36 ksi yield. This beam falls within the criteria for Category A lifters, so require design factors of 2.0 for yielding and buckling and 2.4 for fracture and connections.

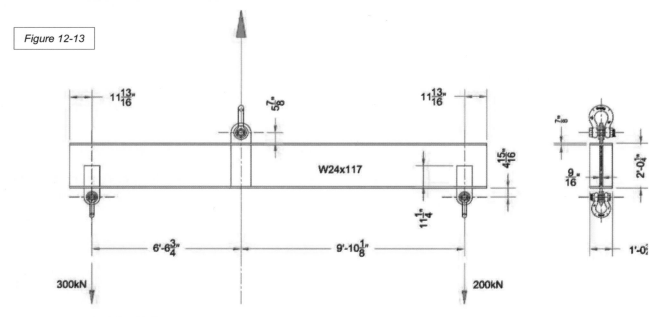

Figure 12-13

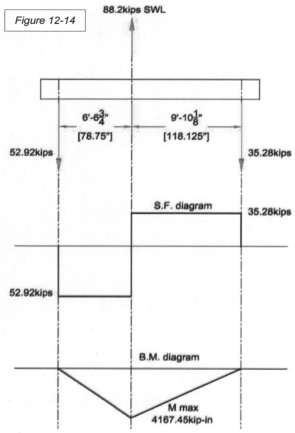

Figure 12-14

The beam proposed is a W24x117 beam section which is virtually identical to the 610x305 x179 kg/m UB proposed above.

Properties of the W24 beam section are as follows:

- Area $A = 34.4in^2$
- Depth $d = 24.3in$
- Web thickness $t_w = 0.55in$
- Flange width $b_f = 12.8in$
- Flange thickness $t_f = 0.85in$
- Clear web depth $T = 20.75in$
- Compact section criteria $bf/2tf = 7.53$, $h/tw = 39.2$
- Moment of inertia $I_{xx} = 3540in^4$
- Section modulus $S_{xx} = 291in^3$
- Radius of gyration $rxx = 10.1in$
- Plastic modulus $Z_{xx} = 327in^3$
- Moment of inertia $I_{yy} = 297in^4$
- Section modulus $S_{yy} = 46.5in^3$
- Radius of gyration $r_{yy} = 2.94in$
- Plastic modulus $Z_{yy} = 71.4in^3$

The beam is to be rated at 88,200# (88.2 kips)

The LH lug sees 88.2x118.125 / (78.75+118.125) = 52.92 kips

The RH lug sees the remainder = 88.2 - 52.92 = 35.28 kips

Max shear force (design) = 52.92 kips

Beam bending

For a beam formed from a rolled section to be considered "compact" for bending, it's (half) flange width / thickness ratio ($b_f/2t_f$) must not exceed:

$0.38\sqrt{E/F_y}$, where E=the modulus of elasticity = 29,000 ksi (200,000 MPa or N/mm$^2$) and $F_y$ = the minimum yield stress for the steel to be used, in this case A36 with min yield = 36 ksi

$0.38\sqrt{E/F_y} = 0.38\sqrt{29000/36} = 10.8$; from above $b_f/2t_f$ = 7.53, $\therefore$ flange is OK

Its clear web height / thickness ratio ($h/t_w$) must not exceed:

$3.76\sqrt{E/F_y} = 3.76\sqrt{29000/36} = 107$; from above $h/t_w$ = 39.2, $\therefore$ web is OK,

$\therefore$ section can be considered "compact".

Note: the vast majority of all current ASTM W shapes have compact flanges for Fy $\leq$ 50 ksi (350 MPa), the few are very lightweight sections; all have compact webs. We could have avoided this step.

$L_p$, the maximum laterally unbraced length (in) of a bending member for which the full plastic bending capacity can be realized, is given by:

$L_p = 1.76r_y\sqrt{E/F_y} = 1.76 \times 2.94\sqrt{29000/36} = 147$ in

As our beam is unbraced at approximately 197 in long we cannot use the full plastic bending capacity and need to check out the next limiting condition $L_r$.

$L_r$, the laterally unbraced length of a bending member above which the limit state will be lateral-torsional buckling is given by:

$L_r = \sqrt{(3.19r_T^2EC_b/F_y)}$, where $r_T$ is the radius of gyration of a section comprising the compression flange plus one 1/3rd of the compression web area taken about an axis in the plane of the web.

$r_T$ can be approximated accurately and conservatively as:

$r_T = b_f/\sqrt{12(1 + (ht_w/6b_ft_f))}$, where $b_f$ = flange width, $t_f$ = flange thickness, h = height of web, $t_w$ = thickness of web

$r_T = \dfrac{12.8}{\sqrt{12\left(1 + \left(\frac{(22.6 \times 0.55)}{(6 \times 12.8 \times 0.85)}\right)\right)}} = 3.39$ in

$C_b$ may be taken conservatively as unity.

$\therefore L_r = \sqrt{(3.19 \times 3.39^2 \times 29000 \times 1/ 36)} = 172$ in,

As our beam is unbraced at approximately 197' long we cannot use the simple yield stress over design factor formula $F_b = F_y/N_d$ and will be limited by lateral buckling conditions and formulae.

Per BTH-1 formula (3-13), if $\left(\sqrt{(3.19EC_b/F_y)}\right) \leq L_b/r_T \leq \left(\sqrt{(17.59EC_b/F_y)}\right)$ then the permissible compressive bending stress is the larger of the values given by formulae (3-14) or (3-17). If $L_b/r_T$ is > the RH term above, then it is the larger of the values given by (3-16) or (3-17) that applies.

Check out $L_b/r_T$ versus the conditions given in formula (3-13)

$L_b$, the unbraced length in our case is equal to the distance between the lift lugs = 197 in, $r_T$ = 3.39 in

$\therefore L_b / r_T = 197/3.39 = 58.1$

$\sqrt{(3.19EC_b/F_y)} = \sqrt{(3.19 \times 29000 \times 1/36)} = 50.7$

$$\sqrt{(17.59EC_b/F_y)} = \sqrt{(17.59 \times 29000 \times 1/36)} = 119$$

∴ Our condition falls within the conditions given in (3-13), so the permissible bending stress is the larger of the values given by (3-14) or (3-17)

Formula BTH-1 (3-14),

$F_b = (1.10 - (F_y(L_b/r_T)^2 / 31.9EC_b) ) F_y/N_d$

$F_b = (1.10 - (36x(197/3.39)^2/(31.9x29000x1))) \times F_y/N_d$

$F_b = (1.10 - 0.13) \times F_y/N_d = 0.97 F_y/N_d$ ; it cannot be greater than $F_y/N_d$ (and isn't)

$0.97 F_y/N_d = 0.97x36/2 = 17.46$ ksi

∴ The permitted bending stress (elastic) is 17.46 ksi per (3-14)

Formula BTH-1 (3-17):

$F_b = 0.66EC_b / N_d(Lb_d/A_f) \leq F_y/N_d$ , where $A_f$ is the area of the compression flange.

$F_b = 0.66 \times 29000 \times 1 / 2x(197x24.3/12.8x0.85) = 21.8$ ksi, which is greater than $F_y/N_d$, ∴ $F_y/N_d$ governs

$F_y/N_d = 36/2 = 18$ ksi

∴ $F_b$ is governed by the RH term of (3-17) and is 18 ksi

We have a max B.M. of 4167 kip-in and a section modulus = 291 in$^3$

$F_{b (compressive)} = M_{max} / S_{xx} = 14.3$ ksi, which is $0.79P_b$, OK

<u>Beam shear</u>

The average shear stress on unstiffened plates for which $h/t \leq 2.45 \sqrt{E/F_y}$ shall not exceed $f_v = F_y/N_d\sqrt{3}$

$h/t = 39.2; \ 2.45\sqrt{29000/36} = 69.5$

∴ h/t is less than the criteria and $f_v = F_y/N_d\sqrt{3}$ applies, $N_d = 2.0$ for a Category A lifter (3-1.3)

$f_v = F_y/N_d\sqrt{3} = 36/(2x1.732) = 10.4$ ksi (max permitted)

$f_v = 52.92 / (24.3 x 0.55) = 3.96$ ksi  OK

<u>Lugs - upper</u>

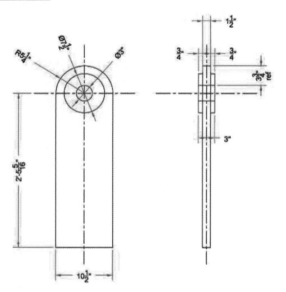
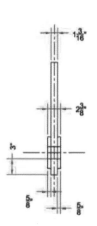
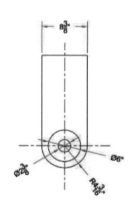

**Upper lug**

Lower lug

Figure 12-15

Static Strength of the Plates; per BTH-1, the strength of a pin-connected plate in the region of the pin hole shall be taken as the least value of:

— the tensile strength of the effective area on a plane through the center of the pin hole perpendicular to the line of action of the applied load,

— the fracture strength beyond the pin hole on a single plane parallel to the line of action of the applied load and,

— the double plane shear strength beyond the pin hole parallel to the line of action of the applied load.

The allowable tensile strength through the pin hole Pt shall be calculated as follows:

$$P_t = C_r(F_u/1.2N_d)2tb_{eff}$$

where:

$b_{eff}$ = effective width to each side of the pin hole

$$C_r = 1 - 0.275\sqrt{\left(1 - (D_p^2/D_h^2)\right)}$$

where:

$D_h$ = hole diameter

$D_p$ = pin diameter

The value of $C_r$ may be taken as 1.00 for values of $D_p/D_h$ greater than 0.90 – this will generally be the case if following the guidelines herein.

The effective width shall be taken as the smaller of the values calculated as follows.

$$b_{eff} \leq 4t \leq b_e$$

$$b_{eff} \leq b_e 0.6 \frac{F_u}{F_y}\sqrt{\frac{D_h}{b_e}} \leq b_e$$

In our example, $C_r$ = 1, $F_u$ = 58 ksi, $N_d$ = 2,

For the upper lug, t = 1.5 in, $b_e$ = 3.75 in

$$b_{eff} \leq 4 \times 1.5 \leq 3.75$$

Hence $b_{eff}$ = $b_e$ = 3.75 in (per the first condition)

$$b_{eff} \leq 3.75 \times 0.6 \frac{58}{36}\sqrt{\frac{3}{3.75}} \leq 3.75$$

$$b_{eff} \leq 3.24 \leq 3.75 \text{ in (per the second condition)}$$

∴ this is the limiting condition, $b_{eff}$ = 3.24 in

$P_t$ = 1 x (58/1.2x2) x 2 x 1.5 x 3.24 = 235 kips; (versus 88.2 kips rating)

The allowable single plane fracture strength beyond the pin hole $P_b$ is:

$$P_b = C_r \frac{F_u}{1.2N_d}\left[1.13\left(R - \frac{D_h}{2}\right) + \frac{0.92b_e}{1 + b_e/D_h}\right]t$$

Where R is the distance from the center of the hole to the edge of the plate in the direction of the applied load.

In our example, $F_u$ = 58 ksi, $N_d$ = 2, R = 5.25 in, $D_h$ = 3 in, $b_e$ = 3.24 in, $C_r$ = 1

$$P_b = 1.0 \left(\frac{58}{1.2 \times 2}\right)\left[1.13\left(5.25 - \frac{3}{2}\right) + \frac{0.92 \times 3.24}{1 + (3.24/3)}\right] \times 1.5$$

$P_b$ = 205.6 kips; (versus 88.2 kips rating)

The allowable double plane shear strength beyond the pin hole $P_v$ is:

$$P_v = \frac{0.7F_u}{1.2N_d} A_v$$

Where $A_v$ = total area of two shear planes beyond the pinhole

$$A_v = 2\left[a + \frac{D_p}{2}(1 - \cos \emptyset)\right]t$$

Where a is the distance from the edge of the pinhole to the edge of the plate in the direction of the applied load and $\emptyset = 55D_p/D_h$

In our example, $D_p$ = 2.75 in, $D_h$ = 3.00 in

$\emptyset$ = 55x2.75/3.00 = 50.4°

$$A_v = 2\left[3.75 + \frac{2.75}{2}(1 - \cos 55)\right] \times 1.5 = 13.00 \text{ in}^2$$

Note: Conservatively, you could take Av = 2at

$$P_v = \frac{0.7 \times 58}{1.2 \times 2} \times 13 = 219.9 \text{ kips}$$

The governing condition is $P_b$, which limits the permitted force to 205.6 kips (versus 88.2 kips rating).

*Note, that the doublers were not considered in the strength calculation.*

We also need to check bearing; this is not a strength limit, but we want to control deformation. $F_p$ is the bearing stress between the plate and pin based on the projected area of the pin.

For connections that are not required to rotate under load for a large number of cycles;

$$F_{p\,max} = \frac{1.25F_y}{N_d} \text{ (ksi)} \quad = \frac{1.25 \times 36}{2} \quad = 22.5 \text{ ksi}$$

$$F_{p\,actual} = \frac{88.2}{3 \times 2.75} \text{ (based on full width)} = 10.7 \text{ ksi}$$

$\therefore$ the top lug design satisfies BTH-1 with ample reserves

Lugs – lower

Check allowable tensile strength $P_t$ through the pin hole.

The effective width shall be taken as the smaller of the values calculated as follows.

$$b_{eff} \leq 4t \leq b_e$$

$$b_{eff} \leq b_e 0.6\frac{F_u}{F_y}\sqrt{\frac{D_h}{b_e}} \leq b_e$$

In our example, $C_r$ = 1, $F_u$ = 58 ksi, $N_d$ = 2,

For the lower lug, t = 1.25 in, $b_e$ = 3.00 in

$$b_{eff} \leq 4 \times 1.25 \leq 3.00$$

Hence $b_{eff} = b_e = 3.00$ in (per first condition)

$$b_{eff} \leq 3.00 \times 0.6 \frac{58}{36}\sqrt{\frac{2.375}{3.00}} \leq 3.00 \text{ in}$$

$b_{eff} \leq 2.58 \leq 3.00$ (per the second condition)

$\therefore$ this is the limiting condition, $b_{eff} = 2.58$ in

$P_t = 1 \times (58/1.2 \times 2) \times 2 \times 1.25 \times 2.58 = 155$ kips; (versus 52.9 kips rating)

The allowable single plane fracture strength beyond the pin hole $P_b$ is:

$$P_b = C_r \frac{F_u}{1.2 N_d}\left[1.13\left(R - \frac{D_h}{2}\right) + \frac{0.92 b_e}{1 + b_e/D_h}\right] t$$

where R is the distance from the center of the hole to the edge of the plate in the direction of the applied load. In our example, $F_u = 58$ ksi, $N_d = 2$, R = 4.19 in, $D_h = 2.375$ in, $b_e = 2.58$ in, Cr = 1

$$P_b = 1.0 \times \frac{58}{1.2 \times 2}\left[1.13\left(4.19 - \frac{2.375}{2}\right) + \frac{0.92 \times 2.58}{1 + (2.58/2.375)}\right] \times 1.25$$

$P_b = 136.9$ kips; (versus 52.9 kips rating)

The allowable double plane shear strength beyond the pin hole $P_v$ is:

$$P_v = \frac{0.7 F_u}{1.2 N_d} A_v$$

Where $A_v$ = total area of two shear planes beyond the pinhole

$$A_v = 2\left[a + \frac{D_p}{2}(1 - \cos\emptyset)\right] t$$

Where a is the distance from the edge of the pinhole to the edge of the plate in the direction of the applied load and $\emptyset = 55 D_p/D_h$

In our example, $D_p = 2.25$ in, $D_h = 2.50$ in

$\emptyset = 55 \times 2.25/2.50 = 49.5°$

$$A_v = 2\left[3.00 + \frac{2.25}{2}(1 - \cos 49.5)\right] \times 1.25 = 8.49 \text{ in}^2$$

$$P_v = \frac{0.7 \times 58}{1.2 \times 2} \times 8.49 = 143.6 \text{ kips}$$

The governing condition is $P_b$, which limits the permitted force to 136.9 kips (versus 52.9 kips rating).

*Note, that the doublers were not considered in the strength calculation.*

We also need to check bearing; this is not a strength limit, but we want to control deformation. $F_p$ is the bearing stress between the plate and pin based on the projected area of the pin.

For connections that are not required to rotate under load for a large number of cycles;

$$F_{p\,max} = \frac{1.25 F_y}{N_d} \text{ (ksi)} = \frac{1.25 \times 36}{2} = 22.5 \text{ ksi}$$

$$F_{p\,actual} = \frac{52.9}{2.5 \times 2.25} \text{ (based on full width)} = 9.4 \text{ ksi}$$

$\therefore$ the lower lug design satisfies BTH-1 with ample reserves.

## Conclusion

The design checks out conservatively versus BTH-1 but is not highly efficient in material use. If I was to make these commercially I should want to refine it. The analysis suggests that designing conservatively using BTH-1 principles and an elastic code will also yield a sound result, probably with a lot less design steps.

## 12.3 Spreader bars

What is a spreader bar as against a lift beam?

Figure 12-16

- A spreader (bar) is a structural member used to hold apart two inclined slings, allowing 2 vertical slings to be turned and combined together for attachment to say a crane hook
- Typically the vectors acting on it are inclined above and are vertical below; the spreader resists the equal and opposite horizontal components of the inclined vectors, acting primarily in compression
- Like a lift beam it can be used to combine or split forces equally or unequally
- Also like lift beams, multiple spreaders can be cascaded combining differing forces from multiple vertical lift lugs up to a single support point
- As a compression member it has relatively light weight
- As it requires inclined slings at a minimum 45° angle, it has a longer suspension length (height) than the equivalent lift beam
- As the "hinge" point where the inclined slings meet is relatively high, it provides a stable arrangement that will lift closer to level for a given inaccuracy in locating the C of G

This 300 t Generator is being lifted and placed using a 3-spreader arrangement. The crane's lifting effort is firstly split in two to suit the longitudinal spacing of the lifting points, allowing for any offset of the C of G in that direction and adjusting inclined sling lengths to suit. It appears central as no extra shackles are used. A second tier of spreaders is then used at 90° to the first to further split the loads two ways to suit the lateral centers of the lifting points. Again the C of G is central in that direction. Four basketed slings are used to cradle the lifting trunnions. As this whole systems can articulate at the hinge points and equalize out, you are assured with an arrangement such as this that all slings will carry the intended proportion of total load regardless of slight discrepancies in sling lengths and the like.

### 12.3.1 Different types of spreaders

Conventional spreaders

With the majority of spreaders, the suspension slings are discontinuous at the spreader, i.e. you have (essentially) vertical slings below the spreader to the load and separate inclined slings above the spreader to the crane hook (or other) suspension point. They would ideally never be flatter than 45° to the horizontal and preferably 60° or better. In the purest form, the lines of action of the slings intersect on the axis of the spreader, ensuring the spreader is loaded axially in pure compression (no bending induced). Most usually, the attachment of the slings to the spreader is by means of shackles, although link plates and/or sheaves may be used. This typical arrangement is as shown in the picture above – Versabar end caps and pipe inserts are used.

Note: As the forces in the inclined slings see a greater force than the vertical slings (+15.5% at 60°, +41.4% at 45° to the horizontal), the upper shackles are often a size greater than the lower ones.

Unless you exactly know the angle at which the inclined slings will operate and it always remains the same, the only way in which you can be sure the forces will intersect at a common point regardless of angle is to place the upper (shackle) pins at that intersection point, so the inclined slings hinge around that point. The lower slings being vertical (or very close to it) can be pinned anywhere along the line of action of the force without fundamentally changing the point of intersection.

Typically a single plate will be used with holes in it for the upper and lower shackles providing a continuous load path with no structural joints; it will be sized according to the same principles outlined in the preceding section as the considerations are the same as for lift lugs.

The plates need to be mated to a suitable compression member to resist the horizontal components of the inclined sling forces. If making a fixed length spreader for a specific purpose, you might simply let the plate end-on into the end of a suitable pipe section with adequate weld to transfer the compressive force into the pipe. Many spreader arrangements are designed for multiple uses at variable lengths, so it is common practice to design the end plates and transitions as node assemblies that can be mated to suitable compression members of varying (or variable) length. A large variety of proprietary spreader designs are available, from a number of suppliers. You are encouraged to investigate the links at the start of this section.

Unless the span is large the bending stresses in the spreader due to its self-weight are usually insignificant and it can be sized for the compression forces alone. This is not necessarily so for very long spreaders. Deflection (sag) due to self-weight (or joints) in long spreaders needs to be considered as it will cause the compression force to act eccentrically to the centroid of the member at mid span causing bending moments that will reduce the compression capacity of the member.

As regards compression members; one of the most convenient solutions for general use spreaders is to use a pipe (tube / round hollow) section. Pipes are available in a wide variety of diameters and wall thicknesses; they have uniform properties in all directions which make them very efficient as compression members and keeps them light. The end assemblies can be made to slip over the pipe end and the pipe cut to length to suit; alternatively the end assemblies may be flanged; the pipe is similarly flanged to form inserts of varying lengths to can be selected to give the required span. Rolled column sections or box sections are sometimes used. Square or rectangular hollow or box sections may be used; there are adjustable designs in which the pipe or hollow section used at one end is smaller than that used at the other allowing one to slide inside the other and be pinned at the required extension. See later.

Figure 12-17

To the left is a (very) heavy duty MorBar offered by Holloway Houston. The green items are the end "caps". The grey item is the pipe insert over which the end caps slip. As the forces are compressive only light weight retention of the caps is required.

The lower shackle hole is on a separate drop link plate whose upper hole is pinned in the end cap using the (wide body) shackles provided for the inclined slings.

Note that everything comes to a node point on the axis of the spreader.

You may be able to rent proprietary spreaders suitable for your needs more economically than making or purchasing one. They will all come fully load tested.

For all spreaders, you want to keep the compression load as concentric as possible; for that reason, you don't want the compression element to sag under its self-weight very much, so deflection is a consideration. Selecting a pipe size for the capacity required at the span intended requires a balance of diameter and wall thickness. You also might consider using a lattice section such as a light crane jib section with suitable ends as the compression member if a very long / heavy spreader is required.

<u>Selecting a proprietary spreader</u>

As with every piece of rigging, spreaders have a rating. Modulift, for instance, offers a range of models of off-the-shelf spreaders to similar (scaled up or down) designs; the following selection chart is an aid to determining which spreader type is required. It gives Safe Working Loads versus span (in tonnes and metres). Select a span and a SWL; the colored area in which they intersect indicates the system required.

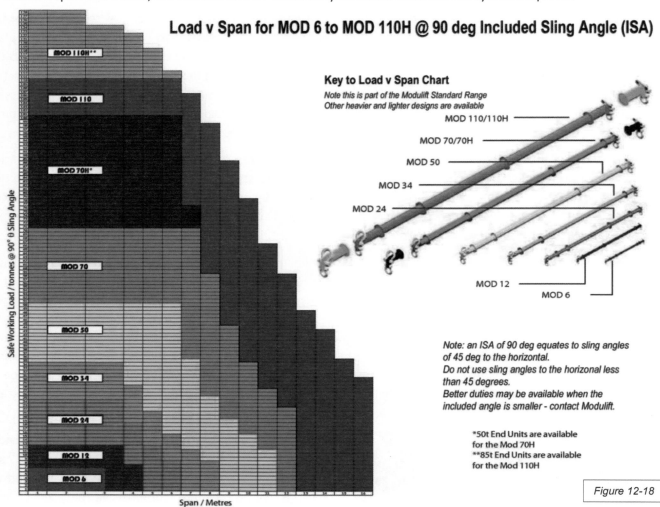

Figure 12-18

These types have a design limitation for the end assemblies and limitations on the pipe determined by compressive strength (at short spans) or buckling at longer spans.

The compressive force induced in the spreader is a function of inclined sling angle as well as sling tension. So spreader capacity is related not only to load and span but also to sling angle. Typically, manufacturers will provide capacity graphs / charts for 60° and 45° angles (to the horizontal), some also offer 30°. Note that the above selection chart (Fig 12-18) is for slings at 45° to horizontal or vertical.  All manufacturers will be able to provide similar information for their products.

Note: the US practice has always been to been to quote sling angles to the horizontal, some regions of the world traditionally use angles to the vertical or the included sling angle (ISA) at the top – make sure you carefully check that point when reading capacities.

Sample Modulift 70H specifications.

Following is some sample information relating to the Modulift 70H.

Note that a long span may dictate the use of a heavy pipe but the matching ends may be overkill for the rated capacity at those long spans. Modulift offer lighter, reduced capacity end units for use with the MOD100 & MOD70 ranges in such cases. This helps to minimize the rigging weight.

The Modulift Spreader is modular in length. Every spreader consists of 1 pair of End Units & Drop Links, with intermediate struts that can be bolted into the assembly to achieve different spans. The MOD 70H has an assembled span ranging from 1 metre to 12 metres in 0.5 metre increments.

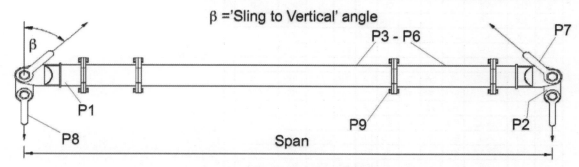

β ='Sling to Vertical' angle

Typical Spreader Assembly.

| TABLE 1: COMPONENT LIST | | |
|---|---|---|
| PART REF: | DESCRIPTION | WEIGHT / ITEM |
| P1 | END UNIT | 58kg |
| P2 | DROP LINK | 32kg |
| P3 | 4.0m STRUT | 240kg |
| P4 | 2.0m STRUT | 136kg |
| P5 | 1.0m STRUT | 85kg |
| P6 | 0.5m STRUT | 61kg |
| P7 | 85t SHACKLE | 62kg |
| P8 | 55t SHACKLE | 40kg |
| P9 | M20x65, GRADE 8.8 HT BOLTS, NUTS & WASHERS | |

STRUT

DROP LINK

END UNIT SUB-ASSY

Larger shackle

Drop Link

Smaller shackle

MOD 70H - Beam specification.

- 'Sling to vertical' angle, β, 45 degrees or less.
- End Units & Drop Links are rated at 50 tonnes WLL each (100 tonnes combined capacity).

*Figure 12-18a*

Note the Modulift spreader design incorporates drop links to which the lower shackles are pinned. The links are retained by the upper shackle pins and can articulate +/- 6 degrees from the vertical about the upper shackle pin. The design ensures that no moment is induced in the end cap even if the lower vertical slings are not truly plumb.

## Modulift 70H Load v Span Table – for example only, do not use!

Figure 12-19

### MOD 70H Load v Span

| 45° STV | | | Recommended Configuration. EU - End Unit (0.5m) STV = 'Sling to Verticle' angle, β | | | | | | 30° STV | | |
|---|---|---|---|---|---|---|---|---|---|---|---|
| Span /m | SWL /t | Min Top Sling Length/m | | | | | | | Span /m | SWL /t | Min Top Sling Length/m |
| 1 | 100 | 0.7 | EU | EU | | | | | 1 | 100 | 1.0 |
| 1.5 | 100 | 1.1 | EU | 0.5 | EU | | | | 1.5 | 100 | 1.5 |
| 2 | 100 | 1.5 | EU | 1 | EU | | | | 2 | 100 | 2.0 |
| 2.5 | 100 | 1.8 | EU | 1 | 0.5 | EU | | | 2.5 | 100 | 2.5 |
| 3 | 100 | 2.2 | EU | 2 | EU | | | | 3 | 100 | 3.0 |
| 3.5 | 100 | 2.5 | EU | 2 | 0.5 | EU | | | 3.5 | 100 | 3.5 |
| 4 | 100 | 2.9 | EU | 2 | 1 | EU | | | 4 | 100 | 4.0 |
| 4.5 | 100 | 3.2 | EU | 0.5 | 2 | 1 | EU | | 4.5 | 100 | 4.5 |
| 5 | 100 | 3.6 | EU | 2 | 2 | EU | | | 5 | 100 | 5.0 |
| 5.5 | 100 | 3.9 | EU | 2 | 2 | 0.5 | EU | | 5.5 | 100 | 5.5 |
| 6 | 100 | 4.3 | EU | 2 | 2 | 1 | EU | | 6 | 100 | 6.0 |
| 6.5 | 88 | 4.6 | EU | 0.5 | 2 | 2 | 1 | EU | 6.5 | 100 | 6.5 |
| 7 | 76 | 5.0 | EU | 2 | 2 | 2 | EU | | 7 | 100 | 7.0 |
| 7.5 | 67 | 5.3 | EU | 0.5 | 2 | 2 | 2 | EU | 7.5 | 100 | 7.5 |
| 8 | 58 | 5.7 | EU | 2 | 2 | 2 | 1 | EU | 8 | 100 | 8.0 |
| 8.5 | 51 | 6.0 | EU | 0.5 | 1 | 4 | 2 | EU | 8.5 | 89 | 8.5 |
| 9 | 44 | 6.4 | EU | 4 | 4 | EU | | | 9 | 77 | 9.0 |
| 9.5 | 39 | 6.8 | EU | 4 | 4 | 0.5 | EU | | 9.5 | 68 | 9.5 |
| 10 | 34 | 7.1 | EU | 4 | 4 | 1 | EU | | 10 | 59 | 10.0 |
| 10.5 | 30 | 7.5 | EU | 1 | 4 | 4 | 0.5 | EU | 10.5 | 53 | 10.5 |
| 11 | 27 | 7.8 | EU | 2 | 4 | 4 | EU | | 11 | 47 | 11.0 |
| 11.5 | 25 | 8.2 | EU | 2 | 4 | 4 | 0.5 | EU | 11.5 | 43 | 11.5 |
| 12 | 22 | 8.5 | EU | 2 | 4 | 4 | 1 | EU | 12 | 38 | 12.0 |

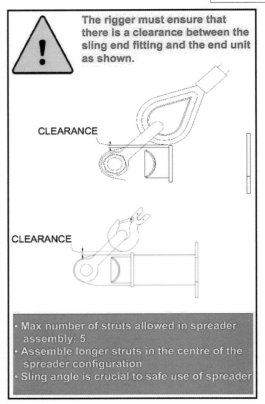

The rigger must ensure that there is a clearance between the sling end fitting and the end unit as shown.

CLEARANCE

CLEARANCE

- Max number of struts allowed in spreader assembly: 5
- Assemble longer struts in the centre of the spreader configuration
- Sling angle is crucial to safe use of spreader

## Variations on the pipe and cap theme

Using custom corner end caps and intermediate connectors with pipe inserts, custom lifting frames may be assembled on similar principles. The system pictured was provided by Carol Crane & Rigging.

Figure 12-20

In this case, the module had 15 lift points at the column tops, all of which required vertical suspension.

The upper level of the suspension was a simple pipe spreader with end caps. This provides 2 suspension points centrally over the 6 points in each of the end bays. A frame was formed at each end to pick up on the 6 points. Each comprised 4 corner pieces (in which the suspension attachment plates are orientated to the center of pick) picking up on the outer 4 points, and 2 intermediate connectors for the central 2 points, together with pipe inserts. The suspension is 4 slings from the corners inclined in 2 planes pyramid fashion to the end of the primary spreader and 2 slings inclined in one plane from the intermediate connectors to the same point.

The central 3 points are supported using a separate conventional spreader direct to the crane hook to pick up the outer 2 points; the central point is taken directly from the hook through an intermediate connector. Turnbuckles are used throughout to get the suspension lengths correct.

## Fixed length custom spreader

Figure 12-21

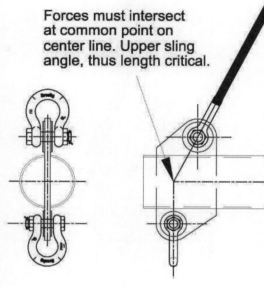

**Forces must intersect at common point on center line. Upper sling angle, thus length critical.**

Figure 12-22

A simple solution for a custom spreader for a specific use is to slot a plate (with holes for the upper and lower shackles) through a pipe and weld it up.

Knowing the sling lengths to be used, the geometry can (and must) be arranged so that the forces intersect on the axis of the pipe.

This 3-spreader rig was supplied with the module. The other holes are for a 2nd module of different length.

## Continuous sling spreaders

All the preceding variations have a node at which the slings are discontinuous; there is a further variation in which there is no node and the spreader truly spreads continuous slings.

There are designs in which the suspension slings are continuous; the ends of the spreader are provided with rounded bearing surfaces over which the vertical slings are diverted to meet the crane hook. Assuming the bearing on the spreader ends to be frictionless, the tension in the suspension slings will be constant and each equal to 50% of the lift weight. The resolution of the vertical and inclined elements of the sling acts inwards and slightly downwards. These downwards components would squeeze the spreader downwards if not resisted. In order to provide this resistance, two smaller holding slings are used from the crane hook shackled to the spreader close to the ends. As with earlier designs the ends including the shackle point are made as assemblies and are flanged; bolted inserts of varying lengths make up the rest of the required span. Rolled column sections are usually used rather than pipe sections.

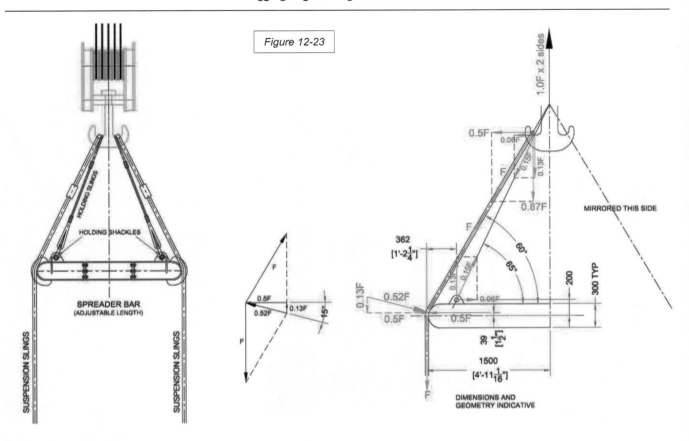

Figure 12-23

The following analysis is indicative only, to illustrate the concepts.

If the sling tension = F, and the sling is diverted through 30° (sling angle is 60° to the horizontal), the force required to hold that situation in equilibrium is a vector = 0.52F acting through the intersection of the forces at -15° to the horizontal. That vector acts through the center of curvature of the end. That force in turn can be resolved into a horizontal component = 0.5F and a vertical (downwards) component of 0.13F. The horizontal forces coming in from either end directly oppose each other in compression. However, unlike the earlier examples, you can note that they do not act on the exact center line of the member but, in this case, 1.5" (39 mm) above it. The 0.13F downward force is resisted in shear through the beam by the equal and opposite vertical component of the holding sling tension. Knowing that and the sling angle, we can determine the holding sling tension to be 0.15F and its horizontal component to be 0.06F.

Taking this up to the crane hook, resolving the main sling force you have a horizontal component of 0.5F acting outwards balanced by the horizontal component of the other main sling, and a vertical component of 0.87F acting downwards resisted by the crane hook. The holding sling resolved applies 0.06F outwards, opposed by the other holding sling horizontal component and 0.13F downwards resisted by the crane hook. Summing the vertical components, the crane hook has to provide 0.87F + 0.13F = F (either side), which = the suspension forces.

The spreader has to resist 0.5F compression (and the small tension force of 0.06F), the moments induced by those forces being offset & 0.13F shear between the end and the holding lug.

This type of spreader has the advantage of requiring less shackles, the load path is direct, the length of the main slings is not critical as you can ring the changes merely by altering the holding sling length. Disadvantages are that you need to de-rate the main slings some according to how tight the bend over the end is, the end bearing is not actually frictionless which possibly loads the holding slings more than the theory suggests, it is not as positive a connection.

As with all spreaders, it will have a capacity chart based on sling angle, vertical load and span. Analysis to derive this is not as straightforward as for other types.

This particular type has bolted inserts; changing length requires unbolting it all and replacing sections.

Note: As a reality check, as we saw above, if the suspension slings were discontinuous the inclined leg (when at 60°) would have 15.5% more tension than the vertical leg. However our slings are continuous, therefore (ignoring friction), the tension is constant and they can't provide that extra force. We are short of sling tension; the holding sling provides that. If directly alongside the inclined leg it would have to provide 15.5% of the vertical force. Giving our geometry it works out at 15%. As a ready-reckoner, when using this type of spreader, you can expect the holding slings to see 15% or so of the vertical force when the sling angles are 60°. Size them more conservatively.

## Pinned spreaders

When making multiple relatively light lifts of varying size it can be a great advantage to use a pinned adjustable length spreader. Changing spans is quick and easy and does not require removal of the rigging.

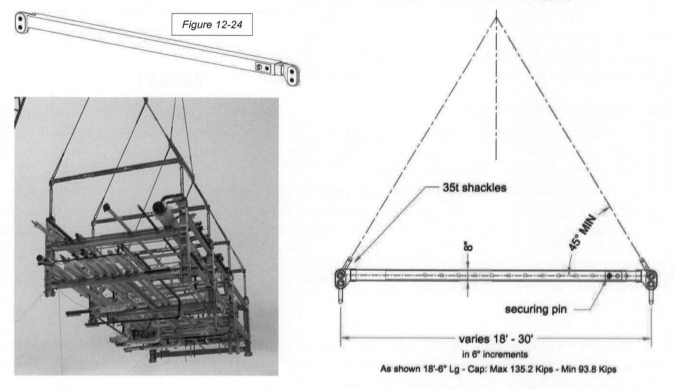

Figure 12-24

35t shackles

8"

45° MIN

securing pin

varies 18' - 30'
in 6" increments
As shown 18'-6" Lg - Cap: Max 135.2 Kips - Min 93.8 Kips

The particular spreader illustrated uses a rectangular rolled hollow section inside a slightly larger one. Holes allow the required extension to be pinned in 6" increments from 18' to 30'. Similar spreaders are available in a range of capacities. Myshak in Canada would be one source. Most rigging supply companies carry something somewhat similar. There are variations that use hydraulic rams to extend and retract them.

### 12.3.2  Design standards for spreaders

Spreaders like lifting beams are structural lifting devices and as such, in the USA, are covered under ASME B30.20 – 2006 "Below the hook lifting devices" and its related design code BTH-1. As noted above, those documents are probably the most practical and comprehensive on the subject and I would recommend that you design in accordance with their principles.

As with lifting beams, spreaders need to be designed with greater factors of safety than regular structural steel design codes provide. Per ASME B30.20 BTH-1, two use-determined design categories are specified. For a spreader with a specific well controlled purpose and limited use, you can use Category A. For every other application including "use-and-abuse" spreaders use Category B. Read BTH-1 carefully for the details.

BTH-1 specifies that:

- Design factors for Design Category A lifting devices shall be not less than 2.00 for limit states of yielding or buckling and 2.40 for limit states of fracture and for connection design.
- Design factors for Design Category B lifting devices shall be not less than 3.00 for limit states of yielding or buckling and 3.60 for limit states of fracture and for connection design.

This is approximately 1.25x and 1.8x respectively more conservative than using a regular structural steel design code.

You have a couple of options, either apply a 1.25x or 1.8x "impact / dynamic" factor to the required rating up front as a factor and then design to that design load using a regular structural code for permissibles or, use BTH-1 with actual required rating using the BTH-1 design factors.

### 12.3.3 Design process

You have to go through a similar process to designing a lifting beam, i.e. establish the required rating and operational parameters, decide if you want it adjustable or fixed length, establish the appropriate design Category, decide what design code to use, figure out the forces (and moments) acting on the spreader in the worst conditions (noting the range of operational parameters).

Compression member selection

- Knowing the span and compression load it has to withstand (possibly some moments and shears also), and the type of service you have in mind, make a judgment as to whether you will be best served using a pipe, rectangular box section or lattice member.
- Decide what steel grade is to be used and hence determine the yield stress and modulus of elasticity.
- With compression members, the concept of "compact" or "non-compact" isn't really applicable. The section will act inelastically (it will fail in compression and/or some buckling) up to a certain critical point defined by its slenderness ratio after which it will buckle elastically, the border being when Kl/r = Cc,

$$C_c = \sqrt{\frac{2\pi^2 E}{F_y}}$$

where K is the effective length factor based on the degree of fixity of the ends (1 if a pin-ended strut), l is the actual unbraced length and r is the radius of gyration of the member about the axis in question. E is the modulus of elasticity (ksi) and $F_y$ is the yield stress of the material. The critical slenderness ratio works out at about 126 for 36 ksi yield material.

- BTH-1 provides two formulae for allowable axial compression stress on gross area Fa; one where the slenderness ratio is less than the critical figure (inelastic); Kl/r<Cc

$$F_a = \frac{\left[1 - \frac{(Kl/r)^2}{2C_c^2}\right] F_y}{N_d \left[1 + \frac{9(Kl/r)}{40C_c} - \frac{3(Kl/r)^3}{40C_c^3}\right]}$$

and the other where it is greater than critical (elastic); Kl/r=>$C_c$

$$F_a = \frac{\pi^2 E}{1.15 N_d (Kl/r)^2}$$

- At the point of Kl/r criticality (126 if A36), the design factor works out at 1.15N$_d$. The formulae give equal results at that point. As Kl/r decreases it tends towards 1N$_d$. As it increases above the threshold, it remains at 1.15N$_d$.

- Some elastic codes will have done the work for you and tabulated it, at least up to 500 mm (20") diameter or so. After that you are on your own to work it out. Start by applying the appropriate 1.25x or 1.8x factor to your required SWL, work out the compression force, then select a section that provides a greater safe load figure. Note that effective length is actual length x the end fixity factor K; for a non-uniform section r is the lesser radius of gyration.

Attachment lug design

Lug design needs to follow the same guidelines as used in the lifting beam section. Note the upper slings will be angled and make sure shackle and sling eye don't foul on the plate or pipe.

### 12.3.4  Sample spreader design

This simple pipe spreader is typical of what you might find on a project for general handling of any number of light items. In this case the boilermakers intended to lift the permanent plant electric hoist up the lifting well into the roof of the boiler building of a coal fired power plant using a tugger. The hoist was supported from beneath and secured to a custom frame provided with four lift lugs. A custom 8' (2.4 m) spreader good for 13.2 tons (12 t) was required.

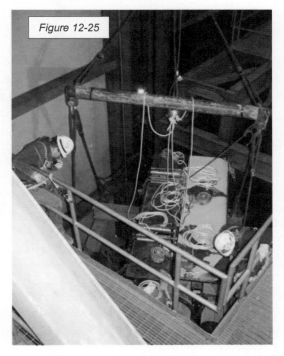

Figure 12-25

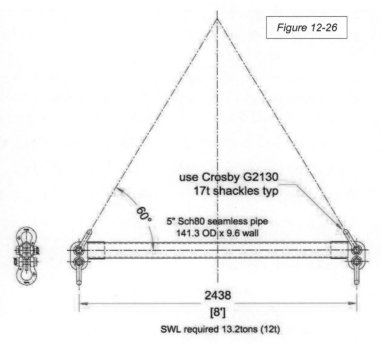

Figure 12-26

use Crosby G2130
17t shackles typ

60°

5" Sch80 seamless pipe
141.3 OD x 9.6 wall

2438
[8']

SWL required 13.2tons (12t)

On the basis of the oversize sling diameters they had available and intended to use, it was decided to specify 17 t shackles; various lengths of pipe were available including a quantity of 5" diameter Schedule 80 seamless (141.2 mm OD x 9.6 mm wall) in A36 equivalent grade. A36 plate was freely available. Inclined slings were available at lengths that would give sling angles of 60° or greater.

In this case, for simplicity, the structural code BS449 was used with BTH-1 conservatism. BS449 is retired but still yields perfectly acceptable results. You could use a current structural code or better still BTH-1.

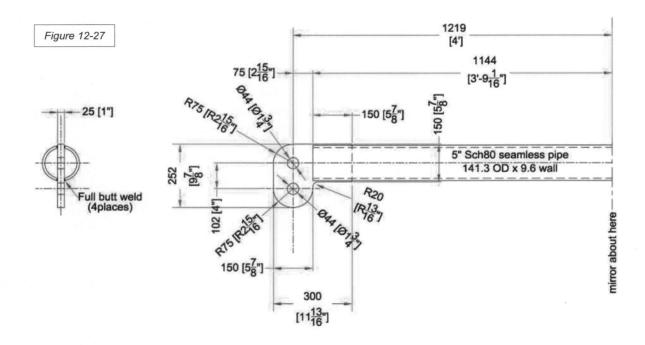

Figure 12-27

The inclined sling forces at 60° (unfactored) = 1.155x120/2 kN = 69.3 kN $\cong$ 7 t, the slings and shackles need to be rated at this as a min, the shackles at 17 t are therefore good. Note slings and shackles are rated at 5:1 safety factor over failure.

It was thought likely that this spreader might be used in the future for other general purposes, so checking it's structural design to Category B criteria was deemed appropriate. We intended to use an elastic code, so a 1.8x factor was applied up front with the intention of then using regular structural permissibles.

With a required rated load of 12 t $\cong$ 120 kN, design load = 1.8x120 = 216 kN $\equiv$ 108 kN per side vertical

The inclined sling forces at 60° (design) = 1.155x108 kN = 125 kN

The compressive force in the spreader (design) = 50% x 125 kN = 62.5 kN

The fixity factor K=1 and l = span = 2.43 m, $\therefore$ effective length = 2.43 m, use 2.5 m

Check compressive strength

To check the capacity of the pipe section in compression, the following table will be used; it tabulates the Safe Compressive Loads per BS449 for steel to BS4360 grade 43 (255 N/mm², or 36 ksi yield), which is closely equivalent to A36.

For checking the rating, use D = 139.7 mm x 8 mm thick wall as the closest (more conservative) metric size).

At 2.5 m effective span, safe axial compressive loading is 441 kN versus our design compression load of 62.5 kN, a factor of 0.14. Therefore compression strength is OK.

## CIRCULAR HOLLOW SECTIONS IN TENSION AND COMPRESSION
Safe axial loads (kN) for BS 4360 grade 43C steel (255N/mm2 yield) per BS449-2:1969
Values shown for l/r < 180

Figure 12-28

| OD (mm) | t (mm) | ID(mm) | A (cm2) | I (cm4) | r (cm) | Max Tensile | 2.5 | 3 | 3.5 | 4 | 4.5 | 5 | 6 | 7 | 8 | 9 | 10 |
|---|---|---|---|---|---|---|---|---|---|---|---|---|---|---|---|---|---|
| 76.1 | 3.2 | 69.7 | 7.33 | 48.8 | 2.58 | 114 | 61 | 46 | 36 | 28 | 33 | | | | | | |
| | 4.0 | 68.1 | 9.06 | 59.1 | 2.55 | 140 | 75 | 56 | 43 | 34 | 36 | | | | | | |
| | 5.0 | 66.1 | 11.17 | 70.9 | 2.52 | 173 | 90 | 68 | 52 | 41 | 43 | | | | | | |
| 88.9 | 3.2 | 82.5 | 8.62 | 79.2 | 3.03 | 134 | 88 | 70 | 55 | 44 | 53 | 29 | | | | | |
| | 4.0 | 80.9 | 10.67 | 96.4 | 3.00 | 165 | 108 | 86 | 67 | 54 | 81 | 36 | | | | | |
| | 5.0 | 78.9 | 13.18 | 116.4 | 2.97 | 204 | 131 | 104 | 82 | 65 | 109 | 43 | | | | | |
| 114.3 | 3.6 | 107.1 | 12.52 | 192 | 3.92 | 194 | 155 | 137 | 116 | 97 | 133 | 68 | 49 | 37 | | | |
| | 5.0 | 104.3 | 17.17 | 257 | 3.87 | 266 | 212 | 186 | 157 | 131 | 183 | 91 | 66 | | | | |
| | 6.3 | 101.7 | 21.38 | 313 | 3.82 | 331 | 262 | 229 | 193 | 160 | 226 | 111 | 80 | | | | |
| 139.7 | 5.0 | 129.7 | 21.16 | 481 | 4.77 | 328 | 284 | 264 | 240 | 212 | 279 | 158 | 117 | 89 | 70 | | |
| | 6.3 | 127.1 | 26.41 | 589 | 4.72 | 409 | 353 | 328 | 297 | 261 | 337 | 194 | 144 | 110 | 86 | | |
| | 8.0 | 123.7 | 33.10 | 720 | 4.66 | 513 | 441 | 409 | 369 | 323 | 276 | 239 | 177 | 134 | 105 | | |
| | 10.0 | 119.7 | 40.75 | 862 | 4.60 | 632 | 541 | 500 | 448 | 391 | 343 | 288 | 213 | 161 | 126 | | |
| 168.3 | 5.0 | 158.3 | 25.65 | 856 | 5.78 | 398 | 359 | 345 | 327 | 303 | 427 | 248 | 194 | 152 | 120 | 97 | 80 |
| | 6.3 | 155.7 | 32.07 | 1054 | 5.73 | 497 | 448 | 430 | 407 | 377 | 521 | 307 | 240 | 187 | 148 | 120 | 98 |
| | 8.0 | 152.3 | 40.29 | 1297 | 5.67 | 625 | 562 | 539 | 509 | 471 | 384 | 381 | 297 | 231 | 183 | 148 | 121 |
| | 10.0 | 148.3 | 49.74 | 1564 | 5.61 | 771 | 693 | 663 | 624 | 576 | 444 | 464 | 360 | 280 | 221 | 178 | 146 |
| 193.7 | 5.4 | 182.9 | 31.95 | 1417 | 6.66 | 495 | 456 | 444 | 428 | 408 | 556 | 355 | 294 | 238 | 192 | 157 | 130 |
| | 6.3 | 181.1 | 37.10 | 1630 | 6.63 | 575 | 529 | 515 | 497 | 473 | 683 | 411 | 340 | 274 | 221 | 180 | 149 |
| | 8.0 | 177.7 | 46.68 | 2016 | 6.57 | 724 | 665 | 647 | 623 | 593 | 835 | 514 | 423 | 340 | 274 | 223 | 185 |
| | 10.0 | 173.7 | 57.72 | 2442 | 6.50 | 895 | 822 | 799 | 768 | 730 | 1,034 | 629 | 516 | 414 | 333 | 271 | 224 |
| | 12.5 | 168.7 | 71.17 | 2935 | 6.42 | 1103 | 1,012 | 982 | 943 | 894 | 539 | 767 | 626 | 501 | 402 | 327 | 270 |
| | 16.0 | 161.7 | 89.33 | 3555 | 6.31 | 1385 | 1,267 | 1228 | 1,177 | 1112 | 677 | 947 | 767 | 611 | 489 | 397 | 328 |
| 219.1 | 6.3 | 206.5 | 42.12 | 2386 | 7.53 | 653 | 609 | 597 | 582 | 563 | 835 | 511 | 444 | 373 | 308 | 255 | 213 |
| | 8.0 | 203.1 | 53.06 | 2960 | 7.47 | 822 | 766 | 751 | 732 | 707 | 1026 | 641 | 555 | 465 | 384 | 317 | 264 |
| | 10.0 | 199.1 | 65.70 | 3599 | 7.40 | 1018 | 948 | 929 | 904 | 873 | 1281 | 789 | 681 | 568 | 468 | 387 | 322 |
| | 12.5 | 194.1 | 81.14 | 4345 | 7.32 | 1258 | 1170 | 1145 | 1114 | 1075 | 1555 | 968 | 832 | 691 | 568 | 468 | 390 |
| | 16.0 | 187.1 | 102.10 | 5297 | 7.20 | 1583 | 1470 | 1438 | 1397 | 1345 | 629 | 1205 | 1029 | 851 | 697 | 574 | 477 |
| | 20.0 | 179.1 | 125.11 | 6262 | 7.07 | 1939 | 1798 | 1757 | 1704 | 1638 | 791 | 1458 | 1237 | 1017 | 830 | 682 | 566 |
| 244.5 | 6.3 | 231.9 | 47.15 | 3346 | 8.42 | 731 | 687 | 677 | 664 | 648 | 978 | 606 | 547 | 477 | 406 | 342 | 289 |
| | 8.0 | 228.5 | 59.45 | 4161 | 8.37 | 921 | 866 | 853 | 837 | 816 | 1206 | 761 | 686 | 596 | 507 | 427 | 360 |
| | 10.0 | 224.5 | 73.68 | 5074 | 8.30 | 1142 | 1072 | 1056 | 1036 | 1010 | 1513 | 940 | 845 | 733 | 621 | 522 | 440 |
| | 12.5 | 219.5 | 91.12 | 6148 | 8.21 | 1412 | 1325 | 1305 | 1279 | 1246 | 1847 | 1157 | 1037 | 896 | 757 | 636 | 535 |
| | 16.0 | 212.5 | 114.87 | 7534 | 8.10 | 1781 | 1669 | 1642 | 1608 | 1566 | 725 | 1449 | 1292 | 1111 | 936 | 784 | 659 |
| | 20.0 | 204.5 | 141.08 | 8958 | 7.97 | 2187 | 2048 | 2013 | 1970 | 1915 | 914 | 1766 | 1566 | 1339 | 1123 | 938 | 787 |
| 273 | 6.3 | 260.4 | 52.79 | 4696 | 9.43 | 818 | 774 | 765 | 755 | 741 | 1132 | 706 | 656 | 593 | 522 | 451 | 388 |
| | 8.0 | 257.0 | 66.61 | 5852 | 9.37 | 1032 | 976 | 965 | 952 | 935 | 1398 | 889 | 825 | 744 | 654 | 565 | 484 |
| | 10.0 | 253.0 | 82.63 | 7155 | 9.31 | 1281 | 1211 | 1197 | 1180 | 1158 | 1760 | 1100 | 1020 | 918 | 804 | 693 | 594 |
| | 12.5 | 248.0 | 102.31 | 8699 | 9.22 | 1586 | 1498 | 1481 | 1459 | 1432 | 2159 | 1358 | 1256 | 1128 | 986 | 848 | 725 |
| | 16.0 | 241.0 | 129.20 | 10708 | 9.10 | 2003 | 1891 | 1868 | 1839 | 1804 | 2632 | 1708 | 1575 | 1408 | 1226 | 1052 | 898 |
| | 20.0 | 233.0 | 158.99 | 12800 | 8.97 | 2464 | 2325 | 2296 | 2259 | 2214 | 890 | 2092 | 1922 | 1710 | 1483 | 1267 | 1080 |
| | 25.0 | 223.0 | 194.80 | 15129 | 8.81 | 3019 | 2846 | 2809 | 2762 | 2704 | 1124 | 2547 | 2329 | 2061 | 1777 | 1513 | 1285 |
| 323.9 | 6.3 | 311.3 | 62.87 | 7930 | 11.23 | 974 | 928 | 921 | 913 | 903 | 1395 | 876 | 839 | 790 | 729 | 659 | 587 |
| | 8.0 | 307.9 | 79.40 | 9911 | 11.17 | 1231 | 1172 | 1164 | 1153 | 1139 | 1727 | 1105 | 1058 | 995 | 917 | 828 | 737 |
| | 10.0 | 303.9 | 98.63 | 12160 | 11.10 | 1529 | 1456 | 1445 | 1431 | 1414 | 2183 | 1371 | 1311 | 1232 | 1134 | 1023 | 909 |
| | 12.5 | 298.9 | 122.30 | 14848 | 11.02 | 1896 | 1805 | 1791 | 1774 | 1753 | 2688 | 1698 | 1622 | 1521 | 1398 | 1258 | 1116 |
| | 16.0 | 291.9 | 154.79 | 18392 | 10.90 | 2399 | 2283 | 2265 | 2243 | 2216 | 3297 | 2144 | 2045 | 1915 | 1754 | 1575 | 1393 |
| | 20.0 | 283.9 | 190.97 | 22142 | 10.77 | 2960 | 2816 | 2793 | 2764 | 2730 | 1251 | 2639 | 2513 | 2346 | 2143 | 1918 | 1692 |
| | 25.0 | 273.9 | 234.79 | 26404 | 10.60 | 3639 | 3460 | 3431 | 3394 | 3350 | 1554 | 3234 | 3072 | 2860 | 2602 | 2319 | 2039 |
| 355.6 | 8.0 | 339.6 | 87.37 | 13203 | 12.29 | 1354 | 1294 | 1286 | 1276 | 1265 | 1927 | 1235 | 1194 | 1141 | 1073 | 992 | 903 |
| | 10.0 | 335.6 | 108.59 | 16226 | 12.22 | 1683 | 1608 | 1598 | 1586 | 1571 | 2438 | 1533 | 1482 | 1415 | 1329 | 1228 | 1115 |
| | 12.5 | 330.6 | 134.75 | 19855 | 12.14 | 2089 | 1995 | 1982 | 1967 | 1948 | 3008 | 1901 | 1836 | 1751 | 1643 | 1515 | 1374 |
| | 16.0 | 323.6 | 170.72 | 24666 | 12.02 | 2646 | 2526 | 2510 | 2490 | 2467 | 3698 | 2405 | 2321 | 2210 | 2069 | 1904 | 1723 |
| | 20.0 | 315.6 | 210.89 | 29796 | 11.89 | 3269 | 3120 | 3099 | 3074 | 3044 | 1805 | 2966 | 2859 | 2717 | 2539 | 2330 | 2103 |
| | 25.0 | 305.6 | 259.69 | 35681 | 11.72 | 4025 | 3840 | 3814 | 3782 | 3744 | 2241 | 3644 | 3507 | 3326 | 3099 | 2834 | 2550 |
| 406.4 | 10.0 | 386.4 | 124.55 | 24479 | 14.02 | 1931 | 1850 | 1841 | 1831 | 1819 | 2840 | 1788 | 1747 | 1693 | 1625 | 1541 | 1442 |
| | 12.5 | 381.4 | 154.70 | 30035 | 13.93 | 2398 | 2297 | 2287 | 2274 | 2259 | 3511 | 2220 | 2167 | 2100 | 2013 | 1908 | 1783 |
| | 16.0 | 374.4 | 196.26 | 37454 | 13.81 | 3042 | 2914 | 2900 | 2884 | 2864 | 4328 | 2813 | 2746 | 2658 | 2546 | 2409 | 2248 |
| | 20.0 | 366.4 | 242.81 | 45438 | 13.68 | 3764 | 3605 | 3587 | 3566 | 3541 | 5430 | 3477 | 3391 | 3279 | 3137 | 2963 | 2760 |
| | 25.0 | 356.4 | 299.59 | 54709 | 13.51 | 4644 | 4446 | 4424 | 4398 | 4366 | 2051 | 4284 | 4175 | 4033 | 3852 | 3630 | 3373 |
| | 32.0 | 342.4 | 376.44 | 66441 | 13.29 | 5835 | 5585 | 5556 | 5521 | 5479 | 2549 | 5373 | 5230 | 5042 | 4804 | 4514 | 4179 |

Note the above table is derived from the following formula:

$$p_C = \frac{\dfrac{Y_s + (\eta + 1)C_O}{2} - \sqrt{\left[\left(\dfrac{Y_s + (\eta + 1)C_O}{2}\right)^2 - Y_s C_O\right]}}{K_2}$$

Where $p_c$ = the permissible average stress, N/mm$^2$

$K_2$ = load factor or co-efficient (taken as 1.7 in BS449)

$Y_s$ = minimum yield stress, N/mm$^2$, (255 N/mm$^2$ in this case)

$$C_o = \text{Euler critical stress} = \frac{\pi^2 E}{(l/r)^2} = \frac{\pi^2 210000}{(l/r)^2} \; N/mm^2$$

$$\eta = 0.3(l/100r)^2$$

l/r = slenderness ratio = effective length / radius of gyration

Knowing $p_c$, (the permissible average stress on gross sectional area of the compression member), the permissible load can be determined by multiplying $p_c$ x the gross sectional area for each section. The results expressed in kN are tabulated.

Check shear out of shackle pins

Max design load = 125 kN, assume 2 shear planes based on min distance hole to head radius

$f_q$ = 125x$10^3$/ 2x25x53 = 47.2 N/mm$^2$, $p_q$ = 115 N/mm$^2$, a factor of 0.41 OK

Check tensile failure of lugs

Apply max load (upper) to min area (lower)

Max design load = 125 kN

$F_t$ = 125x$10^3$/ 2x25x53 = 47.2 N/mm$^2$, $p_t$ = 155 N/mm$^2$, a factor of 0.30 OK

Check pin bearing

Shackle pin diameter = 41.4 mm (17t Crosby G2130)

$f_b$ = 125x$10^3$ / 41.4x25 = 121 N/mm$^2$, $p_b$ = 190 N/mm$^2$, a factor of 0.64 OK

Check weld plate to pipe

Full butt welds are specified

Weld length = 4x150 mm = 600 mm

Weld area = 600x9.6 = 5760 mm$^2$

$p_q$ = 115 N/mm$^2$, $\therefore$ weld is good for 5760x115/1000 kN = 662 kN, compressive force is 62.5 kN, factor = 0.09

Conclusion

This design is more than adequate for the purpose, in fact is rather over-designed. Pin bearing (which isn't a failure mode) governs at 64% of permissible, lug shear governs next at 41%, the shackles are at about 41% of rating. The beam could have been rated at 2x12 t = 24 t, although if doing so adding some donuts to ease pin bearing would be recommended.

## 12.4 Testing and marking of lift beams and spreaders

Note that if you design and manufacture a lifting beam or spreader yourself, you assume the responsibilities of the manufacturer.

Any below the hook lifting device, including devices such as these, needs to be marked with:

- The rated load
- The manufacturers name
- A serial number to identify it
- Self-weight if more than 100 lbs (45 kg)
- Safety labels / instructions

In Europe a CE mark is required.

Some areas of the world require proof load testing before use, others do not. You need to prove the item is fit for service before putting it to use and I would recommend you always proof load test below-the-hook lifting devices whether absolutely required or not. The appropriate over load is 125%.

## 12.5 Using spreaders back to back

There are occasions when you need to convert a narrow vertical 2-leg suspension into a wider 2-leg suspension. You could use a beam to do that or use a pair of spreader bars back to back to achieve the same end.

Shown here is the test lift of a 450 ton overhead crane to 125% using water bags. Carol Crane designed the test arrangement using standard components in a non-standard (but verified) way.

Note that the upper spreader is being used in an unconventional manner; rather than being in compression, it is in tension. This could be a problem for many designs which rely on compression joints. Also, the inclination of the lower links results in the three forces acting on the end cap not intersecting at a common point. This will induce a small amount of bending. If intending to use a spreader in an unconventional manner, the designer / manufacturer must first be consulted.

Figure 12-29

Figure 12-30

Figure 12-31

Where loads such as this turbine require vertical suspension, a rectangular arrangement such as this using 4 spreaders (2 over 2) can be useful.

Note the two crossed wires used to maintain the rectangular plan shape.

Without those wires, a 2 over 2 arrangement like this can "fold up" creating an extremely dangerous situation.

# 13 Slings

The subject of slings, their design, construction, selection, use and maintenance is an enormous topic. However, it is one that is well covered; there is a wealth of information on slings available from manufacturers & industry bodies and within consensus standards and statutory regulations.

Good sources include:

- ASME B30.9 - Slings. This is a US industry safety standard formulated under the general auspices of the American National Standards Institute. Complying with its "shall" provisions and treating it's "shoulds" as "shalls" as far as is possible should keep you in line with OSHA legislation on the subject.
- OSHA Code of Federal Regulations 29 CFR Subpart H §1926.251 Rigging equipment for material handling
- Euronorm standard EN13414 – steel wire rope slings
- LOLER and PUWER regulations (UK)
- The Wire Rope Technical Board and their sponsors – specifically the Wire Rope Sling Users Manual
- Certex
- SLINGMAX® (Catalog and Riggers Handbook)
- United Offshore Services (for heavy hand spliced wire rope slings and grommets primarily for offshore use)
- The Web Sling and Tie-down Association (various publications and manuals)

See also the reference list at the back of this volume.

I propose to concentrate on those aspects of primary interest & concern to persons planning & engineering rigging activities, specifying rigging tackle rather than those that apply primarily to those manufacturing rigging, using it in the field or inspecting it. I will highlight the most common types of slings used in construction; their characteristics, design & construction; the primary considerations to be made when selecting slings and engineering for their use, including factors that affect their usable strength.

When it comes to slings, you have a number of basic choices each with their own characteristics, advantages and disadvantages.

The primary types used in construction are:
- Wire rope slings
- Synthetic rope slings
- Alloy chain slings

Each has its own sub-set of varieties, attachments and so on.

## 13.1 Wire rope slings (single part)

Until more recent times with the advent of synthetic slings, wire rope slings were the most common type used on construction sites. The most basic sling is a length of stranded wire rope terminated at each end with an eye or fitting for attachment purposes. We will start there, and then briefly discuss variations such as endless slings, cable laid slings, braided slings, grommets and so on.

### 13.1.1 Wire rope

Before discussing wire rope slings, a brief overview of wire rope construction and terminology is needed.

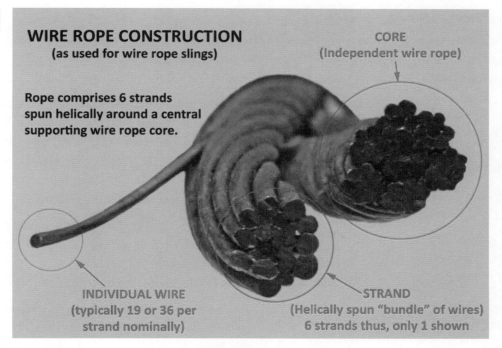

Figure 13-1

**WIRE ROPE CONSTRUCTION**
(as used for wire rope slings)

**CORE**
(Independent wire rope)

Rope comprises 6 strands
spun helically around a central
supporting wire rope core.

**INDIVIDUAL WIRE**
(typically 19 or 36 per
strand nominally)

**STRAND**
(Helically spun "bundle" of wires)
6 strands thus, only 1 shown

Wire ropes from which slings are made consist of three basic components:

- A core around which the rope is formed
- Individual wires spun around a center wire to form a multi-wire strand
- Strands spun helically around the core

For slings, wires will be drawn high-carbon steel. A variety of steel grades are used; increasing in strength, in the USA these would commonly be IPS (Improved Plow Steel), EIPS (Extra Improved Plow Steel) or EEIPS (Extra Extra Improved Plow Steel). In Europe, grades 1770 or 1960 are common.

The strands are formed in multiple layers of wires of varying diameters. A combination of larger wires and smaller "filler" wires may be used. A wide variety of strand patterns are available designed for different purposes. For slings, typically Seale or Warrington Seale patterns are used.

The core provides support for the strands and helps maintain them in their correct relative positions under bending and loading. The core may be fiber or a wire strand or rope. For slings for lifting, I would recommend specifying an Independent Wire Rope Core (IWRC) construction.

Ropes may be spun (layed) around the core in Right Hand or Left Hand directions; then there are different styles of lay, primarily Regular Lay or Langs Lay. A RRL (right hand regular) looks as per the above diagram and has the strands spun around the core in the opposite direction to the way the individual wires are spun around the center. This helps to balance the torques in the rope. As you look at it, the wires appear to lie along the axis of the rope. This is the type of construction used for slings. (With Langs Lay, the strands and the rope are spun in the same direction and this causes the wires to appear to lie across the axis of the rope). Langs Lay is not used for sling construction as it may unwind under load. Note: a "lay" is the distance along the rope it takes for one strand to make a 360° rotation of the core.

There are a number of classifications of wire rope based on the numbers of strands and the <u>nominal</u> number of wires in each strand. Rope for slings would typically be classified as 6x19 or 6x36. Within these classifications, various patterns are possible. e.g. 6x31 Warrington Seale IWRC, 6x36 Seal Filler Wire IWRC, 6x36 Warrington Seale FC (and more) up to 6x49 Filler Wire Seal IWRC are all classified as 6x36 construction. For a given rope diameter, a 6x19 will be a stiffer rope than one with a 6x36 construction. 6x19 tends to be used for smaller diameter wire rope slings and 6x36 class for the larger diameters.

### 13.1.2  End terminations

To use a single part wire rope as a tension member, you need some form of end termination to be able to attach a load to it. There are many options with their own scope of application. A number of them are shown in the following illustration. The following four types are NOT used for sling applications.

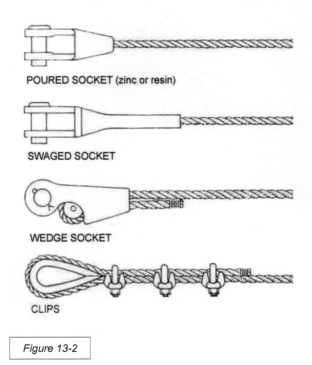

Figure 13-2

In a poured socket, the body incorporates a conical recess; the wire is passed through the socket body and opened out in the recess to form an included angle of approximately 60°. Zinc spelter or resin is poured into the socket forming a conical wedge (incorporating the wire ends) that seats into the conical recess.

With swaged sockets, the fitting is crimped on the end of the rope in a hydraulic press. Socket terminations may be seen in applications such as crane pendant ropes. Clevis ends (as here) or loop ends are possible.

Wedge sockets are typically used to terminate a hoist line on a crane at the block or boom head where the attachment needs to be removed/replaced. The rope passes around a wedge that seats in the becket. More tension, more seating. A safety clip is used to prevent unseating in the event of load reversal. Various patterns are available; refer to manufacturers such as Crosby for details.

"Crosby" clips (as here) or fist grip type clips can be used to terminate a guy or wire or lashing; <u>you may not form a lifting sling using them.</u> Use of a thimble (hard) eye is recommended.

Figure 13-3

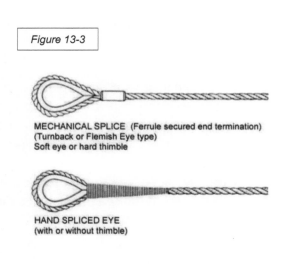

MECHANICAL SPLICE  (Ferrule secured end termination)
(Turnback or Flemish Eye type)
Soft eye or hard thimble

HAND SPLICED EYE
(with or without thimble)

Figure 13-4

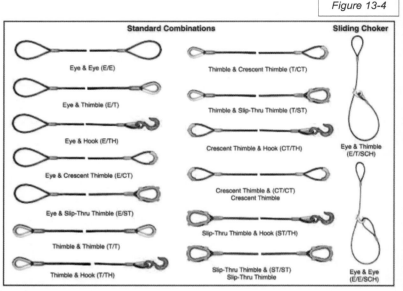

For slings, the most common form of end termination is to form an eye using either a mechanical splice or the traditional hand splice method as shown above left. Thereafter you have a number of options for thimbles and / or attached end fittings to choose from including links, shackles and hooks (as shown above right from Lift-All range).

### 13.1.3  Hand spliced eye

To form an eye and secure it with a hand tucked splice, the wire is first looped back to itself, often around a thimble with sufficient length to allow the dead end to be spliced back into the live side of the rope. Each strand is then given one forming tuck and a three or more full tucks around the same strand. The forming tuck is formed by prying two adjacent strands apart, inserting a dead end strand in the opening and passing it under up to three adjacent strands in the body of the rope. A full tuck is made by taking a strand through a complete 360° turn around the live strand. At each stage, the tucks need to be set by pulling the end of the strand end with considerable force. The completed splice may be "served" or "wrapped" as shown above. This does not improve the strength any. The strength of the splice is derived from friction between the strands, the greater the load, the greater the gripping effect.

Figure 13-5

The efficiency of this type of termination is not as great as with a mechanical splice and, not having a positive lock, it could open up if rotated. For that reason they must never be used singly. Some prefer slings with hand-spliced eyes for handling loads such as bundles of pipe as they have no ferrule to get caught up when extracting the sling from under the load. I would generally not recommend using hand spliced eyes unless there is an over-riding reason to do so.

### 13.1.4  Mechanically spliced eyes or ferrule secured end terminations (FSET)

There are two basic types of mechanically spliced eyes:

- The turnback eye
- The Flemish eye

Figure 13-6

#### Turnback eye

To form a turnback eye, the rope is passed through a sleeve or sleeves, looped back to itself (a thimble may be incorporated) and passed back through the sleeve(s). The sleeve is then pressed (swaged) between dies in a hydraulic press to secure the eye. This type of eye is what you will likely get if you just order a sling without specifying the eye type. Its integrity depends entirely on the quality of the swaging of the sleeve. If it cracks and fails (or is incorrectly pressed), the eye is lost.

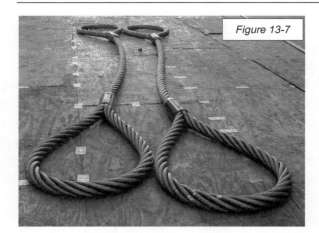

Figure 13-7

## Flemish eye

To form a Flemish Eye, the end of the rope is unlayed an appropriate length to form the eye. Three of the strands are looped (say) clockwise whilst the core and remaining three strands are looped anti-clockwise. The strands are re-layed around each other around the eye to reform the rope. A metal sleeve is slipped over the area where the tails of the strands lay back against the body of the rope and is swaged. Most of the strength of this type of eye is derived from friction between the strands in the eye. If the swaging were to fail, the eye would still likely hold.

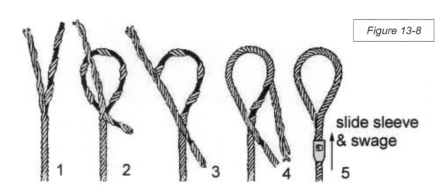

Figure 13-8

slide sleeve & swage

The sequence is shown schematically above. To the right an eye in the process of being formed.

Figure 13-9

Figure 13-10

Close up of one of the die sets for swaging ferrules mounted in the hydraulic press shown right. Photo courtesy of Holloway Houston.

Presently they can swage wire ropes up to a maximum of 6" diameter (as shown left).

Figure 13-11

### 13.1.5  Efficiencies of end terminations

Generally speaking wire rope end terminations will fail before the rope itself does. The efficiencies of splices of different types have been measured extensively over the years and form the basis for the following table (quoted from the WRTB). Only splices in ropes of 9x19 and 6x36 IWRC RRL construction in IPS, EIPS or EEIPS are shown as they are the most common grades used for slings.

| Termination | Efficiency | |
|---|---|---|
| **Hand tucked splices 7/8" dia and above** | | |
| 7/8" dia and above (22 mm +) | 80% | |
| | | |
| **Mechanical splice (inc turnback or Flemish Eye)** | | |
| IPS or EIPS 1/4" to 1" dia (6 mm – 26 mm) | 95% | |
| IPS or EIPS 1-1/8" to 2" dia (28 mm – 50 mm) | 92.5% | |
| IPS or EIPS >2" dia and above (>50 mm) | 90% | |
| | | |
| **Note also not used for slings** | | |
| Wedge sockets | 75% - 80% | See manufacturer's info. |
| Clips | 80% | See manufacturer's info. |
| Wire rope socket (resin or spelter or swaged) | 100% | |

### 13.1.6   Designing a wire rope sling

You will not normally be designing wire rope slings, nor should you be back-calculating what an existing sling is good for; if it is not tagged with a WLL, don't use it. However an understanding of how a manufacturer designs slings will give you an appreciation that will help you specify them correctly and assist you in using them.

A wire rope sling is rated based on the Minimum Breaking Load (MBL) of the wire rope from which it is made, the efficiency of the end termination and a design factor established by code.

WLL = MBL x efficiency / design factor

For general use wire rope slings in construction the design factor is 5 per most codes worldwide. If terminal fittings are used with a lesser Factor of Safety, the WLL of the sling assembly must be reduced accordingly. For engineered lifts with large diameter cable laid slings and grommets, codes may allow less (e.g. EN13414-3 reduces to a minimum of 3 on failure). For heavy offshore lifting, different codes apply; IMCA M179 "Guidance on the use of cable laid slings and grommets" is recommended reading.

Example of single leg wire rope sling design calculation

If a manufacturer was to design a sling to ASME B30.9 using $1\frac{1}{8}$" 6x36 IWRC EIP grade RRL lay wire rope with a Flemish eye termination, the rating would be calculated as follows:

—   Start with the MBL of the wire rope. A sling manufacturer will use a load test certificate provided by the mill from testing a sample of the actual rope supplied to destruction. In lieu of that, we will use the Wire Rope Sling Users Manual as a reference for the example; $1\frac{1}{8}$" 6x36 IWRC EIP grade wire rope is rated to break at not less than 65 tons (US).

—   Next the end efficiency; the end efficiency of a Flemish eye of this size is 92.5% (see above)

—   The Design Factor is 5 per code (ASME B30.9 in this case).

—   WLL = 65 x 92.5% / 5 = 12 tons; this confirms the actual minimum rating of a sling of this type in the same volume.

### 13.1.7  Specifying a wire rope sling

When specifying a wire rope sling, you need to consider the intended manner of use which includes not only the required strength, but also the following:

<u>Eye type</u>

As noted earlier, you have a choice of eye types & fittings; the type you want depends on the duty you intend.

When the wire rope is terminated with a loop, there is a risk that it will bend too tightly, especially when the loop is connected to a device that spreads the load over a relatively small area. A thimble can be installed inside the loop to preserve the natural shape of the loop, and protect the cable from pinching and abrading on the inside of the loop. The use of thimbles in loops is industry best practice. The thimble prevents the load from coming into direct contact with the wires

Soft eyes should never be used over a surface (shackle pin or whatever) of lesser diameter than the rope body diameter. Note that the pin diameter of a high alloy shackle may be less than the rope diameter of a similarly rated sling. In such cases, specify a larger capacity shackle, or use a hard eye (thimble). If attaching to the pin of a shackle rather than the bow, you could use a profiled bobbin over the pin to increase the bearing diameter. If using a soft eye to a shackle, consider specifying a wide-body shackle (available over about 35 t capacity). These have a greater radius on the bearing surface and are kinder on the sling eye.

<u>Eye size</u>

Natural soft eye dimensions (i.e. unloaded) will <u>typically</u> be 8D wide x 16D long (inside), where D is the rope diameter. Note that if using a Flemish eye, the length of the ferrule securing the splice (the swaging sleeve) will be a further 4D or so long. Hence the total splice length for a FSET splice is about 20D. There is no code requirement as such for eye sizes; if a smaller eye size is used without a thimble, a reduction may apply. The maximum pin diameter should not be any greater than the natural width of the eye.

The maximum pin diameter = (2L + W) x 0.2, where L = eye length and W = eye length

If you intend to use a sling eye over say a large crane hook, you may want to specify a larger size eye; you should not have to force the sling eye onto the hook.

If eye size is important to you, be sure to specify it.

Note that eyes formed with hard eyes (thimbles) will be much smaller. Inside length will only be about 6D.

Make sure if using a thimble and need to bear in the body of the shackle rather than the pin, e.g. at a lifting lug, that the bow of the shackle you intend to use can physically be fitted through the thimble eye. There are different sorts of thimbles available that could get you round this if you note the issue early enough to specify them in the sling construction.

<u>Length</u>

Length is measured from bearing point to bearing point in the eyes (or eye fittings) or to the pin center in the case of a clevis; it is measured under nominal tension only. Having slings of a specific length or a set of matched length slings, may or may not be critical to your particular application. If so, be sure to specify those facts when ordering a sling (and make note on the rigging arrangement).

Note that slings have a tolerance on permissible length; typically +/-2d or 0.5% whichever is greater. (Codes for cable laid slings may permit up to 1%). Matched slings will be expected to be within this tolerance and within about 50% of that tolerance to each other. Note also that slings stretch in use and if one or more of a matched set is used more than the others, you may get slings that differ significantly in length.

Figure 13-12

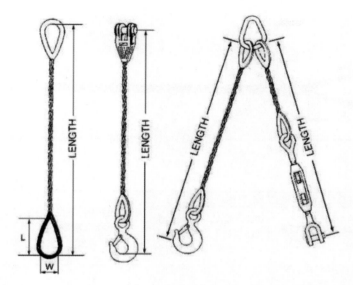

Note also that there needs to be a minimum sling body length of 10 rope diameters between splices, sleeves or fittings (which equates to about 1.5 rope lays for a single part wire rope sling). There is therefore a minimum length that a sling with eyes can be made to. If requiring a shorter sling, using a grommet sling may get you there.

If using a sling over a rolling block, you can only work within the sling body length and don't want the eye splices, sleeves or fittings to come too close to the rolling block at the required extremes of travel. Eye size may be important to you here. Don't bend a sling close to the eye.

For information only, the following table shows standard eye sizes (with and without thimbles) and minimum eye-eye sling lengths for wire rope slings made by Holloway Houston. Others will publish their similar standard information. The ratings are for a mechanical splice 6x19 or 6x36 IWRC and are in US tons.

### 13.1.8 Calculating the weight of a wire rope sling

If you do not know the weight of a wire rope sling and need to estimate it, note that the total length of wire used in making a sling with Ferrule Secured End Terminated eyes (mechanical splice) is approximately:

- "Standard" Hard Eyes: Sling length + 30D
- "Standard" Soft Eyes: Sling length + 54D

where D is the rope diameter.

If you do not have access to wire rope tables, note that wire rope weight (6x19 or 6x36 IWRC) is <u>approximately</u> $1.85D^2$ lbs/ft (D in inches), $4.25 \times 10^{-3}D^2$ kg/m (D in mm).

Weights of ferrules (sleeves) and thimbles (hard eyes) can be found in manufacturers catalogs (Crosby for instance). Alternatively, sleeves weigh approximately $2D^{2.6}$ lbs and heavy duty thimbles (to 2.25" wire size) weigh about $3.3D^3$ lbs (where D is in inches); that is $202 \times 10^{-6} \times D^{2.6}$ & $97 \times 10^{-6} \times D^3$ respectively in kg and mm. You rarely will be concerned with <u>absolute</u> accuracy; the above guidance will give you an adequately accurate estimation where the sling weight is unknown.

Figure 13-13

# HHI HOLLOWAY HOUSTON, INC.

## EYE & EYE WIRE ROPE SLINGS

## HH-105-E

LENGTH OF SLING

| WIRE ROPE DIAMETER | RATED CAPACITIES IN TONS | | | CROSBY S-320 HOOK (TONS) | STANDARD EYE DIMENSIONS (W" X L") | | G-414 HEAVY DUTY THIMBLE (W" X L") | | Min. EYE & EYE SLING LENGTH |
|---|---|---|---|---|---|---|---|---|---|
| | VERTICAL HITCH | CHOKER HITCH | VERTICAL BASKET HITCH | | | | | | |
| 1/4 | 0.65 | 0.48 | 1.3 | 3/4-C | 2" | 4" | 7/8" | 1-5/8" | 1' 6" |
| 5/16 | 1 | 0.74 | 2 | 1-C | 2-1/2" | 5" | 1 -1/16" | 1-7/8" | 1' 9" |
| 3/8 | 1.4 | 1.1 | 2.8 | 1-1/2-C | 3" | 6" | 1-1/8" | 2-1/8" | 2" |
| 1/2 | 2.5 | 1.9 | 5 | 3-C | 4" | 8" | 1-1/2" | 2-3/4" | 2' 6" |
| 9/16 | 3.2 | 2.4 | 6.4 | 5-A | 4-1/2" | 8" | 1-1/2" | 2-3/4" | 2' 9" |
| 5/8 | 3.9 | 2.9 | 7.8 | 5-A | 5" | 8" | 1-3/4" | 3-1/4" | 3' |
| 3/4 | 5.6 | 4.1 | 11 | 7-A | 6" | 12" | 2" | 3-3/4" | 3' 6" |
| 7/8 | 7.6 | 5.6 | 15 | 11-A | 7" | 14" | 2-1/4" | 4-1/4" | 4' |
| 1 | 9.8 | 7.2 | 20 | 11-A | 8" | 14" | 2-1/2" | 4-1/2" | 4' 6" |
| 1 1/8 | 12 | 9.1 | 24 | 15-A | 9" | 18 | 2-7/8" | 5-1/8" | 5' |
| 1 1/4 | 15 | 11 | 30 | 15-A | 10" | 20 | 2-7/8" | 5-1/8" | 5' 6" |
| 1 3/8 | 18 | 13 | 36 | 22-A | 11" | 22 | 3-1/2" | 6-1/4" | 6' |
| 1 1/2 | 21 | 16 | 42 | 22-A | 12" | 24 | 3-1/2" | 6-1/4" | 7' |
| 1 3/4 | 28 | 21 | 56 | 30-A | 14" | 28 | 4-1/2" | 9" | 8' |
| 2 | 37 | 28 | 74 | 37-A | 16" | 32 | 6" | 12" | 9' |
| 2 1/4 | 44 | 35 | 88 | 45-A | 18" | 36 | 7" | 14" | 10' |
| 2 1/2 | 54 | 42 | 108 | 60-A | 20" | 40 | - | - | 11' |
| 2 3/4 | 65 | 51 | 130 | - | 22" | 44 | - | - | 12' |
| 3 | 77 | 60 | 154 | - | 24" | 48 | - | - | 13' |
| 3 1/2 | 102 | 79 | 204 | - | 28" | 56 | - | - | 16' 6" |
| 3 3/4 | 115 | 90 | 230 | - | 30" | 60 | - | - | 18' |
| 4 | 130 | 101 | 260 | - | 32" | 64 | - | - | 20' |
| 4 1/2 | 160 | 124 | 320 | - | 36" | 72 | - | - | 24' |

*RATED CAPACITIES OF BASKET HITCHES ARE CALCULATED BASED
ON 40 TIMES THE ROPE DIAMETER FOR SLINGS 1/4" THROUGH 1" IN DIAMETER
AND 25 TIMES THE ROPE DIAMETER FOR SLINGS 1-1/8" DIAMETER, AND LARGER.

WWW.HOLLOWAYHOUSTON.COM

## 13.1.9 Different types of hitches

There are three basic hitches and variations thereon for single leg IWRC slings. Each has its own rating, which can be found on the sling tag and in manufacturer's literature.

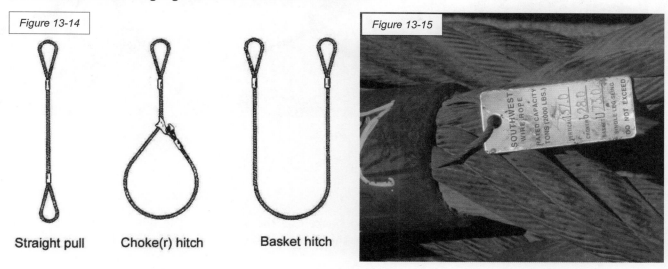

Figure 13-14    |    Straight pull    |    Choke(r) hitch    |    Basket hitch

Figure 13-15

### Single leg – straight pull

With this hitch the sling is loaded axially and its SWL is the WLL of the sling. Note that if you suspend a load using a single sling, as tension is applied the sling may want to rotate as a result of the way in which it is constructed; this may open up its construction. It is therefore not recommended; normally two or more slings will be used, often in a bridle arrangement, see later.

### Choke or choker hitch

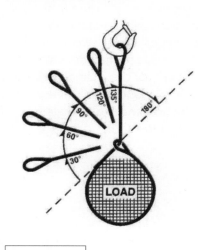

Figure 13-16

With this type of hitch, a loop is formed around the load by passing one eye of a sling through the other. As you come up on the load, the loop tightens and forms a natural angle of about 135° at the choke – see sketch left. Slings will generally have a rating quoted for this type of hitch (at this natural angle); in the US, this will be about 75% of the straight pull capacity for wire rope slings. If the choke angle is less than 135°, a reduction for must be taken:

| | |
|---|---|
| 121 - 135° | 100% of rated choke capacity |
| 90 - 120° | 87% |
| 60 - 89° | 74% |
| 30 - 59° | 62% |
| < 30° | 49% |

Do not beat the choke down, use a wrapped choke if you require better contact with the load.

The capacity reduction with a choke hitch results from this method of rigging affecting the ability of the wire rope components to adjust during the lift, placing angular loading on the body of the sling and creating a sharp bend at the point of choke.

Note it is recommended that you form the choke by shackling the eye to the body of the sling rather than passing the sling through its own eye as shown on the LH picture below. It will be less likely to be damaged or kinked. The eye should be taken to the pin with the sling body to the bow, so that the pin cannot unscrew as you come up on the load. Use of a wide-body shackle would reduce the severity of the bend and be kinder to the sling.

Figure 13-17

Figure 13-18

Figure 13-19

Wrong!

– No shackle
– No protection where the slings are bent over the flange
– The sling is bent very close to the eye splice

Wrong!

– The pin could slacken as the wire runs through the shackle as it is tensioned.

Correct!

– The eye is to the pin to the eye with the body in the bow; it would be better if the eye was centered on the pin so the load doesn't go down one side of the shackle so much.

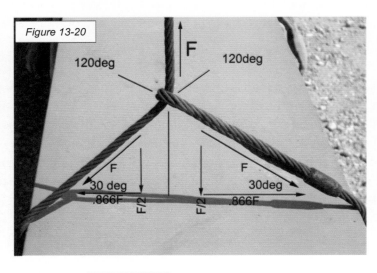

Figure 13-20

If the system was frictionless, the tension "F" in the sling would be constant throughout and the choke would come to equilibrium forming 3 equal angles of 120°; each vector would bisect the included angle opposite. The two inclined legs would form 30° angles to the horizontal; the vertical components of the inclined forces would each be F/2 which balances the single vertical leg. As a result of friction, the choke angle (top left) is actually closer to 130 - 135°.

Figure 13-21

Wrapped choke hitch

With a basic choker hitch, the load is not gripped effectively at the top by the choke. For loose loads such as a bundle of pipe or rebar this would be insecure. For most loads, and these in particular it is a good idea to use a longer sling and double wrap it as shown to the left. This arrangement will compact around the load and keep it secure. For long loads in particular, you should use a pair of slings hitched like this rather than a single sling.

The capacity of this arrangement remains the capacity of the basic choke hitch, wrapping does not affect that.

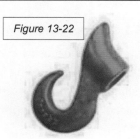

Figure 13-22

If you intend using a sling regularly in a choke hitch as say 1 leg of a 2 or more legged bridle, you could specify incorporation of a shackle hook as shown in the graphic above. Patterns such as that shown here or ones with latches are available. They are fitted permanently during manufacture. Thimble hard eyes should be used with them.

## Basket

Figure 13-23

With a basic basket hitch as shown above, the load is cradled by the sling with both eyes going vertically to the lifting mechanism. The tension is constant through the sling and there are effectively two vertical parts of rope supporting the load. So long as the sling is not bent around the load tighter than about 20 - 25x the rope diameter (see section following), the basket hitch will be good for 2x the single leg straight pull capacity.

With this basic hitch, the load is not gripped at all. For many loads, loose bundle of pipe or rebar in particular this would be insecure. It is a good idea to use a longer sling and double wrap it as shown to the right. This arrangement will contract around the load and keep it secure. For long loads in particular, you should use a pair of slings hitched like this rather than a single sling.

The capacity of this arrangement remains the capacity of the basic basket hitch, wrapping does not affect that.

**Double wrapped
Vertical basket hitch**

Figure 13-24

**Double wrapped
Angled basket hitch**

In many cases the two eyes of the sling will be brought to a common point, say a crane hook or shackle and the legs of the sling will thus be angled. The capacity of this arrangement is determined by the angle the sling legs make, the more vertical the legs are, the more effective the sling is and the closer to the full basket hitch capacity it will be rated for.

The effectiveness of the sling is the sine of the angle <u>each leg makes to the horizontal</u>. e.g. at 60° to the horizontal the SWL of the hitch is sin60° = 0.866 x the basic basket hitch; at 45° it is 0.707x.

Note that in Europe, they define efficiency on the basis of the included angle between the slings.

Efficiency = cos(included angle/2). The result is the same.

### 13.1.10 Slings used at an angle

When slings are used at an angle, as for instance in this case where a pair of slings connects to a spreader, the usefulness of each sling in supporting a vertical load is the vertical component of the sling's tension. The flatter a sling is to the horizontal, the less effective it is (vertically); the greater the tension has to be to get the desired vertical component and the greater the horizontal component of the sling tension that the spreader has to resist is.

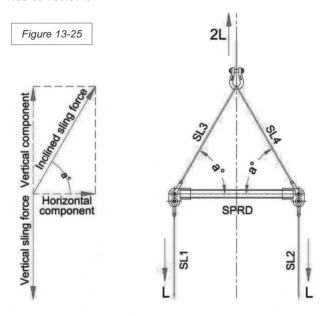

Figure 13-25

If the tension in vertical sling SL1 = L, and it's angle to the horizontal = a°, then:

- The tension in inclined sling SL3 = L x (1 / sin(a))
- The horizontal component (which is the compression in the spreader in this case) = L / tan(a)

These relationships are tabulated below for reference. To determine the inclined sling force at say 60°, go up until the 60 grid crosses the green line, then read the factor = 1.15 approximately. The inclined sling force at 60° is thus 1.15 x the vertical force. At 45°, it is 1.4x; at 30°, it is 2x.

Note: 60° is preferred, 45° is max recommended; do not go flatter than 30° ever.

You can do similar with the purple line to figure out the horizontal components for say spreader design.

Knowing the required vertical forces, you can determine the tension in the inclined slings at a specific angle and thus specify them (with adequate margin). e.g. if $L_{vertical}$ = 10 t; with a 60° spreader arrangement $SL3_{actual}$ = 10x1.15 factor = 11.5 t; use at least a 12 t sling, 15 t would be better.

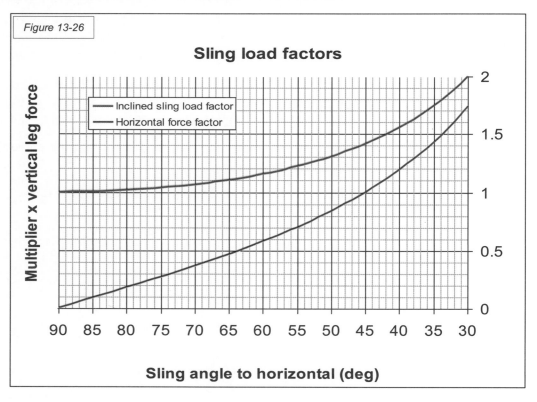

Figure 13-26

## 13.1.11 Typical IWRC sling chart capacities for different hitches

| Figure 13-27 |

# CAPACITIES OF MECHANICAL SPLICE IWRC SLINGS
## (EXTRA IMPROVED PLOW STEEL GRADE)

| ROPE DIAMETER (INCHES) | SINGLE LEG SLING CAPACITIES BY HITCH TYPE | | | ANGLED SINGLE LEG BASKET OR 2-LEG BRIDLE CAPACITIES | | |
|---|---|---|---|---|---|---|
| | VERTICAL | CHOKER | VERTICAL BASKET | BASKET AT DEGREES | | |
| | | | | 30 DEGREE | 45 DEGREE | 60 DEGREE |
| 1/4 | 0.65 | 0.48 | 1.3 | 0.65 | 0.91 | 1.1 |
| 5/16 | 1.0 | 0.74 | 2.0 | 1.0 | 1.4 | 1.7 |
| 3/8 | 1.4 | 1.1 | 2.9 | 1.4 | 2.0 | 2.5 |
| 7/16 | 1.9 | 1.4 | 3.9 | 1.9 | 2.7 | 3.4 |
| 1/2 | 2.5 | 1.9 | 5.1 | 2.5 | 3.6 | 4.4 |
| 9/16 | 3.2 | 2.4 | 6.4 | 3.2 | 4.5 | 5.5 |
| 5/8 | 3.9 | 2.9 | 7.8 | 3.9 | 5.5 | 6.8 |
| 3/4 | 5.6 | 4.1 | 11 | 5.6 | 7.9 | 9.7 |
| 7/8 | 7.6 | 5.6 | 15 | 7.6 | 11 | 13 |
| 1 | 9.8 | 7.2 | 20 | 9.8 | 14 | 17 |
| 1 1/8 | 12 | 9.1 | 24 | 12 | 17 | 21 |
| 1 1/4 | 15 | 11 | 30 | 15 | 21 | 26 |
| 1 3/8 | 18 | 13 | 36 | 18 | 25 | 31 |
| 1 1/2 | 21 | 16 | 42 | 21 | 30 | 37 |
| 1 5/8 | 24 | 18 | 49 | 24 | 35 | 42 |
| 1 3/4 | 28 | 21 | 57 | 28 | 40 | 49 |
| 1 7/8 | 32 | 24 | 64 | 32 | 46 | 56 |
| 2 | 37 | 28 | 73 | 37 | 52 | 63 |
| 2 1/8 | 40 | 31 | 80 | 40 | 56 | 69 |
| 2 1/4 | 44 | 35 | 89 | 44 | 63 | 77 |
| 2 3/8 | 49 | 38 | 99 | 49 | 70 | 85 |
| 2 1/2 | 54 | 42 | 109 | 54 | 77 | 94 |
| 2 5/8 | 60 | 46 | 119 | 60 | 84 | 103 |
| 2 3/4 | 65 | 51 | 130 | 65 | 92 | 113 |
| 2 7/8 | 71 | 55 | 141 | 71 | 100 | 122 |
| 3 | 77 | 60 | 153 | 77 | 108 | 132 |
| 3 1/8 | 82 | 64 | 165 | 82 | 117 | 143 |
| 3 1/4 | 89 | 69 | 177 | 89 | 125 | 153 |
| 3 3/8 | 95 | 74 | 190 | 95 | 135 | 165 |
| 3 1/2 | 102 | 79 | 203 | 102 | 144 | 176 |
| 4 | 130 | 101 | 260 | 130 | 183 | 224 |
| 4 1/2 | 160 | 124 | 320 | 160 | 225 | 276 |

BASKET HITCH RATED CAPACITIES BASED ON D/d RATIO OF 25
RATED CAPACITIES BASED ON PIN DIAMETER NO LARGER THAN NATURAL EYE WIDTH OR LESS THAN THE NOMINAL SLING DIAMETER
RATED CAPACITIES BASED ON A DESIGN FACTOR OF 5
HORIZONTAL SLING ANGLES LESS THAN 30 DEGREES SHALL NOT BE USED
RATED CAPACITIES SHOWN APPLY ON TO 6X19 AND 6X37 CLASSIFICATION WIRE ROPE
**CAPACITIES IN TONS (2000lb)**

The above is a typical capacity chart for Mechanical Splice IWRC 6x19 of 6x37 steel wire rope slings to EIPS grade (based on Certex). <u>For example only, do not use for lift planning.</u>

The first three columns quote the capacities for a single leg sling in the three most common hitches. The wrapped versions of choke and basket are the same as the basic hitches. The next three are for a single leg sling in a basket hitch with the legs angled. You could work out a reduced capacity for the angled basket hitch using the principles in the preceding section (and that is acceptable), but the chart has it readily figured for you for three most angles (30° is the absolute minimum). If between angles, use the more conservative angle. The three RH columns also apply to a pair of single leg slings used as a bridle. See following.

## 13.1.12 Bridles (types)

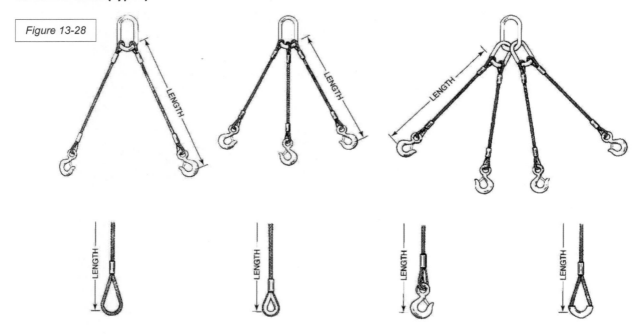

Figure 13-28

Bridles are available as matched sets of 2, 3 or 4 single-leg slings permanently attached to a master link for suspension from a crane hook or similar. They may be fitted with hooks or simply hard or soft eyes according to intended application. Bridle slings are rated as sets and, as with single leg slings, capacities may be quoted for vertical, 30°, 45° and 60° to the horizontal (or the equivalent included angles depending on locale). These capacities are based on all of the legs of the bridle being equally loaded.

<u>2-leg bridles</u>

For 2-legged bridles the leg loads will be equal if the attachment points are at the same height and equidistant about the C of G. The load will be level and the angles to the horizontal equal. If the attachment points are at different heights or are not equal about the C of G, then the required leg lengths will be different, the horizontal angles will be different and the loads unequal.

<u>3-leg bridles</u>

With 3-legged bridles, the legs will be equally loaded if the attachment points are at the same height, the same distance from the C of G and equally disposed around the C of G at 120° to each other. Of course in the real world, you don't get too many lifts like that. If the attachment points are at different heights, are at different distances from the C of G and/or are not at 120° to each other, then the required leg lengths will be different, the horizontal angles will be different and the loads will be unequal. You ideally want sling lengths that will give you close to 60° to the horizontal in the worst case. You will get that if you use a sling length about 2x the distance from the C of G to the furthest lug. The leg with the shortest distance from lug to hook will use its sling with no extra shackles or whatever, whilst those further away will need some form of length adjustment device to make up the length difference. As regards the required capacity, the surest method is to work out the actual sling loads in each leg knowing the lug and C of G locations and the length of the slings. Having determined the worst load, multiply it by 3 to derive the minimum 3-leg bridle capacity (in a straight pull). Choose a bridle that exceeds that with some margin for factors such as possible weight growth.

How do we figure out the sling loads? The first thing to do is identify the relative lug locations and the relative position of the C of G. To do that, use the principles outlined in 3.4. Note the legs of the 2-beam "T" analogy do not have to be normal to each other for the principle to work. You could crank out the answers by hand individually or use a spreadsheet to automate the work as shown below.

In this case, we used metric units and all 3 lugs are level and disposed at 6m from each other, the C of G is central. The load is taken as 36 t (for the sake of a figure). The vertical lug loads are equal at 12.0 t. The distance from each lug to the C of G is about 3.5 m, so could have used 7 m slings, but had 6 m available so used those. This gives equal sling angles of 54.7° to the horizontal and a suspension drop of 4.9 m. Knowing that geometry, we can determine the sling tensions to be 14.7 t. You'd want to use slings individually rated for say 16 t (17.6 US tons) in a straight pull, or 48 t (52 US tons) as a 3-leg bridle in straight pull. $1^3/_8$" (26 mm) diameter slings in EIPS grade would be about right.

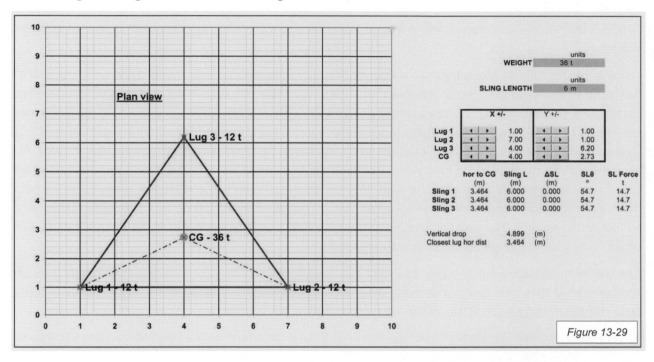

Figure 13-29

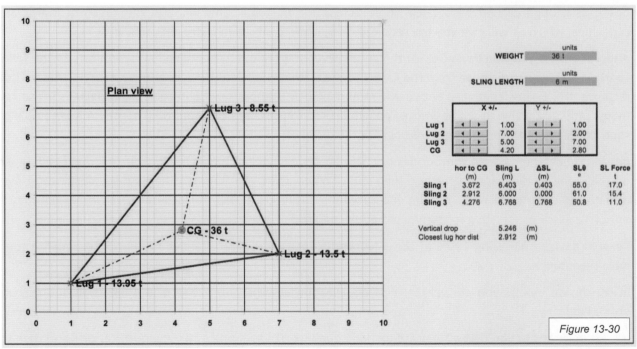

Figure 13-30

If our 36 t piece looked more like the above in plan, with a C of G location as shown, then using the same principles, we can determine the vertical lug loads to be different, ranging from 9 t to 14 t. The distance from each lug to the C of G varies from 2.9 m to 4.3 m. Lug 2 being closest gets the basic length sling – again 6 m slings are proposed. Lugs 1 and 3 require extra suspension lengths of approximately 0.4 m & 0.8 m respectively in order to lift level. The flattest sling angle is Sling 3 at 50.8° - that is OK. <u>Note: the lugs should ideally be orientated in plan to point towards the C of G so that the slings lie in their plane and side loading is not induced across the lug.</u> Knowing the geometry, we can determine the max sling tension to be 17.0 t. $1^1/_2$" (38 mm) diameter slings in EIPS grade would be good for about 19 t (21 tons) each and would be about right. This requires a capacity of 57 t (63 US tons) as a 3-leg bridle in straight pull.

<u>4-leg bridles</u>

Whilst 3-leg bridles are determinate, 4-legged bridles are not; there is thus a problem in assessing the loads in the slings.

Using a master link, all four slings can be considered to come directly to a single common upper point which has zero articulation. You might imagine that if the lifting lugs are level with each other and disposed on a rectangular grid with the C of G dead center and you used 4 matched slings that you would get equal loading in the slings. In an ideal world you might, but are much more likely not to. If the load is rigid (such as a turbine upper casing) and the slings are considered to be inelastic, then any slight difference in sling length / dimensional discrepancy in the load will result in all the load being taken by diagonally opposite slings with the other two slings merely balancing the load. In practice slings have some elasticity; many loads can deflect a little, you can possibly use turnbuckles or chain falls in the suspension to take out the length tolerances and try to load them equally. The point is, that unless you take very specific measures to equalize out the loads, they could be as much as 2x greater than you anticipated.

The safest approach with a rigid load and no specific measures taken to equalize loads is to assume conservatively that only two are carrying the load and double the capacity of the bridle used. <u>This is a code requirement in certain countries.</u> I strongly recommend it.

Knowing the relative locations of the lugs, the C of G location and the sling lengths, you can use geometry to calculate the sling angles in true plane (through the diagonal basically). You can then determine the sling loads based as though carried by a 2-leg bridle across the diagonal. This will size the required individual sling capacities, which x4 will give you the required 4-leg bridle capacity in a straight pull.

Alternatively, if you don't want to do the geometry and work out actual sling loads, you can do the following. Firstly, measure the distance from the C of G to the furthest lug. Your sling lengths need to be at least 1.4x that distance. If the sling length lies between 1.4x and 2x the distance, look up 2-leg bridle capacities in the capacity tables until you arrive at a size whose capacity at 45° exceeds the payload; then specify a 4-leg bridle of that rope size & type. If your sling lengths are > 2x the distance, use the capacities at 60°.

If using similarly tensioned turnbuckles or chain-falls in each leg, it <u>may</u> a reasonable judgment call to use 75% of the 4-leg bridle capacity rather than 50%. When using turnbuckles in multi-leg suspension systems, monitoring sling loads with shackles incorporating strain gauge load pins (Strainsert or similar) may be an option to assist in adjusting for somewhat equal loading.

I would advise only using 100% of the 4-leg bridle capacity where effective measures to equalize the loads have been taken.

In conclusion, unless you are very sure of equalization assume only 2 legs of a 4-leg bridle are carrying the entire load.

If it is important to you that all legs are loaded equally, consider using a two-leg bridle at one end then using a double length sling over a snatch block at the other to the other two lugs. This will bring it to a 3-point support which is determinate.

Figure 13-31

Nobles in Australia did some interesting testing on the subject.

The photo left shows one of the investigations conducted by Nobles into load equalization in multi-leg slings. This particular arrangement uses a 2-leg bridle (chain actually but same principle) to the left and a single leg wire rope sling over a snatch block to the right. Digital load cells were used in each leg. As you might expect this showed very close to equal loading in each (26% max).

Note: The equivalent test with a 4-leg bridle with legs of equal length showed the heaviest loaded sling to be carrying 31% of the total of the sling loads i.e. $\approx \frac{1}{3}^{rd}$. A test with a 4-leg bridle when one chain leg was reduced by only 1 link gave them a maximum of 47% in the heaviest loaded sling. i.e. approximately ½.

Using 2 x 2-leg bridles and a rams-horn hook (which has some articulation) gave them a max 26% with equal length legs and 40% with 1 leg reduced by 1 link. This obviously helped equalize to some degree, but you can't rely on that alone to make a significant improvement.

### 13.1.13 Bending of wire rope slings

Rope breaking strength is determined in standard tests with the rope pulled in a straight line. When a wire rope is bent (statically) over a pin the various components of it have to move relative to each other to accommodate the bend and differential loadings are set up within the rope. As a result, the wire rope will fail at a lesser load. The reduction in strength of a rope is a function of how severely it is bent. Some years ago the reduction was graphed (by others) expressed as efficiency against D/d ratio, where "d" is the diameter of the rope and "D" is the diameter of the pin over which it is bent.

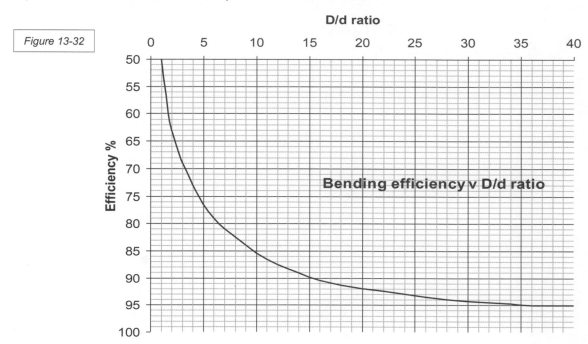

Figure 13-32

This graph (MacWhytes efficiency curve) is based on empirical measurements in numerous tests and is an average for 6x19 and 6x36 classification ropes, fiber core or IWRC, regular lay or Langs lay.

From the above, you can see that if a wire rope sling is bent over a pin of equal diameter to itself, the D/d ratio will be 1 and the efficiency of the wire rope will only be 50%.

If you note the Holloway chart preceding, their basket hitch ratings are based on a D/d ratio of 25 or better (some use 20:1). From the chart above, you can see than this equates to a wire rope efficiency of about 93%. Slings up to 2" diameter with this type of splice have an eye efficiency of 92.5% which was accounted for by the manufacturer in determining the WLL marked on the sling. So as long as the bend is no worse than 25:1, the eye will be the most exacting condition and no further capacity reduction is required. However, if you bend the rope tighter than 25:1 the bend becomes the governing condition and you have to start taking capacity deductions to determine the SWL.

e.g. per the preceding table, so long as it is not bent tighter than 25:1, a 2" sling in a basket hitch (both legs vertical) is rated at 74 tons (US), which is 2x the quoted straight line pull of 37 tons. This makes sense as when doubled, there are two parts supporting the load with equal tension of 37 tons.

If you now basket a 2" sling over a 30" diameter pin, the D/d becomes 15 and the efficiency is only 90%. D/d, being less than 25:1, governs and a reduction is required.  The simplest (and most conservative) thing to do is to multiply the basket capacity by 90% to give a SWL of 90% of the WLL <u>of the basket hitch</u> = 0.9 x 74 = 66.6 tons.

Strictly speaking it should be 90% of the sling capacity <u>before the eye efficiency was taken into account.</u> You don't really want to take a factor on a factor as they occur in different places; rather you want to take the more exacting reduction i.e. the eye or the bend. To determine the capacity on that basis, you'd have to divide the 74 tons by 92.5% eye efficiency to determine the rope capacity in a basket (at 5:1 SF) = 74 / 0.925 = 80 tons; then multiply that by the governing reduction determined from the bend ratio = 90%; this gives 80 x 0.9 = 72 tons. Quite a difference!

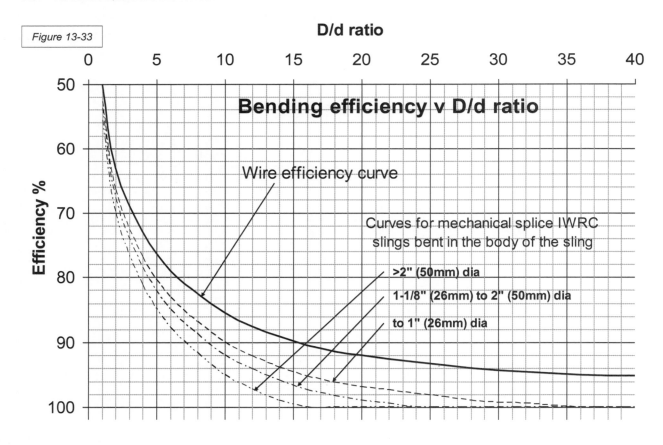

Figure 13-33

Based on the above, a series of curves can be developed to enable you to down rate the basic basket hitch capacities of an IWRC sling when you bend its body over pins of different diameters. As you can see a 2" (50 mm) IWRC sling with mechanical splice eyes will max out at 100% of rated basket hitch capacity when bent at a D/d ratio of about 25; anything tighter than this and you need to derate per the corrected curve. For larger diameter slings, you could use the rated basket hitch capacity above D/d ratios of about 18.

If in doubt, and you have plenty of sling capacity, take the preceding more conservative approach. Don't use these curves for anything other than IWRC single body slings.

## 13.2 Cable laid wire rope slings

When it comes to specifying wire rope slings of increasing capacity, there eventually comes a practical size limit to the diameter of a single wire rope. Whilst a mechanically spliced end can be formed from a single wire up to 6" diameter, the excessive stiffness of a rope above about 3" diameter for general construction purposes (even of 6x36 construction) makes it sensible to look at slings made of multiple parts of ropes, either cable-laid or braided construction. Both of these types will be considerably more flexible (but less abrasion resistant). Cable laid slings are not generally seen much in the USA in the larger sizes; braided slings are much more common there (see later).

A cable-laid rope is formed by spinning 6 unit ropes around an inner core rope. The nominal diameter of the core unit rope will be at least 12% but not greater than 25% larger than the nominal diameter of the outer unit ropes. All the unit ropes will be IWRC and of stranded construction say 6x36. Thus a cable might for instance be classified as 7x6x36 IWRC.

EN13414-3 defines a cable-laid sling as a sling formed from a wire rope constructed of six unit ropes laid as outers over one core unit rope, with a termination at each end, usually in the form of a spliced eye. Normally mechanical splices will be used at smaller sizes, whereas hand slices are likely at larger diameters.

The (UK) Lifting Equipment Engineers Association (LEEA) Code of Practice for the Safe Use of Lifting Equipment also contains good information on the subject.

For further information, refer to EN13414-3; IMCA M 179, the International Marine Contractors Association Guidance on the Use of Cable Laid Slings and Grommets, although aimed at offshore lifting (where the factors of safety may be less), it contains much useful information. Although all the principles and formulae are valid, be aware that for general use on-shore you will likely need to use a greater factor of safety than prescribed therein. There is logically a case to be made for using lesser factors of safety, as they do for offshore lifting, when making one-off ultra-heavy engineered lifts with new (tested) slings, but you would need to check legislation.

Note: EN13414-3 requires a 5:1 safety factor for cable laid slings up to 60 mm diameter; from 60-150 mm it is 6.33-0.022d; above 150 mm, it is 3:1.

As with all slings, a cable-laid sling is required to be tagged with its rated capacity. Typically basket capacities are based on 10:1. If a cable laid sling is basketed over say a crane hook or a lift point, the WLL needs to be reduced by a bending factor if the bending efficiency is more exacting than the eye efficiency.

Per heavy slings within the scope of IMCA, per IMCA the bending factor would be calculated as:

$$E_B = 1 - \frac{0.5}{\sqrt{D/d}}$$

Where D is the diameter being bent over and d is the rope (cable) diameter.

The bending efficiency is not additive to the eye efficiency. If for instance a hand spliced eye is used with an efficiency of 0.75, then the bending efficiency would only govern the sling capacity for D/d ratios that give a bending efficiency of less than 0.75. This equates to a D/d of 4:1. If a mechanical splice with say 0.8 efficiency were used, the limiting D/d would calculate out at 6.25: 1.

The eye must never be used over a pin diameter less than "d"; at least 2d is recommended.

For cable laid slings, per IMCA, the length is measured bearing point in the eye to bearing point under a nominal tension of 3% of breaking strength using pins of a prescribed diameter (approximately 2d)

Be aware that the minimum sling length needs to provide for at least 15d between the last splice tucks.

## 13.3 Braided & other multi-part wire rope slings

Where a high degree of flexibility is required in slings with smaller capacities or where high capacity slings are required, multi-part wire rope slings are an alternative to cable-laid slings. There are many varieties on the basic theme and many manufacturers with their own patent constructions. The following extract illustrates the types made by SLINGMAX® for instance and highlights the characteristics of each.

## Wire Rope Slings

Figure 13-34

GATOR-LAID® WIRE ROPE SLING

This is identical to the GATOR-MAX® sling with the parallel eyes except it has metal sleeves for the splice connection. This is the product when a big lift but shorter sling is required. It also has twelve parts of wire rope in the loop and has great flexibility.

GATOR-MAX® SLING

This sling also has parallel eyes like the GATOR-LAID® sling but it has hand spliced metal sleeves. Another sling with great flexibility and the same high strength and efficiency as the GATOR-LAID® sling.

GATOR-FLEX® WIRE ROPE SLING

This sling has a nine part body style but the eyes are crossed or interwoven. The eyes are terminated in a hand-tuck type construction. High flexibility and strength also feature in this nine-part sling.

GATOR-FLEX® GROMMETS

Ultra flexible slings for that short heavy lift connection. These slings can be made shorter than standard multipart slings but maintain all of the advantages.

TRI-FLEX® WIRE ROPE SLING

This is a three part sling was created to replace large diameter single part wire rope slings which proved awkward and stiff. Steel erectors, millwrights and riggers use Tri-Flex® slings for everything from steel erection or machinery moving to any type of heavy lift. These slings are made in matching lengths.

T&D ULTRA-FLEX WIRE ROPE SLING

This wire rope sling is an extremely flexible product with great applications for general rigging purposes in the utility industry. It makes a fantastic choker sling especially when lifting poles.

## 13.4 Construction of braided wire rope slings

Braided slings are an option where flexibility in (generally) larger slings is important. They are formed by firstly making a long single part stranded sling as described above with (usually) mechanical splice soft eyes. This sling is then hand braided back and forth several times around itself to form a shorter multi-part sling. To form a 3-part sling, you would double it back on itself twice; this gives 3 parts in the body and 4 parts in the eye. With an odd number of parts each end of the sling gets 1 component rope eye and one loop, typically they may be seized together to form an eye. The below graphic (courtesy of Yarbrough illustrates the concept.

Figure 13-35

These slings can be either flat or round and are very flexible and versatile. They are made with different numbers of parts; 3, 6, & 9 parts are common in round types.

The minimum sling length between loops, sockets or sleeves is recommended to be 40 times the component rope diameter of the braided body.

The rated capacity for a basket hitch is typically based on a minimum D/d ratio of 25, where "d" is the component rope diameter (not the completed sling diameter).

Figure 13-36

The picture left is of Yarbrough testing a 3 part sling, you can see the eye comprises 1 ferrule secured eye plus a loop.

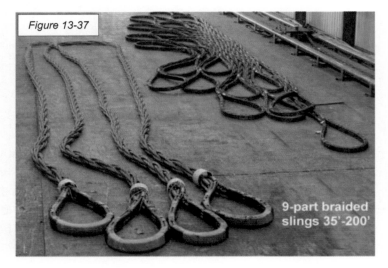

Figure 13-37

The picture left is of a selection of 9-part braided slings made by Holloway Houston. Each is formed from 3 matched 3-part braided slings laid helically around each other with the eyes seized together. This gives 9 parts in the body and 12 in the eyes.

With these particular slings, the pin diameter in the eyes must be at least 4x the component rope diameter.

There are many variations on the theme offered by different manufacturers. Each has its own ratings and characteristics. You need to carefully consult the manufacturer's literature to understand their intended manner of use before specifying these types of slings.

## 13.5 Wire rope slings (endless)

In addition to single-leg wire rope slings there are a number of types of endless slings. These are particularly useful in low-headroom applications.

### Strand laid hand tucked grommet

These slings are made from a single continuous length of strand laid to make a rope body composed of six strands around a strand core. The strand ends are tucked into the body to form the core, with the tuck position diametrically opposite the core butt position. No sleeves (ferrules) are used so it has a smooth appearance. The core butt position is to be clearly marked with paint (red usually).

Grommets are defined by the length of their circumference <u>not by inside length</u>.

The circumference is a minimum of 96 x body diameter (USA) to avoid bending at the splice. Per EN13414-3 it shall be at least 5x the grommet lay length which, given a lay is 6d to 7.5d works out to be a lot less.

D/d is very important with these types of slings; it is to be a minimum of 5:1 including at the crane hook or other bearing point. The sling is not to be bent at the locations of the tuck or core butt, keep these locations in the vertical legs.

The rating chart to the right is typical (courtesy of Lift-All®). For information only.

### Strand laid mechanical splice grommet

These slings are made from a single continuous length of strand laid wire rope body with a lap joint secured by a number of swaged sleeves / ferrules.

The rating chart to the right is typical (courtesy of Lift-All). For information only. Below are mechanical splice grommets by Yarbrough ready for testing.

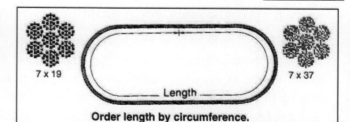

Figure 13-38

Order length by circumference.

| Rope Dia. (in.) | Rated Capacity (tons)* | | | Minimum Sling Length | Splice Length (in.) |
|---|---|---|---|---|---|
| | Vertical | Choker | Vertical Basket | | |
| 3/8 | 2.1 | 1.5 | 4.2 | 3' 0" | 2 7/16 |
| 7/16 | 2.8 | 2.0 | 5.7 | 3' 6" | 2 7/8 |
| 1/2 | 3.7 | 2.6 | 7.3 | 4' 0" | 3 1/4 |
| 9/16 | 4.6 | 3.2 | 9.3 | 4' 6" | 3 11/16 |
| 5/8 | 5.7 | 4.0 | 11 | 5' 0" | 4 1/16 |
| 3/4 | 8.2 | 5.7 | 16 | 6' 0" | 4 7/8 |
| 7/8 | 11 | 7.7 | 22 | 7' 0" | 5 11/16 |
| 1 | 14 | 10 | 29 | 8' 0" | 6 1/2 |

Vertical and Basket ratings are based on a minimum D/d of 5.

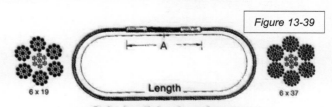

Figure 13-39

Order length by circumference.

| Rope Dia. (in.) | Rated Capacity (tons)* | | | Minimum Sling Length | Splice Length A (in.) |
|---|---|---|---|---|---|
| | Vertical | Choker | Vertical Basket | | |
| 1/4 | 1.0 | .71 | 2.0 | 3' 0" | 8 |
| 5/16 | 1.6 | 1.1 | 3.1 | 3' 0" | 8 |
| 3/8 | 2.3 | 1.6 | 4.5 | 3' 0" | 8 |
| 7/16 | 3.1 | 2.1 | 6.1 | 6' 0" | 10 |
| 1/2 | 3.9 | 2.8 | 7.9 | 6' 0" | 10 |
| 9/16 | 5.0 | 3.5 | 10 | 6' 0" | 10 |
| 5/8 | 6.1 | 4.3 | 12 | 6' 0" | 10 |
| 3/4 | 8.8 | 6.2 | 18 | 8' 0" | 16 |
| 7/8 | 12 | 8.3 | 24 | 8' 0" | 18 |
| 1 | 15 | 11 | 31 | 8' 0" | 20 |

Note: 3 sleeves used on 3/4" and larger.
Vertical and Basket ratings are based on a minimum D/d of 5.

Figure 13-40

## 13.6 Cable laid grommet slings

Cable laid hand tucked grommet

A cable laid grommet is an endless loop of wire rope cable.

Size for size, a cable laid grommet will be more flexible than a strand laid grommet as a result of its multiple parts. It will not be as abrasion resistant.

These slings are formed in much the same way as strand laid hand tucked grommets except that it is a long single continuous length of wire rope that is used. The rope is laid up helically continuously around itself to make a rope body composed of six parts of rope around the core rope. A temporary rigid former is required during this process. Note that as one piece of rope is used, the core will be the same diameter as the body parts unlike a cable laid sling in which the core has a larger diameter.

The rope ends are tucked into the body to form the core, with the tuck position diametrically opposite the core butt position. No sleeves (ferrules) are used so it has a smooth appearance. The core butt position is to be clearly marked with paint (red usually). The grommet is never to be bent at that location.

As with other types of grommets, these are defined by the length of their circumference not by inside length.

D/d is very important with these types of slings; refer to the manufacturers for guidance.

Cable laid mechanical splice grommet

Cable laid mechanical splice grommets are made using a single length of wire rope cable looped and secured using one or more mechanically swaged sleeves / ferrules.

## 13.7 Double part leg wire rope slings

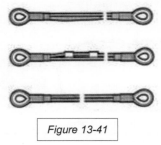

Figure 13-41

Double part leg wire rope slings are slings, whose body has two parts of wire. They are formed from endless slings or grommets The loop of rope is drawn together to form two eyes which are seized around a thimble. This gives two eyes in parallel and two legs in the body. The splices are located in the leg parts. Capacity is limited by the splice efficiency or the bend efficiency in the eye, whichever is worse.

## 13.8 Synthetic slings

Slings made from synthetic materials provide alternatives to wire rope slings in many applications.

They have the advantage over wire rope slings of light weight, flexibility, and easy stowage; they provide softer bearing onto sensitive loads and their strength is basically not affected by bending over tight radii. However they are much more easily cut / damaged, may degrade when exposed to UV or chemicals or high temperatures and are more bulky, (which may be a consideration when attaching to predetermined shackle sizes / trunnions on chemical vessels and the like). Single sling capacities are currently available up to about 250 tons in a straight pull.

There are two primary types of synthetic slings, namely:

- webbing slings
- round slings

### 13.8.1 Webbing slings

Webbing slings are flat slings formed from woven nylon, polyester or polypropylene type yarns; they may be endless or single part with stitched looped ends forming eyes; a variety of fittings may be used. There are many permutations possible. I recommend the Web Sling & Tie Down Association to you as a source of further information. One of the primary manufacturers is Lift-All whose information is duplicated below.

## STANDARD WEB SLING TYPES

Figure 13-42

### Hardware Slings

*Unilink* and *Web-Trap* hardware can help to extend sling life by protecting the webbing from abrasion on rough crane hooks. Hardware can often be reused, lowering sling replacement costs.

**Type U (UU)** - Has the preferred and economical *Unilink* fitting on each end for use in a vertical, choker or basket hitch. *Unilinks* allow choking from either end to save time and vary wear points. See page 22.

Type U

**Type 1 (TC)** - Has a *Web-Trap* triangle and choker fitting on either end. Typical use is in a choker hitch. Can also be used in vertical and basket hitches.

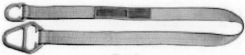

Type 1

**Type 2 (TT)** - Has a *Web-Trap* triangle on each end. Normally used in a basket hitch, but can also be used in a vertical hitch. They cannot be used as a choker.

Type 2

### Eye Type

**Type 3 (EE)** - Flat Eye slings are very popular and can be used in all three types of hitches. They are easier to remove from beneath the load than sling Types 1, 2 and 4. Unless Type 4 is requested, Type 3 will be supplied as the standard EE sling.

Type 3

**Type 4 (EE)** - Twisted Eye slings are similar to Type 3 except the eyes are turned 90° to form a better choker hitch. The eyes of a Type 4 nest better on the crane hook.

Type 4

### Endless Type

**Type 5 (EN)** - Endless slings are versatile and the most economically priced. They can be used in all three types of hitches. The sling can be rotated to minimize wear. The sling legs can be spread for improved load balance.

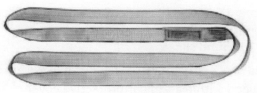

Type 5

### Reverse Eye Type

**Type 6 (RE)**-An endless sling with butted edges sewn together to double the sling width. They have reinforced eyes and wear pads on both sides of body and eyes. The result is an extremely strong and durable sling.

Type 6

To the above, you have the option of different eye treatments including lined bearing points, lined eyes, and wrapped bearing points. They may also be provided as bridle assemblies of 2 or more slings permanently attached to a link. Refer to manufacturer's information to check all the options.

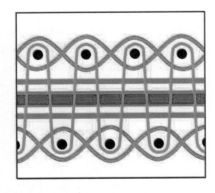

Figure 13-43

**Lift-All Sling Webbing**

● Transverse pick yarns inter-relate with binder/surface yarns.

● Woven surface yarns cover each side and carry a portion of the load.

● Strip of longitudinal core yarns bears majority of load.

● Binder yarns secure the surface yarns to web core yarns.

● Red core warning yarns.

The webbing itself may be woven in a number of ways. The way Lift-All do it is shown left.

The type of weave they use for their sling webbing has the surface yarns connected from side to side, which not only protects the core yarns, but positions all the surface and tensile yarns to work together to support the load.

Wear and damage is a major concern with any type of synthetic sling as it will cause an immediate strength loss. Their webbing has red core yarn to visually reveal damage and act as a basis for sling rejection.

Webbing slings are ideal for use handling loads that require a uniformity of support when being lifted as the load is spread well across the entire width of the sling avoiding point loading. They are unlikely to abrade or otherwise damage finished surfaces. There are a number of different materials used; which you choose depends on intended duty. Nylon will stretch more and absorb shock loading; polyester stretches less for better load control and has better abrasion resistance. Abrasion resistant yarns may be used on the surface; surface treatments for better abrasion resistance are also possible.

The rated capacity of these slings is based on the minimum breaking load of the sewn webbing component and is based on a FOS of 7:1 in the EU; in the USA, the FOS is 5:1. In the USA, webbing slings are not color coded by capacity. In the EU it is understood that it is the intention to do that. Do not rely on color, check the tag!

To increase capacity, 2, 3 or 4 ply slings are manufactured. Widths of up to 18" (450 mm) are available.

As with all slings, the manufacturer will affix a tag indicating ratings for the three regular hitches and will provide information as to the safe use of the sling (including environmental conditions). As with wire rope slings, useful capacity is dependent on the hitch used and sling angle; there are no D/d deductions, but bends should be softened as best possible.

Be aware that these types of slings can stretch significantly (from about 3% to 10% dependent on material and treatment).

### 13.8.2 Round slings

Round slings are endless slings formed with a core of multiple loops of synthetic yarn (polyester or similar) contained within a tubular protective cover of similar material (woven somewhat similarly to a webbing sling). The cover or covers are non-load carrying; the core yarns are the load-carrying elements and move independently of the cover. The covers protect the core yarns against UV and against damage. There are a number of companies making synthetic round slings each with their own proprietary materials, construction and safety features.

The advantages of these types of sling are that they are available to very high capacities; they are light and flexible and are easy to handle and store. They are however susceptible to damage and difficult to inspect for internal damage. Their bulk needs to be accounted for in the design of rigging arrangements.

As with all slings, they should have tags and published capacities for the standard hitches; the useable vertical capacity is dependent on the hitch used and the sling angle.

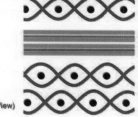

Figure 13-44

## Tuflex Roundslings

- Transverse pick yarns position surface yarns and protect core yarns
- Woven surface yarns also protect core yarns, carry no load
- Longitudinal core yarns carry 100% of load
- Red core warning yarns

*Tuflex* (Side View)

Roundsling construction, as shown above, protects all load carrying core yarns from abrasion with an independent, woven jacket. Replacement is not necessary until the red striped white core yarns can be seen through holes in the jacket. When core yarns are visible, sling must be removed from service. *Tuflex* roundslings provide double wall protection for extended sling life.

The graphic left shows the general construction and features of Lift-All's range of Tuflex Roundslings. They use polyester yarn for the core. Red fibers are included as a warning of damage. A double wall protective cover made of bulked nylon is used.

Stretch with these slings is up to approximately 3%.

The below is a Lift-All extract showing the characteristics of their range of Tuflex endless round slings.

For information only, do not use for lifting purposes. All manufacturers produce the equivalent.

Note that these slings are color coded. Not all manufacturers use the same colors, so do not rely on color alone – check the tag!

| WSTDA Sling Size | Part No. | Color | Vertical | Choker | Basket | Minimum Length (ft.) | Weight (lbs. / ft.) | Body Dia. Relaxed (in.) | Width at Load (in.) | Mimimum Hardware Dia. ** (in.) |
|---|---|---|---|---|---|---|---|---|---|---|
| 1 | EN30 | Purple | 2,600 | 2,100 | 5,200 | 1 1/2 | .2 | 5/8 | 1 1/8 | 1/2 |
| 2 | EN60 | Green | 5,300 | 4,200 | 10,600 | 1 1/2 | .3 | 7/8 | 1 1/2 | 5/8 |
| 3 | EN90 | Yellow | 8,400 | 6,700 | 16,800 | 3 | .5 | 1 1/8 | 1 7/8 | 3/4 |
| 4 | EN120 | Tan | 10,600 | 8,500 | 21,200 | 3 | .6 | 1 1/8 | 2 1/8 | 7/8 |
| 5 | EN150 | Red | 13,200 | 10,600 | 26,400 | 3 | .8 | 1 3/8 | 2 1/4 | 1 |
| 6 | EN180 | White | 16,800 | 13,400 | 33,600 | 3 | .9 | 1 3/8 | 2 1/2 | 1 1/8 |
| 7 | EN240 | Blue | 21,200 | 17,000 | 42,400 | 3 | 1.3 | 1 3/4 | 3 | 1 1/4 |
| 9 | EN360 | Grey | 31,000 | 24,800 | 62,000 | 3 | 1.7 | 2 1/4 | 3 3/4 | 1 1/2 |
| 11 | EN600 | Brown | 53,000 | 42,400 | 106,000 | 8 | 2.8 | 2 3/4 | 4 5/8 | 1 7/8 |
| 12 | EN800 | Olive | 66,000 | 52,800 | 132,000 | 8 | 3.4 | 3 1/8 | 5 1/4 | 2 1/8 |
| 13 | EN1000 | Black | 90,000 | 72,000 | 180,000 | 8 | 4.3 | 3 5/8 | 6 | 2 1/2 |

Rated Capacity (lbs.)* — Vertical / Choker / Basket. Approximate Measurements. Figure 13-45

Note that the Web Sling & Tie Down Association allocates standard sling sizes to Synthetic Polyester Round Slings which tie in with the Lift-All information as shown in the LH column. (They also specify a Size 10, which is rated at 40,000# in a vertical hitch).

When a round sling is loaded, the presumption is that it will become somewhat elliptical at an aspect ratio of about 3:1. The loaded width will therefore be about 1.7x the unloaded body diameter.

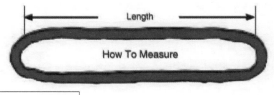

Figure 13-46

Notes:

(i) unlike wire rope grommets, sling lengths are measured bearing point to bearing point.

(ii) capacity in the USA is based on a FOS of 5 (ASME B30.9) but is based on a FOS of 7 in the E.U.

Another manufacturer, SLINGMAX®, makes a range of slings that feature two independent parallel round slings within a common cover, marketed as "Twin-Path®" slings. The core yarn composition is their patented specification; the cover is a bulked nylon construction. All these slings feature overload tell-tails, which if sucked up into the cover are a cause for sling rejection. A fiber optic cable is also (optionally) provided; if broken, it will not transmit light and is a sign of possible overload. The independent paths provide a degree of security; if one path should fail in use, one remains (albeit with a reduced but sufficient FOS of 2.5). Standard details are shown above. Twin-Path® slings are also available as a 2-leg bridle and as an eye-eye type sling. A self-adjusting bridle design is also available where odd length legs are needed.

## Twin-Path® Extra Check-Fast® Sling

Figure 13-47

US Patent #7,926,859, #7,661,737, #7,568,333   CA #2,547,632
EP #1,899,255   Japan #4,864,965   China #ZL200680017605.5

**TPXCF** These slings have overload indicators, Covermax® covers for superior abrasion resistance and inner red covers. They are used worldwide in place of steel rigging for heavy lifts. They are approximately 10% of the weight of a steel sling and products are repairable. The Twin-Path® patented design provides the rigger with two independent connections between the hook and the load for protection assurance. These slings have less than 1% elongation at rated capacity. If ergonomics, productivity and safety are important, then these slings are your best choice. Independent testing shows that K-Spec® is the longest lasting load bearing core yarn in any sling.

NOTE: Capacities shown include both paths and are for one complete sling. Sling ratings based on commercial fittings of equal or greater capacity. Conforms to ANSI/ASME B30.9 chapter 6, NAVFAC P-307 section 14.7.4.3, and the Cordage Institute Roundsling Standard. This chart is based on a 5:1 Design Factor (DF); but any other DF can be fabricated. Higher capacity slings are available. **CAPACITIES ARE IN POUNDS (LBS.).**

| Twin-Path® Sling Stock No. | Vertical | Choker | Vertical Basket 90° | Basket Hitches 60° | Basket Hitches 45° | Approximate Weight (Lbs. per Ft.) (Bearing-Bearing) | Nominal Body Width (Inches)* |
|---|---|---|---|---|---|---|---|
| TPXCF/TPXC 1000 | 10,000 | 8,000 | 20,000 | 17,320 | 14,140 | .40 | 1.5 - 3" |
| TPXCF/TPXC 1500 | 15,000 | 12,000 | 30,000 | 25,980 | 21,210 | .45 | 1.5 - 3" |
| TPXCF/TPXC 2000 | 20,000 | 16,000 | 40,000 | 34,640 | 28,280 | .51 | 1.5 - 3" |
| TPXCF/TPXC 2500 | 25,000 | 20,000 | 50,000 | 43,300 | 35,350 | .57 | 2.0 - 4" |
| TPXCF/TPXC 3000 | 30,000 | 24,000 | 60,000 | 51,960 | 42,420 | .71 | 2.0 - 4" |
| TPXCF/TPXC 4000 | 40,000 | 32,000 | 80,000 | 69,280 | 56,560 | .83 | 2.0 - 4" |
| TPXCF/TPXC 5000 | 50,000 | 40,000 | 100,000 | 86,600 | 70,700 | 1.14 | 2.5 - 5" |
| TPXCF/TPXC 6000 | 60,000 | 48,000 | 120,000 | 103,920 | 84,840 | 1.27 | 2.5 - 5" |
| TPXCF/TPXC 7000 | 70,000 | 56,000 | 140,000 | 121,240 | 98,980 | 1.39 | 2.5 - 5" |
| TPXCF/TPXC 8500 | 85,000 | 68,000 | 170,000 | 147,220 | 120,190 | 1.65 | 3.0 - 6" |
| TPXCF/TPXC 10000 | 100,000 | 80,000 | 200,000 | 173,200 | 141,400 | 1.84 | 3.0 - 6" |
| TPXCF/TPXC 12500 | 125,000 | 100,000 | 250,000 | 216,500 | 176,750 | 2.35 | 4.0 - 8" |
| TPXCF/TPXC 15000 | 150,000 | 120,000 | 300,000 | 259,800 | 212,100 | 2.66 | 4.0 - 8" |
| TPXCF/TPXC 17500 | 175,000 | 140,000 | 350,000 | 303,100 | 247,450 | 3.14 | 4.0 - 8" |
| TPXCF/TPXC 20000 | 200,000 | 160,000 | 400,000 | 346,400 | 282,800 | 3.45 | 5.0 - 10" |
| TPXCF/TPXC 25000 | 250,000 | 200,000 | 500,000 | 433,000 | 353,500 | 4.07 | 5.0 - 10" |
| TPXCF/TPXC 27500 | 275,000 | 220,000 | 550,000 | 476,300 | 388,850 | 4.61 | 6.0 - 12" |
| TPXCF/TPXC 30000 | 300,000 | 240,000 | 600,000 | 519,600 | 424,200 | 4.92 | 6.0 - 12" |
| TPXCF/TPXC 40000 | 400,000 | 320,000 | 800,000 | 692,800 | 565,600 | 6.54 | 7.0 - 14" |
| TPXCF/TPXC 50000 | 500,000 | 400,000 | 1,000,000 | 866,000 | 707,000 | 8.15 | 7.0 - 14" |
| TPXCF/TPXC 60000 | 600,000 | 480,000 | 1,200,000 | 1,039,000 | 848,000 | 10.20 | 11.0 - 22" |

*Dimensions can vary according to the hardware or bearing points the slings are used with.   **METRIC SLINGS AVAILABLE**
Minimum is "tapered" width; Maximum is the flat tubing width.

Metric charts are available at 5:1 and 7:1 factors of safety (note local code requirements).

Refer to the SLINGMAX® website for up-to-date information and detailed product information.

Note: Always refer to manufacturer's product warnings and comply with them.

### 13.8.3  Hitches in synthetic slings

As you can see from the above tables, you have the same basic hitches available with synthetic slings as you have with wire rope slings, i.e. vertical (straight pull), choke (basic or wrapped), basket (vertical or inclined legs, basic or wrapped).

Figure 13-48

Figure 13-49

Basic choke hitch

The basic choke will tighten around a load but will not properly secure items located in the angle by the choke. There is a real risk of insecure items slipping out, particularly if only a single hitch is used as here and the load is unstable.

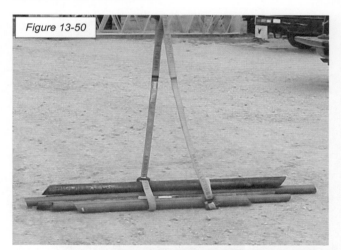

Figure 13-50

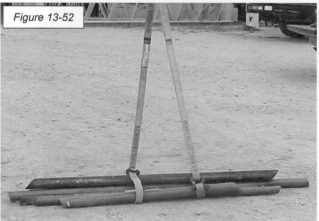

Figure 13-52

Figure 13-51

A pair of basic chokes will tighten around a load (as you can see above) and will be much more stable, but will still not properly secure loose items located in the angle by the choke (see right). Note if the load could be affected by torsion between the two chokes, but you can tolerate a little rolling as the choke tightens, make the choke on the same side of the load as here. If the load can tolerate a little torsion, but you don't want it to roll any as the chokes tighten, (for instance a steel beam) oppose the chokes on opposite sides of the load.

Figure 13-53

Wrapped choke – the sling has full 360° contact and the choke will secure loose items against slipping, even when inclined.

A wrapped choke hitch has no better or worse capacity than a basic choke.

Note that a choked synthetic sling (in the USA at least) has a capacity of about 80% of the vertical (straight pull) capacity of the sling, as against a wire rope sling where the choke capacity is about 75%.

Basket hitches with basically vertical legs as here are rated at twice the WLL (rated capacity) of the sling in a straight pull.

Figure 13-54

Figure 13-55

### Basic Basket Hitch – paired

The basic basket hitch cradles the load and will not secure a number of loose items. A single basketed sling would be fundamentally unstable. Always use in pairs and wrap them if bundling loads or where the C of G is uncertain and the load could slide.

Figure 13-56

Figure 13-57

Wrapped Basket Hitch – paired

This arrangement has full 360° contact and will secure loose items against slipping. The load will be stable and secure.

### 13.8.4   Use factors that affect the capacity of synthetic slings

Angle of use

As with wire rope slings, the angle at which you use synthetic slings affects the force you induce in them (the less vertical the sling, the less effective it is in supporting a vertical load and therefore the greater the tension). It is a purely a matter of trigonometry and nothing to do with the sling itself. You can either:

a.  Do the math, work out the tensions and select slings whose basic rated capacities (WLL) exceed those forces. e.g. a pair of slings (located equidistant about the C of G) used at 60° to lift a 17,320 lb load will each need to contribute 8,660 lbs vertical. The induced sling tension = 8,660 / sin(60) = 10,000 lbs. As a minimum you therefore need a pair of slings such as the SLINGMAX® TPXC1000 (see preceding table) round sling which is rated at 10,000 lbs in a straight pull.

b.  Look up the effective vertical capacity of paired slings in the manufacturer's tables. e.g. in the SLINGMAX® table above look for a basketed sling whose effective vertical capacity at 60° is 10,000 lbs or better, i.e. a TPXC1000. Note: a basketed sling is effectively the same as a pair of individual slings so far as capacity goes. If the slings were at 45° (to the horizontal), you'd need to go up a size and choose a pair of TPXC1500 slings whose basket capacity is 21,210 lbs. If between angles, go to the more conservative quoted angular capacity.

Bending

Unlike wire rope slings, the construction of a synthetic sling is not severely disturbed by a tight bend and high local stresses are not induced. There is as yet, no equivalent of McWhyte's efficiency curve (D/d deductions) for synthetic slings that I am aware of and no requirement to reduce the capacity of a synthetic sling when it is bent around an object. That said, to claim they are totally unaffected by a tight bend cannot be true and (in addition to the need to protect the sling against cutting) it is good practice to "soften" the edge / corner to give the sling a reasonably generous radius for it to bend around and bear on. *Note that SLINGMAX® has recently published a table of minimum recommended diameters for hardware over which their TwinPath® slings are bent. Contact them for details.*

## 13.9 Protection of slings at bearing points

Whenever you bend a sling around a corner or over a sharp edge, you must protect it.

Note that ASME B30.9 requires that "Slings in contact with edges, corners, protrusions, or abrasive surfaces shall be protected with a material of sufficient strength, thickness, and construction to prevent damage."

With synthetic slings, the main concern is damage; it is vital that they be protected against cuts at sharp edges; abrasion protection is also very important at bearing points. Wire rope slings need to be protected against cutting, kinking and distortion. For them to work correctly their strands need to maintain their correct relative locations around the core – if you bend them too tightly, the construction is disturbed and the capacity reduced. So, with wire rope slings maintaining a decent bend ratio (D/d) is important also.

Figure 13-58

Wire rope slings.

A generous radius is required at bearing points when a sling is diverted to avoid damage and required capacity reduction. This edge is not sharp, but the radius is too small and the sling will be kinked and its capacity reduced.

Figure 13-59

Synthetic sling hitches.

Synthetic slings are very vulnerable to damage including cutting. You must be especially careful to protect them at sharp edges. This edge is not particularly sharp but would benefit from a protector.

Note the sharpness of the bend does not reduce capacity of synthetic slings unlike wire rope slings.

Figure 13-60

Figure 13-61

### Synthetic web sling protection.

Above - this edge is not particularly sharp, but it would be better to provide some protection and softening of the bend radius.

Top right – edge is sharp, belting may help some, but this belting is likely to be of little use.

Right - using a length of split steel tube / pipe over a sharp corner is an effective and cost-effective way of providing a smooth rounded bearing surface that will protect the sling and soften bending.

Figure 13-62

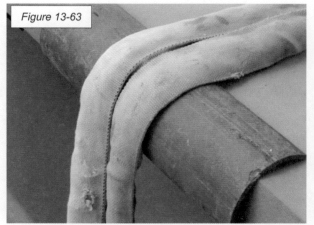

Figure 13-63

Figure 13-64

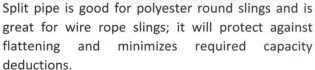

Split pipe is good for polyester round slings and is great for wire rope slings; it will protect against flattening and minimizes required capacity deductions.

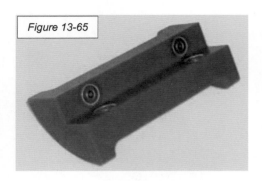

Figure 13-65

This Magnetic Sling Protector is manufactured by Linton Rigging Gear Supply LLC and is available from leading rigging suppliers. Made from nylon in 6", 9", 12" and 18" versions, it is provided with four imbedded magnets allowing it to be easily attached to the corner of a steel section or fabrication at a sling bearing point. It will protect against wear and cutting and "softens" the severity of bending in both wire rope and synthetic sling applications.

Many sling manufacturers have their own patent protection and/or softening products / devices; check them out.

Be aware that some devices are intended to protect against wear or abrasion but will not protect against cutting. Where bending a sling over a sharp corner, you are recommended to use substantial corner protectors, not simply a device described as a "softener". Synthetic slings are particularly susceptible to cutting, wire rope slings can be severely damaged if bent too tightly.

# 14 Shackles

When it comes to specifying shackles to attach your slings to a lug, spreader bar, lift beam or similar, you have a variety of types and manufacturers to choose from. The following will give you a brief overview on the characteristics of the different sorts of shackles, how to make an appropriate selection and what to watch out for in designing for their use. If you want to get into more depth on the topic, the manufacturers and industry associations have great information; there is a wealth of information in the ASME and other standards and there are many publications describing field considerations for their use. See the reference list to the rear.

## 14.1 Nomenclature

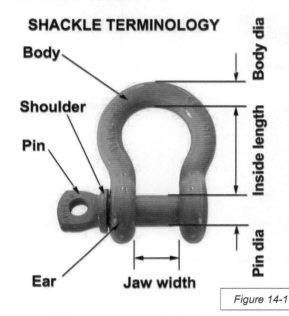

Figure 14-1

It helps when discussing shackles (or anything in fact) to understand the terminology. Much of rigging terminology goes back to the days of sailing ships and varies some according to local custom.

The body of the shackle itself may be referred to as the bow; the curved part of the body may be referred to as the bow, bail (bale), dee or bowl.

In the UK, an anchor shackle is a bow shackle; a chain shackle is a dee shackle.

Dimensions that are of particular interest are noted. Note that a 2" shackle refers to the body diameter, not the pin diameter (which would likely be 2.25").

## 14.2 Manufacturers

There are a number of preeminent manufacturers of shackles including, but not restricted to, Crosby, Columbus McKinnon (Midland), Skookum (Ulven), Van Beest (Green Pin), Gunnebo, Chicago Hardware & Fixture. This list is by no means exhaustive and is not meant to imply that only these companies make quality products; however, what you want from a shackle manufacturer is guaranteed quality at a fair price and this is not a place to cut corners on price. I am still a believer in ordering shackles load tested; I think it is relatively cheap insurance and would hopefully detect a gross manufacturing defect or deficiency.

On the subject of load testing, understand its limitations. Successfully testing something to say 2x rated capacity doesn't prove it would have failed at, or greater than, the required 5x. It just proves it held together on that occasion at 2x; it may be cracked and have been about to fail at 2.1x. It does however give you some confidence it won't fail on you when you use it later at 1x. Load testing is not enough in its own right and isn't a substitute for quality processes or proper inspection.

## 14.3 Standard shackle patterns and options

Traditional styles are shown below (images are of Columbus McKinnon shackles).

As noted above, you have quite a number of options. Basic varieties of "body type" are the chain (Dee) shackle and the anchor (Bow) type. Pin types include screw pin, bolt type and round pin. The types you don't want to use for lifting purposes are the round pin types as the security of the pin in the body relies entirely on a cotter (split) pin. Material types include carbon steel (quenched and tempered) and high alloy steel. (Carbon steel shackles may still have alloy pins). Finish options include self-color, painted and galvanized. For most lifting applications using wire rope or synthetic slings, you would need the space in the bow that the anchor type affords. Do not specify a screw pin type for a long term application or for any application where there is a chance of the pin unscrewing in use.

Figure 14-2

**Screw pin chain shackle**

**Bolt type chain shackle**

**Round pin chain shackle**

**Screw pin anchor shackle**

**Bolt type anchor shackle**

**Round pin anchor shackle**

Figure 14-3

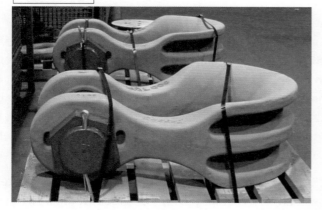

Figure 14-4

More recent developments include Wide-Body shackles such as these made by Crosby. They provide a generously radiused bearing surface that is much kinder on the sling or sling eye. I would recommend these, particularly when basketing a sling over a shackle. It will help to avoid permanent kinks in the sling and you won't have to derate the hitch as much for the D/d considerations. They are now available from 7 t to 1550 t. Note that they are high strength and the shackle pin is relatively smaller. Check the lug!

Figure 14-5

Another useful type when lifting using synthetic web slings is the Sling Saver type such as the Crosby example shown. This provides a wide bearing surface for the web sling avoiding pinching or bunching of the sling ensuring proper load distribution within the sling's fibers.

These are available up to about 50 tons in screw pin or bolt type patterns. Various fittings and accessories are available.

## 14.4 Specials

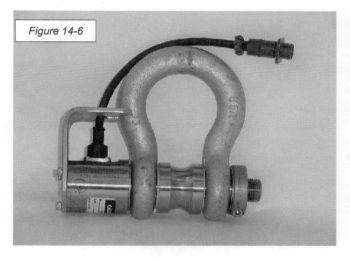

Figure 14-6

Strainsert offer a range of Force Sensing Shackle bolts that can be used to replace the standard bolts or pins in Crosby or Skookum shackles up to 4" size (220,000#). The pin incorporates a strain gauge bridge circuit cable-linked to remote instrumentation to provide a load readout wherever you need it.

This can be a good option where you want to weigh a load or determine tension in a system to a fair degree of accuracy. Claimed accuracy of these is approximately 1%. Refer to the manufacturers for details.

There are other less common specialist varieties available from various manufacturers including large bow and wide mouth shackles; low temperature shackles are available. Sea-fit Inc in the USA offers a "Super Shackle" which is a wide body variety with even greater bearing diameter. Skookum offers a number of quality niche products including shackles for handling sheet piles including a "ground-release" option. Stainless steel shackles are available. Make sure any shackle you use for lifting is rated for lifting.

Some manufacturers are offering RFID (radio frequency ID) chipping of certain of their shackles for tracking purposes and inspection record keeping.

## 14.5 Specifying a shackle

Figure 14-7

You will often see a rigging plan specify something like "12 ton shackle" or "$1\frac{1}{4}$ in shackle". It is not enough information to get what you want!

Both these shackles (left) are 12 ton shackles. Plainly they are physically different: that might matter – say to fit a lug, other times maybe not. Specifying just the capacity is not enough.

If you specify just a 2" shackle, you might get a 35 ton G2130 or maybe a 55 ton G2140 alloy shackle.

You might need 45 tons, so quoting size alone isn't enough either. You need to quote size, capacity (WLL), screw pin type and bow type, say "35 ton Crosby G2130 (2")". The environment is important also, if you intend to use the shackle in extreme temperatures or acidic / caustic environments specify shackles intended for those applications. Finish may be important too; if you want a galvanized shackle for instance (as against self-color), be sure to specify it. (The "G" in G2130 for instance indicates galvanized).

## 14.6 Standards

The US industry standard relating to Rigging Hardware (including shackles) for lifting purposes is ASME B30.26. Key provisions include:

- A minimum Factor of Safety of 5:1 on shackles up to 150 ton (136 t), 4:1 above that.

- No statutory requirement to load test shackles, but if specified, the proof load for shackles up to 150 tons (136 t) is a min of 2x and a max of 2.2x; above that it is a minimum of 1.33x and a max of 2x. *(I would recommend specifying that shackles are supplied load tested, particularly at the larger sizes where it is not such a significant cost penalty – it is cheap insurance; I do not advocate periodic load testing).*

- Shackles to be marked with the name of mark of the manufacturer, rated load and size. Do not use a shackle that does not have the required markings.

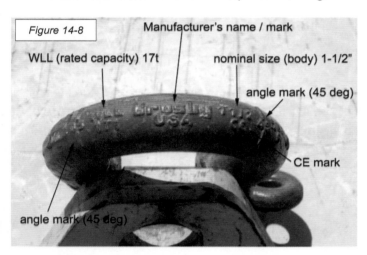

Figure 14-8
Manufacturer's name / mark
WLL (rated capacity) 17t
nominal size (body) 1-1/2"
angle mark (45 deg)
CE mark
angle mark (45 deg)

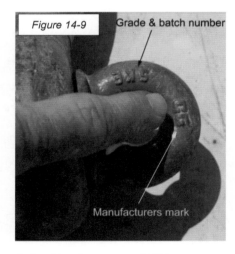

Figure 14-9
Grade & batch number
Manufacturers mark

In Europe, shackles may be manufactured to EN 13889 – Forged steel shackles for general lifting purposes or other national or ISO standards. European shackles (to a harmonized standard) are not required to be load tested either, but do have to be CE marked and supplied with an EC declaration of conformity (which is the manufacturer asserting the standards to which it was made and its quality). I still recommend they are supplied tested.

Beware of caustic or acid environments, both can affect strength; check with the manufacturers if intending to use shackles below -4F or over 400F.

Most manufacturer's carbon steel shackles are actually rated at 6:1, with alloy shackles being rated at 5:1 (or 4:1) at the heavier sizes).

## 14.7 Proper use of shackles

### 14.7.1  Side loading

Figure 14-10

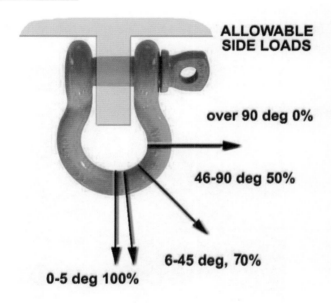

**ALLOWABLE SIDE LOADS**

over 90 deg 0%

46-90 deg 50%

6-45 deg, 70%

0-5 deg 100%

Shackles are designed for in-line loading and you should design your lift so that, so far as it is possible, you load them that way.

However if for instance you are suspending a load with two lugs from a spreader, the standard width intervals on the spreader may not match exactly the span between your lugs and you may have a slight fleet angle on the suspension. Shackles to ASME B30.26 allow for up to 5° inclination without loss of capacity. Although strongly not recommended, if there is no option but to side load a shackle worse than 5°, B30.26 allows reduced loads per the graphic.

If you intend to side load shackles supplied to standards other than ASME B30.26, check that it is permitted, and if so, what reductions apply.

Figure 14-11

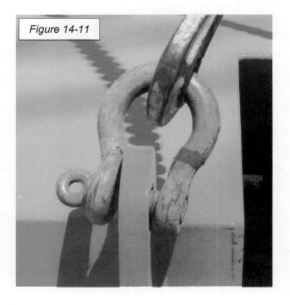

If you have to side load a shackle, you'd be well advised to make the hole a relatively close fit for the shackle pin so that the shackle doesn't rotate too much in the "slop", resulting in very high point loads on the shackle pin and outside edges of the hole in the lug (as is shown here).

You should note that although the shackle may be OK for the bending induced in it, the lug (and its fixing) may <u>not</u>. As noted in the section on lug design, I recommend that the design of lugs intended for in-line loading never-the-less allow for up to 10% lateral force applied at the pin center.

### 14.7.2  Included angle

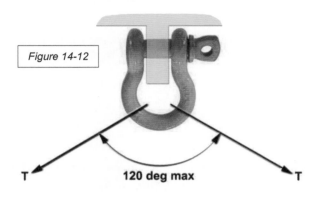

Figure 14-12

120 deg max

If slinging a load from a shackle using two (+/- equally loaded) slings, per ASME B30.26 the maximum included angle between the slings is 120°. Even though the resolution of the two forces is in line and there is no nett rotation on the shackle, you are trying to pull the bow apart. The 120° is compatible with the maximum allowed included angle between a pair of slings (equivalent to each being a minimum 30° to the horizontal). Ideally you want to aim for the included angle to be about 60° or less.

No deration of the shackle applies as long as the two forces are basically the same as the resultant is in-line loading.

Figure 14-13

Neither of these practices is acceptable.

Figure 14-14

### 14.7.3  Wire rope slings – selecting a shackle

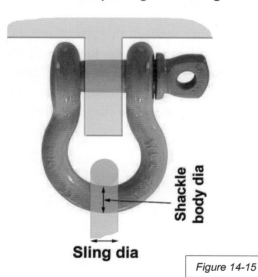

Shackle body dia

Sling dia

Figure 14-15

When using a shackle to attach to the eye of a wire rope sling, you need to check to make sure that you are not bending the wire rope too tightly over the shackle body to the point where you are damaging the eye.

At the point of bearing in the eye, you have two parts of wire and what is the equivalent of a mini (inverted) basket hitch. So long as the D/d ratio (bearing dia / sling dia) at that point is 1 or greater, the bending of the wire rope in the eye will not be the determining factor for the Safe Working Load of the sling. Why is that? At D/d = 1, the bend efficiency is 50% of the basket hitch capacity. The basket hitch capacity is 2x the capacity of the single part wire in the sling body. So the eye capacity = 50% x 2 = the same as the body capacity.

As long as you use a shackle with a body size equal or greater than the wire rope sling diameter, you will be OK. The eye will still likely flatten if used to capacity; it would be kinder on the sling eye to use a wide body shackle and the sling will repay you with an extended life.

As noted earlier, shackles are sized by body diameter, not by pin diameter, which is convenient for this check. A 1" EIPS sling has a capacity of about 8.5 tons (US); a 1" Crosby G2130 shackle is rated for 8.5 tons. A 2" G2130 is rated at 35 tons, a 2" EIPS sling about 32 tons. Size for size, EIPS slings and G2130 (or G209) shackles are comparable.

Where you might hit a problem is fitting a lower grade (say IPS) sling to a higher grade alloy shackle, say a Crosby G-2140.

A 2" Crosby G2140 shackle is rated at 55 tons. An IPS sling rated for 55 tons would have a diameter of approximately 2.875". i.e. capacity for capacity, an IPS sling will have a diameter greater than the body diameter of a high alloy shackle. That would yield a D/d ratio of less than 1, which would be a problem for capacity and would be very detrimental to the shackle eye; an instance for considering a wide-body shackle.

### 14.7.4 Round slings – selecting a shackle

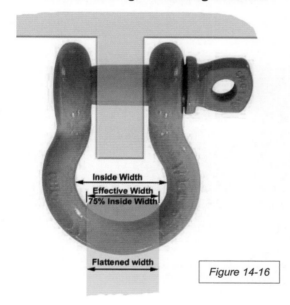

Inside Width

Effective Width
75% Inside Width

Flattened width

Figure 14-16

When attaching to a Polyester Roundsling using a shackle (or similar item of rigging hardware), there are a few considerations to take into account.

Per WSTDA guidelines, there is a minimum pin diameter (shackle body diameter in this case) and a minimum effective contact width. See table below.

For a vertical / choke hitch, the shackle body diameter needs to be a minimum of approximately 0.7x the sling's unloaded diameter and the minimum effective contact width (which approximates to the flattened width of the sling) needs to be about 1.7x the unloaded diameter.

For a basket hitch (where there are two parts of sling in the shackle) those figures are about 1x the sling body diameter for the shackle body and about 3x the sling body diameter for the effective contact width.

For an anchor shackle such as this, the effective bearing width (sling to shackle) will be the flattened width of the sling up to a maximum of 75% of the inside width of the bow. Bunching of the sling up the sides of the bow beyond that width doesn't contribute! Also, the bearing stress = the sling load / (the effective bearing width x the shackle body diameter). This figure must not exceed 7000 psi; if it does, increase the size of the hardware or reduce the permissible sling load.

The above size requirements may dictate the use of a larger shackle than capacity requires (right). If the lug dimensions are already fixed, that may or may not be possible. As noted earlier, consider the use of a Slingsaver (left) or wide-body shackle as a better alternative – that would give better bearing without enlarging the shackle pin diameter and jaw width.

Figure 14-17

Figure 14-18

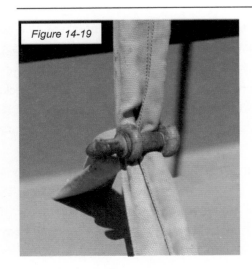

*Figure 14-19*

Synthetic sling choke hitch.

When choking a synthetic sling, the eye goes to the pin not the body as shown here. Neither should the sling be bunched up as is shown here; the shackle needs to be physically large enough to accommodate the sling without doing so.

WSTDA suitable hardware connection sizes for synthetic polyester round slings (single path). Ref WSTDA-RS-2.

*Figure 14-20*

| WSTDA sling size | Vertical / choker hitches | | | Basket hitches | | |
|---|---|---|---|---|---|---|
| | WLL (lbs) | Min pin dia (in) | Min effective contact width (in) | WLL (lbs) | Min pin dia (in) | Min effective contact width (in) |
| 1 | 2,600 | 0.50 | 1.00 | 5,200 | 0.62 | 1.25 |
| 2 | 5,300 | 0.62 | 1.25 | 10,600 | 0.88 | 1.75 |
| 3 | 8,400 | 0.75 | 1.62 | 16,800 | 1.00 | 2.25 |
| 4 | 10,600 | 0.88 | 1.75 | 21,200 | 1.25 | 2.50 |
| 5 | 13,200 | 1.00 | 2.00 | 26,400 | 1.38 | 2.75 |
| 6 | 16,800 | 1.12 | 2.12 | 33,600 | 1.62 | 3.00 |
| 7 | 21,200 | 1.25 | 2.62 | 42,400 | 1.75 | 3.62 |
| 8 | 25,000 | 1.25 | 2.88 | 50,000 | 1.88 | 4.00 |
| 9 | 31,000 | 1.50 | 3.12 | 62,000 | 2.00 | 4.38 |
| 10 | 40,000 | 1.62 | 3.50 | 80,000 | 2.38 | 5.00 |
| 11 | 53,000 | 1.88 | 4.00 | 106,000 | 2.75 | 5.50 |
| 12 | 66,000 | 2.12 | 4.50 | 132,000 | 3.00 | 6.50 |
| 13 | 90,000 | 2.50 | 5.12 | 180,000 | 3.50 | 7.38 |

WSTDA -RS-2

### 14.7.5 Selecting a shackle – load rating

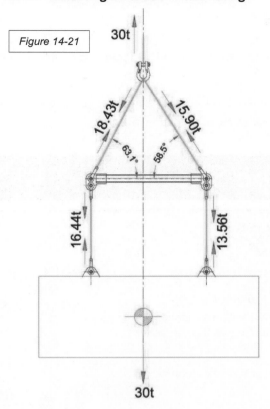

Figure 14-21

Don't forget that when using an arrangement such as this, the tension in the inclined slings will be higher than the tension in the vertical legs. The inclined shackles see the same tension as the inclined slings and need to be rated according.

In this example, the 30 t load has a slightly offset C of G that results in the LH vertical lift lug reaction being 16.44 t and the RH reaction being 13.56 t. Slings and shackles rated at 17 t would be adequate in the vertical legs.

The tension in the inclined slings and shackles = the vertical reaction / the SIN of the angle to the horizontal.

Noting the angles of inclination of the upper slings, this gives 18.43 t to the LHS and 15.90 t to the RHS. The LH tension is greater than 17 t and it will be necessary (as a minimum) to use the next greater rated shackle which is 25 t.

### 14.7.6 Summary - selecting a shackle

When selecting a shackle and planning for its use, you need to:

- Select a type and finish appropriate to the environment and duty
- Specify an adequately rated shackle considering factors such as increase in sling tension when inclined
- Ensure it fits the lug you have in mind; jaw width, pin size, adequate inside length for the sling
- Aim for a diametrical pin hole clearance of about $^1/_8$" to ¼" for larger shackles
- Avoid significant side loading (>5°) if at all possible, check the lift lug can accept any side load you intend
- Aim for the included angle between a pair of slings to be about 60° (or better); never can it be greater than 120°
- Consider using wide body shackles if their physical size is compatible with the lugs you have.
- Consider using Slingsaver shackles for synthetic slings
- Ensure the shackle body diameter is greater than the sling diameter when using wire rope slings
- When using synthetic slings, make sure the sling body diameter is greater than the figure in the table above (noting the type of hitch); that the effective bearing width is greater than the minimums quoted in the table: that the bearing pressure at the point of contact does not exceed 7000 psi
- Fully specify the shackle you intend to use to make sure you get what you wanted
- Note that nominally similar shackles to different standards may vary in physical size
- Check the lugs you have to work with to make sure your intended shackle fits and meets the various criteria outlined in this section
- Note manufacturing tolerances on these items; they are forged (or cast). Do not design lugs etc too tightly

## 14.8 Shackle data

### 14.8.1 Crosby G2130

For reference, an extract of the Crosby® catalog for the G2130 pattern shackles is attached for reference (Fig 14-22).

While current at the time of writing, this information may be subject to change at any time; you are advised to consult the latest Crosby catalog for current details of these shackles and their other products.

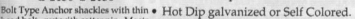

Figure 14-22

# Crosby® Bolt Type Shackles

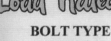   

**BOLT TYPE ANCHOR SHACKLES**

**G-2130 S-2130**

Bolt Type Anchor shackles with thin head bolt - nut with cotter pin. Meets the performance requirements of Federal Specification RR-C-271D Type IVA, Grade A, Class 3, except for those provisions required of the contractor.

- Working Load Limit permantently shown on every shackle. Capacities 1/3 thru 150 metrics tons.
- Forged — Quenched and Tempered, with alloy pins.
- Look for the Red Pin®... the mark of genuine Crosby quality.
- Shackles 55 metric tons and smaller can be furnished proof tested with certificates to designated standards, such as ABS, DNV, Lloyds, or other certification.
- Shackles 85 metric tons and larger can be provided as follows.
  - Non Destructive Tested
  - Serialized Pin and Bow
  - Material Certification (Chemical) Certification must be requested at time of order.
- Hot Dip galvanized or Self Colored.
- Fatigue rated.

**BOLT TYPE CHAIN SHACKLES**

**G-2150 S-2150**

Bolt Type Chain shackles. Thin hex head bolt - nut with cotter pin. Meets the performance requirements of Federal Specification RR-C271D Type IVB, Grade A, Class 3, except for those provisions required of the contractors.

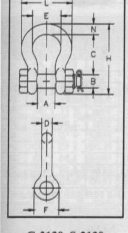

**G-2130 S-2130**

| Nominal Size (in.) | Working Load Limit (t)* | Stock No. G-2130 | Stock No. S-2130 | Weight Each (lbs.) | Dimensions (in.) A | B | C | D | E | F | H | L | N | Tolerance +/- C | Tolerance +/- A |
|---|---|---|---|---|---|---|---|---|---|---|---|---|---|---|---|
| 3/16 | 1/3‡ | 1019464 | - | .06 | .38 | .25 | .88 | .19 | .60 | .56 | 1.47 | .98 | .19 | .06 | .06 |
| 1/4 | 1/2 | 1019466 | - | .11 | .47 | .31 | 1.13 | .25 | .78 | .61 | 1.84 | 1.28 | .25 | .06 | .06 |
| 5/16 | 3/4 | 1019468 | - | .22 | .53 | .38 | 1.22 | .31 | .84 | .75 | 2.09 | 1.47 | .31 | .06 | .06 |
| 3/8 | 1 | 1019470 | - | .33 | .66 | .44 | 1.44 | .38 | 1.03 | .91 | 2.49 | 1.78 | .38 | .13 | .06 |
| 7/16 | 1-1/2 | 1019471 | - | .49 | .75 | .50 | 1.69 | .44 | 1.16 | 1.06 | 2.91 | 2.03 | .44 | .13 | .06 |
| 1/2 | 2 | 1019472 | 1019481 | .79 | .81 | .63 | 1.88 | .50 | 1.31 | 1.19 | 3.28 | 2.31 | .50 | .13 | .06 |
| 5/8 | 3-1/4 | 1019490 | 1019506 | 1.68 | 1.06 | .75 | 2.38 | .63 | 1.69 | 1.50 | 4.19 | 2.94 | .69 | .13 | .06 |
| 3/4 | 4-3/4 | 1019515 | 1019524 | 2.72 | 1.25 | .88 | 2.81 | .75 | 2.00 | 1.81 | 4.97 | 3.50 | .81 | .25 | .06 |
| 7/8 | 6-1/2 | 1019533 | 1019542 | 3.95 | 1.44 | 1.00 | 3.31 | .88 | 2.28 | 2.09 | 5.83 | 4.03 | .97 | .25 | .06 |
| 1 | 8-1/2 | 1019551 | 1019560 | 5.66 | 1.69 | 1.13 | 3.75 | 1.00 | 2.69 | 2.38 | 6.56 | 4.69 | 1.06 | .25 | .06 |
| 1-1/8 | 9-1/2 | 1019579 | 1019588 | 8.27 | 1.81 | 1.25 | 4.25 | 1.13 | 2.91 | 2.69 | 7.47 | 5.16 | 1.25 | .25 | .06 |
| 1-1/4 | 12 | 1019597 | 1019604 | 11.71 | 2.03 | 1.38 | 4.69 | 1.25 | 3.25 | 3.00 | 8.25 | 5.75 | 1.38 | .25 | .06 |
| 1-3/8 | 13-1/2 | 1019613 | 1019622 | 15.83 | 2.25 | 1.50 | 5.25 | 1.38 | 3.63 | 3.31 | 9.16 | 6.38 | 1.50 | .25 | .13 |
| 1-1/2 | 17 | 1019631 | 1019640 | 20.80 | 2.38 | 1.63 | 5.75 | 1.50 | 3.88 | 3.63 | 10.00 | 6.88 | 1.62 | .25 | .13 |
| 1-3/4 | 25 | 1019659 | 1019668 | 33.91 | 2.88 | 2.00 | 7.00 | 1.75 | 5.00 | 4.19 | 12.34 | 8.86 | 2.25 | .25 | .13 |
| 2 | 35 | 1019677 | 1019686 | 52.25 | 3.25 | 2.25 | 7.75 | 2.00 | 5.75 | 4.81 | 13.68 | 9.97 | 2.40 | .25 | .13 |
| 2-1/2 | 55 | 1019695 | 1019702 | 98.25 | 4.13 | 2.75 | 10.50 | 2.62 | 7.25 | 5.69 | 17.84 | 12.87 | 3.13 | .25 | .25 |
| 3 | † 85 | 1019711 | - | 154.00 | 5.00 | 3.25 | 13.00 | 3.00 | 7.88 | 6.50 | 21.50 | 14.36 | 3.62 | .25 | .25 |
| 3-1/2 | † 120 ‡ | 1019739 | - | 265.00 | 5.25 | 3.75 | 14.63 | 3.62 | 9.00 | 8.00 | 24.63 | 16.50 | 4.12 | .25 | .25 |
| 4 | † 150 ‡ | 1019757 | - | 338.00 | 5.50 | 4.25 | 14.50 | 4.10 | 10.00 | 9.00 | 25.69 | 18.42 | 4.56 | .25 | .25 |

Note an 85 ton G2140 alloy shackle is the same size as a 55 ton G2130 shackle: a 120 ton G2140 is the same size as an 85 ton G2130. There are a few other matches too.

### 14.8.2 Green pin standard shackles

For reference, an extract of the Green pin catalog for their Standard pattern shackles (bow shackles with safety bolt type) is attached hereafter (Fig 14-23). Dimensions are very close to Crosby's metric equivalents, but not identical.

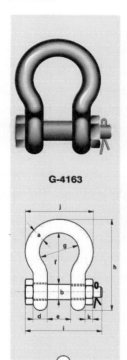

G-4163

## Green Pin® Standard Shackles
### bow shackles with safety bolt

Figure 14-23

- **Material** : bow and pin high tensile steel, Grade 6, quenched and tempered
- **Safety Factor** : MBL equals 6 x WLL
- **Standard** : EN 13889 and
  meets performance requirements of US Fed. Spec. RR-C-271 Type IVA Class 3, Grade A
- **Finish** : hot dipped galvanized
- **Temperature Range** : -20°C up to +200°C
- **Certification** : at no extra charges this product can be supplied with a works certificate, certificate of basic raw material, manufacturer test certificate and/or EC Declaration of Conformity

| working load limit | diameter bow | diameter pin | diameter eye | width eye | width inside | length inside | width bow | length | length bolt | width | thickness nut | weight each |
|---|---|---|---|---|---|---|---|---|---|---|---|---|
| | a | b | c | d | e | f | g | h | i | j | k | |
| tons | mm | mm | mm | mm | mm | mm | mm | mm | mm | mm | mm | kg |
| 0.5 | 7 | 8 | 17 | 7 | 12 | 29 | 20 | 54 | 43 | 37 | 4 | 0.06 |
| 0.75 | 9 | 10 | 21 | 9 | 13.5 | 32 | 22 | 61 | 51 | 42 | 5 | 0.11 |
| 1 | 10 | 11 | 23 | 10 | 17 | 36.5 | 26 | 71 | 61 | 49 | 8 | 0.16 |
| 1.5 | 11 | 13 | 26 | 11 | 19 | 43 | 29 | 80 | 68 | 54 | 11 | 0.22 |
| 2 | 13.5 | 16 | 34 | 13.5 | 22 | 51 | 32 | 91 | 83 | 63 | 13 | 0.42 |
| 3.25 | 16 | 19 | 40 | 16 | 27 | 64 | 43 | 114 | 99 | 79 | 17 | 0.74 |
| 4.75 | 19 | 22 | 47 | 19 | 31 | 76 | 51 | 136 | 115 | 94 | 20 | 1.18 |
| 6.5 | 22 | 25 | 53 | 22 | 36 | 83 | 58 | 157 | 131 | 107 | 23 | 1.77 |
| 8.5 | 25 | 28 | 60 | 25 | 43 | 95 | 68 | 176 | 151 | 124 | 25 | 2.58 |
| 9.5 | 28 | 32 | 67 | 28 | 47 | 108 | 75 | 197 | 167 | 137 | 28 | 3.66 |
| 12 | 32 | 35 | 74 | 32 | 51 | 115 | 83 | 218 | 179 | 154 | 31 | 4.91 |
| 13.5 | 35 | 38 | 80 | 35 | 57 | 133 | 92 | 240 | 198 | 170 | 34 | 6.54 |
| 17 | 38 | 42 | 89 | 38 | 60 | 146 | 99 | 262 | 202 | 183 | 19 | 8.19 |
| 25 | 45 | 50 | 104 | 45 | 74 | 178 | 126 | 314 | 244 | 226 | 24 | 14.22 |
| 35 | 50 | 57 | 111 | 50 | 83 | 197 | 138 | 358 | 270 | 250 | 27 | 19.85 |
| 42.5 | 57 | 65 | 134 | 57 | 95 | 222 | 160 | 414 | 302 | 287 | 30 | 28.33 |
| 55 | 65 | 70 | 145 | 65 | 105 | 260 | 180 | 463 | 330 | 329 | 33 | 39.59 |
| 85 | 75 | 83 | 163 | 75 | 127 | 329 | 190 | 556 | 376 | 355 | 40 | 62 |

While current at the time of writing, this information may be subject to change at any time; you are advised to check with Van Beest for current details of these shackles, their Heavy Duty shackles and their other products.

In your rigging arrangements, you should always note the pattern of the shackles you intend, and acceptable alternatives where applicable. Simply specifying a required WLL is insufficient information as there can be a lot of variation dimensionally between similarly rated shackles of different types. Also note that different types of shackles have different intended uses – your selection needs to be appropriate.

# 15 Assessing support reactions

We know from earlier that we can determine the location of the C of G (in plan at least) if we know the support reactions. Does it work the other way round? If we know the location of the C of G, can we predict the support reactions? It's a bit of yes, no and maybe.

## 15.1 Determining support reactions knowing C of G location

Turning our earlier skid example on its head, if we know the location of the C of G, how can we determine the vertical support reactions at the 6 legs? The simple answer is that there is no simple answer to that question. If the skid is stiff and the supports are similarly very stiff, then it could well be that as a result of tolerances, one or more supports points have air gaps. You can only really guarantee that three supports carry load; even then only two diagonal supports might be doing all the work and the third balancing it.

In practice nothing is infinitely stiff; if the situation warrants it, the structure and its supports can be modeled using a finite element program such as STAAD Pro and the theoretical support loads determined. The way in which the loads & stresses within the structure change if support heights vary can be investigated.

So, what do we do in the field if we need to figure out say temporary supports? In the case of 6 legs, if the C of G is fairly central, I would estimate that anyone could carry 25% of the load and size my supports and load-spreading accordingly. As the load is just touching down, you should shim out the supports with steel / plywood to a sliding fit, and then lower off. There should be enough compliance in the system to ensure that all points carry useful load and enough reserve in the design to cope with it if they don't.

Note:

i.   the designers of the skid may well have assumed that in all its journeys, the skid is supported at every support point per the theoretical loadings – not supporting one or more points may well over-stress the piece.

ii.  when designing say sea-fastenings and grillages and the like where marine dynamic effects come into play, accelerations due to pitch, roll, heave need to be considered. These accelerations increase the apparent weight and vary by locale and carrying vessel type. Refer to Noble Denton or other applicable guidelines as a design basis.

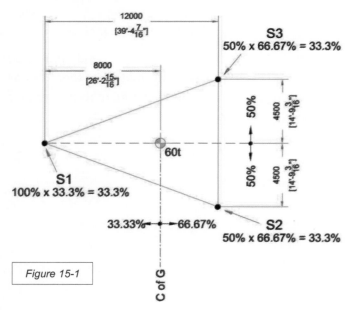

Figure 15-1

A 3-point support can be determined. You could think of this as a T-shaped beam arrangement. Looking in plan, firstly we have a single 12 m beam spanning from S1 to a support at the midpoint of a second beam spanning from S2-S3. The 60 t load is supported on the first beam 8m distant from S1, so S1 supports 4 m/12 m = 33.3% of the load. The beam end supported on S2-S3 sees the remaining 66.7%. This is equally divided between S2 and S3, so they also see 33.3%. If the load is applied on the center line of a triangle 1/3 of the height from the base, as here, the three loads will always be equal. Support elevation differences will not affect this unless they are sufficient to throw the C of G off line in plan.

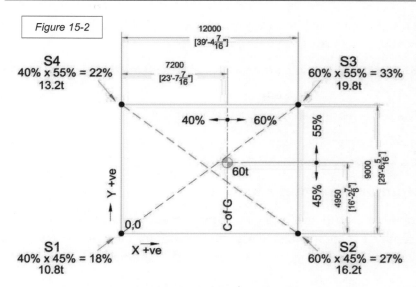

Figure 15-2

Without doing a finite element analysis considering the stiffness of the load and its supports, a 4-point support can only be estimated on the basis that the supports are absolutely level, which they won't be, and the load is flexible enough to load all the supports accommodating tolerances.

You can think of this an H-shaped beam arrangement. We have a single 12 m beam carrying the 60 t load supported at one end by a 9 m beam S1-S4 and at the other end by a 9 m beam S2-S3. The location of the C of G is off center in this case.

By calculation, the 60 t is split 40% to line S1-S4 and 60% to line S2-S3. Each of these 2 reactions is then split 55% to line S4-S3 and 45% to line S1-S2. Multiplying this out gives a theoretical 18%, 27%, 33%, and 22%. S3 at 19.8 t is the maximum as it is closest to the C of G. S1 being furthest away sees only 10.8 t.

Let's consider what happens if the skid is stiff, support S4 is low and we don't shim it out.

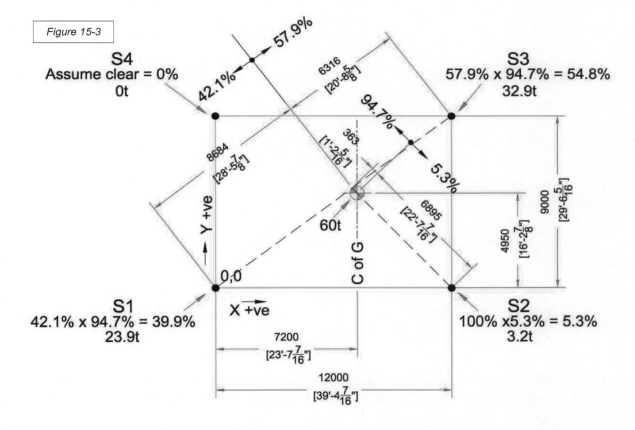

Figure 15-3

There is now a situation in which the load is only supported on S1-S2-S3; it becomes a 3-point support exercise. We can think of the support as a 2-beam arrangement, Beam 1 spanning from S1 to S3 and Beam 2 from S2 through the C of G to a support point on Beam1. Beam 2 initially carries the load; it has a total length of 7258 mm and the load is applied 363 mm from Beam 1. By calc, 94.7% of the load goes to the support on S1-S3 and only the remaining 5.3% goes to S2. The S1-S3 "beam" is 15000 mm long and the point at which the 94.7% "support" load is applied is 6316 mm from S3. By calculation, 42.1% of that load goes to S1 and 57.9% to

S3. Multiplying it out gives 42.1% x 94.7% = 39.9% of the 60 t weight = 23.9 t goes to S1; 57.9% x 94.7% = 54.8% x 60t = 32.9 t goes to point S3 and 5.3% of 60 t = 3.2 t goes to S2.

The load is thus basically balancing on S1-S3 with S2 providing the balance load. You might expect this as the C of G is very close to the S1-S3 line.

S3 was theoretically 19.8 t but is actually 32.9 t – more than half of the total load on one point only!

It pays to be realistically conservative when assessing loads. It is not unusual to go to a support under something in a laydown area and find it is loose or you can see daylight.

## 15.2 Multiple supports on a common line under a load

If a uniform relatively flexible load is supported on stiff level supports, it may be a reasonable approximation (if not 100% correct) to consider that the supports share the load in accordance with load concentration i.e. each will take the weight attributable to the zone it is supporting. Simplistically it looks something like the below.

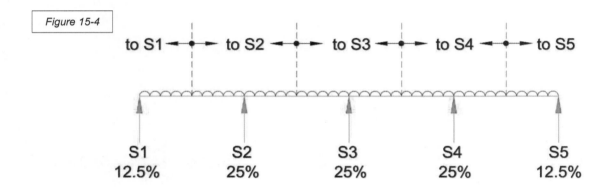

Figure 15-4

What happens if you lose a support, say S3? Is the load S3 was carrying shared equally between S2 and S4 so that they now get 37.5% each? It's not likely that it will be so.

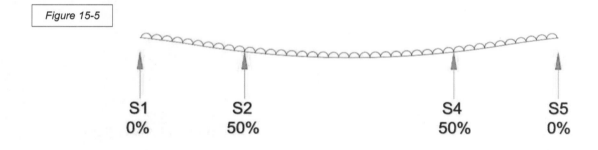

Figure 15-5

To exaggerate, it will sag where S3 was and, being continuous over the supports S2 and S4 will tend to lift at the ends, reducing load at S1 and S5. It may not lift totally clear, but that is the tendency. If it does lift clear, S2 and S4 could each get 50% of the load, a doubling of their initial load.

# 16 Lift Lug Design

## 16.1 Caution

Let's start by saying that this is definitely an area in which a little knowledge can be dangerous. The whole integrity of your lift can hang on this detail (literally). So if you don't have the necessary structural engineering competence, get with someone who has – bring your rigging expertise to the table.

That said, we see many lift lugs that are apparently designed by well qualified structural engineers but are not fit for purpose. Examples include suiting no known shackle or failing to account for the magnitude and/or direction of the forces that will be induced during handling or being located in such a place that the shackles or slings will bind up or be forced to bend over a sharp corner. Sometimes we see lugs that are massively overdesigned. Some understanding of rigging is therefore required in addition to structural expertise.

This section will not make lift lug designers out of you, but should point you in the right direction.

## 16.2 What do you want the lift lug to do?

It is important that you establish:

- The intended slinging arrangement
- The part the lug plays including its location
- The maximum load is has to take
- The direction(s) of the load(s)
- The hardware that has to fit to it

### 16.2.1 Slinging arrangement

For example, a load such as the below may be slung in a number of ways. How it is to be slung affects the lift lug design.

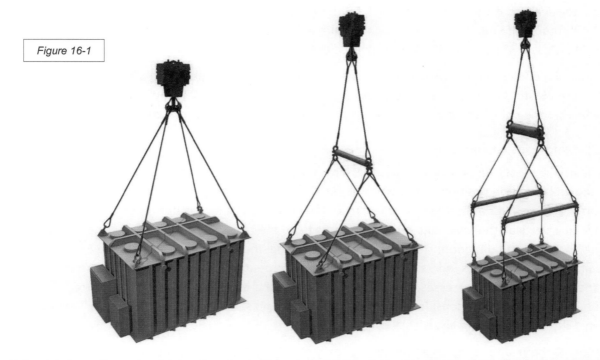

Figure 16-1

Left, the four slings are taken directly to the suspension point with no attempt made to equalize loads. The lugs need to be orientated in plan towards the C of G and the loads act in the plane of the lug at an "in plane" angle to the horizontal determined by the sling lengths.

As noted elsewhere, it is recommended that you assess this situation as though only two slings (and the lugs to which they are attached) are carrying the entire load. If the C of G is offset, the angles "a" that the slings make to the horizontal in true plane will not be equal and one of the slings will be more highly loaded than the other. Knowing the dimensions, you can assess angle "a" and thus the tension in the slings. Let's assume that the load is 100 t and the slings all make an angle in true plane of 60° to the horizontal. You need to size the lugs on the basis that the vertical load at any one will be 50% x 100 t = 50 t. The tension in the sling will be 50 t/sin(60°) = 57.7 t. This is too much for a standard 55 t shackle, so you'll have to go to say an 85 t Crosby G2130 or similar at each point. You might want to rate the lug at 60 t. You have already been fairly conservative in considering only two carrying the load, and the 100 t design load should have some conservatism in it, so adding on too much more conservatism is not appropriate unless you are really not sure of the real weight.

Center, a single spreader bar is used across the width of the piece. The slings are paired in the plane of the long faces to the ends of the spreader. Two inclined slings from the spreader go to the suspension point. The lugs need to be orientated in the plane of the long faces and the loads will act in the planes of the lugs at an angle to the horizontal determined by the sling lengths. If the C of G is offset, the sling lengths will need to be adjusted accordingly and the sling loads (and angles) will vary slightly. All four slings will take load even if their lengths are not quite accurate.

Assuming once again that the load is 100 t and the slings all make an angle 60° to the horizontal in the plane of the lug. You need to size the lugs on the basis that the vertical load at any one will be 25% x 100 t = 25 t (plus a reasonable design margin). The tension in the sling will be 25 t/sin(60°) = 28.9 t. You would probably use a 35 t Crosby G2130 or similar at each point. You might want to rate the lug at 35 t.

Right, a three-spreader arrangement is used with two bars along the piece and one across it. All four slings are truly vertical. The orientation of the lugs is unimportant; the angle of application of the force will be at 90° to the horizontal. If the C of G is offset, the inclined spreader sling lengths will need to be adjusted accordingly and the vertical sling loads will vary slightly. All four slings will take load even is their lengths are not quite accurate.

Assuming once again that the load is 100 t and the four suspension slings are all vertical, the tension in each will be 25 t. In theory, if your 100 t had enough reserve in it, you could use 25 t shackles and lugs. In practice, you would likely use a 35 t Crosby G2130 or similar at each point and rate at say 30 t.

In conclusion, depending on how this load is to be sling, you could be looking at sizing the lugs for shackles anywhere from 25 t to 85t and designing the lugs from anywhere between 25 t and 60 t. You can see how if it was designed per the right-hand graphic, but used per the left-hand graphic, you could be in trouble.

### 16.2.2  Changing loads and direction

When tailing up a vessel (upending it), you might have lugs at the head and a single lug at the tail. In the example shown below the position of the C of G and the 64 t load would give you 31.2 t at the tail and a total of 32.8 t on the pair of lugs at the head at the start of the lift when the load is horizontal. At the end of the lift when the load is vertical, the head lugs get the entire 64 t and the tail lug has none. During the lift, the tail load is decaying and changing direction; the head load is increasing and changing direction. See Section 19 which deals specifically with how that works. Initially there is no moment (rotation) induced into the tail lug (in the plane of the lug. As the lift progresses, rotation is induced. At the extreme end of the lift, there is no load, so no rotation. It is not enough to consider only the situation and the start and end of the lift, the worst condition could be mid-lift. You need to analyze it say every 5°.

The situation at the head is somewhat similar; at the start of the lift, there is a considerable moment to the weld group securing the lug. As the lift progresses the load increases, but the moment arm reduces. Eventually you have the total load but no moment arm. Again you need to consider the situation every 5° or so.

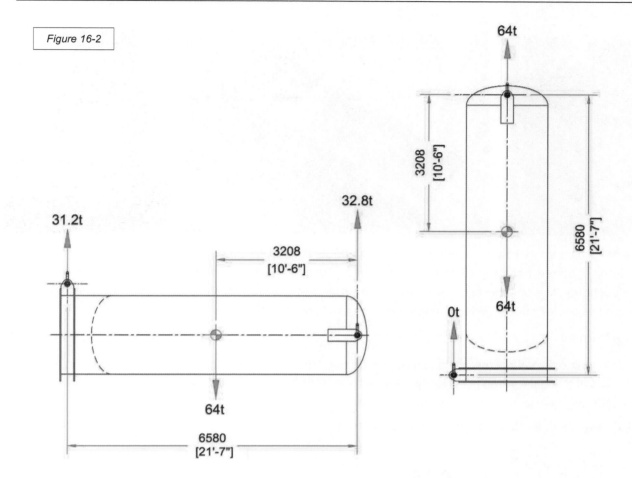

Figure 16-2

### 16.2.3 Side loading lugs

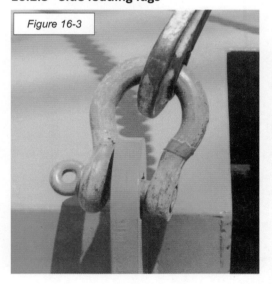

Figure 16-3

Do not side a shackle / lift lug like this. Neither the shackle nor the lug is designed for it. You can bend/distort the lug or even peel it off; the shackle can be damaged.

The other issue here is that the shackle pin is not a good fit in the hole. When side loading like this the shackle rotates to take up the slack; this concentrates the load on a point on the pin (to one side) and on a single point on the lug. This will likely cause local overstress and permanent deformation in the lug at that point.

Rigging arrangements should always be designed so that the lifting loads lie in the plane of the lug and not across it. However, there will be instances where the slings will be slightly inclined, say if the standard length intervals of a spreader bar do not exactly match the span between the lifting lugs. So it is always prudent to consider some side loading on the lug. I recommend you use 10% applied laterally at the pin center.

Figure 16-4  Figure 16-5  Figure 16-6

This steel column was to be upended by hinging about its bottom corner (on a wood mat) while lifting the head using a bolted head lug to attach. During the process, the lug's attitude was to be per the LH photo. While upending, the column became unstable and rolled to the side on the mat so that it lay in the attitude shown in the center photo. This side loaded the lug and broke it off above the stiffeners.

Lessons learned:

- Rolling up a tall narrow steel column on its bottom corner is not stable – it is better (but more costly) to tail it using a crane from a point above the center line
- Lift lugs do not accept side loading well

What sling angle does 10% load at the pin equate to?

Figure 16-7

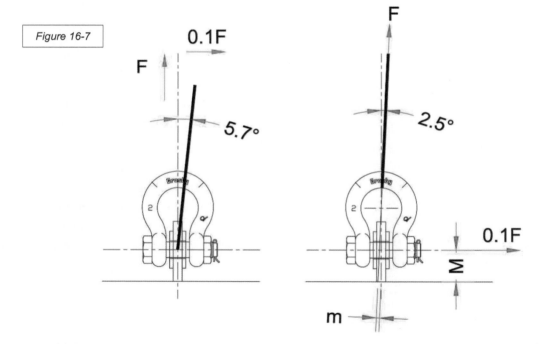

You might imagine that the sling angle to give you a 10% side load would be an angle of tan$^{-1}$(0.1) = 5.7°. That would be the case if the line of action of the sling intersected at the center of the lug / center of the pin as shown left. What will actually tend to happen is that the line of action of the sling will act through the center of the bow of the shackle. The max lateral moment on the lug (where it is affixed) = 10% of the vertical sling load (approximately equal to the sling tension at these small angles) applied laterally at the pin x M. This is equivalent to the sling tension F x the small moment arm "m".

Therefore Fm = 0.1FM or m =0.1M. (This assumes the shackle is a fairly close fit in the lug).

You can draw a line acting through the center of the bow that passes the center of the lug at the point of attachment at a distance of 0.1M. Given the geometry of my sample lug and shackle (typical 35 t), this is actually an angle of only about 2.5°. i.e. in my example a sling angle of 2.5° results in a lateral moment in the lug equivalent to 10% of the sling tension applied laterally at the pin. This is actually not as generous as the 5° out of line the shackle manufacturers allow without derating.

If you design your lugs for 10% lateral load, and they are proportioned much as above, keep your out-of-plumb within 2.5°.

### 16.2.4  Hardware in lugs

It is important that the designer of a lug and the users of the lug have a common type of shackle in mind. Take for instance 120 t shackles; a Crosby G2130 has a pin diameter of 95.5 mm and a jaw width of 133 mm, a G2140 alloy shackle has a pin diameter of 82.5 mm and a jaw width of +/- 127 mm, a 125 t G2160 wide body shackle has a pin diameter of 80 mm and a jaw width of +/- 130 mm. A lug suitable for one type will likely not be suitable for the others. The tailing lug below has a relatively small hole diameter with a lot of metal around it. It only suits a wide body shackle.

Figure 16-8

Figure 16-9

Make sure that the lug design does not result in the sling being trapped & pinched between the lug and shackle at the extremes of required movement. You can see one of the concerns with this design on the lug on the right. When you get near vertical, as a result of the rake of the lug there is little or no room left for the sling. You run a real risk or deforming or cutting the sling, particularly if using a bulky synthetic sling (see below). Note the ideal use of a SlingSaver shackle with this TwinPath sling.

Figure 16-10

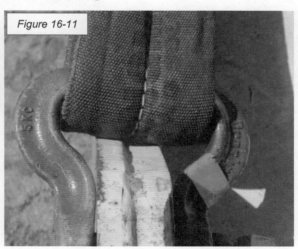
Figure 16-11

As noted earlier, you need to design the lug with a particular shackle or shackles in mind. The hole in the lug needs to be well matched to the shackle pin diameter in order that the bearing stress is not excessive and the loads do not result in permanent deformation of the lug at the point of bearing. Shackles are generally forged and therefore not precision made; you need to be able to fit and remove the shackle easily in the field. As noted later, I recommend that the pin holes are about $1/8$" (3 mm) larger than the intended shackle diameter up to 55 t and ¼" (6 mm) larger above that.

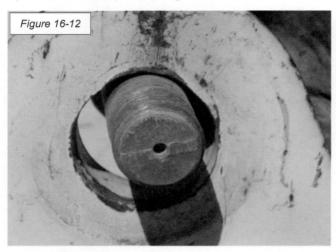
Figure 16-12

Figure 16-13

Left – the clearance is too great, high local bearing stresses will cause permanent deformation of the hole in the lug if the pin is not a good fit on diameter. Right - when the proper clearance is specified, the pin will not cause permanent deformation of the hole. Note high alloy shackles will be physically smaller than "regular" shackles for a given capacity.

It is also important that the lug thickness is well matched to the jaw width of the intended shackle to keep the shackle well centered.

Figure 16-14

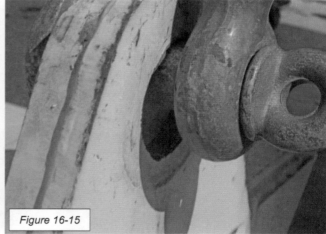
Figure 16-15

Left – the shackle pin is a reasonable fit in the hole but the shackle jaw width is too large for the shackle to be well centered. If critical, washers can be used. Right - The shackle jaw width is a good fit for the lug thickness but the hole is excessively large for the pin diameter.

## 16.3 Patterns of lugs

You will need to decide where (and how) your lug is to be attached and what vectors it has to deal with. That will help you decide on a suitable pattern to design to.

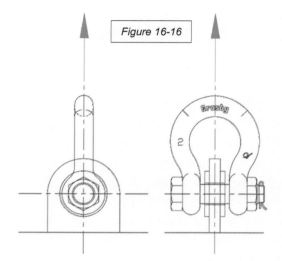

Figure 16-16

The most basic type of lug is designed for a straight line pull only without any consideration of inclined loads or bending across the plane of the lug.

So long as the hole is centered in the lug and you size the double plane shear out conservatively, the tension across the pin hole will check out OK and thus the tension in the lug below the pin will also be OK. Make sure the bearing width is adequate and add doubler (cheek) plates if required. Occupying 70% or so of the jaw width will virtually assure the bearing stress will be OK and the shackle will remain well centered.

When using doublers, provide enough fillet weld to transmit the proportion of load carried by each doubler plate into the center plate.

The lug may be directly welded to the load or form part of an assembly that is bolted to the load.

Note that is considering lateral moments, the height of the pin above the weld plane is important and should be no more than is reasonably required. I would always recommend using full penetration welds between the lug and whatever it is affixed to. Where lateral moments are involved you require enough weld to develop sufficient lateral elastic modulus to resist the moment at an adequately low stress level (in addition to carrying the tension). For that you likely need the full lug plate strength.

Beware of welding to laminated plate, ensure through thickness properties. If you have purely linear load, the center plate may not need to be as thick (as lateral bending is no longer a consideration) and fillet welds may be an acceptable attachment method.

An alternative to welding on the lug is to extend the structure itself to form the center plate or carry the center plate into the structure of the load.

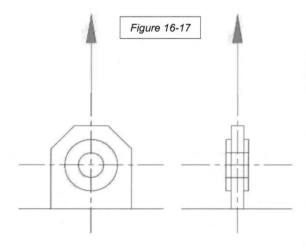

Figure 16-17

If you want to "square off" the lug and crop the corners, that works too and is cheaper to make. The cropping should enclose the equivalent round head you calculated.

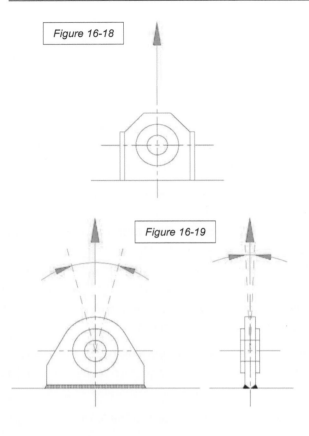

Figure 16-18

If you want to resist lateral loads by means other than relying on the lateral strength of the lug plate, you can provide stiffeners or provide plates as shown here to form an "I" in plan.

You may not need as thick a center plate taking this approach.

Whatever you do must not interfere with the fitting and operation of the rigging tackle.

Figure 16-19

If you intend to resist lateral loads using only the lateral strength of the lug plate, noting the elastic modulus $=bd^2/6$ where "b" is the breadth of the plate and "d" is its thickness, you need the lug plate to be relatively thick. If you make it about 35% of the jaw width (give or take), to keep the proportions reasonable, you'll probably need to make the breadth of the plate greater than the diameter of the head determined from shear considerations. Something like this would work and give you some limited in-plane inclination tolerance.

Again you could stiffen the plate with lateral "ribs" to keep the plate thinner if the shear and other considerations allow.

You might find a lug like this as one of a pair at the head of a chemical vessel. The shackle rotates through 90° during upending. Typically the shell of the vessel would re locally reinforced and the lug would be welded to the reinforcing plate. The weld group has to resist the rotation as the line of action of the applied force changes. In the photo on the left, the lug plate is shaped to maximize weld length.

Figure 16-20

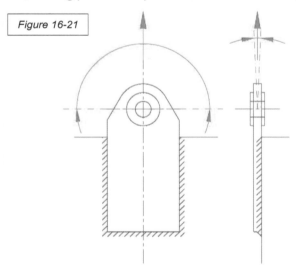

Figure 16-21

You may see a lug like this bolted to an item. If the forces are inclined, the bolt group would have to resist the rotation and the shear forces.

Figure 16-22

This lug is tied back circumferentially to the vessel shell to take lifting loads normal to the center line of the vessel directly into the shell avoiding the tendency to rotate the lug.

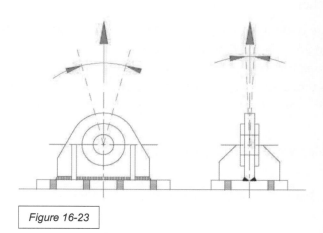

Figure 16-23

You might typically use (and re-use) a removable lug such as this when lifting say multiple piperack modules. You can make the case that lugs that are welded to a piece are part of the piece and "belong" to it and are not below the hook lifting devices even though you may have used BTH-1 to design them. Similarly bolted on lugs that are dedicated to a particular piece and a particular function could be considered part of the piece, whereas bolted-on lugs that could have multiple uses are below-the-hook lifting devices. However, all lift lugs need to be proved in some way; in particular 100% NDT should be applied to all attachment welds. I would recommend that bolted lifting lugs are load tested as pieces of rigging tackle. All lift lugs should have their rated capacity hard stamped on them. Check applicable regulations!

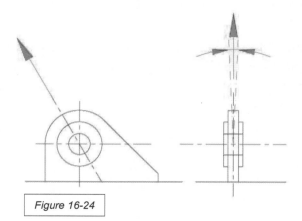

Figure 16-24

Where you intend to incline the slings (in the plane of the lug), such as shown at say 60°, you might use an arrangement such as this. Stiffeners could be incorporated to take out lateral bending.

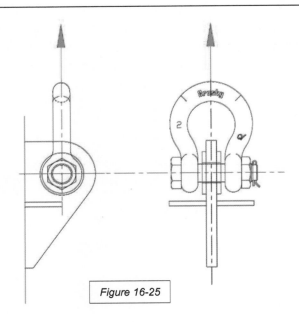

Figure 16-25

A lug welded to the side of a skid and subject to only vertical loading might look something like this. You need enough depth in the plate to give you the elastic modulus you need to withstand the bending induced by the suspension force x the offstand. Lateral stiffener plates are definitely recommended in these instances.

## 16.4 Design basis

### 16.4.1  Design code

It is recommended that lift lugs are designed in accordance with the provisions of ASME B30.20 BTH-1 (Below-the-hook lifting devices design standard). See also the section on spreader design with worked example.

BTH-1 allows two design categories. For low-frequency use under controlled conditions, Design Category A, the design factor is 2 for limit states of yielding or buckling and 2.4 for limit states of fracture and connection design. Most lugs you are likely to be involved with in a construction environment will be Category A. If you are designing lugs on something that will be used numerous times as general rigging tackle where you don't have control over its later use, you should use Category B which requires factors of 3 and 3.6 respectively. Refer to BTH-1 for details.

As noted preceding, it is recommended that the pin holes are $^1/_8$" (3 mm) larger than the intended shackle diameter up to 55 t and ¼" (6 mm) larger above that.

I would recommend that all pin holes are machined not flame cut. Where cheek plates (doublers or donuts) are fitted, the holes should be in line bored / drilled.

As noted earlier, I recommend that 10% lateral load, applied at the pin hole is considered in the design. If this results in the plate sizes becoming excessive, stiffeners may be incorporated to take out the lateral bending. Their location must not interfere with the fitting or use of the shackle through its intended range of movement.

You must allow enough room between the lug and the bow of the shackle for the sling you intend to use considering the full potential range of movement – see above. Heads of lugs may be rounded or be rectangular with their corners clipped to clear sling and shackle movement.

### 16.4.2  Failure modes

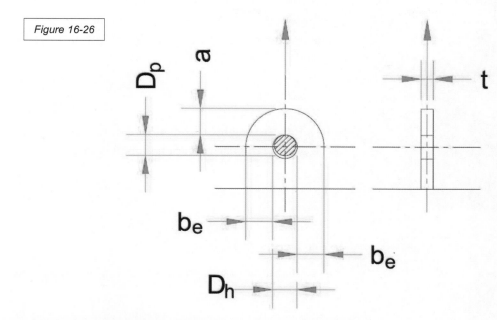

Figure 16-26

There are a number of potential failure modes you need to consider.

Per BTH-1, the strength of a pin-connected plate in the region of the pin hole shall be taken as the least value of:

- the tensile strength of the effective area on a plane through the center of the pin hole perpendicular to the line of action of the applied load,
- the fracture strength beyond the pin hole on a single plane parallel to the line of action of the applied load and,
- the double plane shear strength beyond the pin hole parallel to the line of action of the applied load.

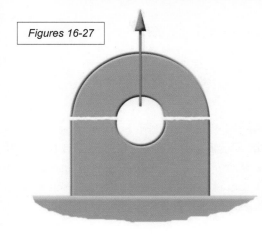

Figures 16-27

Tensile failure of the head

The allowable tensile strength through the pin hole $P_t$ shall be calculated as follows:

$$P_t = C_r(F_u/1.2N_d)2tb_{eff}$$

The value of Cr may be taken as 1.00 for values of $D_p/D_h$ greater than 0.90 – this will generally be the case if following the guidelines herein.

$b_{eff}$ = effective width to each side of the pin hole and is the smaller of the values calculated as follows.

$$b_{eff} \leq 4t \leq b_e$$

$$b_{eff} \leq b_e 0.6\frac{F_u}{F_y}\sqrt{\frac{D_h}{b_e}} \leq b_e$$

$N_d$= is the design factor for yield or buckling (2 for Category A)

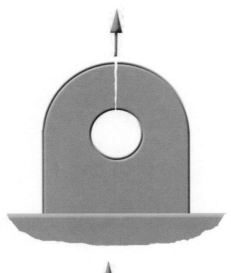

### Fracture strength of the head

The allowable single plane fracture strength beyond the pin hole $P_b$ is:

$$P_b = C_r \frac{F_u}{1.2N_d} \left[ 1.13 \left( R - \frac{D_h}{2} \right) + \frac{0.92b_e}{1 + b_e/D_h} \right] t$$

Where R is the distance from the center of the hole to the edge of the plate in the direction of the applied load

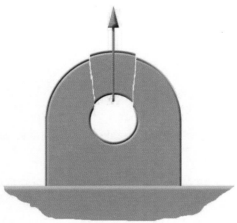

### Double plane shear strength

The allowable double plane shear strength beyond the pin hole $P_v$ is:

$$P_v = \frac{0.70F_u}{1.2N_d} A_v$$

Where $A_v$ = total area of two shear planes beyond the pinhole

$$A_v = 2 \left[ a + \frac{D_p}{2} (1 - \cos \emptyset) \right] t$$

Where "a" is the distance from the edge of the pinhole to the edge of the plate in the direction of the applied load and $\emptyset = 55D_p/D_h$ (deg).

You could conservatively use $A_v = 2at$

### Tensile failure of the body

If the breadth of the lug plate => 2 x the head radius, and the tensile stress at the pin checks out, tensile stresses in the body will not govern design. If you have high bending stresses at the attachment point, you should consider the effect of the tensile stress in combination with the bending stresses.

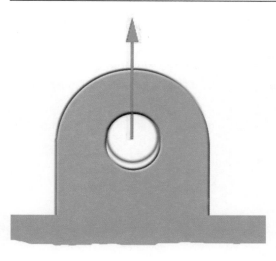

### Bearing

We also need to check bearing; this is not a strength limit, but we want to control deformation. $F_p$ is the bearing stress between the plate and pin based on the projected area of the pin.

For connections that are not required to rotate under load for a large number of cycles; $F_{p\,max} = 1.25F_y/N_d$

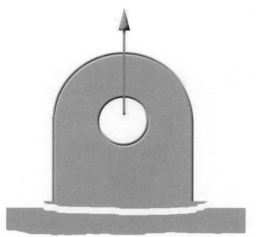

### Failure of the attaching weld

Full pen butt welds are recommended. Ensure the piece you are welding to has through thickness properties or you may find you have simply welded to a lamination.

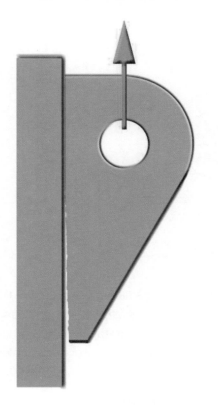

### In-plane bending failure

The offset of the force creates a moment about the attachment weld in addition to shear and possibly lateral bending. You may need to check combined stresses.

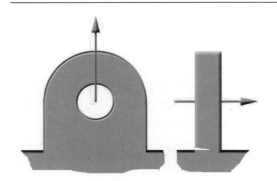

### Lateral bending failure

If lateral bending is to be considered, you need enough bending resistance in the lug plate and its attachment. This may require a full penetration butt weld.

Suggested proportions & dimensions

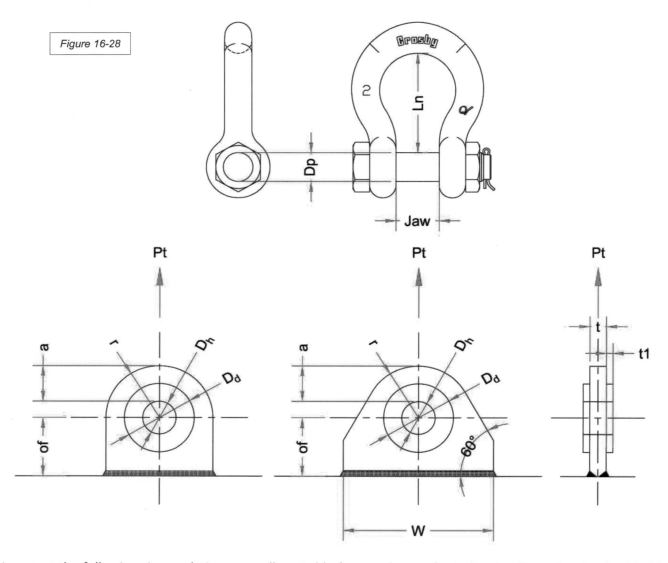

Figure 16-28

I suggest the following sizes as being generally suitable for attachment for in-line loading using Crosby G2130 type shackles or the Green Pin equivalents in the range 12-150 ton (or 12-150 t) range. Full penetration butt welding of the lug to the load is recommended (and would likely be required if 10% lateral load capability is to be achieved). If lateral loading is not to be considered a plate breadth = 2r is sufficient, otherwise make the breadth = W as shown in the center graphic.

I suggest the following proportions as a starting point. Head radius = 1.8x pin dia; plate thickness = 37.5% of jaw width; total bearing width = 70% of jaw width; plate breadth W = 2.8 x the head radius; doubler diameter =

2.35 x pin diameter. If 10% lateral loading is to be considered, it is recommended that the pin hole center is about 2x the pin diameter above the attachment point. If you start your design from these proportions, the shackle will fit, you should have adequate room for the sling and you should be in compliance with BTH-1. It will not necessarily be the most economic design you could achieve.

If you intend to incline the sling in the plane of the lug, the head detail will be OK, but you will need to adjust the shape of the lugs as shown in the preceding section. Similarly, if the lug is to be welded to the side of the piece, you will need to increase the depth of the plate to obtain the required bending strength. Consider lateral stability / dishing of the plate and provide stiffeners if required to provide lateral stability / resist lateral loads. Use this table as a basis only and design considering your particular situation. The lug designer needs to be suitably qualified.

*Figure 16-29*

| WLL | Shackle | | | Lug | | | | | | | | |
|---|---|---|---|---|---|---|---|---|---|---|---|---|
| (t) | Dp | Jaw | Ln | Dh | t | r | W | t1 | Dd | weld | a | of |
| 12 | 35.1 | 51.5 | 119 | 38.1 | 19.1 | 63 | 177 | 9.5 | 82 | 3 | 44.1 | 70 |
| 13.5 | 38.1 | 57 | 133 | 41.1 | 22.2 | 69 | 192 | 9.5 | 89 | 3 | 48.0 | 76 |
| 17 | 41.4 | 60.5 | 146 | 44.4 | 22.2 | 75 | 209 | 9.5 | 98 | 4 | 52.3 | 83 |
| 25 | 51 | 73 | 178 | 54 | 25.4 | 92 | 257 | 11.1 | 121 | 4 | 64.8 | 102 |
| 35 | 57 | 82.5 | 197 | 63 | 31.8 | 103 | 287 | 12.7 | 133 | 4 | 71.1 | 114 |
| 55 | 70 | 105 | 267 | 76 | 38.1 | 126 | 353 | 15.9 | 165 | 6 | 88.0 | 140 |
| 85 | 82.5 | 127 | 330 | 88.5 | 47.6 | 149 | 416 | 19.1 | 194 | 6 | 104.3 | 165 |
| 120 | 95.5 | 133 | 372 | 101.5 | 57.2 | 172 | 481 | 22.2 | 225 | 8 | 121.2 | 191 |
| 150 | 108 | 140 | 368 | 114 | 63.5 | 194 | 544 | 22.2 | 254 | 8 | 137.4 | 216 |

*Dimension in millimetres*

| WLL | Shackle | | | Lug | | | | | | | | |
|---|---|---|---|---|---|---|---|---|---|---|---|---|
| (tons) | Dp | Jaw | Ln | Dh | t | r | W | t1 | Dd | weld | a | of |
| 12 | 1.38 | 2.03 | 4.69 | 1.500 | 0.750 | 2.49 | 6.96 | 0.375 | 3.25 | 1/8" | 1.74 | 2.75 |
| 13.5 | 1.50 | 2.24 | 5.24 | 1.625 | 0.875 | 2.70 | 7.56 | 0.375 | 3.50 | 1/8" | 1.89 | 3 |
| 17 | 1.63 | 2.38 | 5.75 | 1.748 | 0.875 | 2.93 | 8.21 | 0.375 | 3.88 | 3/16" | 2.06 | 3.25 |
| 25 | 2.01 | 2.87 | 7.01 | 2.125 | 1.000 | 3.61 | 10.12 | 0.438 | 4.75 | 3/16" | 2.55 | 4 |
| 35 | 2.24 | 3.25 | 7.76 | 2.500 | 1.250 | 4.04 | 11.31 | 0.500 | 5.25 | 3/16" | 2.79 | 4.5 |
| 55 | 2.76 | 4.13 | 10.51 | 3.000 | 1.500 | 4.96 | 13.89 | 0.625 | 6.50 | 1/4" | 3.46 | 5.5 |
| 85 | 3.25 | 5.00 | 12.99 | 3.500 | 1.875 | 5.85 | 16.37 | 0.750 | 7.63 | 1/4" | 4.10 | 6.5 |
| 120 | 3.76 | 5.24 | 14.65 | 4.000 | 2.250 | 6.77 | 18.95 | 0.875 | 8.88 | 5/16" | 4.77 | 7.5 |
| 150 | 4.25 | 5.51 | 14.49 | 4.500 | 2.500 | 7.65 | 21.43 | 0.875 | 10.00 | 5/16" | 5.40 | 8.5 |

*Dimension in inches*

*Weld size refers to the doubler attachment.*

Note: Some nuclear standards may require you to take a capacity reduction for shackles >85t if the total lug width is less than 80% of the jaw width. Check! The above may not give you quite that.

### 16.4.3 Check out design for 35 ton shackle to BTH-1

Check out design per table above for 35 ton (70 kips) against BTH-1, ignore doubler plates for head strength; assume straight sided design for head strength.

<u>Tensile failure of head</u>

$P_t = C_r(F_u/1.2N_d)2tb_{eff}$

$C_r = 1$, $F_u = 58ksi$, $F_y = 36ksi$, $N_d = 2$, t=1.25", $b_e$ = dim "a" = 2.79"

The effective width shall be taken as the smaller of the values calculated as follows.

Per first criterion, $b_{eff} \leq 4t \leq b_e$; $b_{eff} \leq 5 \leq 2.79$; therefore $b_{eff} = 2.79"$

Per second criterion, $b_{eff} \leq b_e 0.6\frac{F_u}{F_y}\sqrt{\frac{D_h}{b_e}} \leq b_e$

$$b_{eff} \leq 2.79 \times 0.6 \frac{58}{36} \sqrt{\frac{2.5}{2.79}} \leq 2.79$$

$$b_{eff} \leq 2.55 \leq 2.79$$

Criterion 2 governs, $b_{eff}$ = 2.55"

$$P_t = 1.0(58/1.2 \times 2)2 \times 1.25 \times 2.55$$

$P_t$ = 154 kips (versus required rating of 70 kips)

The allowable tensile strength through the pin hole $P_t$ is 154 kips.

## Single plane fracture strength

The allowable single plane fracture strength beyond the pin hole $P_b$ is:

$$P_b = C_r \frac{F_u}{1.2N_d} \left[ 1.13 \left( R - \frac{D_h}{2} \right) + \frac{0.92b_e}{1 + b_e/D_h} \right] t$$

where R is the distance from the center of the hole to the edge of the plate in the direction of the applied load.

In our example, $F_u$ = 58 ksi, $N_d$ = 2, R = 4.05 in, $D_h$ = 2.5 in, $b_e$ = 2.79 in, $C_r$ = 1, t = 1.25 in.

$$P_b = 1.0 \frac{58}{1.2 \times 2} \left[ 1.13 \left( 4.05 - \frac{2.5}{2} \right) + \frac{0.92 \times 2.79}{1 + (2.79/2.5)} \right] 1.25$$

$P_b$ = 24.167 x [3.164+1.213] x 1.25

$P_b$ = 132.2 kips (versus 70 kips required rating)

The allowable single plane fracture strength beyond the pin hole $P_b$ is 132.2 kips.

## Allowable double plane shear strength beyond the pin hole

The allowable double plane shear strength beyond the pin hole $P_v$ is:

$$P_v = \frac{0.70F_u}{1.2N_d} A_v$$

$$A_v = 2 \left[ a + \frac{D_p}{2} (1 - \cos \emptyset) \right] t$$

Where a is the distance from the edge of the pinhole to the edge of the plate in the direction of the applied load = 2.79" , $\emptyset$ = 55$D_p$/$D_h$ = 55x(2.24/2.5) = 49.3°

$$A_v = 2 \left[ 2.79 + \frac{2.24}{2} (1 - \cos 49.3) \right] 1.25 = 7.95 in^2$$

$$P_v = \frac{0.70 \times 58}{1.2 \times 2} 7.95 = 134.5 kips$$

The allowable double plane shear strength beyond the pin hole $P_v$ is 134.5 kips

## Head strength

The governing condition is $P_b$, which limits the permitted force to 132.2 kips (versus required 70 kips rating). Note, that the doublers were not considered in the strength calculation.

## Pin bearing

We also need to check bearing; this is not a strength limit, but we want to control deformation. $F_p$ is the bearing stress between the plate and pin based on the projected area of the pin.

$F_{p\ max} = 1.25F_y/N_d$ (ksi)

$F_{p\ max} = 1.25 \times 36/2 = 22.5$ ksi

$F_{p\ actual} = 70 / 2.25 \times 2.24$ (based on full width) = 13.9 ksi

$\therefore$ the head strength and bearing of the lug design satisfies BTH-1 with ample reserves

## Body tensile

The tensile area of the body > the tensile area of the head and the load is the same, $\therefore$ OK

## Lateral bending

If the lug is subject to 10% lateral bending, consider the width W and the attachment as being a full pen weld.

Elastic modulus = $bd^2/6 = 11.31 \times 1.25^2/6 = 2.945$ in$^3$

M = $0.1 \times 70 \times 4.5 = 31.5$ kip-in

Actual $f_{bc/t} = 31.5 / 2.945 = 10.7$ ksi, allowable = 36/2 = 18 ksi.

### 16.4.4  Check out design for 35 t shackle to BS449

Check out design per table above for 35 t (343 kN) using material to BS4360 grd 43 (36 ksi yield material). Reduce permissibles by a design factor of 1.25 to arrive at a factor of about 2 over yield.

## Double plane shear strength beyond the pin hole

Consider shear area = 2 a t = $(2 \times 71.1 \times 31.8) + 2(35 \times 12.7 \times 2) = 6300$ mm$^2$

$f_q = 343 \times 10^3 / 6300 = 54.4$ N/mm$^2$, $p_q = 105/1.25 = 84$ N/mm$^2$ OK

## Tensile strength beyond the pin hole

Tensile stress area is the same as the shear area, therefore $f_t = 54.4$ N/mm$^2$, $p_t = 155/1.25 = 124$ N/mm$^2$, OK

## Tensile strength in body

Tensile stress in body < $f_t$, therefore OK

## Doubler weld strength

Load carried by 1 doubler = $343 \times 12.7 / ((2 \times 12.7) + 31.8) = 76.2$ kN.

Weld length = $3.142 \times 133 = 418$ mm

Load/mm = 76.2 / 418 = 0.18 kN/mm; 4 mm weld OK.

## Bearing

Bearing stress = $343 \times 10^3 / 57 \times 57.2 = 105.2$ N/mm$^2$; $p_b = 190/1.25 = 152$ N/mm$^2$ OK

### Lateral strength

$$z_{xx} = bd^2/6 = 287 \times 31.8^2 / 6 = 48.371 \times 10^3 \, mm^3$$

$$M = 0.1 \times 343 \times 0.114 = 3.91 \, kNm$$

$$f_{bc/t} = 3.91 \times 10^6 / 48.371 \times 10^3 = 80.8 \, N/mm^2, \quad p_{bc/t} = 165/1.25 = 132 \, N/mm^2, \, OK$$

### Combined stresses

Combined stresses may need to be calculated where percentages of individual stresses (particularly shear) approach allowables. They don't here.

### Conclusion

The design for a 35 t lug in a straight pull checks out conservatively versus BTH-1; it is not highly efficient in material use; you may choose to refine it for your specific application.

The metric check shows that designing using BTH-1 principles using an allowable stress (elastic) code and conservative design is going to yield a sound result, probably with a lot less design steps.

## 16.5 Lifting concrete panels and beams

### 16.5.1 General

When planning a lifting operation you may be required to produce rigging arrangements to handle precast concrete beams, panels, slabs or units. The task may be relocation, loading / offloading, tilt-up of (say) panels or an overhead lifting operation to place the item. As with any lift, you will want to lift the piece in a manner that is stable, keeps the load in basically level (or in the required attitude) and does not overstress it. There are therefore choices to be made regarding the number and type of lifting points.

Depending on what you are intending to do, you may be able to basket sling the item, although you need to be concerned about factors such as:

- Security of sling location
- Bending / chafing of slings at corners and edge protection
- Forces you are inducing in the piece, e.g. side forces on the tops of walls of box units
- Stability against rolling

To that end, you may be able to get the designer / manufacturer of the piece to provide grooves for slings. e.g. The casting forms may be designed to create grooves in (say) the end walls of box-shaped products, such as utility vaults and septic tanks in which lifting slings may be securely located. The advantages of this approach are that it is inexpensive, uncomplicated, easy to install and requires no special handling equipment. There are no problems with concrete spalling and no holes are made through the product.

In many cases, however, actual lifting points will be required to which you can attach your rigging. You may have an opportunity to influence the design to best suit your intentions and get a properly engineered solution. On the other hand you may be simply confronted with a piece that has a couple of non-engineered rebar loops sticking out of it and you have to make a judgment as to whether you can safely use those for your purposes.

### 16.5.2 Use of rebar loops - caution!

Manufacturers of precast concrete items often provide strategically placed lifting points for handling and manipulating the items in manufacture. Several types of "home-made" devices are routinely used, including bent reinforcing steel bar, pre-stressed strand as loops and recessed bars (countersunk with temporary blockouts). This type of attachment is likely non-engineered, won't be load-tested or "proved" in any way. They are however inexpensive, simple to use, and don't require any special lifting hardware. Whilst these types of "home-made" devices may suffice in the casting yard, I don't recommend using them in the field when handling or placing these items. See below.

Apart from the lack of proof of fitness-for-purpose, a major problem with using bent rebar is that lifting devices are subject to dynamic loads and thus ductility of the material is a requirement. The position of the Precast / Pre-stressed Concrete Institute is that "deformed reinforcing bars should not be used as the deformations result in stress concentrations from the shackle pin. Also, reinforcing bars may be hard grade or re-rolled rail steel with little ductility and low impact strength at cold temperatures. Strain hardening from bending the bars may also cause embrittlement.

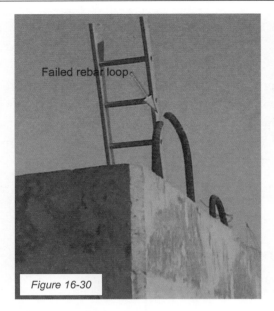

*Figure 16-30*

*Figure 16-31*

Smooth bars of a known steel grade may be used if adequate embedment or mechanical anchorage is provided. The diameter must be such that localized failure will not occur by bearing on the shackle pin". Other problems are sloppiness in placing the loops and inadequate tying in to the rebar within the structure. I would recommend, and in some places it is a requirement, that you do not use rebar loops as attachments for overhead lifting purposes. Although it may not be the cheapest option, I would recommend that you always use appropriate, properly rated, proprietary lifting devices.

### 16.5.3  Lifting attachment options

So what options are there for engineered proprietary lifting devices to be incorporated in the piece for handling and placing purposes? The answer to that is that there are a multitude of types and variations each tailored to a particular application. So, which one should be used? As a lift planner, you are often involved after these decisions have been made, however you may have a chance to influence the choice to best suit your purposes if you get in early enough with the designer. At the least, you need to have a brief overview of the characteristics of the various types to understand how to use them.

In selecting an appropriate, safe and efficient type of anchor for lifting precast concrete products there are a number of factors to be considered including the type of load, type of lift, concrete thickness, edge distance, reinforcement, ease of attachment to product, compliance with safety requirements, ease of use and cost.

In establishing the required rating per insert for handling and installation purposes, the following factors need to be considered:

- Weight and location of C of G
- Type of concrete (normal, light weight, etc.)
- Dynamic loads
- Concrete compressive strength at time of lift
- Number of lifting points and type of rigging to be used.
- Direction of lift forces relative to attachment (sling angles etc)
- Flexural stresses of thin concrete shapes

Note that per OSHA (Part 1910), ANSI and ASTM in the USA, lifting devices embedded in precast concrete must support at least four times the maximum intended load applied or transmitted to them (as against rigging tackle which, generally speaking, is rated at a factor of 5:1). If there are dynamic effects you may need to allow a design factor before applying the 4:1. Also do not forget static indeterminacy; e.g. that when taking four slings directly to a single suspension point without equalization, you can only count on two of them doing useful work.

### 16.5.4  Coil threaded inserts

Coil threaded inserts are an attachment method that has been used for many years. The insert has a "thread" formed from a helically wound wire contained within (and welded to) two or more wire "struts". It has to be located and properly secured (by bolts or brackets or by tying in to the reinforcing steel) prior to casting the concrete.

The concept is that a "shear cone" is developed in the concrete resisting the applied tension; anything that affects development of a full shear cone greatly reduces the capacity of the insert.

A wide variety of types of inserts are available including coil loop types, flared loops, double flared loops and so on to suit particular applications such as thin or thick slabs, lightweight concrete, to straddle reinforcing bars and so on.  Refer to the manufacturer's information for details of applications, methods of use and rated capacities.

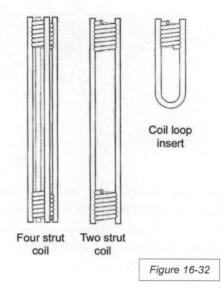

Coil loop insert

Four strut coil    Two strut coil

Figure 16-32

There are different options for securing the insert depending on the thickness / depth of the piece etc.

The head of the insert needs to be about ½" below the concrete and the insert needs to be correctly aligned. Check this before use.

Figure 16-33

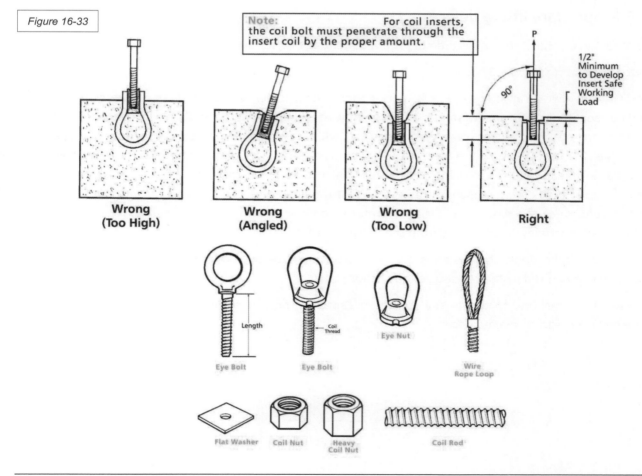

Note: For coil inserts, the coil bolt must penetrate through the insert coil by the proper amount.

P

1/2" Minimum to Develop Insert Safe Working Load

90°

**Wrong (Too High)**    **Wrong (Angled)**    **Wrong (Too Low)**    **Right**

Length

Coil Thread

Eye Nut

Eye Bolt    Eye Bolt    Wire Rope Loop

Flat Washer    Coil Nut    Heavy Coil Nut    Coil Rod

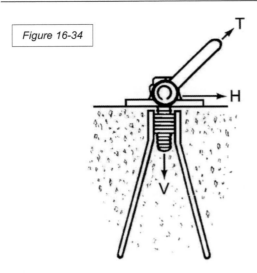

Figure 16-34

To form a lifting point, you can screw eye bolts with a shank having a matching thread form into the insert or use coil rods (with nuts) or coil bolts to secure a lifting eye or lifting plate (lug). Wire rope loops are also available with a threaded shank. All these are intended for a straight pull only.

Angled loading will require a swivel lifting plate bolted to the insert – see left.

*Illustrations based on Dayton Superior®*

The inserts, rods, eyes and so on all have rated capacities. The capacity is of course dependent on correct location and installation and all being in accordance with the manufacturer's stipulations. The rated capacity may need to be reduced in some cases, e.g. lightweight concrete, reduced edge distance, sling angle, dynamic effects. Therefore the useful Assessed Capacity in a particular application may be less; you may need to up the size of the insert or increase numbers of inserts to obtain the capacity you require.

Note that it is essential that there is a sufficient length of thread engagement; that the thread is not bottoming out in the concrete preventing proper flush tightening; that the attachments are secured using the correct torque.

Refer to the manufacturer's information.

## 16.6 Proprietary lifting devices

As noted earlier, there are a multitude of proprietary lifting devices available; I'll briefly describe a few options.

Dayton Superior® Swift Lift System

The Swift Lift Universal lifting eye is a quick-connect device that allows precast concrete elements to be handled repeatedly, with speed, safety, and economy. At its heart is hot forged carbon steel anchor that is cast into the concrete. The anchor has a cylindrical shaft with a head formed that provides spherical seating for a Lifting Eye that engages it. At the base of the anchor is a disc shaped foot that engages the concrete to form the required shear cone to resist the applied tension. The anchor is cast into the concrete with a disposable former around the head; the anchor is affixed so that the head of the former is flush with the finished face of the concrete. Once the concrete is set, the former is removed leaving a semi-spherical recess into which the anchor head protrudes, inset slightly from the finished surface.

For thin wall applications, anchors are available with a hole in the bottom instead of a foot. This allows a rebar tension link to be used instead to secure the anchor.

As with other anchors, to obtain the full rated capacity, there is a minimum edge distance and spacing between anchors to be maintained.

# P-52 Swift Lift Anchor and Recess Plug Dimensions

*Figure 16-35*

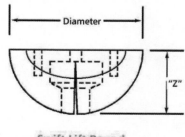

Swift Lift Round Recess Plug

P-52 Swift Lift Anchor

| Swift Lift Round Recess Plug Dimensions | | |
|---|---|---|
| Swift Lift Anchor | Diameter of Recess Plug | Dimension "Z" |
| 1 | 2-7/16" | 1-3/16" |
| 2 | 3-5/16" | 1-7/16" |
| 4 | 4" | 1-13/16" |
| 8 | 5" | 2-5/16" |
| 20 Tons | 6-3/8" | 3-1/8" |

Note: The diameter of the narrow recess plug is the same as the diameter of the round recess plug.

| P-52 Swift Lift Anchor Dimensions | | | | | |
|---|---|---|---|---|---|
| Swift Lift Anchor | Dimension "X" | Dimension "Y" | Shaft Diameter | Foot Diameter | Head Diameter |
| 1 | 5/16" | 7/8" | 3/8" | 1" | 11/16" |
| 2 | 7/16" | 1-1/16" | 9/16" | 1-3/8" | 1-1/32" |
| 4 | 9/16" | 1-5/16" | 3/4" | 1-7/8" | 1-11/32" |
| 8 | 9/16" | 1-5/8" | 1-3/32" | 2-5/8" | 1-7/8" |
| 20 Tons | 9/16" | 2-5/8" | 1-1/2" | 3-3/4" | 2-3/4" |

## P-52 Swift Lift Anchors for Edge Lifting

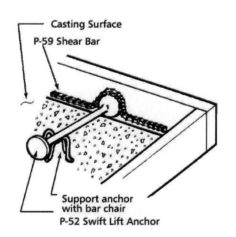

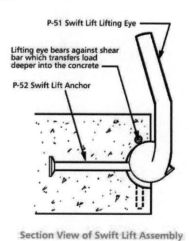

Section View of Swift Lift Assembly

When lifting thin panels or where shear loads (across the anchor) are developed, a shear bar should be used to spread the shear loads into the concrete.

Attachment to the anchor is by a Lifting Eye, of which there are a few varieties.

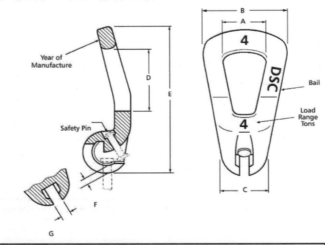

*Figure 16-36*

P-51 Swift Lift Lifting Eye

| P-51 Swift Lift Lifting Eye Selection Chart | | | | | |
|---|---|---|---|---|---|
| Safe Working Loads (tons) | A (Inches) | B (Inches) | C (Inches) | D (Inches) | E (Inches) |
| 2 | 2.64 | 4.52 | 2.36 | 3.74 | 8.43 |
| 4 | 3.00 | 5.06 | 2.83 | 4.96 | 10.35 |
| 8 | 3.54 | 5.98 | 3.70 | 5.60 | 12.87 |

Safe Working Load provides a factor of safety of approximately 5 to 1.

The Dayton Superior P51 type Lifting Eye is a steel casting with a ball-shaped lower end that fits into the spherical void left by the casting former. A T-shaped slot in the ball end engages the head of the anchor allowing rapid attachment and release. A gravity operated safety pin ensures the eye cannot accidentally disengage. The design of the lifting eye permits the bail to rotate 180 degrees, while the eye may rotate through a 360-degree arc, while allowing the precast pieces to be turned, tilted, or rotated under load. The P51 is restricted to 8 tons (at 5:1 SF); the slightly differently designed P50 Lifting Eye goes up to 20 tons.

## How to Install The P-51 Swift Lift Lifting Eye

*Figure 16-37*

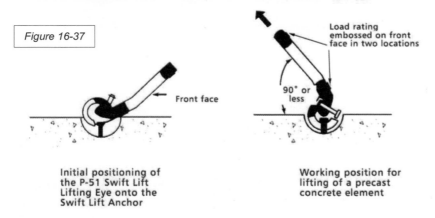

Initial positioning of the P-51 Swift Lift Lifting Eye onto the Swift Lift Anchor

Working position for lifting of a precast concrete element

The eye is engaged with the front facing the concrete and rotated to its operating attitude, automatically allowing the safety pin to drop into place.

When the slings are inclined the front face must always face away from the concrete with the load rating visible on top.

It is important that the attitude is as shown or it will overload the anchor and possibly break it.

It is necessary to read the manufacturer's do's and don'ts carefully when designing a slinging arrangement with these anchors, particularly when tilting up/down thin panels. The friction between the ball of the Lifting Eye and the concrete recess can be a limiting issue; use of soap solution is recommended in some cases.

On completion, the lifting eye is removed and the recess patched flush (with the pin in place).

Other Swift Link options offered by Dayton include 3-way chain slings fitted with 4 ton P50 Swift Link Universal Lifting Eyes for lifting and placing pre-cast concrete pipe. Using the chain's shortening clutches allows asymmetrical lifting.

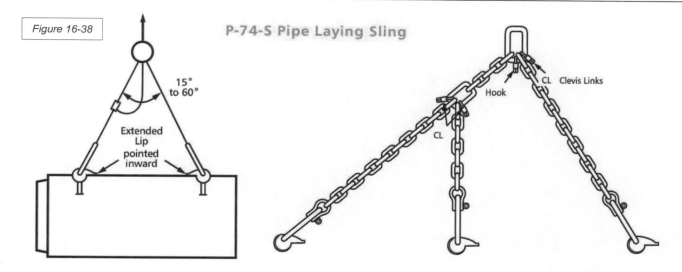

Figure 16-38

P-74-S Pipe Laying Sling

15°
to 60°

Extended
Lip
pointed
inward

CL   Clevis Links

Hook

CL

## Clutch systems

Other options include Ring Clutch systems such as the Dayton Superior Fleet-Lift system. This comprises an anchor cast into the concrete and a clutch that locks onto it. The clutch comprises a body, a curved bolt and a heavy-duty bail (to lift from).

To use, the ring clutch is pushed onto the head of the anchor that is located in a recess created by a Fleet-Lift recess plug; the ring clutch's curved bolt can then be rotated through the engagement hole in the anchor, locking the ring clutch and anchor into a single unit ready to lift the precast concrete element. Once installed the bail can rotate within the body to align.

To disengage, the curved bolt is pulled free of the anchor allowing the ring clutch to be easily removed from the head of the anchor.

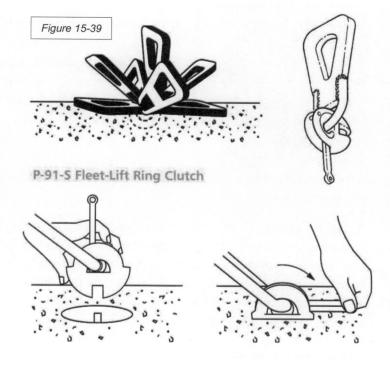

Figure 15-39

P-91-S Fleet-Lift Ring Clutch

Both the anchor and ring clutch are rated with a safe working load which is based on a factor of safety of 4 to 1 (ultimate to safe). Each ring clutch has a Load Range embossed on it, which shows the anchors it can be used with. A factor of safety of 5 to 1 is applied to the highest load in the range for each size of ring clutch. Anchor plates used with clutch systems can take a variety of forms to suit particular applications.

For deep members, the tension forces may typically be taken by tension bars (rebar) passing through a hole in the plate, while shear loads are passed into horizontal shear bars engaged in cutouts in the sides of the plate. These devices may have a rated capacity as high as 22 tons, with reductions for thin panels or close edge distances. Supplemental reinforcement may be required to achieve these values.

For thin members, the base of the plate may be split and turned to form a spread foot bearing up against rebar (running in two directions) taking the tension and shear loads. These devices may be rated up to 8 tons.

These attachments do not swivel and, being pocketed, are only suitable for vertical in-plane lifting.

Manufacturer recommendations must be rigorously followed when using any of these devices.

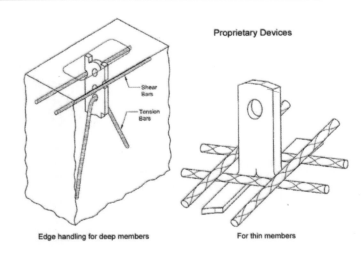

Figure 16-40

Proprietary Devices

Edge handling for deep members | For thin members

## Other systems

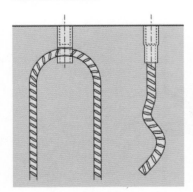

Other options include threaded Lifting Inserts such as by Artéon available from Technique Béton. The inserts are used in conjunction with threaded wire lifting loops or with special lifting devices. There are a number of options for securing the inserts into the concrete including the reinforcing stirrup shown left or by use of a long wavy rebar as shown right.

Figure 16-41

## Caution

As noted earlier, there are many ways of securing to concrete. Not all of them are intended for lifting purposes. In devising lifting arrangements, make sure that you are using an attachment point appropriately and where necessary, taking the appropriate deductions as advised by the manufacturers. Note the FOS of concrete attachments is 4:1, which is less than the rigging that attaches to it; add a dynamic load factor to the load as appropriate to the handling method; be conservative in assessing the loads involved considering the slinging method and the operation to be conducted.

### 16.6.1 References & resources

The following list is by no means exhaustive

- National Precast Concrete Association – Lifting Systems for Precast Concrete Products
- Precast Concrete Institute – Design Handbook
- OSHA CFR 29 Section 1926
- ANSI: Standard A10.9-1983: Concrete and Masonry Work – Safety Requirements
- Technique Beton
- Pfeifer Lifting Anchor Systems
- Dayton Superior (precast product handbook)
- Lok and Key, A-Lok Products Inc. *www.a-lok.com*
- Seifert *www.seifert.de*

# 17 Rigging Arrangement Principles

## 17.1 Objectives

When designing an arrangement to suspend or otherwise support a load there are a few basic objectives:

- The load must be stable when lifted
- The load must be level when lifted (or hang at the required inclination)
- The load itself must be capable of being supported in the intended manner without being over-stressed locally or globally
- Rigging tackle must be appropriate to its use and rated for the loads induced

## 17.2 Stability and equilibrium

What do we mean by "stable"? Before that can be explained, it is necessary to understand the concept of equilibrium.

### 17.2.1 Equilibrium

Equilibrium is the state of a body or physical system at rest or in unaccelerated motion in which the resultant of all forces acting on it is zero and the sum of all torques about any axis is zero. i.e. all forces and all moments balance out; there is no nett force or rotation acting on the piece to make it want to change its location or its attitude.

As applies to lifting, a load hanging freely will always attempt to attain a state of static equilibrium. i.e. it will try to move or rotate to find a condition, a state of equilibrium, in which the sum of the forces acting on it in all directions is zero and the sum of the moments acting on it is zero. In such a state it no longer wants to move in any direction or rotate.

e.g. If you try to suspend a load (on a single line) out of plumb, there will be a horizontal component to the suspension force that will cause the load to want to move sideways towards the suspension point; as it moves the suspension angle is reduced, which in turn reduces the sideways force until it achieves a position where the C of G is directly under the suspension point, the suspension angle is zero, the lateral component is zero; it no longer wants to go anywhere and is in equilibrium. The principle of the plumb bob.

### 17.2.2 Stability

Stability is a property of a body that causes it, when disturbed from a condition of equilibrium, to develop forces or moments that restore the original condition. i.e. an object suspended in equilibrium in a stable manner will always try to regain that original state of equilibrium if you attempt to move it. It resists change – the more stable it is, the more it resists change.

If you move a plumb bob sideways and release it, it will eventually settle back to being plumb.

Someone walking a tight rope is fundamentally in a state of instability. When truly vertical with the body's C of G directly above the rope, the walker is in a state of equilibrium; the rope provides vertical support directly equal and opposite to the walker's weight, there are no side loads and no moments. However, if the walker deviates even slightly from being directly over the rope, his/her C of G develops a horizontal offset from the wire which causes a moment to be developed that wants to rotate him/her around the rope; this rotation has the effect of increasing the offset of the body's C of G from the rope, ever increasing the moment and the tendency to rotate. Far from self-correcting, the situation gets ever worse – this is instability and a situation we need to avoid when designing rigging arrangements. You may have equilibrium but you might not have stability; both need to be considered.

### 17.2.3 Example of instability

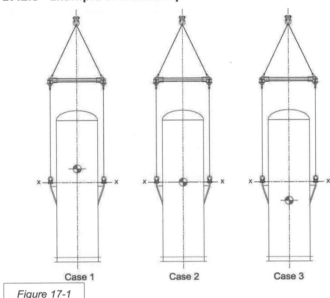

Case 1          Case 2          Case 3

Figure 17-1

In a case such as this, the load can rotate on an axis x-x which passes through the holes in the lift lugs. It is a hinge basically and is analogous to our tightrope above. In Case 1, the C of G is above the axis of support. It is unstable in that condition and with the least excuse will just attempt to roll in the rigging 180º until the C of G is directly below, at which point it becomes stable, but upside down. Case 2 is marginally stable / unstable, the C of G is on the axis of support and it could rotate anywhere.

Case 3 is stable; the load is hanging from x-x rather than balancing on it. Beware however of locating the lift lugs too close above the C of G as wind forces could be sufficient to overturn the relatively small restoring effect the C of G would provide.

I will discuss stability further as we look at specific rigging arrangements.

### 17.2.4 Lifting from below the C of G

Figure 17-2

It is very important when lifting from below the C of G to ensure that the lifting arrangement is stable.

In this case, a process plant module is being loaded onto a ship using two ship's derricks. The module is narrow and tall with a high C of G. It is being lifted from temporary lifting attachments at the base. How is stability maintained?

Let's consider a simplified example looking on one end of a similar load.

Figure 17-3

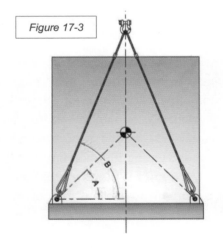
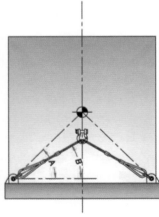

The point at which the two inclined slings meet at the shackle is the point from which the load is suspended and it can act as a hinge.

If the C of G is below that point it acts as a plum bob and is stable; if it is above, it is trying to act like a tight rope walker balancing on the support and is unstable.

We can say that angle "B" has to be larger than angle "A" for stability.

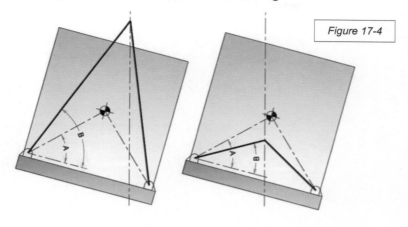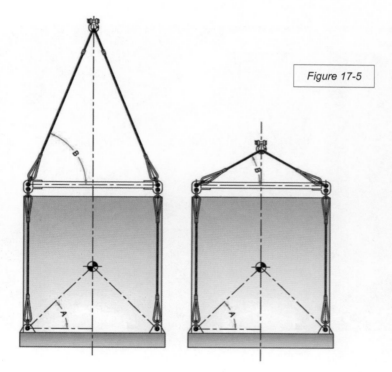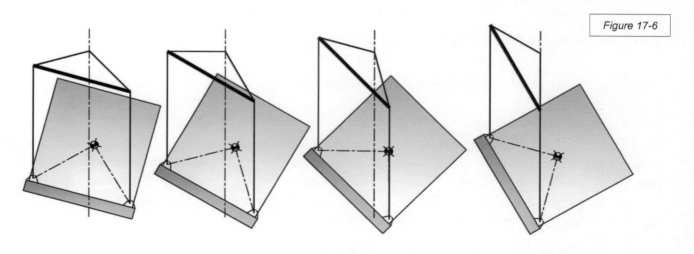

**Rigging Engineering Basics**

How does that work? Consider the following.

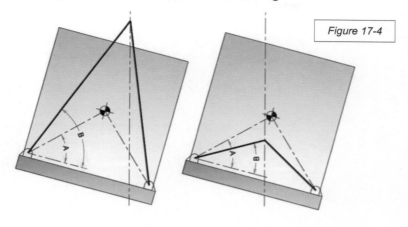

Figure 17-4

If, with the long slings, you rotate the load clockwise (say 15°), the C of G moves left of the line of support. It tries to rotate anti-clockwise when released countering the initial rotation, coming back plumb.

If, with the short slings, you rotate the load clockwise, the C of G moves right of the line of support. It tries to rotate clockwise when released making the rotation increasingly worse.

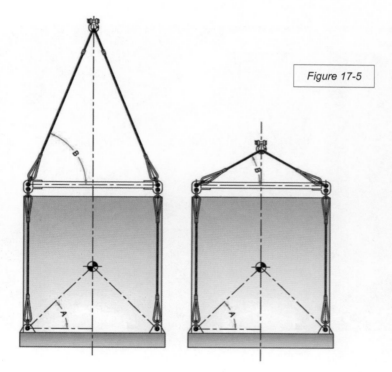

Figure 17-5

What happens if we use long slings and a spreader to get the suspension point high above the C of G?

Angle "B" must still be bigger than "A" for stability.

The situation is exactly the same as Figure 17-3. The vertical lower slings just transfer the loads at the base directly up to the spreader. It is as though the C of G was transposed up to the spreader upper shackles at the same relationship it has to the lift lugs.

I know the slings foul on the RH sketch - artistic license!

Assume such an arrangement is possible for illustration.

If, when using short slings, you disturb the load and rotate it a little clockwise, the C of G moves right of the line of support. This offset further tries to rotate the load clockwise making it increasingly worse. It is unstable!

Figure 17-6

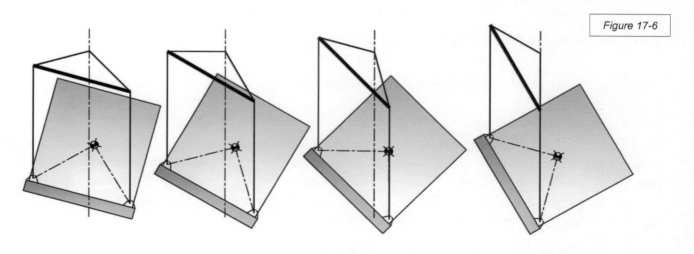

Page 295

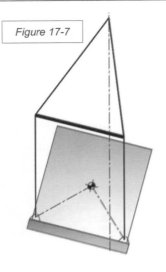

Figure 17-7

If, with the long slings, you rotate the load clockwise (say 15°), the C of G moves left of the line of support. It tries to rotate anti-clockwise when released countering the initial rotation, coming back plumb.

Figure 17-8

Figure 17-9

The smaller excavator was lifted successfully (Figure 17-8), but the larger one was unstable when lifted in a similar manner (Figure 17-9). A major contributing factor was likely the shallowness of the upper sling angles versus the height of the C of G – longer upper slings would have helped avoid this issue. The angle at which the boom is set is also important to ensure the C of G is in the correct location. You need to be very aware of such situations and carefully evaluate the stability.

I will discuss stability further as we look at specific rigging arrangements.

## 17.3 Equilibrium of loads in free suspension

### 17.3.1 Single crane suspension

As noted above, a load hanging freely will always attempt to attain a state of static equilibrium. i.e. a condition in which the sum of the forces acting on it in all directions is zero and the sum of the moments acting on it is zero. In such a state it neither wants to move in any direction or rotate. For a load hanging freely from a single suspension point e.g. a single crane hook, this means the C of G will always attempt to align itself directly under the crane hook and its suspension point e.g. boom tip; the suspension will be vertical and the force in the suspension will equal the sum of the weights hanging below that point.

### 17.3.2 Boom head not over load

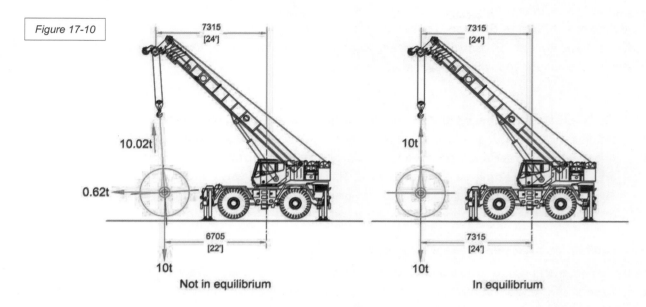

Figure 17-10

Not in equilibrium                    In equilibrium

In this case a 10 t rotor is lifted with the boom head of the crane 2' ahead of the load (referred to as outhaul). As the load line is not plumb, the force it exerts to provide the vertical lift also has a lateral component that isn't resisted by anything. It is not in static equilibrium. The load will move laterally away from the crane reducing the load line angle until it is plumb and has no lateral component at which point the load is now in equilibrium. Note that this can happen if boom deflection is not accounted for as the load is applied by booming back – particularly so with long telescopic booms. The uncontrolled movement is potentially hazardous and the margins of safety compromised as the crane may not have the required capacity at the greater radius. Note also that once movement starts, inertia may carry the load past vertical before it stabilizes, further increasing radius.

### 17.3.3 Load subject to side force

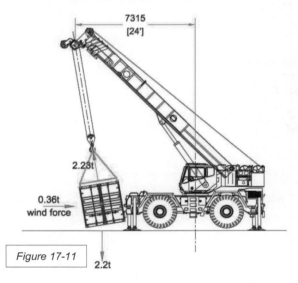

Figure 17-11

If a freely suspended load is subjected to a steady lateral force (such as wind or a restraint wire), it will swing out of plumb to a particular angle at which it attains a new state of equilibrium; in this condition the vertical component of the suspension force equals the total suspended weight and the horizontal component of the suspension force equals the lateral force applied. By Pythagorus, the tension in the out-of-plumb suspension is equal to the square root of the sum of the squares of the vertical and horizontal loads.

In this case an empty 40' shipping container with tare weight of 2.2 tons (US) is lifted in a steady wind of 30 mph (for the example block & rigging weight ignored).

Wind pressure @ 30mph = 2.25 lbf/ft$^2$; shape factor taken as 1; frontal area = 20' x 8' = 320 ft$^2$

Force = 2.25x1x320 = 720 lbf = 720/2000 = 0.36 US ton.

The angle adopted by the load line = tan$^{-1}$(0.36/2.2) = 9.35°.

The lateral component of the load line force = 2.23 sin(9.35°) = 0.36 t which directly opposes the wind force, balancing it; the vertical component of the load line force = 2.23 cos(9.35°) = 2.2 t which directly opposes the vertical downward force of the load. Thus all is in equilibrium (as long as the wind remains steady). However, the load is basically out of control. In gusting conditions, the load will move under the influence of the changing wind pressure and will start swinging.

Notes:

i.    If the container had been loaded it would not have swung so far, the greater weight results in a much smaller angle being required to provide the necessary lateral force to balance the load.

ii.   A load with different areas on its elevations (side to end for instance) will always try to present its least area to the wind, acting like a weather vane. This needs to be resisted with tag lines

iii.  Two guys on tag lines would not be able to prevent the load swinging, the best they might be able to do would be to stop it wind-vaning on the crane hook.

### 17.3.4  Equilibrium principles in a real life application

For ease of construction, the large stainless steel duct inlet section you see here was assembled with its mating face horizontal on the fabrication "table". It needed to be upended (90° anti-clockwise), then lifted to height, swung 180° and mated to a large duct high in the structure to the left.

It was provided with four lift lugs, two at the upper end of the inclined face, two at the lower end. As the piece had little inherent strength, all the lugs had to be loaded throughout the operation. To assist in upending, two "tailing" lugs were provided at the top LH corner (as currently shown).

Figure 17-12

It was decided to use an arrangement as indicated on the sketch to the right. A long sling basketed over a rolling block was shackled to the upper and lower lugs at each of two locations. The two rolling blocks were suspended from a spreader bar with upper inclined slings to the hook-block of the main lift crane. A tail crane with spreader arrangement was slung to the two 2 tail lugs.

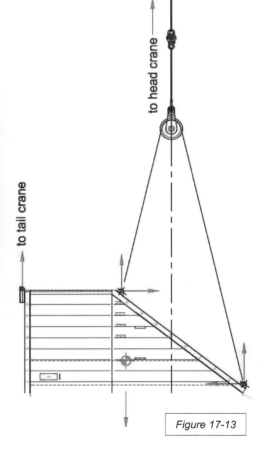

Figure 17-13

The concept was that as the inlet duct was upended, the main lift slings would pay around the rolling blocks, maintaining equal loading to the main lift lugs. Eventually, the C of G would align under the hook and the load would be suspended freely off the main lift crane, at which point the tail crane would be detached and the load lifted to height and placed. As the inlet section has to be attached to the open face of the duct, it has to hang with the mating face plumb when upended; will it do so? What will its natural attitude be when freely hanging from the main crane and how can that be determined?

The inlet duct will try to achieve a state of equilibrium when freely suspended. As noted above:

> *A body is in mechanical equilibrium when the sum of all forces acting on the system is zero, and also the sum of all moments acting on the system is zero.*

i.e. The freely suspended load will hang in an attitude in which the sum of the moments acting on it are zero; we want it to do this with the flange vertical as it has to mate up.

For the forces to equal out, the C of G has firstly to align under the hook-block, next it will rotate until the moments acting on it are zero. So, noting where the C of G is, what is the attitude when the moments are zero?

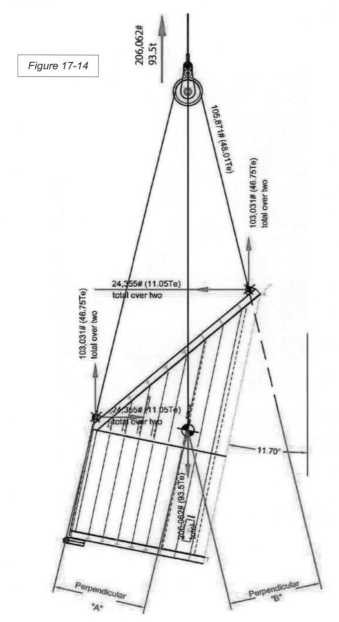

Figure 17-14

First locate the C of G directly under the rolling block (say vertically) and adjust the relative heights to get the total length of the slings correct.

For equilibrium, the moments about the C of G have to be equal.

The forces acting are the tensions in the two inclined slings. They are of course the same tension as the sling is continuous and the rolling block assumed frictionless. So the two inclined forces are equal.

The moments each induces about the C of G is its magnitude x the distance it acts normal from the C of G. As the moments have to equal for equilibrium and the forces are equal, the distances they act perpendicular from the C of G have also to be equal and it will rotate until they are. i.e. when Dist "A" = Dist "B". It will be seen that it is necessary to rotate the duct clockwise.

I find it easiest just to rotate the piece graphically about the C of G until those distances are found to be equal. You will have to adjust the relative heights a bit to keep the total sling length correct.

In this case, the natural angle is found to be when the duct is about 11.7° off plumb.

That is too much to accommodate, so it is necessary to correct the attitude somehow.

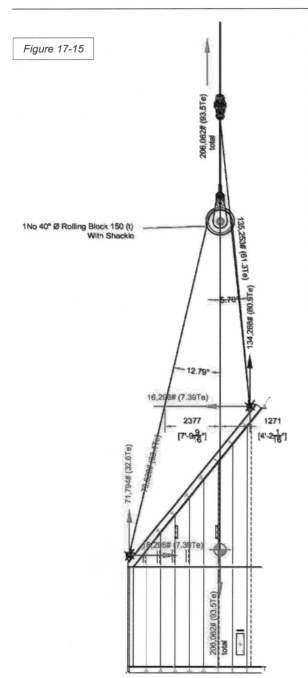

Figure 17-15

1No 40" Ø Rolling Block 150 (t)
With Shackle

206,062# (93.5Te) total

135,255# (61.3Te)

134,298# (60.9Te)

5.78°

12.79°

16,296# (7.39Te)

2377 [7'-9 9/16"]    1271 [4'-2 1/16"]

71,794# (32.6Te)

70,629# (32.4Te)

16,296# (7.39Te)

206,062# (93.5Te) total

To correct the attitude, it is necessary to provide some anti-clockwise moment.

The duct was drawn in the required attitude and the sling tensions calculated as though they were individual slings. Probably the easiest way to do that is to strike a horizontal line from the upper lug to intersect the line of the sling to the lower lug. The relative horizontal distances can be measured from which the vertical components of the sling tensions can be calculated (by inverse proportion) to be 65% (right) : 35% (left), which, given the total weight of 93.5 t, equates to totals of 32.6 t (L) & 60.9 t (R). Knowing the sling angles to be 12.79° and 5.7° yields required sling tensions (total) of 33.4 t (L) and 61.2 t (R). However the sling tension will actually be 33.4 t (total) throughout (as the sling is continuous), which leaves a shortfall of 27.8 t total in the two RH sling legs.

Figure 17-16

The chosen solution was to use 2 x 15 t chain falls from the upper lugs to the ends of the spreader bar, closely mirroring the line of the RH legs of the main lift slings. By synchronous operation of the chain falls, the duct could be rotated to align vertically.

## 17.4 Lifting level and stable

In the following case the crew have to lift and place a 100 t duct section; having estimated approximately where the C of G is, and having determined that they are to use suitably rated lifting lugs positioned as shown, the rigging crew have selected a 50' sling for the LH side and a 30' sling for the RH side. This will give sling angles better than 60° (to the horizontal). However, with the slings taut and the load line plumb, the C of G is in fact about 500 mm left of the line of action of the load line. When they go to lift, the load will not initially be in equilibrium as there is a moment resulting from the weight acting eccentrically from the load line. As they lift, the load will swing until the C of G aligns under the crane hook at which time it will be stable but will not be level.

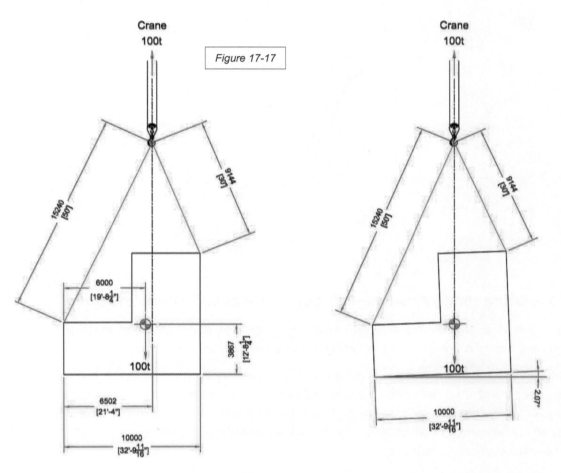

Figure 17-17

This relatively small angle may not be an issue and it might be decided that it is OK to proceed. If it is important to level it up (to make the joint to the mating section for instance) it will be necessary to shorten the LH sling or lengthen the RH sling. It is usually easier to do the latter. If you know the C of G, you can sketch it out, use a standard length sling on one side (50' to the LH side in this case), strike an arc at that length to intersect a vertical line passing through the C of G and determine the length required from that intersection to the second lug (in this case 31'-4"). We can make that length up using a standard 30' sling and make the additional 1'-4" using a couple of suitably rated shackles in a chain. Crosby or other manufacturers specify the inside lengths of their shackles in their catalogs. If the distance to be made up is more than 2 or 3 shackles, you might want to consider using link plates or other arrangements. If you don't exactly know where the C of G is, you may have to use trial and error adding shackles one at a time and re-picking it until acceptable.

Note: Crosby, in general, permits point to point loading of their shackles, connecting them pin-pin, bow-to bow or bow-pin so long as the loads are well centered. Other manufacturers may prohibit this practice for some or all of their patterns of shackles. Check this point before "daisy-chaining" shackles.

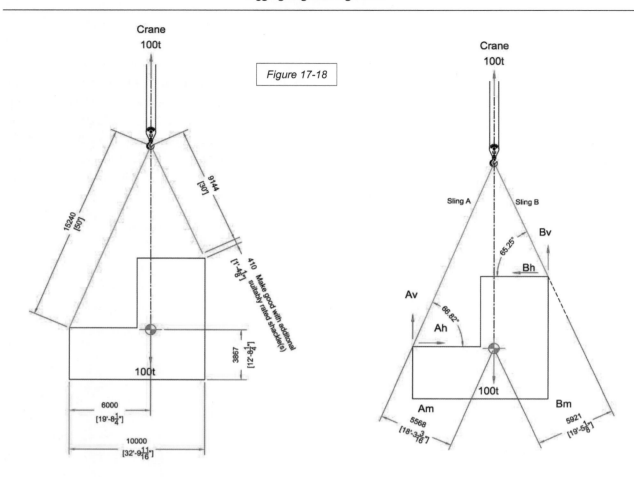

Figure 17-18

## 17.5 Assessing sling loads when lift points are at different elevations

We now have an arrangement that will lift level, the suspension points are comfortably above the C of G so we have no concerns that it will roll in the rigging; how do we assess the loadings? (See also 4.3).

Normally we'd start by assessing the vertical support loads by proportioning the horizontal distances to the support points and then figure the sling forces required to provide those knowing the sling angles, finally knowing all that, we can determine the horizontal components. However in this case, the attachment points are not at the same height which gives rise to moments deriving from the horizontal components as well as those from the vertical components.

For equilibrium, nett forces and moments have to be zero, i.e.

$Ah = Bh$

$Av + Bv = Wt$

$A \times Am = B \times Bm$

$Ah = A \cos(66.82°) = 0.3936A, \quad Bh = B \cos(65.25°) = 0.4186B$

$Av = A \sin(66.82°) = 0.9193A, \quad Bv = B \sin(65.25°) = 0.9081B$

$0.9193A + 0.9081B = 100$

$0.3936A = 0.4186B, \quad A = (0.4186/0.3936)B = 1.0635B$

$(0.9193 \times 1.0635B) + 0.9081B = 100, \quad 1.886B = 100, \quad B = 53.0\,t, \quad A = 1.0635 \times 53 = 56.4\,t$

Therefore

$Av = 0.9193 \times 56.4 = 51.8\,t$

Bv = 0.9081 x 53.0 = 48.2 t

Ah = 0.3936 x 56.4 = 22.2 t

Bh = 0.4186 x 53 = 22.2 t

Therefore the forces balance.

Checking moments,

A x Am = 56.4 x 5.568 = 314 t.m

B x Bm = 53.0 x 5.921 = 314 t.m

They agree, so the load is in equilibrium.

Whilst this approach will give an answer, there is an easier way to analyze it.

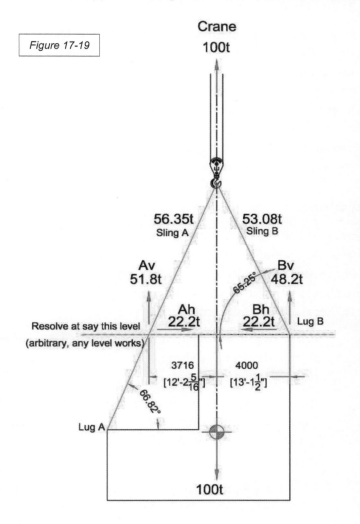

Figure 17-19

The forces in the slings are vectors and each may be resolved at any point along their line of action into a vertical component and a horizontal component. It does not matter at what point the resolution is made as it is simply the result of a force acting at a specific angle.

The load does not know where along the line of action of sling A lug A is located; it merely knows a load of a certain magnitude is being applied along a certain line of action. The lug could be anywhere along that line as far as forces are concerned; its location is immaterial as regards analyzing the forces.

It simplifies the analysis if the forces in the two slings are resolved at the same vertical level, as the horizontal components of the two slings will directly oppose each other without inducing a moment.

For convenience, we have chosen an axis through Lug B; it could be anywhere, the proportions of the horizontal distances will be unaffected.

We can now assess the vertical components by inverse proportion of the horizontal distances either side of the C of G at that level.

Bv = 100 x 3.716 / 7.716 = 48.2 t

Av = 100 x 4.000 / 7.716 = 51.8 t

Ah = 51.8 / tan(66.82) = 22.2 t

Bh = 48.2 / tan(65.25) = 22.2 t

A = $(51.8^2 + 22.2^2)^{0.5}$ = 56.3 t

B = $(48.2^2 + 22.2^2)^{0.5}$ = 53.1 t

Note that A is calculated at the green axis but acts on a line through Lug A and is applied to the load at Lug A.

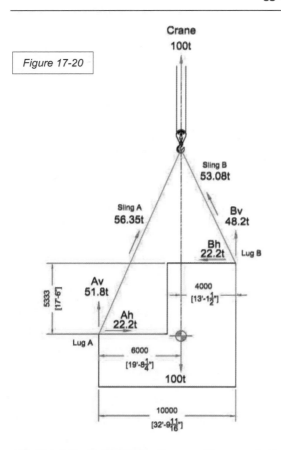

Figure 17-20

Considering the resolved components of Forces A and B and checking equilibrium

Ah = 22.2t = Bh

Av + Bv = 51.8 + 48.2 = 100 t = Wt

Taking moments about say Lug A (to eliminate Av and Ah as they have no moment about that point),

M = (100x6) – (22.2x5.333) – (48.2x10)

M = 600 – 118 – 482 = 0

Therefore, the load is in equilibrium.

In conclusion, where inclined slings are attached at different elevations, take a horizontal line representing a plane through the slings at a convenient elevation (say through one of the lugs) and calculate the vertical loads in each by proportioning the horizontal distances from the C of G to the slings on that plane. Knowing the sling angles, derive the horizontal components and the sling forces. Apply the loads calculated at the lift lugs.

## 17.6 Non vertical suspension – 2 lines of support

Consider a situation like this. There is a 4000 kg packaged skid located on a floor in a building; it is provided with lift points on the frame; the C of G is not central between the lift points. It needs to be lifted a few inches directly vertically, keeping it level to clear its holding down bolts. There is no crane access and noting that there is a substantial steel floor structure above, you choose to use chain falls. The more substantial members run in and out of the page and are your first choice to use; the unit is not central between them.

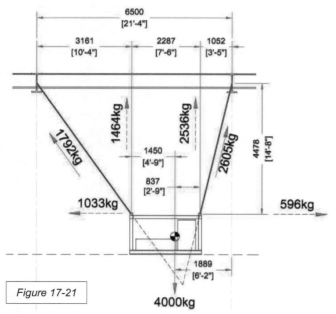

Figure 17-21

If it is rigged as shown, how will it react? We know that all the forces and moments need to balance out for equilibrium.

By inverse proportion we can derive that the vertical forces at the lift points need to be 4000 x (837/2287) = 1464 kg (left) and 4000 x (1450/2287) = 2536 kg (right).

With the LH sling at the angle shown, the horizontal component of the sling force = 1464 x (3161/4478) = 1033 kg. The RH horizontal component = 2536 x (1052/4478) = 596 kg. They are not in balance, the load wants to move to the left until the horizontal components equal out. (Note that the three vectors, the weight down and the two inclined slings do not intersect at a common point as they need to).

Forgive my calling kg "forces", it would have been more correct to use "kN" as units of force. However, this works well enough for our purposes.

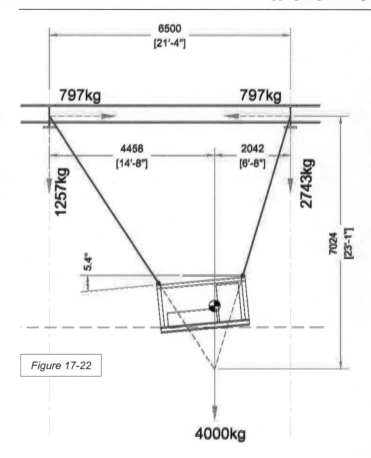

Figure 17-22

As the load moves left, the RH lug moves upwards and the LH lug moves downwards causing the load to rotate. It becomes stable when the three vectors find a position at which they intersect as shown left. The load has moved 153 mm (6") left and rotated 5.4°. At that point, the loads and moments all balance out.

Note that, in the process of adjusting, the suspension loads have changed.

This situation is obviously not want we need, so what can we do about it? It is not simply a case where we can shorten the RH leg to move it to the right as it will rotate even further. If the LH leg is shortened in an attempt to level it up, it will move even further to the left.

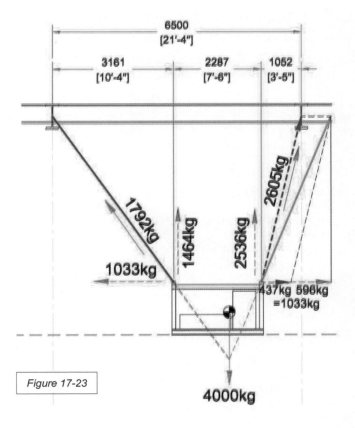

Figure 17-23

The first option is to provide an extra 437 kg horizontal restraint at the RH lug (acting to the right) so that the horizontal loads all balance out directly and oppositely resulting in no moment.

The RH sling tension is $\sqrt{(2536^2 + 596^2)}$ = 2605 kg. That vector and the 437 kg vector can be resolved into a single resultant vector shown by the magenta line. Its line of action intersects the other two vectors at a common point. Thus there are no nett moments acting on the load.

The resolution of the new vector gives us the required 1033 kg to oppose the 1033 kg horizontal component of the LH sling in an equal and opposite manner; the vertical component is the required 2536 kg at the RH lug which together with the 1464 kg vertical component of the LH sling equal out the vertical load of the piece and have it held in balance.

Thus all the loads and moments balance out; it is in equilibrium.

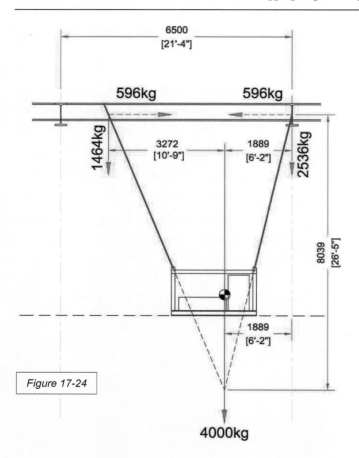

6500
[21'-4"]

596kg    596kg

1464kg

3272
[10'-9"]    1889
[6'-2"]

2536kg

8039
[26'-5"]

1889
[6'-2"]

*Figure 17-24*

4000kg

Another option you have is to shift the inclined vectors so they intersect where you want them to, on the vertical line through the C of G of the load.

We can't do much about the lift lug locations but we can perhaps shift the point in the roof where we attach the LH chain fall.

If you take the point at which the line of action of the RH sling crosses the vertical line through the C of G and draw a line from that point through the LH lug, it will give you the required line of action of the LH force for it all to balance out. Where that line meets the beam to which you are attaching the LH chain fall gives you the required point in the roof. If it can take the load, all is well.

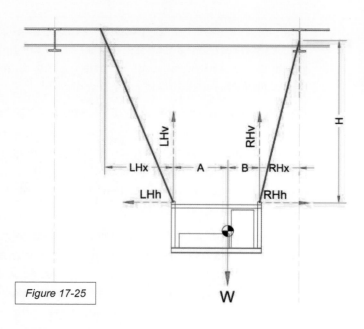

LHv    RHv

LHx — A — B — RHx

LHh    RHh

H

W

*Figure 17-25*

If you would rather work the required offset $LH_x$ mathematically than do it graphically, you can approach the problem this way. With the lift lugs at the same elevation,

$$RH_v = W \times A / (A+B)$$
$$LH_v = W \times B / (A+B)$$
$$RH_h = RH_v \times RH_x / Y$$
$$LH_h = LH_v \times LH_x / Y$$

For equilibrium, $RH_h = LH_h$,

Therefore, $RH_v \times RH_x = LH_v \times LH_x$,

Substituting for $RH_v$ and $LH_v$ and eliminating common terms,

$A \times RH_x = B \times LH_x$

$LH_x = RH_x \times A/B$

Substituting for this example,

$LH_x = 1052 \times 1450 / 837 = \underline{1822 \text{ mm}}$

= 1822 + 1450 = 3272 mm from the C of G, which agrees exactly with the graphical method.

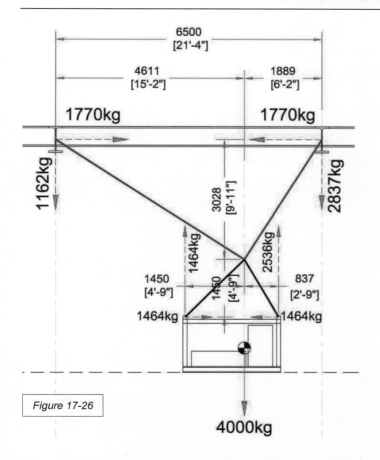

Figure 17-26

Another solution to consider if you have the height would be to bring the two legs with the chain falls to a common point from which you suspend the load.

As the slings get working at a flatter angle, the slings get less effective at supporting the load and their tensions ever higher. The horizontal components start to get to be ever bigger and something you need to be concerned about and have checked out.

## 17.7 Selecting lift points – stability & equilibrium considerations

A compound duct section is formed from two separate assemblies and lift lugs are provided to the top left of the lower section and the top left of the upper section. Slings are selected as shown.

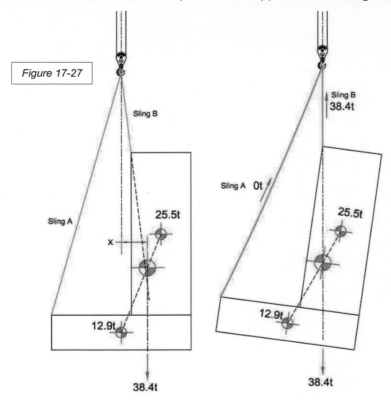

Figure 17-27

The load is not in equilibrium when lifted as the C of G is offset from the hook by a distance "X".

As it lifts it rotates under the influence of this moment until the C of G comes under the hook at which points it stabilizes. However ALL the load is in sling B, sling A is slack. This will always happen if the C of G is not enclosed between the lines of action of the two slings. By inspection you can see that it lies just outside the line of sling B.

This load could never be lifted level from these lift points; if the crane hook is brought over the C of G both Sling A and Sling B are on the same side of the line of action. No amount of extra shackles will help; the line of action of sling B has to be altered, attachment to the top right corner would be a possible option.

*Note: If you have choice in where and how to rig a load, i.e. lift points and manner of slinging are not dictated, you have to not only consider the stability of the load and its equilibrium in the required attitude, but the ability of the load to withstand being supported in the manner intended.*

## 17.8 Lift points provided

Where lift points are provided, you also need to ask the following questions:

- Are the lift points designed for lifting the whole item (or just say the top cover)?
- What are the lift points rated for, is my intended loading within the rating?
- What direction of loading is permitted, are the lugs (for instance) designed for vertical loading only (which may require use of a spreader, lift beam or frame) or can I apply loads in the plane of the lugs; if so down to what minimum angle (say 45 degrees to the horizontal or greater)?

If an item is provided with four lugs, are they inclined in plan towards a single central point or do they lie in the planes of the sides of the item, which would require a spreader?

Do I intend to side load a lifting lug, if so by how much, is the lug designed to take this?

## 17.9 Other considerations

In any slinging arrangement you need to also ensure that:

- The rigging is being used as intended within rating and the worst loading conditions are considered
- The rigging tackle does not foul up on the load or bear on it in places that can't take it
- Bending over sharp edges is avoided

# 18 Tandem lifts

## 18.1 Assessment of loads to support points

If a load is suspended from two lines <u>and they are maintained plumb</u> then there are only 3 forces to consider, namely the weight acting vertically downwards and the two support forces A and B acting vertically upwards. For equilibrium there has to be zero nett moment on the load, therefore the clockwise moment = the anti (counter) clockwise moment. Taking moments about say the C of G to eliminate Wt from the equation (as it acts through the C of G) yields A x X1 = B x X2. This can be re-written as A/B = X2/X1, i.e. the total weight is shared between two support loads <u>in inverse proportion</u> to the horizontal distances of the load lines from the C of G. The greater the distance (proportionally) the support is from the C of G, the smaller proportion of the load it takes. The load sharing is in proportion to the horizontal distances.

The nett vertical load is zero, so the forces acting down = the support forces acting upwards and therefore A+B = total weight.

There are no lateral forces so it is in balance in the horizontal direction.

The easiest way to figure the loads is to take moments about one of the attachment points, say A to eliminate A from the equation,

Wt x X1 = B x L

Therefore B = Wt x (X1/L)

Similarly, A = Wt x (X2/L)

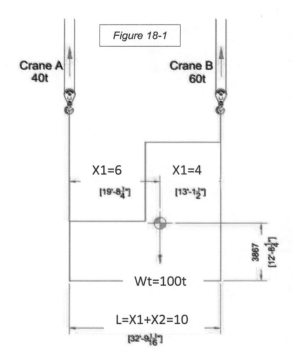

Figure 18-1

In this case a complex duct section 10 m long is being lifted with two cranes. The C of G is known to be 6 m from Crane A and 4 m from Crane B.

To determine the support loads, we can take moments about the Crane A attachment point to eliminate Crane A from the equation,

Clockwise must equal anti-clockwise, so:

100 t x 6 m = Crane B x 10 m

Crane B = 100 t x 6 m / 10 m = 60 t

Crane A = 100 t – 60 t = 40 t

Note: if in doubt, the greater load is always taken by the crane closest to the C of G.

The C of G is 6 m / 10 m = 60% of the horizontal distance between attachment points towards B. Crane B therefore takes 60% of the load. As the loads are all vertical, for moment calculation, all we are concerned about are horizontal distances, the vertical location of the C of G or of the attachment points does not affect the load sharing calculation but may be important for ensuring stability.

The moment of a force about a point is the product of the magnitude of that force x the perpendicular distance from the point to the line of direction of the force. In the above example the forces are all vertical, therefore the perpendicular distances we are interested in are all horizontal distances. So long as the support loads continue to act vertically and the load is not rotated any changing the geometry, the attachment points could be located anywhere along the line of action of the support forces without affecting the result as the moments are unchanged.

## 18.2 Inclining loads

If the load is lifted so that one end is raised higher than the other and the load lines are maintained vertical, the support loads are unaffected so long as the attachment points and the C of G are on a common axis. The important horizontal distances are changed as the load is rotated, but the ratio Dist A : Dist B is unchanged, so the proportional load sharing is unaffected. If however, the attachment points and the C of G are not on a common axis and one end is raised relative to another, then the horizontal distances are not changed proportionally and the load sharing changes. This is particularly so when upending a chemical vessel or similar.

Here a 24 m bridge beam is being placed by two cranes. The C of G is central, therefore the loads are equally shared. The attachment points and C of G are all on the longitudinal axis of the beam. (Assume this is stable).

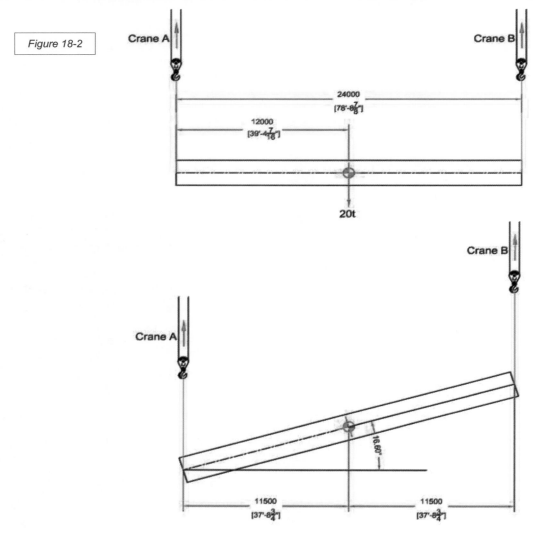

Figure 18-2

In order the place the beam, one end has to be raised approximately 6.9 m to obtain the necessary clearances. The suspension is maintained plumb. How is the load sharing affected?

With the beam at an inclination of about 16.6° the horizontal distances between the C of G and each of the two cranes is reduced to 11.5 m, but as the lines of support are still equidistant about the C of G, they still share the load equally. As long as the attachment points and C of G are on the center line, inclining the object does not change the relative horizontal distances and thus doesn't change load sharing.

In practice if the lift points are say on the top flange of a long shallow beam, inclining it will only make a minor difference to the load sharing.

Figure 18-3

It is best practice when making tandem lifts not to exceed 75% of chart with either machine to avoid load shedding overloading one of them. In cases like this however, significant load shedding is unlikely and it would be reasonable to extend this percentage if required. I would recommend never exceeding 90% of chart.

## 18.3 Using two cranes on the head of a vessel

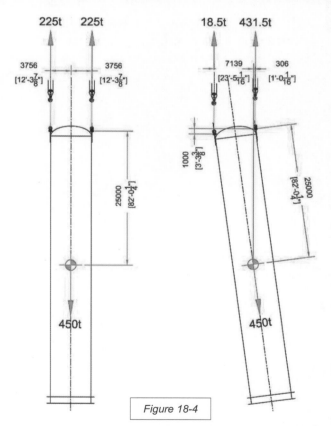

Figure 18-4

It is necessary to be very careful when using two cranes to support a load where the attachments points are close together and the C of G is significantly below the attachment points. The closer the lift centers are and the lower the C of G is, the greater the risk.

In this case two independent cranes are being used to place a 450 t Reactor. Lift lugs are provided on the top tangent line. In ideal world, the Reactor is maintained plumb and the lift lugs totally level with each other. However as a result of slightly different hoisting speeds, one crane has hoisted higher than the other. In this example, the lift points are 7.4 m apart, the C of G is 25 m below the lugs and the difference in hoist height is 1 m.

The result is that the C of G now lies virtually directly below the RH crane resulting in that crane getting 431 t and the LH crane a mere 18 t.

When using two cranes in this manner, use similar cranes with similar hoisting speeds, similar amount of wire on the drums, plan on using up to 75% of the rated chart capacity of the machines, have good communication between the operators and monitor loads carefully (preferably at one central location). Ideally design an equalizing system that allows for the cranes to get a little out of step whilst hoisting without affecting load-sharing.

Figure 18-5

This 450 ton Reactor is being upended using two telescopic boom cranes to the head and two similar cranes to the tail. The vessel has a single head lug bolted on the top nozzle outlet and a single tail lug at the base ring. At the head, the crane hook-blocks pin directly into a lift attachment that incorporates a swivel to which the lug is pinned. Within a limited range, the attachment acts as an equalizing beam, all three attachment points are on a common axis.

At the tail, the lifting efforts of the two tail cranes are unified using an inverted spreader. This will unify but not equalize well. If those two cranes were to get high / low relative to each other the spreader would rotate about the tail lug and change the load balance between the two cranes. However, the spreader is always going to be relatively low and fairly easy to keep relatively level.

You might spot that the tail spreader is being used incorrectly. The inclined slings must be attached to the holes on the center line of the spreader and the vertical slings to the offset holes so that all forces intersect on the axis of the compression member. As shown, some bending is induced in the spreader.

# 19 Upending and inverting loads – general notes

## 19.1 Load sharing during upending operations

### 19.1.1 Effect of positive offset of tail lugs

Typically large vertical chemical vessels and similar items are delivered horizontally and need to be upended; a lifting device (crane or lifting rig) is used to raise the head while a second crane holds the tail of the vessel just clear of the ground and moves it towards the head as the lift progresses, keeping the head and tail suspension vertical. There are many variations on the theme that will be discussed later.

These items are usually fairly symmetrical and the C of G will typically be on the longitudinal axis (or as close as makes little difference) and the attachment points (lugs or trunnions) at the head will also be located on the longitudinal axis so that the vessel hangs plumb when upended.

The tail lug however is usually offset from the longitudinal axis and is often incorporated into the base ring of the vessel (up-over as delivered). Locating it here keeps the tail suspension from fouling the vessel when vertical.

How do the head and tail loads change during upending?

Figure 19-1

We know that at the start of a lift, the main lift crane and the tail crane share the load in inverse proportion to their horizontal distances from the C of G. We know that at the end of the lift, the main lift crane at the head supports 100% of the load and the tail crane 0%, but how does the tail load decay as the vessel is being upended (and why does it decay)?

When presented with a typical lift in the field and asked to predict how the tail load will decay, most people guess that it will decay much more quickly than it actually does and are surprised when shown how it actually reacts. This understanding is important as many people believe that they can afford to let the tail crane radius increase as the lift progresses and let the load block fleet out at the end on the basis that they have lost a lot of load and don't therefore require as much capacity.

As a vessel is upended, the horizontal distances of the head and tail suspensions from the C of G change; if the attachment points and the C of G are all on a common axis, they change proportionally and the load sharing is unchanged throughout upending.

If they do not lie on a common axis, then as the lift progresses, the horizontal distances change disproportionately to each other and the proportion of load carried by the head and tail suspensions change accordingly.

Let's look at an example and analyze what is happening.

In this case a 450 t chemical vessel is being upended using two cranes. The main lift crane (which will ultimately get all the load) is attached to a pair of lugs provided at the top tangent line, whilst the weight of the tail is being taken by a smaller crawler crane which crawls towards the head crane as the lift progresses to keep the suspensions plumb at all times.

The head and tail cranes are equidistantly spaced at 25 m either side of the C of G and the tail lug is attached to the base ring offset 8.333 m from the center line. The head lug is on the center line.

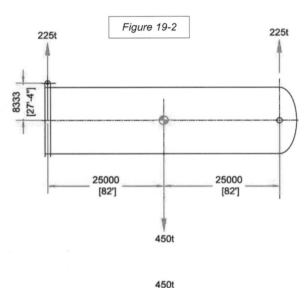

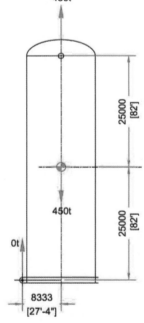

By inspection we know that at the start of the lift, the two cranes are equal distances horizontally either side of the C of G so the loads must be equal at 225 t each. We know that by the end of the lift, the load is freely hanging on the head crane which must be carrying the full load of 450 t and therefore the load to the tail crane must now be 0 t – see the two cases left. In what manner did the head crane load increase from 225 t to 450 t and the tail load decrease from 225 t to 0 t throughout the lift?

Considering the situation at 37° upended.

The head lug will be 25 m x cos37° = 20 m horizontally from the C of G. If the tail lug were on the center line and not offset, it would also be 25 m x cos37° = 20 m horizontally from the C of G. Both distances would be reduced but still equal, so the load share would still be equal. The head and tail loads wouldn't change at all until the last moment when the head crane would suddenly get it all.

However, the tail lug is in fact offset from the center line; as you upend the vessel an additional small horizontal distance is developed to the tail lug, 8.333 m x sin37° = 5 m in this case. This means the head is now 20 m horizontally from the C of G but the tail is 25 m away. By inversely proportioning the distances as shown earlier, we can show that the head gets (25 m/45 m) x 450 t = 250 t and tail the remaining 200 t. The head has only gained 25 t when upended through 37°.

For typically proportioned vessels and reactors, you don't see a significant reduction until upended by about 70°.

The greater the offset of the tail lug, the more pronounced is the effect and the tail load drops off more rapidly than it would with a smaller offset.

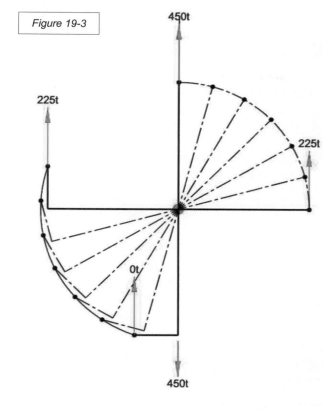

Figure 19-3

For ease of understanding what is going on, we can reduce the problem to a simple L-shaped line representation as shown and we will consider the vessel as being rotated about its C of G in order to upend it. The suspension forces are considered vertical at all times.

For the piece to be in equilibrium:

- the forces must be in balance
  - vertically, the head load + tail load (acting up) = the weight (acting down)
  - there are no horizontal forces
- there must be no nett moment acting
  - therefore $L_h.X_h = L_t.X_t$
  - or $L_h/L_t = X_t/X_h$ ............ Eq1

<u>i.e. the weight is shared by the head and tail lugs in inverse proportion to their distances from the C of G.</u>

It can be seen that as you start to rotate, initially the tail lug actually gets further away from the C of G horizontally, while the head lug gets closer. The proportions of the distances are thus changing. When vertical, $X_h = 0$ while $X_t$ is still +ve and = the offset. At that point, the head obviously gets 100% and the tail 0%.

To determine how the head and tail loads change, it is necessary to calculate the horizontal distances from the head and tail lugs to the C of G as the angle changes (and proportion them).

Considering the vessel at 37° upended.

$$X_h = 25m \times \cos(37°) = 20 \text{ m}$$

$$X_{ta} = 25m \times \cos(37°) = 20 \text{ m}$$

$$X_{to} = 8.33m \times \sin(37°) = 5 \text{ m}$$

$$X_t = X_{ta} + X_{to} = 25 \text{ m}$$

Sub in Eq1, $L_h/L_t = 25/20$, therefore $20L_h = 25L_t$

$L_h + L_t = 450$ t, therefore $L_h = 450 - L_t$

$9000L_h - 20L_t = 25L_t$; $45L_t = 9000$

$L_t = 200$ t, therefore $L_h = 250$ t; the tail has lost 25 t and the head gained it.

Note that $X_t = X_{ta} + X_{to}$, where $X_{ta}$ is the horizontal distance to where the tail lug would be if it had NO offset and $X_{to}$ is a little extra horizontal distance derived from having an offset.

The changing proportions are solely the result of $X_{to}$. If there is no offset, then $X_{to} = 0$ and $X_t = X_{ta}$

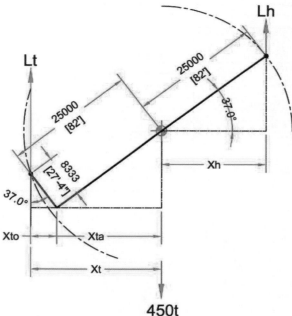

The tail load can be calculated at any angle using the below formula:

$$L_t = Wt \left( \frac{X_{ho} . \cos \alpha}{\text{Offset}. \sin \alpha + X_{ta0} . \cos \alpha + X_{ho} . \cos \alpha} \right)$$

Where $L_t$ = tail load, $\alpha$=angle

$X_{ho} = X_h$ @ $\alpha=0$;   $X_{ta0} = X_{ta}$ @ $\alpha=0$

As the ratio $X_h/X_{ta}$ is unchanged with angle, if there is no offset, then there is no small extra distance $X_{to}$ and the ratio of the head and tail loads does not change with angle. <u>The decay of the tail load is a direct result of the offset of the tail lug, the greater the offset, the quicker it decays. No offset, no decay until the load is truly vertical and the head crane hoists to take all the weight.</u>

There are spreadsheets available that will help you figure out the tailing loads. If you don't have access to such spreadsheets and/or don't want to do the calculations, draw the vessel to scale and measure the horizontal distances at the angle of interest then inversely proportion the load accordingly.

The following extract from a spreadsheet shows graphically how the head and tail loads change through the whole upending process <u>for the above example</u>. Note verification of loads at 37° as calculated above.

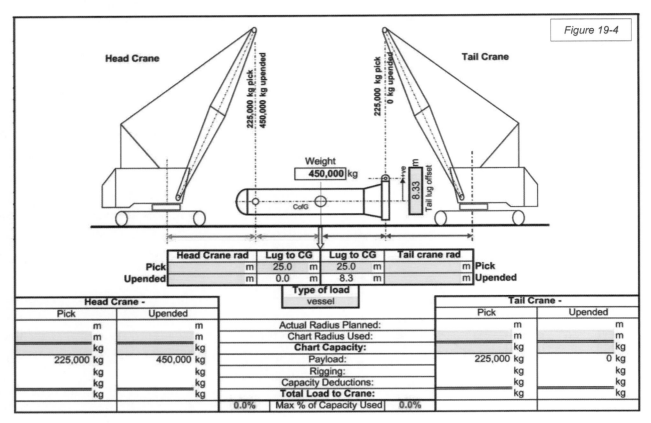

Figure 19-4

| | Head Crane rad | Lug to CG | Lug to CG | Tail crane rad | |
|---|---|---|---|---|---|
| Pick | m | 25.0 m | 25.0 m | m | Pick |
| Upended | m | 0.0 m | 8.3 m | m | Upended |

Type of load: vessel

| Head Crane - | | | | Tail Crane - | |
|---|---|---|---|---|---|
| Pick | Upended | | | Pick | Upended |
| m | m | Actual Radius Planned: | m | m |
| m | m | Chart Radius Used: | m | m |
| kg | kg | Chart Capacity: | kg | kg |
| 225,000 kg | 450,000 kg | Payload: | 225,000 kg | 0 kg |
| kg | kg | Rigging: | kg | kg |
| kg | kg | Capacity Deductions: | kg | kg |
| kg | kg | Total Load to Crane: | kg | kg |
| | | 0.0% Max % of Capacity Used 0.0% | | |

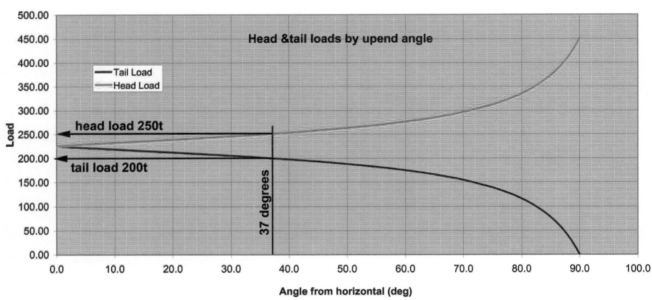

As noted above, the greater the offset of the tail lug, the more pronounced is the effect and the tail load drops off more rapidly than it would with a smaller offset. The tail load when upending the vessel in the example was plotted for five different offsets from 0m to 12m. The effect of the offset on the rate of decay can be seen. The smaller the offset, the more the profile trends towards a rectangle. At zero offset, it remains constant until 90° at which point, the head crane takes the whole load.

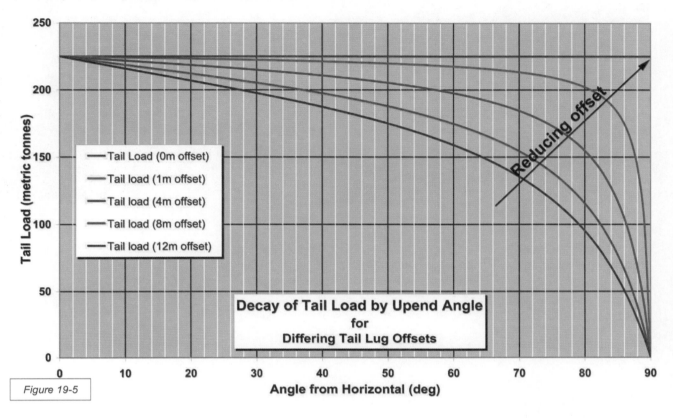

Figure 19-5

## 19.1.2 Effect of negative offset of tail lugs

So far we have seen how positive offset of a tail lug affects load distribution between head and tail cranes during upending – the tail load decays as the item is upended; we have seen how the magnitude of the offset affects the rate of decay – the greater the offset, the sooner and more uniformly the tail load decays; we have seen that with zero offset, the tail load does not decay at all until the load is plumb at which point the tail load suddenly drops to zero.

What happens if the offset is negative, i.e. if the tailing point is a hinge below the longitudinal axis of the vessel? This is much like what happens when you roll say a fridge up to the vertical on its bottom corner. You can be faced with this kind of situation when you want to upend a heavy vessel using a base mounted tailing device mounted on skids or trailers as an alternative to using a crane.

The following two photos illustrate such a case. The assembly is basically a hinge. One part of the frame attaches to the base of the piece to be upended, the lower part is supported (in this case) on a Self-Propelled-Modular-Transporter (SPMT), skids or rollers are sometimes used instead. The two parts of the frame are pinned together to form the hinge. They could have put the hinge point on the longitudinal axis of the piece or even above it, but that would have resulted in a very tall arrangement which adds to the lift height when vertical and is less stable on the trailer. To keep the overall height down, they have started with the bottom hinge point at basically the bottom corner of the piece which is of course well below the axis of the piece which is where the C of G is.

What effect does this have on the tail load and how it changes during upending?

Figure 19-6

Figure 19-7

Let's consider our 450 t chemical vessel again as though it was being tailed using a trailer mounted tilt-up frame in the manner shown above.

The head crane attachment point is again 25 m above the C of G and on the center line while the tailing hinge point is 25 m below the C of G and is negatively offset 8.333 m from the center line.

Figure 19-8

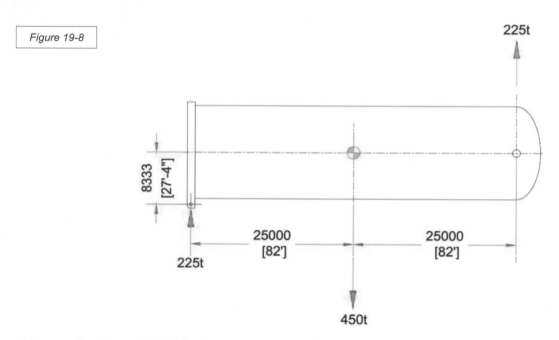

Again, at the start of the lift, the two means of support (the crane and the tilt frame) are equal distances horizontally either side of the C of G so the loads must be equal at 225 t each.

What happens as the vessel is upended?

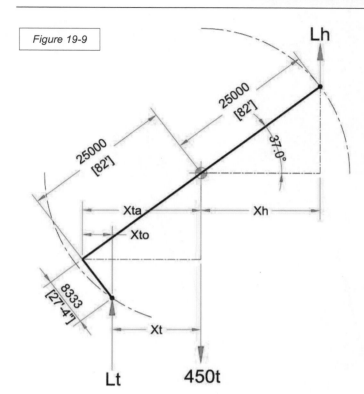

Figure 19-9

Let us consider our vessel at 37° upended.

$$X_h = 25\text{ m} \times \cos(37°) = 20\text{ m}$$

$$X_{ta} = 25\text{ m} \times \cos(37°) = 20\text{ m}$$

$$X_{to} = 8.33\text{ m} \times \sin(37°) = 5\text{ m}$$

$$X_t = X_{ta} - X_{to} = 15\text{ m} \quad \text{Note the minus!}$$

Thus by inverse proportion, the head load is:

$$= (15/35) \times 450\text{ t} = 193\text{ t}$$

and the tail load is

$$= (20/35) \times 450\text{ t} = 257\text{ t}$$

Therefore the tail has gained 32 t and the head lost 32 t.

The effect of a negative offset of the tailing point is that instead of decaying, the tail load will actually increase with angle.

The situation is like two people carrying a fridge up a flight of stairs, the person on the bottom corner gets the majority of the weight as the load is more over him/her (proportionally) when the fridge is inclined. Given a choice you would likely instinctively choose to take the top without necessarily knowing exactly why it would be lighter.

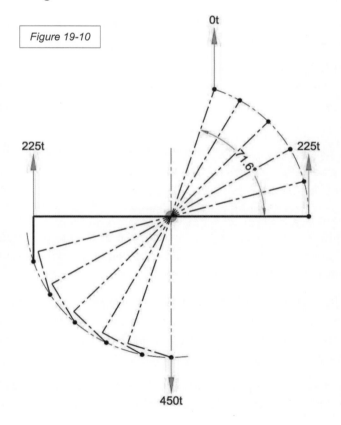

Figure 19-10

What happens as we continue to upend the vessel?

For ease of understanding, we can again reduce the problem to a simple L-shaped line representation as shown and we will consider the vessel as being rotated about its C of G in order to upend it. The suspension forces are considered vertical at all times.

As you continue rotating, the tailing point gets ever closer to the line of action of the weight and is doing it at a greater rate than the head lug is approaching it. The tailing load continues to increase until there comes a point at which the C of G is directly over the tailing point while the head point is still some distance away. At that point the tail has 100% of the load and the head crane is doing nothing more than balancing the load.

In this example it happens at 71.6° to the horizontal as shown left.

What happens if continue to lift further?

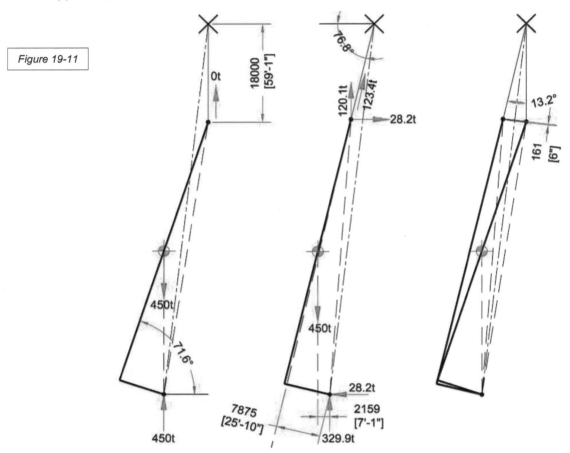

Figure 19-11

As shown left, the vessel is balanced on the tailing rig, any further attempt to lift will cause it to flip over-center as the C of G crosses over the line of support. We are at a point of instability.

The straight line distance between the tail point and the boom head of the crane is obviously the shortest distance between those points. The distance between the tail point to the head lug to the boom head exceeds it by 6" (150mm) if we assume for the purpose of the example that we have 18m (59') of total suspension length. The suspension thus goes slack.

The eccentricity of the C of G about the tail point causes the load to rotate counter-clockwise until the suspension once again becomes taut. That happens when the suspension has mirrored itself about the line joining the tail point to the boom head, a total flip of the suspension of 13.2°. The load rotates uncontrolled through 4.7°.

As a result of the flip, assuming the boom head stays where it was, the suspension goes out of plumb, the head crane load goes suddenly from 0t to 123.4t (plus dynamic effects) and the tail load reduces by the same amount; there is a horizontal load developed at the tail equal and opposite to the resolved head load of 28.2 t.

The load would like to act like a plumb bob and align its C of G under the boom head; however, it can't rotate freely as the tail point has yet to reach its lowest point on its arc of movement relative to the boom head. Thus as you cautiously lift, the tail will be able to move and the load will gradually align itself until the tail point lies directly under the boom head, approximately another 6.2°, reducing the horizontal load as it does.

If you lift further, the tail point has passed its lowest point and is now rising, and unless restrained in some way in the tail rig, the vessel will quickly freely rotate the last 7° or so until everything lines up plumb with the whole load on the main crane.

Inputting the offset into the spreadsheet to obtain the changing load profile shows how the head load starts at 225 t and drops to 0 t by 71.6°, while the tail load increases from 225 t to 450 t over the same angle; it shows how you have instability over the next 18.4°, then the head load increases to 450 t and the tail load drops to zero.

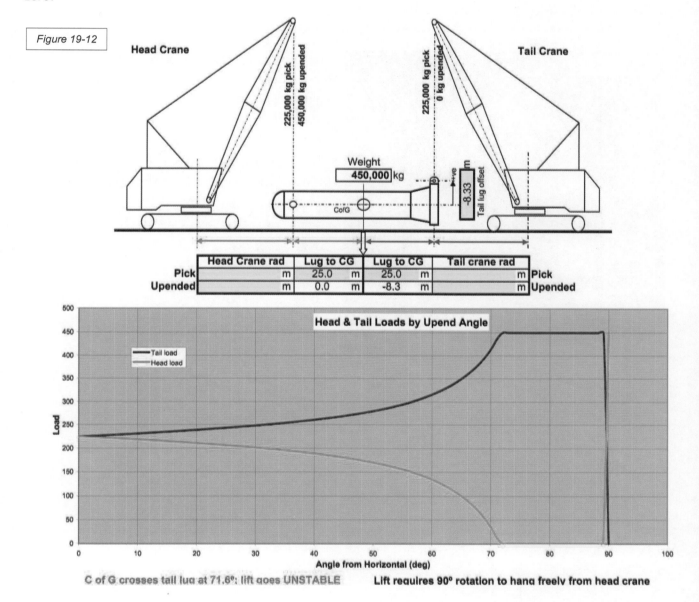

| | Head Crane rad | | Lug to CG | | Lug to CG | | Tail crane rad | | |
|---|---|---|---|---|---|---|---|---|---|
| Pick | | m | 25.0 | m | 25.0 | m | | m | Pick |
| Upended | | m | 0.0 | m | -8.3 | m | | m | Upended |

**Head & Tail Loads by Upend Angle**

C of G crosses tail lug at 71.6°: lift goes UNSTABLE          Lift requires 90° rotation to hang freely from head crane

It is obviously unacceptable for the load to go into free-fall during upending, for the suspension to go out of plumb and for the crane to have to catch the roll inducing all sorts of dynamic effects, so it is necessary to avoid this situation. How do we do that?

Basically you have to prevent the C of G crossing a vertical line passing through the lower support point and there are a number of ways to do that.

### 2-hinge arrangements

The way in which it was done in the preceding photographs was to provide a second hinge point on, or slightly above, the axis of the vessel. Shortly before the point of criticality, the second set of pins engages in their support yokes and the tail weight transfers onto them. As lifting continues, the first set of pins automatically disengages from their yokes, completing the transfer. The second set of supports needs to be slightly higher to account for the fact that the base is still inclined at the time of transfer.

Points to be aware of include:

- The support trailer will see virtually all the load of the vessel at one stage
- The tail load will change (reduce) at the time of transfer
- The point of application of the tail load to the trailer changes which will change the distribution of load in the pressure fields and may require adjustment of the trailer

Figure 19-13

In this case, the crane is making all the head movement, the tail rig is static. The second set of pins has just engaged and the pins in the upper part of the frame are just lifting clear of their support yokes.

The second line of support is well offset (+ve) from the axis which will keep it comfortably stable.

A number of contractors have two-hinge varieties of tailing frames that can be made adjustable to suit different base ring diameters. Such a design is shown here.

J-skids

Another option is to use a J-skid as shown below.

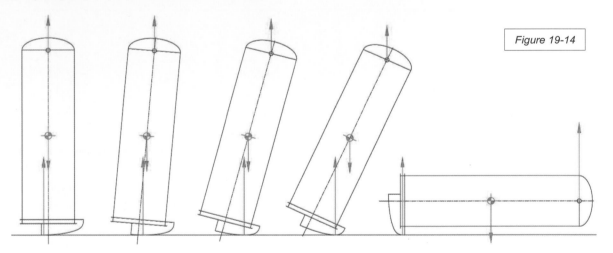

Figure 19-14

With a J-skid, an attachment with a semi-elliptical profile is bolted to the base ring. It may be trailer, skid or roller mounted. Sometimes it may use a peg and hole arrangement as a kind of primitive gear to locate it to the surface on which it rolls. It may be static with the head crane doing all the rolling.

As the vessel rolls up, the point of contact on the skid keeps changing and shifting the axis of support such that it is always to the left of the C of G maintaining stability. As stability doesn't become an issue typically till about 70° or so, you can keep the initial profile fairly tight to start with and only need to let it significantly "unwind" thereafter. This keeps the profile relatively low. The J-skid type of arrangement is of course specific to a particular lift and needs to be designed on a case by case basis.

<u>Tailing on, or above the center line</u>

It may be possible to locate the tail hinge point at, or slightly above, the axis of the vessel. The problem with this is the height that the arrangement needs to be and the stability issues that result, particularly with large diameter vessels.

Figure 19-15

Figure 19-16

This roller mounted tailing frame is being used to lower a Steam Generator to the horizontal within a Nuclear Containment Building to allow it to be removed from the building horizontally and replaced. The head is being lowered by a lifting device mounted on the permanent polar crane in the building; the tail hinge point is on the center line.

## 19.2 Upending HRSG modules

Combined Cycle Power Plants use steam generated from the waste heat from the Combustion Turbines used to power Generators to drive a Steam Turbine coupled to another Generator. The steam is generated in a Heat Recovery Steam Generator. This is a large enclosed casing through which the flue gases flow. Suspended from the roof of the structure into the gas flow are a number of long HRSG modules each of which is basically a bundle of heat exchanger tubes attached to headers.

The modules arrive horizontally in a relatively light weight shipping frame and need to be upended for installation. They have little or no bending strength in their own right and need to be supported during the upending process until vertical and freely hanging. There are a number of ways in which this is done according to who the manufacturer is. The following describes one method that does not require a tailing crane. It is worth examining in detail as it raises some points that can catch you out.

The HRSG module is loaded horizontally into an upending frame (the yellow pieces), L-shaped in side elevation. The long leg starts off horizontal and supports the HRSG module in the horizontal. The short leg is a head piece that pins to the long leg and is braced to it. The HRSG is rigged to the head section such that when vertical it hangs from it. The head is rigged to the main lift crane hook-block using a rolling block arrangement. The frame is laid out with the bottom end towards the lift crane; as upending progresses, the crane booms back to bring the head towards itself. To facilitate the rolling, the bottom end of the frame is provided with a rounded profile to form a hinge point.

As it is upended, the weight of the HRSG transfers gradually to the head slings. The concept is that, once vertical, the HRSG is free hanging from the frame head and the long vertical leg can be detached and lowered back to the ground using a second crane (the red one), without it ever leaving the ground. The yellow crane now has the head with suspended module which it can lift into the boiler structure.

Figure 19-17

Figure 19-18

Figure 19-19

Figure 19-20

The upending operation may appear relatively straightforward at first glance, apart from the difficulty of detaching the frame head and lowering the remainder of the frame whilst the load is hanging from the main lift crane; there are however some aspects of this arrangement that cause it to be less than straightforward.

For installation you want the module to hang plumb when upended and choose lift points on the head so that it will do so; but when initially upended, you have the weight of the long leg of the frame located off-center. This means that the combined frame and load would hang freely slightly inclined (at 89.3° for this particular module), noting that you don't actually want to lift the whole assembly clear as you have to remove the long leg of the frame first; plus you want neutral load balance on the head attachment pins to be able to remove them. The module is still leaning slightly into the frame at this time. As you lower off the frame, the module peels away from the frame and starts to hang plumb. See RH picture above.

The following sketch indicates the "freely-hanging" attitude of the frame and module.

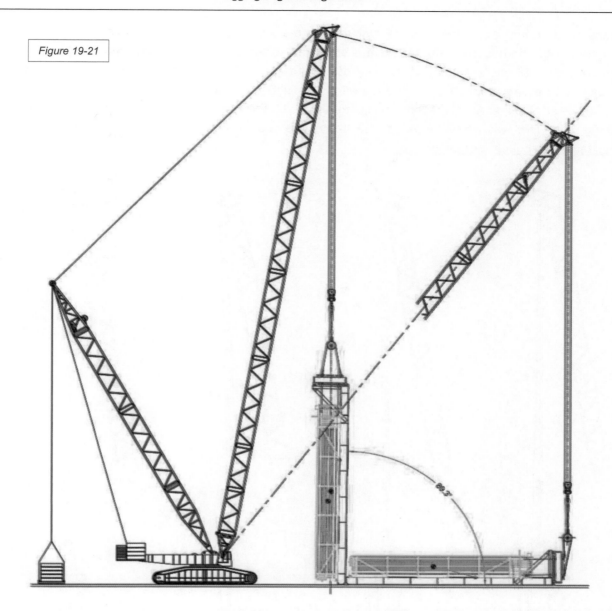

Figure 19-21

A bigger issue however is that, as we saw earlier, with negative tail offsets, there comes a point where the C of G crosses the vertical axis of support. At that time the combined frame and load is balancing on the tail point and the main lift crane is only providing stability. That happens in this case at 82.4°, which is several degrees before where we need to be.

The distance from the tail point to the rolling block to the crane boom head is slightly longer than the straight line distance between the tail point and the boom head. If the load wants to go over-center, there is nothing to stop it until the rigging once again becomes taut, which it will do when the rigging is mirrored about the line from the tail to the boom head. The rigging goes slack and the load rolls freely from 82.4° to 87.2°, a head movement of approximately 7 ft (2.1 m) at which point it is caught by the rigging. See the following diagram (working from right to left).

This movement is to say the least, somewhat unnerving to the crane operator, particularly when it is rolling towards him as in this case. The instinctive reaction of the operator is to boom up to get himself out of trouble at which point he gets the whole load including the frame, a situation that is unplanned and could overload the crane.

Assuming a crane operator with strong nerves what happens next? At 87.2° the suspension is no longer plumb and we have shock loaded the crane. The suspension is inclined which causes a horizontal load at the tail (and crane head). If lifting continues, the tail will drag across the ground as the load tries to go plumb. When the load is at 88.2° (in this case), the tail point is at its lowest point of its arc in relation to the boom head as it is directly below it. There is still 1.1° of load rotation to go. As lifting further continues, the load rotates, the suspension becomes more vertical and the tail rises slightly. As it was already at its lowest point, the tail lifts slightly clear of the ground, the load swings the last 1.1°, the suspension goes plumb and the crane gets the whole load. This was never intended, the frame was supposed to stay on the ground; however it is an inevitable consequence of the design.

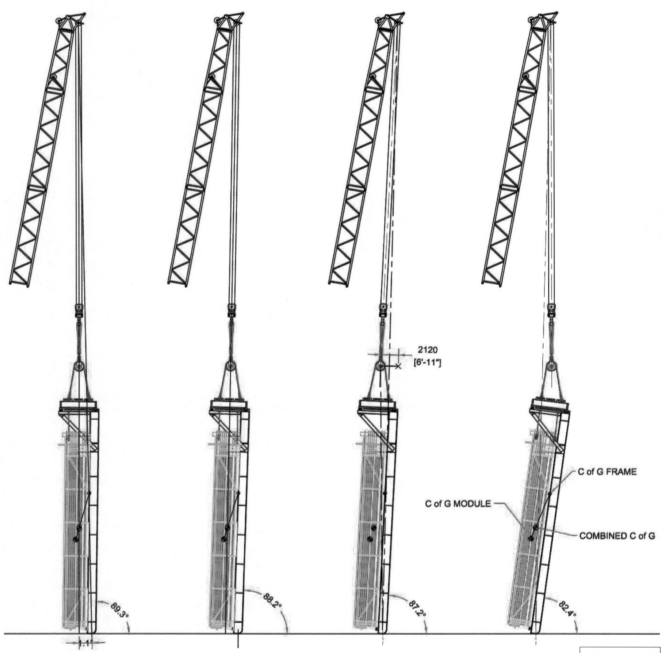

Figure 19-22

This arrangement leads to:

- an unstable load
- uncontrolled rolling of the load
- shock loading
- out of plumb suspension

How might this have been avoided? By:

- Incorporating a J-profile into the rolling point, or
- Using a second hinge point on the tail above the center and allowing the tail load to transfer, or
- Upending in a box structure and tailing with a crane off the top corner of the upending box

Note that some vertical vessels incorporate tube bundles that hang internally from a heavy flange. These need periodic replacement. They are shipped to site in a transport can which is typically upended using a tail crane and is then bolted down to a foundation for stability. The cap is removed and the bundle assembly is lifted clear out of the can and into the vertical body of the vessel.

## 19.3 Tail movement during upending operations

It is important to note the speed at which the tail moves when upending a chemical vessel (for instance).

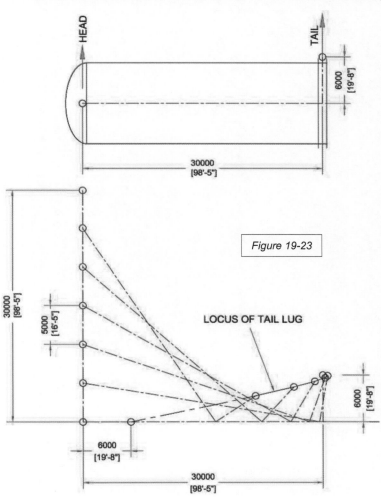

Figure 19-23

We can show what happens by considering a vessel such as this one, 30 m long with 6 m tail offset.

As you upend a vessel the head to tail distance shortens and you need to move the tail (or head) to maintain vertical suspension. It does not move at a constant rate, but more like a sine curve.

At the start of the lift, the tail doesn't move much at all. In fact when there is a positive tail offset, as there is here, the tail actually moves back towards the tail crane slightly. As the lift continues, the tail reaches its maximum distance from the tail crane and starts to move forwards towards the main lift crane. As the lift progresses the rate of movement of the tail accelerates. By the end of the lift, a small rate of lift requires a very rapid rate of tailing to maintain vertical suspension.

With long suspension lengths, a foot or so lag in tailing doesn't result in a large suspension angle and thus doesn't result in a large horizontal force being developed in to the cranes. This can be spotted and easily corrected to control it.

When using a tilt-up tailing frame, there is no tail suspension length to take up any lag, so the entire discrepancy appears at the head and results in the head suspension being dragged out of line towards the tail. That results in a horizontal load into the crane head trying to drag it towards the tail and an equal and opposite horizontal force trying to drag the tail rig to the crane. If using a roller / rail mounted tail device 2% or so out of line may be enough to overcome rolling friction and allow the vessel to self-tail; with trailers it won't and they will have to be driven in.

If you are using a strand jack or similar system on the head, the head suspension length will likely be short at the end of the lift, so any lag in tailing can result in a large suspension angle at the head; this can happen very quickly at the end of the lift and could topple the rig if not recognized and accounted for. The issue is compounded as the lifting speed of hydraulic lifting systems is often not readily adjusted unlike cranes where you can slow the hoist speed to dead slow if needed.

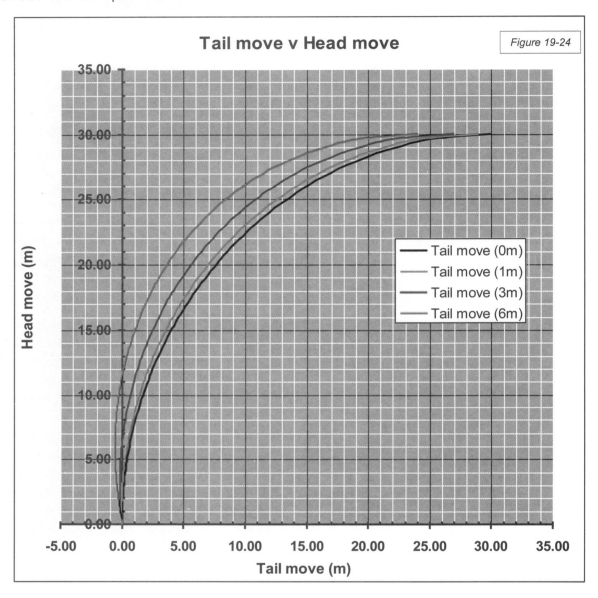

Here I plotted the head movement versus tail movement for the example vessel with four different offsets. You can see that with a 6 m offset, the last 1 m of lift requires about 13 m of tail movement.

Note that you have about 0.75 m backwards movements at the start of the lift. With zero offset, it's a pure sine curve with no backwards movement; the tail movement in the last 1 m of lift is less at about 8.5 m.

## 19.4 "Flipping" a Turbine Casing

There are occasions when pieces are assembled or shipped face down and need to be rolled through 180° to bring them face up for installation – Lower Turbine Casings are such pieces. The 'flipping' operation needs careful consideration and there are some aspects to it that are not always well understood and can get you in trouble, as happened here.

Figure 19-25

Figure 19-26

These Turbine Casings are constructed as two semi-cylindrical pieces with a heavy horizontal flanged joint. Both the Upper and Lower Casings are transported with the flat flanged joint down-over on the trailer and therefore the Lower Casings need to be inverted for installation. For handling purposes, two pairs of lifting trunnions, cast into the horizontal flange, are typically provided.

The plan here was to lift the Casing off the trailer horizontally using two cranes (Step 1), to tail it up (Step 2) until Crane A had the entire load freely hanging (Step 3), to disconnect Crane B and rotate the piece 180° on Crane A crane hook until the lift points once again faced Crane B (Step 4), at which point it could be tailed up to the horizontal using the two cranes (Step 5).

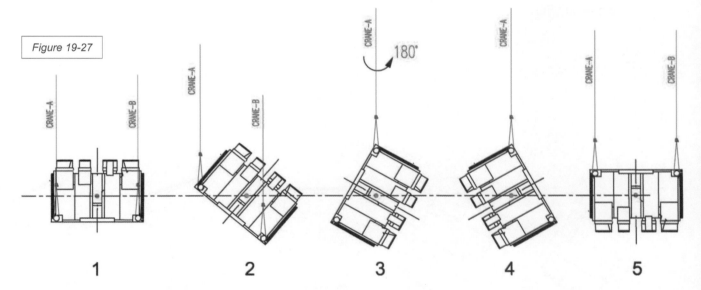

Figure 19-27

1          2          3          4          5

Sounds OK in principle, doesn't it?

There is a fundamental flaw; the tailing point is negatively offset relative to the axis running through the head trunnion and the C of G. The head load decreases & tail load increases as you rotate; there comes a point where the C of G has to pass over the tailing point and it gets outside the two lines of support. At that point the tail crane gets the entire load and the lift goes unstable. It only becomes stable again when the piece is freely hanging with the C of G directly under Crane A. This is after an uncontrolled further rotation of 58°.

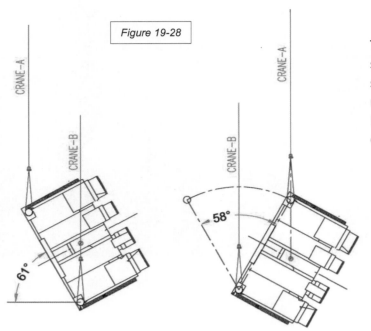

*Figure 19-28*

Through that rotation, Crane A suspension goes slack and somehow has to pass by Crane B suspension which has the load. I In fact, Crane A rigging actually came off the trunnions and the load came to rest on the ground leaning on Crane A.

How can this problem be averted to invert these casings safely? Somehow it is necessary to find a way to get from Step 1 to Step 3 without the C of G crossing the line of support. Steps 1 and 3-5 are stable.

A tail lug on top would be nice but unavailable. The method adopted was to roll the Casing up on its end flange on a pile of wooden cribbing so that the hinge point kept moving and the C of G never crossed it. This kept the load stable at all times.

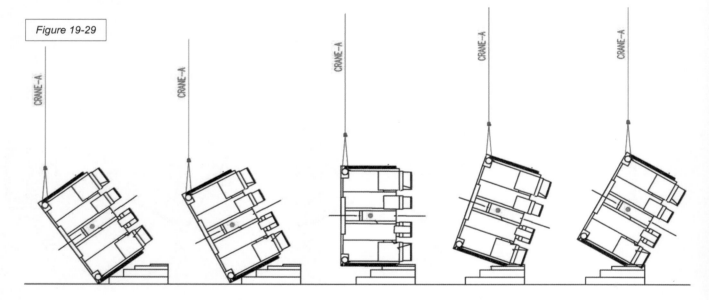

*Figure 19-29*

## 19.5 Inverting hopper assemblies

The task in this case was to safely invert an assembly of three hoppers for installation. A total of eight lift lugs (2 lines of 4) were provided on the flange face. Again, we had to be inventive to maintain the C of G within the lines of support at all times. Two heavy lift cranes were available; the assembly weighing 68 t (metric tons) was delivered face down on a multi-axle trailer.

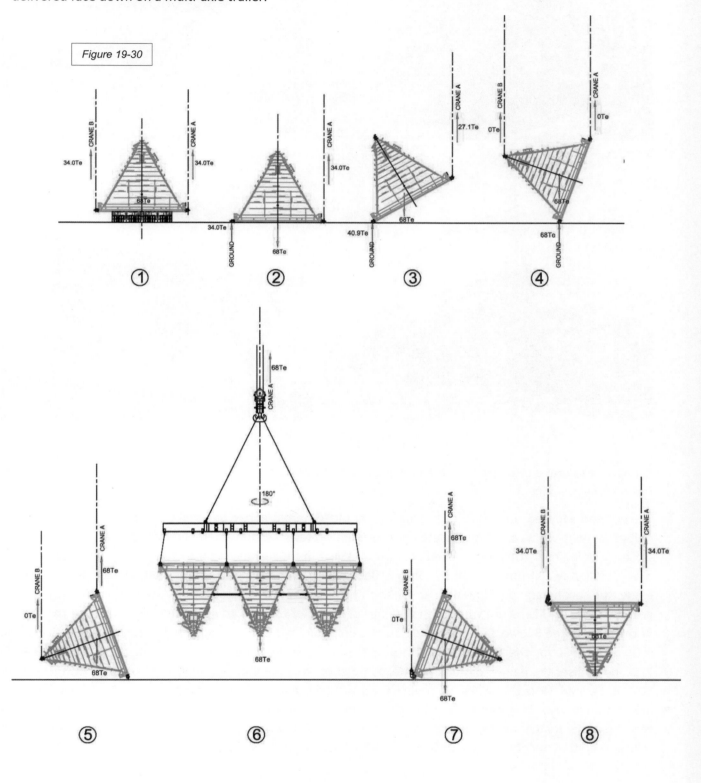

Figure 19-30

Step 1

Figure 19-31

Step 4

Figure 19-32

Step 5

Figure 19-33

Step 8

Figure 19-34

It was agreed that a temporary bolted lift lug could be fitted to the bottom nozzle of each of the three hoppers forming the assembly.

The method adopted was to attach the main lift crane (Crane A) to one line of lift lugs and to use the other line of lugs as hinge points bearing on plate on the ground – Step 2. As the assembly rolls up, the C of G moves ever closer to being over the ground hinge, the ground gets more weight and the Crane A less; the nozzle outlets move further away from the C of G – Step 3. Before getting to the point where the C of G crosses the ground hinge, the second crane (Crane B) is attached to the nozzle outlet lugs – Step 4. The load is lifted clear of the ground, the C of G is securely between the lines of action of the two cranes with Crane A getting the majority of the load. Crane B lowers off the nozzle outlets until the load is freely hanging off Crane A – Step 5. The load is then spun 180° on the hook of Crane A – Step 6 until the second line of lugs on the flange face Crane B – Step 7. Crane B raises the flange to the horizontal completing the operation – Step 8, at which point both cranes get 50% of the load. Note that while we could have attached Crane B earlier between Steps 3 & 4, doing it this way means that it never sees more than 50% of the load which allows use of a lesser rated crane. Crane A of course gets the entire load at one stage and has to be rated accordingly. Shifting the tailing points like this during the rolling operation maintains the C of G between the lines of action of the supports at all times.

## 19.6 Rotating a roll mill housing

Some years ago, I was tasked with figuring out a way to turn over a number of 300 t steel rolling mill housings inside a factory for machining purposes. In elevation these castings are a kind of open rectangle with rounded corners; mounted vertically in pairs they form the main frame of rolling mills used to roll steel plate. The long vertical side members of the housings contain the large forces trying to separate the rolls and are required to be of very heavy construction

For machining the castings were laid horizontally on a large machine bed. As both sides needed to be machined, the castings needed to be turned over.

There was no way to get a heavy crane anywhere close and there was restricted headroom; there was however an available area adjacent to the milling machine that could be used. The solution we came up with was to provide a lifting gantry inside the factory spanning the machine bed and the available area to the side of it. The casting was to be moved sideways off the machine bed and rolled about its longitudinal axis through 180° in the working area, then returned to the machine.

Figure 19-35

Figure 19-36

Figure 19-37

To handle the castings, special cradles were designed; they were located at two positions along the length equidistant about the C of G. Each cradle comprised two identical "J" shaped frames which were clamped back to back around the side legs of the casting using heavy screwed tie rods. See the following sketches which are an end section through the casting at each lift location.

As with any load that needs to be inverted, there was the consideration of how to avoid any instability with the C of G crossing the tail support. It was also necessary to figure out a very short head suspension arrangement that would pick up on the two halves of the cradle.

It was decided to use a rolling block arrangement on the head, picking off the ends of the two cradle halves and sharing the load equally into them. When horizontal, we had to devise a way to keep a horizontal offset between the two legs of the sling to avoid interference and concluded it was best to aim to keep the legs vertical (or close to it). This required the lower pick point to be further out than the upper one, which could be done; however that would pose an even greater problem when rotated. The solution was to use link plates with restricted movement. The links would be capable of moving from in line with the cradle through 90° (to point away from the casting). Beyond that range, they would be bearing on stops. At first pick, the lower links are in line with the lower cradle and bearing on their stops, the upper links are free to point directly upwards. This provides the required offset for the rolling block. As the casting is rotated, the lower link still bears on its stops while the upper link rotates towards being more in line with the cradle. The sling pays over the rolling block. By the time the casting is vertical, the upper and lower links are both on the stops and the sling makes equal angles to both sets of links. As you rotate further, the links which are now upwards rotate away from their stops, while other links stay on the stops. This maintains the required offset for the rolling block throughout the roll.

On the tail, a large hole was provided in the cradle half in the short leg of the "J" through which a pin could be passed; the ends of each pin are supported by a tailing carriage mounted on rollers. Initially the hole on the upper cradle half is used. This provides a small positive offset for tailing. As lifting progresses, the weight of the casting transfers more and more from the long leg of the lower "J" onto the short legs. The head is lifted and the tail rolls towards the head. When vertical, the entire weight is taken on the head and the entire assembly is lifted clear of the tail device, which is relocated (with the pin) to the equivalent hole in the other cradle half. This effectively shifts the hinge point to the other side of the line of action and provides a positive tail offset for the remaining 90° of rotation to complete the operation. For the rest of the rotation, the tail is kept in fixed location and the head is moved laterally and lowered using the lift rig. This minimizes the space required.

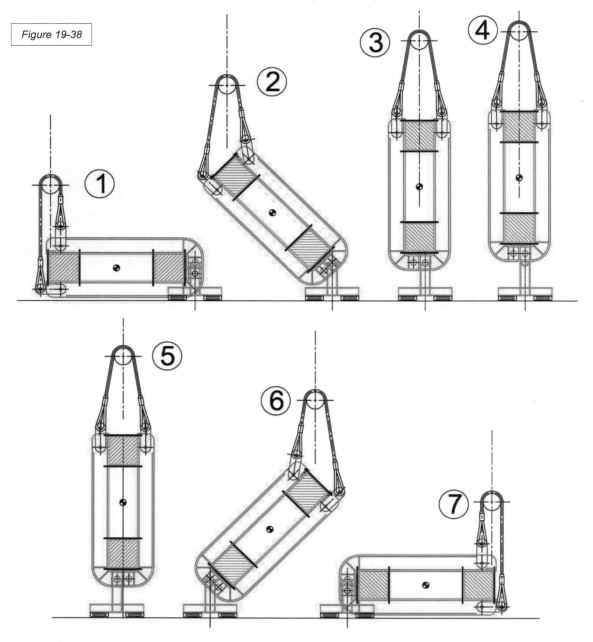

Figure 19-38

Although this operation is specific, it illustrates head and tail techniques, variations of which may be useful in other applications.

## 19.7 Upending a load using diagonally opposed lift points

Large vertical ducts / modules and the like often need to be delivered horizontally to minimize transport height. They will either be built horizontally or built as installed and laid down for transport; at site, these pieces will require to be rolled up to the vertical.

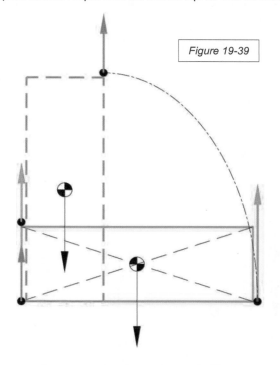

Figure 19-39

A good stable lifting arrangement can often be devised using two cranes and diagonally opposed lifting points as shown here.

The C of G is always contained within the two lines of support and never wants to go "over-center". If the load is symmetrical and the C of G is somewhat central as shown here, then it will lie on or close to the line joining the two lifting points and the balance of load between the two cranes will change little (if at all) as the load is upended.

There is therefore no need for one crane to be sized for the entire load, as would be the case if the RH lifting point was located in the center of the short face or if rolling blocks were used attaching to both of the top corners.

When lifting like this, temporary bracing of the structure may be required and any fitted equipment / piping etc adequately supported.

In a similar vein, you may want to upend a load using a single crane and the ground as a hinge point.

If doing that, the C of G has to pass over the hinge point and you'll want to devise an arrangement in which it does so in a controlled manner. The best way to achieve that is to try to arrange to locate the head lift points on the diagonally opposite corner of the load such that the C of G lies on a line joining the hinge point to the head lugs. In that way, as it rolls the C of G and the lift point will be directly above the rolling point simultaneously. See the green phase. If the load is symmetrical, this may well be possible to achieve.

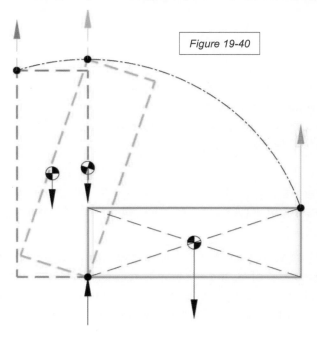

Figure 19-40

As the C of G passes over the hinge, the entire load will be on the rolling point, the head will have none, and the head lift point will be on the apex of its arc (so long as the C of G lies on the line joining head and tail).

At that point it is balancing but doesn't want to flip as the C of G is under the head crane and the suspension length is as short as it can be at that point. (It may sway a bit as moving a few degrees either way does not change the suspension length much but it is not unstable so long as the suspension is maintained plumb).

Despite the theory, taking a load over-center like this is still a skilled operation and great care is required at the apex to ensure good control.

Once over the top, you can continue to roll the load lowering off the head and getting ever more stable until the short face is sitting on the ground – see the blue phase.

If you want to continue and lay it down on its other long face, you would have to relocate your head rigging to the other top corner and roll it down on the other bottom corner as a mirror image of the upending shown above. Once again, there will be a point at which the C of G passes over the second rolling point at which particular care needs to be taken.

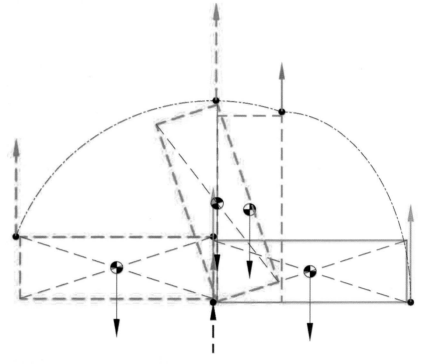

Figure 19-41

An option you may have if you wish to roll the load over the full 180° that avoids having to re-rig is to combine the two previous techniques; i.e. roll it up to the vertical using two cranes, then continue the rest of the way with one crane and the ground as shown below.

This requires being able to put the tail lugs on the extreme corner and providing them with a rounded profile on which you can roll for the later phases.

## 19.8 Location of lift points when upending

When upending a vessel, you may have the option of reducing the magnitude of the tail load by locating the head lifting point(s) closer to the C of G. The closer the head attachments are, the greater the proportion of load taken by the head crane and the less the tail crane has to carry. As the head crane supports the <u>entire</u> load anyway when upending is complete, there is rarely a penalty there, but there is the advantage that the tail crane may be down-sized.

In this case, the initial proposal was for a pair of lifting lugs at the top tan line. Given the geometry of this vessel, the weight and the location of the C of G, the head load will be 225 t at "pick" and the tail load will also be 225 t.

It was suggested to relocate the head attachment points to reduce the required capacity of the tail crane saving money. By providing lifting trunnions 10 m above the C of G, the tail load is reduced by nearly 50% to 129 t bringing the tail weight within the range of a much more cost-effective crawler crane. The head weight has increased but this has not affected the required size of the main lift crane at the head as it has to deal with 450 t when vertical.

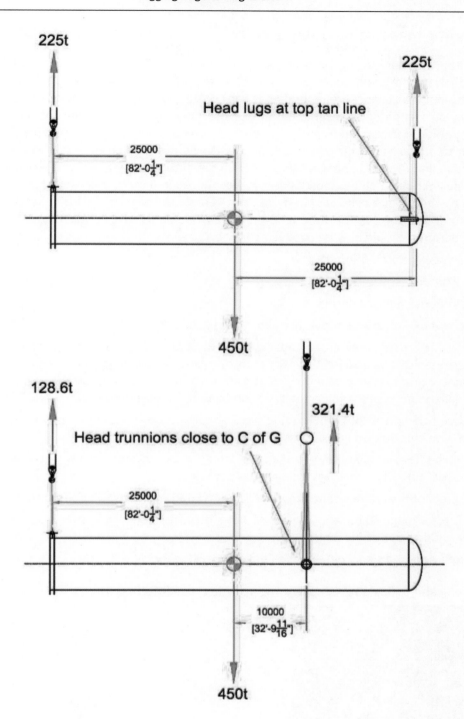

Figure 19-42

Points to note:

- The slings to the head require a clear 90 degree arc to swing through so the locations of ladders and platforms, outlet nozzles and the like above the lift points need to be considered. It may be possible to orientate the lift points in plan so that the slings miss everything, although the vessel may require rotation when vertical to orientate it correctly.
- Do not locate the lift points too close to the C of G that the stability becomes marginal. Aim for at least 20% of the weight on the tail when horizontal.

The vessel engineer has to consider local and global stress effects resulting from the location of the lift points when assessing the viability of particular locations – this isn't the rigging engineers call.

## 19.9 Upending loads using a single crane

There are instances where it <u>may</u> be permissible to "top and tail" an item using a single crane by suspending the "head" off (say) the main boom point and the "tail" off a whip line using a rooster sheave or jib. This technique is sometimes used when upending rebar cages, tilting up precast panels and like operations. It has advantages in not requiring a second tail crane and may allow offloading, upending and placing as one continuous operation; it also keeps the arrangement compact and is more cost effective. It can be however more difficult to analyze and this may result in unwittingly overloading the rigging or elements of the cranes such as the whip line / rooster sheave. Dependant on the exact arrangement, this type of operation may result in the hoist lines not being plumb, odd loads may be induced in unnatural angles, the head of the load may get very close to the boom, the control system may not be able to monitor what is going on everywhere and may not be able to effectively control the operation within safe limits, the radius may be greater than indicated. This kind of operation should only be conducted when:

- Prevailing legislation permits it.

- Your insurer permits it.

- Your in-house policies permit it.

- The crane manufacturer allows it and provides guidance.

- There is adequate rated crane capacity at both boom and jib to suspend the entire load from either point within crane capacity. For a lift of this nature, I would suggest not exceeding 90% of either chart capacity. Conservatively take the radius as though the C of G is below the jib/rooster point rather than the main boom point. It will actually lie somewhere between the two.

- The boom length is long, minimizing the in-haul and out-haul angles of the hoist lines (and keeping them within permitted limits).

- The hoist line in-haul and out-haul angles can be safely accommodated without rubbing or fouling the crane structure or unnaturally loading it in any way.

- The safety of the crane's control system is not compromised by the operation.

- The forces, magnitudes and directions have been assessed by a competent person and verified as being within permissible limits.

- The operator and signal person have the skills necessary.

### 19.9.1 Topping and tailing a rebar cage using a single crane (Method A)

Figure 19-43

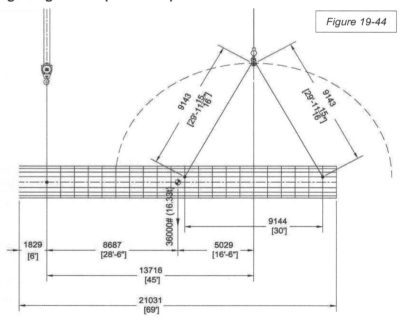

Figure 19-44

Rebar cages, flare stacks and other similarly "floppy" loads have little bending strength when horizontal and require multiple support points along their length to avoid collapsing under their own weight when being handled. This presents some design challenges when conducting an upending operation.

One possible solution for upending a rebar cage is shown above. The diagram to the right is loosely based on the real rebar cage lift made on the left. In this case the load was "topped and tailed" using a single crane. The Cage weight is 36000# (16.33 t); the head load was taken to the main hoist, while the tail support (from the jib) is split into two using a sling basketed over a rolling block.

So how are the forces analyzed and evaluated in such cases?

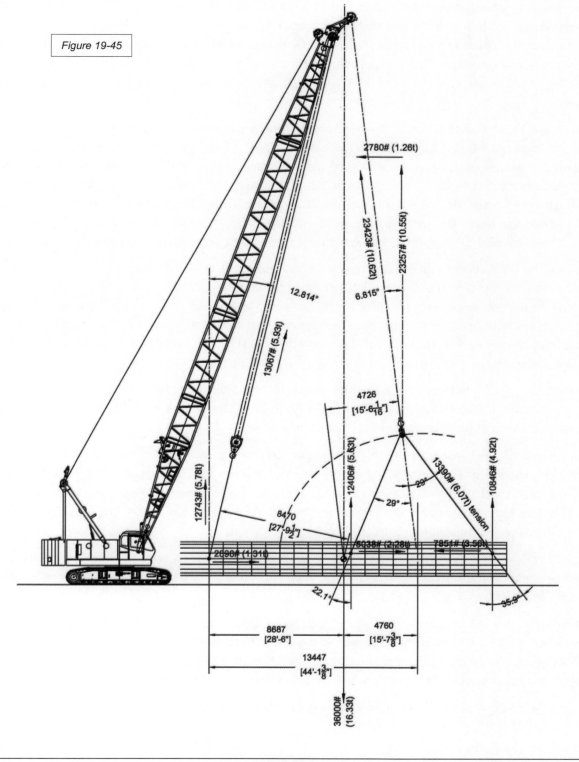

Figure 19-45

A 60' sling is used basketed over a pulley (rolling block) at the tail. The sling is obviously continuous and of a fixed length so as the cage is upended the pulley block will follow a locus that is an ellipse with foci at the two attachment points. (The semi-major axis = 50% x total sling length). The distance from Attachment 1 to the ellipse and back to Attachment 2 is constant at 60'.

By inspection, the C of G at pick will be closer to the tail, about $^1/_3{}^{rd}$ to $^2/_3{}^{rd}$ so we will estimate the C of G to lie on a vertical line located in similar horizontal proportions between the crane suspension points. At pick it will be horizontal at grade; this locates the cage.

The head suspension is on a line from the main boom sheaves to the head lift point. At the tail, the pulley pays along its locus until it comes to equilibrium at a point where the two parts of the sling make equal angles either side of the line of action of the tail suspension. (As the tension in the tail sling is a constant this is required for the sheave to be in equilibrium). This will be so when the tail suspension is normal (90°) to the ellipse; so, draw the ellipse, then construct a line from the rooster sheave normal to it. Draw the two parts of the sling from the attachment points to the pulley; they make an equal (29°) angle either side of the line of action.

Next, project the lines of action of the head and tail suspension forces down to a common horizontal line and note the points of intersection with it. In this case, the center line of the cage was used (any line would do, the proportions we are evaluating will always be the same) and measure the horizontal distances from the C of G to the points of intersection, 8.687 m & 4.760 m in this case. The C of G is thus located closer to the tail than the head in the proportions 8.687 / (8.687 + 4.760) = 0.646 or 64.6% to the tail; 4.76 / (8.687 + 4.760) = 0.354 or 35.4% to the head. Knowing this the head and tail loads (vertical) can then be evaluated to be 5.78 t & 10.55 t respectively. (See Section 6.1 in which load sharing by inverse proportion of distance is discussed).

Knowing the head and tail suspension angles we can now determine the head and tail tensions to be 5.93 t & 10.62 t respectively. (For those who wish to follow in USCU units refer to the diagram where equivalents are shown). As we now know primary force magnitudes and angles, we have the total vector information for the head and tail load lines. Factoring those vectors, we can next determine the horizontal components to be approximately equal and opposite at 1.3 t, which validates the estimated C of G location between the suspension points.

The moments acting on the load are the magnitude of the head and tail load vectors x the distances from the C of G normal to the lines of action = 5.93 t x 8.47 m = 50.2 t.m clockwise and 10.62 t x 4.726 m = 50.2 m; so as all forces and moments balance, the load is in equilibrium.

Finally, we can investigate how the tail load is split. Each of the two parts of the tail sling provides 50% of the force along the line of action and we know the angle each side = 29°, so we can evaluate the sling tension to be = 50% x 10.62 t / cos(29°) = 6.07 t. Knowing the sling tension and the two angles the sling makes to the cage (22.1° & 35.9°) we can evaluate the vertical and horizontal components of the sling tension at the attachment points. This gives us the whole picture at "pick".

Note: the self-weight of the main hook-block is not considered in analyzing how the load will hang. In practice it will be significant and will tend to make the main suspension more vertical than indicated pushing the load away from the crane a bit.

Conclusions: now we have evaluated all this and drawn it out, there is an obvious concern that the main hoist lines, when working at this angle, may foul at the boom head (even noting it is an open throat construction). We can already say that a longer boom or entirely different arrangement may be required. However, before making that call, we will next investigate the situation as the cage is upended. See diagram following.

On a similar basis, what is the situation when the cage is partially upended – say at 45°?

By inspection the C of G is now going to lie proportionally closer to the line of action of the tail sling, about $^1/_4$th to $^3/_4$th so we will estimate the C of G to lie on a vertical line located between the crane suspension points in those proportions, a little closer to the rooster sheave. This won't make a huge difference if we get it slightly wrong, our estimate will be vindicated (or not) later when we calculate the horizontal components.

Knowing the line of the C of G, the angle at 45° and the need to keep the tail close to the ground, we can locate the cage. As previously, the head suspension will be on a line joining the main boom sheaves to the head lift point.

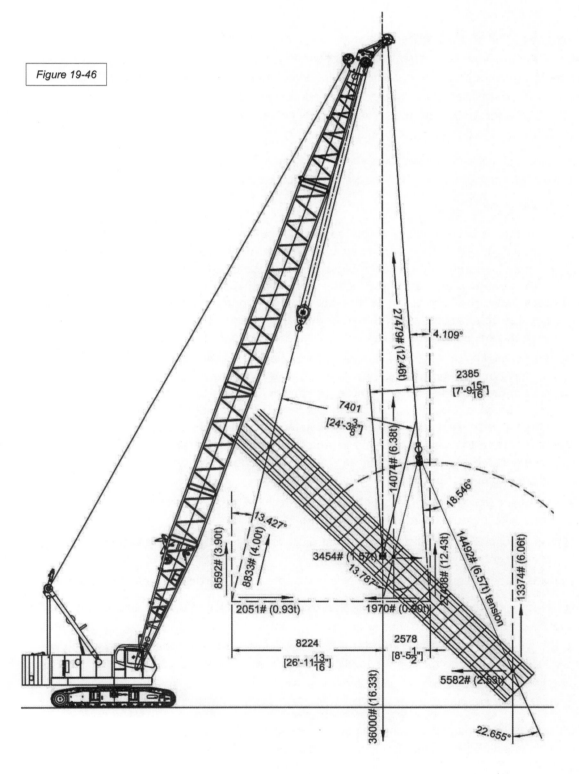

Figure 19-46

At the tail, again draw a line from the rooster sheave normal to the ellipse; this is where the pulley comes to equilibrium with the two parts of the sling making equal angles of about 18.5° either side of the line of action of the tail suspension. This establishes the lines of action of the head and tail slings.

To complete the vectors, we need to establish the tension in the slings. Once again project the lines of action down to a common horizontal line (in this case I used the intersection of the line of action of the tail sling with the center line of the cage) and measure the horizontal distances from the points of intersection to the line of action of the C of G (8.224 m & 2.578 m). This yields vertical components of the head and tail loads to be 3.90 t & 12.43 t respectively.

Knowing the head and tail suspension angles we can now determine the head and tail tensions to be 4.00 t & 12.46 t. The horizontal components are approximately equal and opposite at 0.9 t. The moments acting on the load are the magnitude of the head and tail load vectors x the distances from the C of G normal to the lines of action = 4.00 t x 7.40 m = 29.6 t.m clockwise and 12.46 t x 2.385 m = 29.7 t.m; so we were a small amount off with the C of G location, it should be very slightly nearer the rooster, but within practical limits, all forces and moments balance and the load is in equilibrium.

Splitting the tail load into its two parts shows the sling tension to be 6.57 t; from that we can derive the vertical and horizontal components of the tension at the attachment points.

What can we say at this point?

- The cage is way too close to the boom; in fact it may already be interfering. Certain innovative, but misguided, people have in the past been known to rotate it plan view (using an excavator or whatever to drag it round) so it comes up alongside the boom as it is lifted until past the point of interference. This is unacceptable as it side loads the sheaves, which will damage the rope, wear the sheaves and may cause the wire to jump the sheave; it also puts unnatural loads into the crane and creates a considerable torsion which if inadvertently released will cause the cage to crash into the boom. We probably need a greater radius and/or longer boom or a totally different arrangement.

- By rigging like this we have induced vertical support components of 3.90 t / 6.38 t / 6.06 t, which may or may not be what the cage would ideally like to see as a distribution, in fact it would probably prefer a bit more on the head and a little less on the extreme tail. This isn't likely an issue in this case, but could be when (say) lifting a flare. In the case of a load that isn't very stiff the differential between the ideal support reactions and those actually induced could cause significant deflections in order to redistribute the load in the way in which we are forcing it to do. If deflected excessively it could be overstressed. Hence it is important to choose lift point locations carefully to most closely duplicate a neutral load distribution.

- A longer boom would be a better idea to reduce the in-haul and out haul angles; the head reeving looks like it would be into the boom head.

- Approximately 76% of the load of the piece is being carried on the whip line on the rooster (tail), we may be getting very close to its capacity.

If we now consider the situation when the cage is approaching vertical – say at 75°. (See following diagram).

Using the same methodology, we can see that the head is starting to pick up a little more load, the C of G is still relatively closer to the rooster sheave and the in-haul and out-haul angles are much improved. At about this point, the whip line will be lowered off, the C of G will swing to under the hook, the load will rotate to plumb, the head sling will start to take all the load and the line become plumb and the tail load disappear and that line become slack. The radius of the load is now the radius of the head. The load is freely hanging from the main boom via the head rigging.

Note that the head rigging attachment points are inside the cage allowing the head slings free movement between rebars without fouling during upending as would be case if they were rigged outside the cage.

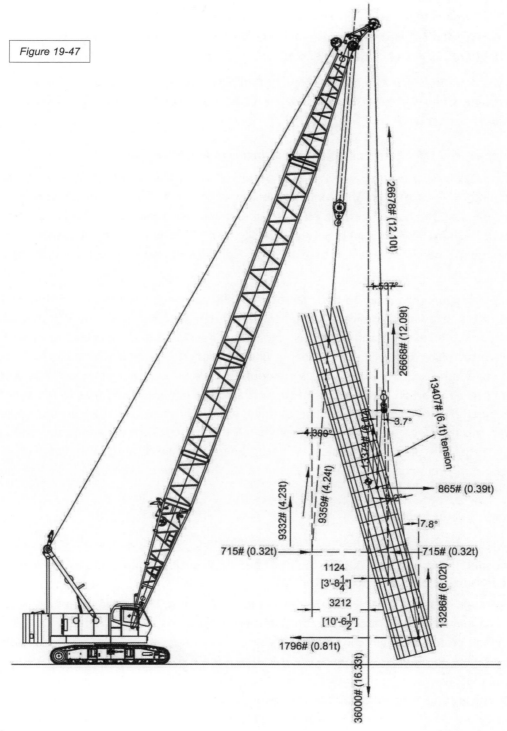

Figure 19-47

In conclusion:

- This arrangement requires a lot of analysis to figure out; it would be easy to unwittingly induce excessive loads and/or load in unacceptable directions.

- It won't work safely as drawn as there is a cage /boom foul and likely a boom head / reeving foul; if using this methodology, a longer boom and/or greater radius is required.

- The two suspension points being close together do not provide much resistance / stability against the load rotating in plan; using a short jib rather than the rooster sheave would have provided a better spread and kept the load more stable, it would also have kept the load further away from the crane boom and improved in-haul and out-haul angles.

— Using a small tail crane would have eliminated a lot of risk, been simple to figure, and would have kept all the vectors in directions intended by the crane manufacturer.

If you are determined to use a single crane, alternative arrangements that allow the cage to be kept normal to the crane boom rather than in line with it should be investigated.

*Note: You are recommended to read the excellent American Society of Civil Engineers (ASCE) publication "Rebar Cage Construction and Safety – Best Practices" by Casey and Urgessa before planning a lifting operation to "trip" (upend) a rebar cage.*

### 19.9.2  Topping and tailing a rebar cage using a single crane (Method B)

Siefert Associates were presented with a similar problem in upending a series of even larger rebar cages. These pieces required 5 lines of support along the length and 4 lateral points of support on each line. Space restrictions dictated the use of a single crane to upend and place the cages. They took the afore-mentioned technique to the next level of complexity with a slight modification that has advantages (which come with added engineering responsibilities). I thank Siefert for allowing me to use their drawings to illustrate the concept.

The slinging arrangement proposed had the load initially suspended entirely from the auxiliary boom head. The C of G of the load was thus directly under the aux boom head sheaves. Line 1 (the head of the cage) was taken to the main boom head and initially is unloaded. Lines 2 and 3 are shackled to opposite ends of a sling basketed over a rolling block. Similarly Lines 4 & 5 are basketed over a rolling block. The afore-mentioned blocks are shackled to opposite ends of a sling doubled over yet another block which is suspended from the aux boom head hook-block. All four lines of support are thus equalized and free to roll over the blocks as the load is upended. (The support is also split laterally, which I'll ignore for the purpose of description). Being equalized in this manner, the load is effectively balancing and could freely adopt any attitude. The aux hoist line is truly vertical. By operation of the main hoist, the load can be rotated as though hinged about its C of G; the load essentially remains all on the aux hoist until nearly completely vertical at which point it transfers all to the main hoist.

This approach has the benefit of:

— keeping the load lines to the aux head vertical (or very near vertical) at all times
— knowing the load split (100% to the aux head until vertical, then 100% to the main) which makes the operation easier to monitor and control

The disadvantage is that you can't push with the main hoist lines; they need to remain in tension so that the load will only roll when pulled around. To do that it is necessary to make sure that the location of the C of G is well known and preferably slightly inside the effective line of support provided by the tail hoist. i.e. choose the attachment points carefully. If not, there is a risk that, if the C of G is actually outside the lines of support, the load will roll of its own volition. As well as careful calculation of the C of G and attachment choice, keeping the load low to the ground will help guard against uncontrolled movement as any slight tendency to self-rotate will be resisted by the cage "scraping" the ground. If this is the case, note that as the attachment points are on the "top" face, the C of G will eventually move inside the line of action of the tailing as upending progresses and the self-rotation tendency will stop; at what angle depends on the actual C of G location and the geometry of the piece.

Engineered and executed carefully (and of course sanctioned by the crane manufacturer et al), this is another approach to be considered. All the previously mentioned clearance and (main hoist) fleet angle considerations remain of course.

Figure 19-48

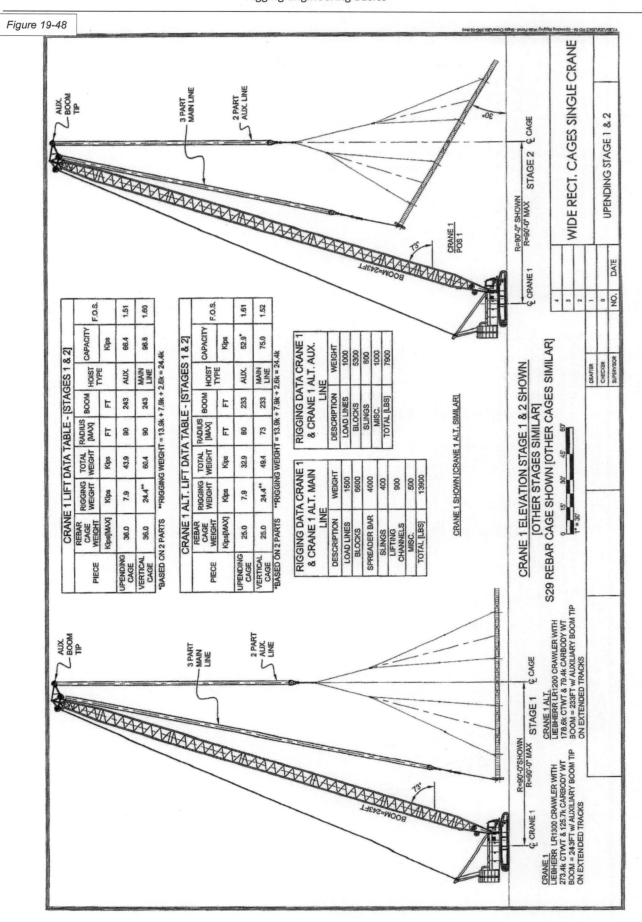

**CRANE 1 LIFT DATA TABLE - [STAGES 1 & 2]**

| PIECE | REBAR CAGE WEIGHT Kips[MAX] | RIGGING WEIGHT Kips | TOTAL WEIGHT Kips | RADIUS [MAX] FT | BOOM FT | HOIST TYPE | CAPACITY Kips | F.O.S. |
|---|---|---|---|---|---|---|---|---|
| UPENDING CAGE | 36.0 | 7.9 | 43.9 | 90 | 243 | AUX. | 66.4 | 1.51 |
| VERTICAL CAGE | 36.0 | 24.4** | 60.4 | 90 | 243 | MAIN LINE | 96.8 | 1.60 |

*BASED ON 2 PARTS    **RIGGING WEIGHT = 13.9k + 7.9k + 2.6k = 24.4k

**CRANE 1 ALT. LIFT DATA TABLE - [STAGES 1 & 2]**

| PIECE | REBAR CAGE WEIGHT Kips[MAX] | RIGGING WEIGHT Kips | TOTAL WEIGHT Kips | RADIUS [MAX] FT | BOOM FT | HOIST TYPE | CAPACITY Kips | F.O.S. |
|---|---|---|---|---|---|---|---|---|
| UPENDING CAGE | 25.0 | 7.9 | 32.9 | 80 | 233 | AUX. | 52.9* | 1.61 |
| VERTICAL CAGE | 25.0 | 24.4** | 49.4 | 73 | 233 | MAIN LINE | 75.0 | 1.52 |

*BASED ON 2 PARTS    **RIGGING WEIGHT = 13.9k + 7.9k + 2.6k = 24.4k

**RIGGING DATA CRANE 1 & CRANE 1 ALT. AUX. LINE**

| DESCRIPTION | WEIGHT |
|---|---|
| LOAD LINES | 1000 |
| BLOCKS | 5300 |
| SLINGS | 600 |
| MISC. | 1000 |
| TOTAL [LBS] | 7900 |

**RIGGING DATA CRANE 1 & CRANE 1 ALT. MAIN LINE**

| DESCRIPTION | WEIGHT |
|---|---|
| LOAD LINES | 1500 |
| BLOCKS | 6600 |
| SPREADER BAR | 4000 |
| SLINGS | 400 |
| LIFTING CHANNELS | 900 |
| MISC. | 500 |
| TOTAL [LBS] | 13900 |

CRANE 1 SHOWN [CRANE 1 ALT. SIMILAR]

CRANE 1 ELEVATION STAGE 1 & 2 SHOWN
[OTHER STAGES SIMILAR]

S29 REBAR CAGE SHOWN [OTHER CAGES SIMILAR]

0  15'  30'  45'  60'
1" = 30'

CRANE 1
LIEBHERR LR1300 CRAWLER WITH
273.4k CTWT & 125.7k CARBODY WT
BOOM = 243FT w/ AUXILIARY BOOM TIP
ON EXTENDED TRACKS

CRANE 1 ALT.
LIEBHERR LR1200 CRAWLER WITH
178.6k CTWT & 79.4k CARBODY WT
BOOM = 233FT w/ AUXILIARY BOOM TIP
ON EXTENDED TRACKS

WIDE RECT. CAGES SINGLE CRANE

UPENDING STAGE 1 & 2

| | | | DRAFTER | | |
|---|---|---|---|---|---|
| 4 | | | CHECKER | | |
| 3 | | | SUPERVISOR | | |
| 2 | | | | | |
| 1 | | | | | |
| 0 | | | | | |
| NO. | DATE | | | | |

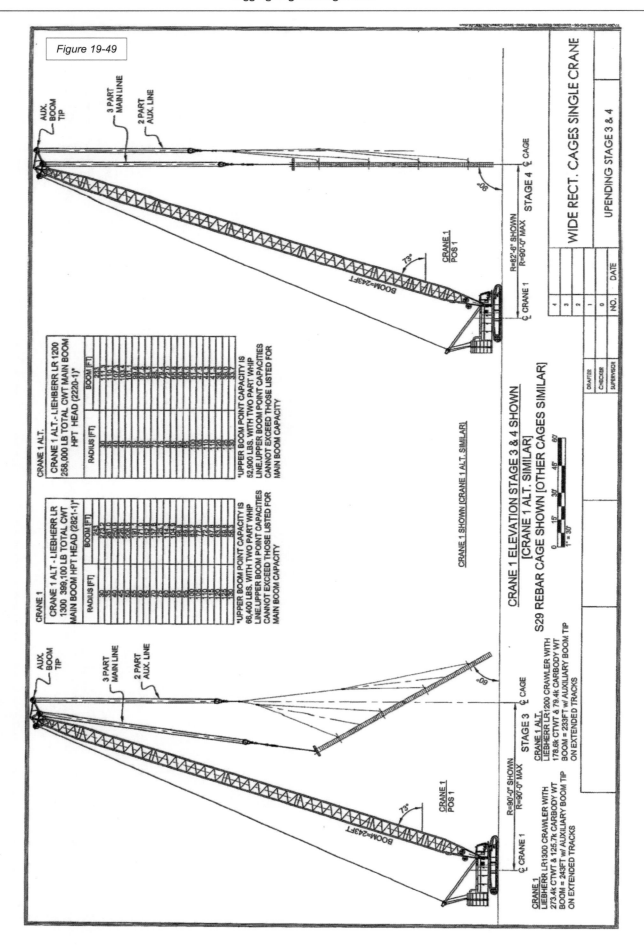

Figure 19-49

Figure 19-50

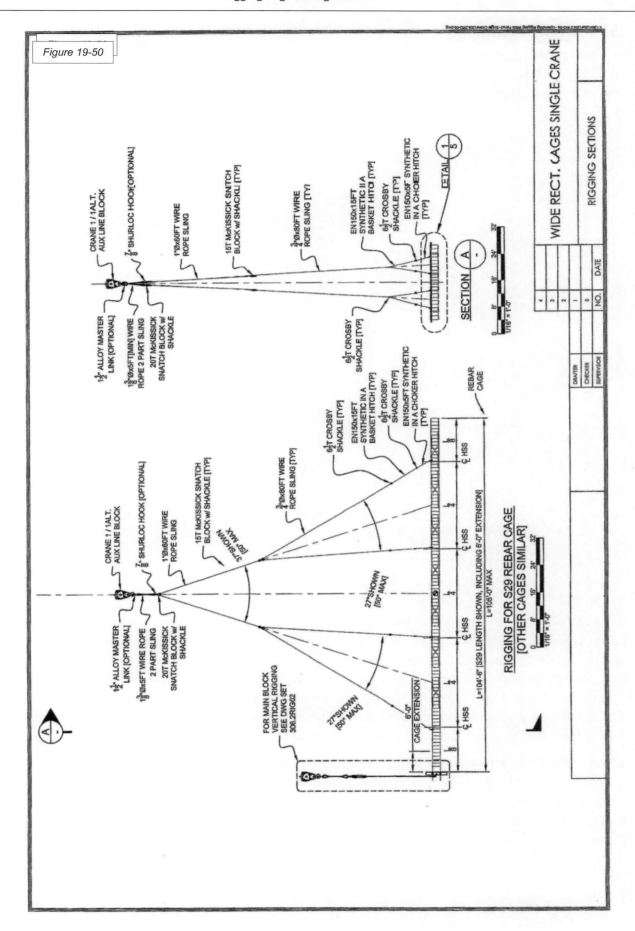

### 19.9.3 Alternative single crane "topping and tailing" arrangements

An alternative arrangement that would have allowed the cage in Method "A" to be upended normal to the boom (rather than in line with it) is shown schematically below. If we had used it on our cage lift, it might have looked something like the left hand view.

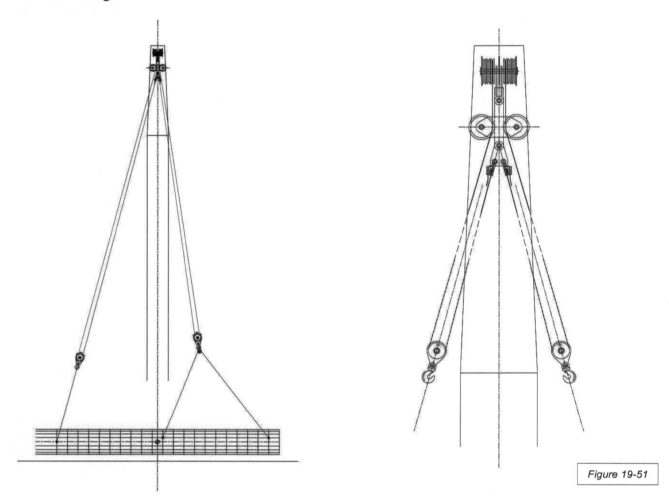

Figure 19-51

Working with the crane manufacturer, the contractor designed a special lift attachment that fitted to the boom head sheave nest. Both winch lines were taken over sheaves in the same sheave nest; each was taken around a diverter, reeved to a crane block and dead-ended back at the attachment. Links and pins were incorporated to allow the components to align themselves and find equilibrium as the forces changed magnitude and direction. By doing it this way, clearance issues between the cage and boom are totally avoided, in-haul and out-haul forces are taken in the attachment and oppose each other and issues of reeving fouling the boom head eliminated. The cage can now be lifted at close radius.

Another alternative arrangement (lifting a vessel) is shown below. The head arrangement is of fixed length and is suspended from the main hook. The whip line is taken over one of the boom head sheaves, down alongside the main hoist lines, round a diverter sheave anchored back to the main block, to a pulley block shackled to the tail lug and back to the main hook-block where it is dead-ended. The tail can be lowered off independently as the head is raised using the main hoist.

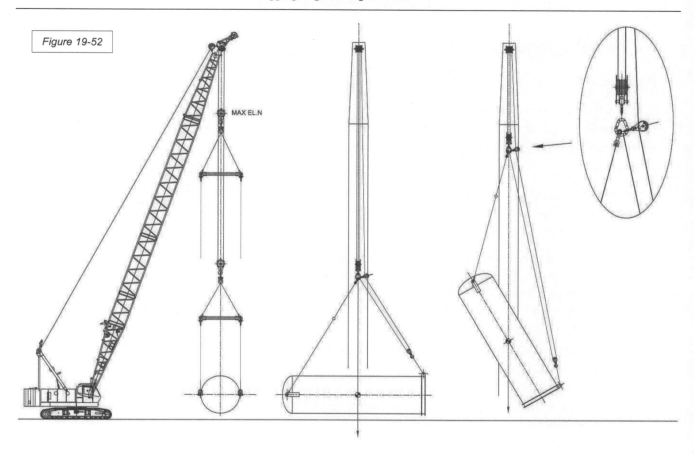

Figure 19-52

This has the advantage of allowing the load to be upended across the beam, avoids all the in-haul and out-haul issues on the boom head, requires no special head attachment, but does require a long head suspension as it has to make a 60° horizontal angle at pick. Thus it only works for short items and long booms. You need to be able to work both winches simultaneously.

The manufacturer would still need to approve use of both winches in this manner and not all will do so.

Note: Barnhart have a proprietary "Tri-block" arrangement working on similar principles; contact them for details.

Figure 19-53

Figure 19-54

Figure 19-55

The Tri-block is seen here handling a "screw". The head is held at fixed length from the Tri-block and the tail is reeved to the Tri-block using the auxiliary hoist, allowing the attitude to be adjusted. The whole arrangement is lifted / lowered using the main hoist.

# 20 Vessel upending techniques

## 20.1 Basics

When upending a vessel or similar, there are a number of options commonly available when choosing how to lift the head including cranes (various types), strand jack rigs, gantries (telescoping and fixed), climbing jack systems and so on; similarly when tailing there are options including cranes, gantries, trailer or skid mounted tilt-up frames.

When designing a lifting operation with two cranes, you have to visualize how their operation needs to be coordinated to achieve the movements of the load that you require; when upending a load with two cranes you have a number of specific concerns to address:

- Keep it simple, don't design a lift sequence that requires either of the cranes to make multiple movements at the same time, booming up whilst cabling down and swinging all at the same time – it's too complex to manage and direct, keep it to two functions at most; don't design an arrangement that requires a very complex dance between the two cranes, one needs to lead and the other follow at any one time – you can change which leads and which follows mid-lift if you need to

- Consider the potential for side-loading the booms if the coordination is not as perfect as you intended

- Try to get the booms pointing at each other (or relatively close to it) by the end of the lift; any in-haul or out-haul (out of plumb of the hoist lines) you get as the load approaches vertical, when the tail needs to move a long way quickly, will then be in the plane of the booms and not acting across them. Crane booms / jibs are relatively weak laterally and it is bad practice to side load them as you will inevitably do if you tail across the boom / jib, particularly at the end of the operation when you need to let the tail fleet out

- If the load is already at its pick location before the cranes are located, remember to allow the space required for the saddles / grillages / mats used to support it and consider how to remove them when the load is free hanging on the two cranes; if the load has to be delivered with the cranes already in place and directly lifted, consider the space required for the trailers and how to remove them when the load is hanging on the cranes

## 20.2 Tailing in line with a crawler crane

Probably the most basic arrangement is to use a static main lift crane to hoist the head in fixed location and a crawler crane at the tail. As the lift progresses and the horizontal head to tail distance shortens, the tail crane crawls forward to maintain vertical suspension. At the very end when the tail load is reduced, the tail may be allowed to fleet out slightly.

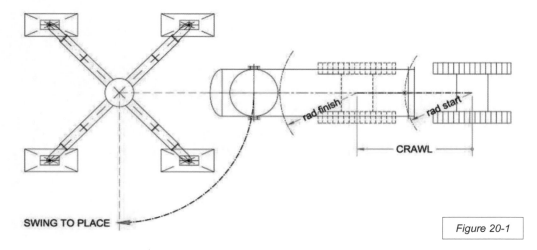

Figure 20-1

Advantages are:

- – Simplicity, easy to coordinate & signal.
- – Loads all in the plane of the booms.

Disadvantages are:

- – Need extended matting or prepared ground for tail crane.
- – May need to offload vessel before positioning tail crane as it could be difficult to remove trailer with tail crane in place.

If you don't get the set-up quite right, the tail crane radius may swing out as the load comes clear and the suspensions adjust.

Figure 20-2

This 640 t $CO_2$ Absorber was upended in this manner with a Demag CC6800 (with Superlift) on the head and a CC2800 on the tail.

Once vertical the tail crane was disconnected and the head crane with suspended load was swung 90° counter-clockwise, the vessel re-orientated and placed.

Figure 20-3

Foundation

Figure 20-4

## 20.3 Tailing over the side with a crawler crane

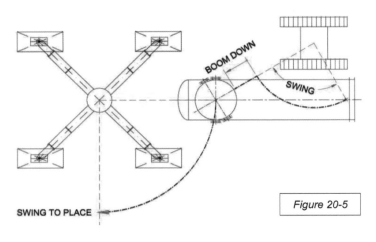

Alternatively, there may be the option to locate the tail crane to the side of the vessel. As you lift, you reduce the head to tail distance by swinging (slewing) the tail crane initially; once the booms are somewhat lined up you may have to crawl some for longer vessels; towards the end as the load drops off, you can usually boom down and let the load fleet out a little.

If a fly jib is fitted to the tail crane when lifting from the main boom, watch where the jib ends up relative to the vessel, rigging and the main lift crane to make sure you don't have a clash. You might need to keep the booms slightly out of line for that reason.

*Figure 20-5*

Note: some crane models may restrict crawling to only with the boom over the front or rear – check!

Advantages are:

- Keeps matting to a minimum
- Allows the delivery trailer to be readily removed
- Load is spread uniformly along tail crane tracks at pick
- If the slew brake is off, the tail crane can swing to align itself up correctly without affecting the radii if the set up is not perfect
- Takes up a minimum of space

Disadvantages are:

- Needs to be designed such that you get the tail out from under the boom before it gets too vertical when it could possibly cause a boom foul to the tail crane.
- The tail load gets over one corner of the tail crane at one stage, which is the worst place for it to be

## 20.4 Tailing over the side with an outrigger mounted crane

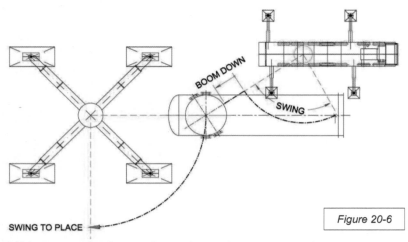

If a suitably sized crawler crane is unavailable for the tail, an AT, RT or mobile telescopic crane may provide a good solution when the vessel is not too long. Longer vessels will require a crawler tail crane or the capacity in the main lift crane to bring the head to the tail crane.

By locating it to the side, you can accommodate a lot of tail movement merely by swinging (slewing) with maybe some booming down as the load decays.

*Figure 20-6*

Advantages of using a telescopic outrigger mounted crane are:

- Quick and easy to set up
- Minimal matting
- Likely to be cheaper for a one-off operation than bringing in a crawler crane specially

Disadvantages over using a crawler tail crane are:

- Only good when the required tail movement (and load) is small enough to be accommodated by the swing motion of an economically available (and physically small enough) telescopic crane.
- Not likely to be economic when large tail radii are required

## 20.5 Tailing using the head crane

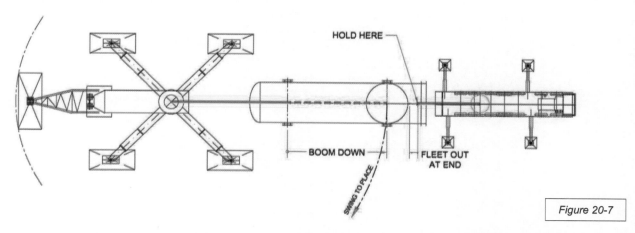

Figure 20-7

An option you have when using a main lift crane with plenty of capacity is to hold the tail lug in fixed position with the tail crane and roll the vessel up towards the tail crane using the head crane. This may well be the case when the vessel is ultimately to be placed at considerable radius. You have the capacity; you may as well use it and minimize the required capacity of the tail crane.

Figure 20-8

Advantages of this arrangement are:

- Tail crane just has to hold the tail
- Tail radius is minimal, so the tail crane can be minimized
- Minimal matting
- Makes best use of the head crane, keeps the costs down

Disadvantages over using a crawler tail crane are:

- As drawn it may be difficult to remove "conventional" trailers unless the vessel is delivered beforehand and offloaded onto temporary supports
- If a main lift crane using a Superlift tray is used you cannot swing the head anywhere until the head crane has the entire weight at the completion of upending and the Superlift tray lifts clear of the ground. This is not an issue if you don't need Superlift or use a Superlift bogie or ring crane or similar

For a long vessel, you could combine this with one of the over-the-side tailing methods, doing the tailing with the tail crane so far as you can, and then completing with the head crane.

Similarly, you could combine it with in-line tailing, doing as much as you can with the head crane and completing with the crawler tail crane.

## 20.6 Head with crane, tailing using tilt-up frame

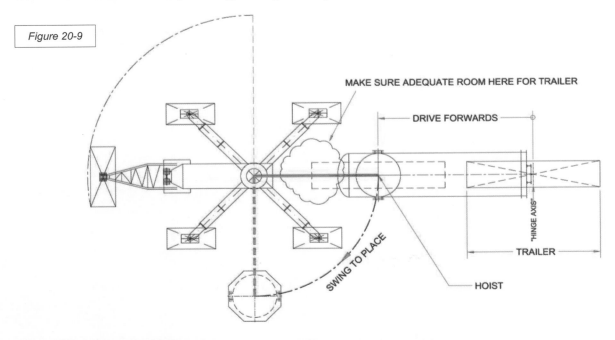

Figure 20-9

MAKE SURE ADEQUATE ROOM HERE FOR TRAILER
DRIVE FORWARDS
"HINGE AXIS"
TRAILER
SWING TO PLACE
HOIST

Figure 20-10

If using a crane to the vessel head and a tilt-up frame on trailers for the tail, there are a few considerations to address:

— After delivering the vessel, it will be necessary to release the trailers to relocate them to the tail and to fit the tailing device. This will likely require a height adjustment (upwards). You might be able to use the lift crane at the head but at the tail you may need to lower the rear transport saddle onto blocking outside the trailer width and use the trailer hydraulics to adjust the height by jack and pack method. Alternatively you might use a small lifting gantry or other means.

— Ideally you want to tail towards the crane for reasons noted earlier. You need to consider the space required by the trailers at the end of the operation, it can be considerable.

For this lift, the crane and vessel foundation were inside an area bounded by piperacks; the only place to upend the vessel was in the road on the other side of one of the racks. This put the tailing across the crane boom which isn't ideal but is an option. Careful control was required to ensure that the suspension remained acceptably plumb, particularly when near vertical. When upended, the frame was released and the vessel lifted over the rack and swung to location inside the bounded area.

## 20.7 Head with lift system, tailing by crawler crane

### 20.7.1 Tail in line

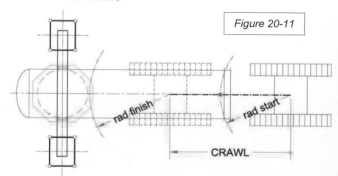

Figure 20-11

CRAWL

Figure 20-12

When using a basic lift system to raise the head, you typically don't have the facility to move the suspension anywhere other than up. A swivel may be included as shown in the photo or the lugs may be suspended directly from the lift beam if rotation is not needed. This is the Sarens Sarlift system which is a hydraulic push up arrangement.

Typically the vessel head is delivered with the head lift points directly over the center of the foundation.

The masts straddle the foundation; often piles to support the mast lift reactions will be incorporated in the foundation raft design. This particular rig uses no guy wires but has structural stays to mid height to resist wind and other horizontal forces (stability, tailing etc).

As the head is raised, the tail is (in this case) crawled in using a crawler crane. Note that the tail crane is "in-line"; you can't commence tailing with the tail crane over the side unless a swivel is fitted to the rig and you still may not be able to do it if the angle the vessel has to swing through in plan view would cause it to foul the masts / stays – see following series of photos.

Considerations include:

- As the head has generally to be over the foundation, this arrangement doesn't work well for raised foundations. Even ground level foundations will be raised to some extent and there will be holding down bolts to consider. If the trailers delivering the vessel need to be driven over the foundation, the foundation / bolt height needs to be considered. You may need to ramp up over the foundation and bolts and/or use removable holding down bolts.

- You need to consider how to get the delivery trailer(s) out if the tail crane is at the rear. Not so much of an issue with SPMTs but could be with conventional trailers. You may possibly be able to drive through the rig and out the other side but often there will be a connecting pipe-rack there.

- Unless you can get the lift lugs and the lift rig in very specific orientations, the vessel will likely not be in the correct orientation when vertical and a swivel will be needed.

Advantages of this type of arrangement are:

- If you have only one or two heavy vessels, you might use a lift system for those and use the crane you have as the main lift crane for the rest of the lifts as your tail crane. The main lift crane can thus be sized smaller; using a lift system avoids bringing in a heavy crane for a limited number of lifts.

- Lift systems are relatively cheap by comparison with ultra-heavy cranes, particularly in more remote locations.

- Lift systems are relatively compact for their capacity.

- Distributing lifting reactions is generally easier (and cheaper) than doing so for heavy cranes.

- As lift systems straddle the load, they don't require the huge amounts of balancing counterweight that a heavy crane requires. This is a transport cost saving and also reduces the magnitude of the loads to be distributed.

Disadvantages of this type of arrangement include:

- Labor intensive, slow to erect (as are ultra-big cranes), working at height to build, slow to lift.

### 20.7.2 Lift rig at head, crane tail over the side

Figure 20-14

Figure 20-15

Figure 20-13

Figure 20-16

Here it was possible to tail over the side when using a lifting rig at the head. This 700 t vessel is being upended with a strand jack lifting rig and a crawler crane on the tail. A swivel is incorporated into the suspension. Delivery is by self-propelled modular transporters; with the head over the foundation, the SPMTs stop just short of the vessel foundation.

The vessel is lifted bodily, having the tail crane over the side on free slew allows the vessel to align without the suspension going out of plumb or the radius increasing. The SPMTs are turned on the spot and driven out. As lifting progresses, the tail is initially swung round in front of the tail crane pivoting on the swivel so that the boom points directly at the head suspension point. Note the use of a Superlift tray on the tail crane; it can only slew at the start of the lift. As the tail weight reduces, the SL tray comes down on the ground and the tail crane booms down to complete the operation. For a while, if required to slew or travel, the SL tray can be kept floating by increasing the tail radius as the tail load reduces.

### 20.7.3 Cross-slide the head

Figure 20-17

If the foundation is considerably elevated as here, you may have to upend the vessel alongside the foundation, lift it above foundation height, then cross-slide it and lower to location. This requires the lift system to straddle the foundation and the upending zone and thus requires a longer (and heavier) lift beam.

This rig is an 800 t climbing jack system, in which the lift beam (and suspended load) is raised by jacks climbing the front faces of the masts. The lift beam is fitted with a sliding bogie from which the suspension is hung. The bogie uses Teflon pads and a small climbing jack is used horizontally to move the bogie along the beam.

Because the load shifts from one end of the lift beam to the other, each end of the lift system has to support the majority of the load at different times and the rig has to be rated accordingly.

## 20.8 Head with lift system, trailer tailing

### 20.8.1 Fixed head suspension

Figure 20-18

This heavy Vacuum Column was upended using a strand jack rig to the head and a trailer mounted tilt-up frame to the tail. Note that no external guys are stays were required for this lift.

In this particular case, no swivel was provided, a strand jack was provided for each lift trunnion; therefore no rotation of the upended vessel was possible on the lifting rig. The trunnions therefore had to be positioned, and the lifting rig orientated, such that the vessel would be correctly positioned when vertical.

As the vessel was to be directly placed on its foundation with no cross-slide facility provided, the tailing trailers end up directly over the vessel foundation on completion of the lift which can be an issue if the foundation is elevated or long holding down bolts are used. Here, removable holding down bolts were used and the ground was ramped up the 300 mm (1 ft) or so to the foundation.

## 20.9 Strand jacks on structure, trailer tailing

Where a vessel is surrounded by a substantial steel structure it may be possible to locate strand jacks on it to lift the vessel and avoid the need for masts or heavy cranes.

Figure 20-19

Figure 20-20

In this case, four very heavy reactors were to be located in a steel structure. The designers were able to leave the front face of each bay open in turn and beef up the structure somewhat to take the lifting loads. A movable temporary strand jack support structure was located on the top of the permanent steel. After lifting one reactor, the bracing was fitted and the strand jacks skidded across to the next bay to repeat the process. The delivery trailers were reconfigured and used to support the tilt-up tailing device. As they had to drive over the vessel foundations, removable anchor bolts were used. This lifting arrangement provided a convenient and economical solution.

# 21 Load sharing & equalizing arrangements

## 21.1 Concepts of equalization

When supporting a stiff load on four or more stiff support points (or lifting from four or more lift points), there is a real risk that one or more of the support points will not be contributing as much as it should to supporting the load. In the real world it is very difficult, if not impossible, to maintain the support points truly level with each other and the load will go to whichever points are highest. If the whole system is stiff you could end up in a situation where, when using four points on a rectangular grid, the load is taken across diagonal corners with one of the other corners providing balance only, as with a 4-legged stool on an uneven floor. It is likely that the designers intended equal loading and designed the load and lift lugs accordingly. The way in which load-sharing varies in practice from the theoretical in such cases may be referred to as "load-shedding".

Certainly if using four or more cranes to lift a load, you want to ensure that all four carry their fair share of the load. If not, you run the risk of severely overloading some of them, possibly to the point of collapse – and it has happened. There are measures that can be taken including matching cranes so that the hoist speed is similar, monitoring support loads with load cells and so on in order to lift level, however a simpler, more robust method that can be used in cases such as the below is to use equalizing systems.

Figure 21-1

In this case, a 105 t dredger needed to be refloated after refurbishment. Two Grove 5130 GMK 130 t mobile cranes were used to lead the lift, with two Manitowoc M12000 crawler cranes following.

At each end of the dredger, vertical rigging was used to the ends of a lift beam with a single central lift point, unifying the load at that point. A similar inverted arrangement was shackled to that point, splitting the load equally to the 2 cranes.

Minor differences in sling length or in hoist height will not fundamentally alter the load sharing. In fact, it can be seen that the cranes to the left are slightly out of phase with each other but carrying nominally correct load.

## 21.2 Unequal load sharing arrangements

If you using two cranes of different capacity to lift a load in tandem, you likely won't want to share the load equally to the cranes but will want to make sure that they take their designed share even if they get slightly out of phase with each other. One way to do this is to use a lift beam to split the load unequally by arranging the crane attachment points at different distances from a single point from which the load is suspended. The load will be shared in inverse proportion to their distance from the suspension point.

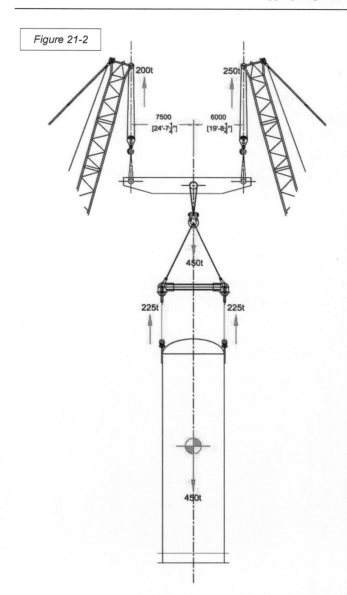

Figure 21-2

In this case, a 450 t vessel is to be lifted with two similar, but not identical cranes. It has been determined that one crane can safely support 200 t and the other 250 t; however both cranes will be at approximately 85% of chart capacity. Neither crane has the capacity to make the lift alone. Any load shedding between the cranes could overload them, so a rigging arrangement is required to ensure that any slight inequality of lifting does not alter the load sharing significantly. The lift lugs can only accept loads within the plane of the lug +/- 5%, so the slings must be nominally vertical.

We have elected here to bring the weight of the suspended vessel to a single point using a spreader bar & slings, then to use a lift beam to split that load in the required proportions by locating the stronger crane 6 m from the suspension point and the other 7.5 m away.

Ignoring rigging weight,

Crane A sees: (450 t x 6 m) / 13.5 m = 250 t

Crane B sees: (450 t x 7.5 m) / 13.5 m = 200 t

Any slight inclination of the lift beam will not alter the proportions significantly as the 3 support points are close to being on a common line.

Whilst this arrangement takes a lot of risk out of the lift, be aware that the weight of the lift beam and spreader may be significant and will eat into your available capacities. Lifts of this type using 2 cranes should ideally be designed such that neither crane is loaded to more than 75% of chart. It is permissible to go higher if steps such as the above have been taken to minimize load shedding, the cranes are static, the lifting wind speeds are low, the loads are accurately determined before lifting and the lift is thoroughly planned by a competent person. I would not recommend ever going higher than 90% of chart on either crane when making a tandem lift.

## 21.3 Equalizing plates

Triangular equalizing plates can be a useful tool to combine or split two forces.

In the below example , on the left (a), in a "tugger" (base-mounted drum hoist / lifting winch) system, the two drums of the hoist are reeved independently to a load. In order to ensure that the line pulls remain basically equal even if one drum pulls in slightly less wire than the other, a triangular link plate is used. If the drums get slightly out of phase, the plate will rotate slightly to accommodate it. The geometry is slightly changed and the load sharing will no longer be exactly 50:50, but so long as the plate is kept within fairly close limits, they will be similar.

In the next example, two nominally matched 10' slings are used to attach to closely spaced lugs on a load. To ensure that they are both loaded equally a triangular equalizing plate is used with the upper hole in the plate shackled to a single sling. If the two longer slings are of exactly equal length, the plate will be level and the load in the upper sling will be shared equally. This type of arrangement can sometimes be seen in crane pendant systems. See (b).

If one sling is actually 2.5" shorter than the other, the plate will rotate a little (5 degrees with this geometry) and the load sharing will change to 42% : 58%, which in this case is acceptable within the limits of the lug design and rigging capacity. See (c).

There are limits to this however, to take it to an extreme, if one sling were 1'-2" shorter than the other, the plate would rotate to such an extent that the entire load would be passing down one sling and none down the other. You need to design these plates with proportions sufficiently large that differences you can reasonably expect and manage within will not change the load split beyond determined permissible limits. See (d).

Plates or beams can also be used to change the load split when you want something different than 50:50. An offset plate such as that shown in (e) for instance will share the load nominally 60:40.

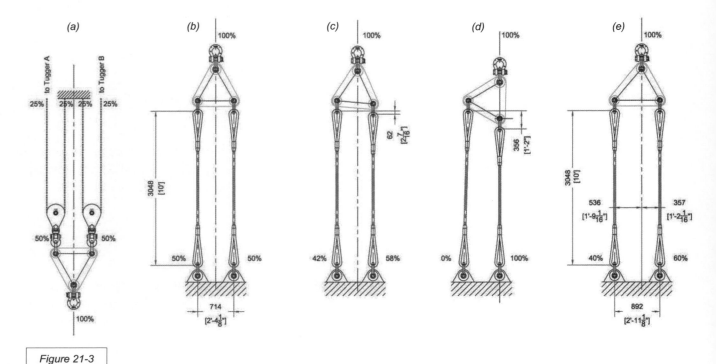

Figure 21-3

## 21.4 Handing-off loads using triangular plates

It can sometimes be necessary to hand-off a load from one crane to another or from a crane to say a strand jack rig whilst the load is free-hanging. An example might be a coal-fired boiler where a boiler wall panel is prefabricated and transported into the boiler cavity horizontally. A crane is used to upend it, then it is handed off to a strand jack system mounted on the boiler steelwork to raise it high into the structure (where the crane boom could not get to). A triangular plate might be used at each suspension point to allow the hand-off.

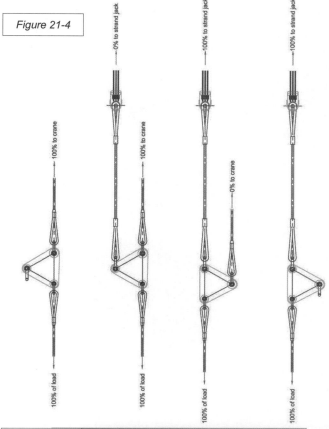

Figure 21-4

In this case, the load is lifted into the boiler with the crane.

The plates at each point have 3 holes, one for the load, one for the crane and one provided with a shackle to be used later to attach the strand jack. The load initially passes straight through the plate which acts as a pure link. When in the boiler, the strand jack is attached to the "spare" hole. The crane then lowers off and the link starts to rotate progressively transferring load from the crane to the strand jack until ultimately it is all on the strand jack and the crane can be disconnected.

Figure 21-5

In a similar manner, a triangular "spreader-like" frame can be used to pass a load from one crane to another. In this case, the load would be suspended from the sling attached to the bottom right attachment lug of the frame. With the load taken by the crane to the right, the left hand crane can hoist rotating the frame until it has the entire load.

## 21.5 Load splitting & combining using spreaders and lift beams

There are many instances where the single lifting effort provided by a lifting device (crane for instance) needs to be split into multiple smaller forces down at the level of the piece being lifted or (looking at it from bottom up rather than top down) multiple support reactions need to be combined to a single support point.

In the simplest of cases (below) a chemical vessel may be provided with two lifting lugs or trunnions at its head, requiring vertical slinging. A single spreader or lift beam is used to combine those two vertical forces bringing them to a single point for attachment to a crane hook.

Figure 21-7

Figure 21-6

A transformer (above) might be provided with four trunnions with only vertical loading permitted. A 3-spreader arrangement can be used to combine the four to two and then the two to one for attachment to the crane hook.

So you can see that a spreader can be used to split a load two ways (or combine two loads). If the upper inclined slings are of equal length and the spreader is kept horizontal, then the vertical support provided by the crane is divided equally into two vertical forces at the spreader ends. To further divide those forces, another level of spreaders can be provided and so on. One force can be split to 2, then 4, then 8 then 16 by cascading additional levels of spreaders.

This kind of arrangement is required where a payload is provided with multiple lift points.

In the case of the transformer lift shown, the C of G is central between the lugs, the load will lift level and the reactions at the four lift lugs will be equal.

Note that even if the sling lengths are not <u>quite</u> the same, all of the slings will be loaded and the arrangement cannot go to a diagonally loaded situation as could be the situation if the spreaders were not used and four inclined slings were used pyramid-fashion directly to the crane hook. Use of the spreaders ensures articulation and correctness of loading.

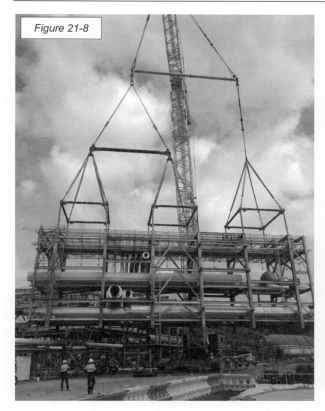

Figure 21-8

In the case shown here, the module has 12 lift points and it is apparently acceptable (or required even) that they are all equally loaded. How to split the crane's effort equally 12 ways?

The lift reactions were grouped into 3 groups of 4. Each group used a rectangular spreader frame to bring the 4 vertical slings to a common point. Note the use of equalizing plates at the apex of each. These ensure equal loading in the 4 inclined slings.

At this level, there are now 3 lift points with equal load. A spreader is used to combine two adjacent points while the remaining singleton is taken directly up to the same level.

At this upper level, there are now two points, one with twice the load of the other. A spreader is used to combine them. Odd-length inclined slings are used to bring the point at which they meet directly over the C of G. In the horizontal sense, the line of suspension splits the length of the spreader in the ratio 1:2. i.e. inverse proportion of the vertical load carried by the ends.

As noted, if the inclined sling lengths are equal, then the forces will be split equally at each spreader; at the lowest level of a 3-level arrangement as shown right (the vertical slings attached to the load) will carry an exact 1/8th of the force applied by the crane, i.e. the weight of the load will be shared as equal forces at the lift lugs.

The problem arises when the designers of the payload do not want equal force applied to each lug, i.e. to lift level and planar it is necessary to apply different forces at each support point. If you use equal length slings you will force the lugs to accept equal force and the payload will deflect until it sheds load between the lugs to an extent that could overstress the loads members.

Figure 21-9

A flexible load requires a lot of support points to prevent excessive deflection. Each one of those points needs to take a specific share of the weight if the load is to remain planar. It is complex to design a slinging arrangement to do this. If the spreader arrangement forces a different load sharing than ideal, the load will deflect to shed load between lift points. If the load is flexible, it can deflect excessively to achieve this.

Figure 21-10

This large, heavy and very flexible module was provided with 12 lift lugs. It was to be lifted onto a heavy lift ship using the two ships derricks (which always have limited headroom). Heavy lift ships often carry heavy lift beams as seen here for use in loading operations. They have multiple lift attachments to suit different situations. In this case, each derrick's lifting effort had to be split six ways. The solution adopted was to use one of the yellow beams on each and sling from it on three lines with a spreader on each line. The issues were firstly that 3 lines of support from a beams like this is statically indeterminate and secondly that the arrangement impose too much load at the center of the module and not enough at the ends. It deflected until it came to an over-deflected equilibrium. The solution was to stiffen the module and go for an eight point support that was determinate. You can see a much improved (and acceptable) situation resulted.

Figure 21-11

For that module to lift level as originally designed, each lift point would have had to carry a different and specific proportion of the total weight. How can we split the effort provided by the lift crane(s) in different and specific proportions to suit the requirements at the lift points? Let us consider this as a 2D problem.

By using odd length inclined slings the forces can be split unequally through the levels until you arrive at the required load distribution at the attachment points. In this case, a 100 t load needs to be supported as 10 t / 30 t / 35 t / 25 t (working from left to right). Starting at the left, choose sling lengths whose intersection splits L2 in the (inverse) proportions 30:10. Similarly on the right choose sling lengths that split L3 in the inverse proportion 35:25. Use standard length slings on both sides but add length on the lighter side with extra shackles / turnbuckles to get the right split. Arrange for the two intersections to be at the same level using extra shackles if required. Now strike a line up through the C of G and provide slings whose lengths intersect on that line, again using same length slings and adding shackles on the light side. Aim for sling angles (to the horizontal) of about 60° or better (45° min).

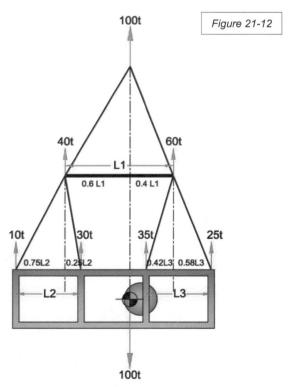

Figure 21-12

It can get complicated. This module had 17 lift points and a specific load to be applied at each. Every one of these inclined slings required length adjustment using turnbuckles or extra shackles.

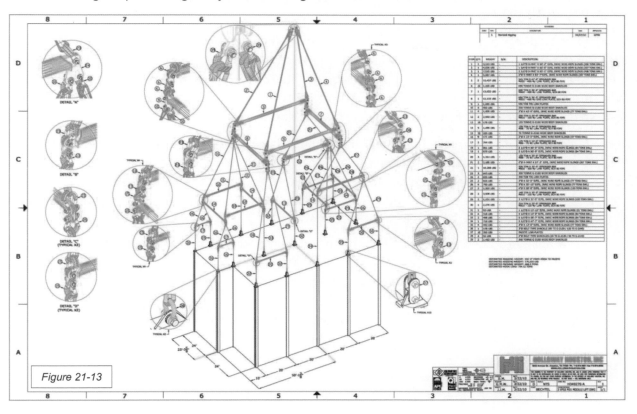

Figure 21-13

A similar lift on the same project.

Figure 21-14

Note that lifting beams can also be used to split loads unequally or to combine unequal loads. See 21.2 and 18.3.

# 22 Modularization

## 22.1 Introduction

As a rigging engineer or someone concerned with lifting / moving things, you may be called upon to advise on the lifting / transport aspects of modularization. e.g. What is the optimum size or weight to make something? If I make an item this big / heavy, can it be moved and lifted? How? At what cost? Does it make sense to do so? What are the gains and risks? Note: I am using the term "module" very loosely to refer to anything that can be preassembled "large" off site. It could be a very large chemical vessel.

There is a constant drive to make things bigger and thus heavier as it is perceived to be more efficient to do so. Process plants are built as skids or modules; pipe racks or stair towers are modularized, electrical facilities are made as buildings, offshore oil rigs are built as complete topsides, chemical vessels are made bigger and completed offsite, ships are built as modules in "factories" and so on. It is true that there are many advantages to be gained from doing this including:

- The ability to build in a controlled production facility or "factory" leading to better productivity and quality, fewer weather delays
- The use of skilled, available and economic workers, working in their home environment, reducing costs and improving quality
- The ability to work on parallel fronts in several facilities, shortening production time
- The ability to test before dispatch
- Fewer persons required at site with resulting reductions in temporary facilities, less environmental issues / social disruption in the area of the worksite
- A shorter site schedule
- Improved safety with fabrication at low level in a controlled environment as against stick building which requires numerous lifts to height
- Risk reduction (financial and physical)

e.g. a large chemical vessel that can be built in one piece in a factory rather than two will not need a field weld, scaffolding to mid height for access, fitting up, aligning and welding in the field and can be pressure tested before dispatch. That is a considerable benefit.

It is not all good news however; there are prices to pay.

- You need to be very organized up front
- You have to create "modules" whose size and weight is optimized (more later)
- The equipment to transport and lift these large and heavy items is larger, more expensive and less available, however the duration of requirement is shorter
- The whole project has to be coordinated to come together like a jigsaw puzzle, things have to fit together and arrive on time
- You can't work at site on as many different fronts (a delayed delivery has everyone waiting around)
- Modules often arrive on barges or ships in "deliveries" rather than individually as required. A delivery will include immediately required items, the remainder have to be stored till needed
- Lose one module and it is catastrophic; so in some ways, risk can be escalated and has to be well managed to realize the benefits
- There are significant temporary works (stiffening etc) required to make modules transportable, storable and liftable, to secure pipes etc against dynamic forces
- Significant space is required to transport, store and lift large modules
- Site roads, quaysides, crane foundations and so on all require to be stronger
- If planning for very large / heavy modules, you likely won't be able to move them very far on land and you will probably require marine transport with suitable load-out / load-in facilities local to the

production facility and the project site. Sites not local to suitable ports / quays will be limited as to the size of modules that can be transported there.

So you need to balance cost, safety, quality, schedule, environmental, risk and other considerations when deciding whether to modularize or not, if you decide to do so, the optimum extent of modularization to realize the maximum benefits.

Note that what makes best sense in one situation doesn't necessarily make the same sense if doing the exact same thing somewhere else.

Factors that will affect the judgment include:

- Where the jobsite is, logistical considerations
- What labor force (and skills) is available
- What infrastructure exists
- The cost of local labor, cost of ex-pat expertise where needed
- The cost of temporary site accommodation, labor camp and other facilities
- The availability of heavy equipment
- Political considerations (required local content for instance)
- Prevailing weather conditions (temperature, wind etc)
- Access to deep water
- Proximity to suitable production facilities
- Environmental restrictions
- The premium placed on a "fast-track" project delivery; penalties on being late

Figure 22-1

Figure 22-2

e.g. A smelter in Iceland was heavily modularized, a similar smelter in the Middle East was not modularized. Seen here one of the Iceland modules being moved and loaded at the fabricator's facility in Europe.

## 22.2 Handling considerations in module design

So, say you have decided that some degree of modularization is appropriate, what practical handling considerations to you have to account for?

**MODULARIZATION - PRACTICAL HANDLING CONSIDERATIONS**

Figure 22-3

| | General | Size | Weight and C of G |
|---|---|---|---|
| **Fabrication** | | | |
| **Under cover** | Building a module in (say) a fabrication hall has advantages including better productivity & quality, no weather issues. Craneage can be a limiting factor & the size of the hall is a constraint. Often pre-assemblies are formed inside and united outside where more space and heavy duty cranes are available. | | |
| | Size, available headroom<br>Permissible ground loadings?<br>Overhead cranes?<br>Other cranes?<br>How many "hooks' to service lifting?<br>Component delivery method / lifting zone | Height to overhead cranes v transport height<br>Can preassemblies be formed?<br>Door height versus max transport height<br>Door width versus max transport width | Capacity of available cranes<br>Use of over head cranes? Capacity?<br>Support loads? |
| **Outside** | Building a module in a module "yard" can provide good all-round access and opportunity to use multiple cranes. Good ground bearing and a well prepared surface are required. The module requires level solid support. | | |
| | Size of area available<br>Prevailing weather conditions<br>Available cranes, operating space required<br>Suitably prepared ground | Layout of module(s) on the "yard" | Number of support points?<br>Support loads v ground capacity?<br>Lift loads v capacity of available cranes? |
| **Facility** | You need to be able to move the module within the fabrication facility once assembled and export it. For very large modules, export usually requires access to deep water. | | |
| | Suitability for onward transport<br>  Road access?<br>  Rail spur?<br>  Deep water access?<br>Physical restrictions to movement at facility | | |

| | General | Size | Weight and C of G |
|---|---|---|---|
| **Land transport (at origin)** | | | |
| **Trailers** | Whatever you fabricate needs to be transported to site and this will most likely involve an element of land transport. Large/heavy modules are often moved on hydraulic platform trailers; for site moves, self propelled modular trailers (SPMTs) are often used; for road transport, regular platform trailers. or special heavy haul trailers (towed) are used. | | |
| | Type of trailers to be used? Width, height range, capacity? Availability? | Required extent of support of a large (plan) area module may determine required numbers of trailers / axles<br>Sufficient area beneath the module to locate required trailers<br>Sufficient load carrying beams or other means of supporting the module and correctly loading trailers<br>Large sail areas and high winds affect trailer loadings and stability<br>Long trailer arrangements require very flat surfaces to operate on; changes in grade combined with humps/hollows, cross-falls, deflections etc may cause the trailer suspension to "bottom out"<br>Tall narrow loads (particularly on long narrow trailer arrangements) may not be stable<br>Support grillages / loadspreading arranging need to allow clear access beneath for trailers if self-loading<br>Support height needs to be determined by trailer type and interface with module; it is critical to ensure enough reserve of stroke at either end of suspension travel<br>Route to be taken; width / height restrictions, corners; negotiations required<br>Permit size restrictions | Weight and C of G determines min required number of axles per trailer type<br>Max permitted axle loadings / pressures on the route may determine numbers of axles<br>Heavier the load, the fewer axles can be cantilevered beyond (or between) lines of support to the load<br>High C of G and long / narrow trailer arrangements = poor stability<br>Changes in longitudinal / lateral level of trailer as a result of say gradients or cross-falls will move the C of G around in plan view and affect trailer loading and stability; worse if the C of G is high<br>How is "module" to be loaded to the trailers? Craned on or using trailer suspension hydraulic stroke? What are the lift points & loads; what craneage is available, at what radii?<br><br>Bridges, culverts, services to be crossed; weight restrictions<br>Permit weight restrictions |
| **Skids / rollers** | A very heavy load to be moved a relatively short distance in a straight line(s) may be skidded or rolled along steel or concrete tracks. e.g. a oil rig jacket may be skidded onto a barge using teflon skid shoes on steel beams and strand jacks as the motive force. Articulation or hydraulic equalization may be required to account for minor height discrepancies / deflections to ensure correct loading at all times. | | |
| | Is there an existing track system, or does it require something temporary / custom? | Tracks under "strong points" of structure?<br>How many tracks required?<br>How is module supported during fabrication? On the tracks? Is a transfer required? How?<br>Is a change of direction required? If so, how? | Use rollers or skids? Capacity of each?<br>How many support points are required?<br>Load equalization required? Hydraulic or mechanical?<br>How is load transferred from fabrication supports to tracks?<br>Loads can be very concentrated, what track support is needed? |
| **Rail transport** | It may be possible to move a heavy or oversized load from point of origin to site (rail spur) using a Schnabel type railcar. You should check with forwarders / rail companies. You will still likely need land transport to the rail spur and a means of loading to the car. | | |
| | What sort or rail car? | Overall width, height on rail car.<br>How to load to rail car? | What is the carrying capacity?<br>Route weight retrictions<br>Lift on with gantry or crane(s)? What available capacity? |

| | General | Size | Weight and C of G |
|---|---|---|---|
| **Marine transport** | | | |
| **Barging** | *River/canal barging from the fabrication facility directly to site or to a port where the load can be transferred to ocean going transport may be a possibility. River barges are limited in width by lock sizes. Water depth, bridges, tidal effects can all determine max envelope size and carrying capacity. Barges may be combined between bridges / locks to give a larger area / capacity. Stability must be considered.* | | |
| | River/canal or sea-going? | What is the maximum size of module that can be accommodated on the max size barge? | Type of quay construction? Permissible quay loadings: apron, quay wall, strong points, roadway? |
| | What water-side facilities exist? How close to fabrication facility? | What size barge is proposed / available / possible? | Barge deck loadings, uniform and concentrated? |
| | Is there a quay? | Is there adequate clear height on route considering water height, ballast etc | How much ballast is required? |
| | Water depth, quay height, tide range, current? | | How stable is the arrangement? |
| | What size barges can be accommodated? Is ro-ro possible? Check compatibility of heights. | | Is there adequate water depth considering low water height and submerged barge depth? |
| | Is module to be craned on to barge or is ro-ro intended? Crane capacities & location versus suitability for ro-ro operations. | | What loadings will the carrying trailers impose? |
| | Is a transfer to a ship required in deeper water? By free-floating ro-ro, ships gear or floating crane? | | What line loads will ro-ro ramps impose (where used), in what location? |
| | Are levee crossings involved? Permits & approvals may be required. (U.S. Corps of Engineers). A temporary "bridge" may be required. | | |
| | *Some References: McDonough, Crowley, SMIT, Intermarine, Canal Barge.* | | What crane loads will be imposed (where used) and location? |
| **Ro-ro ships** | What options are possible? | Does module have to go below decks? | Imposed trailer pressure to ship. |
| | Ramp width, ramp height, required dock height? | Height / width / length (on trailer) versus ship? | Number of supports, size and location, do they interfere with trailers? |
| | Permitted deck loadings? Required water depth? | | Imposed loads and pressures through supports? Seafastening required, forces and locations? |
| | Length of ramp, imposed loads to quay? | | Check dynamic accelerations required by insurers / marine surveyors e.g. Noble Denton / Norsk Veritas or whoever for this type of load on this type of barge in this sea/ocean. |
| | Hatch covers over the hold? | | |
| | Means of offloading module from trailers onto hold? Cranes or trailer hydraulics, jacking systems? | | |
| | Availability and cost; an extra foot or two on size may take you to a different class and cost of ship. | | |
| | Check marine insurance versus say heavy lift ship. Barging may be restricted to inland waterways or coastal waters. | *Some shipping References: Jumbo, Rolldock, BigLift, Dockwise, Ocean Heavylift.* | |
| **Heavy lift ships** | What options are possible? Don't forget submersible options. | Pick points on module, location and number. | Single crane or tandem pick? Radii? |
| | Deck loadings, hatch cover loadings? On which deck? Below deck? | Required slinging arrangement. Stability during loading. | Crane capacities versus module weight and C of G. Available hoist height, swing path. |
| | Required water depth? | Height / width / length in hold or on deck / hatch covers. | |
| | Availability and cost; an extra foot or two on size may take you to a different class and cost of ship. | Size of ship versus entrances to harbors etc | |

| | General | Size | Weight and C of G |
|---|---|---|---|
| **Other transport means** | | | |
| **Hover barges** | Hover or air cushion barges (ACB) are barges that can rise clear of the water and and traverse poor or environmentally sensitive ground on a cushion of air like a hovercraft. They can be used for transporting payloads of several hundred tons over swamps, shallow water, soft mud, ground fast ice, tundra, permafrost, sandbars, wet sand, deep water and land; conditions that might be would be impossible for more conventional means. Exerting only 1psi ground pressure when on hover, they have minimal impact on the environment. When not required to hover, they float like a standard marine barge. | | |
| | Suitably level route?  Loading means?  Shallow ramp or similar may be required.  May be used for one leg of a longer journey into remote territory e.g. Alaska  *Reference: Hovertrans* | Deck size of current largest design is 9000ft2  Modular and custom designs are possible. | Practically, weights from 50t to 2500t can be moved. Current existing design (max) is good for 450t at a transit height of 5' (check with Hovertrans). |
| **Helicopters** | Helicopters can and are used to lift and place relatively light loads to inaccessible locations and/or extreme heights. Typical uses include placing flare tips or communications equipment or HVAC units on high buildings. | | |
| | | Sail areas need to be well considered - contact operators. | Greatest capacities are the Russian Mil Mi-26 with a max payload of 44,000lbs (20t); the Mil-12 with 88,000lbs (40t).  The Sikorsky S-64 Skycrane has a capacity of 25,000lbs (11.34t). |
| **Aircraft** | Aircraft may be an option to transport an item quickly over large distances, but weight and size are restricted. | | |
| | Availability of airfields. | The Antonov An-124 is available with a hold width of 21' (6.4m) and a height of 14.4' (4.3m), less if the crane is used.  The Skylifter SL-150 is a proposed lighter-than-air heavy lift aircraft (airship) with a capacity of 150t. It may in time provide options and would be better suited to heavy lift / carry than conventional planes. | The Antonov An-124 has a max 150t payload. |

| | General | Size | Weight and C of G |
|---|---|---|---|
| **Receipt at site** | | | |
| **Barging/shipping** | Considerations at the end of the journey are much the reverse of those at the start. Refer to those sections. Can the module be received directly by road or rail; is there a port close by? Can it be shipped directly, is a marine transfer required? What about a beach landing and so on? | | |
| | What water-side facilities exist? How close to jobsite?  Water depth, quay height, tide range, current?  What size barges / ships can be accommodated?  Is ro-ro possible? Check compatibility of heights.  Is module to be craned off by ships gear or land cranes? Is quay suitable? | Area of quay available for use?  Is quayside storage required? How much area?  Jetty width restrictions (where applicable).  Parallel use / other activities | Type of quay construction? Permissible quay loadings: apron, quay wall, strong points, roadway?  What line loads will ro-ro ramps impose (where used), in what location?  What crane loads will be imposed (where used) and location?  Storage loads and locations? |
| **Land transport** | Route from receipt to placing? Direct to foundation or storage required?  Route width / height restrictions.  Corners to be negotiated.  Grade changes and cross-falls.  Permitted loadings / upgrades proposed? | Height of load on transport versus absolute height restrictions?  Swept area of transport versus restrictions?  There may be a need to place holds on construction to reserve necessary space; the larger the load, the more the holds.  Ability to store loads in a manner that facilitates moving them out when required. | Imposed trailer (or other) loadings versus permitted GBP on route? |
| | Note: if moving on SPMTs, the suspension stroke is limited to a max of about 600mm. This, with reserves either end of travel) has to cater for the max difference in elevation between any set of wheels in the whole arrangement due to: gradient changes, cross falls, humps and hollows, trailer deflections etc. This can be very difficult to achieve with large trailer arrangements (length in particular being an issue). | | |
| **Offloading** | You may need to offload a "module" to storage or you may be able to take it direct to the foundation. It might be possible to design so that the module can be rough placed directly on the foundation using trailer hydraulics. Alternatively, it may need to be offloaded with a lift system or crane and lifted / lowered and/or | | |
| | | Adequate space is required at the foundation or storage area for delivery, the handling means and any storage equipment. | If a crane / lift system is to be used, adequate capacity is required. See "lifting" later.  The area has to be prepared level and adequately "strong" to withstand imposed loads and pressures from transport, offloading and storage equipment. |

| | General | Size | Weight and C of G |
|---|---|---|---|
| **Lifting** | | | |
| **Means** | As noted elsewhere in the course, there are numerous options for lifting large/heavy modules including cranes, jacking systems, strand jack systems, gantries and so on. What is used depends on weight / required lift height / need to move the load at height (or not). There are few limitations on height and weight in lifting if cost is no object; the restriction is likely to be driven by other practical (and financial) considerations. | | |
| | Decide on a suitable type of crane or alternative means of lifting considering the site conditions. | Use course guidance to select a suitable type of crane or alternative means of lifting considering the size. | Use course guidance to select a suitable type of crane or alternative means of lifting considering the weight. |
| **Lift arrangement** | Lift arrangement has to be stable, within the capacity of the lifting system, rigging and the supporting surface. | | |
| | Decide on the design basis for the lift arrangement. | | Conceptually design the approved rigging arrangement with the lifting method in mind. e.g. will a very long truss be a single crane or a 2-crane pick. |

| | | General | Size | Weight and C of G |
|---|---|---|---|---|
| **Module - design for handling** | | | | |
| **General** | | The handling method needs to be compatible with the limitations of the module design, i.e. the module shall not be overstressed or over-deflected during transport and lifting. Conversely the module should be designed to accommodate the intended handling method without being overstressed or over-deflected. | | |
| **Structure** | Transport | | Try not to design very tall narrow modules as they have to stable in handling. Maybe splitting them into two stacked modules makes better sense. | The members into which the transport forces are imposed must be designed to suit, including appropriate dynamic effects. |
| | | | Try to optimize height and width to suit particular classes of ships if close to being over-size and this is driving the selection. | Note: Trailers are not infinitely stiff and deflect in use. Deflections are dependant on relative stiffnesses of load and trailer . Temporary steel may be required to increase module stiffness. |
| | | | Don't make modules so long that you have suspension stroke issues when trying to negotiate the real world transport route. | Globally, the module must be capable of being supported in the intended manner in transport without over-stress considering static loads and dynamic accelerations (lateral and longitudinal). Shipping accelerations are dependent on shipping method. |
| | | | Try to design modules so that they can self-load and self-unload (preferably direct to foundation) using trailer hydraulics. It's much more efficient. | Sometimes modules need to be laid on their side for shipping, in which case all the contents need securing and the structure needs to consider upending forces. |
| | Lifting | | Consider the size of the module. It may for instance be better to lift a 12000t hanger roof as 2 x 6000t lifts rather than a single lift.<br>If stacking modules, lower ones can be larger and heavier, whereas higher ones should be kept smaller and lighter to be compatible with reducing crane capabilities. | Lift attachments should reflect the intended lifting method. |
| | | | | Lifting points need to consider stability during lifting, not just be ideal from a module design perspective - there is an optimum. Keep lift points above the C of G where possible. |
| | | | Try to make module to module connections as easy as possible with some tolerance on fit up. | Try to minimize numbers of lift attachment points. It may keep the module as light as possible but be virtually impossible to rig, particularly if they all want different loads. Try to stick to even numbers. |
| | | | Provide adequate stiffening in items such as large duct sections to maintain shape during lifting. | Consider the magnitude and direction of induced forces at all stages of lifting reflecting the lifting method. Stresses can be different (and worse) than in service. |
| | | | Try not to design top-heavy modules; they may not be adequately stable during handling. | Orientate lifting lugs to suit intended slinging method, standardize shackles to be used. |
| | | | | Do not forget that you can get load transfer / unequal load sharing between lift points when the load is stiff and the lifting forces independent of each other. |

Note that some limitations are absolute restrictions and cannot be engineered out or avoided in any practical / economic manner. Others can be engineered out at a price (that you might not want to pay). e.g. if there is only one entrance to site and it is under a live piperack, it may present a practical height restriction, although at a cost and some elevated risk, you may be able to lift a module over it.

Note that weight in itself does not present much in the way of a limitation against something being moved at grade by one means or another. Offshore modules of over 10,000 t have been moved on trailers and lifted offshore; jackets weighing considerably more than that have been skidded out onto launch barges and upended in the sea. Weight does however pose some practical limitations when lifting to significant height. We have seen that hanger roofs weighing up to about 10,000 t have been lifted onshore using strand jacks (but not to great height). Given enough masts and strand jacks, you can lift just about anything; controlling them is the real limitation. Lifting something straight up is much easier than moving it suspended at height. Size can present some real challenges and may well govern. Then the work you have to do to say make a process module strong enough to handle may not justify it and you may decide that particular area should not be modularized.

## 22.3 Optimizing modularization

Having decided that some degree of modularization is likely to bring benefit, you can see that, from a practical perspective there are some things you cannot do at any cost, then there are things that can be done at major cost and difficulty, then there are things that can be done at a manageable cost and difficulty. These options can be investigated, costed and balanced against the benefits they bring to arrive at an optimum solution.

# 23 Hanging loads from horizontal lines

## 23.1 Basics

### 23.1.1 Catenaries

When a chain or flexible wire is suspended with "sag" between two level points, it adopts a curved shape called a catenary, similar but not to be confused with the parabola.

The equation for the catenary curve is:

$y = a \cosh(x/a)$,

where a is a constant that determines the sag between the suspension points.

x = 0 corresponds to the vertex (the lowest point of the curve); the suspension points correspond to +/- span/2.

The length of the curve is:

$s = a \sinh(t/a)$

The tangential angle at any point is:

$\emptyset = 2 \tan^{-1}[\tanh(x/2a)]$

Using the above to figure the slope of the wire at the supports, and knowing that the vertical support load at each point needs to be 50% of the weight of the suspended wire, enables you to determine the wire tension and the horizontal component / restraint force.

### 23.1.2 Parabolas

When a wire is suspended between two level suspension points and is used to support a uniformly distributed hanging load, such as is the case in a suspension bridge, the shape the wire adopts is a parabola.

The equation for the basic curve when the vertex is at 0,0 is:

$y = ax^2$

where a is a constant; the parabola sags if a<0 as is the case with a wire; x will be between +/- span/2.

Calculating the length of the parabolic curve is surprisingly difficult, if you want to go there, the true formulae are available on the web, an approximation for the length offered in the civil engineers pocket book is the following:

Length = $2 \times \sqrt{((0.5 \times base)^2 + 1.333 \times (height)^2)}$

### 23.1.3 The difference between Parabolas and Catenaries

For the sake of comparison, I plotted the parabolic curve $y=ax^2$ from x = -1 to +1 as shown below and compared it to a plot of a catenary curve for the same wire length.

It can be shown that the length of the parabolic curve is 2.958; "a" was adjusted in the catenary curve until the lengths agreed;

The catenary formula becomes: $y=0.629 \cosh(x/0.629)$

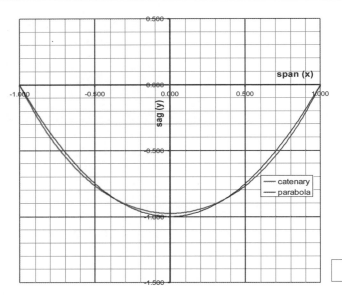

It does not sag quite so much (0.977 versus 1) but the curve is fuller towards the supports.

Why the difference in profile? With the catenary, the load is constant along the length of the wire, which from a horizontal perspective makes the load distribution more concentrated towards the supports as the slope gets steeper; the parabola has constant load distribution in the horizontal sense.

Figure 23-1

With a suspension bridge, the unloaded cable has a catenary shape, which changes towards parabolic as the road deck is hung from the cable (the deck weighing much more than the cable).

Note that for a sag of 1 and a span of 2, the civil engineers pocket book approximation yields:

Length = 2 x √ ((0.5x2)$^2$ + 1.333x(1)$^2$) = 2√2.333 = 3.055,

or 3.3% over-estimate

For most applications with which the rigging engineer is likely to be concerned the sag will not be as much (proportionally) as this and there will be little difference between the curves. For say sag = span / 10, a true circular curve would approximate well enough. The length approximation calculation above gets more accurate as the sag gets less proportionally.

### 23.1.4 Suspending loads from rat lines

There are occasions when you need to suspend a load or loads over a void where there are no strong points overhead, say in a valley or a large building. A solution may be to string a line across the void from two suitably strong points and suspend the load(s) from that.

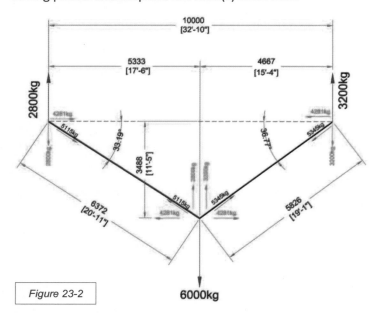

Figure 23-2

If it is a single load, it is relatively simple to figure out. In this case, the RH reaction

= 6000 x 5333 / 10000 = 3200 kg

LH reaction = 6000 - 3200 = 2800 kg,

Horizontal components = 2800 x 5333 / 3488 = 4281 kg.

Knowing H and V, the tensions can be derived from the square root of the sum of the squares.

LH$_t$ = 5115 kg, RH$_t$ = 5345 kg.

The combined length of the two slings used for this exercise is 12192 mm (40'); the LH sling is 6372 mm long, the RH is 5826 mm long.

The horizontal components, sling lengths and sling tensions will vary according to the "drop" you choose. You don't want it too shallow or the tensions get enormous.

Note an unloaded sling of total length 12.192 m (40') would have a sag of 3.08 m compared with the loaded sag of 3.49 m above. This ignores elastic stretch of the loaded cable.

## Two loads

If suspending more than one load from the wire, the analysis gets more complex.

Let us consider the above case where we substitute a load of 4000 kg at 4 m from the LH end and a second load of 2000 kg at 8 m from the LH end. There are many ways to look at this, perhaps the best approach is to start by figuring out what is effectively the C of G of the combined pay-loads. The distance between the two loads is 4 m; the single equivalent load of 6000 kg would act on a line that splits the 4 m distance in inverse proportion to the loads at either end. The LH load represents 4000/6000 = $^2/_3^{rd}$ of the total, therefore the line of action is $^2/_3^{rd}$ of 4 m away from the RH end as shown below.

Alternatively, taking moments about the LH support, (4000 kg x 4 m) + (2000 kg x 8 m) = 6000 kg x dist

Dist = 32000 kg.m / 6000 kg = 5333 mm from the LH support.

Thus, whichever way you get there, as far as the supports are concerned the two loads can be considered the same as one load of 6000 kg acting at 5.333 m from the LH end.

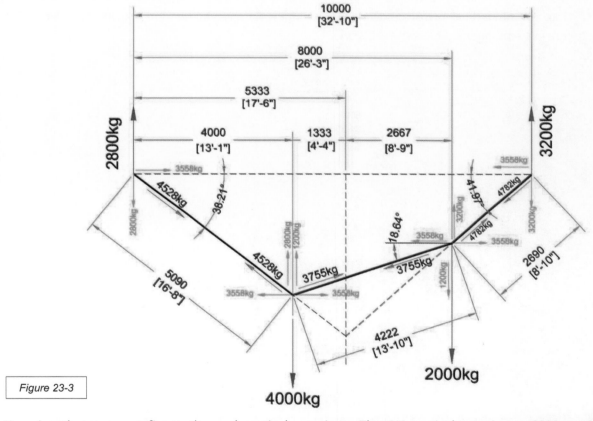

Figure 23-3

Knowing that, we can figure the end vertical reactions. The RH vertical reaction = 6000 x 5333/10000 = 3200 kg, therefore the LH vertical reaction is 6000 - 3200 = 2800 kg.

For equilibrium, the LH leg and the RH leg will adopt angles at which they intersect the axis of the 6000 kg equivalent load at a common point. Where those lines of action cross the lines of action of the 4000 kg and 2000 kg loads gives you two intersections which determine the ends of the central leg. You can therefore draw the line of (say) the LH leg first choosing an angle, or a length to the first load to suit your needs; project the line till it crosses the axis of the equivalent 6000 kg load; draw a line from that intersection to the RH support point; note where that intersects the line of the 2000 kg load; complete the arrangement by drawing the central leg between the two intersection points. If this doesn't give you the leg lengths you want, adjust and repeat till it does. In this case, the sum of the three legs is again 12192 mm (40').

Knowing the end vertical reactions and the angles of the end legs, you can determine the tensions in those legs and the horizontal components of the tensions. The equal and opposite components of the tension act at the nodes from which the loads are suspended. Looking at the equilibrium of the nodes allows you to determine the vertical and horizontal components provided by the central leg and thus figure out its tension. As can be seen everything balances out.

Note that, except for the case where a single load is suspended from the center of the span using a pulley or similar where the load will find the low point and be stable, the tensions in the system change at each node point and the arrangements shown only work if each leg is a separate tension member (wire, chain, lifting device or whatever) of the required calculated length. Suspension bridges do use a single cable but have hangers that clamp around the cable at each node locations; this will allow a change in cable tension at each node.

If using a single wire and rolling blocks, the wire tension would need to be constant throughout the system, which it isn't. If you tried to use a single wire and rolling blocks, the loads would just run down hill to the lowest point. You could devise a system where the tension in the wire is 3755 kg and you provide a separate holding line from the LH anchor to the LH rolling block that provides the required difference of 4528 kg – 3755 kg = 773 kg and similarly at the RH end where the holding wire would need to provide 4782 kg – 3755 kg = 1027 kg in much the manner that a cable car works.

Multiple loads

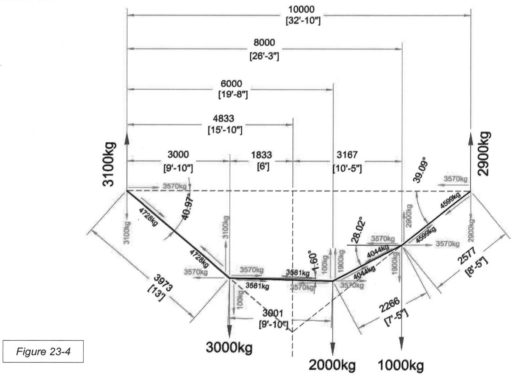

Figure 23-4

You can follow the same principles for multiple loads; calculate the line of action of the "C of G" of all the suspended loads, the lines of action of the wires at the two supports must intersect on that axis (in this case 4833 mm from the LH support). Knowing the C of G location, the end vertical reactions can be determined, knowing the angles, the horizontal components can be determined. Work from say left to right, at each node the vertical and horizontal components must equal – the horizontal loads are constant throughout the system, the vertical components of each leg change as loads are imposed. Knowing the vertical and horizontal components, the tensions can be calculated. This works for any number of imposed loads.

# 24 The rationale for Lift Planning

## 24.1 The importance of planning load handling operations

What are the benefits of planning? Why is thorough planning of lifting and other load handling operations so particularly important?

Planning (anything) allows you to:

- Analyze the task and identify / avoid key issues that could trip you up, avoiding crisis management
- Balance options and make informed choices
- Focus on the task and establish a logical and seamless progression of steps that will lead to success and effective, efficient management of the process

In short, we plan these operations for the reason we plan anything – it goes much better that way. A lifting operation that is not planned (or is poorly planned) stands a much higher chance of going badly. With the potential consequences of it "going badly" being so severe and the opportunities to take corrective measures very limited, "going badly" is not an option when lifting - all lifting operations have to go as well as they can <u>first time</u> and that requires good planning. A well planned lifting operation is a much safer (and more efficient) operation.

Good planning is of course not the only essential element in successful lifting, the other side of the coin is skilled execution using good equipment and qualified people. This volume is concerned only with the planning aspect; the execution side is well covered elsewhere.

## 24.2 Accidents – four basic categories

Every day we see headlines such as:

- "Crane falls into nursing home"
- "Crane collapse at East 51st Street"
- "Crane topples into Gulf of Mexico"
- "Worker killed, 3 injured in crane collapse"
- "Crane electrocution - Lakeland, FL"
- "Crane load block drops on work platform, killing worker"
- "Falling crane kills senior citizen, injures three"

and many more.

I reckon that just about every crane related accident you will have ever been involved with, or hear about, falls into one (or more) of four fundamental categories, namely:

- The crane collapses
- The load drops
- The crane or load strikes something or somebody
- The crane or load contacts high voltage electricity

Primary in the drive to eliminate crane-related accidents is thinking the task through, identifying where risk lies and <u>planning</u> least-risk (cost-effective) methods. Proper planning is vital! The rationale for writing this book is specifically to assist persons planning lifting operations.

In working to reduce Risk in lifting there are two aspects you need to consider:

- Causes (and the attendant probability of the cause occurring), i.e. the preventative side, working towards elimination of accidents

- Consequences (and their severity dependent on the presence of risk factors), i.e. minimizing the potential consequences should an accident occur

## 24.3 Causes of lifting related accidents

If you can eliminate the causes, you don't have an accident and there are no consequences! So that is always a good place to initially concentrate attention; what are the causes?

Each of the four fundamental categories of accidents has several potential underlying causes, many of which can be influenced for good or bad by the Lift Planner. e.g. the Lift Planner can ensure that the loadings imposed by the crane are correctly assessed and adequately catered for in the stipulated ground preparation, reducing the risk significantly of crane collapse due to ground failure.

In the following table I have attempted to break down the basic types of accidents into their primary and root causes. *(I don't guarantee this list is exhaustive).*

e.g. working from the root cause,

> Improper ground preparation or matting → Ground Failure → Crane toppling

> > or

> Failure to assess wind loads on payload in high winds → Excessive wind loads → Crane toppling

By properly identifying potential root causes of accidents and having means in place to deal with those causes up front before they are a problem, you can eliminate (or at least very much reduce) the likelihood of an accident.

e.g. working from the (resolved) root cause,

> Proper ground preparation or matting → No Ground Failure → Crane remains stable

> > or

> Properly assessed wind loads on payload → Wind speed limited → Crane remains stable

Of course, many people other than the Lift Planner have a part to play in eliminating causes of accidents:

- The Assembly/Disassembly Director has the make sure the crane is assembled correctly
- The Crane Operator has to operate the crane correctly
- Geotechnical Engineers have to determine permissible ground loadings

and so on.

Here however we are concerned with those factors that can be influenced by the Lift Planner.

Associated with causes are <u>Risk Factors</u>, factors which if present will make it more likely that an accident deriving from that cause will happen. e.g. a crane is more likely to tip when conducting a tandem lift over 75% and moving with the load on poor ground conditions with a long boom/jib combinations in high winds than conducting a single crane pick at 50% of capacity in low wind conditions on good ground.

So the first thing you are going to want to do is to look for the presence of Risk Factors and attempt to eliminate them or reduce (control) them as far as is reasonable and practical.

*Is weight a Risk Factor? Traditionally there has always been a lot of concentration on categorizing lifts by their weight and prescribing the required extent of lift planning accordingly. In my view, weight in itself is not a Risk Factor - just being heavy doesn't increase the probability of an accident if everything is sized accordingly. What is important is the percentage of capacity everything (the crane, rigging, ground etc) is working at – that definitely has an effect on probability. Of course, a heavy load may well be a large load and have a large sail area which will give larger lateral wind forces – you will need to consider that. Also, a heavy load is more likely to require a heavy crane and have you pushing the boundaries of the ground's capability, but that is a ground bearing issue that you will need to consider.*

*On the consequence side, a heavy load will do more damage when dropped, but the height from which you drop it is also important (and rarely considered). That said, even a relatively light load such as a wrench may have sufficient potential energy to kill if dropped from height onto a person at ground level. Destruction is however a consequence not a risk – so weight should appear in the consequence side of the equation!*

*I therefore advocate considering magnitude of weight as a Consequence Severity factor rather than a Risk Factor. The primary drive should be to prevent an accident which requires putting emphasis first on actual Risk Factors – consequences are applied to the residual risk.*

## 24.4 Consequences of lifting related accidents

Every accident has consequences; some of the major ones are listed in the table following. How consequential an accident is, is largely dependent on whether certain severity factors are present. e.g. a crane collapse in a field will likely have less severe consequences than the same accident happening in tight quarters in a live petrochemical plant. Therefore in planning a lifting operation in a live petrochemical plant, it would be appropriate that policy should require a more stringent investigation into ground conditions, more conservative matting and a more comprehensive lift plan with greater oversight.

## 24.5 Introducing Risk and Severity Factors

The following table breaks down the four fundamental types of crane accidents by their primary causes and their root causes. The blue highlight indicates those causes that could possibly be influenced by the lift planner; those things that he/she could be expected to know about and account for in a lift plan. In addition to root causes, there are factors, which if present, will increase the risk of an operation; they are highlighted grey. Some potential consequences are listed by accident type; finally those consequences are likely to be more severe if certain severity factors (highlighted grey) are present.

This list is by no means totally exhaustive – you may need to expand it for your own purposes or modify it to suit your situation.

Figure 24-1

| Primary causes | Root causes | Increased Risk factors | Consequences | Severity factors |
|---|---|---|---|---|
| **The crane or lifting apparatus collapses** | | | | |
| Tip or fail due to overload / excessive radius | Excessive weight / incorrect C of G | Tandem lifts over (say) 75% | • Crane damaged or destroyed | – Proximity to equipment, plant, buildings |
| | Poor / no plan | Lifts over say 85% of chart | • Load damaged or destroyed | – Proximity to pressurized lines or vessels |
| | Planner misread crane chart | Weight and/or C of G uncertain | • Collateral damage to equipment, plant, buildings etc | – Proximity to pipelines carrying flammable or explosive gases, liquids |
| | Unaccounted load transfer between cranes | Lifts "on rubber" | • Release of pressurized gases | – Proximity to toxic materials |
| | Load shift | Lifts moving with the load | • Release of flammable or explosive liquids or gases | – Power lines within fall zone |
| | Excessive lateral loadings | Multi-crane lifts | • Release of toxic materials | – Length of boom/jib |
| | Incorrect set-up | Use of land-based cranes on barges | • Contact made with power lines etc | – Proximity of people |
| | Errors in radius measurement | Poor ground conditions | • People killed or maimed | – Cost of crane |
| Mechanical / structural failure (except overload) | Previous misuses | Lifting out of water | • Schedule slippage | – Cost of load |
| | Poor maintenance / inspection | Demolition work | • Financial costs | – Replacement time of crane |
| | Manufacturing defect | Use of narrow tracks | | – Replacement time of load |
| | Improper training | Use of short outrigger duties | | – Item on critical schedule |
| | Wilful mis-operation / failure to follow plan | Upending or "inverting" operations | | |
| Operating error | Incorrect coding of computer | Topping and tailing with a single crane | | |
| | Inattention / misunderstanding signals | Long boom / jib | | |
| | Excessive dynamic loads | High winds | | |
| Ground failure | Improper ground / mat prep.n | Custom lifting equipment or techniques | | |
| | Failure to assess loads | | | |
| | Failure to assess ground | | | |
| Excessive wind loads | Failure to understand crane chart wind restrictions in preparing plan | | | |
| | Failure to comply with plan | | | |
| | Failure to assess wind loads on payload | | | |
| Incorrect assembly | Failure to follow procedures | | | |
| | Lack of training | | | |
| | No procedure | | | |
| As result of load dropping | Failure to check before use | | | |
| | (See below) | | | |
| Control system failure | Defective system, welding, lightning or high voltage damage | | | |

| Hazard | Cause | Contributing factors | Consequences | Outcome factors |
|---|---|---|---|---|
| **The load drops** | Crane failure | (See above) | • Load damaged or destroyed | – Weight of load |
| | Rigging failure | – Failure to assess loads correctly<br>– Undersized for load<br>– Defective tackle<br>– Cut / damaged slings or other tackle<br>– Improperly used<br>– Failure to understand limitations on use | • Crane damaged or destroyed<br>• Collateral damage to equipment, plant, buildings etc<br>• Release of pressurized gases<br>• Release of flammable or explosive liquids or gases<br>• Release of toxic materials | – Height of load<br>– Proximity to equipment, plant, buildings<br>– Proximity to pressurized lines or vessels<br>– Proximity to pipelines carrying flammable or explosive gases, liquids<br>– Proximity to toxic materials |
| | Instability due to improper slinging | – Failure to correctly assess the stability of the slinging arrangement<br>– Failure to account for effects of dynamic and wind loads on marginally stable loads | • Contact made with power lines etc<br>• People killed or maimed<br>• Schedule slippage<br>• Financial costs | – Power lines within fall zone<br>– Length of boom/jib<br>– Proximity of people<br>– Cost of crane<br>– Cost of load |
| | Lift lug failure | – Incorrect design of attachments<br>– Improper use including excessive side loading<br>– Weld failure / lack of inspection / laminations in metal<br>– Bolt failure inc incorrect torque<br>– Defective material / fabrication | | – Replacement time of crane<br>– Replacement time of load<br>– Item on critical schedule |
| | Failure of the load itself | – Failure to check load for stresses (local and global) induced in lifting<br>– Not slinging the load as the designer intended<br>– Disconnect between the lift planner and the designer of the load | | |
| | *(Load factors)* | – Multiple pick points<br>– Requirement for complex slinging arrangement<br>– Awkward, odd-shaped, brittle or otherwise sensitive load<br>– Lift loads result in compression in members designed for tension in use<br>– Weight and/or C of G of load uncertain<br>– Where condition of load is uncertain / deterioration<br>– Hostile lifting environments, extremes of temperature, acid/alkali etc<br>– Pick points below the C of G<br>– Top-heavy / unstable load | | |
| **The crane becomes energized with high voltage electricity** | Load or crane touches live power line<br><br>or<br><br>Load or crane becomes energized without contact | – Failure to identify power lines / other sources of high voltage<br>– Failure to plan or to follow a good plan<br>– Failure to check voltage and plan to maintain appropriate required clearances<br>– Failure to ensure power is switched off and grounded (if planned so)<br>– Failure to consider the entire crane, load, load lines, tail swing etc<br>– Planning to lift too close to power lines or other sources of electrical energy etc<br><br>– Presence of power lines within fall zone of crane<br>– Presence of power lines closer than mandated min operating clearance distance<br>– Inability to relocate the lifting operation to maintain required clearances<br>– Inability to shut power off<br>– Voltage | • Electrocution of crane operator or other persons<br>• Fire / explosion<br>• Damage to, or destruction of, the crane or load<br>• Damage to surrounding plant, buildings, equipment etc<br>• Shutdown of power supply | – Direct and indirect cost of power line being shut off<br>– Presence of flammable / explosive gases or liquids<br>– Presence of people<br>– The location of the operation<br>– Sensitivity of the load to high voltage electricity |

| The load or crane strikes something | | | |
|---|---|---|---|
| **Crane or load strikes fixed structure or other obstruction** | - Failure to identify obstructions<br>- Failure to consider the entire crane, load, load lines, tail swing etc<br>- Failure to plan for adequate clearances<br>- Failure to consider the movements of load and crane required adequately<br>- Failure to follow plan in placing and operating the crane, improper set up<br>- Failure to clear planned load path<br>- Inaccurate survey information<br>- Obstructions put in place after plan preparation<br>- Load swings during operation<br>- Improper signaling / miscommunication | – Working in tight locations<br>– High winds, funneling, gusting<br>– Poor illumination<br>– High noise areas<br>– Cross language issues | • Damage to, or destruction of, the crane or load / collapse<br>• Damage to, or destruction of, surrounding plant, buildings, equipment etc<br>• Fire / explosion<br>• Release of pressurized gases<br>• Release of flammable or explosive liquids or gases<br>• Release of toxic materials |
| | | | – Proximity to equipment plant, buildings<br>– Proximity to pressurized lines or vessels<br>– Proximity to pipelines carrying flammable or explosive gases, liquids<br>– Proximity to toxic materials<br>– Cost of crane<br>– Cost of load<br>– Replacement time of crane, load or items hit |
| **Persons struck or trapped by crane or load** | - Persons working under load<br>- No planned means of egress from danger<br>- Trapped in a pinch point<br>- Lack of awareness | – Persons working under a load or in the fall zone<br>– Persons required to work in pinch zones without proper means of egress | • Persons killed or maimed |
| | | | – Severity of injuries |

## 24.6 Establishing a lift planning policy

To deal properly with the risks posed by lifting activities, it is necessary that there is a policy in place that stipulates (amongst other things) how lift planning is to be executed. This may be a corporate policy, a statutory policy or even one of your own devising as appropriate to the particular situation. As regards lift planning, it should:

- include a standardized means of assessing the risk the operation poses
- define a process of categorizing lifts by the residual risk they pose
- stipulate the minimum required content of a lift plan (by risk category)
- define minimum qualifications for persons who prepare lift plans (by risk category)
- stipulate the extent of review and approval required (by risk category)

### 24.6.1 Assessing Risk

To paraphrase the various definitions risk assessment professionals use, Risk can be defined as something along the lines of:

*(the <u>probability</u> of something unwanted happening) x (the severity of the <u>consequences</u> if it does so)*

Probability can be assessed by the presence or otherwise of Risk Factors such as those tabulated above and consequences can be assessed by the presence or otherwise of Severity Factors.

Naturally, your plan should have been devised to minimize the Risk Factors thereby driving Risk down to its lowest practical level; what remains is residual risk. The final assessed risk level drives the actions to be taken to mitigate the residual Risk (control measures).

*Note the words "lowest practical level". Every human activity, including lifting, has some degree of risk associated with it; we can do much to reduce that risk but we cannot totally eliminate it. There will always be <u>some</u> degree of residual risk no matter how good the lift plan. This fact must not lead us to conclude that statistically accidents are inherently inevitable and therefore acceptable, but must serve to keep us ever vigilant to the possibility of things going off track.*

There are a number of approaches you could take to assess risk.

You might devise a "score" system for each Risk Factor dependent on the risk it poses if present and you may "score" the Severity Factors based on the severity of the consequences if that eventuality happened. Multiplying the Risk x the Severity yields a measure of Risk. There may of course be multiple risks present, in which case sum the whole lot up. You could then say if the score is greater than a certain threshold, you will deal with it in a certain manner, if it's greater than another threshold, you will deal with it in another more exacting manner.

Alternatively, you may simply say that if any of certain Risk or Severity factors are present you will deal with it as being a "Critical Lift", "High-Risk Lift" or whatever. If none of the factors are present you will deal with it as a "Routine Lift" or "Low-risk Lift". (I am not keen on the term "Routine" as I believe it can lead to complacency). If only certain lesser risk factors are present you might deal with it as something between the two.

However you choose to assess risk and categorize lifts, you need to ensure that the extent of planning and oversight and the skills of the persons involved are commensurate with the risk that the operation poses.

### 24.6.2 Requirements by Risk Category

Having categorized a lifting operation according to the risk it poses, the policy needs to define requirements for lift planning. Let us assume that you define three risk categories, say Low, Medium, High Risk; they may be called "Routine", "Engineered", "Critical" or whatever works for you. Your policy might look something like the following:

<u>Low Risk Lift</u>

— A lift that presents none of the defined Risk or Severity Factors and is (say) less than 10 tons.

*Typically a Low-Risk lift might be jointly planned by the (Qualified) Crane Operator and Qualified Rigger. The record of the lift could simply be a line entry in a crane lift log.*

<u>Medium Risk Lift</u>

— A lift that presents only one or two of the lesser Risk or Severity Factors and does not weigh more than say 50 tons.

*You may decide that the appropriate extent of lift planning is that a Rigging Supervisor or other Competent Person completes a Lift Data Sheet laying out the essentials of the lift and a Rigging Engineer or other suitably qualified person reviews and approves it. The Data sheet would be supplemented by any sketches (such as rigging hook up) necessary to adequately explain the intent. Appending a crane chart extract is always a good idea.*

<u>High-Risk or Critical Lifts</u>

— All lifts that cannot be categorized as "Low" or "Medium" risk are considered High Risk or Critical.

*Typically you would want to see a full-blown lift plan for these lifts including full plan and elevation drawings, hook up sketches, brief method statement, lift data sheet (if information is not presented on the drawings), calculations where applicable, crane chart extracts and so on. Preparation needs to be someone with the requisite skills such as a rigging engineer. A qualified person needs to review and approve the plan. The risks may require approval by say a Site Manager or similar. In some jurisdictions, the plan may need to be stamped by a Professional Engineer.*

## 24.7 Lift planners – required knowledge

You can see from the preceding that the lift planner has a vital role to play in ensuring that lifting operations are conducted safely. To discharge that duty properly there is a considerable amount of required knowledge (and experience). This includes:

— Being able to identify hazards and circumvent or address them in the lift plan

— Assessing lift reactions, understanding the effects of C of G and lift lug locations

— Understanding and quantifying how lift reactions change during upending and manipulating loads

— Understanding and quantifying load transfer between support points

— Knowing the characteristics of rigging components, how to select and specify them

— Assessing the loads in the components of different types of rigging arrangements

— Knowing how to design and/or specify and use lift beams and spreader bars

— Ability to correctly design and use lift lugs

— Understanding concepts of stability in rigging arrangements

— Knowing the importance of checking the ability of the payload to withstand being lifted

— Knowing the characteristics of the various types of cranes and alternative lifting devices available

— Knowing how to read a crane chart, assess the loads acting on the crane (and applicable deductions), and make an appropriate selection

— Knowing how to assess track and outrigger loads

- Understanding concepts of matting & load distribution, being able to design load spreading arrangements
- Understanding options re ground preparation
- Understanding the effects of wind loads on crane and payload
- Knowing the importance of maintaining adequate clearances to power lines
- Maintaining adequate clearances to structures etc
- Knowing how to appropriately document (and communicate) a lift plan

## 24.8 Summary

- Good planning is one of the key tools in attacking the causes of lifting related accidents and their probability. You may also be able to attack consequences through planning by measures such as relocating lifting operations away from live power lives or live process pipelines, requiring areas to be cleared of people and equipment and so on.
- All lifting operations need to be planned!
- All lift plans need to be prepared by someone who has the requisite skills – an appropriately qualified person.
- The rigor of lift planning needs to be appropriate to the complexity of the operation and the risks the operation poses. e.g. the lifting of a 2 t valve over a live piperack may be considered high risk and require a comprehensive lift plan by virtue of the consequences if the load was dropped and a pipe breached, despite the crane only operating at 50% capacity. The same lift in a laydown yard may be considered low risk and not require a formal lift plan.
- The content of the lift plan needs to address the risks that operation poses. e.g. if the ground is poor, the plan needs to show that the distributed loadings are within the ground bearing capacity; if there are adjacent power lines, the plan needs to show that the minimum clearance distances are planned to be maintained; and so on.
- The skills required of a lift planner depend on the complexity of the operation and the nature of the task. A person well versed in planning for heavy crane operations may know little of lifting with strand jacks or general "bull-rigging". Qualified means qualified for the task in hand.
- The Lift Planner, (be that a Rigging Engineer, Rigger, Supervisor or whatever) has the responsibility to plan the operation and to communicate that plan by means of written or verbal instructions to those persons who have to execute the work. I have highlighted some of the root causes of crane accidents that should be considered and addressed by the Lift Planner. Your particular situation may require more or less or different topics. The complexity of the Lift Plan, who would be qualified to be the Lift Planner, the depth and scope of the Lift Plan, whether it is a formally recorded written plan or merely verbal instruction depends on the complexity of the operation and the Risk the operation poses.
- Your company or client or legislation may mandate what they consider appropriate – as a lift planner, you of course as a professional still have a duty to plan the work to the level of detail necessary to mitigate the risks as far as is possible and to ensure that the plan is fully communicated to those who have to execute the work. Just because your employer does not require you to produce a rigging hookup sketch for a lift in a certain risk band does not mean that you shouldn't produce one, if one is required to adequately explain your intentions.
- All lift plans should be verified.

This volume is intended to address each of the above bullet points (and more) and should provide useful information (and sources of information) that will be helpful to lift planners.

# 25 Lift plan content

## 25.1 Purpose

As noted earlier, planning allows you to:

- Analyze the task and identify / avoid key issues that could trip you up, avoiding crisis management
- Balance options and make informed choices
- Focus on the task and establish a logical and seamless progression of steps that will lead to success and effective, efficient management of the process

The process of lift planning should therefore address all the above.

## 25.2 Process

The basic steps in the planning process are bulleted following:

- Understand the task
  - What the load is, what it weighs, how big it is, where it's C of G is
  - Know where it has to go from and to and any manipulation required e.g. upending or flipping
  - Understand the working environment, the limitations and the hazards it presents
  - Understand the applicable rules governing the activity
- Review the options
  - Review available lifting techniques appropriate to the task
  - Review available lifting equipment
  - Make a least-risk selection of equipment and methodology
- Develop a good plan
  - Determine crane (or alternate) location(s), required configuration, boom and jib length etc, operating radii
  - Determine the load path, sequence of the operation and manipulations involved
  - Devise a stable rigging arrangement and specified appropriate and suitably rated rigging equipment
  - Check loads and capacities and verify required clearances
  - Check ground bearing pressures and matting requirements
- Based on the residual risks associated with the plan, categorize the risk band it falls within
- Document the plan to a level of detail appropriate to the risk the operation poses; describe how the work is to be conducted, the progression of steps to be taken and detail the measures to be taken to control the risks

## 25.3 Content

While a less complex low-risk operation may not need a formally documented plan, operations that are either complex or are in a high risk band or entail pre-planning will require documented plans to a greater or lesser extent.

The policy you are operating under will define the <u>minimum</u> extent of documentation required by the Risk category into which the operation falls and the extent of review and approval needed. You should include any information that those persons conducting the operation will need to execute it efficiently and safely per your intentions. The policy you devise might define something like the following for content requirements.

### 25.3.1  Low Risk Lifts

As noted earlier, a Low-Risk lift (my definition – you may use other terminology in your organization) may typically be jointly planned by the (Qualified) Crane Operator and Qualified Rigger who are going to undertake the work and often won't be pre-planned or require any further review and approval. (Terminology for these positions varies from country to country).

The low risk and lack of complexity posed by this type of operation will likely not require any formal written lift plan or drawings. That doesn't mean that you don't need to have a plan – all lifting operations need to be planned. The plan would usually be figured out at the time of the lift by the participants (see above) and communication in such cases will likely just be verbal. Although formal approval would not be required, I would however recommend that you require that a daily crane log is maintained in the crane cab in which the basic details of each executed lift (or series of similar lifts) are kept. The record of the lift may simply be a line entry with description, weight (inc deductions), crane configuration, radius and capacity. This simple discipline will encourage proper verification of capacities.

The lift plan to lift 40' long pieces of pipe off a truck into laydown using a Grove RT865B rough terrain crane might simply be (for example):

- Offload 20 no. 40' x 5000# pipes in laydown area 1.
- 65' main boom, stowed jib, 45 t block x 4 parts, full outrigger c/s, full cwt.
- Lift and place at max 35' rad – capacity 32500#.
- Use 2 x 5 ton WLL (min) synthetic slings x 20', wrapped choke 10' either side of C of G.

### 25.3.2  Medium Risk Lifts

As noted earlier a Medium Risk lift may be one that presents only one or two of the lesser Risk or Severity Factors. It might for instance have more complexity about it (than a basic low-risk lift) or be working at high percentages of capacity or the load may be particularly sensitive. It therefore merits a more detailed plan that properly addresses those things that made it "Medium Risk". It will likely require review and approval (by a suitably qualified person) and will need someone with more than basic skills to prepare the plan. In this case a Rigging Supervisor or Advanced Rigger might possibly be considered qualified to prepare the plan.

Typically a Medium Risk lift plan might simply be a completed Lift Data sheet summarizing the essentials of the lift. The Data sheet may need to be supplemented with say a rigging hook up sketch if the hook-up is complex or by a simple drawing if necessary to explain where the crane or load is to go, or the movements to be made, or to demonstrate clearances. Appending a crane chart extract is always a good idea for reference by those reading the plan. Typically, a Rigging Engineer or other suitably qualified person reviews and approves it.

The sort of output you get from Compu-Crane or other graphics based lift planning software might represent sufficient of a plan for a medium risk lift. It would contain the crane configuration, radius, outrigger loads, show obstructions and critical clearances; RiggingPro might be used to illustrate a less-than-straightforward rigging hook up arrangement.

## 25.4 Critical Lifts

As noted earlier a Critical Risk lift will present one or more of the higher order Risk or Severity Factors and will probably be a more complex operation. It will therefore require a much more detailed plan in order to properly address those things that made it "Critical Risk". Policy will probably require detailed scrutiny and multiple approvals of the plan and will require someone with advanced drafting, engineering and field skills to prepare it. In this case a Rigging Engineer would be considered qualified to prepare the plan.

### 25.4.1  Rigging Plan Content (critical lifts)

Typically, a Critical lift plan might include:

- Lift studies (drawings)
- Plan and elevation views
- Rigging hook-up detailed arrangements
- Matting arrangement
- Detailed clearance checks (where applicable)
- Sequence drawing (if required to explain the phases of a complex operation)
- A brief method statement explaining how the operation is to be undertaken (if not readily apparent from the drawings)
- Completed Lift Data Sheet (unless this information appears on the drawings)
- Crane chart extract(s)
- Supporting documentation / rating charts for equipment such as spreader bars or lift beams
- Calculations for any custom items of rigging
- Ground bearing pressure estimates, load distribution design calculations

The information that you need to include on a lift study for a critical lift plan depends a lot on the task in hand. You could use the following as a general content guide, adding or subtracting as appropriate.

Figure 25-1

## CONTENT OF CRITICAL LIFT STUDIES

**Drawing utilities**
Job description, client, job no., drawing no., revision no., date
Site North
Plan, elevations, end views
Notes & limiting conditions

**Load to be handled**
Reference No. / description
Reference to vendor / other drawing of item
Leading dimensions of load
Extent of ladders, platforms shown, weight included
Erection weight of load defined, factor added as required
Position of C of G shown
Head / tail loads shown (where appropriate)
Location / type of lifting points shown and checked v rigging
Delivery direction / laydown shown
Transport envelope shown (as appropriate)
Temporary supports / grillages shown

**Main lift crane(s)**
Crane manufacturer / model
Config.n (inc boom / jib lengths & type, jib/ boom angles)
Machine and auxiliary counterweight
Crawler c/s, outrigger c/s, ring dia (as appropriate)
Leading dimensions of crane, tail swing radius
Superlift (where used) back mast radius / length / type
Hoist block capacity, number of parts used
Two block minimum distance

**Main crane location and moves**
Erection location of crane and area required (if appropriate)
Boom laydown area & direction (where appropriate)
All crane locations referenced, movements defined
Crane radii at all phases of the operation
Path of load movement defined
Zone of tail swing defined and affected zone
Zone of Superlift swing defined
Foundation holds required
Undergrounds near imposed loads shown
Matting arrangements required
Crawler / outrigger loads & pressures at all phases
Site permissible GPB / ground prep. defined

**Rigging**
Slings (type, constr.n, eye type, length, dia., grade, WLL)
Spreader (type / ref, span, WLL)
Shackle details (type, WLL)
Other rigging details as required
Hook up drawing

**Tailing (where required)**
Method to be used (crane/trailer/other)
Details of tailing frame attachment if any (inc WLL)
Crane & rigging details as main crane (or alt equip.t details)
Tail height at commencement and completion
Required clearance over bolts

**Operation details**
Exclusion (working) zones defined
Limiting wind speeds for operation
Special operational restrictions (visibility, temperature etc)
Clearances to power lines, rail lines, live plant etc
Plan showing load path, tail and superlift swing
Elevation showing min clearances load & rigging to crane
Critical clearances load and rigging to surrounding plant.
Path of tail and tailing crane / trailer
Elev.n of load at max height, confirm head clearance >ATB dist

**Load table (repeat for all phases)**
Payload weight (inc contingencies, contents / attachments)
Load factors e.g. dynamic effects, suction etc (as apply)
Crane fixed weights (hook blocks, hoist line, jibs etc)
Rigging weights
Total lift load
Crane capacity & percent used at all phases

The information contained in the lift plan should be relevant and succinct and aimed at communicating (and justifying) the intent of the Lift Planner. As well as containing all the planning information the people in the field need to execute the operation, it should specifically address all the factors that made the operation "critical" in the first place. i.e. the control measures to mitigate the risk. Standard corporate safety, quality information, organization charts and the like should not be included unless directly relevant. The aim should not be to maximize the paper content but to create a complete, lean and totally relevant, easily read document of real value. You want to create the road map to a seamlessly executed, safe and efficient operation, in which all the potential glitches have been considered and designed out (or at least catered for).

The following sheets show a lift study prepared as part of the lift plan for a Crude Colum upending operation. The content is generally compatible with the above list. The style of presentation is of course your own choice; this used 2-D Autocad. Note the crane load tables are included on the drawing in this case. You could equally have included that information on a Lift Data Sheet instead.

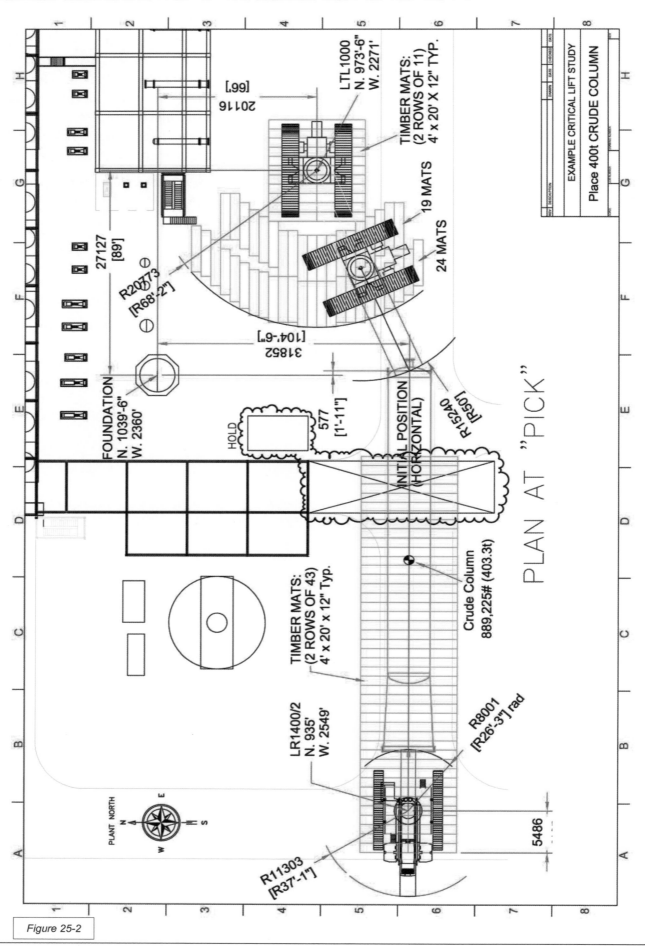

PLAN AT "PICK"

EXAMPLE CRITICAL LIFT STUDY

Place 400t CRUDE COLUMN

LTL1000
N. 973'-6"
W. 2271'

TIMBER MATS:
(2 ROWS OF 11)
4' x 20' X 12" TYP.

19 MATS

24 MATS

FOUNDATION
N. 1039'-6"
W. 2360'

27127
[89']

R20773
[R68'-2"]

31852
[104'-6"]

R1524
[R50']

577
[1'-11"]

INITIAL POSITION
(HORIZONTAL)

HOLD

20116

[66']

Crude Column
889,225# (403.3t)

TIMBER MATS:
(2 ROWS OF 43)
4' x 20' x 12" Typ.

LR1400/2
N. 935'
W. 2549'

R8001
[R26'-3"] rad

5486

R11303
[R37'-1"]

PLANT NORTH

N
E
W
S

Figure 25-2

Page 390

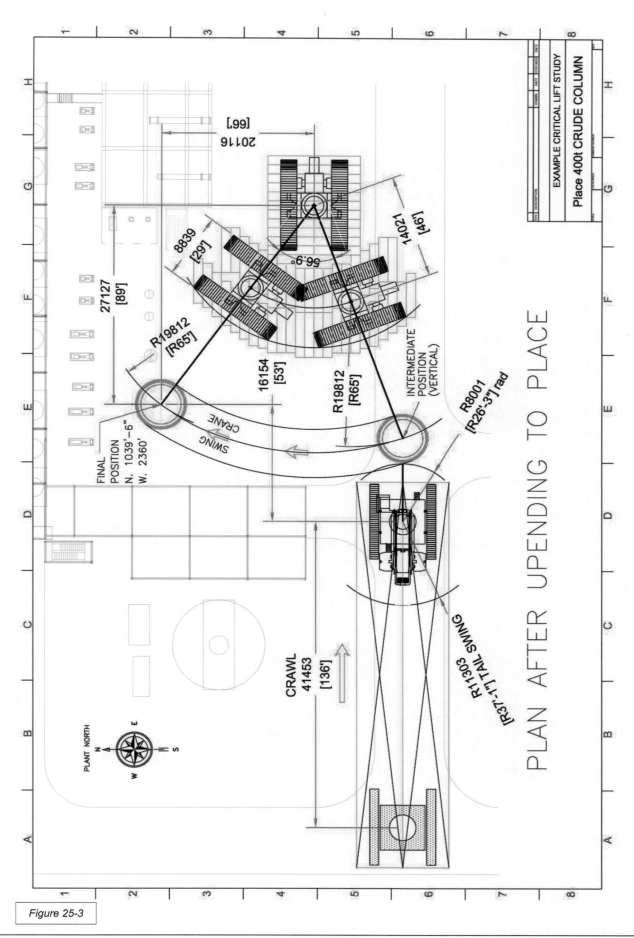

PLAN AFTER UPENDING TO PLACE

EXAMPLE CRITICAL LIFT STUDY

Place 400t CRUDE COLUMN

Figure 25-3

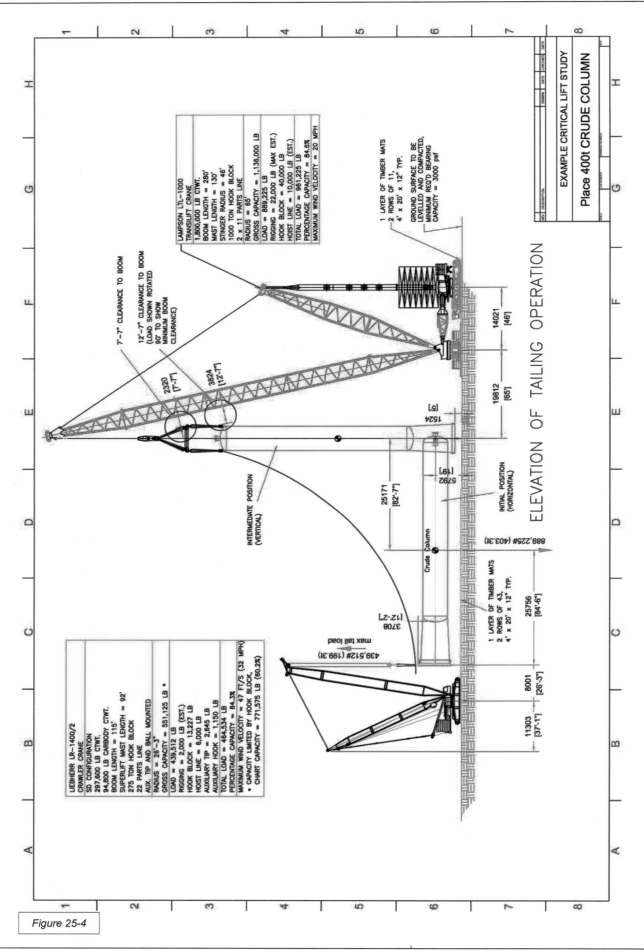

ELEVATION OF TAILING OPERATION

Figure 25-4

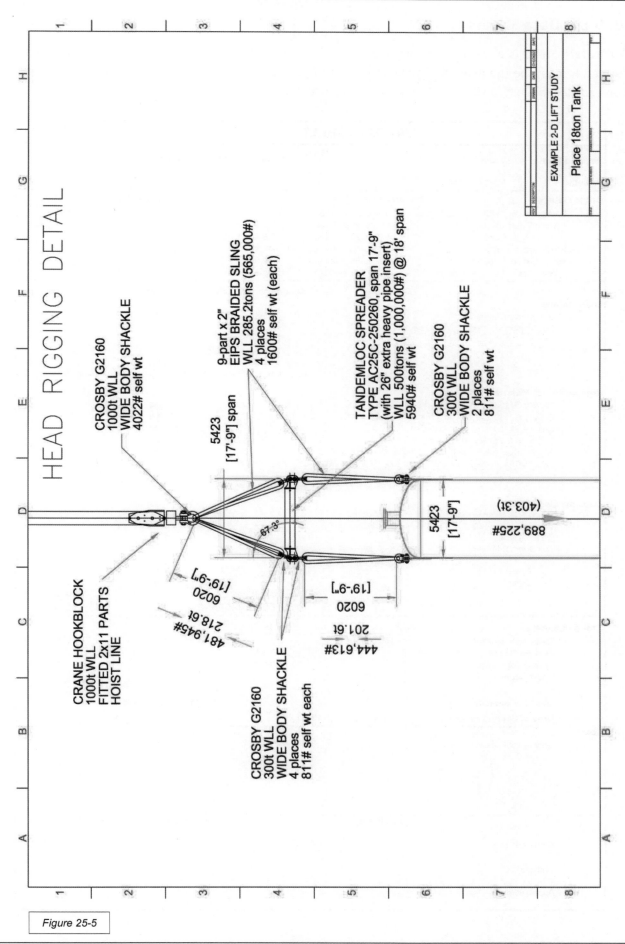

HEAD RIGGING DETAIL

CRANE HOOKBLOCK
1000t WLL
FITTED 2x11 PARTS
HOIST LINE

CROSBY G2160
1000t WLL
WIDE BODY SHACKLE
4022# self wt

9-part x 2"
EIPS BRAIDED SLING
WLL 285.2tons (565,000#)
4 places
1600# self wt (each)

TANDEMLOC SPREADER
TYPE AC25C-250260, span 17'-9"
(with 26" extra heavy pipe insert)
WLL 500tons (1,000,000#) @ 18' span
5940# self wt

CROSBY G2160
300t WLL
WIDE BODY SHACKLE
2 places
811# self wt

CROSBY G2160
300t WLL
WIDE BODY SHACKLE
4 places
811# self wt each

5423
[17'-9"] span

67.3°

6020 [19'-9"]
481,945# 218.6t

6020 [19'-9"]
444,613# 201.6t

5423 [17'-9"]
889,225# (403.3t)

EXAMPLE 2-D LIFT STUDY
Place 18ton Tank

Figure 25-5

## 25.5 Lift Data Sheets

A Lift Data Sheet is a means of summarizing the essentials of a lifting operation on one page in a standard format. It might <u>be</u> the plan for a medium risk lift or possibly one of the components of a Critical risk lift plan. For a single crane lift, a LDS might look something like this.

Figure 25-6

| LIFT DATA SHEET | | #: 113 |
|---|---|---|

**Payload Name:** Truss T11    **Lift Description:** Installation of Truss T11

**Project:** Power project    **Units:** U.S. (ft - lbs)

**Crane Details**   **Manufacturer:** Demag   **Model No.** CC-2800

| | | |
|---|---|---|
| Configuration: SWSL-Main, Luffer, SL. | Base Mount Type: Crawlers | Track c/s: 27.5 ft |
| Boom Type: Lattice | Length Used: 236.2 ft | Main Boom Angle: 85 degrees |
| Jib Type: Luffing | Jib Length Used: 137.8 ft | |
| Superlift Apparatus: Tray | Superlift Radius: 49 ft | Superlift: 220,500 lbs |
| Machine ballast: 396,828 lbs | Aux counterweight: 0 lbs | Hoist Line Pull: 30,000 lbs |
| Block Cap'y: 400 tons | Line Size: 1.125 in | Parts Line Used: 8 |

**Load Details**

| | Quantity | Wt./each | Weight | Totals |
|---|---|---|---|---|
| Basic weight of item | 1 | 144,427 | 144,427 lbs | |
| (total suspended weight after upending) | | | 0 lbs | |
| | | | 0 lbs | |
| | | | 0 lbs | |
| | | | 0 lbs | |
| Total weight of item to be lifted | | | | 144,427 lbs |

**Rigging Bill of Materials**

| | Quantity | Wt./each | Weight | Totals |
|---|---|---|---|---|
| Crosby G2130 3" bolt anchor shackle 85tons WLL | 2 | 154 | 308 lbs | |
| Crosby G2130 2.5" bolt anchor shackle 55tons WLL | 2 | 98 | 197 lbs | |
| Crosby G2140 3" anchor shackle 120tons WLL | 2 | 178 | 356 lbs | |
| 52ft span Modulift 250 spreader 110ton WLL | 1 | 8,200 | 8,200 lbs | |
| 11' IWRS sling 2.5" dia EIPS, 52.5tons WLL @5:1 SF | 2 | 325 | 650 lbs | |
| 52'-6" LiftAll braided polyester round sling 67.55 tons WLL | 2 | 500 | 1,000 lbs | |
| | | | 0 lbs | |
| Total Rigging Weight | | | | 10,711 lbs |

**Capacity Deductions**

| | | Quantity | Wt./each | Weight | Totals |
|---|---|---|---|---|---|
| Load Block Used to make lift | 400ton | 1 | 22,046 | 22,046 lbs | |
| Wire Rope | qty x wt per length | | | 0 lbs | |
| Optional Block | | 1 | 6,614 | 6,614 lbs | |
| Aux Boom Sheaves | | | | 0 lbs | |
| Jib | | | | 0 lbs | |
| Other | runner | 1 | 2,205 | 2,205 lbs | |
| Other | | | | 0 lbs | |
| Total Deductions: | | | | | 30,865 lbs |
| TOTAL LOAD TO CRANE | | | | | 186,003 lbs |

**Crane capacities**

| | Hoist | Place | |
|---|---|---|---|
| Total load to crane: | 186,003 lbs | 186,003 lbs | lbs |
| Planned Radius: | 85.3 ft | 98.4 ft | ft |
| Chart Radius Used: | 85.3 ft | 98.4 ft | ft |
| Chart Capacity: | 264,600 lbs | 246,960 lbs | lbs |
| | 70.3% | 75.3% | |

**Max % of capacity used:** 75.3%    **% Line Pull Capacity:** 73.8%

**Ground Bearing Pressure:** Actual: 16 ksf    Allowable: 19 ksf

**Notes**

Double hookblock required

| | Name (Print) | Signature | Date |
|---|---|---|---|
| Prepared by: | | | |
| Checked by: | | | |
| Approved by: | | | |

Whatever the format of choice, a Lift Data sheet should specify:

- The crane to be used and it's configuration
- The load details and its weight including any attachments / internals / insulation etc
- The rigging to be used and its self-weight
- The applicable crane capacity deductions

The load, rigging and capacity deductions need to be summed to give the total load to the crane which can then be compared to the capacity of the crane at the various radii at which it will operate. Percentages of crane capacity and of hoisting capacity being used are metrics that an approver will want to review as is the ground bearing pressure being imposed versus the allowable. An area in which you can add a few brief operational notes if required is useful.

This is by no means the only way you could present this type of information; you should come up with something equivalent that does what you need in your particular situation.

As noted above attach any sketches required to explain the intent and include the relevant crane chart extract(s).

For an upending operation that is a "medium lift" you would need to create a version that accommodates the changing head and tail loads and the second (tail) crane; similarly tandem lifts that are not "critical" would require a split sheet that reflects the situation for both cranes.

As a lift requiring a LDS is likely to require documenting and review, it should be planned adequately in advance of the projected lift date. It is possible that the person planning this category of lift will not be one of those executing it so the Lift Data sheet and its attachments should therefore be sufficient to communicate the intent of the Lift Planner to those executing the work.

## 25.6 Communicating the plan

The importance of communicating the plan whether it is verbal or written cannot be over-emphasized. After all, having a plan isn't any good if you don't tell people what it is and enforce it. How often do you see a paper exercise that is the plan completely divorced from what is going on in the field? You need to communicate the plan to those who are going to execute the lifting operation in the field and you need to ensure the plan is followed.

# 26 Preparing a lift plan

## 26.1 Investigating options

Once you fully understand the task and are as informed as you can be, you are going to want to investigate your options and plan your lift.

The things you need to fix on include:

- The technique(s) to be used.
- The location of the load at the start of the lift.
- The location of the crane(s) throughout the operation.
- The required configurations of the crane(s).
- The movements of the crane(s) and load.
- The radii of the crane(s).
- Slinging arrangements.
- Loads imposed and matting arrangements.
- Critical clearances.

So the first phase is investigative, how might I best do this?

Lift planning is often iterative; you have a number of options, you check out the implications of each, go round in circles a bit and then home in on what works best. There may be practical and/or commercial restrictions placed on you; for instance you may have only certain cranes readily available to you. You might check out tandem lifting versus single crane lifting; a longer boom may let you get closer and so on. You might find that your first great idea is supplanted by your second even greater idea – take some time to think it through properly.

There are a number of tools available to help you with this investigative phase.

It might be that a crane chart, piece of paper, pencil and maybe range diagram are all you need, however there are now software applications that can help with crane selection and lift planning.

There are applications that will:

- Search databases and suggest suitable crane and crane configuration options.
- Figure out crane loadings and matting arrangements.
- Verify clearances.
- Help figure out slinging arrangements.
- Print out lift data, ground bearing information and slinging arrangements.

Many of these crane selection tools will be integrated with graphics packages or CAD programs to produce 2-D or 3-D graphical representations or working drawings of your lift, from simple block and stick representations to highly sophisticated CAD drawings. Using one of these programs can greatly speed up the selection process against thumbing through crane charts and can produce something quickly that can be sent to a client with a proposal, used to explain a plan or even be used in the field for construction.

## 26.2 Lift planning software

As noted, there are a number of software tools for lift planning available to you. They vary to some degree in their intended scope of application. Some are simple aids to selecting cranes and documenting the basics of a lift that can be used by anyone, others are more sophisticated graphic based packages that require some skill to use, others are CAD based aimed at selection followed by production of high end construction drawings. The following is a brief over view of the lift planning applications that are currently available and their features. This review is a moving target as these products are constantly evolving.

### 26.2.1  Compu-Crane & Rigging Pro

Compu-Crane

Compu-Crane is a software tool intended for industrial lift planning <u>and crane selection</u>; it is owned and distributed by Manitowoc and is offered free of charge to all affiliates of Manitowoc. The standard version includes current Grove models with a capacity over 60 US tons (50 metric tonnes) and current Manitowoc cranes with a capacity of 120 US tons (100 tonnes) and above.

With Compu-Crane, you can:

- Plan lifts and select crane(s)
- Automatically generate lists of appropriate cranes and configurations
- Generate crane specs, load charts and site views
- Detect potential collisions for boom, jib, and tail swing

The software:

- Allows rotation of carrier to any relative load position
- Has dimensioning to identify objects and obstructions
- Displays rear obstacles
- Allows you to see the lift before you start the job

Also available (currently for GMK cranes only) is an outrigger pad load estimator.

This program requires no drafting skills or expensive CAD packages and can be operated by any lift planner with basic computer skills.

Advantages are:

- Ease of use
- Price
- The ability to sort quickly through current Manitowoc  models to identify suitable cranes and configurations
- No need for paper charts for capacities
- A clear cut uncluttered, easy to read output with all the basic information you need on a single sheet

Disadvantages are:

- It is really only best suited to relatively simple lifting operations (for which it is good), more complex operations will require a more sophisticated tool, but Compu-Crane could help you hone in on a suitable crane in the first place.
- Having decided on a crane, you still need to know what the required deductions and self-weight of hook-blocks etc are.
- It is currently geared only to cranes that the Manitowoc group makes.

<u>My</u> opinion is that this is a fairly basic, easy to use tool suited to simpler lifts, bids, presentations and the like. For actually conducting a more complex lift or using some of the larger cranes, you would probably need to use a more sophisticated program to properly address the challenges the lift presents.

The two sample sheets following are indicative of the type of output you get from Compu-Crane.

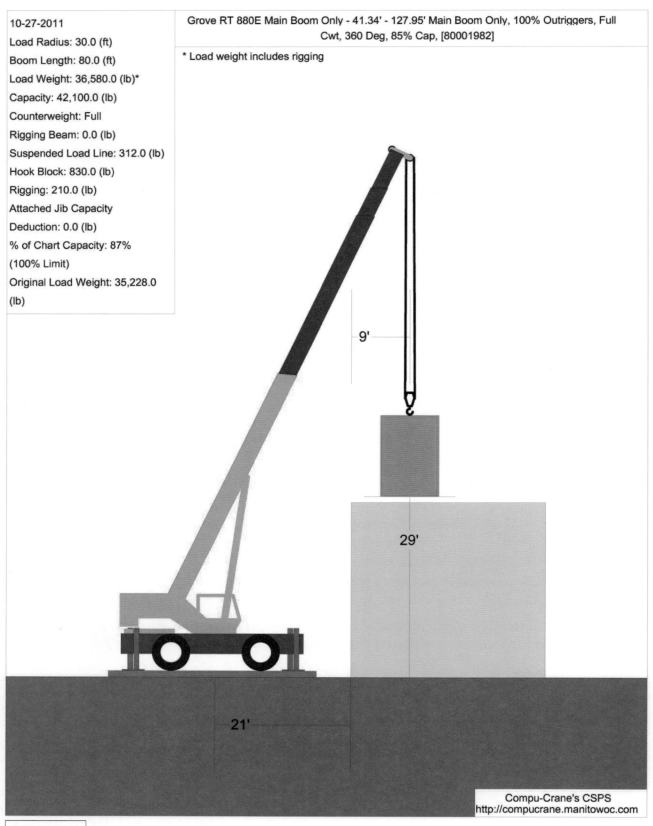

10-27-2011
Load Radius: 30.0 (ft)
Boom Length: 80.0 (ft)
Load Weight: 36,580.0 (lb)*
Capacity: 42,100.0 (lb)
Counterweight: Full
Rigging Beam: 0.0 (lb)
Suspended Load Line: 312.0 (lb)
Hook Block: 830.0 (lb)
Rigging: 210.0 (lb)
Attached Jib Capacity
Deduction: 0.0 (lb)
% of Chart Capacity: 87%
(100% Limit)
Original Load Weight: 35,228.0
(lb)

Grove RT 880E Main Boom Only - 41.34' - 127.95' Main Boom Only, 100% Outriggers, Full Cwt, 360 Deg, 85% Cap, [80001982]

* Load weight includes rigging

9'

29'

21'

Compu-Crane's CSPS
http://compucrane.manitowoc.com

Figure 26-1

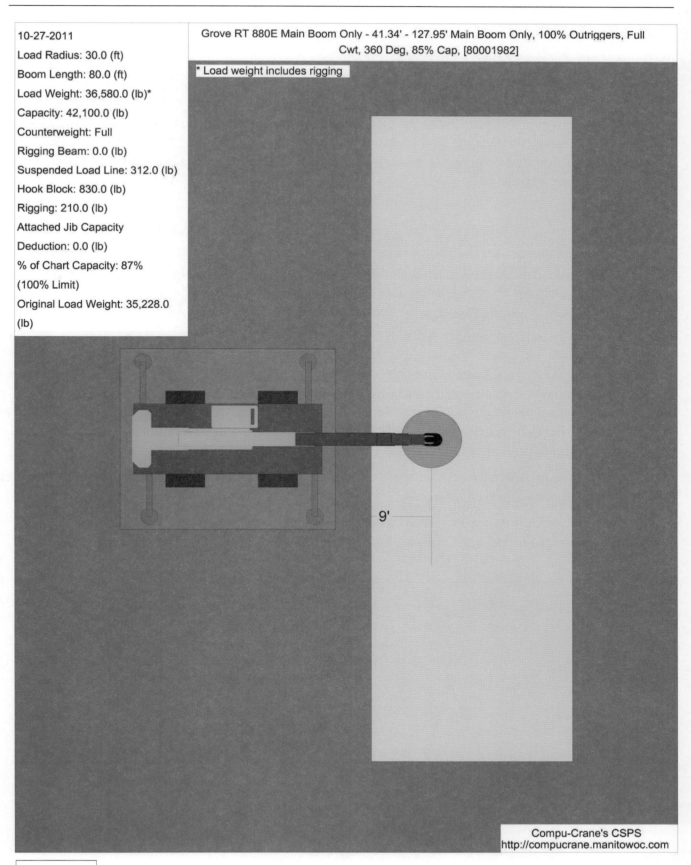

10-27-2011

Load Radius: 30.0 (ft)

Boom Length: 80.0 (ft)

Load Weight: 36,580.0 (lb)*

Capacity: 42,100.0 (lb)

Counterweight: Full

Rigging Beam: 0.0 (lb)

Suspended Load Line: 312.0 (lb)

Hook Block: 830.0 (lb)

Rigging: 210.0 (lb)

Attached Jib Capacity

Deduction: 0.0 (lb)

% of Chart Capacity: 87%

(100% Limit)

Original Load Weight: 35,228.0

(lb)

Grove RT 880E Main Boom Only - 41.34' - 127.95' Main Boom Only, 100% Outriggers, Full Cwt, 360 Deg, 85% Cap, [80001982]

* Load weight includes rigging

9'

Compu-Crane's CSPS
http://compucrane.manitowoc.com

Figure 26-2

Rigging Pro

If your slinging arrangement is more complex, there is another tool available to assist you. Rigging Pro is a suite of three rigging design programs that integrate with Compu-Crane; it is owned and distributed by SkyAzul Equipment Solutions.

A 3D design program lets you specify the load and hitch type, gives you tensions on each of the slings, and checks to see which hardware in your inventory can handle the load. In the 2D SketchPad program you can quickly create a professional rigging drawing for any rigging situation, complete with title block, text, and detailed rigging components.

The program:

- Automatically develops sling model and applies sling and hardware properties
- Structurally analyzes each element and provides quick confirmation through a color-coded 3D image
- Define load dimensions, hitch type and add hardware such as collector rings, shackles and fittings to the rigging plan through a simple user interface
- Customized inventory manager
- Provides accurate detailed working drawings of the load and rigging with specifications and bill of materials

If you specify the load parameters and hitch type, Rigging Pro can calculate the center of gravity of the load and sling tensions and display your rigging assembly in 3D. The load can be viewed from all sides; you can experiment with different rigging components and ensure that your hardware will do the job. Rigging Pro automatically develops the rigging model, calculates loads and evaluates capacities and will alert you to potentially hazardous situations.

Components can be selected from a database of Crosby® hardware or you can enter hardware and fabrications into a customized inventory for reference.

Rigging Pro lets you create accurate drawings of the load and rigging, allowing you to effectively communicate your plan to accomplish the rigging task to those in the field. The sort of output you get is shown below.

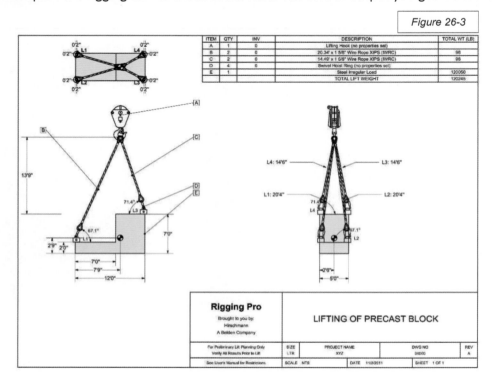

Figure 26-3

### 26.2.2  3D Lift Plan by A1A Software

3D Lift Plan is a graphics based crane selection and lift planning application in similar mode to Compu-Crane but is considerably more developed and has many more advanced features; it does not require a CAD program or CAD expertise. 3D Lift Plan provides true 3D lift planning, crane selection and rigging design; it claims to be user-friendly and easy-to navigate with step-by-step design making it easy enough for a novice to use. I'd say the novice would need to be relatively computer-savvy and crane-knowledgeable to get the best out of it.

The program is not installed on your computer but is run on-line through your web browser. As a corporate user, you basically purchase a number of "seats" with the right to run the program for a period of time. This has the advantages that you are always running the latest version and don't need to support or update it; however it does require you to have fast web access and be on line. Lift plans you create are stored on the 3D Lift Plan server.

3D Lift Plan is not restricted to any specific manufacturer and currently has a large library of cranes of over 700 cranes available on its server. Link-Belt sponsors all of their cranes so they are free of charge to use as are current production Terex cranes. The use of other cranes such as Kobelco, Manitowoc, Terex, Tadano, Liebherr, and others is purchased for a period of time and you can quickly add other available cranes to your "fleet" as required.

The program features:

- Advanced Crane Selection
- Ground Bearing Pressure calculation
- Crane Mat Calculator
- Critical Lift Worksheet
- Sling Tension and Dimension Calculator
- Advanced Rigging Designs

and it has the ability to:

- Plan Multiple Crane Lifts
- Export to CAD
- Use Multiple Parts of Line
- Calculate the area needed to assemble the Crane
- Display images of your jobsite

Using the program you can:

- Build 3D jobsites and loads.
- Create detailed rigging designs with hooks, shackles, slings, and more.
- Determine sling lengths, heights, and angles.
- Simulate your lift while monitoring the crane's capacity.
- View the lift in 3D from any angle.
- Account for obstructions on your jobsite using the powerful crane selection algorithm.
- Plan your lift with multiple cranes and equipment including tower cranes, mobile cranes, aerial lifts and more.
- Handle tandem lifts, tailing operations, and three-crane lifts.
- Export jobsites for use in CAD programs.
- Develop and print multiple views of your lift plan and rigging designs in 3D.

The following "snapshots" are examples of the sort of outputs you can develop with 3D Lift Plan.

Figure 26-4

Figure 26-5

Figure 26-6

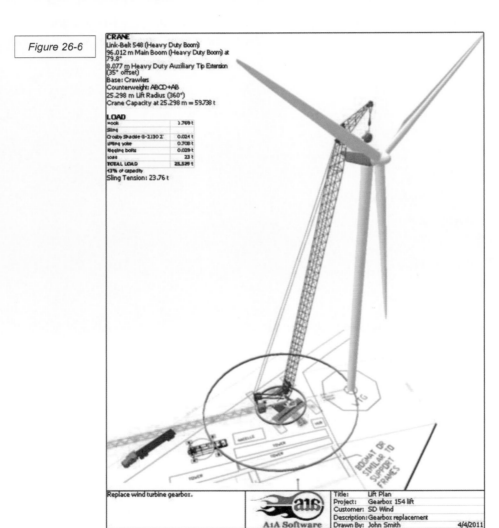

CRANE
Link-Belt 548 (Heavy Duty Boom)
96.012 m Main Boom (Heavy Duty Boom) at 79.8°
8.077 m Heavy Duty Auxiliary Tip Extension (35° offset)
Base: Crawlers
Counterweight: ABCD+AB
25.298 m Lift Radius (360°)
Crane Capacity at 25.298 m = 59.738 t

| LOAD | |
|---|---|
| Hook | 1.769 t |
| Sling | |
| Crosby Shackle G-2130 2' | 0.024 t |
| Lifting yoke | 0.708 t |
| Rigging bolts | 0.029 t |
| Load | 23 t |
| TOTAL LOAD | 25.529 t |
| 43% of capacity | |

Sling Tension: 23.76 t

Replace wind turbine gearbox.

| Title: | Lift Plan |
|---|---|
| Project: | Gearbox 154 lift |
| Customer: | SD Wind |
| Description: | Gearbox replacement |
| Drawn By: | John Smith  4/4/2011 |

A1A Software

In my opinion, this program is strong graphically; it is more sophisticated than you may require for the simplest jobs and the more complex jobs might be done more easily and better with a 3-D CAD package. As noted, you would need to be fairly computer literate to get the best out of this package.

### 26.2.3 KranXpert

KranXpert is another graphics based lift planning program. It falls somewhere between Compucrane and 3-D Lift Plan in terms of sophistication and capabilities; it exists in 3 forms, the full version, a free version and a pocket PC version; as with other graphics based programs, it does not run on a CAD platform or require you to have CAD expertise.

The program is capable of producing 2-D plan and elevation views and generating 3-D isometric "images".

You commence by selecting a crane from your "fleet" using a drop-down menu, it won't suggest suitable options. There is a fairly extensive range of cranes available in the database, notably many Liebherr, Terex-Demag and Tadano products; alternatively you can create your own using kranFileEditor. Originating in Germany, this program has more metric cranes than imperial. The crane can then be manipulated for boom length, radius etc. The crane graphics are fairly basic but plenty adequate.

Using the drawing tools, you can create your payload and size it.

You can then create your virtual lifting environment using the 2-D and 3-D drawing tools provided; alternatively you can import existing satellite images or site plans, scale them and use them as your background to plan over.

If you wish, you can add more cranes.

Everything you need to do is driven from one page and is easy to navigate with buttons and drop down menus. The program is fairly intuitive.

The welcome page looks like this.

Figure 26-7

The planner windows with load grid look like this.

Figure 26-8

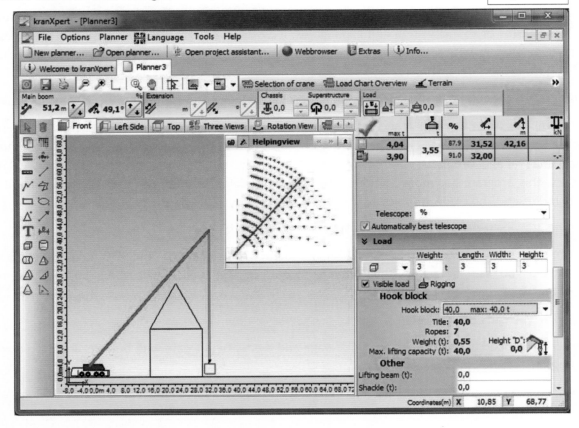

Your terrain options screen looks like this. You have style options and can scale your selection.

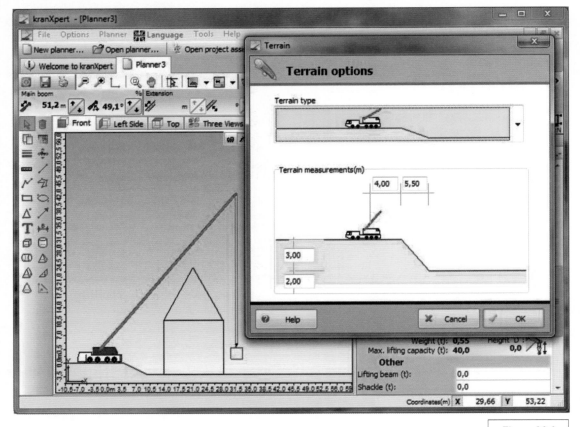

Figure 26-9

The plan view with range diagram and crane details might look something like this. Note you can click between the two cranes in the plan.

Figure 26-10

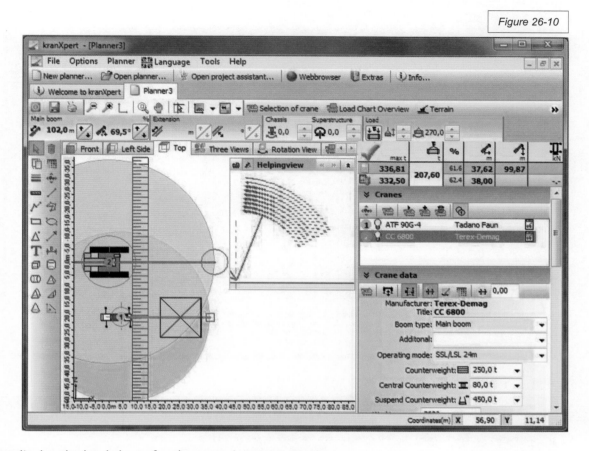

You can display the load charts for the crane in use at any time.

Figure 26-11

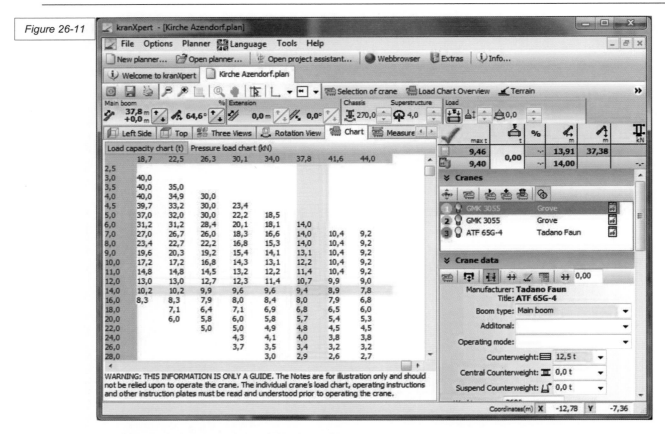

The "3 views" option gives you a result such as this.

Figure 26-12

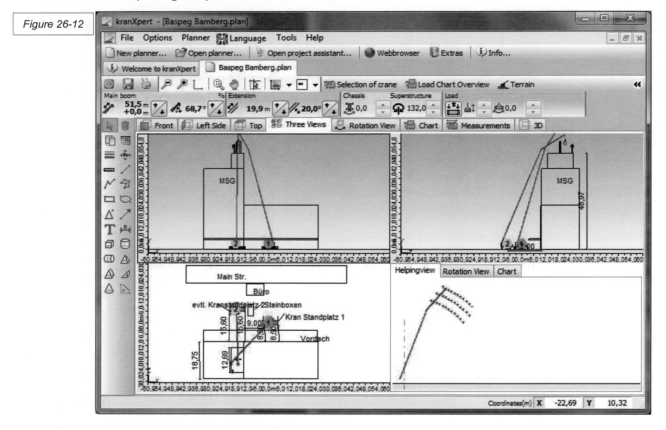

The 3-D view you can produce looks something like this. Wire frame and solid options are available.

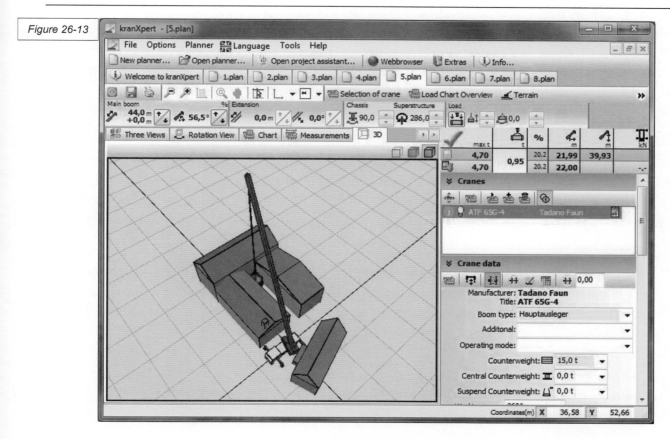

Figure 26-13

Basic rigging can be designed; the rigging screen might look something like this.

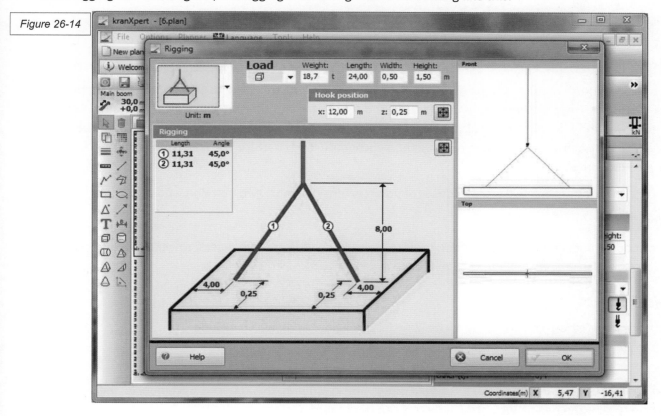

Figure 26-14

This program may not offer as many features as others or be as sophisticated as some graphics based programs, but it is simpler to use; it doesn't seek to do what is better done with a CAD based program and fills a middle ground in lift planning software very well.

### 26.2.4 LiftPlanner

LiftPlanner is a 3-D Crane and Rigging lift planning system that runs inside AutoCAD©. It is a customization of Autocad with routines created to automate many of the processes necessary to produce a 3-D lift study. It looks and feels like AutoCAD, just with custom drop down menus. You need to be proficient in using 3-D AutoCAD to use LiftPlanner.

<u>Environment</u>

You firstly need to create your 3-D lift environment. That may already exist in the form of an AutoCAD compatible CAD "model" of the environment or a file created from a laser scan "cloud" or a 2-D plan drawing that is extruded vertically in the areas of interest, or you may simply draw it. LiftPlanner includes programs to assist in generating the lift environment including libraries of standard steel profiles, piping and so on.

<u>Lift equipment</u>

LiftPlanner includes an extensive library of cranes, gantries and platform trailers. Using the drop down menus you select and place the basic crane within your drawing. The program does not feature a sort routine to offer you up a list of cranes having the required capacity. Once in the drawing LiftPlanner has routines that allow you to:

- Configure the crane
- Move the crane
- Swing
- Set the hook elevation
- Boom up or down
- Telescope
- Add or change jib
- Change jib angle

and provides gross capacity

As you configure the crane, you are prompted to input known or trial data such as boom length, radius and hook elevation. The program automatically returns boom angle and tip sheave height to the user. Conversely you can snap the hook to a particular point and the program will adjust all the crane movements accordingly and advise you. At any time you can retrieve the appropriate load chart for the crane configuration and input it into your drawing.

LiftProgram monitors and will warn the user of boom extension limits, two blocking, and angle limitations.

<u>Payload</u>

Having got a crane, LiftPlanner offers you tools to help create vessels, exchangers, towers and other objects in 3-D and to add trunnions or lift lugs.

<u>Rigging</u>

Another useful feature of LiftPlanner is the libraries of rigging tackle which include:

- 275 pre-built slings with weight and rating data attached.
- Shackles from 6 tons through 700 tons with weight and rating data.

There is also a program that inserts skewed slings and calculates the reduced SWL due to the angle and a program to sum the rigging weights. Lift beams can be created.

All the standard features of AutoCAD are available, so the look and feel of the drawings you produce, the views you produce and the level of information included are very much down to you, LiftPlanner just facilitates production.

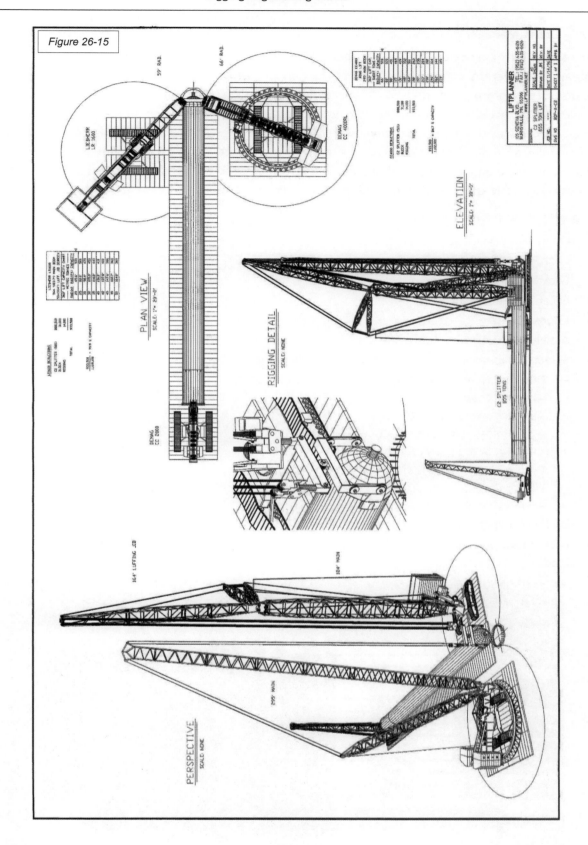

Figure 26-15

## Lift Movie

Lift Movie is a 3-D Crane and Rigging lift simulation system that works in tandem with LiftPlanner. It is used to prepare realistic animations for client presentation or for briefing of the crew prior to the lift. Lift Movie includes software for rendering and animation.

### 26.2.5 Crane Manager by Cranimax

Cranimax of Germany offers Crane Manager, a 2-part lift planning software program. The first application contains all the crane charts and allows calculation of outrigger loadings and mat pressures using actual manufacturer's information; the second application is a graphics program that runs in a CAD environment to produce CAD drawings of your lift. The data application is always running behind the graphics package to verify crane capacities as the cranes are manipulated in the drawing. Multi-crane lifts are possible. There are also CAD modules to facilitate the creation of the lifting environment and to design your rigging arrangement. Both contain libraries of standard pre-defined items that can be used to speed the process. (I believe the graphics side was previously known as Cranimation and was originally developed for Demag cranes).

The process is somewhat like this;

- Open Crane Manager Explorer Page
- Click Projects > Create a new project
- Click Crane selection
- Enter Job Information
- Choose Units
- Assign a CAD drawing (optional)
- Select a crane from list, you have filter options including,
    - Min radius, min hook height, min boom extension
    - Min chart capacity
    - Allow crawlers / outriggers
    - Allow telescopic boom / lattice booms
- You can switch to graphical mode and
    - Define obstructions, adjust the crane configuration
    - Filter to exclude certain boom / jib configurations
    - Enter parameters (weight rad boom tip) and search
- Crane Manager will offer up options that work
- Click on the one you want and it brings up the crane characteristics, load chart, configuration, outrigger loads.

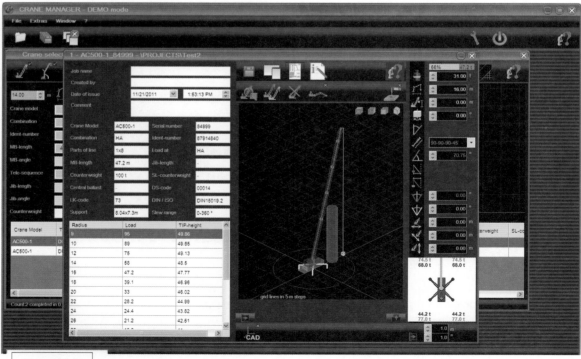

Figure 26-16

You can add mats, change the views to show 2-D plan and or elevations or a 3-D representation and can change the configuration using Liebherr-like icons, change the xyz of the crane, rotate it, swing the upper works. The crane chart and data will adjust according to the changes you make.

Once satisfied, print results that look somewhat like this:

Figure 26-17

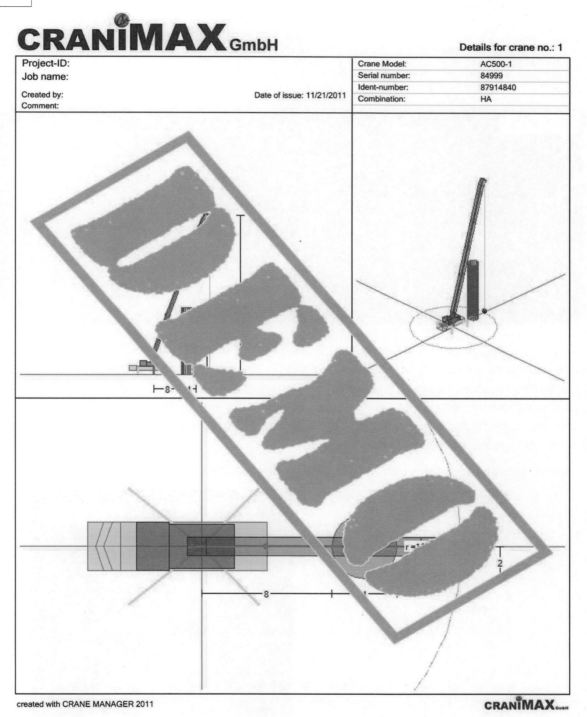

This might be enough for what you are doing. However using CAD, you can take it to the next level.

On the Crane Manager screen, you can activate or deactivate the CAD connection. If activated, you have the option to relocate the crane, change the radius and/or add rigging to the CAD drawing from within the Crane Manager.

Within your CAD package (such as AutoCAD), you have Crane Manager tools available which allow you to:

- Work with multi-cranes
- Build obstacles
- Define Rigging Hook and Load from standards (or use your own)

The following graphics are the sort of result you can produce from the Crane Manager 2011 (graphics) package.

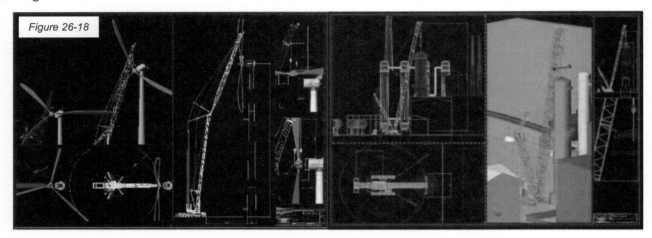

Figure 26-18

Cranimax also offers ToM Tower Manager, which is for the graphical representation of tower cranes in an 3D environment such as AutoCAD® or BricsCad®. With ToM you select the specific crane from the database at the program start and then assign it to an actual project. All cranes can be manipulated in 3-D using the control menu. The 3D functionality of the CAD-systems enables the creation of a virtual worksite with a realistic, true to scale representation of the cranes and allows for collision detection. Selected views as required can be produced and documented in a scaled drawing.

The following graphic is the sort of result you can produce with ToM.

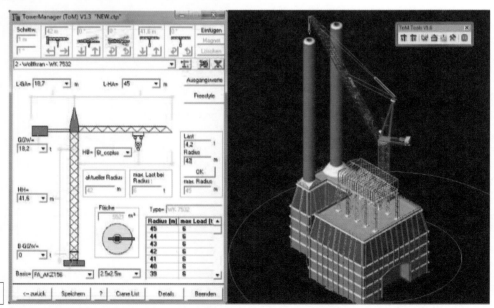

Figure 26-19

As with Crane Manager, there are modules that can be integrated into your CAD system:

- – MCC - Multi Crane Control for layer control for the final plotting
- – OBB - Obstacle Builder for creating your scale 3-D virtual environment
- – RHL - Rigging, Hook and Load to create complex three-dimensional load cases
- – REC - Rope Equipment Creator for the creation of your own lifting accessories.

Both OBB and RHL include a library of pre-defined shapes and components which speeds the creation of your projects (see following).

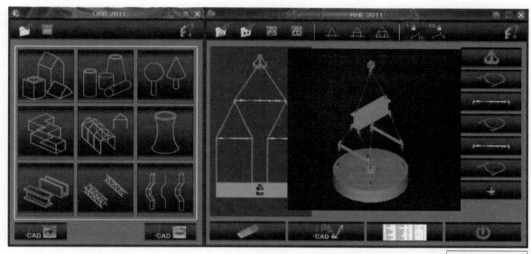

Figure 26-20

Crane Manager can:

- – Help you select cranes
- – Quickly produce a graphic representation of your lift and calculate ground loadings and matting arrangements
- – Use the data package as a front end to a CAD package to automate and speed up the production of 3-D CAD drawings.

The quality of the result is limited only by your CAD proficiency and the CAD package used. You do need to be CAD proficient to use the CAD graphics well.

### 26.2.6  CAD packages

The industry CAD package of choice when it comes to lift planning is AutoCAD®.

For planning purposes, you need the crane (or other lifting / moving machinery) in the form of drawing blocks representing the various major sub-assemblies that move relative to each other during lifting in order to be able to readily manipulate them in your drawing simulating real world use. Some of those drawing blocks may themselves be built up from blocks representing the major components of that sub-assembly e.g. a long boom is built from a number of standard inserts, a root and a head section; each of the components is a block and the assembly is blocked to allow you to move the boom as one items. Ideally, you want the blocks detailed enough for the purpose and not unnecessarily over-detailed; in earlier years, when drawing was almost exclusively 2-D, blocks would be produced for plans and standard elevations, now you are more likely to produce a single block in 3-D. Insertion points should be chosen at a standard reference point about which the block rotates and/or where it mates to another assembly.

To date crane manufacturers have not been very forthcoming in providing CAD drawings of their cranes to the end users who have to plan for their use, at least not in a ready-to-use 3-D "blocked" form suitable for lift planning. So that task of creating drawing blocks has generally fallen to the crane companies or those producing lift planning software as described above. Doing it yourself may be a viable option if you have the information, keep it relatively simple and are likely to use it repeatedly; otherwise you might be better going another route.

Regarding the environment in which you are lifting, you may be able to use an existing 3-D CAD model of the (say) plant in which you are working as an environment or use parts of 2-D CAD drawings for a 2-D lift study. Site plans are often produced using Bentley MicroStation; bringing them in to AutoCAD doesn't always work too well – the converted file often has numerous layers and consists of polylines requiring quite a lot of cleaning up to use; that be almost as much work sometimes as drawing the areas you are interested in from scratch.

Other options include using a 3-D electronic site survey with software that works with the site survey equipment to generate a very accurate "as-built" 3-D representation that will link with AutoCAD® Civil 3D® software. Check out the Leica, Trimble and Bentley MicroStation web sites for more information.

Further options include using satellite images as a 2-D background for your drawing.

Failing all those options, you can draw the portion of the environment you are interested in from scratch from paper or electronic site plans.

The load itself you need to create as a drawing block or blocks.

Some manufacturers such as Crosby make drawing blocks of their rigging freely available; other items you may have to create as blocks. You are then pretty much ready to go.

The following 3 views are indicative of the sort of drawings you might produce in 2-D AutoCAD® for the simple placement of an 18ton tank onto a raised foundation using a Grove RT crane. Subject to you adding ground bearing information this would give you all you needed to know to execute that operation. Compare this to the somewhat similar earlier Compucrane example, which would give you enough information to confirm that the crane could make the lift but could leave you a little short on information to make the lift. What you use all depends on what you intend the lift study for, what tools you have available to you and the skills of the personnel involved.

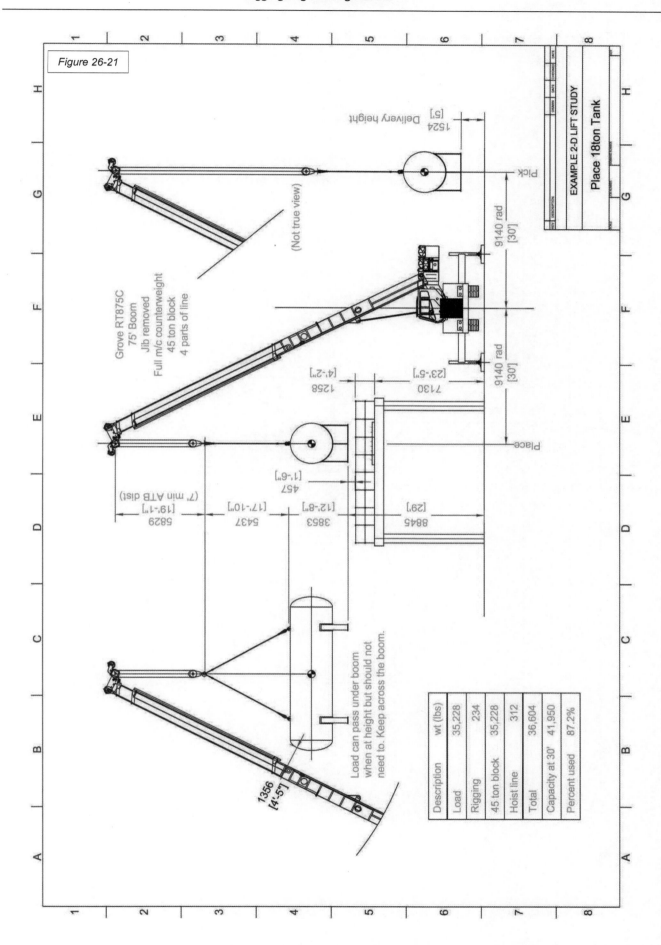

Figure 26-21

(Not true view)

Grove RT875C
75' Boom
Jib removed
Full m/c counterweight
45 ton block
4 parts of line

Load can pass under boom
when at height but should not
need to. Keep across the boom.

Delivery height
1524 [5']

9140 rad [30']

Pick

9140 rad [30']

7130 [23'-5"]

1258 [4'-2"]

Place

5829 [19'-1"] (7' min ATB dist)

5437 [17'-10"]

3853 [12'-8"]

8845 [29']

457 [1'-6"]

1356 [4'-5"]

EXAMPLE 2-D LIFT STUDY

Place 18ton Tank

| Description | wt (lbs) |
|---|---|
| Load | 35,228 |
| Rigging | 234 |
| 45 ton block | 35,228 |
| Hoist line | 312 |
| Total | 36,604 |
| Capacity at 30' | 41,950 |
| Percent used | 87.2% |

Figure 26-22

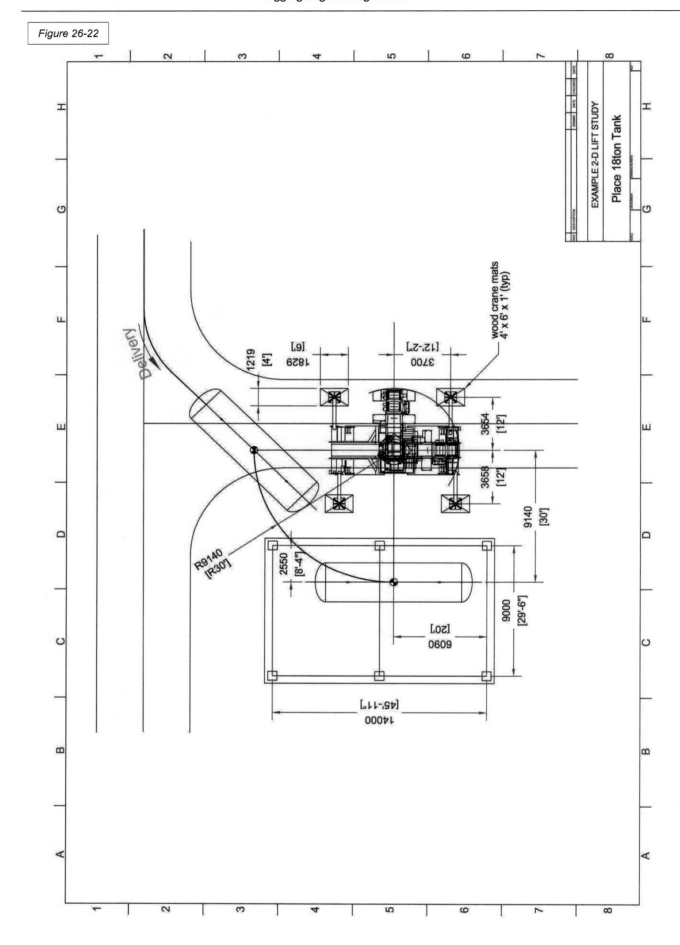

Figure 26-23

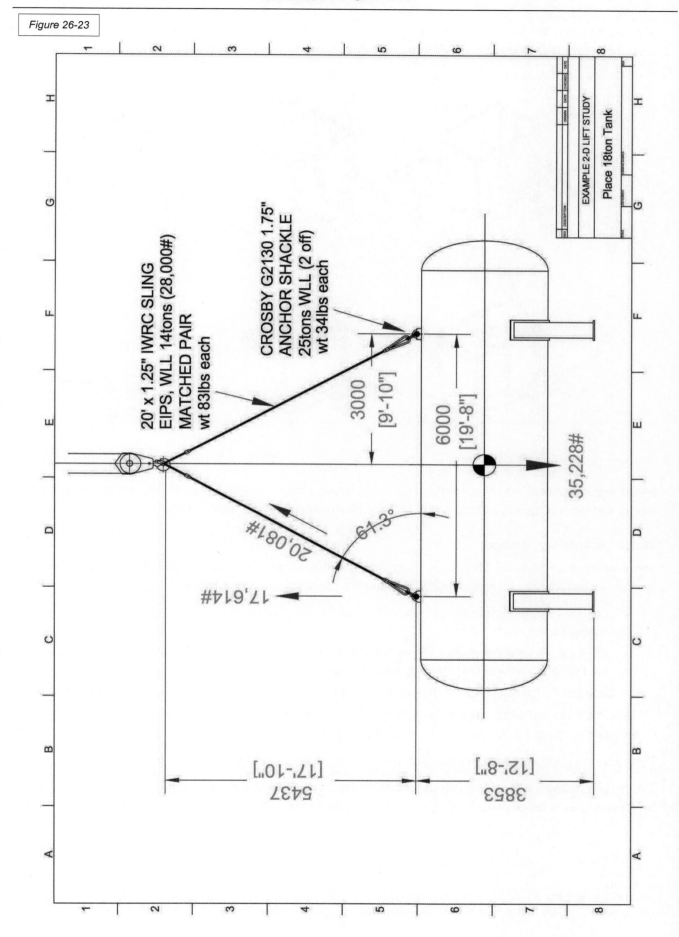

20' x 1.25" IWRC SLING EIPS, WLL 14tons (28,000#) MATCHED PAIR wt 83lbs each

CROSBY G2130 1.75" ANCHOR SHACKLE 25tons WLL (2 off) wt 34lbs each

3000 [9'-10"]

6000 [19'-8"]

35,228#

20,081#

61.3°

17,614#

5437 [17'-10"]

3853 [12'-8"]

EXAMPLE 2-D LIFT STUDY

Place 18ton Tank

3-D drafting can be useful to explain your intent; the below for instance illustrates the intended lifting sequence of the 2-D study above. For more complex lifts (unlike this one), this can be worthwhile.

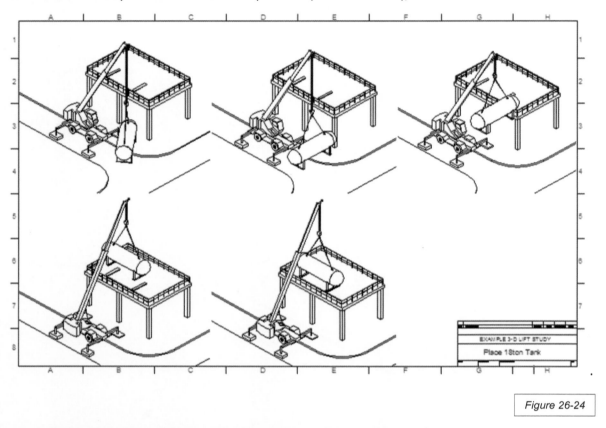

Figure 26-24

If you require photo quality renderings for say a presentation, you would start with more detailed drawing blocks and use a program such as 3D Studio Max. The results can be almost life-like.

### 26.2.7 Proprietary packages

Some companies such as Mammoet have developed their own software packages to assist them in the production of lift studies. Mammoet's Autocrane is a crane selection tool that will:

- Search a filtered database of cranes to allow the lift planner to select an appropriate crane and crane configuration
- Produce a single sheet that contains the essentials of the lift including graphical plan and elevation, load details, crane details, outrigger loads and mat pressures.
- Integrate with AutoCAD® to export the crane in the selected configuration into a 3-D CAD drawing.

The graphical side includes basic drawing tools. On the CAD side, the crane can be manipulated with AutoCAD or returned to the graphical package for reconfiguration if you want to change something.

This tool is only internal to Mammoet but its inclusion herein illustrates what is possible.

The graphic following is the sort of output Mammoet can produce in the graphics side. It allows a non-CAD draftsman to very quickly check what works and produce something for illustration and discussion.

Figure 26-25

Worldwide specialists in heavy lifting and transport

## MAMMOET

**RT875**

| | | |
|---|---|---|
| Client | SAP Nr. | Page  1/1 |
| Project | Doc. Nr.  N/A | Date  17/11/2011 |
| Subject  Max GBP | Ref. | Rev.  00 |

**Crane configuration:**

Make: *Grove*
Type: *RT875*
Selected chart: *SH*

Boomlength: *78.0*
Carrier: *24ft Front*
Ballast: *14,000*

Upper rotation: *-46.7*
Lift height: *49.2*

Lift radius: *30.0*
Lift capacity: *42,800*

**Elevation**

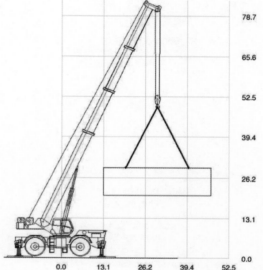

**Load configuration:**

Title: *Lift*
Load name: *Tank*
:
Load: *35,200*
Hook block: *1,900*
Auxiliary: *0*
Rigging: *200*

Total: *37,400*
Percentage[%]: *87.5*

**Plan view**

11,800        29,300

31,100        77,100

**Ground bearing pressures:**

Mat height: *0.4*
Mat length: *7.9*
Mat width: *3.1*

Max. GBP under mats: *3,109*

*Measurements in Feet, Weights & Capacities in Lbs, GBP in Psf*

*AutoCRANE version 1.18.4.240 Datasheet version: 28/06/2011*

Figure 26-26

*Worldwide specialists in heavy lifting and transport*

# MAMMOET

## RT875

| | | |
|---|---|---|
| Client | SAP Nr. | Page 1/1 |
| Project | Doc. Nr. N/A | Date 17/11/2011 |
| Subject Max GBP | Ref. | Rev. 00 |

**Elevation**

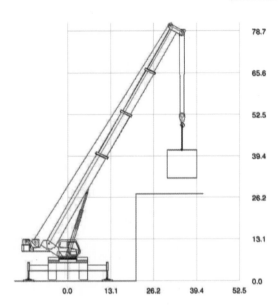

**Crane configuration:**

Make: *Grove*
Type: *RT875*
Selected chart: *SH*

Boomlength: *78.0*
Carrier: *24ft Front*
Ballast: *14,000.0*

Upper rotation: *-46.7*
Lift height: *49.2*

Lift radius: *34.9*
Lift capacity: *37,400.0*

**Plan view**

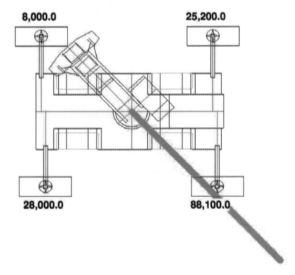

**Load configuration:**

Title: *Lift*
Load name: *Tank*
:
Load: *35,200.0*
Hook block: *1,900.0*
Auxiliary: *0.0*
Rigging: *200.0*

Total: *37,400.0*
Percentage[%]: *100*

**Ground bearing pressures:**

Mat height: *0.4*
Mat length: *7.9*
Mat width: *3.1*

Max. GBP under mats: *3,552*

*Measurements in Feet, Weights & Capacities in Lbs, GBP in Psf*

*AutoCRANE version 1.18.4.240 Datasheet version: 28/06/2011*

## 26.3 What software do I use?

As you can see you have options, no one of them is the universal tool. You need to consider what suits you best in your situation; whether it is outrigger loads / ground bearing pressures you want to calculate, whether it is crane selection that is important, whether you just want to check something out, whether you want construction drawings or something to present to a client, whether animation is required, what cranes you will be working with, who is going to use the software and many more considerations.

Regarding lift studies, before you produce a lift study, you need to consider its purpose. Producing a drawing that overwhelms you with a whole lot of unnecessary information is wasteful of time and effort and is as bad in its own way as a drawing that doesn't give you the information you need. Similarly a beautiful 3D "picture" may look great and be good for explaining a concept but be no use to the guy in the field who has to do the work.

So firstly, decide the purpose, it may be:

- To investigate options
- To check boom clearances, operating radii
- To verify a crane will "fit"
- To accompany a bid to illustrate general intent
- For presentation purposes to a non-technical audience
- For actual execution in the field, say as part of a critical lift plan

The purpose of your lift study will determine the whether you require to produce a nicely rendered "picture", a sophisticated 3D animation, a simple hand sketch, a graphic output or a full-blown CAD study for construction. When it comes to lift planning, you have a number of options ranging from a simple paper and pencil line drawing or acetate overlays (over plot plans), through various proprietary lift planning software programs of differing sophistication through to use of computer drafting programs of varying complexity. There is no one universal lift-planning option that is appropriate to all situations, some will suit your purpose better than others; you might use any or all of the above methods at different times depending on what you want to do.

# 27 "Abnormal" transportation using modular trailers

## 27.1 Introduction

Closely allied to "abnormal" lifting operations are "abnormal" transportation operations. Both would be considered "load handling activities" per ASME P30.1 parlance and there is often an interface between them.

"Abnormal" transportation could be considered any non-routine engineered movement of a load by means of equipment and techniques such as skidding, crawler transporters, custom wheeled transporters, air/water/grease skates, forklifts, roller skates, wheeled dollies, low-boys, hovercraft, barges, ships of many varieties, helicopters, planes, dirigibles, Schnabel type railcars and so on. However, useful as it is to know something of some or all these options, the majority of abnormal transportation operations encountered in construction or heavy engineering are conducted using modular hydraulic trailers; rigging engineers and those planning load handling activities should, as a minimum have some basic knowledge of this type of equipment.

Accordingly, this section will be devoted to an overview of (standard range) modular trailers and self-propelled modular transporters (SPMTs) as used to move "abnormal" loads, particularly on construction sites and other private facilities.

Even when discussions of abnormal transport are restricted to this narrow window, it is still a very large topic and it is my intent simply to briefly discuss the types of equipment available, their operating characteristics and some important things to watch out for when thinking of making use of them. For the detail, I commend you to Marco van Daal's excellent book "The Art of Heavy Transport" in which anything you could want to know is discussed in depth.

## 27.2 Overview of modular hydraulic transport equipment

There are two primary types of heavy duty modular wheeled transport equipment using hydraulic suspension, namely:

– Modular platform trailers
– Self-drive transporters a.k.a self-propelled modular transporters (SPMTs)

### 27.2.1 Modular platform trailers

Figure 27-1

Originally developed primarily to haul heavy and large loads over the road, these trailers:

- Are towed by a prime mover (ballasted tractor unit typically) using a drawbar or a gooseneck attachment bearing on the 5th wheel of a tractor unit
- Are road-going and travel at highway speeds
- Are typically 3 m (10') or 3.6 m (12') wide
- Typically have (longitudinal) axle spacings of 1.5 m (5') although many options are available to suit differing legislative requirements
- Are modular in units of typically 4, 5 or 6 axle lines; modules are coupled to form trailers of the required length / carrying capacity; trailers can be arranged side by side to form wider arrangements
- Have hydraulically assisted mechanical steering with limited steering options
- Have hydraulic suspension allowing load equalization between axles and a variable deck height
- Have a carrying capacity of between 15 t to 45 t per axle line depending on model

## 27.2.2  Self-propelled modular transporters (SPMTs)

Figure 27-2

*Mammoet – BP Clair loadout*

A further evolution of modular trailers, Self-Propelled Modular Transporters (SPMTs) were developed primarily to meet the requirements of the offshore fabrication industry when loading out modules onto barges. SPMTs:

- Have hydrostatically driven axles
- Are not intended for extended road use
- Travel at low speeds
- Are typically 2.4 m (8') wide (for economy of shipping), although wider 3 m (10') and other options exist
- Have axle spacings typically 1.4 m (4.6') although other options available

- Are modular in units of typically 4, 5 or 6 axle lines; modules are coupled to form trailers of the required length / carrying capacity; trailers can be arranged side by side to form wider arrangements
- Mainly feature electronic multi-mode steering and are highly maneuverable
- Have hydraulic suspension / load equalization, variable deck height
- Have a carrying capacity from about 36 t to 60 t per axle line depending on model

Advantages/disadvantages

The advantages SPMTs have over modular platform trailers are:

- They are self-driven and do not require a separate prime mover or winches or other form of external tractive effort. The tractive effort is applied by the driven wheels in the direction those wheels are pointing. Drive is bi-directional.
- They are highly maneuverable and controllable. The swept area is less as a result of this and the lack of a prime mover.
- Single person operation.
- Electronic steering (where so equipped) does not require the time consuming setup that mechanical steering does.
- Types are available with very high carrying capacity per axle line.

The advantages modular platform trailers have over SPMTs are:

- They are less complex with less to go wrong.
- They are cheaper to purchase and maintain and could be more economic when they are a viable solution.
- A single width standard (10' wide) modular trailer is more stable than a single width standard (8' wide) SPMT.
- They are designed for road-going use for which SPMTs are generally unsuitable.
- They can travel at higher speed.
- The tractive effort provided by an SPMT is dependent on having sufficient weight on the driven wheels which is a function of the weight of the payload versus the number of axle lines being used; with modular trailers, the tractive effort is independent of the payload weight but is instead simply dependent on having adequate ballast weight over the driven axles of the prime mover.

### 27.2.3  Primary suppliers of modular trailers and SPMTs

Primary suppliers of modular trailers and SPMTs include:

- Tii Group
  - Scheuerle
  - Kamag
  - Nicolas
- Goldhofer
- Cometto
- Faymonville

## 27.2.4 Characteristics of model ranges

The following graphics tabulate the characteristics of the various model ranges offered by the Tii Group, Goldhofer and Faymonville. Note that this information is indicative and not all-inclusive; further, specifications change and evolve. Contact the manufacturers for full up-to-date details.

Figure 27-3

**GOLDHOFER**

| | THP/ET | THP/UT | THP/UT | THP/MT | THP/SL-S | THP/SL-S | THP/SL-L | THP/SL | THP/SL (1800) | THP/HL | THP/H |
|---|---|---|---|---|---|---|---|---|---|---|---|
| Single tires | ✓ | | | | ✓ | ✓ | | | | | |
| Tire size | 285/70 R 19.5 | 205/65 R 17.5 | 215/75 R 17.5 | 215/75 R 17.5 | 245/70 R 17.5 | 285/70 R 19.5 | 215/75 R 17.5 | 215/75 R 17.5 | 215/75 R 17.5 | 245/75 R 17.5 | 235/75 R 17.5 |
| Twin tires | | ✓ | ✓ | ✓ | | | ✓ | ✓ | ✓ | ✓ | ✓ |
| Pivot bearing | ✓ | ✓ | ✓ | ✓ | | | | | | | |
| Ball bearing race | | | | | ✓ | ✓ | ✓ | ✓ | ✓ | ✓ | ✓ |
| Hydrostatic drive | | | | | | | | | | | |
| Tractive force | | | | | | | | | | | |
| Mechanical steering | ✓ | ✓ | ✓ | ✓ | ✓ | ✓ | ✓ | ✓ | ✓ | ✓ | ✓ |
| Electronic steering | | | | | | | | | | | |
| Public roads | ✓ | ✓ | ✓ | ✓ | ✓ | ✓ | ✓ | ✓ | ✓ | ✓ | |
| Construction sites | ✓ | | | | ✓ | ✓ | | ✓ | | ✓ | ✓ |
| Inside plants | | | | ✓ | | | ✓ | ✓ | | | |
| Height (mm) | 1250 | 1070 | 1120 | 1120 | 1190 | 1190 | 1175 | 1175 | 1175 | 1208 | 1250 |
| Travel (mm) | +/- 300 | +/- 300 | +/- 300 | +/- 300 | +/- 300 | +/- 300 | +/- 300 | +/- 300 | +/- 300 | +/- 300 | +/- 300 |
| Width (mm) | 2750 (2500 alt) | 3000 (2750 alt) mechanical width adjust | 3000 (2750 alt) mechanical width adjust | 3000 | 3000 | 3000 | 3000 | 3000 | 3000 | 3200 | 3600 |
| Axle spacing (mm) | 1400 | 1500 | 1500 | 1500 | 1500 | 1500 | 1500 | 1500 | 1800 | 1500 (choice) | 1600 |
| Steering angle | +/-60° | +/-60° | +/-60° | +/-60° | +/-60° | +/-60° | +/-60° | +/-60° | +/-60° | +/-60° | +/-60° |
| Self wt | | | | | | | | | | | |
| Axle load | 23t @ 10km/hr | 25t @ 10km/hr | 25t @ 10km/hr | 25t @ 20km/hr | 15.6t @ 20km/hr | 23t @ 10km/hr | 26.1t @ 20km/hr | 45t @ 1km/hr | 45t @ 1km/hr | 45t @ 1km/hr | 45t @ 5km/hr |
| Comments | | Low height | Low height | High B.M. / low height | Light as possible, concentrated loads, high BM | Light as possible, concentrated loads, high BM | High BM, closed loading platform | High BM, closed loading platform | Split module for highway, hydraulic width adjustment optional | High BM for off-road. Wider. | Heavy duty off-road. Widest for optimum stability. |

Figure 27-4

**GOLDHOFER**

| | PST/SL | PST/H | PST/SL-E | PST/ES-E (285) | PST/ES-E (315) | PST/ES-E (385) |
|---|---|---|---|---|---|---|
| Single tires | | | | ✓ | ✓ | ✓ |
| Tire size | 215/75 R 17.5 | 235/75 R 17.5 | 215/75 R 17.5 | 285/70 R 19.5 | 315/60 R 22.5 | 385/55 R 22.5 |
| Twin tires | ✓ | ✓ | ✓ | | | |
| Pivot bearing | | | | | | |
| Ball bearing race | ✓ | ✓ | ✓ | ✓ | ✓ | ✓ |
| Hydrostatic drive | ✓ | ✓ | ✓ | ✓ | ✓ | ✓ |
| Tractive force | 160kN/axle | 160kN/axle | 160kN/axle | 165kN/axle | 153kN/axle | 153kN/axle |
| Mechanical steering | ✓ | ✓ | | | | |
| Electronic steering | | | ✓ | ✓ | ✓ | ✓ |
| Public roads | | | | | | |
| Construction sites | ✓ | ✓ | ✓ | ✓ | ✓ | ✓ |
| Inside plants | ✓ | ✓ | ✓ | ✓ | ✓ | ✓ |
| Height (mm) | 1175 | 1250 | 1220 | 1500 | 1500 | 1515 |
| Travel (mm) | +/- 300 | +/- 300 | +/- 300 | +/- 325 | +/- 350 | +/- 350 |
| Width (mm) | 3000 | 3600 | 3000 | 2430/2730 | 2430 | 2430 |
| Axle spacing (mm) | 1500 | 1600 | 1500 | 1400 | 1400 | 1600 |
| Steering angle | +/-60° | +/-60° | +/-135° | +/-135° | +/-135° | +/-135° |
| Self wt | | | | | | |
| Axle load | 45t @ 1km/hr | 45t @ 5km/hr | 45t @ 1km/hr | 40t @ 0.4km/hr | 45t @ 1km/hr | 60t @ 1km/hr |
| Comments | Closed laoding platform, high BM | Heavy duty off-road. Widest for optimum stability. | Closed loading platform, high BM | Closed loading platform, high BM | Closed loading platform, high BM | Closed loading platform, high BM |

Figure 27-5

**FAYMONVILLE**

| | TOWED (drawbar or gooseneck) | | | | |
|---|---|---|---|---|---|
| | **S-ST** | **G-ST** | **G-MT** | **G-UT** | **G-UT** |
| Single tires | | | | | |
| Tire size | 215/75 R 17.5 | 215/75 R 17.5 | 215/75 R 17.5 | 205/65 R 17.5 or 215/75 R 17.5 | 215/75 R 17.5 |
| Twin tires | ✓ | ✓ | ✓ | ✓ | ✓ |
| Pivot bearing | ✓ | ✓ | ✓ | ✓ | ✓ |
| Ball bearing race | | | | | |
| Hydrostatic drive | available | available | available | available | available |
| Tractive force | | | | | |
| Mechanical steering | ✓ | ✓ | ✓ | ✓ | ✓ |
| Electronic steering | | | | | |
| Public roads | ✓ | ✓ | ✓ | ✓ | ✓ |
| Construction sites | | | | | |
| Inside plants | ✓ | ✓ | ✓ | ✓ | ✓ |
| | | | | | |
| Height (mm) | 1190 | 1120 | 1120 | 1020 | 1175 |
| Travel (mm) | +/- 325 | +/- 300 | +/- 300 | +350/- 250 | +/- 300 |
| Width (mm) | 3000 | 3000 | 3000 | 3000 | 3000 |
| | | | | | |
| Axle spacing (mm) | 1500 | 1500 | 1500 | 1500 | 1500 |
| Steering angle | +/-60° | +/-60° | +/-60° | +/-60° | +/-60° |
| Self wt | 13.12t (4 axle) | 11.4t (4 axle) | 13.4t (4 axle) | 13.4t (4 axle) | 14.0t (4 axle) |
| Axle load | 36t @ 1km/hr | 36t @ 1km/hr | 25t @ 5km/hr | 25t @ 1km/hr | 45t @ 0.5km/hr |
| Comments | Split bogies available (for 3 file 1+1/2) | Split bogies available (for 3 file 1+1/2) | Split bogies available (for 3 file 1+1/2) | | |

Fully compatible with Goldhofer equivalent trailers
ModulMAX

Figure 27-6

**SCHEUERLE (modular trailer)**

| | Scheuerle Combi road-going trailers | | | | |
|---|---|---|---|---|---|
| | **Eurocombi** | **Eurocombi ES** | **FlatCombi M₀/M₁** | **FlatCombi M₃** | **InterCombi S₀/S₁** |
| Single tires | ✓ | ✓ | | | |
| Tire size | 285/70 R 19.5 | 285/70 R 19.5 | 205/65 R 17.5 | 205/65 R 17.5 | 215/75 R 17.5 235/75 R 17.5 |
| Twin tires | | | ✓ | ✓ | ✓ |
| Pivot bearing | ✓ | ✓ | ✓ | ✓ | ✓ |
| Ball bearing race | | | | | |
| Hydrostatic drive | | | | | |
| Tractive force | | | | | |
| Mechanical steering | ✓ | ✓ | ✓ | ✓ | ✓ |
| Electronic steering | | | | | |
| Public roads | ✓ | ✓ | ✓ | ✓ | ✓ |
| Construction sites | limited use | limited use | | | |
| Inside plants | ✓ | ✓ | ✓ | ✓ | ✓ |
| | | | | | |
| Height (mm) | 1260 | 1260 | 1030 | 1020 | 1190/1270 |
| Travel (mm) | +/-300 | +/-300 | +/-250 | +350/-250 | +/-325 |
| Width (mm) | 2750/2430 | 2750/2430 | 3000/2750 | 3000 | 3000/3100 |
| | | | | | |
| Axle spacing (mm) | 1500 | 1500 | 1500 | 1500 | 1500 |
| Steering angle (deg) | +/-60 | +/-60 | +/-60 | +/-60 | +/-60 |
| Self wt | 2.875t | 2.875t | 2.9t | 3.075t | 3.350t |
| Axle load | 20t/axle | 20t/axle | 23t/axle | 23t/axle | 36t/axle |
| | | | | | |
| Comments | Up to 80 km/hr | ES version has much higher bending strength spine beam. | | | Long distance road, heavy loads. Available with powerpack as SP or PB variants. Split versions available for widths to 4m or 3-file combinations. |

Figure 27-7

**SCHEUERLE & KAMAG SPMTs**

| | Scheuerle SPMT | | Kamag SPMT | |
|---|---|---|---|---|
| | G3 | G4 | K24** | K24** ST |
| Single tires | ✓ | ✓ | ✓ | ✓ |
| Tire size | ? | ? foam filled or solid | ? | foam filled |
| Twin tires | | | | |
| Pivot bearing | | | | |
| Ball bearing race | ✓ | ✓ | ✓ | ✓ |
| Hydrostatic drive | ✓ | ✓ | ✓ | ✓ |
| Tractive force | 240kN/ 4 or 6 module | 240kN/ 4 or 6 module | 120kN (4) / 240kN (6) | 120kN (4) / 240kN (6) |
| Mechanical steering | | | | |
| Electronic steering | ✓ | ✓ | ✓ | ✓ |
| Public roads | restricted use | restricted use | restricted use | restricted use |
| Construction sites | ✓ | ✓ | ✓ | ✓ |
| Inside plants | ✓ | ✓ | ✓ | ✓ |
| | | | | |
| Height (mm) | 1500 | 1500 | 1500 | 1500 |
| Travel (mm) | +/- 350 | +/- 350 | +/- 350 | +/- 350 |
| Width (mm) | 2430 | 2430 | 2430 | 2430 |
| | | | | |
| Axle spacing (mm) | 1400 | 1400 | 1400 | 1400 |
| Steering angle (deg) | +130/-100 | +130/-100 | +130/-100 | +130/-100 |
| Self wt | 4t/axle | 4.45t/axle | 4.45t/axle | 4.75t/axle |
| Axle load | 40t/axle | 48t/axle | 40t/axle | 48t/axle |
| | | | | |
| Comments | Rated at 0.5 km/hr speed | Rated at 0.5 km/hr speed | Rated at 0.5 km/hr speed | Rated at 0.5 km/hr speed |

Figure 27-8

**KAMAG (modular and self-propelled)**

| | K25H (Kamag) road-going range (self-drive and towed) | | | | | | |
|---|---|---|---|---|---|---|---|
| | K25 H 3.2 | K25 H SL3.2 | K25 H | K25 H PB | K25 H SP | K25 H SPE | K25 H SL |
| Single tires | | | | | | | |
| Tire size | 245/70 R 17.5 | 245/70 R 17.5 | 215/75 R 17.5 | 215/75 R 17.6 | 215/75 R 17.5 | 215/75 R 17.6 | 215/75 R 17.5 |
| Twin tires | ✓ | ✓ | ✓ | ✓ | ✓ | ✓ | ✓ |
| Pivot bearing | ✓ | ✓ | ✓ | ✓ | ✓ | ✓ | ✓ |
| Ball bearing race | | | | | | | |
| Hydrostatic drive | | | | ✓ | ✓ | ✓ | |
| Tractive force | | | | | ? | ? | |
| Mechanical steering | ✓ | ✓ | ✓ | | ✓ | | ✓ |
| Electronic steering | | | | | | ✓ | |
| Public roads | ✓ | ✓ | ✓ | ✓ | ✓ | ✓ | ✓ |
| Construction sites | limited use | limited use | limited use | limited use | limited use | limited use | limited use |
| Inside plants | ✓ | ✓ | ✓ | ✓ | ✓ | ✓ | ✓ |
| | | | | | | | |
| Height (mm) | 1250 | 1250 | 1175 | 1175 | 1175 | 1220 | 1175 |
| Travel (mm) | +/-300 | +/-300 | +/-300 | +/-300 | +/-300 | +/-300 | +/-300 |
| Width (mm) | 3200 | 3200 | 3000 | 3000 | 3000 | 3000 | see below |
| | | | | | | | |
| Axle spacing (mm) | 1500 | 1500 | 1500 | 1500 | 1500 | 1500 | 1500 |
| Steering angle (deg) | +/-60 | +/-60 | +/-60 | +/-60 | +/-60 | +/-140 | +/-60 |
| Self wt | 3.4t | 3.6t | 3.33t | 3.5t | 3.5t | 4.03t | 3.5t |
| Axle load | 36t/axle | 36t/axle | 45t/axle | 45t/axle | 45t/axle | 45t/axle | see below |
| | | | | | | | |
| Comments | | | Also a K25 H ES with extra strong spine beam. | Has drive axles, can be self-propelled or used with K25 H axles; can "assist". | Is self-propelled. Can be coupled to the electronic steered SPE. | Self-propelled, electronic steering. Compatible with entire K25 range | Split longitudinally, can be made into 3-file with K25 H or use spacers for widths to 4m. |

So you can see that there are many options. In some cases you may be able to mix and match within a transport arrangement. Faymonville products may, for instance, possibly be used with Goldhofer products. It might be possible to mix Tii products. If intending to do so, you should check whether there are compromises to be made, whether there is any loss of functionality, control software issues and so on.

## 27.3 General construction features

### 27.3.1 Frame

Modular trailers and SPMTs are all built around a frame which has bending and shear strength. The principle is common but details vary.

The frame comprises:

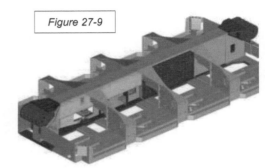
Figure 27-9

- a spine beam (a box beam in this case, others use a lattice design)
- cantilevered cross beams
- a reinforced loading platform (deck) which can be open (as shown here) or closed
- multi-plate tension connections to allow modular units to be pinned together

*Goldhofer THP 4-line frame (shown upside down for clarity)*

### 27.3.2 Wheel sets

Wheel sets are mounted on bearings on either side of the spine between stiffener beams, they comprise:

- a bearing (ball type or pivot type) supporting
- an upper arm to which is pinned a lower arm (forming a knuckle)
- a double acting hydraulic ram between the upper and lower arms
- a pendulum axle articulating (rocking) on the lower arm
- a single wheel (or pairs of wheels) at either end of the axle
- a brake (some axle sets)
- a hydrostatic drive motor (some axles, some designs)
- electronic steering system or mechanical linkage

Normal travel direction is with the knuckles leading so the wheels trail, riding the undulations.

Figure 27-10

Scheuerle    Figure 27-11

Note the tires can be pneumatic, foam filled or solid. The ram is not directly above wheels and is not necessarily vertical, so the ram force can be different to the wheel load.

The pivot type bearing shown right is generally used on road-going modular trailers, whereas SPMTs will generally use a ball bearing race ring design similar to that shown below.

Figure 27-12

Figure 27-13

Goldhofer

The way in which the axles articulate to accommodate lateral ground undulations is shown below. This of course is extreme, for illustration purposes only – your ground preparation needs to be a whole lot better than this!

Figure 27-14

Goldhofer

### 27.3.3 Suspension

The suspension rams are connected hydraulically into groups (more later). All the rams within a group are at equal pressure (static) and thus support equal load regardless of their extension. The closed oil volume averages ram extensions in a group to accommodate longitudinal ground undulations and cross falls. Fluid can be pumped in/out to increase/reduce the closed volume to level out the deck.

This photo shows a loaded SPMT negotiating a loadout ramp between land and a free-floating barge; the suspension is able to accommodate the height differences keeping the load level with all axles correctly loaded.

Bechtel

Figure 27-15

The suspension rams apply basically equal loads to the trailer (which acts as a beam and has a certain stiffness); the load (which has its stiffness) is supported on the trailer deck at designated support points. The loads come to equilibrium with the trailer and load deflected to an extent dependent on their relative stiffnesses.

Figure 27-16

It is often the presumption of designers of modules and other items requiring to be moved that hydraulic trailers will provide a totally planar support to their payload; conversely it is often the assumption of the people responsible for the transport operation that the module or whatever will remain totally planar when supported by the trailer. In practice both trailer and load deflect; how much each deflects is a function of their relative stiffnesses. The above foreshortened view graphically illustrates the rippled deflection of this loaded SPMT. It may be necessary to add temporary bracings in say a module to stiffen it up and keep deflections within acceptable limits when moving it.

### 27.3.4 Imposed pressures

The weight of the loaded transporter is passed into the ground through the contact the tires make with the ground. At the point of contact the tires flatten until an area is developed sufficient to support the tire load at the internal pressure of the tire which is usually about 150 psi (or about 10 bars). The contact pressure = the tire pressure. The imposed loads dissipates from those "contact patches" at say 45 degrees until at about 575 mm or so below the surface the pressure can be considered uniform and is equal to the total traveling load divided by the distributed area. See below - note a 2.4 m wide (8') Kamag SPMT is shown for the sake of the exercise.

Figure 27-17

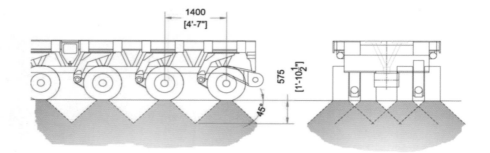

It is unrealistic (and unnecessary) to prepare a roadway for a uniform pressure of the magnitude of the localized "patch" contact pressure. So long as the surface can take the traveling contact pressures without creating ruts, the pressure usually considered for roadbed preparation is the uniformly distributed pressure.

By convention, and simplistically, the imposed pressure is taken as being equal to the total travelling load divided by the projected deck area of the transporter(s) i.e. the total shadow area.

You should not use this uniform pressure approach when analyzing the loadings into barge decks or load-out ramps. Instead, consider the loading as multiples of traveling line loads of trailer width.

### 27.3.5 Required tractive effort

The rolling friction of a platform trailer or SPMT on an asphalt roadway is about 2 or 3%. So, on a level roadway you will require, as a minimum, 3% of the total loaded weight of the transporter as tractive effort provided from the prime mover or the SPMT driven axles. If you are driving up/down a hill, there is a component, acting down the slope, of the traveling weight equal to the gradient x the weight. That force has to be additionally opposed in order to climb the hill. So, if negotiating an upward gradient of say 8%, a total tractive effort of approximately 11% of the traveling weight will be required as a minimum. If using a platform trailer towed by a ballasted tractor unit (prime mover), the tractive effort that the tractor unit can provide = the number of driven axles x the load on those axles x the friction factor (rubber to road of about 0.8). For example, a ballasted prime mover with three driven axles each loaded to 12 t will be capable of a tractive effort of 3 x 12 x 0.8 = 28 t or so, subject to it having sufficient horsepower.  A 150 t transformer on a double width 6 axle platform trailer might weigh all up about 200 t; if traveling on asphalt up a 5% slope, the require tractive effort will be about 8% x 200 t = 16 t. The aforementioned ballasted tractor unit would be sufficient. Note that gravel site road will for instance likely not provide as high a friction factor.

*Figure 27-18*

*600 t test load on double 15-axle Goldhofer SPMT on site road*

For SPMTs, refer to the data sheets for the units you are using, noting that the quoted tractive efforts for a driven unit will be based on the driven axles carrying a minimum load. Too little load on the driven axles will result in spinning the wheels when attempting to apply higher tractive efforts.

# 27.4 Lashing and securing (generally)

### 27.4.1 Forces acting during road transportation

It is obviously very important that loads are adequately secured to the transport equipment on which they are being moved. While heavy specialized transport is different in many ways from conventional road-going transport (equipment characteristics, speed of travel, braking and so on), the following principles apply universally.

Forces acting on the load during road transportation include:

- Static forces
    - The weight of the load acting downwards
    - Components of the weight acting along the length of the transporter as a result of inclines and declines
    - Components of the weight acting across the transporter as a result of inclination of the transporter resulting from cross falls
- Dynamic effects
    - Forces resulting from longitudinal accelerations and decelerations of the transporter (speeding up and braking) acting on the mass of the load
    - Horizontal centripetal forces resulting from the outward acceleration engendered when turning corners acting on the mass of the load; changing lanes at speed will also create lateral accelerations
    - Vertical forces resulting from vertical accelerations/decelerations acting on the load caused by traveling at speed over bumps; these will act to reduce or increase the apparent weight of the load
    - Transverse rocking of the transporter and load may be induced by negotiating bumps (at even quite slow speeds)

All the above can be considered to act at the C of G of the load.

REMINDER: the C of G of an object is the average of the mass distribution within that object. It is the notional location at which the load would be in perfect balance if supported there. The weight of the object can be considered as a single force acting vertically downwards from that point. The center of gravity of an object is not necessarily within the object; examples would be where the object is curved or L-shaped.

In transit, these forces are constantly engendered and can act in unison. The only time no horizontal forces are acting is when the load is traveling at constant speed in a consistent direction on a perfectly level road – which never happens!

NOTE: Wind forces may be a significant factor on larger loads. They will act through the center of area of the load as presented to the wind. This is most likely not the same location as the C of G.

### 27.4.2 Effects resulting from these forces

Things you don't want to happen resulting from these forces can include:

- Sliding
- Tilting and tipping

So lashing and possibly blocking is used to restrain the load to the transporter.

Sliding

Friction between the load and transporter will resist movement but alone is insufficient to prevent an unsecured load from sliding. Further, when the transporter is moving, vertical movements caused by bumps and vibrations from the road will reduce the restraining force due to friction. First, the load needs to be held down to the transporter using direct (essentially vertical) lashings or top-over lashings or other restraining methods. Plywood or other materials are recommended at bearing points to prevent steel to steel contact and enhance the friction factor. Second the load needs to be blocked and/or lashed to the transporter to prevent horizontal movement both laterally and longitudinally. These measures taken together contribute to adequate securing against sliding.

Tilting and Tipping

The other primary concern is tilting (and ultimately tipping). Even if the load is prevented from sliding, additional restraining methods may be necessary to avoid tilting. As noted, loads with high centers of gravity and narrow bases are more susceptible to tilting and tipping.

### 27.4.3 Restraining methods

Tensioned chains are the primary method used for direct lashing of heavy and abnormal loads on platform trailers and SPMTs.

Two properties determine the strength of a chain: the thickness of the links and the quality of the metal used. Refer to standards such as EN 12195. In the USA, transport chain is designated grade 70. The chain used should be compatible with the requirements of the load carried. Lashing chains shall never be used when knotted or connected with a pin or screws. Where necessary, corner protectors should be used on corners or sharp edges to protect lashing chains and the edges of the loads against abrasion and damage. Chains are not to be bent tightly around corners; using generously proportioned corner protectors increases the radius around which they bend maintaining their effective strength.

Tensioning is usually by means of ratchet (turnbuckle type) load binders.

### 27.4.4 Calculating lashing forces

The accelerations and decelerations used to determine acceleration, braking and centrifugal forces acting on loads under normal conditions on the public highway were determined through scientific measurements. EN12195 recommends the following:

1. 0.8 g deceleration in the forward direction;
2. 0.5 g acceleration in the rearward direction and
3. 0.5 g acceleration in the lateral direction.

Note: for other transportation modes like rail or sea, other acceleration coefficients must be used.

THESE ACCELERATIONS ARE NOT APPLICABLE TO "ABNORMAL" TRANSPORT OPERATIONS ON SPECIALIST TRANSPORT EQUIPMENT. Mostly this is so because "abnormal" operations, particularly those on SPMTs, are conducted at so much slower speeds

## 27.5 Characteristics of SPMTs

### 27.5.1 Scope of use

SPMTs are typically used for movement of abnormally heavy and/or large loads such as modules, vessels, generators, bridge structures, pre-assemblies (ships) over short distances on private facilities. They are used extensively for load-outs/load-in & site movements.

Figure 27-19

Figure 27-20

### 27.5.2 Steering & steering modes

The wheel-sets of modern electronically steered SPMTs (such as the Goldhofer PST/SL-E types shown here and the PST/ES-E types) can be individually turned more than +/- 90° from "normal" straight ahead and can be computer controlled to allow synchronized complex steering arrangements.

Figure 27-21

Figure 27-22

Electronic multiway steering

Electronically steered wheel set

The following two graphics illustrate the steering mode possibilities of the Goldhofer PST/SL-E types.

Figure 27-23

*Goldhofer*

## MAIN STEERING MODES
## PST/SL-E – PST/ES-E

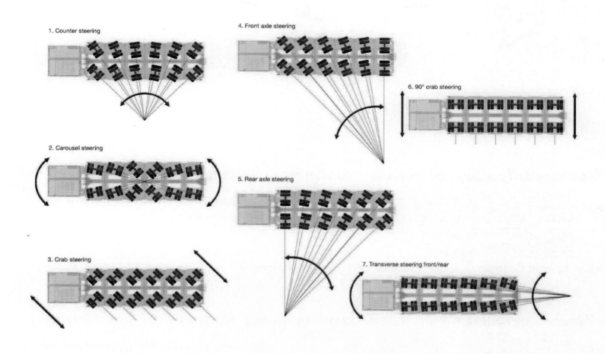

## MAIN STEERING MODES
## PST/SL-E – PST/ES-E

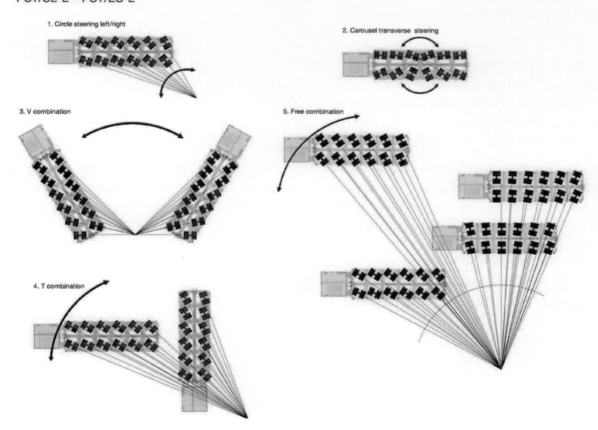

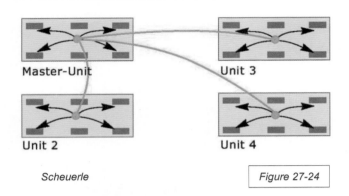

Electronically controlled SPMTs (such as this type) may be linked to act as one even though they may not be physically connected. One transporter unit is designated the Master unit. All other transport units – regardless of how many are in the coupling mode – receive their corresponding control commands for steering system, drive system, brake, etc. from this Master via data connections.

Scheuerle

Figure 27-24

Figure 27-25

## Mechanically coupled vehicle combination (example of combination)

Connection elements (spacers) are used for mechanical side-by-side coupling of transport units.

RC = Remote Control      MU = Master Unit      ▌ = Spacer

## Vehicle combination in loose coupling mode (example of combination)

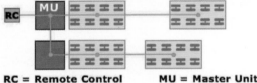

All transport units are positioned freely and connected to the Master Unit (MU) only by a data line. The transport units can be set up in an area of 600m x 600m.

RC = Remote Control      MU = Master Unit

Scheuerle

The extent to which the individual wheel sets have to be rotated to make a coordinated steering movement is determined by the master power unit's computer considering the steering mode and the relative locations of the transporter modules. An X and Y coordinate system is used relative to a datum on the master unit. To some extent the modules (in a train) can be sensed, whereas the locations of unconnected trains have to be entered manually.

It is vital (particularly with loose coupled modules) that the coordinates are correctly entered in order that the whole transport arrangement acts as one and, for instance, turns about a common center point. To have individual transporters heading in different directions risks imposing heavy side loads into the payload and/or one or more transporters moving under the load.

### 27.5.3  SPMT module combinations

As an example, the following tabulates the weight, payload and tractive force for various Scheuerle G3/G4 transporter combinations.

Figure 27-26

**Technical data**

| Axles | Combinations (examples) | Total weight G3 | Total weight G4 | Max. payload G3 | Max. payload G4 | Tractive force | Gradient |
|---|---|---|---|---|---|---|---|
| 4 | | 160 t | 192 t | 144.0 t | 174.2 t | 240 kN | 12.0 % |
| 6 | | 240 t | 288 t | 216.3 t | 262.0 t | 240 kN | 7.0 % |
| 14 | | 560 t | 672 t | 504.3 t | 610.4 t | 720 kN | 9.8 % |
| 20 | | 800 t | 960 t | 720.6 t | 872.4 t | 960 kN | 9.0 % |
| 30 | | 1200 t | 1440 t | 1080.9 t | 1308.6 t | 1440 kN | 9.0 % |
| 40 | | 1600 t | 1920 t | 1441.2 t | 1744.8 t | 1920 kN | 9.0 % |
| 48 | | 1920 t | 2304 t | 1729.8 t | 2094.6 t | 2160 kN | 8.2 % |

Data on the following figures:
Speed 0.5 km/h · Rolling resistance 0.025 · Acceleration 0.005 m/s2

4-axle module type PKEZ 140.8.4   Empty weight   16.0 t
6-axle module type PKEZ 210.12.4   Empty weight   23.5 t

\* The respective payload must be reduced by the weight of the applied PowerPackUnit (PPU).
The dead weight for the PPU Z 100 is 3.5 t, for the PPU Z 350 7.2 t.

Note that this date is indicative only; also that payload is an absolute maximum and does not consider site conditions or limitations of the load itself.

### 27.5.4  Tractive effort

Figure 27-27

Not every wheel-set on a hydrostatically driven SPMT is driven. On the Scheuerle SPMTs a 4-axle or a 6-axle module usually has two driven axle lines, i.e. 4 driven pendulum wheel-sets per the picture.

The max tractive force per driven line (of this type) is 120 kN, i.e. 60 kN per wheel-set. To develop this, there needs to be adequate friction tire to running surface and enough weight on the tires.

Required tractive effort is determined by gradient, rolling friction, turning resistance and the need to accelerate the arrangement.

*Scheuerle*

This Goldhofer graphic indicates how the driven axles are "plumbed" to the powerpack on their PST-E transporters.

Hydrostatic drive

Figure 27-28

Hydrostatic drive

Figure 27-29

### 27.5.5 Connecting SPMTs

To provide a transport arrangement that:

- Has the required load carrying capacity
- Supports the payload as required
- Imposes adequately low pressures on the ground,

SMPT modules are connected longitudinally to form transporters of the required length. The trailer is subject to bending in use; the lower tension connections are pinned multi-plate lugs; the pin is hydraulically driven for installation/removal in this case.

Multiple Transporters may be connected side by side using spacers or may be distributed (with no mechanical connection) as required under the load to adequately support it.

The total number of axle lines is determined by the bulleted points.

*Scheuerle*

Hydraulic vehicle coupling system

Figure 27-30

### 27.5.6 Suspension zones

The transport arrangement is divided into hydraulic zones or areas; the suspension rams within a zone are connected hydraulically and thus at a common pressure (ignoring dynamic effects). The rams within a zone extend/retract about the mean displacing fluid within the group to accommodate ground undulations keeping the wheel sets (nominally) equally loaded and the deck support height averaged.

Each zone provides effectively a single point of support to the transport arrangement at the hydraulic center (the point at which a single load would be notionally balanced). This is a fulcrum point for loading.

The preference in most cases is to divide the transport arrangement into 3 zones providing three-point triangulated support (in plan) to the load. This ensures all zones remain loaded with planar (but necessarily level) support for the load. Transverse level can be maintained by pumping fluid into, or out of, one of the side zones.

A triangle can be drawn joining the hydraulic centers of area of the three zones. This is the triangle of stability and its boundaries are the tipping lines. For the load to be stable, the center of gravity has to remain (in plan) securely within the stability triangle.

The proportion of load carried by each zone is dependent on the relative proximity of the C of G to the corners of the triangle. The C of G can move around within the triangle (in plan) if the trailer deck tilts laterally or longitudinally; wind loads will have a similar effect. This changes the hydraulic zone load distribution.

Figure 27-31

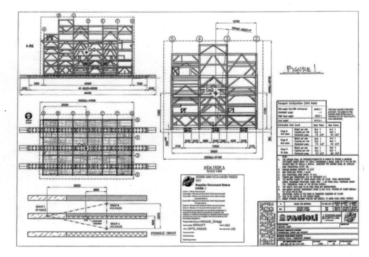

### 27.5.7 Hydraulic Stability

As noted, the default suspension arrangement is to use 3 hydraulic zones; the support is analogous to that provided by a 3-legged stool. Keep the C of G within the triangle formed by the legs and the load will not tip.

The hydraulic zones average out the suspension extensions and the transporter deck takes its level accordingly following the averaged profile of the roadway. If there is significant cross fall, the deck (and load) tilts laterally, gradients cause a longitudinal incline of the deck. Dynamic effects can cause the load to rock laterally, wind loads can create an overturning effect. Turning causes lateral centripetal forces.

All these factors have the effect of moving the C of G in plan view relative to the triangle of support.

As well as affecting stability, movement of the C of G changes the load balance to the zones.

If the trailer were to tip, the fulcrum would be the pivot points where the pendulum axles attach to the lower arms. Stability is by convention considered at the height of that pivot point. In practice it makes little difference to the angle of stability whether taken there or at ground level.

*Figure 27-32*

*Figure 27-33*

If the C of G is allowed to cross outside the triangle of hydraulic support, the point of no return has been reached and the load and trailer will tip. What angle of tilt is required to bring the C of G over the boundary of the triangle? The distance of the C of G normal to the closest boundary is the amount of shift required (in plan view). The angle "A" is the inverse tangent of that distance / the height of the C of G above the pivot points.

Typically, the stability angle is required to be at least 7 degrees.

Note that the location of the C of G used is that of the payload itself and does not consider the weight of the trailers / SPMTs themselves. If that weight is required to be taken into consideration to lower the C of G, then there has to be adequate connection (securing) between the load and trailer to make them act as one, at least as far as the point at which hydraulic tipping occurs (by which time all is lost anyway).

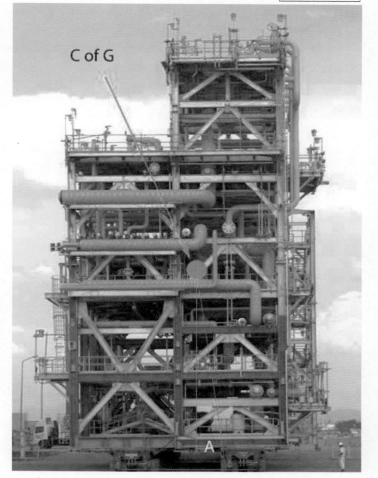

In the instance shown below, the inclined panel is one half of the bottom of an Ash Hopper (together they form a V). It was built horizontally, inclined and lifted onto a transport frame for movement into the boiler building through the side wall using Goldhofer self-drive trailers. A custom frame was built to support it in transit. This in turn sat on two longitudinal transport beams centered over the two trailers. Lateral beams were placed between said beams and the trailers allowing the trailers to self-load and off-load from support "cans". Physical height and width constraints entering the building located the load and frame on the trailers.

Figure 27-34

The issue was that that this placed the C of G of the load very much to one side of the arrangement and too close for comfort to the hydraulic support triangle. The solution was to place crane counterweight (the two gray items) on the transport frame to balance the load out. Two additional beams were sat on the transport frame and two counterweight slabs placed across the two. The whole arrangement was lashed to secure it. By this means we were able to arrange a balanced load during transport and keep trailers and load within the very tight size constraints.

Incidentally, once in the building and lowered onto support cans, the trailers were removed and house-moving hydraulic dollies inserted under the main transport beams to move the load to the right inside the building to location. The second mirror image panel was then brought in in like manner through the same entrance.

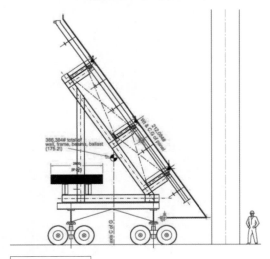

Figure 27-35

Figure 27-36

### 27.5.8  3-point versus 4 point suspension

The advantages of a three-point suspension include:

—  Guaranteed loading of all axles

—  Planar support

—  Ease of adjustment of lateral level

Sometimes an adequately large stability angle cannot be achieved with 3-point suspension due to the height of the C of G of the load or the narrowness of the transport arrangement. In such cases it may be necessary to go to a 4-point arrangement.

For 4-point, the suspensions are arranged as 4 independent zones on a (typically) rectangular grid. The advantage is increase of the distance to the stability boundary and thus improved stability angle. The disadvantages are:

—  The possibility of diagonal loading with one or more zones carrying less than they should and others carrying more than intended.

—  Potential overload of load and/or transporters.

—  Criticality of monitoring and adjustment of level

### 27.5.9  Limitations on suspension travel

Figure 27-37

As noted earlier, the suspension rams typically have a total stroke of about 600mm with travel height being nominally at mid stroke. The stroke has to accommodate a number of things:

—  Cross falls (you want to keep the transport level side to side)

—  Humps and depressions

—  Changes in gradients

—  Deflections,

without "bottoming out" at either end of the stroke.

(The transporter will typically not be kept level longitudinally when say negotiating inclines but will follow the slope).

The longer the transport arrangement, the more difficult it is to work within the stroke limitations; the route has to be very flat and level, changes in gradient very slight.

Figure 27-38

## 27.5.10 Transporter Loading

Transporters have to be loaded such that the permissible bending stress in the spine beam is not exceeded. This may require multiple lines of support such as the three saddles used here.

Also note shear limitations and requirements re localized loadings on the trailer deck.

Figure 27-39

Figure 27-40

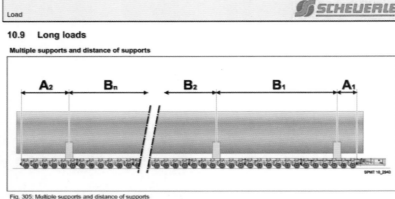

Load                                                                    SCHEUERLE

### 10.9   Long loads

**Multiple supports and distance of supports**

Fig. 305: Multiple supports and distance of supports

In order not to exceed the permissible bending moment of the platform trailer, several supports may be required for the load.

**Requirements:**

Positioning of supports.

- The projections A1 and A2 must not exceed A max.
- The distances B1 / B2 /..... Bn may not exceed B max.
- Both requirements must be complied with.

– Bending resistance of load must be higher than that of transporters.
– The load must consist of one piece.
– The load must be at least as long as the vehicle combination.

▶ Position load on vehicle in such a way that overload of individual pendulum axles as well as of the entire combination is impossible.
▶ Take shifting of the payload COG during transport due to inclines/declines of the road into consideration.
⇨ The position of the payload COG must be within the overturn lines of the entire vehicle combination in any operating condition.

▶ Connect supports torsion-resistant with load.
▶ Secure load and supports in suitable manner on platform trailer against shifting.

**SPMT**

| Axle load [t] | | A max [m] | B max [m] |
|---|---|---|---|
| 2-file | 4- file | | |
| 48 | 96 | 6,3 | 14 |
| 40 | 80 | 7 | 15,4 |
| 30 | 60 | 8 | 18 |
| 20 | 40 | 10 | 22,5 |

| Axle load [t] | A max [m] | B max [m] |
|---|---|---|
| 3- file | | |
| 72 | 5,5 | 12,5 |
| 60 | 6 | 13,5 |
| 45 | 7 | 16 |
| 30 | 8,5 | 20 |

Knowing the axle loads and the properties of the trailer, the numbers of supports through which the payload is supported and their location can be determined using manufacturer's information such as the above (which is indicative only). Software is also available to help with this.

The transporter manufacturers can provide purchasers with structural strength properties for the specific products they have purchased.

For a module such as this, the transport arrangement will usually be developed in collaboration with the module designers; they will advise the number of lines of support required, the permissible support locations and the anticipated support reactions (and permissible tolerances there-from). The loads are usually calculated on the basis of level support. If the module is deflected, the loadings are redistributed according to the stiffness of the module.

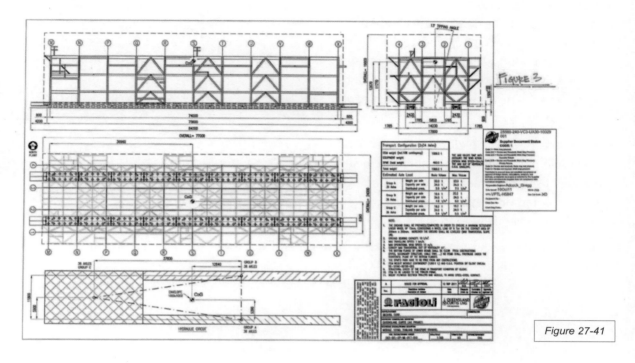

Figure 27-41

## 27.5.11 Deflection analysis

Structurally, the loaded hydraulic trailer or SPMT can be considered as a beam supported from beneath at regular intervals by essentially equal loads (from the wheels through the suspension rams); imposed on the beam from above are support reactions from the payload at every line of support of which there can be multiples. The suspension ensures the lower loads remain constant and equal (within each zone) regardless of deflection so long as the suspension remains within permitted travel range i.e. not bottomed out either end of the ram stroke.

How is this loading regime reconciled? Through deflection of trailer beam and payload.

How to figure that out? With great difficulty – it's a job for a computer and a competent structural engineer.

The ram loads are usually modeled in analysis programs as springs. The trailer beam has its moment of inertia (second moment of area), modulus of elasticity and so on and can be modeled. The module properties can be modeled. The whole arrangement will come to equilibrium with both the trailer and module deflected somewhat. The module support reactions will likely differ from those theoretical reactions you would see if the modular support was planar; as noted, the module will very likely be deflected somewhat in transport.

Try to design the transport arrangement such that the loads the trailer will impart through the interfaces with the payload do not differ markedly from the loads the payload would theoretically impose through those interfaces if supported totally rigidly level (undeflected). If the payload (module or whatever) is relatively stiff any load shedding that has to happen in the module to bring it to equilibrium when transported will not excessively deflect it.

### 27.5.12 Self-loading / unloading

An advantage of hydraulic suspension is the ability of the transporter to self-load/unload.

If a payload to be transported is supported at a height that allows the trailers to be driven beneath (with the suspension low), the trailer decks, once in position, can be raised to uplift the load from its supports allowing the trailer and load to be driven clear. Offloading is possible by reverse process if suitable height supports are once again provided. Note the steel support "cans" here.

If the piece is to be directly installed on raised piers, it might be possible to elevate the load using the trailer hydraulics and jack and pack methodology, then drive it directly over the piers and lower to place.

Figure 27-42

This module is being loaded out onto a barge; it will be lowered onto the sea-fastening using the trailer hydraulics and secured for the marine voyage.

Figure 27-43

It is vital to get the support heights right so that the trailer (when low) has enough clearance to get beneath the load and, when high, lifts clear over the supports onto which the payload is supported / is to be lowered. Not all trailers / SPMTs have the same mean height and/or stroke. This must be established early.

It is also necessary to ensure that, when loading out onto a barge, the trailers can be removed from beneath the load over the linkspan.

The height of the underside of the module when lowered to the supports may cause the trailers to bind up on the module when trying to negotiate the hump that the linkspan between barge and land presents.  This is really only an issue if the trailer directly bears on the module support beams (as in the right photo). If packers are required between trailer and the module support beams, they can be removed before taking the trailer out to give better clearance to the module.

Figure 27-45

Figure 27-44

### 27.5.13 Acceleration / deceleration forces on SPMTs

SPMTs moving heavy loads travel relatively slowly and acceleration is not a major concern.  There is however a possibility of conducting an emergency stop that could give rise to significant deceleration forces. Assuming a travel speed of say 3.6km/hr (1m/s) and a stop to zero over 1 sec, the deceleration rate would be 1 m/s$^2$. With gravity at 9.81 m/s$^2$, this equates to a deceleration of 0.1g.

i.e. in this instance, there is a force of 10% of the weight of the payload trying to slide the load forwards relative to the trailer deck during braking. It acts through the C of G of the payload.

If negotiating a decline at the same time, there will be a static component of the weight of the payload also acting forwards along the trailer deck.

Plywood (or similar) is generally used between the load and trailer deck to improve friction; lashing and securing design does not usually consider this.

Conventionally lashing/securing on these types of moves considers 0.1g acting in any direction. Tipping, where a concern, should be considered separately - as should forces from gradients and wind forces.

## 27.6 In conclusion

Figure 27-46

Figure 27-47

Although the majority of the preceding has concentrated on moving modules and vessels, load out work and so on, SPMTs and modular trailers are used in wide ranging applications in construction and elsewhere. Left they are being used with a tilt-up frame to tail a vessel they earlier delivered; above a large Absorber ring is being moved to the lift crane.

As noted, this section can only scratch the surface and provide a few pointers. I reiterate that you are commended to Marco van Daal's book "The Art of Heavy Transport" for a learned study of the subject.

# 28 References

Following is a list of some references you may find useful; no claim of all-inclusivity (or accuracy) is made. Many manufacturers also have very good information on their products online.

| Description | Publisher | ISBN |
|---|---|---|
| **Legislation, codes & standards** | | |
| **Australia (Workplace Health & Safety - Queensland)** | | |
| Mobile Crane Code of Practice (2006) | WHS | |
| **Canada (Canadian Standards Association)** | | |
| CSA Z248-04    Code for Tower Cranes | CSA | 1-55397-551-0 |
| CSA B167-08    Overhead Travelling Cranes - Design, Inspection, Testing, Maintenance, and Safe Operation | CSA | 978-1-55436-508-1 |
| CSA Z150-98    Safety Code on Mobile Cranes | CSA | 0317-5669 |
| **Europe (Federation Europeene de la Manutention)** | | |
| 98/37/EC    Machinery Directive - Classification of equipment used for Lifting Loads with Lifting Machinery | EU | |
| FEM 1.002    Illustrated Terminology of Heavy Lifting Equipment | FEM | |
| **International (International Organization for Standardization)** | | |
| ISO 2408:2004    Steel wire ropes for general purposes – Minimum requirements | ISO | |
| ISO 2415:2004    Forged shackles for general lifting purposes – Dee shackles and bow shackles | ISO | |
| ISO 3266:1984    Eyebolts for general lifting purposes | ISO | |
| ISO 4301-1:1986    Cranes and lifting appliances -- Classification -- Part 1: General | ISO | |
| ISO 4301-2:2009    Cranes -- Classification -- Part 2: Mobile cranes | ISO | |
| ISO 4301-3:1993    Cranes -- Classification -- Part 3: Tower cranes | ISO | |
| ISO 4301-4:1989    Cranes and related equipment -- Classification -- Part 4: Jib cranes | ISO | |
| ISO 4301-5:1991    Cranes -- Classification -- Part 5: Overhead travelling and portal bridge cranes | ISO | |
| ISO 4302:1981    Cranes -- Wind load assessment | ISO | |
| ISO 4304:1987    Cranes other than mobile and floating cranes -- General requirements for stability | ISO | |
| ISO 4305:1991    Mobile cranes -- Determination of stability | ISO | |
| ISO 4306-1:2007    Cranes -- Vocabulary -- Part 1: General | ISO | |
| ISO 4306-2:1994    Cranes -- Vocabulary -- Part 2: Mobile cranes | ISO | |
| ISO 4306-3:2003    Cranes -- Vocabulary -- Part 3: Tower cranes | ISO | |
| ISO 4306-5:2005    Cranes -- Vocabulary -- Part 5: Bridge and gantry cranes | ISO | |
| ISO 4308-1:2003    Cranes and lifting appliances -- Selection of wire ropes -- | ISO | |

Part 1: General

| ISO 4308-2:1988 | Cranes and lifting appliances -- Selection of wire ropes -- Part 2: Mobile cranes -- Coefficient of utilization | ISO |
| --- | --- | --- |
| ISO 4309:2004 | Cranes -- Wire ropes -- Care, maintenance, installation, examination and discard | ISO |
| ISO 4309:2004 /Amd 1:2008 | Cranes -- Wire ropes -- Care, maintenance, installation, examination and discard -- Amendment 1 | ISO |
| ISO 4310:2009 | Cranes -- Test code and procedures | ISO |
| ISO 8686-1:1989 | Cranes -- Design principles for loads and load combinations -- Part 1: General | ISO |
| ISO 8686-2:2004 | Cranes -- Design principles for loads and load combinations -- Part 2: Mobile cranes | ISO |
| ISO 8686-3:1998 | Cranes -- Design principles for loads and load combinations -- Part 3: Tower cranes | ISO |
| ISO 8686-4:2005 | Cranes -- Design principles for loads and load combinations -- Part 4: Jib cranes | ISO |
| ISO 8686-5:1992 | Cranes -- Design principles for loads and load combinations -- Part 5: Overhead travelling and portal bridge cranes | ISO |
| ISO 8792:1986 | Wire rope slings -- Safety criteria and inspection procedures for use | ISO |
| ISO 8793:1986 | Steel wire ropes -- Ferrule-secured eye terminations | ISO |
| ISO 8794:1986 | Steel wire ropes – Spliced eye terminations for slings | ISO |
| ISO 9373:1989 | Cranes and related equipment -- Accuracy requirements for measuring parameters during testing | ISO |
| ISO 9927-1:2009 | Cranes -- Inspections -- Part 1: General | ISO |
| ISO 9927-3:2005 | Cranes -- Inspections -- Part 3: Tower cranes | ISO |
| ISO 10245-1:2008 | Cranes -- Limiting and indicating devices -- Part 1: General | ISO |
| ISO 10245-2:1994 | Cranes -- Limiting and indicating devices -- Part 2: Mobile cranes | ISO |
| ISO 10245-3:2008 | Cranes -- Limiting and indicating devices -- Part 3: Tower cranes | ISO |
| ISO 11661:1998 | Mobile cranes -- Presentation of rated capacity charts | ISO |
| ISO 11662-1:1995 | Mobile cranes -- Experimental determination of crane performance -- Part 1: Tipping loads and radii | ISO |
| ISO 12480-1:1997 | Cranes -- Safe use -- Part 1: General | ISO |
| ISO 12480-3:2005 | Cranes -- Safe use -- Part 3: Tower cranes | ISO |
| ISO 12480-4:2007 | Cranes -- Safe use -- Part 4: Jib cranes | ISO |
| ISO 12482-1:1995 | Cranes -- Condition monitoring -- Part 1: General | ISO |
| ISO 12485:1998 | Tower cranes -- Stability requirements | ISO |
| ISO 14518:2005 | Cranes -- Requirements for test loads | ISO |
| ISO 15442:2005 | Cranes -- Safety requirements for loader cranes | ISO |
| ISO 15513:2000 | Cranes -- Competency requirements for crane drivers (operators), slingers, signallers and assessors | ISO |
| ISO 20332:2008 | Cranes -- Proof of competence of steel structures | ISO |
| ISO/TR 19961 :2005 | Cranes -- Safety code on mobile cranes | ISO |

New Zealand

| | | |
|---|---|---|
| | Approved Code of Practice for Cranes | 978-0-487-33384-8 |
| | Approved Code of Practice for Load-Lifting Rigging | 0-477-03595-7 |

United Kingdom (British Standards Institution)

| | | |
|---|---|---|
| BS7121-1:2006 | Code of practice for safe use of cranes. General. | BSI |
| BS7121-2:2003 | Code of practice for safe use of cranes. Inspection, testing and examination | BSI |
| BS7121-3:2000 | Code of practice for safe use of cranes. Mobile cranes | BSI |
| BS7121-4:2010 | Code of practice for safe use of cranes. Lorry loaders | BSI |
| BS7121-5:2006 | Code of practice for safe use of cranes. Tower cranes | BSI |
| BS7121-7 currently BS5744 | Code of practice for safe use of cranes. Overhead cranes | BSI |
| BS7121-11:1998 | Code of practice for Safe use of cranes — Part 11: Offshore cranes | BSI |
| BS7121-13:2009 | Code of practice for safe use of cranes. Hydraulic gantry lifting systems | BSI |
| BS4278:1984 | Specification for eyebolts for lifting purposes. | BSI |
| BS449 | The use of structural steel in building | BSI |
| BS449-2 | The use of structural steel in building Part 2 Metric Units | BSI |
| BS13001-1 | Cranes - general design - Part 1 - General Principles & Requirements | BSI |

United Kingdom (Health & Safety Executive)

| | | |
|---|---|---|
| S.I. 2307 :1998 | LOLER - Lifting Operations Lifting Equipment Regulations 1998 | HSE |
| S.I. 2306 :1998 | PUWER - Provision & Use of Work Equipment Regulations 1998 | HSE |

USA (American Society of Mechanical Engineers)

| | | |
|---|---|---|
| B30.1 | Jacks | ASME |
| B30.2 | Overhead and Gantry Cranes (Top Running Bridge, Single or Multiple Girder, Top Running Trolley Hoist) | ASME |
| B30.3 | Construction Tower Cranes | ASME |
| B30.4 | Portal, Tower, and Pedestal Cranes | ASME |
| B30.5 | Mobile and Locomotive Cranes | ASME |
| B30.6 | Derricks | ASME |
| B30.7 | Base Mounted Drum Hoists | ASME |
| B30.8 | Floating Cranes and Floating Derricks | ASME |
| B30.9 | Slings | ASME |
| B30.10 | Hooks | ASME |
| B30.11 | Monorails and Underhung Cranes | ASME |
| B30.12 | Handling Loads Suspended From Rotorcraft | ASME |
| B30.13 | Storage/Retrieval (S/R) Machines and Associated Equipment | ASME |
| B30.14 | Side Boom Tractors | ASME |
| B30.15 | Mobile Hydraulic Cranes (withdrawn 1982) | ASME |
| B30.16 | Overhead Hoists (Underhung) | ASME |

| | | | |
|---|---|---|---|
| B30.17 | Overhead and Gantry Cranes (Top Running Bridge, Single Girder, Underhung Hoist) | ASME | |
| B30.18 | Stacker Cranes (Top or Under Running Bridge, Multiple Girder With Top or Under Running Trolley Hoist) | ASME | |
| B30.19 | Cableways | ASME | |
| B30.20 | Below-the-Hook Lifting Devices | ASME | |
| BTH-1 | Design of Below-the-Hook Lifting Devices | ASME | |
| B30.21 | Manually Lever Operated Hoists | ASME | |
| B30.22 | Articulating Boom Cranes | ASME | |
| B30.23 | Personnel Lifting Systems | ASME | |
| B30.24 | Container Cranes | ASME | |
| B30.25 | Scrap and Material Handlers | ASME | |
| B30.26 | Rigging Hardware | ASME | |
| B30.27 | Material Placement Systems | ASME | |
| B30.28 | Balance Lifting Units | ASME | |

USA (Occupational Safety & Health Administration )

| | | | |
|---|---|---|---|
| | Cranes and Derricks in Construction | OSHA | |
| 29 CFR 1926 | OSHA Construction Industry Regulations | OSHA | 1-59959-102-2 |
| 29 CFR Part 1926 Sub. CC | Operator Certification | OSHA | |
| 29 CFR Part 1926.1402 | Ground Conditions | OSHA | |
| 29 CFR Part 1926.1403-04-05-06 | Crane Assembly | OSHA | |
| 29 CFR Part 1926.1413 / 1414 | Wire Rope | OSHA | |
| 29 CFR Part 1926.1428 | Rigger Certification | OSHA | |
| 29 CFR Part 1926.1428 | Signal Person Certification | OSHA | |
| 29 CFR Part 1926.1431 | Hoisting Personnel | OSHA | |
| 29 CFR Part 1926.1436 | Derricks | OSHA | |
| 29 CFR Part 1926.1437 | Floating Cranes | OSHA | |
| 29 CFR Part 1926.1438 | Overhead Cranes | OSHA | |
| 29 CFR Part 1926.1440 | Side Booms | OSHA | |
| 29 CFR Part 1926.1501 & 1433 | Mobile Cranes | OSHA | |

USA (American National Standards Institute / American Society of Safety Engineers)

| | | | |
|---|---|---|---|
| A10.13 | Steel Erection | ANSI | |
| A10.19 | Pile Installation and Extraction Operations | ANSI | |
| A10.28 | Platforms Suspended from Cranes or Derricks | ANSI | |
| A10.42 | Rigging Qualifications and Responsibilities in the Construction Industry | ANSI | |

Industry Association Publications & Guides

Canada (Construction Safety Association of Ontario)

| | | | |
|---|---|---|---|
| | Mobile Crane Manual | CSAO | 0-8273-6527-6 |
| | Rigging Manual | CSAO | 0-7726-1574-8 |
| | Slings | CSAO | 0-919465-76-5 |
| | Specialized Rigging - Safety Guidelines for Construction | CSAO | 0-919465-78-1 |

| | | | |
|---|---|---|---|
| | The Wedge Socket for Overhead Lifting | CSAO | 0-919465-68-4 |
| | Helicopter Lifting - Safety Guidelines for Construction | CSAO | 0--919465-75-7 |
| | Hoisting and Rigging Safety Manual | CSAO | 978-0-919465-70-6 |

**Canada (Operating Engineers Training Institute of Ontario)**

| | | | |
|---|---|---|---|
| | Mobile Craning Today | OETIO | 0-8273-5460-6 |

**International (International Marine Contractors Association)**

| | | | |
|---|---|---|---|
| IMCA M 187 | Guidelines for lifting operations | IMCA | |
| IMCA M 179 | Guidance on the use of cable laid slings and grommets | IMCA | |
| IMCA M 171 | Crane specification document | IMCA | |

**United Kingdom (Lifting Equipment Engineers Association)**

| | | | |
|---|---|---|---|
| COPSULE | Code of practice for the safe use of lifting equipment | LEEA | |
| | Lifting Equipment - a users Pocket Guide | LEEA | |
| | Lifting Engineers Handbook | LEEA | |

**USA (Crane Manufacturers Association of America)**

| | | | |
|---|---|---|---|
| CMAA-70 (2010) | Specification for top running bridge and gantry type multiple girder electric overhead traveling cranes | CMAA | |
| CMAA - 78 (2002) | Standards and guidelines for professional services performed on overhead traveling cranes and associated hoisting equipment | CMAA | |
| CMAA - 74 (2010) | Specifications for top running and under running single girder electric overhead cranes utilizing under running trolley hoist | CMAA | |
| CMAA - 79 | Crane operators manual | CMAA | |
| MH27.1 (2009) | Specification for patented track underhung cranes and monorail systems | CMAA | |
| MH27.2 (2009) | Specification for enclosed track underhung cranes and monorail systems | CMAA | |

**USA (Wire Sling & Tie-down Association)**

| | | | |
|---|---|---|---|
| WSTDA-RS-1 | Synthetic Polyester Roundslings Standard | WSTDA | |
| WSTDA-RS-2 | Synthetic Polyester Roundslings Manual | WSTDA | |
| WSTDA-WS-1 | Synthetic Webslings Standard | WSTDA | |
| WSTDA-WS-2 | Synthetic Webslings Manual | WSTDA | |

**USA (Specialist Carriers & Riggers Association)**

| | | |
|---|---|---|
| Glossary of common crane & rigging terms | SCRA | |
| Recommended practices for telescopic hydraulic gantry systems | SCRA | |
| Forklift rigging attachments | SCRA | |
| Lifting Industry: Weights, Measures & Signals | SCRA | |
| Exxon Crane Guide by Bates & Hontz | SCRA | |

**USA (Wire Rope Technical Board)**

| | | |
|---|---|---|
| Wire rope user's manual (4th Ed) | WRTB | |
| Wire rope sling user's manual (3rd Ed) | WRTB | |

Books, papers and publications

   International

| | | |
|---|---|---|
| The Art of Heavy Transport | Marco van Daal | 978184426744-6 |
| Bowles, J.E. (1996). Foundation Analysis and Design (5th Ed), McGraw-Hill. | McGraw-Hill | |
| "Effective Bearing Length of Crane Mats" - D.Duerr | 2DM Associates | |
| "Crane Mats and Ground Bearing Issues" - D.Duerr | 2DM Associates | |
| Mobile Cranes | James Headley | |
| Mobile Craning Today | D.H.Campbell | |
| How to use Load Charts | Crane Institute of America | |
| Bobs Overhead Crane & Rigging Handbook | Pellow Engineering Services | |
| Cranes and Derricks (4th Edition) - Shapiro | McGraw- Hill | |
| Handbook for riggers | W.G. (Bill) Newberry | |
| Bobs Rigging & Crane Handbook (7th Ed) | Pellow Engineering Services | |
| Rigging Handbook (3rd Ed) | Jerry Klinke | |
| Rigging Handbook | James Headley | |
| North American Rigging & Lifting Handbook | North Sea Lifting Ltd | |
| "Lifting Equipment Control and Operation Procedures" (LECOP) | North Sea Lifting Ltd | |
| Working Cranes near Power Lines | Crane Institute of America | |
| Wire Rope Inspection Guidelines | Crane Institute of America | |

Manufacturers catalogs, bulletins, technical information

| | |
|---|---|
| Crosby Catalog | Crosby |
| SLINGMAX® catalog (and other brochures, technical bulletins) | SLINGMAX® |
| SLINGMAX® Riggers Handbook | SLINGMAX® |
| Certex Catalog | Certex USA |
| Green pin catalog (and other info) | Van Beest |

# LIST OF FIGURES

The author wants to thank those who have given permission for their original material to be used and will be glad to correct any errors and omissions in giving credit.